HANDBOOK ON THE ECONOMICS OF RECIPROCITY AND SOCIAL ENTERPRISE

Handbook on the Economics of Reciprocity and Social Enterprise

Edited by

Luigino Bruni

Professor of Economics, Lumsa University, Rome, Italy

Stefano Zamagni

Professor of Economics, University of Bologna and Johns Hopkins University, Bologna Center, Italy

With editorial assistance from Dr Antonella Ferrucci

Edward Elgar
Cheltenham, UK • Northampton, MA, USA

Published by
Edward Elgar Publishing Limited
The Lypiatts
15 Lansdown Road
Cheltenham
Glos GL50 2JA
UK

Edward Elgar Publishing, Inc.
William Pratt House
9 Dewey Court
Northampton
Massachusetts 01060
USA

A catalogue record for this book
is available from the British Library

Library of Congress Control Number: 2012952651

This book is available electronically in the ElgarOnline.com
Economics Subject Collection, E-ISBN 978 1 84980 474 5

ISBN 978 1 84980 463 9 (cased)

Typeset by Servis Filmsetting Ltd, Stockport, Cheshire
Printed by MPG PRINTGROUP, UK

Contents

Figures

Tables

Contributors

Ricardo Abramovay is Professor of Economic Sociology at the Department of Economics and the Institute of International Relations of the University of São Paulo, Brazil. His major research area includes sustainable development and social participation in the transition towards a low carbon economy.

Helen Alford is Dean of the Faculty of Social Sciences at the Pontifical University of St Thomas (Angelicum) in Rome. Her research interests focus on business and economic ethics, corporate social responsibility and Christian social thought.

Antonio Andreoni is Research Associate at the University of Cambridge and Adjunct Professor in Ethical Banking and Microcredit at the University of Bologna. He is also International Consultant for the United Nations Industrial Development Organization, Vienna. He was co-founder of micro.Bo ONLUS and Make a Change. His research focuses on development and institutional economics, structural change and production economics, manufacturing development and industrial policies, microfinance and cooperatives.

Antonio Argandoña is Professor of Economics and holder of the 'la Caixa' Chair of Corporate Social Responsibility and Corporate Governance at IESE Business School, University of Navarra. He is a member of the Royal Academy of Economics and Finance of Spain and has been a member of the Executive Committee of the European Business Ethics Network (EBEN), and Secretary General of EBEN-Spain. His main fields of interests are macroeconomics and monetary economics, business ethics, corporate social responsibility and corporate governance.

Albino Barrera is Professor of Economics and Theology at Providence College, Rhode Island (USA). He has published in the areas of economic ethics, globalization, and theological ethics. His books include *Market Complicity and Christian Ethics* (Cambridge University Press, 2011), *Globalization and Economic Ethics* (Palgrave MacMillan, 2007), *Economic Compulsion and Christian Ethics* (Cambridge University Press, 2005), and *God and the Evil of Scarcity* (Notre Dame, 2005).

Leonardo Becchetti is Professor of Economics at the University of Rome Tor Vergata. President of the Ethical Committee of Banca Popolare Etica, Director of www.bene-comune.net. He is the author of around 345 published works and his main research interests are ethics and economics, sustainable development and subjective well-being.

Nicolò Bellanca is Associate Professor of Economics at the University of Florence and a member of the lab ARCO (Action Research for Co-Development). His recent research has focused on the logic of collective action, comparative institutional analysis, capability approach, relationship between economic development and post-representative democracy.

Dr Elisa Bortoluzzi Dubach is a consultant in the fields of communication, foundations and sponsoring. She has broad experience as a leader of cultural and social sponsoring projects, has contributed to the creation of large grantmaking foundations and is an advisor to CEOs and Presidents of the Board of international companies. She is also a lecturer in sponsoring and foundations at several European universities and institutions.

Carlo Borzaga is Professor of Economic Policy at the University of Trento. He is President of the European Research Institute on Cooperative and Social Enterprises (Euricse). His scientific interests are labour economics, the economic analysis of cooperatives, social enterprises and non-profit organizations and the evolution of this sector in Europe. He is also concerned with welfare systems and the provision of social and health-care services.

Luk Bouckaert is emeritus Professor of ethics at the Catholic University of Leuven (Belgium). He started the interdisciplinary Centre for Economics and Ethics at Leuven (1987) and is founder-president of the European SPES Forum (2004). His most recent publication is *The Palgrave Handbook of Spirituality and Business* (co-edited with L. Zsolnai (2011)).

Samuel Bowles is Research Professor at the Santa Fe Institute where he heads the Behavioral Sciences Program. He is also Professor of Economics at the University of Siena. His recent studies on cultural and genetic evolution have challenged the conventional economic assumption that people are motivated entirely by self-interest. His recent books include *Poverty Traps* (Princeton 2006), *Globalization and Egalitarian Redistribution* (Princeton, 2006), *A Cooperative Species: Human reciprocity and its evolution*, co-authored with Herbert Gintis (2011), and *Machiavelli's Mistake: Why good laws are no substitute for good citizens* (Yale University Press, forthcoming 2013).

Andrea Brandolini is director and economist in the Department for Structural Economic Analysis at the Bank of Italy. He is associate editor of the *Journal of Economic Inequality* and chaired the International Association for Research in Income and Wealth from 2008 to 2010. His research interests include income and wealth distribution, poverty, and measurement of economic well-being.

Luigino Bruni is Professor of Economics at the Lumsa University in Rome, and at the Sophia University of Loppiano (Florence). During the last 15 years his research has covered many areas ranging from microeconomics, ethics and economics, history of economic thought, methodology of economics, sociality and happiness in economics. He has also demonstrated great interest on the civil economy and economic-related categories, such as reciprocity and gratuitousness. His current research focuses on the role of intrinsic motivation in economic and civil life.

Alain Caillé, formerly trained as an economist, is emeritus Professor of Sociology at the University Paris Ouest Nanterre La Défense. He is the director of La Revue du MAUSS (Mouvement anti-utilitariste en science sociale, Anti-Utilitarian Movement in Social Science), an international and interdisciplinary review in sociology, anthropology, economics and political philosophy. His main interest is in general social theory, especially in the wake of Marcel Mauss' Essay on the Gift and Karl Polanyi.

John B. Davis, Professor of Economics, Marquette University, and Professor of Economics, University of Amsterdam, is author of *Keynes's Philosophical Development*

(Cambridge University Press, 1994), *The Theory of the Individual in Economics* (Routledge, 2003), *Individuals and Identity in Economics* (Cambridge University Press, 2011), and co-author with Marcel Boumans of *Economic Methodology: Understanding Economics as a Science* (Palgrave, 2011). He is co-editor with Wade Hands of the *Journal of Economic Methodology*.

Jacques Defourny is Professor of Economics at the University of Liege (Belgium) where he is also a director of the Centre for Social Economy. From 1996 to 2010, he acted as the founding coordinator and then the president of the EMES European Research Network, which gathers 12 university research centres working on the third sector and the emergence of social enterprise. His work currently focuses on comparisons of social enterprise models across the world and on conceptual and quantitative analysis of the third sector in developed as well as developing countries.

Lewis Faulk is an Assistant Professor in the Department of Public Administration and Policy in the School of Public Affairs at American University. His research focuses on non-profit competition, organizational capacity, resource development, and performance.

Bruno S. Frey is Professor at the University of Zurich, Distinguished Professor of Behavioural Science at the Warwick Business School, University of Warwick, UK, and holds honorary doctorates at the University of Gothenburg and four other universities. He has published extensively on public choice and non-market economics including happiness and economics, motivation and knowledge transfer, and arts and economics.

Dr Lorna Gold is Policy and Advocacy Manager for Trócaire, the Irish Catholic International Development Agency. She writes extensively on ethics and public policy, with special focus on international cooperation. She has published two books and numerous articles on the Economy of Communion and is a former member of the international commission for an Economy of Communion.

Herbert Gintis is External Professor at the Santa Fe Institute (Santa Fe, NM) and Professor of Economics, Central European University (Budapest, Hungary). His recent books include, *A Cooperative Species: Human Reciprocity and Evolution* co-authored with Samuel Bowles (Princeton: Princeton University Press, 2011), *The Bounds of Reason: Game Theory and the Unification of the Behavioral Sciences* (Princeton: Princeton University Press, 2009); and *Game Theory Evolving* (Princeton: Princeton University Press, 2009). His recent work on market dynamics includes 'The Emergence of a Price System from Decentralized Bilateral Exchange', *Contributions to Theoretical Economics* 6(1), p. 13 (2006) and 'The Dynamics of General Equilibrium', *Economic Journal* 117, pp. 1289–1309 (2007).

Benedetto Gui is Professor of Economics at the University of Padova (Italy). His research interests include: the economic behaviour of cooperative, non-profit, and social enterprises; the economic implications of interpersonal relations; and the role of non-instrumental motivations in economic organisations. He is a member of the management board of *Annals of Public and Cooperative Economics*.

André Habisch is Professor of Christian Social Ethics and Civil Society at the Catholic University of Eichstaett Ingolstadt's faculty of Business and Economics. As a trained economist and Catholic theologian he teaches Applied Business Ethics, CSR and Catholic Social Thought. As Associate Research Director of ABIS – The Academy of Business in Society (Brussels–New York–Shanghai) – he coordinates the interreligious Project, 'Practical Wisdom in Management from the Religious and Spiritual Traditions'; moreover, he advises the Federation of Catholic Entrepreneurs and serves as a Scientific Advisor in the Study Commission of the German Parliament on 'Growth, well-being and quality of life'.

Shaun P. Hargreaves Heap is Professor of Economics at the University of East Anglia. His recent research has been on the social influences on individual decision making, using experiments, and on media pluralism. He has written previously on hysteresis and wage in equality in macroeconomics, on rational choice in a social and historical context and on the method of experimental economics.

Derek C. Jones is Morris Professor of Economics at Hamilton College, Clinton, New York; Research Director at the Mondragon Co-operative Academic Community; and Faculty Fellow and Mentor, Rutgers University. His research interests include employee ownership and cooperatives, personnel economics and economics of transition.

Panu Kalmi is Professor of Economics at the University of Vaasa, Finland. His research interests include financial institutions, personnel economics and cooperatives.

Elias L. Khalil specializes in behavioural and evolutionary economics. He focuses on rational choice theory with regard to four areas: i) creativity and entrepreneurship; ii) evolutionary change of institutions and technology; iii) emotions and ethical judgements; iv) behaviour of organisms. His articles have appeared in *Economic Inquiry, Behavioral and Brain Sciences, Southern Economic Journal, History of Political Economy*, and *Economics and Philosophy*.

Serge-Christophe Kolm is professor and director at the Ecole des Hautes Etudes en Sciences Sociales, Paris. His main fields of research include normative economics and social ethics (e.g., the comparison and measure of inequalities, 1966; *Justice and Equity*, 1971; *Modern Theories of Justice*, 1996; *Macrojustice*, 2004); public economics (e.g., *The State and the Price System*, 1970; *The Theory of Value Constraints*, 1970; *Optimal Public Prices*, 1968; *Mass Services*, 1970); giving, altruism and reciprocity (e.g., *General Reciprocity*, 1984; *Reciprocity*, 2008); and Oriental philosophy and psychology (e.g., *Happiness-Freedom*, 1982).

Cristian R. Loza Adaui is a Doctoral Researcher at the Ingolstadt School of Management of the Catholic University of Eichstätt-Ingolstadt, a research fellow and project manager at EABIS – The Academy of Business in Society and a researcher of the Center for Corporate Citizenship e.V. (Germany). His research focuses on business ethics, corporate social responsibility, corporate citizenship and Catholic social thought, and spirituality in management.

Jasmine McGinnis is an Assistant Professor at The George Washington University. Her research interests include philanthropy, international grantmaking, governance and issues of wage equity in the nonprofit sector. She has published articles on foundation giving and comparisons of nonprofit/for-profit wage differentials for Generation Y and female employees.

Jean Mercier Ythier is Professor of Economics at Sorbonne University (Panthéon-Assas) and permanent member of the Institut d'Economie Publique. His main fields of interest include the economics of gift-giving, general equilibrium, social contract theory, public economics, and topics of economic anthropology.

Dr Susanne Neckermann, Dipl.-Vw., MBA, studied economics at the University of Cologne, Germany and business administration at the Eastern Illinois University, Charleston, USA. She earned her PhD at the University of Zurich in 2009. From 2009 to 2012 she was a post-doctoral fellow at the Center for European Economic Research and the University of Mannheim. From September 2012 she has been an Assistant Professor at the Erasmus University in Rotterdam.

Vera Negri Zamagni is Professor of Economic History at the University of Bologna and Adjunct Professor of European Economic History at the Bologna Centre of the Johns Hopkins University. Publications include more than 80 essays, 10 volumes and 14 edited volumes. They cover the economic history of Italy from 1860 to the present in the context of European and world economic history of the last two centuries, with special reference to the reconstruction of national income estimates, regional disequilibria, income distribution and wages, state intervention, business history, evolution of the cooperative movement, and European integration.

Avner Offer is Chichele Professor of Economic History and a Fellow of All Souls College at the University of Oxford, emeritus. He has worked on land tenure, the economics of war, consumption and well-being, and obesity. He is currently investigating the Nobel Prize in Economics as part of a study of the transition from social democracy to market liberalism.

Adrian Pabst is Lecturer in Politics at the University of Kent, Canterbury, and Visiting Professor at the Institut d'Etudes Politiques de Lille (Sciences Po). His research focuses on political thought, political economy and religion. Currently he is writing (together with John Milbank) *The Politics of Virtue*. He is also a Trustee of The ResPublica Trust, London, where he works on alternative political economies.

Russell G. Pearce is the Edward & Marilyn Bellet Professor of Legal Ethics, Morality & Religion at Fordham University School of Law. His current research explores the implications of relational ethics for legal, economic, and political culture.

Vittorio Pelligra is Assistant Professor of Economics at the University of Cagliari (Italy), research fellow of CRENoS and Invited Professor at the International University Institute 'Sophia' (Loppiano-Florence). His researches, both theoretical and experimental, deal with the individual, strategic and institutional consequences of non-self-interested behaviour. He has written extensively on trust, reciprocity, empathy and social emotions.

Pier Luigi Porta is Professor of Economics at the University of Milano-Bicocca. He is a Life Member of the Istituto Lombardo (Accademia di Scienze e Lettere) and a Visiting Fellow of Wolfson College at the University of Cambridge. He is the Editor-in-Chief of the *International Review of Economics* (IREC), published by Springer Verlag. His main fields of research are classical political economy, welfare economics, and civil economy.

Pier Luigi Sacco is a Professor of Cultural Economics at IULM University, Milan, where he serves as Deputy Rector for International Affairs. He also teaches Creative Industries at the University of Italian Switzerland (USI), Lugano. He is the author of more than 150 papers on the topics of economic theory, game theory, cultural economics, cultural and creative industries, and cultural policy design at the urban, regional and national level.

Lorenzo Sacconi is Professor of Economic Policy and Unicredit Chair in Economic Ethics and Corporate Social Responsibility at the University of Trento (Italy). He is also the scientific director of EconomEtica, the inter-university centre of research for economic ethics and CSR at the University Milano Bicocca. His research areas focus on ethics and economics, the economic modelling of the social contract, institutional economics, behavioural and experimental game theory, theory of the firm and incomplete contracts, corporate governance, business ethics and social responsibility. His recent books are: *The Social Contract of the Firm* (Springer, 2000); *Corporate Social Responsibility and Corporate Governance* (Palgrave Macmillan, 2010) with Margaret Blair, R. Edward Freeman and Alessandro Vercelli; and *Social Capital, Corporate Social Responsibility, Economic Behaviour and Performance* (Palgrave Macmillan, 2011) with Giacomo Degl Antoni.

Alessandra Smerilli is Associate Professor of Economics at PFSE-Auxilium of Rome. Her publications include: 'We-thinking and vacillation between frames: filling a gap in Bacharach's theory', *Theory and Decision*, Springer, 73(4), pp. 539–560; with Bruni Luigino: 'The value of vocation. The crucial role of intrinsically motivated people in values-based organizations', *Review of Social Economy*, 67, pp. 272–281. She is interested in we-rationality, cooperation, evolutionary game theory.

Amelia J. Uelmen is a Visiting Lecturer at Georgetown University Law Center. From 2001 to 2011 she served as the Director of the Fordham Institute on Religion, Law & Lawyer's Work. Her current research explores the implications of relational ethics for tort law, legal ethics, legal education, and debates about religion in the public square.

Paolo Vanin is Assistant Professor of Economics at the University of Bologna. His research interests include the implications of social capital and social interaction for growth, time allocation and crime. He has also worked on the economics of moral values, international trade and asymmetric information.

Brendan M. Wilson is an attorney at the law firm of Caplin & Drysdale Chartered in Washington, D.C. He specializes in representing tax-exempt organizations and hybrid enterprises that use business to address social and environmental problems.

Dennis R. Young is Bernard B. and Eugenia A. Ramsey Professor of Private Enterprise and Director of the Nonprofit Studies Program at Georgia State University. He is editor of the journal *Nonprofit Policy Forum*. His research interests focus on finance, management and governance of non-profit organizations and social enterprise.

Stefano Zamagni is Professor of Economics at the University of Bologna and Adjunct Professor of International Economics at Johns Hopkins University, Bologna Center. He is the author of several books, including *Microeconomic Theory* (Oxford: Blackwell, 1987) and *Avarice* (Bologna: Il Mulino, 2009). He co-authored *History of Economic Thought* (Oxford: Oxford University Press, 2005) with E. Screpanti; *Relational Complexity and Economic Behaviour* (Bologna, Il Mulino, 2006) with P. Sacco; *Civil Economy* (Oxford: Peter Lang, 2007) with L. Bruni; *Dictionary of Civil Economy* (Rome: Citta' Nuova, 2009) with L. Bruni; *Cooperative Enterprise* (Cheltenham: Edward Elgar 2010) with V. Zamagni and *Family and Work* (Milan: San Paolo, 2012 (ed.) with Vera Negri Zamagni. He edited *Dictionary of Civil Economy* (Rome: Città Nuova, 2009) with L. Bruni and *Markets, Money and Capital* (Cambridge: Cambridge University Press, 2008) with R. Scazzieri and A. Sen.

Luca Zarri is Associate Professor at the Economics Department of the University of Verona. He held the position of visiting scholar at Carnegie Mellon University in 2008 and 2010. His current research interests include behavioural economics and experimental economics, with a special focus on social preferences, social norms and their interplays with incentives and institutions.

Daniel John Zizzo is Professor of Economics, Head of the School of Economics and Associate Dean (Research) in the Faculty of Social Sciences at the University of East Anglia. He is a member of the Centre for Behavioural and Experimental Social Science (CBESS) and a Coordinating Editor of *Theory and Decision*. His primary research areas are experimental and behavioural economics.

Acknowledgments

This handbook is a collective action, fruit of hundreds of relationships. Therefore it is impossible to acknowledge all our intellectual debts, and express all our gratitude to the many who have contributed indirectly to this joint work. Of course, our first thanks go to the 47 authors of the entries of the handbook, who have written their chapters with a genuine academic spirit of gratuitousness.

We also want to thank the various protagonists of the many areas of civil and social economy which have inspired most of the pages of this volume. Last but not least, a sincere and deep thank you to Dr Antonella Ferrucci, the editorial assistant: without her committed and hard work this Handbook would have not be possible.

Introduction
Luigino Bruni and Stefano Zamagni

The political economy is unpopular with the general public. The war, the postwar and the crisis have given many and such denials of what appear strictly to be scientific estimates, advanced by economists. It is no wonder that any layman could believe to be authorized to proclaim the bankruptcy of the political economy. Hence, at times it happens that economists must take a stand against the false news of the death of their science. To the voices, some calumny, not a mitigating factor is lacking. In fact, many economists have sinned by immodesty. On the eve of the world war itself, too many have proclaimed, on behalf of the economic laws, that the war itself could not do or if it could have, the active forces of the nations would have been depleted within the strict limits of time. Nevertheless, the war had run its course for many years, refuting and depleting its deniers. In the early days of the economic crisis, other economists did not hesitate to declare themselves on the basis of the conjuncture of science fallacy that the crisis could not explode or that if it exploded it would soon be quelled. (R. Michels, 'Inaugural Address of the academic year 1933–1934', University of Perugia, 1934)

DOING ECONOMICS IN THE AGE OF CRISIS

This time of crisis (much deeper and more serious than just a financial or economic crisis) calls us back to individual and collective responsibility, even of thought. One dimension of such an appeal to responsibility is the need today to reopen a new, true and profound debate about the nature of business, banks, profit, market and, therefore, of capitalism. The challenge is in being able to speak about these major aspects of civilization while freeing oneself from ideologies and overused words. Over the last 20 years, such ideologies and words have obstructed the reopening of a season of deep review and a highpoint of our economic system, for which people recognize a growing and urgent need.

The main idea underlying the various contributions of this Handbook is the acknowledgment of the civilizing nature of market and firms when and if they are understood as expressions of civil virtues. Civil virtues in relation to markets mean in particular that what is typical of markets and firms is the dimension of reciprocity: the peculiar virtues in the economic domain are social by nature. There are of course also individual virtues (prudence, innovation, creativity . . .), but the actual 'golden rule' of the market is reciprocity, because contracts, business, exchanges are matters of cooperation and of common advantage, i.e. forms, albeit different one from the other, of reciprocity.

We are aware that to speak today of virtues in the market can appear odd or at least controversial in this age of crisis, when an influential part of today's public opinion views market logic as corrupt of civil virtues, as it leads to the commodification of all human relationships. In fact, in previous writings we have highlighted the serious risks associated with fundamentalism in the market and its individual and collective vices (Bruni and Zamagni 2007). In as much as it is a human activity, the market is perfectible and should therefore always be subject to the critique of thought. However, especially in periods of crisis, we believe that it is very important to call people, institutions and human reality back to their 'vocation', inviting them to rediscover, or finally discover, their best part. As those who have lived through serious crises know, and as those who have helped others overcome crises know, it is not possible to get out of these impasses if one does not find his/her own Socratic 'daimon' again, without rediscovering one's profound vocation. Something similar happens for collective realities, institutions and societies. In difficult moments, pessimism will not help. Instead, we need to know how to look deeper and draw from purer waters.

In fact, we should remember that the current phase of the market economy (which we might call financial-individualistic capitalism) arises from an anthropological pessimism that dates back to Guicciardini, Machiavelli, Luther, Calvin and Hobbes. The great premise or anthropological hypothesis on which both economic theory and the western economic system rest is the assumption that human beings are radically opportunists and too self-interested to think that they can commit themselves because of higher motivations (like the common good). The Italian economist, Maffeo Pantaleoni, one of the great figures of 20th-century economics, wrote a very eloquent passage in this regard. In a writing from the beginning of the 1900s, he challenges the 'optimists' to show that the motivations that lead:

> street sweepers to sweep, tailors to make suits, the tram conductor to work 12 hours of service on the tram, the miner to descend into the mine, the stockbroker to follow orders, the miller to buy and sell grain, the farmer to hoe the earth, etc., be they honours, dignity, spirit of sacrifice, the waiting for heavenly rewards, patriotism, love of neighbour, spirit of solidarity, imitation of ancestors and the good of descendants and not only a kind of benefit that is called economic. (Pantaleoni 1925)

Such anthropological cynicism is one of the building stones of the contemporary economics system, that we would like to challenge with this Handbook.

This Handbook, in fact, does not share this cynical or pessimistic view. We are convinced that there is today an ethical responsibility of thought to propose and foster a more positive outlook on the world, on mankind, on politics and on the economy. This different and positive outlook can start from a reflection on how the market 'should be', on its moral task in edifying a good and just social order – a civil society that dies when community life is regulated only by the market but also dies or does not flourish without the market and its typical virtues. They are virtues that seem, and often are, far from the economic praxis of our time, and that is why they ought to be called back into our personal and collective consciousness.

The cultural vision that inspires the architecture of this Handbook is that of *Civil Economy*, a tradition of thought that has its roots in the late Middle Ages, and that in modern times includes among its founders economists such as Antonio Genovesi, Giacinto Dragonetti, Pietro Verri, Adam Smith, John S. Mill, Alfred Marshall, Luigi Einaudi, Giorgio Fuà and many others. For these authors, even in different gradients due to the diverse cultural backgrounds, historical contexts, etc., market exchange is also and above all a form of reciprocity and social tie, a branch of common living, where at work are the same passions, the same vices and the same virtues of the entire life in common, because 'political economy or economics is the study of mankind in the ordinary business of life; it examines that part of individual and social action which is most closely connected with the attainment and use of the material requisites of well-being' (Marshall 1890, p. 1).

IN SEARCH OF THE 21ST-CENTURY PARADIGM

The main ambition of this Handbook is to face and overcome one of the most profound dichotomy of modern economic and social thought, in particular in the 20th century, namely that between the Anglo-Saxon (US-Protestant in particular) and the European (Latin-Catholic) economic and social systems. The former is based on the principles of individual freedom and a sharp distinction-separation between the logic of the market and that of solidarity: business is business and what is associated to solidarity is something that does not belong to the economic domain. In the Anglo-Saxon culture, philanthropy has been the *link* between the world of business and that of solidarity, and the non profit sector is a consistent economic and social expression of this humanism. The Latin-Catholic economic and social culture, on the other hand, has been built in Europe upon community and a weak (or no) distinction between market and (civil and political) society. In this system the link between business and solidarity has been the Welfare State, and the strong European cooperative movement on the one hand, and the industrial district model on the other, are just natural consequences of this communitarian model. In the European system, in fact, the economic dimension has been embedded into the community (local and national). In the US model business is business, and philanthropy cares about the social dimension; in Latin and Catholic culture, business has never been only business, because strong communitarian ties have always impeded market and firms from being really distinct – let alone separated – from both community and society. The Latin/catholic market has never been 'pure', because it has tried to 'save' something of the communitarian model of the first Medieval foundations of markets within the *comuni*, where market economy came out from the hearth of the Christian *communitas* (Todeschini 2002).

The 20th century has been the century that has exalted this dichotomy, where two different models of market economy have been alternatives. In this dawn of the 21st century it is evident that both systems of market economy and society are both in crisis. Many people feel the need for something new, capable of building a bridge between these two humanisms. Globalization has in fact radically changed the scenario, and neither philanthropy nor the welfare state is enough to face the new challenges successfully. Indeed, the Anglo-Saxon model based on philanthropy is failing in the area of community and social belonging, as the various paradoxes of opulent unhappiness are more and more evident (Bruni and Porta 2005). On the other hand, the welfare state system has flopped because of its inability to keep up with the growing costs (the enormous public debt in Europe is at the basis of the many financial difficulties of most countries, in particular in the Latin/Mediterranean ones) and for not being able to develop an appropriate market culture. Too little community and too much individualism in the Aglon-Saxon world; too much statism and an immature market mentality in the European one. In the search of something new, of a post-capitalistic market economy, we think that the paradigms of Reciprocity and Social Entrepreneurship can offer new hints and indicate viable paths of research. Reciprocity, in fact, is neither philanthropy nor solidarity, being the social and economic translation of the 18th-century keyword fraternity. Fraternity is in fact the forgotten principle of Modernity: equality has been at the centre of the welfare state system; freedom in the Anglo-Saxon world, but fraternity is still waiting its moment. We read this new interest within economics for the issues of reciprocity, relational goods, and public happiness as important signs that the time of the fraternity principle is again forthcoming. In fact, when the founders of Modernity announced the new principles of the new world – *liberté, égalité, fraternité* – they said something crucial: individual freedom and social equality are not enough to build the new post-*ancient régime* society, because neither liberty nor equality denotes a 'link', relationships *among* persons. Certainly the fraternity we are referring to is not the one that refers to shared bloodlines, nor exclusively to family and clan ties. Neither is it the fraternity often used by closed and discriminating communities. Rather, it is the kind of fraternity, grouped with freedom and equality, that is close to the notion of 'open impartiality' used by Sen (2002). This kind of fraternity on the part of members of a community means feeling part of a common destiny, of being united by a link less exclusive and elective than friendship, but which is capable of generating feelings of reciprocal sympathy, and which can and should be expressed even in ordinary market transactions. Better said, the construction of a market economy was understood by Enlightenment thinkers as a pre-condition so that fraternity would not remain an abstract principle or a mere utopia but would become a general, everyday praxis.

How does the vision of the economy and the market change if we take fraternity into serious consideration? How can we reconcile the idea of the market envisioned as a locus of possible fraternity with price mechanism? This Handbook aims at answering these questions. To choose reciprocity as a keyword of contemporary economics means to conceive market interactions as fully human and moral, builders of fraternal relationships. Ultimately, the aim is to help economics overcome the acute reductionism from which it suffers – a reductionism which represents a serious obstacle to the entry of new ideas and a dangerous form of protectionism against innovations stemming from other social sciences.

THE TRUE ENTREPRENEUR IS SOCIAL

Another keyword of this Handbook is *social enterprise*. We are convinced that being a social entrepreneur is the rule not the exception of entrepreneurship. In fact, when the market functions correctly, it is a place in which innovation and human creativity are favoured and rewarded. Market competition (as it emerges from many entries of the Handbook) can be – and if we want to understand it in its truest nature, should be – seen as a race to innovation. Those who innovate grow and live, while those who do not innovate remain behind and leave the economic and civil game.

The author who has most caught this virtuous dynamic of the market (the capacity to innovate is undoubtedly a virtue, because it is an expression of *arête*, of excellence) is J.A. Schumpeter. In 1911, he published *The Theory of Economic Development*. There, Schumpeter masterfully describes the dynamics of the market as a 'run' between innovators and imitators. To explain the nature and role of innovation, Schumpeter draws upon a model where the starting point is the 'stationary state', the situation in which businesses only carry out routine activities and the economic system perfectly replicates itself over time, without profits and loses, without creation of added values and true wealth. Economic development then starts when the entrepreneur breaks from the stationary state by introducing innovation, which can be a technical invention, a new organizational formula, the creation of new products or new markets, which reduce costs and make it possible for the business to create new wealth.

The entrepreneur-innovator is the protagonist of economic development, as he/she creates real added value and makes the social system dynamic. The innovator is then followed by a 'swarm' of imitators attracted by that created added value, just as bees are attracted by nectar. When they enter into those sectors that verify the innovation, they cause the market price of that given product to decrease, to the point that all the profit generated by the innovation is entirely absorbed. The economy and society return to the stationary state until a new innovation restarts the cycle of economic development. Therefore, for Schumpeter, profit has a transitory nature, as it subsists as long as there is innovation, in that time lapse between the initial innovation and the imitation.

This classic text of economics reminds us that the truest nature of the entrepreneur and the entrepreneurial function is the capacity to innovate. The entrepreneur is not a profit-seeker: profit is only a signal that innovation is present. When the entrepreneur (including the social entrepreneur) complains because he/she is imitated, his/her vocation is already in crisis. He/she must be reminded that imitation also plays an important role, as it ensures that derivative advantages that come from an innovation do not remain in the innovating business alone but are spread throughout society (for example, through the reduction of market prices, which increases collective well-being). The entrepreneur is not a 'rational' agent as understood in neoclassical economics. In fact, what motivates her or him is 'the dream and the will to found a private kingdom. . . the will to conquer; the impulse to fight, to prove oneself superior to others. . . the joy of creating' (Schumpeter 1911, p.93). Many other economists belonging to this 'broad' civil economy tradition believe in this thesis: what is typical of entrepreneurship is not profit-seeking per se but innovation, and in doing this she or he also promotes the common good, is a social entrepreneur. When an entrepreneur stops innovating, he/she dies as an entrepreneur (perhaps transforming himself/herself into a spectator or a rent-seeker), and so blocks the innovation-imitation relay race, which is the true virtuous dynamics that pushes society ahead, not only the economy.

One of the deepest reasons for the current crisis was the progressive transformation of many entrepreneurs into mere speculators, which took place in the past decades following the financial boom. The entrepreneur-innovator, compared to the speculator, thanks to his/her vocation, sees the world as a dynamic place that can be changed. He/she doesn't simply think of increasing his/her own piece of a given 'pie'. He/she creates new 'pies', welcomes new opportunities, looks ahead and not beside him/her in search of rivals to battle with so that he/she can hoard the pie.

THE IDEA OF A CIVIL ECONOMY

From the period of civil humanism in the 15th century up until today, western civilization has been capable of economic and civil development when cultural and institutional conditions have allowed people to cultivate the virtue of creativity and innovation. The civil vision of the market as an institution that awards innovation places the accent on people and not so much on capital, finance or technology. Innovation is first of all a matter of vision, of a different outlook on things and on the world, and therefore a matter of people that see reality differently. And, in fact, in the 1940s, Schumpeter himself foresaw that the passage of innovation from persons to research offices and development of large businesses would change the nature of capitalism. It would cause capitalism to lose contact with the personal dimension – the only one that can really favour innovation. And still today, after decades of getting drunk over what's 'big' and anonymous, we're realizing that the businesses that are able to grow and be leaders in the globalized economy are, increasingly, those where there is one or more persons capable of seeing reality differently, capable of innovation.

The only true key to innovation and creation of economic value is people's intelligence (that is, their capability to 'read and see inside' things), as an Italian economist even older than Schumpeter said. We are referring to Milanese Carlo Cattaneo (1859), who, in the mid 19th century, wrote one of the most beautiful and humanistic theses on economic action, in which he reminds us that the virtue of innovation is founded on an even more radical virtue (because more universal): creativity. 'There is not job or capital that does not begin with an act of intelligence,' he wrote. 'Before every job, before all capital. . .it's the intelligence that begins the work and stamps the character of wealth into it for the first time.' The notions, recently introduced in economic discourse, of 'connective capital' (Ichiniowski and Show 2009) and 'shared capitalism' (Kruse et al 2006) are clear indication of a revival of attention to the argument sketched above. What induces workers and firms to invest in connective capital, intended as the sum of the person's own capital and the knowledge capital of others who he/she taps into to solve problems? Why should each worker tap into the skill of others and how much should others be willing to share their skills? Why is shared capitalism – conceived as an organizational system which seeks to align the interests of the employee with the owner by sharing participation in decisions and the residual return – today increasing and spreading in many different places? These are only some of the questions that are being raised in the current economic debate.

The virtuous relay race of innovation-imitation is greater than just the economic environment. This gives us a beautiful and original key to understanding not only the market but also the civil history of peoples. When societies and markets favour people who innovate, when these people do not lament but delight in being imitated, when even institutions universalize these innovations, then common living and the market work, and they are beautiful places in which to live. Finally, from such a perspective comes an idea of market seen basically as cooperation before and more deeply than pure competition. When economists such as Smith, Genovesi, Mill, Edgeworth or Marshall thought of market interactions, for them it was normal to depict such relationships in terms of cooperative competition.

This Handbook reminds us that the world is a place where water falls from mountains to valleys, and where human relationships are founded on the law of reciprocity, including the reciprocity as market relationship. Mill, for instance, was convinced that over time the market would develop and strengthen people's capacity for cooperation, and therefore their civic virtue. He wrote in his *Principles of Political Economy*:

> One of the changes which most infallibly attend the progress of modern society, is an improvement in the business capacities of the general mass of mankind . . . Works of all sorts, impracticable to the savage or the half-civilized, are daily accomplished by civilized nations [. . .]. The peculiar characteristic, in short, of civilized beings, is the capacity of co-operation. (Mill (1920[1848]), p. 698)

Today, more than a century and a half after Mill wrote these words, looking at cooperation in the market and at the culture it has produced, would Mill still consider the market in the same way? In light of his thought, were he to observe a company, a commercial centre and ordinary social and economic life (from air travel to a football league), we believe that he would not have second thoughts, and would see his insights and his predictions confirmed. On the other hand, we would begin to have some doubt about his answer if Mill, or one of the fellow economists or liberal philosophers of his generation (as well as those that have followed), encountered the digital, financial, and technological world of our time. In fact, he would understand immediately that there is an ever increasing fundamental alliance between market and technology, and after brief reflection he would see that the logic of these relationships in a network differs little from that which drives the relationships within a multinational company or in the supermarkets in our cities. He would understand, that is, that the market has not only increased relationships, human contacts, and cooperation, as compared to the pre-modern world; it has also changed their *nature*, becoming more and more a great 'mediator' that makes interpersonal relationships and common life 'immune', a change in relation to which ethical judgement is complex and ambivalent.

Ambivalence is, perhaps, the most characteristic dimension of the ethos of the market, since ambivalence is the characteristic that marks all great human words (which are great *because* of this ambivalence). The great linguist Émile Benveniste (1971, p. 272) reminds us that even the word gift, a word that should be free from any ambivalence, is instead marked by 'a curious semantic ambivalence', because in many Indo-European languages the concept carried by the verb 'to give' can be expressed also by the verb 'to take'. The market, in fact can also be a social mechanism that, when working properly, is not in contrast with the authentic gift and can be read also as remuneration for civic virtues.

The civil economy perspective – as several of the entries in this Handbook indicate – is founded on the premise that the market is capable of hosting not only the principles of exchange of equivalents and redistribution, but also the principle of reciprocity. This implies that markets can serve multiple functions, not just one, i.e. efficiency, as the 'institutional mono-tasking' school of thought advocates, provided it makes room for the gift principle. An economy that loses contact with the spirit of gift does not have a future as an economy, for it will not attract those people with high vocation. If the enterprise becomes only a business (in the sense of 'a machine to make money') and excludes the passions and moral sentiments, it will only attract those people with a low capacity for human relations, meaning poor managers and workers. Money and profits are weak incentives if we want to move people at the level of their most noble and most powerful energies. Not only this, but when we act because we are motivated only by monetary incentives, freedom becomes of little value, until it fades away. That is why good businesses, those that give value to ideals, passions, reciprocity are so important: they foster personal and collective freedom. And from freedom all wealth is created.

We would like to conclude this Introduction with an ancient thought by the Latin author Seneca that vividly conveys the general idea of reciprocity. In his *De Beneficiis*, he wrote:

> Why are the Graces three in number and why are they sisters, why do they have their hands interlocked, and why are they smiling and youthful? Some would have it appear that there is one for bestowing a benefit, another for receiving it, and a third for returning it; others hold that there are three classes of benefactors – those who earn benefits, those who return them, those who receive and return them at the same time. But of the two explanations do you accept as true whichever you like? Yet what profit is there in such knowledge? Why do the sisters hand in hand dance in a ring which returns upon itself? For the reason that a benefit passing in its course from hand to hand returns nevertheless to the giver, the beauty if it is continuous and maintains and uninterrupted succession. (Seneca 1985, p. 13)

Those with no hope in the future have only the present; and those who have only the present have no compelling reason to be interested either in reciprocity or in innovative endeavours. But, fortunately, people who continue to entertain a hope in the future and who do not suffer the whims of the 'gloomy passions' (in the sense of Baruch Spinoza) have not disappeared altogether.

REFERENCES

Benveniste, E. (1971), *Problems in general linguistics*, University of Miami Press, Miami.
Bruni, L. and P. Porta (eds) (2005), *Economics and Happiness*, Oxford University Press, Oxford.
Bruni, L. and S. Zamagni (2007), *Civil Economy*, Peter Lang, Oxford.
Cattaneo C. (1956[1859]), *Sul pensiero come principio dell'economia pubblica*, in A. Bertolino (ed.) *Scritti*, vol. III, Le Monnier, Florence.
Ichiniowski, C. and K. Show (2009), 'Connective capital as social capital', *NBER*, December, 15619.
Kruse, D., J. Blasi and R. Park (2006), 'Shared capitalism in the US economy', *NBER*, October, 12315.
Marshall, A. (1890), *Principles of Economics*, Macmillan, London.
Mill, J.S. (1920[1848]), *Principles of political economy*, Macmillan, London.
Pantaleoni, M. (1925), *Erotemi di Economia*, vol. II, Laterza, Bari.
Schumpeter, J.A. (1961[1911]), *The theory of economic development*, Oxford University Press, New York.
Sen, A. (2002), 'Open and Closed Impartiality', *The Journal of Philosophy*, 99, 445–469.
Seneca, L. (1985), *De Beneficiis*, Book I, iii, 1–5, trans. J.W. Basore, Harvard University Press, Cambridge, Mass.
Todeschini, G. (2002), *Il mercante e il tempio*, Il Mulino, Bologna.

1. Altruism
Luca Zarri

THE ECONOMICS OF ALTRUISTIC BEHAVIOR

In naturally occurring environments, altruism is a widespread phenomenon. People often decide to sacrifice time, give away money and make other valuable gifts (e.g. blood and organ donations) to others. Data on charitable giving indicate that, in the US, roughly 90 percent of individuals donate money every year, also thanks to numerous capital campaigns, with fundraising techniques such as phoneathons, door-to-door drives, and mail solicitations being more and more popular. The time devoted to charities by volunteers is a vital resource for many organizations providing services in important domains such as education, health care or childcare. Free and open-source software developers (e.g. Linux) and volunteers contributing to the implementation of collaborative web-based projects perform a similar function on line. The multilingual encyclopedia Wikipedia is a well-known example of a global public good (accessed by 365 million readers) which has been mainly voluntarily provided and maintained for several years. But altruism also manifests itself in the workplace, with employees going beyond their duties and providing unpaid efforts unrelated to bonuses or promotions. Tipping takes place even when patrons are far away from home in restaurants never likely to be visited again. Similar one-shot interactions may occur for responses to survey requests by researchers (e.g. on a train or a plane) or to questions posed by Internet search services users. Sometimes individuals even save unknown people at the risk of their own life. One-off appeals for disaster relief often raise a great deal of money from contributions from a large number of individuals. Altruistic behavior can also take subtler forms. Let us think about tax compliance: paying taxes is a duty for each citizen and, therefore, paying taxes should not be viewed as a voluntary, altruistic act in itself. However, since in many countries measures of enforcement aimed at deterring evasion (such as audit rates and expected penalties) are weak or absent, the relatively high levels of actual tax compliance observed over time can be accounted for (at least to some extent) in terms of so called 'tax morale', that is, an altruistic attitude towards the community one lives in. As Hirshleifer (1985) pointed out: 'from the most primitive to the most advanced societies, a higher degree of cooperation takes place than can be explained as a merely pragmatic strategy for egoistic man' (p. 55; quoted in Dawes and Thaler, 1988).

Why, then, do so many people in different countries and social domains donate? What factors drive their decision to give to others? Do givers derive utility from giving? This chapter aims to provide an answer to these questions by referring to some key contributions developed in the last years within the huge and growing economics literature offering empirical evidence on altruistic behavior. Since shortcomings exist in both lab-generated data and data from natural settings (Levitt and List, 2007), I will report results from a variety of complementary approaches, namely economic and neuro-economic laboratory experiments, field experiments and more classic empirical methods. By necessity, however, I will address only a small subset of the important works of which the generous economic literature on altruism today consists, by leaving aside not only classical contributions from other disciplines (such as social psychology, sociology and evolutionary biology),[1] but also relevant issues such as the feedback that the reviewed empirical evidence has been producing on economic theories aimed at rationalizing this phenomenon. In particular, even though I am aware that altruistic behavior has a context-dependent nature and is often contingent on several environmental factors, I will restrict my attention to what I refer to as its major *internal* determinants, focusing on the *motivational* dimension underlying individuals' decisions to act altruistically.

In line with the real-life examples recalled above, I define individual i's behavior as 'altruistic' insofar as it possesses the two following features: (1) it confers benefits to (at least) another individual j (with $j \neq i$) and (2) it entails material costs for individual i.[2] In what follows, I will review some significant findings which contributed to shedding light on some key motivational drives of altruistic behavior. In particular, two broad classes of motivational determinants have been identified: *pure* and *impure* (or *warm glow*) *altruism*, incorporating the role of emotions, and in particular of empathy, in affecting one's decision to behave altruistically, and *social image concerns*.

PURE AND IMPURE ALTRUISM

A first important point to be made is that the above economic definition of other-regarding behavior is silent about the possibility that individual i derives non-monetary benefits from acting altruistically towards individual j. Andreoni's (1989; 1990) well-known distinction between 'pure' and 'impure' altruism provides a key contribution to address this issue. A *pure* altruist is a subject driven by a utility function directly depending not only on one's material well-being but also on another individual's (or group of individuals') utility:[3] as Dawes and Thaler (1988) observed, such an agent takes pleasure in others' pleasure. An *impure* altruist, by contrast, takes pleasure from the 'warm glow' of giving, that is from the act of giving *in itself*.[4] Hence, behaving pro-socially positively affects both pure and impure altruists' utility function. However, different implications can often be drawn depending on the pure vs. impure nature of donors' altruism. One of these regards the relevant issue of so called *crowding-out*. With no warm glow, increased giving by others induces people to reduce their gifts, as others' donations are a perfect substitute for one's own. By contrast, with warm glow an individual is no longer willing to decrease his own donation if others increase their contributions. In other words, warm glow makes giving 'sticky', with individuals being no more indifferent to the source of the gift (Andreoni, 2006).

Empirical evidence supports the view that both pure and impure altruism are utility-enhancing motives underlying altruistic behavior (Andreoni and Miller, 2002; Andreoni, 2006). In order to isolate the mechanisms that trigger other-regarding behavior, lab experiments have mainly relied on what is known today as the classical workhorse for the experimental analysis of altruism: the Dictator Game (hereafter, DG; Kahneman et al, 1986). In the DG, there is only one player (the dictator) who is endowed with a certain amount of money and is free to decide whether to keep it or to transfer a positive amount to another person (the Recipient), who is forced to accept his offer.[5] On average, subjects give about 20 percent of their endowment to the recipient (Forsythe et al, 1994; List, 2007; Levitt and List, 2007), so revealing that a non-negligible amount of pro-social behavior emerges in the lab. By using the DG, Konow and Earley (2008) offered lab evidence on the pleasure of giving money to others, finding that generous dictators experience higher overall happiness as well as higher levels of other dimensions of subjective well-being. With regard to the issue of causality, their investigation suggests that the positive correlation linking dictators' generosity and happiness underlies a common cause such as psychological well-being (i.e. healthy psychological functioning).

As to the relationship between gifts of time (i.e. volunteering activities) and happiness, Thoits and Hewitt (2001) showed that happier people are more inclined to volunteer, but also that volunteer work increases happiness as well as other dimensions of psychological and physical well-being. Meier and Stutzer (2008), by means of a natural experiment based on an 'exogenous shock' such as the collapse of East Germany and its infrastructure of volunteering, provided evidence that volunteers are more satisfied with their life than non-volunteers. Bruni and Stanca's (2008) econometric analysis based on a large sample of individuals from the *World Value Survey* reached similar conclusions, as they found that active participation in voluntary organizations is positively and significantly associated with life satisfaction.

Levitt and List (2007) asserted that 'Although leaving a tip imposes a financial cost on the diner, tipping provides an offsetting nonpecuniary reward' (pp. 157–158). Laboratory evidence from neuro-economic experiments confirms that costly altruistic choices are often associated with non-monetary rewards. Neuro-scientific knowledge is available today about the key components of the brain's reward circuits (see Singer and Fehr, 2005). Moll et al (2006) found activation in the stratum – a midbrain area which seems to constitute a fundamental component of reward-related neural circuits – on donating to charities. Drawing on Andreoni's (1990) distinction, Harbaugh et al (2007) tested for the pure altruism and warm glow motives by using functional magnetic resonance imaging while subjects played a DG. Interestingly they found that in terms of both reported satisfaction ratings and reward-related neural activity, voluntary giving led to better results compared to mandatory transfers. Finally, Fehr et al's (2005) results indicate that people derive nonpecuniary utility (i) from mutual cooperation in social dilemma games and (ii) from punishing unfair behavior.

Altruism and Tax Compliance

As far as fiscal behavior is concerned, the canonical model of *homo oeconomicus* predicts that a taxpayer driven by narrow self-interest will only have his net income as an argument in his utility function and, therefore, will systematically attempt to cheat on taxes. Undetected tax evasion yields pecuniary benefits to the free rider, who saves money and gets access to public (hence, non-excludable) goods. As a consequence, since in many countries measures of enforcement aimed at deterring evasion are weak, it has been difficult to understand why relatively high levels of compliance prevail in the Western world. As Andreoni et al (1998) put it: why are so many households honest, and why don't cheaters cheat more? How can we satisfactorily deal with this 'puzzle of compliance'? Recent work within the economic literature on tax compliance suggests that many people view tax cheating as something different from an independently-made amoral gamble. In particular, individuals' *tax morale* – taxpayers' intrinsic motivation to pay taxes – may provide the answer to the above question: insofar as people are morally committed towards paying taxes – regardless of risk-return calculations – the actual level of compliance can be expected to be relatively high even when deterrence measures are weak or absent.

In the neuro-economic experiment run by Harbaugh et al (2007), it turned out that not only voluntary donations but also mandatory, tax-like transfers to a charity elicit neural activity in areas related to reward processing. Using data on roughly 3,800 Italian households for 2004, Lubian and Zarri's (2011) empirical analysis confirmed Harbaugh et al's findings, adducing strong evidence that people with higher tax morale experience higher levels of subjective well-being than the others, even after controlling for the main demographic and socioeconomic determinants of happiness. Instrumental variable estimation suggests that this correlation reflects an independent causal effect of tax morale on happiness. We showed that fiscal honesty generates a higher hedonic payoff than cheating by considering two composite indices of fiscal morality as well as several single tax morale items including some unconditional moral attitudes towards taxation. In particular, we uncovered a positive correlation between happiness and fiscal morality also when considering morally demanding items, capturing a strong altruistic orientation towards others, such as 'Paying taxes is one of the basic duties of citizenship', 'Not paying taxes is one of the worst crimes a person can commit as it harms the whole community' and 'It is right to pay taxes because it helps the weak'.[6] As we noted in the paper, these results suggest that the hedonic return experienced by citizens with higher tax morale might be a reason why so many people report honestly even when effective deterrence measures are lacking: insofar as morally concerned people are characterized by a high degree of subjective well-being, a relatively high level of compliance turns out to be far less paradoxical than it seems to be at first glance.

Empathy

To what extent do *emotional* factors play a role in affecting individuals' choice to behave non-selfishly? How do emotions interact with the human proclivity to act altruistically? As Bowles and Gintis (2005) observed, so called 'pro-social emotions' – i.e. physiological and psychological reactions that induce agents to engage in cooperative behaviors – seem to play an important part in inducing individuals to undertake constructive social interactions. Some studies have focused on the impact of a pro-social emotion like *empathy* on altruistic behavior. Empathy can be viewed as an experience of communal feelings that promotes concern for the other person's welfare and, therefore, fosters pro-social behavior (Kirman and Teschl, 2010). Kirman and Teschl made clear that:

> if empathy leads not only to a better understanding of the other person's beliefs, intentions and motivations, but to a feeling of shared experience with the other person's sensations and emotions, this may well undermine purely self-interested choices and instead promote other-regarding behavior. That is, empathy may be the basis for 'social' preferences and lead to altruistic and other-regarding behavior.' (Kirman and Teschl, 2010, p. 305)

In this regard, Batson (1991) famously proposed the so called 'empathy-altruism' hypothesis, which stipulates that helping behavior is caused by the prior experience of empathic concern for the other person.[7]

Within the framework of the DG, Andreoni and Rao (2011) tested the hypothesis that communication from the Receiver is effective in blocking self-serving behavior on the part of the Dictator: their results confirmed that this was actually the case and allowed them to conclude that a feeling of empathy acted as a proximate factor. Communication led the Dictator to actively think about the Receiver's position and put himself in the other player's shoes. However, it is important to observe, as the two authors correctly pointed out, that whether communication and empathy generate a genuine concern for the welfare of others or not is a subtler and still open question, to be addressed by future research on the theme.

Identification with the Recipient

In many situations, empathy seems to play a role in inducing givers to identify themselves with potential recipients. Several studies on alumni giving to universities suggest that attachment to the organization turns out to be crucial in activating pro-social behavior (Clotfelter, 2003; Frey and Meier, 2004). Andreoni (2006) pointed out that the closer is the charity to their ideal, the more donors are willing to donate. This identification phenomenon appears to closely parallel the well-known 'identifiable victim effect' (Jenni and Loewenstein, 1997; Small and Loewenstein, 2003), which in turn is conceptually related to Schelling's (1968) distinction between an *individual* life and a *statistical* life. Jenni and Loewenstein (1997) reported that in late 1987, Americans were extremely generous towards a child – the 18-month old Jessica McClure – who spent 58 hours trapped in a well, and her family. This famous example of generosity contrasts with the difficulties typically faced in raising money for *preventative* health care for children, which could save hundreds of lives. As the two authors highlighted: 'Identifiable victims seem to produce a greater empathic response, accompanied by greater willingness to make personal sacrifices to provide aid' (p. 236). This empathy seems to play a crucial role in inducing the giver to make significant and seemingly irrational personal sacrifices to help others.

Jenni and Loewenstein (1997) conducted the first experimental test of the identifiable victim effect and focused on its psychological underpinnings. A first potential factor accounting for this effect is *vividness*: when an identifiable individual is at risk of death, the media will provide us with a lot of information on him, so that we may feel as if we know him. As they remarked:

> Situations with identifiable victims are often characterized by all the major factors that convey vividness: the stories are very emotional (victims featured in the media are often particularly sympathetic, helpless, or blameless), we see visual images of the victim in newspapers and on television, and we see the events unfold in real-time – without the emotional distance provided by a historical perspective. For example, we see the picture of the small girl who is trapped in the well, interviews with her tearful parents on television, and live coverage of the desperate attempt to rescue her. These vivid details may result in a perceived familiarity with the victim, making it seem more important to undertake extraordinary measures to save that person. (p. 237)

They further noted that many marketing and fundraising tactics – e.g. the pictures and life stories that accompany requests for money to prevent malnutrition – appear to be based on the view that vividness of an identifiable victim will raise the public's concern and desire to act generously to solve the problem.

Loewenstein et al (2008) stated that people often react to other people at both an emotional and a more deliberative level: tragic events such as mass calamities 'if they occur in distant parts of the world to people with whom we are not familiar, can barely touch our heartstrings, even if we realize at an intellectual level that those victims are highly deserving of our sympathy and aid' (p. 661).[8] Surprisingly, in their experimental investigation Jenni and Loewenstein (1997) did not find that vividness exerted a significant effect on subjects' willingness to support helping actions. By contrast, they discovered that an important factor contributing to explain why people care more about identifiable victims is the so called 'reference group effect': individuals are far more concerned about risks that are concentrated within a geographical region or population (e.g. a disease killing 100 people out of a group of 100) than about risks that are dispersed. Small and Loewenstein (2003) conducted a lab experiment and a field experiment to test the hypothesis that determined victims are perceived as more tangible and hence evoke greater sympathy than indeterminate victims. Their experimental studies, based on subtle manipulations inducing a weak form of identifiability, provided strong support to the hypothesis that identifiability impacts other-regarding behavior.

As far as generous behavior in the lab is concerned, it is important to note that a pure 'taste for altruism' interpretation of the major regularities characterizing the DG has been disputed by Hoffman et al (1994) and Hoffman et al (1996), who hypothesized that by increasing the social distance between the dictator and the experimenters, the amount of transfers would diminish. Their insightful analysis based on a double blind procedure confirmed that an increase in social distance actually led to a decrease to 36 percent of participants who gave something and to 9 percent of the average donation.[9] However, Johannesson and Persson (2000) showed that altruistic behavior does not disappear even after removing any possible form of reciprocity between dictators and recipients. They further increased the social distance between the dictators and the recipients by randomly drawing recipients from the adult general population in Sweden and found that about one third of the dictators still deviated from the standard narrow material self-interest assumption, in line with previous evidence on the emergence of non-reciprocal, other-regarding behavior in the DG.

Some authors claimed that also Hoffman et al's (1996) experimental results on the role of social distance in affecting giving behavior in the DG naturally lend themselves to be interpreted in terms of identifiability. According to Bohnet and Frey (1999), the key effect of a decrease in social distance is the 'other' being transformed from some unknown individual into an 'identifiable victim'. They conducted a DG experiment by varying the degree of social distance and, in line with Small and Loewenstein's (2003) analysis, discovered that with one-sided visual identification, other-regarding behavior is more pronounced if dictators are provided with some information on who their respective recipient is. They viewed their finding as matching the experimental results obtained by Eckel and Grossman (1996), showing that many more dictators (over 73 percent) donated when the recipient was an established charity like the American Red Cross, compared to an anonymous student (only 27 percent). In a similar vein, Branas Garza (2006) found that recipients from poor countries attract a higher level of donations than anonymous subjects.

SOCIAL IMAGE CONCERNS

In interpreting their own laboratory findings, Hoffman et al (1994) interestingly argued that they may depend not on other-regarding preferences, but on a social concern for what others think, and for being held in high regard by others (p. 371; cited in Levitt and List, 2007, p. 161). Ariely et al (2009) proceeded along these lines and, in their experimental work, focused on *image motivation* as a possible motive behind individuals' choice to behave pro-socially. Image (or signaling) motivation refers to an agent's tendency to be motivated to some extent by others' perceptions, that is, her desire to be liked and respected by others. Their argument is that people who care about gaining social approval of their behavior, will try to signal traits defined as 'good' on the basis of the community's prevailing norms and values. Since being altruistic is often seen as 'good' – while being selfish is not – pro-social behavior may follow, as it turns out to be a potentially effective way to signal to others that one is good: 'The desire for social approval implies that, conditional on prosocial activity yielding a positive image, people will act more prosocially in the public sphere than in private settings' (p. 544). They also observed that several field and laboratory studies have found such a pattern, which also helps to shed light on the fact that people seldom donate *anonymously* to charities and several organizations decide to make donors' contributions *visible* to others, sometimes by giving them tokens, such as coffee mugs, as a means to provide public recognition. Ariely et al's (2009) experiment tested the possible detrimental effects that extrinsic incentives can have on pro-social behavior by diluting the signaling value of altruistic behavior (see Bénabou and Tirole, 2006). They found that image motivation has an impact on the decision to act altruistically and that private monetary incentives partially crowd out image motivation. Their results have relevant policy implications: as the authors noted, if a government aims at facilitating the adoption of, say, a new environmentally friendly technology through tax benefits, it should expect the policy to work better if the technology is nonvisible (e.g. water heaters) rather than visible (e.g. hybrid cars).

Lacetera and Macis (2010a) focused on the role of symbolic, non-monetary rewards, such as medals for the donors, affecting blood donation decisions. Their findings indicated that such an incentive scheme, characterized by social recognition value but not by economic value, appears to work fairly well, provided that the prizes are publicly awarded and the recipients' names are published in the local newspaper.[10] Ellingsen and Johannesson (2011) developed a general theoretical model of 'conspicuous generosity' based on the assumption that some individuals are generous, but all of us want to *appear* generous, especially in the eyes of other generous people. By supposing that both donors and recipients are mainly concerned about social esteem (or prestige), they proved that even though non-monetary donations are inefficient, they frequently prevail in equilibrium as they favor signaling.[11] Relatedly, Glazer and Konrad (1996) referred to donors' search for social prestige to explain charities' announcements about received donations. In their work, a charitable gift is characterized as a means to signal one's wealth to others, thus requiring public disclosure of private donations. In a similar vein, Harbaugh (1998) noted that clever charities can capitalize on donors' desire for prestige by manipulating the reports of donors (e.g. reporting donations in categories, rather than reporting exact amounts donated).[12] As suggested by Andreoni (2006), it is even possible that announcing donations triggers competition among donors to appear generous.

As emphasized by Andreoni and Bernheim (2009), studies of field data confirm that the presence of an audience increases charitable giving (Soetevent, 2005). In their paper, they incorporated people's desire to be *perceived* as fair into their utility function and found that in the lab subjects exhibited the predicted behavior to a striking degree: in the DG, their subjects were far more likely to behave fairly as scrutiny increased.[13] Based on personnel, field-generated data from a UK-based fruit farm, Bandiera et al (2005) showed that when other employees can observe their productivity, workers internalize the negative externality imposed on others under a relative compensation scheme. By contrast, such an effect does not occur when employees are prevented from monitoring each other: this reveals that also in the field observability plays a key role in influencing other-regarding behavior. List et al (2004) presented further evidence that the degree of anonymity (both between the experimenter and the subjects as well as among participants) negatively affects individuals' decision to give. Similarly, Haley and Fessler (2005) discovered that introducing in a DG a simple manipulation such as showing a pair of eyes on the computer screen to the dictators significantly increased the level of transfers.

CONCLUSION

Despite the availability of ample evidence on the role played by internal determinants of other-regarding behavior, many important questions remain unanswered. In particular, more work needs to be done on the relationship between motivational factors and social and institutional determinants of altruism. Recent evidence suggests that, in real-world situations, pro-social acts not only depend on individual preferences, but are also contingent on external forces such as social norms (Fershtman et al, 2012) and social pressure (e.g. solicitation efforts by fundraisers; see on this Della Vigna et al, 2012). Further, people's proclivity to behave unselfishly seems to be sensitive to default options (Johnson and Goldstein, 2003) and other people's choices (Martin and Randal, 2008). Though in the last years growing empirical evidence on the channels through which internal and external determinants of giving interact (see e.g. Ariely et al, 2009; Lacetera and Macis, 2010b; Andreoni and Rao, 2011) has been emerging, the nature and extent of such interplays still remain a largely open empirical issue, to be investigated by future research.

NOTES

1. See in particular the central literature in evolutionary biology (Hamilton, 1964; Trivers, 1971; Maynard Smith, 1998) about altruism and its role.
2. Throughout this chapter, expressions such as 'altruism', 'other-regarding' behavior, 'pro-social behavior' and 'non-selfish behavior' will be used interchangeably.
3. See on this Becker's (1974) seminal article.
4. In other words, if individual i is a pure altruist towards individual j, this means that i's utility positively depends on j's utility regardless of the reasons why j's utility grows. By contrast, if i is an impure altruist, j's utility positively affects i's utility only insofar as the increase in j's utility depends on i's own contribution. As noted by some scholars, the notion of warm glow giving risks being elusive due to its being excessively broad, as it potentially includes rather different feelings and emotional states, such as empathy, gratitude, recognition and relief from guilt (Andreoni, 2006; see on this also pp. 12–14, in this chapter). Andreoni and Bernheim (2009) provided possible microfoundations for a theory of warm glow giving based on people's desire to be perceived as fair (see on this pp. 15–16, in this chapter).

5. Therefore, due to its structural features, strictly speaking the DG is not even an experimental game, but a non-strategic individual decision problem.
6. In light of this, Lubian and Zarri (2011) also argued that finding a positive and strong correlation between happiness and tax morale makes it possible to gain further insights on the so called 'hedonistic paradox', stating that *homo oeconomicus*, who seeks happiness for himself, will not find it, while the person who helps others will (Konow and Earley, 2008): the two empirical studies cited in this section confirm this with regard to tax morale, as non-selfish individuals turned out to be happier than less morally concerned ones.
7. However, it is worth noting that today, even though the close relationship between empathy and other-regarding behavior is repeatedly stressed in social and cognitive psychology as well as in neuroscience, the exact mechanism governing the passage from empathy to altruistic behavior is not clear yet (Kirman and Teschl, 2010; Singer and Lamm, 2009).
8. Loewenstein and Small (2007) developed a dual-system model of other-regarding behavior based on the interaction of a highly immature emotional system and a more mature but uncaring deliberative system.
9. Also Levitt and List's (2007) model predicts that, other things equal, the absence of anonymity will be associated with a higher level of pro-social behavior. Cherry et al (2002) showed experimentally that a further decrease in subjects transferring positive amounts takes place when double blind anonymity is coupled with a 'legitimacy' factor. In their study, the dictator's role is made legitimate as dictators earn money answering the questions of a GMAT quiz.
10. The importance of awards – and especially of public awards – in stimulating altruistic action through a boost in the social image of the donors has been neglected for a long time by economists, but has been increasingly investigated in a variety of contexts in the last few years (see on this Neckermann and Frey, 2008).
11. As Ellingsen and Johannesson (2011) remarked, in Andreoni's (1989) classic model of pure and impure altruism, there is no explicit role for the opinion of others.
12. He showed this effect empirically, and Andreoni and Petrie (2004) verified it experimentally.
13. In a similar vein, the model outlined by Levitt and List (2007) assumes that individual moral costs can be affected not only by a concern for others, but also by a concern for one's own appearance. For methodological considerations on the appropriateness of the DG as a tool to measure altruism, see Chapter 10 in this volume.

REFERENCES

Andreoni, J. (1989), 'Giving with impure altruism: applications to charity and Ricardian Equivalence', *Journal of Political Economy*, **97**(6), 1447–1458.
Andreoni, J. (1990), 'Impure altruism and donations to public goods: a theory of warm-glow giving', *Economic Journal*, **100**(401), 464–477.
Andreoni, J. (2006), 'Philanthropy', in Kolm, S.C. and J.M. Ythier (eds), *Handbook of Giving, Reciprocity and Altruism*, volume 2, Amsterdam, Elsevier Science North Holland, pp. 1201–1269.
Andreoni, J., and J. Miller (2002), 'Giving according to GARP: an experimental test of the consistency of preferences for altruism', *Econometrica*, **70**(2), 737–753.
Andreoni, J. and R. Petrie (2004), 'Public goods experiments without confidentiality: a glimpse into fund-raising', *Journal of Public Economics*, **88**, 1605–1623.
Andreoni, J. and B.D. Bernheim (2009), 'Social image and the 50–50 norm: A theoretical and experimental analysis of audience effects', *Econometrica*, **77**, 1607–1636.
Andreoni, J. and J.M. Rao (2011), 'The power of asking: how communication affects selfishness, empathy, and altruism', *Journal of Public Economics*, **95**(7–8), 513–520.
Andreoni, J., Erard, B. and J. Feinstein (1998), 'Tax compliance', *Journal of Economic Literature*, **36**, 818–860.
Ariely, D., Bracha, A. and S. Meier (2009), 'Doing good or doing well? Image motivation and monetary incentives in behaving prosocially', *American Economic Review*, **99**(1), 544–555.
Bandiera, O., Rasul, I. and I. Barankay (2005), 'Social preferences and the response to incentives: evidence from personnel data', *Quarterly Journal of Economics*, **120**(3), 917–962.
Batson, C.D. (1991), *The altruism question: towards a social-psychological answer*, Hillsdale, NJ, USA: Erlbaum.
Becker, G. (1974), 'A theory of social interactions', *Journal of Political Economy*, **82**(6), 1063–1093.
Bénabou, R. and J. Tirole (2006), 'Incentives and prosocial behavior', *American Economic Review*, **96**(5), 1652–1678.

Bohnet, I. and B. Frey (1999), 'Social distance and other-regarding behavior in dictator games: comment', *American Economic Review*, **89**(1), 335–340.

Bowles, S., Gintis, H. (2005), 'Prosocial emotions', in Blume, L. and S. Durlauf (eds), *The Economy as an Evolving Complex System III*, Oxford: Oxford University Press, pp. 339–366.

Branas Garza, P. (2006), 'Poverty in dictator games: awakening solidarity', *Journal of Economic Behavior and Organization*, **60**, 306–320.

Bruni, L. and L. Stanca (2008), 'Watching alone: relational goods, television and happiness', *Journal of Economic Behavior and Organization*, **65**, 506–528.

Cherry, T.L., Frykblom, P. and J.F. Shogren (2002), 'Hardnose the dictator', *American Economic Review*, **92**, 1218–1221.

Clotfelter, C.T. (2003), 'Alumni giving to elite private colleges and universities', *Economics of Education Review*, **22**, 109–120.

Dawes, R. and R.H. Thaler (1988), 'Anomalies: cooperation', *Journal of Economic Perspectives*, **2**(3), 187–197.

Della Vigna, S., List, J. and U. Malmendier (2012), 'Testing for altruism and social pressure in charitable giving', *Quarterly Journal of Economics*, **127**(1), 1–56.

Eckel, C.C. and P.J. Grossman (1996), 'Altruism in anonymous dictator games', *Games and Economic Behavior*, **16**, 181–191.

Ellingsen, T. and M. Johannesson (2011), 'Conspicuous generosity', *Journal of Public Economics*, **95**(9–10), 1131–1143.

Fehr, E., Fischbacher, U. and M. Kosfeld (2005),'Neuroeconomic foundations of trust and social preferences', *American Economic Review*, **95**(2), 346–351.

Fershtman, C., Gneezy, U. and J. List (2012), 'Equity aversion: social norms and the desire to be ahead', *American Economic Journal: Microeconomics*, **4**(4), 131–144.

Forsythe, R., Horowitz, J.L., Savin, N.E. and M. Sefton (1994), 'Fairness in simple bargaining experiments', *Games and Economic Behavior*, **6**(3), 348–369.

Frey, B.S. and S. Meier (2004), 'Social comparisons and pro-social behavior: testing 'conditional cooperation' in a field experiment', *American Economic Review*, **94**(5), 1717–1722.

Glazer, A. and K.A. Konrad (1996), 'A signaling explanation for charity', *American Economic Review*, **86**, 1019–1028.

Haley, K.J. and D.M.T. Fessler (2005), 'Nobody's watching? Subtle cues affect generosity in an anonymous economic game', *Evolution and Human Behavior*, **26**(3), 245–256.

Hamilton, W.D. (1964), 'The genetical evolution of social behaviour I and II', *Journal of Theoretical Biology*, **7**, 1–32.

Harbaugh, W.T. (1998), 'The prestige motive for making charitable transfers', *American Economic Review*, **88**, 277–282.

Harbaugh, W.T., Mayr, U. and D.R. Burghart (2007), 'Neural responses to taxation and voluntary giving reveal motives for charitable donations', *Science*, **316**, 1622–1625.

Hirshleifer, J. (1985), 'The expanding domain of economics', *American Economic Review*, **75**(6), 53–68.

Hoffman, E., McCabe, K., Shachat, K. and V.L. Smith (1994), 'Preferences, property rights and anonymity in bargaining games', *Games and Economic Behavior*, **7**(3), 346–380.

Hoffman, E., McCabe, K. and V.L. Smith (1996), 'Social distance and other-regarding behavior in dictator games', *American Economic Review*, **86**, 653–660.

Jenni, K.E. and G. Loewenstein (1997), 'Explaining the "identifiable victim effect"', *Journal of Risk and Uncertainty*, **14**(3), 235–257.

Johannesson, M. and B. Persson (2000), 'Non-reciprocal altruism in dictator games', *Economics Letters*, **69**, 137–142.

Johnson, E.J. and D. Goldstein (2003), 'Do defaults save lives?', *Science*, **302**, 1338–1339.

Kahneman, D., Knetsch, J. and R. Thaler (1986), 'Fairness and the assumptions of economics', in Hogarth, R.M. and M.W. Reder (eds), *Rational Choice*, Chicago, USA: University of Chicago Press, pp. 101–116.

Kirman, A. and M. Teschl (2010), 'Selfish or selfless? The role of empathy in economics', *Philosophical Transactions of the Royal Society B*, **365**, 303–317.

Konow, J. and J. Earley (2008), 'The hedonistic paradox: is *homo economicus* happier?', *Journal of Public Economics*, **92**, 1–33.

Lacetera, N. and M. Macis (2010a), 'Social image concerns and prosocial behavior: field evidence from a non-linear incentive scheme', *Journal of Economic Behavior and Organization*, **76**, 225–237.

Lacetera, N. and M. Macis (2010b), 'Do all material incentives for pro-social activities backfire? The response to cash and non-cash incentives for blood donations', *Journal of Economic Psychology*, **31**, 738–748.

Levitt, S. and J.A. List (2007), 'What do laboratory experiments tell us about the real world?', *Journal of Economic Perspectives*, **21**(2), 153–174.

List, J.A. (2007), 'On the interpretation of giving in dictator games', *Journal of Political Economy*, **115**, 482–493.

List, J.A., Berrens, R., Bohara, A. and J. Kerkvliet (2004), 'Examining the role of social isolation on stated preferences', *American Economic Review*, **94**(3), 741–752.

Loewenstein, G., Rick, S. and J.D. Cohen (2008), 'Neuroeconomics', *Annual Review of Psychology*, **59**, 647–672.

Loewenstein, G. and D.A. Small (2007), 'The scarecrow and the tin man: the vicissitudes of human sympathy and caring', *Review of General Psychology*, **11**, 112–126.

Lubian, D. and L. Zarri (2011), 'Happiness and tax morale: an empirical analysis', *Journal of Economic Behavior and Organization*, **80**(1), 223–243.

Martin, R. and J. Randal (2008), 'How is donation behavior affected by the donations of others?', *Journal of Economic Behavior and Organization*, **67**(1), 228–238.

Maynard Smith, J. (1998), 'The origin of altruism', *Nature*, **393**, 639–640.

Meier, S. and A. Stutzer (2008), 'Is volunteering rewarding in itself?', *Economica*, **75**, 39–59.

Moll, J., Krueger, F., Zahn, R., Pardini, M., de Oliveira-Souza, R. and J. Grafman (2006), 'Human frontomesolimbic networks guide decisions about charitable donation', *Proceedings of the National Academy of Sciences*, **103**, 15623–15628.

Neckermann, S. and B. Frey (2008), 'Awards as incentives', Institute for Empirical Research in Economics Working Paper No. 334.

Schelling, T.C. (1968), 'The life you save may be your own', in S. Chase (ed.), *Problems in Public Expenditure Analysis*, Washington, DC, USA: Brookings Institution, pp. 127–162.

Singer, T. and E. Fehr (2005), 'The neuroeconomics of mind reading and empathy', *American Economic Review*, **95**, 340–345.

Singer, T. and C. Lamm (2009), 'The social neuroscience of empathy', *Annals of the New York Academy of Sciences*, **1156**, 81–96.

Small, D.A. and G. Loewenstein (2003), 'Helping *a* victim or helping *the* victim: altruism and identifiability', *Journal of Risk and Uncertainty*, **26**(1), 5–16.

Soetevent, A.R. (2005), 'Anonymity in giving in a natural context. A field experiment in Churches', *Journal of Public Economics*, **89**, 457–476.

Thoits, P. and L. Hewitt (2001), 'Volunteer work and well-being', *Journal of Health and Social Behavior*, **42**(2), 115–131.

Trivers, R.L. (1971),'The evolution of reciprocal altruism', *Quarterly Review of Biology*, **46**, 35–57.

2. Altruistic reciprocity
Herbert Gintis

OTHER-REGARDING PREFERENCES AND STRONG RECIPROCITY

By a *self-regarding* actor we mean an individual who maximizes his own payoff in social interactions. A self-regarding actor thus cares about the behavior of and payoffs to the other individuals only insofar as these impact his own payoff. The term 'self-regarding' is more accurate than 'self-interested' because an other-regarding individual is still acting to maximize utility and so can be described as self-interested. For instance, if I get great pleasure from your consumption, my gift to you may be self-interested, even though it is surely other-regarding. We can avoid confusion (and much pseudo-philosophical discussion) by employing the self-regarding/other-regarding terminology. One major result of behavioral game theory is that when modeling market processes with well-specified contracts, such as double auctions (supply and demand) and oligopoly, game-theoretic predictions assuming self-regarding actors are accurate under a wide variety of social settings (see Kachelmaier and Shehata, 1992; Davis and Holt, 1993).

The fact that self-regarding behavior explains market dynamics lends credence to the practice in neoclassical economics of assuming that individuals are self-regarding. However, it by no means justifies 'Homo economicus' because many economic transactions do *not* involve anonymous exchange. This includes employer–employee, creditor–debtor, and firm–client relationships. Nor does this result apply to the welfare implications of economic outcomes (e.g., people may care about the overall degree of economic inequality and/or their positions in the income and wealth distribution), to modeling the behavior of taxpayers (e.g., they may be more or less honest than a self-regarding individual, and they may prefer to transfer resources toward or away from other individuals even at an expense to themselves) or to important aspects of economic policy (e.g., dealing with corruption, fraud, and other breaches of fiduciary responsibility).

Other-regarding preferences were virtually ignored until recently in both economics and biology, although they are standard fare in anthropology, sociology, and social psychology. In economics, the notion that enlightened self-interest allows individuals to cooperate in large groups goes back to Bernard Mandeville's 'private vices, public virtues' (1924 [1705]) and Adam Smith's 'invisible hand' (2000[1759]). The great Francis Ysidro Edgeworth considered self-interest 'the first principle of pure economics' (Edgeworth 1925, p. 173). In biology, the selfishness principle has been touted as a central implication of rigorous evolutionary modeling. In *The Selfish Gene* (1976), for instance, Richard Dawkins asserts, 'We are survival machines – robot vehicles blindly programmed to preserve the selfish molecules known as genes . . . . Let us try to teach generosity and altruism, because we are born selfish.' Similarly, in *The Biology of Moral Systems* (1987, p. 3), R.D. Alexander asserts that 'ethics, morality, human conduct, and the human psyche are to be understood only if societies are seen as collections of individuals seeking their own self-interest.' More poetically, Michael Ghiselin (1974) writes: 'No hint of genuine charity ameliorates our vision of society, once sentimentalism has been laid aside. What passes for cooperation turns out to be a mixture of opportunism and exploitation . . . Scratch an altruist, and watch a hypocrite bleed.'

The Darwinian struggle for existence may explain why the concept of virtue does not add to our understanding of animal behavior in general, but by all available evidence, it is a central aspect of human behavior. The reasons for this are the subject of some speculation (Gintis 2003, 2007), but they come down to the plausible insight that human social life is so complex, and the rewards for pro-social behavior so distant and indistinct, that adherence to general rules of propriety, including the strict control of such deadly sins as anger, avarice, gluttony, and lust, is individually fitness-enhancing (Simon 1990; Gintis 2003).

One salient behavior in social dilemmas revealed by behavioral game theory is *strong reciprocity*. Strong reciprocators come to a social dilemma with a propensity to cooperate (*altruistic cooperation*), respond to cooperative behavior by maintaining or increasing their level of cooperation, and respond to non-cooperative behavior by punishing the 'offenders,' even at a cost to themselves and even when they cannot reasonably expect future personal gains to flow therefrom (*altruistic punishment*). When other forms of punishment are not available, the strong reciprocator responds to defection with defection.

The strong reciprocator is thus neither the selfless altruist of utopian theory, nor the self-regarding individual of traditional economics. Rather, he is a conditional cooperator whose penchant for reciprocity can be elicited under circumstances in which self-regard would dictate otherwise. The positive aspect of strong reciprocity is commonly known as *gift exchange*, in which one individual behaves more kindly than required toward another with the hope and expectation that the other will treat him kindly as well (Akerlof 1982). For instance, in a laboratory-simulated work situation in which employers can pay higher than market-clearing wages in hopes that workers will reciprocate by supplying a high level of effort, the generosity of employers was generally amply rewarded by their workers (Fehr et al, 1997).

A second salient behavior in social dilemmas revealed by behavioral game theory is *inequality aversion*. The inequality-averse individual is willing to reduce his own payoff to increase the degree of equality in the group (whence widespread support for charity and social welfare programs). But he is especially displeased when placed on the *losing side* of an unequal relationship. The inequality-averse individual is willing to reduce his own payoff if that reduces the payoff of relatively favored individuals even more. In short, an inequality-averse individual generally exhibits a *weak* urge to reduce inequality when he is the beneficiary and a *strong* urge to reduce inequality when he is the victim (Loewenstein et al, 1989). Inequality aversion differs from strong reciprocity in that the inequality-averse individual cares only about the distribution of final payoffs and not at all about the role of other players in bringing about this distribution. The strong reciprocator, by contrast, does not begrudge others their payoffs but is sensitive to how fairly he is treated by others.

Self-regarding agents are in common parlance called *sociopaths*. A sociopath (e.g., a sexual predator, a recreational cannibal, or a professional killer) treats others instrumentally, caring only about what he derives from an interaction, whatever the cost to the other party. In fact, for most people, interpersonal relations are guided as much by empathy (and hostility) as by self-regard. The principle of *sympathy* is the guiding theme of Adam Smith's great book, *The Theory of Moral Sentiments*, despite the fact that his self-regarding principle of the 'invisible hand' is one of the central insights of economic theory.

We must of course treat individuals' objectives as a matter of *fact*, not *logic*. We can just as well build models of honesty, promise keeping, regret, strong reciprocity, vindictiveness, status seeking, shame, guilt, and addiction as of choosing a bundle of consumption goods subject to a budget constraint (Gintis 1972a, 1972b, 1974, 1975; Becker and Murphy 1988; Bowles and Gintis 1993; Becker 1996; Becker and Mulligan 1997).

AN ANONYMOUS MARKET EXCHANGE

By *neoclassical economics* I mean the standard fare of microeconomics courses, including the Walrasian general equilibrium model, as developed by Kenneth Arrow, Gérard Debreu, Frank Hahn, Tjalling Koopmans, and others (Arrow 1951; Arrow and Hahn 1971; Koopmans 1957). Neoclassical economic theory holds that in a market for a product, the equilibrium price is at the intersection of the supply and demand curves for the good. It is easy to see that at any other point a self-regarding seller could gain by asking a higher price, or a self-regarding buyer could gain by offering a lower price. This situation was among the first to be simulated experimentally, the neoclassical prediction virtually always receiving strong support (Holt 1995). Here is a particularly dramatic example, provided by Holt et al (1986) (reported by Charles Holt in Kagel and Roth 1995).

In the Holt-Langan-Villamil experiment there are four 'buyers' and four 'sellers.' The good is a chip that the seller can redeem for $5.70 (unless it is sold) but a buyer can redeem for $6.80 at the end of the game. In analyzing the game, we assume throughout that buyers and sellers are self-regarding. In each of the first five rounds, each buyer was informed, privately, that he could redeem up to four chips, while 11 chips were distributed to sellers (three sellers were given three chips each, and the fourth was given two chips). Each player knew only the number of chips in his possession, the number he could redeem, and their redemption value, and did not know the value of the chips to others or how many they possessed or were permitted to redeem. Buyers should be willing to pay up to $6.80 per chip for up to four chips each, and sellers should be willing to sell a chip for any amount at or above $5.70. Total demand is thus 16 for all prices at or below $6.80, and total supply is 11 chips at or above $5.70. Because there is an excess demand for chips at every price between $5.70 and $6.80, the only point of intersection of the demand and supply curves is at the price $p = \$6.80$. The subjects in the game, however, have absolutely no knowledge of aggregate demand and supply because each knows only his own supply of or demand for chips.

The rules of the game are that at any time a seller can call out an asking price for a chip, and a buyer can call out an offer price for a chip. This price remains 'on the table' until it is accepted by another player, or a lower asking price is called out, or a higher offer price is called out. When a deal is made, the result is recorded and that chip is removed from the game. As seen in Figure 2.1, in the first period of play, actual prices were about midway between $5.70 and $6.80. Over the succeeding four rounds the

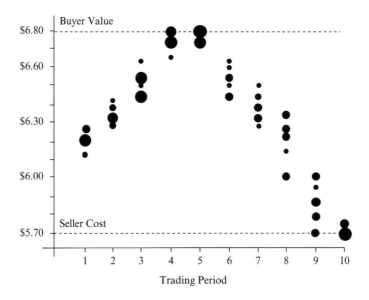

Note: The size of the circle is proportional to the number of trades that occurred at the stated price.

Figure 2.1   The double auction

average price increased until in period 5 prices were very close to the equilibrium price predicted by neoclassical theory.

In period 6 and each of the succeeding four periods, buyers were given the right to redeem a total of 11 chips, and each seller was given four chips. In this new situation, it is clear (to observers who know these facts, though not the subjects in the experiment) that there is now an *excess supply* of chips at each price between $5.70 and $6.80, so supply and demand intersect precisely at $5.70. While sellers, who previously made a profit of about $1.10 per chip in each period, must have been delighted with their additional supplies of chips, succeeding periods witnessed a steady fall in price until in the tenth period the price is close to the neoclassical prediction, and now buyers are earning about $1.10 per chip. We see that even when agents are completely ignorant of macroeconomics conditions of supply and demand, they can move quickly to a market-clearing equilibrium under the appropriate conditions.

THE RATIONALITY OF ALTRUISTIC GIVING

There is nothing irrational about caring for others. But do preferences for altruistic acts entail transitive preferences as required by the notion of rationality in decision theory? Andreoni and Miller (2002) showed that in the case of the Dictator Game, they do. Moreover, there are no known counterexamples.

In the Dictator Game, first studied by Forsythe et al (1994), the experimenter gives a subject, called the Dictator, a certain amount of money and instructs him to give any portion of it he desires to a second, anonymous, subject, called the Receiver. The

Dictator keeps whatever he does not choose to give to the Receiver. Obviously, a self-regarding Dictator will give nothing to the Receiver. Suppose the experimenter gives the Dictator m points (exchangeable at the end of the session for real money) and tells him that the price of giving some of these points to the Receiver is p, meaning that each point the Receiver gets costs the giver p points. For instance, if $p = 4$, then it costs the Dictator four points for each point that he transfers to the Receiver. The Dictator's choices must then satisfy the budget constraint $\pi_s + p\pi_o = m$, where π_s is the amount the Dictator keeps and π_o is the amount the Receiver gets. The question, then, is simply, is there a preference function $u(\pi_s, \pi_o)$ that the Dictator maximizes subject to the budget constraint $\pi_s + p\pi_o = m$? If so, then it is just as rational, from a behavioral standpoint, to care about giving to the Receiver as to care about consuming marketed commodities.

Andreoni and Miller (2002) worked with 176 students in an elementary economics class and had them play the Dictator Game multiple times each, with the price p taking on the values $p = 0.25, 0.33, 0.5, 1, 2, 3$, and 4, with amounts of tokens equaling $m = 40, 60, 75, 80$, and 100. They found that only 18 of the 176 subjects violated GARP (Generalized Axiom of Revealed Preference) at least once and that of these violations, only four were at all significant. By contrast, if choices were randomly generated, we would expect that between 78 percent and 95 percent of subjects would have violated GARP.

As to the degree of altruistic giving in this experiment, Andreoni and Miller found that 22.7 percent of subjects were perfectly selfish, 14.2 percent were perfectly egalitarian at all prices, and 6.2 percent always allocated all the money so as to maximize the total amount won (i.e., when $p > 1$, they kept all the money, and when $p < 1$, they gave all the money to the Receiver).

We conclude from this study that, at least in some cases, and perhaps in all, we can treat altruistic preferences in a manner perfectly parallel to the way we treat money and private goods in individual preference functions. We use this approach in the rest of the problems in this chapter.

CONDITIONAL ALTRUISTIC COOPERATION

Both strong reciprocity and inequality aversion imply *conditional altruistic cooperation* in the form of a predisposition to cooperate in a social dilemma as long as the other players also cooperate, although they have different reasons: the strong reciprocator believes in returning good for good, whatever the distributional implications, whereas the inequality-averse individual simply does not want to create unequal outcomes by making some parties bear a disproportionate share of the costs of cooperation.

Kiyonari et al (2000) ran an experiment with real monetary payoffs using 149 Japanese university students. The experimenters ran three distinct treatments, with about equal numbers of subjects in each treatment. The first treatment was a standard 'simultaneous' Prisoner's Dilemma, the second was a 'second-player' situation in which the subject was told that the first player in the Prisoner's Dilemma had already chosen to cooperate, and the third was a 'first-player' treatment in which the subject was told that his decision to cooperate or defect would be made known to the second player before the latter made his own choice. The experimenters found that 38 percent of the subjects cooperated in the simultaneous treatment, 62 percent cooperated in the second player treatment, and

59 percent cooperated in the first-player treatment. The decision to cooperate in each treatment cost the subject about $5 (600 yen). This shows unambiguously that a majority of subjects were conditional altruistic cooperators (62 percent). Almost as many were not only cooperators, but were also willing to bet that their partners would be (59 percent), provided the latter were assured of not being defected upon, although under standard conditions, without this assurance, only 38 percent would in fact cooperate.

ALTRUISTIC PUNISHMENT

Both strong reciprocity and inequality aversion imply *altruistic punishment* in the form of a predisposition to punish those who fail to cooperate in a social dilemma. The source of this behavior is different in the two cases: the strong reciprocator believes in returning harm for harm, whatever the distributional implications, whereas the inequality-averse individual wants to create a more equal distribution of outcomes even at the cost of lower outcomes for himself and others. The simplest game exhibiting altruistic punishment is the *Ultimatum Game* (Güth et al 1982). Under conditions of anonymity, two players are shown a sum of money, say $10. One of the players, called the Proposer, is instructed to offer any number of dollars, from $1 to $10, to the second player, who is called the Responder. The Proposer can make only one offer and the Responder can either accept or reject this offer. If the Responder accepts the offer, the money is shared accordingly. If the Responder rejects the offer, both players receive nothing. The two players do not face each other again.

There is only *one* Responder strategy that is a best response for a self-regarding individual: accept anything you are offered. Knowing this, a self-regarding Proposer who believes he faces a self-regarding Responder, offers the minimum possible amount, $1, and this is accepted.

However, when actually played, the self-regarding outcome is almost never attained or even approximated. In fact, as many replications of this experiment have documented, under varying conditions and with varying amounts of money, Proposers routinely offer Responders very substantial amounts (50 percent of the total generally being the modal offer) and Responders frequently reject offers below 30 percent (Güth and Tietz 1990; Camerer and Thaler 1995). Are these results culturally dependent? Do they have a strong genetic component or do all successful cultures transmit similar values of reciprocity to individuals? Roth et al (1991) conducted the Ultimatum Game in four different countries (United States, Yugoslavia, Japan, and Israel) and found that while the level of offers differed a small but significant amount in different countries, the probability of an offer being rejected did not. This indicates that both Proposers and Responders share the same notion of what is considered fair in that society and that Proposers adjust their offers to reflect this common notion. The differences in level of offers across countries, by the way, were relatively small. When a much greater degree of cultural diversity is studied, however, large differences in behavior are found, reflecting different standards of what it means to be fair in different types of societies (Henrich et al 2004).

Behavior in the Ultimatum Game thus conforms to the strong reciprocity model: fair behavior in the Ultimatum Game for college students is a 50–50 split. Responders reject offers under 40 percent as a form of altruistic punishment of the norm-violating

Proposer. Proposers offer 50 percent because they are altruistic cooperators, or 40 percent because they fear rejection. To support this interpretation, we note that if the offers in an Ultimatum Game are generated by a computer rather than by the Proposer, and if Responders know this, low offers are rarely rejected (Blount 1995). This suggests that players are motivated by *reciprocity*, reacting to a violation of behavioral norms (Greenberg and Frisch 1972). Moreover, in a variant of the game in which a Responder rejection leads to the Responder getting nothing but allows the Proposer to keep the share he suggested for himself, Responders never reject offers, and proposers make considerably smaller (but still positive) offers (Bolton and Zwick 1995). As a final indication that strong reciprocity motives are operative in this game, after the game is over, when asked why they offered more than the lowest possible amount, Proposers commonly said that they were afraid that Responders will consider low offers unfair and reject them. When Responders rejected offers, they usually claimed they want to punish unfair behavior. In all of the above experiments a significant fraction of subjects (about a quarter, typically) conformed to self-regarding preferences.

STRONG RECIPROCITY IN THE LABOR MARKET

Gintis (1976) and Akerlof (1982) suggested that, in general, employers pay their employees higher wages than necessary in the expectation that workers will respond by providing higher effort than necessary. Fehr et al (1997) (see also Fehr and Gächter 1998) performed an experiment to validate this *legitimation* or *gift exchange* model of the labor market.

The experimenters divided a group of 141 subjects (college students who had agreed to participate in order to earn money) into 'employers' and 'employees.' The rules of the game are as follows. If an employer hires an employee who provides effort e and receives a wage w, his profit is $\pi = 100e - w$. The wage must be between 1 and 100, and the effort is between 0.1 and 1. The payoff to the employee is then $u = w - c(e)$, where $c(e)$ is the cost of effort function shown in Figure 2.2. All payoffs involve real money that the subjects are paid at the end of the experimental session. We call this the *Experimental Labor Market Game*.

The sequence of actions is as follows. The employer first offers a 'contract' specifying a wage w and a desired amount of effort e^*. A contract is made with the first employee who agrees to these terms. An employer can make a contract (w,e^*) with at most one employee. The employee who agrees to these terms receives the wage w and supplies an effort level e that *need not equal the contracted effort* e^*. In effect, there is no penalty if the employee does not keep his promise, so the employee can choose any effort level, $e \in [0.1,1]$, with impunity. Although subjects may play this game several times with different partners, each employer–employee interaction is a one-shot (non-repeated) event. Moreover, the identity of the interacting partners is never revealed.

If employees are self-regarding, they will choose the zero-cost effort level, $e = 0.1$, no matter what wage is offered them. Knowing this, employers will never pay more than the minimum necessary to get the employee to accept a contract, which is 1 (assuming only integer wage offers are permitted).[1] The employee will accept this offer and will set

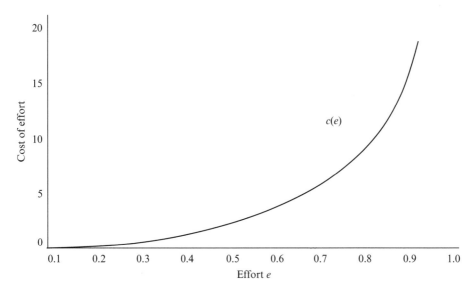

Source: Fehr et al (1997).

Figure 2.2   *The cost-of-effort schedule*

$e = 0.1$. Because $c(0.1) = 0$, the employee's payoff is $u = 1$. The employer's payoff is $\pi = 0.1 \times 00 - 1 = 9$.

In fact, however, this self-regarding outcome rarely occurred in this experiment. The average net payoff to employees was $u = 35$, and the more generous the employer's wage offer to the employee, the higher the effort provided. In effect, employers presumed the strong reciprocity predispositions of the employees, making quite generous wage offers and receiving higher effort, as a means to increase both their own and the employee's payoff, as depicted in Figure 2.3. Similar results have been observed in Fehr, Kirchsteiger, and Riedl (1993, 1998).

Figure 2.3 also shows that, though most employees are strong reciprocators, at any wage rate there still is a significant gap between the amount of effort agreed upon and the amount actually delivered. This is not because there are a few 'bad apples' among the set of employees but because only 26 percent of the employees delivered the level of effort they promised! We conclude that strong reciprocators are inclined to compromise their morality to some extent.

To see if employers are also strong reciprocators, the authors extended the game by allowing the employers to respond reciprocally to the *actual effort choices* of their workers. At a cost of 1, an employer could *increase* or *decrease* his employee's payoff by 2.5. If employers were self-regarding, they would of course do neither because they would not (knowingly) interact with the same worker a second time. However, 68 percent of the time, employers punished employees who did not fulfill their contracts, and 70 percent of the time, employers rewarded employees who overfulfilled their contracts. Employers rewarded 41 percent of employees who *exactly* fulfilled their contracts. Moreover, employees *expected* this behavior on the part of their employers, as shown

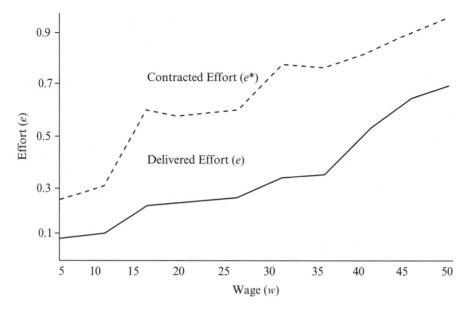

Source: Fehr et al (1997).

Figure 2.3   Relation of contracted and delivered effort to worker wage (141 subjects)

by the fact that their effort levels *increased significantly* when their bosses gained the power to punish and reward them. Underfulfilling contracts dropped from 71 percent to 26 percent of the exchanges, and overfulfilled contracts rose from 3 percent to 38 percent of the total. Finally, allowing employers to reward and punish led to a 40 percent increase in the net payoffs to all subjects, even when the payoff reductions resulting from employer punishment of employees are taken into account.

We conclude from this study that subjects who assume the role of employee conform to internalized standards of reciprocity even when they are certain there are no material repercussions from behaving in a self-regarding manner. Moreover, subjects who assume the role of employer expect this behavior and are rewarded for acting accordingly. Finally, employers reward good behavior and punish bad behavior when they are allowed, and employees expect this behavior and adjust their own effort levels accordingly. In general, then, subjects follow an internalized norm not because it is prudent or useful to do so, or because they will suffer some material loss if they do not, but rather because they desire to do this *for its own sake*.

ALTRUISTIC THIRD-PARTY PUNISHMENT

Pro-social behavior in human society occurs not only because those directly helped and harmed by an individual's actions are likely to reciprocate in kind but also because there are general *social norms* that foster pro-social behavior and many people are willing to bestow favors on someone who conforms to social norms, and to punish someone who does not, even if they are not personally helped or hurt by the individual's actions. In everyday life, third parties who are not the beneficiaries of an individual's pro-social act, help the individual and his family in times of need, preferentially trade favors with the individual, and otherwise reward the individual in ways that are not costly but are nonetheless of great benefit to the cooperator. Similarly, third parties who have not been personally harmed by the selfish behavior of an individual refuse aid even when it is not costly to do so, shun the offender, and approve of the offender's ostracism from beneficial group activities, again at low cost to the third party but at high cost to the offender.

It is hard to conceive of human societies operating at a high level of efficiency in the absence of such third-party reward and punishment. Yet, self-regarding actors will never engage in such behavior if it is at all costly. Fehr and Fischbacher (2004) addressed this question by conducting a series of third-party punishment experiments using the Prisoner's Dilemma and the Dictator Game. The experimenters implemented four experimental treatments in each of which subjects were grouped into threes. In each group, in stage 1, subject A played a Prisoner's Dilemma or the Dictator Game with subject B as the Receiver, and subject C was an outsider whose payoff was not affected by A's decision. Then, in stage two, subject C was endowed with 50 points and allowed to deduct points from subject A such that every three points deducted from A's score cost C one point. In the first treatment, TP-DG, the game was the Dictator Game, in which A was endowed with 100 points, and could give zero, 10, 20, 30, 40, or 50 points to B, who had no endowment.

The second treatment (TP-PD) was the same, except that the game was the Prisoner's Dilemma. Subjects A and B were each endowed with 10 points, and each could either keep the 10 points or transfer them to the other subject, in which case the points were tripled by the experimenter. Thus, if both cooperated, each earned 30 points, and if both defected, each earned 10 points. If one cooperated and one defected, however, the cooperator earned zero points and the defector earned 40 points. In the second stage, C was given an endowment of 40 points, and was allowed to deduct points from A and/or B, just as in the TP-DG treatment.

To compare the relative strengths of second- and third-party punishment in the Dictator Game, the experimenters implemented a third treatment, S&P-DG. In this treatment, subjects were randomly assigned to player A and player B, and A–B pairs were randomly formed. In the first stage of this treatment, each A was endowed with 100 points and each B with none, and the A's played the Dictator Game as before. In the second stage of each treatment, each player was given an additional 50 points, and the B players were permitted to deduct points from A players on the same terms as in the first two treatments. S&P-DG also had two conditions. In the S condition, a B player could punish only his *own* Dictator, whereas in the T condition, a B player could punish only an A player *from another pair*, to which he was randomly assigned by the experimenters. In the T condition, each B player was informed of the behavior of the A player to which he was assigned.

To compare the relative strengths of second and third-party punishment in the Prisoner's Dilemma, the experimenters implemented a fourth treatment, S&P-PG. This was similar to the S&P-DG treatment, except that now they played the Prisoner's Dilemma.[2]

In the first two treatments, because subjects were randomly assigned to positions A, B, and C, the obvious fairness norm is that all should have equal payoffs (an *equality norm*). For instance, if A gave 50 points to B and C deducted no points from A, each subject would end up with 50 points. In the Dictator Game treatment, TP-DG, 60 percent of third parties (Cs) punished Dictators (As) who give less than 50 percent of the endowment to Receivers (Bs). Statistical analysis (ordinary least squares regression) showed that for every point an A kept for himself above the 50–50 split, he was punished an average 0.28 points by C's, leading to a total punishment of $3 \times .28 = 0.84$ points. Thus, a Dictator who kept the whole 100 points would have $0.84 \times 0 = 42$ points deducted by Cs, leaving a meager gain of eight points over equal sharing.

The results for the Prisoner's Dilemma treatment, TP-PD, was similar, with an interesting twist. If one partner in the A–B pair defected and the other cooperated, the defector would have on average 10.05 points deducted by Cs, but if both defected, the punished player lost only an average of 1.75 points. This shows that third parties (Cs) cared not only about the intentions of defectors but also about how much harm they caused and/or how unfair they turned out to be. Overall, 45.8 percent of third parties punished defectors whose partners cooperated, whereas only 20.8 percent of third parties punished defectors whose partners defected.

Turning to the third treatment (S&P-DG), second-party sanctions of selfish Dictators were found to be considerably stronger than third-party sanctions, although both were highly significant. On average, in the first condition, where Receivers could punish their own Dictators, they imposed a deduction of 1.36 points for each point the Dictator kept above the 50–50 split, whereas they imposed a deduction of only 0.62 point per point kept on third-party Dictators. In the final treatment, S&P-PD, defectors were severely punished by both second and third parties, but second-party punishment was again found to be much more severe than third-party punishment. Thus, cooperating subjects deducted on average 8.4 points from a defecting partner, but only 3.09 points from a defecting third party.

This study confirms the general principle that punishing norm violators is very common but not universal, and that individuals are prone to be more harsh in punishing those who hurt them personally, as opposed to violating a social norm that hurts others than themselves.

ALTRUISM AND COOPERATION IN GROUPS

A *Public Goods Game* is an *n*-person game in which, by cooperating, each individual A adds more to the payoff of the other members than A's cost of cooperating, but A's share of the total gains he creates is less than his cost of cooperating. By not contributing, the individual incurs no personal cost and produces no benefit for the group. The Public Goods Game captures many social dilemmas, such as voluntary contribution to team and community goals. Researchers (Ledyard 1995; Yamagishi 1986; Ostrom et al 1992; Gächter and Fehr 1999) uniformly found that groups exhibit a much higher rate of cooperation than can be expected assuming the standard model of the self-regarding actor.

A typical Public Goods Game consists of a number of rounds, say 10. In each round, each subject is grouped with several other subjects – say three others. Each subject is then given a certain number of points, say 20, redeemable at the end of the experimental session for real money. Each subject then places some fraction of his points in a 'common account' and the remainder in the subject's 'private account.' The experimenter then tells the subjects how many points were contributed to the common account and adds to the private account of *each* subject some fraction, say 40 percent, of the total amount in the common account. So if a subject contributes his whole 20 points to the common account, each of the four group members will receive eight points at the end of the round. In effect, by putting the whole endowment into the common account, a player loses 12 points but the other three group members gain in total 24 (8 × 3) points. The players keep whatever is in their private accounts at the end of the round.

A self-regarding player contributes nothing to the common account. However, most of the subjects do not in fact conform to the self-regarding model. Subjects begin by contributing on average about half of their endowments to the public account. The level of contributions decays over the course of the 10 rounds until in the final rounds most players are behaving in a self-regarding manner. This is, of course, exactly what is predicted by the strong reciprocity model. Because they are altruistic contributors, strong reciprocators start out by contributing to the common pool, but in response to the norm violation of the self-regarding types, they begin to refrain from contributing themselves.

How do we know that the decay of cooperation in the Public Goods Game is due to cooperators punishing free riders by refusing to contribute themselves? Subjects often report this behavior retrospectively. More compelling, however, is the fact that when subjects are given a more constructive way of punishing defectors, they use it in a way that helps sustain cooperation (Orbell et al 1986; Sato 1987; Yamagishi 1988a, 1988b, 1992).

Fehr and Gächter (2000) used six- and 10-round Public Goods Games with groups of four, and with costly punishment allowed at the end of each round, employing three different methods of assigning members to groups. There were sufficient subjects to run between 10 and 18 groups simultaneously. Under the Partner treatment, the four subjects remained in the same group for all 10 periods. Under the Stranger treatment, the subjects were randomly reassigned after each round. Finally, under the Perfect Stranger treatment, the subjects were randomly reassigned but assured that they would never meet the same subject more than once.

Fehr and Gächter (2000) performed their experiment for 10 rounds with punishment and 10 rounds without. Their results are illustrated in Figure 2.4. We see that when costly punishment is permitted, cooperation does not deteriorate, and in the Partner game, despite strict anonymity, cooperation increases almost to full cooperation even in the final round. When punishment is not permitted, however, the same subjects experienced the deterioration of cooperation found in previous Public Goods Games. The contrast in cooperation rates between the Partner treatment and the two Stranger treatments is worth noting because the strength of punishment is roughly the same across all treatments. This suggests that the credibility of the punishment threat is greater in the Partner treatment because in this treatment the punished subjects are certain that, once they have been punished in previous rounds, the punishing subjects are in their group. The prosociality impact of strong reciprocity on cooperation is thus more strongly manifested, the more coherent and permanent the group in question.[3]

Many behavioral game theorists have found that, while altruistic punishment increases participation, it often leads to such a high level of punishment that overall average payoffs, net of punishment, are low (Carpenter and Matthews 2005; Page et al 2005; Casari and Luini 2007; Anderson and Putterman 2006; Nikiforakis 2008). Some have

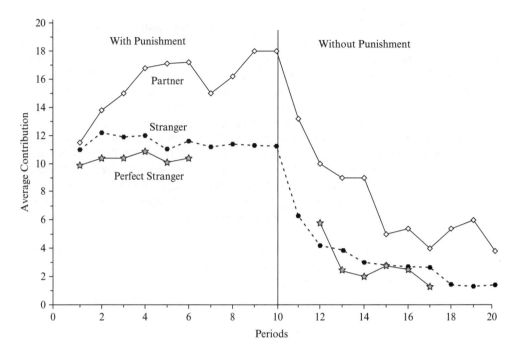

Source: Fehr and Gächter (2000).

Figure 2.4　Average contributions over time in the partner, stranger, and perfect stranger treatments when the punishment condition is played first

interpreted this as showing that strong reciprocity 'could not have evolved,' or 'is not an adaptation.' It is more likely, however, that the problem is with the experiments themselves. These experiments attempt to refute the standard 'homo economicus' model of the self-regarding actor and do not attempt to produce realistic punishment scenarios in the laboratory. In fact, the motive for punishing norm violators is sufficiently strong as to lower overall payoffs when not subject to some social regulation. In real societies, there tends to be collective control over the meting out of punishment, and the excessive zeal of individual punishers is frowned upon and socially punished. Indeed, in one of the rare studies that allowed groups to regulate punishment, Ertan et al (2009) found that groups that voted to permit only punishment of below-average or of average and below-average contributors achieved significantly higher earnings than groups not using punishment.

THE TRUST GAME

In the Trust Game, first studied by Berg et al (1995), subjects are each given a certain endowment, say $10. Subjects are then randomly paired, and one subject in each pair, Alice, is told she can transfer any number of dollars, from zero to 10, to her (anonymous) partner, Bob, and keep the remainder. The amount transferred will be tripled by the experimenter and given to Bob, who can then give any number of dollars back to Alice (this amount is not tripled). If Alice transfers a lot, she is called 'trusting,' and if Bob returns a lot to Alice, he is called 'trustworthy.' In the terminology of this chapter, a trustworthy player is a strong reciprocator, and a trusting player is an individual who expects his partner to be a strong reciprocator.

If all individuals have self-regarding preferences, and if Alice believes Bob has self-regarding preferences, she will give nothing to Bob. On the other hand, if Alice believes Bob can be trusted, she will transfer all $10 to Bob, who will then have $40. To avoid inequality, Bob will give $20 back to Alice. A similar result will obtain if Alice believes Bob is a strong reciprocator. On the other hand, if Alice is altruistic, she may transfer some money to Bob, on the grounds that it is worth more to Bob (because it is tripled) than it is to her, even if she does not expect anything back. It follows that several distinct motivations can lead to a positive transfer of money from Alice to Bob and then back to Alice.

Berg et al (1995) found that, on average, $5.16 was transferred from Alices to Bobs and on average, $4.66 was transferred back from Bobs to Alices. Furthermore, when the experimenters revealed this result to the subjects and had them play the game a second time, $5.36 was transferred from Alices to Bobs, and $6.46 was transferred back from Bobs to Alices. In both sets of games there was a great deal of variability: some Alices transferring everything and some transferring nothing, and some Bobs more than fully repaying their partners, and some giving back nothing.

Note that the term 'trustworthy' applied to Bob is inaccurate because Bob never, either explicitly or implicitly, promised to behave in any particular manner, so there is nothing concrete that Alice might trust him to do. The Trust Game is really a strong reciprocity game in which Alice believes with some probability that Bob is a sufficiently motivated strong reciprocator and Bob either does or does not fulfill this expectation. To turn this into a real Trust Game, the second player should be able to promise to return a certain fraction of the money passed to him.

To tease apart the motivations in the Trust Game, Cox (2004) implemented three treatments, the first of which, treatment *A*, was the Trust Game as described above. Treatment *B* was a Dictator Game exactly like treatment *A*, except that now Bob could not return anything to Alice. Treatment *C* differs from treatment *A* in that each Alice was matched one-to-one with an Alice in treatment *A*, and each Bob was matched one-to-one with a Bob in treatment *A*. Each player in treatment *C* was then given an endowment equal to the amount his corresponding player had after the *A*-to-*B* transfer, but before the *B*-to-*A* transfer in treatment *A*. In other words, in treatment *C*, the Alice group and the Bob group have exactly what they had under treatment *A*, except that Alice now had nothing to do with Bob's endowment, so nothing transferred from Bob to Alice could be accounted for by strong reciprocity.

In all treatments, the rules of the game and the payoffs were accurately revealed to the subjects. However, in order to rule out third-party altruism, the subjects in treatment *C* were not told the reasoning behind the sizes of their endowments. There were about 30 pairs in each treatment, each treatment was played two times, and no subject participated in more than one treatment. The experiment was run double-blind (subjects were anonymous to one another and to the experimenter).

In treatment *B*, the Dictator Game counterpart to the Trust Game, Alice transferred on average $3.63 to player *B*, as opposed to $5.97 in treatment *A*. This shows that $2.34 of the $5.97 transferred to *B* in treatment *A* can be attributed to trust, and the remaining $3.63 to some other motive. Because players *A* and *B* both have endowments of $10 in treatment *B* this other motive cannot be inequality aversion. This transfer may well reflect a reciprocity motive of the form, 'If someone can benefit his partner at a cost that is low compared to the benefit, he should do so, even if he is on the losing end of the proposition.' But we cannot tell from the experiment exactly what the $3.63 represents.

In treatment *C*, the player *B* Dictator Game counterpart to the Trust Game, player *B* returned an average of $2.06, as compared with $4.94 in treatment *A*. In other words, $2.06 of the original $4.94 can be interpreted as a reflection of inequality aversion, and the remaining $2.88 is a reflection of strong reciprocity.

Several other experiments confirm that other-regarding preferences depend on the actions of individuals and not simply on the distribution of payoffs, as is the case with inequality aversion. Charness and Haruvy (2002), for instance, developed a version of the gift exchange labor market capable of testing self-regarding preferences, pure altruism, inequality aversion, and strong reciprocity simultaneously. Strong reciprocity had by far the greatest explanatory value.

CHARACTER VIRTUES

Character virtues are ethically desirable behavioral regularities that individuals value for their own sake, while having the property of facilitating cooperation and enhancing social efficiency. Character virtues include *honesty, loyalty, trustworthiness, promise keeping,* and *fairness.* Unlike such other-regarding preferences as strong reciprocity and empathy, these character virtues operate without concern for the individuals with whom one interacts. An individual is honest in his transactions because this is a desired state of being, not because he has any particular regard for those with whom he transacts. Of course, the sociopath 'Homo economicus' is honest only when it serves his material interests to be so, whereas the rest of us are at times honest even when it is costly to be so and even when no one but us could possibly detect a breach.

Common sense, as well as the experiments described below, indicate that honesty, fairness, and promise keeping are not absolutes. If the cost of virtue is sufficiently high, and the probability of detection of a breach of virtue is sufficiently small, many individuals will behave dishonestly. When one is aware that others are unvirtuous in a particular region of their lives (e.g., marriage, taxpaying, obeying traffic rules, accepting bribes), one is more likely to allow one's own virtue to lapse. Finally, the more easily one can delude oneself into inaccurately classifying an unvirtuous act as virtuous, the more likely one is to allow oneself to carry out such an act.

One might be tempted to model honesty and other character virtues as *self-constituted constraints* on one's set of available actions in a game, but a more fruitful approach is to include the state of being virtuous in a certain way as an argument in one's preference function, to be traded off against other valuable objects of desire and personal goals. In this respect, character virtues are in the same category as ethical and religious preferences and are often considered subcategories of the latter.

Numerous experiments indicate that most subjects are willing to sacrifice material rewards to maintain a virtuous character even under conditions of anonymity. Sally (1995) undertook a meta-analysis of 137 experimental treatments, finding that face-to-face communication, in which subjects are capable of making verbal agreements and promises, was the strongest predictor of cooperation. Of course, face-to-face interaction violates anonymity and has other effects besides the ability to make promises. However, both Bochet et al (2006) and Brosig et al (2003) report that only the ability to exchange verbal information accounts for the increased cooperation.

A particularly clear example of such behavior is reported by Gneezy (2005), who studied 450 undergraduate participants paired off to play three games of the following form, all payoffs to which were of the form (b,a), where player 1, Bob, receives b and player 2, Alice, receives a. In all games, Bob was shown two pairs of payoffs, $A:(x,y)$ and $B:(z,w)$ where x, y, z, and w are amounts of money with $x < z$ and $y > w$, so in all cases B is better for Bob and A is better for Alice. Bob could then say to Alice, who could not see the amounts of money, either 'Option A will earn you more money than option B,' or 'Option B will earn you more money than option A.' The first game was $A:(5,6)$ vs. $B:(6,5)$ so Bob could gain 1 by lying and being believed while imposing a cost of 1 on Alice. The second game was $A:(5,15)$ vs. $B:(6,5)$, so Bob could gain 1 by lying and being believed, while still imposing a cost of 10 on Alice. The third game was $A:(5,15)$ vs. $B:(15,5)$, so Bob could gain 10 by lying and being believed, while imposing a cost of 10 on Alice.

Before starting play, Gneezy asked the various Bobs whether they expected their advice to be followed. He induced honest responses by promising to reward subjects whose guesses were correct. He found that 82 percent of Bobs expected their advice to be followed (the actual number was 78 percent). It follows from the Bobs' expectations that if they were self-regarding, they would always lie and recommend B to Alice.

The experimenters found that, in game 2, where lying was very costly to Alice and the gain from lying was small for Bob, only 17 percent of Bobs lied. In game 1, where the cost of lying to Alice was only 1 but the gain to Bob was the same as in game 2, 36 percent of Bobs lied. In other words, Bobs were loathe to lie but considerably more so when it was costly to Alices. In game 3, where the gain from lying was large for Bob and equal to the loss to Alice, fully 52 percent of Bobs lied. This shows that many subjects are willing to sacrifice material gain to avoid lying in a one-shot anonymous interaction, their willingness to lie increasing with an increased cost to them of truth telling, and decreasing with an increased cost to their partners of being deceived. Similar results were found by Boles et al (2000) and Charness and Dufwenberg (2006). Gunnthorsdottir et al (2002) and Burks et al (2003) have shown that a socio-psychological measure of 'Machiavellianism' predicts which subjects are likely to be trustworthy and trusting.

THE SITUATIONAL CHARACTER OF PREFERENCES

This chapter has deepened the rational actor model, allowing it to apply to situations of strategic interaction. We have found that preferences are other-regarding as well as self-regarding. Humans have social preferences that facilitate cooperation and exchange, as well as moral preferences for such personal character virtues as honesty and loyalty. These extended preferences doubtless contribute to long-run individual well-being

(Konow and Earley, 2008). However, social and moral preferences are certainly not merely instrumental, because individuals exercise these preferences even when no long-run benefits can accrue.

Despite this deepening of rational choice, we have conserved the notion that the individual has an immutable underlying preferences ordering that entails situation-ally specific behaviors, depending on the particular strategic interaction involved. Our analysis, however, is predicated upon the denial of this immutability. Rather, we suggest that generally a social situation, which we call a *frame*, is imbued with a set of custom-ary social norms that individuals often desire to follow simply because these norms are socially appropriate in the given frame. To the extent that this occurs, preferences them-selves, and not just their behavioral implications, are situationally specific. The desire to conform to the moral and conventional standards that people associate with particular social frames thus represents a *meta-preference* that regulates revealed preferences in specific social situations.

We present two studies by Dana et al (2006) that illustrate the situational nature of preferences and the desire to conform to social norms (which we term *normative pre-disposition*. The first study used 80 Carnegie-Mellon University undergraduate subjects who were divided into 40 pairs to play the Dictator Game, one member of each pair being randomly assigned to be the Dictator, the other to be the Receiver. Dictators were given $10, and asked to indicate how many dollars each wanted to give the Receiver, but the Receivers were not informed they were playing a Dictator Game. After making their choices, but before informing the Receivers about the game, the Dictators were presented with the option of accepting $9 rather than playing the game. They were told that if a Dictator took this option, the Receiver would never find out that the game was a possibility and would go home with their show-up fee alone.

Eleven of the 40 Dictators took this exit option, including two who had chosen to keep all of the $10 in the Dictator Game. Indeed, 46 percent of the Dictators who had chosen to give a positive amount to their Receivers took the exit option in which the Receiver got nothing. This behavior is not compatible with the concept of immutable preferences for a division of the $10 between the Dictator and the Receiver because individuals who would have given their Receiver a positive amount in the Dictator Game instead gave them nothing by avoiding playing the game, and individuals who would have kept the whole $10 in the Dictator Game were willing to take a $1 loss not to have to play the game.

To rule out other possible explanations of this behavior, the authors executed a second study in which the Dictator was told that the Receiver would never find out that a Dictator Game had been played. Thus, if the Dictator gave $5 to the Receivers, the latter would be given the $5 but would be given no reason why. In this new study, only one of 24 Dictators chose to take the $9 exit option. Note that in this new situation, the same social situation between Dictator and Receiver obtains both in the Dictator Game and in the exit option. Hence, there is no difference in the norms applying to the two options, and it does not make sense to forfeit $1 simply to have the game not called a Dictator Game.

The most plausible interpretation of these results is that many subjects felt obliged to behave according to certain norms when playing the Dictator Game, or violated these norms in an uncomfortable way, and were willing to pay simply not to be in a situation subject to these norms.

THE DARK SIDE OF ALTRUISTIC COOPERATION

The human capacity to cooperate in large groups by virtue of pro-social preferences extends not only to exploiting nature but also to conquering other human groups as well. Indeed, even a slight hint that there may be a basis for inter-group competition induces individuals to exhibit insider loyalty and outsider hostility (Dawes et al 1988; Tajfel 1970; Tajfel et al 1971; Turner 1984). Group members then show more generous treatment to in-group members than to out-group members even when the basis for group formation is arbitrary and trivial (Yamagishi et al 1999; Rabbie et al 1989).

An experiment conducted by Abbink et al (2010), using undergraduate students recruited at the University of Nottingham, is an especially dramatic example of the tendency for individuals willingly to escalate a conflict well beyond the point of serving their interests in terms of payoffs alone. Experimenters first had pairs of students $i = 1,2$ play the following game. Each individual was given 1000 points and could spend any portion of it, x_i, on 'armaments.' The probability of player i winning was then set to $p_i = x_i/(x_1 + x_2)$.

The teams spent about 600 percent of the optimum in the first few periods, and this declined fairly steadily to 250 percent of the optimum in the final few periods. This experiment showcases the tendency of subjects to overspend vastly for competitive purposes, although familiarity with the game strongly dampens this tendency, and had the participants played another 20 periods, we might have seen an approach to best response behavior.

However, the experimenters followed up the above treatments with another in which, after each round, players were allowed to punish other players based on the level of their contributions in the previous period. The punishment was costly, three tokens taken from the punishee costing the punisher one token. This, of course, mirrors the Public Goods Game with costly punishment, and indeed this game does have a public goods aspect since the more one team member contributes, the less the best response contribution of the others, because the optimal total contribution of team members is 250, no matter how it is divided up among the members.

In this new situation, competition with punishment, spending started at 640 percent of the best response level, rose to a high of 1000 percent of this level, and settled at 900 percent of the best response level in period 7, showing no tendency to increase or decrease in the remaining 13 periods. This striking behavior shows that the internal dynamics of altruistic punishment are capable of sustaining extremely high levels of combat expenditure far in excess of the material payoff-maximizing level. While much more work in this area remains to be done, it appears that the same pro-social preferences that allow humans to cooperate in large groups of unrelated individuals are also turned into the goal of mutual self-destruction with great ease.

NORMS OF COOPERATION: CROSS-CULTURAL VARIATION

Experimental results in the laboratory would not be very interesting if they did not aid us in understanding and modeling real-life behavior. There are strong and consistent indications that the external validity of experimental results is high. For instance,

Binswanger (1980) and Binswanger and Sillers (1983) used survey questions concerning attitudes towards risk and experimental lotteries with real financial rewards to successfully predict the investment decisions of farmers. Glaeser et al (2000) explored whether experimental subjects who trusted others in the Trust Game also behaved in a trusting manner with their own personal belongings. The authors found that experimental behavior was a quite good predictor of behavior outside the laboratory, while the usual measures of trust, based on survey questions, provided virtually no information. Genesove and Mayer (2001) showed that loss aversion determined seller behavior in the 1990s Boston housing market. Condominium owners subject to nominal losses set selling prices equal to the market rate plus 25 percent to 35 percent of the difference between their purchase price and the market price and sold at prices 3 percent to 18 percent of this difference. These findings show that loss aversion is not confined to the laboratory but affects behavior in a market in which very high financial gains and losses can occur.

Similarly, Karlan (2005) used the Trust Game and the Public Goods Game to predict the probability that loans made by a Peruvian microfinance lender would be repaid. He found that individuals who were trustworthy in the Trust Game were less likely to default. Also, Ashraf et al (2006) studied Phillipino women, identifying through a baseline survey those women exhibited a lower discount rate for future relative to current tradeoffs. These women were indeed significantly more likely to open a savings account, and after 12 months, average savings balances increased by 81 percentage points for those clients assigned to a treatment group based on their laboratory performance, relative to those assigned to the control group. In a similar vein, Fehr and Goette (2007) found that in a group of bicycle messengers in Zürich, those and only those who exhibited loss aversion in a laboratory survey also exhibited loss aversion when faced with real-life wage rate changes. For additional external validity studies, see Andreoni et al (1998) on tax compliance, Bewley (2000) on fairness in wage setting, and Fong et al (2005) on support for income redistribution.

In one very important study, Herrmann et al (2008) had subjects play the Public Goods Game with punishment with 16 subject pools in 15 different countries with highly varying social characteristics (one country, Switzerland, was represented by two subject pools, one in Zurich and one in St. Gallen). To minimize the social diversity among subject pools, they used university students in each country. The phenomenon they aimed to study was *antisocial punishment*.

The phenomenon itself was first noted by Cinyabuguma et al (2006), who found that some free riders, when punished, responded not by increasing their contributions, but rather by punishing the high contributors! The ostensible explanation of this perverse behavior is that some free riders believe it is their personal right to free-ride if they so desire, and they respond to the 'bullies' who punish them in a strongly reciprocal manner – they retaliate against their persecutors. The result, of course, is a sharp decline in the level of cooperation for the whole group.

This behavior was later reported by Denant-Boemont et al (2007) and Nikiforakis (2008), but because of its breadth, the Herrmann et al (2008) study is distinctive for its implications for social theory. They found that in some countries, antisocial punishment was very rare, while in others it was quite common. As can be seen in Figure 2.5, there is a strong negative correlation between the amount of anti-punishment exhibited and

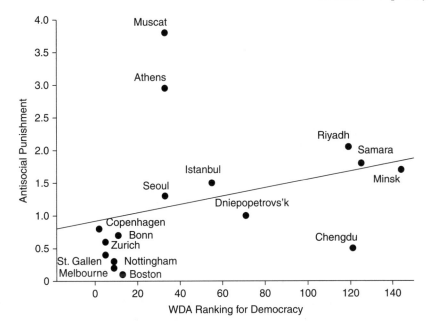

Source: Statistics from Herrmann et al (2008).

Figure 2.5   Countries judged highly democratic

the World Democracy Audit's assessment of the level of democratic development of the society involved.

Figure 2.6 shows that a high level of antisocial punishment in a group translates into a low level of overall cooperation. The researchers first ran 10 rounds of the Public Goods Game without punishment (the *N* condition), and then another 10 rounds with punishment (the *P* condition). The figures show clearly that the more democratic countries enjoy a higher average payoff from payoffs in the Public Goods Game.

How might we explain this highly contrasting social behavior in university students in democratic societies with advanced market economies on the one hand, and more traditional societies based on authoritarian and parochial social institutions on the other? The success of democratic market societies may depend critically upon moral virtues as well as material interests, so the depiction of economic actors as 'homo economicus' is as incorrect in real life as it is in the laboratory. These results indicate that individuals in modern democratic capitalist societies have a deep reservoir of public sentiment that can be exhibited even in the most impersonal interactions with unrelated others. This reservoir of moral predispositions is based upon an innate pro-sociality that is a product of our evolution as a species, as well as the uniquely human capacity to internalize norms of social behavior. Both forces predispose individuals to behave morally, even when this conflicts with their material interests, and to react to public disapprobation for free-riding with shame and penitence rather than antisocial self-aggrandizement.

This experiment shows that laboratory games can be deployed to shed light on real-life

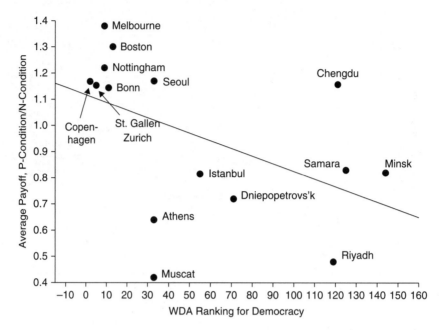

Source: Statistics from Herrmann et al (2008).

Figure 2.6   Antisocial punishment leads to low payoffs

social regularities that cannot be explained by participant observation or cross-country statistical analysis alone.

NOTES

1. This is because the experimenters created more employees than employers, thus ensuring an excess supply of employees.
2. The experimenters never used value-laden terms such as 'punish' but rather used neutral terms, such as 'deduct points.'
3. In Fehr and Gächter (2002), the experimenters reverse the order of the rounds with and without punishment to be sure that the decay in the 'without punishment' phase was not due to its occurring at the end rather than at the start of the game. It was not.

REFERENCES

Abbink, Klaus, Jordi Brandts, Benedikt Herrmann and Henrik Orzen (2010), 'Inter-Group Conflict and Intra-Group Punishment in an Experimental Contest Game,' *American Economic Review* 100,1:420–447.
Akerlof, George A. (1982), 'Labor Contracts as Partial Gift Exchange,' *Quarterly Journal of Economics* 97,4 (November):543–569.
Alexander, R.D. (1987), *The Biology of Moral Systems* (New York: Aldine).
Anderson, Christopher and Louis Putterman (2006), 'Do Non-strategic Sanctions Obey the Law of Demand? The Demand for Punishment in the Voluntary Contribution Mechanism,' *Games and Economic Behavior* 54,1:1–24.

Andreoni, James and John H. Miller (2002), 'Giving According to GARP: An Experimental Test of the Consistency of Preferences for Altruism,' *Econometrica* 70,2:737–753.

Andreoni, James, Brian Erard and Jonathan Feinstein (1998), 'Tax Compliance,' *Journal of Economic Literature* 36,2 (June):818–860.

Arrow, Kenneth J. (1951), 'An Extension of the Basic Theorems of Classical Welfare Economics,' in J. Neyman (ed.) *Proceedings of the Second Berkeley Symposium on Mathematical Statistics and Probability* (Berkeley: University of California Press) pp. 507–532.

Arrow, Kenneth J. and Frank Hahn (1971), *General Competitive Analysis* (San Francisco: Holden-Day).

Ashraf, Nava, Dean S. Karlan and Wesley Yin (2006), 'Tying Odysseus to the Mast: Evidence from a Commitment Savings Product in the Philippines,' *Quarterly Journal of Economics* 121,2:635–672.

Becker, Gary S. (1996), *Accounting for Tastes* (Cambridge: Harvard University Press).

Becker, Gary S. and Kevin M. Murphy (1988), 'A Theory of Rational Addiction,' *Journal of Political Economy* 96,4 (August):675–700.

Becker, Gary S. and Casey B. Mulligan (1997), 'The Endogenous Determination of Time Preference,' *Quarterly Journal of Economics* 112,3 (August):729–759.

Berg, Joyce, John Dickhaut and Kevin McCabe (1995), 'Trust, Reciprocity, and Social History,' *Games and Economic Behavior* 10:122–142.

Bewley, Truman F. (2000), *Why Wages Don't Fall during a Recession* (Cambridge: Cambridge University Press).

Binswanger, Hans (1980), 'Risk Attitudes of Rural Households in Semi-Arid Tropical India,' *American Journal of Agricultural Economics* 62,3:395–407.

Binswanger, Hans and Donald Sillers (1983), 'Risk Aversion and Credit Constraints in Farmers' Decision-Making: A Reinterpretation,' *Journal of Development Studies* 20,1:5–21.

Blount, Sally (1995), 'When Social Outcomes Aren't Fair: The Effect of Causal Attributions on Preferences,' *Organizational Behavior Human Decision Processes* 63,2 (August):131–144.

Bochet, Olivier, Talbot Page and Louis Putterman (2006), 'Communication and Punishment in Voluntary Contribution Experiments,' *Journal of Economic Behavior and Organization* 60,1:11–26.

Boles, Terry L., Rachel T.A. Croson and J. Keith Murnighan (2000), 'Deception and Retribution in Repeated Ultimatum Bargaining,' *Organizational Behavior and Human Decision Processes* 83,2:235–259.

Bolton, Gary E. and Rami Zwick (1995), 'Anonymity versus Punishment in Ultimatum Games,' *Games and Economic Behavior* 10:95–121.

Bowles, Samuel and Herbert Gintis (1993), 'The Revenge of Homo economicus: Contested Exchange and the Revival of Political Economy,' *Journal of Economic Perspectives* 7,1 (Winter):83–102.

Brosig, J., A. Ockenfels and J. Weimann (2003), 'The Effect of Communication Media on Cooperation,' *German Economic Review* 4:217–242.

Burks, Stephen V., Jeffrey P. Carpenter and Eric Verhoogen (2003), 'Playing Both Roles in the Trust Game,' *Journal of Economic Behavior and Organization* 51:195–216.

Camerer, Colin and Richard H. Thaler (1995), 'Ultimatums, Dictators, and Manners,' *Journal of Economic Perspectives* 9,2:209–219.

Carpenter, Jeffrey P. and Peter Matthews (2005), 'Norm Enforcement: Anger, Indignation, or Reciprocity,' Department of Economics, Middlebury College, Working Paper 0503.

Casari, Marco and Luigi Luini (2007), 'Group Cooperation under Alternative Peer Punishment Technologies: An Experiment', Department of Economics, University of Siena.

Charness, Gary and Ernan Haruvy (2002), 'Altruism, Equity, and Reciprocity in a Gift-Exchange Experiment: An Encompassing Approach,' *Games and Economic Behavior* 40:203–231.

Charness, Gary and Martin Dufwenberg (2006), 'Promises and Partnership,' *Econometrica* 74,6 (November):1579–1601.

Cinyabuguma, Matthias, Talbot Page and Louis Putterman (2006), 'Can Second-Order Punishment Deter Perverse Punishment?' *Experimental Economics* 9:265–279.

Cox, James C. (2004), 'How to Identify Trust and Reciprocity,' *Games and Economic Behavior* 46:260–281.

Dana, Justin, Daylian M. Cain and Robyn M. Dawes (2006), 'What You Don't Know Won't Hurt Me: Costly (But Quiet) Exit in Dictator Games,' *Organizational Behavior and Human Decision Processes* 100:193–201.

Davis, Douglas D. and Charles A. Holt (1993), *Experimental Economics* (Princeton: Princeton University Press).

Dawes, Robyn M., A.J.C. van de Kragt and John M. Orbell (1988), 'Not me or Thee but We: The Importance of Group Identity in Eliciting Cooperation in Dilemma Situations: Experimental Manipulations,' *Acta Psychologica* 68:83–97.

Dawkins, Richard (1976), *The Selfish Gene* (Oxford: Oxford University Press).

Denant-Boemont, Laurent, David Masclet and Charles Noussair (2007), 'Punishment, Counterpunishment and Sanction Enforcement in a Social Dilemma Experiment,' *Economic Theory* 33,1 (October):145–167.

Edgeworth, Francis Ysidro (1925), *Papers Relating to Political Economy I* (London: Macmillan).

Ertan, Arhan, Talbot Page and Louis Putterman (2009), 'Who to Punish? Individual Decisions and Majority Rule in the Solution of Free Rider Problems,' *European Economic Review* 3:495–511.

Fehr, Ernst and Simon Gächter (1998), 'How Effective Are Trust- and Reciprocity-Based Incentives?' in Louis Putterman and Avner Ben-Ner (eds) *Economics, Values and Organizations* (New York: Cambridge University Press) pp. 337–363.

Fehr, Ernst and Simon Gächter (2000), 'Cooperation and Punishment,' *American Economic Review* 90,4 (September):980–994.

Fehr, Ernst and Lorenz Goette (2007), 'Do Workers Work More If Wages Are High? Evidence from a Randomized Field Experiment,' *American Economic Review* 97,1 (March):298–317.

Fehr, Ernst and Simon Gächter (2002), 'Altruistic Punishment in Humans,' *Nature* 415 (10 January):137–140.

Fehr, Ernst and Urs Fischbacher (2004), 'Third Party Punishment and Social Norms,' *Evolution Human Behavior* 25:63–87.

Fehr, Ernst, Georg Kirchsteiger and Arno Riedl (1993), 'Does Fairness Prevent Market Clearing?' *Quarterly Journal of Economics* 108,2:437–459.

Fehr, Ernst, Simon Gächter and Georg Kirchsteiger (1997), 'Reciprocity as a Contract Enforcement Device: Experimental Evidence,' *Econometrica* 65,4 (July):833–860.

Fehr, Ernst, Georg Kirchsteiger and Arno Riedl (1998), 'Gift Exchange and Reciprocity in Competitive Experimental Markets,' *European Economic Review* 42,1:1–34.

Fong, Christina M., Samuel Bowles and Herbert Gintis (2005), 'Reciprocity and the Welfare State,' in Herbert Gintis, Samuel Bowles, Robert Boyd and Ernst Fehr (eds) *Moral Sentiments and Material Interests: On the Foundations of Cooperation in Economic Life* (Cambridge, MA: MIT Press).

Forsythe, Robert, Joel Horowitz, N. E. Savin and Martin Sefton (1994), 'Replicability, Fairness and Pay in Experiments with Simple Bargaining Games,' *Games and Economic Behavior* 6,3 (May):347–369.

Gächter, Simon and Ernst Fehr (1999), 'Collective Action as a Social Exchange,' *Journal of Economic Behavior and Organization* 39,4 (July):341–369.

Genesove, David and Christopher Mayer (2001), 'Loss Aversion and Seller Behavior: Evidence from the Housing Market,' *Quarterly Journal of Economics* 116,4 (November):1233–1260.

Ghiselin, Michael T. (1974), *The Economy of Nature and the Evolution of Sex* (Berkeley: University of California Press).

Gintis, Herbert (1972a), 'Consumer Behavior and the Concept of Sovereignty,' *American Economic Review* 62,2 (May):267–278.

Gintis, Herbert (1972b), 'A Radical Analysis of Welfare Economics and Individual Development,' *Quarterly Journal of Economics* 86,4 (November):572–599.

Gintis, Herbert (1974), 'Welfare Criteria with Endogenous Preferences: The Economics of Education,' *International Economic Review* 15,2 (June):415–429.

Gintis, Herbert (1975), 'Welfare Economics and Individual Development: A Reply to Talcott Parsons,' *Quarterly Journal of Economics* 89,2 (February):291–302.

Gintis, Herbert (1976), 'The Nature of the Labor Exchange and the Theory of Capitalist Production,' *Review of Radical Political Economics* 8,2 (Summer):36–54.

Gintis, Herbert (2003), 'The Hitchhiker's Guide to Altruism: Genes, Culture, and the Internalization of Norms,' *Journal of Theoretical Biology* 220,4:407–418.

Gintis, Herbert (2007), 'A Framework for the Unification of the Behavioral Sciences,' *Behavioral and Brain Sciences* 30,1:1–61.

Glaeser, Edward L., David Laibson, Jose A. Scheinkman and Christine L. Soutter (2000), 'Measuring Trust,' *Quarterly Journal of Economics* 65:622–846.

Gneezy, Uri (2005), 'Deception: The Role of Consequences,' *American Economic Review* 95,1 (March):384–394.

Greenberg, M.S. and D.M. Frisch (1972), 'Effect of Intentionality on Willingness to Reciprocate a Favor,' *Journal of Experimental Social Psychology* 8:99–111.

Gunnthorsdottir, Anna, Kevin McCabe and Vernon L. Smith (2002), 'Using the Machiavellianism Instrument to Predict Trustworthiness in a Bargaining Game,' *Journal of Economic Psychology* 23:49–66.

Güth, Werner and Reinhard Tietz (1990), 'Ultimatum Bargaining Behavior: A Survey and Comparison of Experimental Results,' *Journal of Economic Psychology* 11:417–449.

Güth, Werner, R. Schmittberger and B. Schwarze (1982), 'An Experimental Analysis of Ultimatum Bargaining,' *Journal of Economic Behavior and Organization* 3 (May):367–388.

Henrich, Joseph, Robert Boyd, Samuel Bowles, Colin Camerer, Ernst Fehr and Herbert Gintis (2004), *Foundations of Human Sociality: Economic Experiments and Ethnographic Evidence from Fifteen Small-Scale Societies* (Oxford: Oxford University Press).

Herrmann, Benedikt, Christian Thoni and Simon Gächter (2008), 'Anti-Social Punishment across Societies,' *Science* 319 (7 March):1362–1367.

Holt, Charles A. (1995), *Industrial Organization: A Survey of Laboratory Research* (Princeton: Princeton University Press).

Holt, Charles A., Loren Langan and Anne Villamil (1986), 'Market Power in an Oral Double Auction,' *Economic Inquiry* 24:107–123.

Kachelmaier, S.J. and M. Shehata (1992), 'Culture and Competition: A Laboratory Market Comparison between China and the West,' *Journal of Economic Behavior and Organization* 19:145–168.

Kagel, John H. and Alvin E. Roth (1995), *Handbook of Experimental Economics* (Princeton: Princeton University Press).

Karlan, Dean S. (2005), 'Using Experimental Economics to Measure Social Capital and Predict Real Financial Decisions,' *American Economic Review* 95,5 (December):1688–1699.

Kiyonari, Toko, Shigehito Tanida and Toshio Yamagishi (2000), 'Social Exchange and Reciprocity: Confusion or a Heuristic?' *Evolution and Human Behavior* 21:411–427.

Konow, James and Joseph Earley (2008), 'The Hedonistic Paradox: Is Homo Economicus Happier?' *Journal of Public Economics* 92:1–33.

Koopmans, Tjalling (1957), 'Allocation of Resources and the Price System,' in *Three Essays on the State of Economic Science* (New York: McGraw-Hill) pp. 4–95.

Ledyard, J.O. (1995), 'Public Goods: A Survey of Experimental Research,' in John H. Kagel and Alvin E. Roth (eds) *The Handbook of Experimental Economics* (Princeton: Princeton University Press) pp. 111–194.

Loewenstein, George F., Leigh Thompson and Max H. Bazerman (1989), 'Social Utility and Decision Making in Interpersonal Contexts,' *Journal of Personality and Social Psychology* 57,3:426–441.

Mandeville, Bernard (1924[1705]), *The Fable of the Bees: Private Vices, Public Benefits* (Oxford: Clarendon).

Nikiforakis, Nikos S. (2008), 'Punishment and Counter-punishment in Public Goods Games: Can We Still Govern Ourselves?' *Journal of Public Economics* 92,1–2:91–112.

Orbell, John M., Robyn M. Dawes and J.C. van de Kragt (1986), 'Organizing Groups for Collective Action,' *American Political Science Review* 80 (December):1171–1185.

Ostrom, Elinor, James M. Walker and Roy Gardner (1992), 'Covenants with and without a Sword: Self-Governance Is Possible,' *American Political Science Review* 86,2 (June):404–417.

Page, Talbot, Louis Putterman and Bulent Unel (2005), 'Voluntary Association in Public Goods Experiments: Reciprocity, Mimicry, and Efficiency,' *Economic Journal* 115 (October):1032–1053.

Rabbie, J.M., J.C. Schot and L. Visser (1989), 'Social Identity Theory: A Conceptual and Empirical Critique from the Perspective of a Behavioral Interaction Model,' *European Journal of Social Psychology* 19:171–202.

Roth, Alvin E., Vesna Prasnikar, Masahiro Okuno-Fujiwara and Shmuel Zamir (1991), 'Bargaining and Market Behavior in Jerusalem, Ljubljana, Pittsburgh, and Tokyo: An Experimental Study,' *American Economic Review* 81,5 (December):1068–1095.

Sally, David (1995), 'Conversation and Cooperation in Social Dilemmas,' *Rationality and Society* 7,1 (January):58–92.

Sato, Kaori (1987), 'Distribution and the Cost of Maintaining Common Property Resources,' *Journal of Experimental Social Psychology* 23 (January):19–31.

Simon, Herbert (1990), 'A Mechanism for Social Selection and Successful Altruism,' *Science* 250:1665–1668.

Smith, Adam (2000[1759]), *The Theory of Moral Sentiments* (New York: Prometheus).

Tajfel, Henri (1970), 'Experiments in Intercategory Discrimination,' *Annual Review of Psychology* 223,5:96–102.

Tajfel, Henri, M. Billig, R.P. Bundy and Claude Flament (1971), 'Social Categorization and Intergroup Behavior,' *European Journal of Social Psychology* 1:149–177.

Turner, John C. (1984), 'Social Identification and Psychological Group Formation,' in Henri Tajfel (ed.) *The Social Dimension* (Cambridge: Cambridge University Press) pp. 518–538.

Yamagishi, Toshio (1986), 'The Provision of a Sanctioning System as a Public Good,' *Journal of Personality and Social Psychology* 51:110–116.

Yamagishi, Toshio (1988a), 'The Provision of a Sanctioning System in the United States and Japan,' *Social Psychology Quarterly* 51,3:265–271.

Yamagishi, Toshio (1988b), 'Seriousness of Social Dilemmas and the Provision of a Sanctioning System,' *Social Psychology Quarterly* 51,1:32–42.

Yamagishi, Toshio (1992), 'Group Size and the Provision of a Sanctioning System in a Social Dilemma,' in W.B.G. Liebrand, David M. Messick and H.A.M. Wilke (eds) *Social Dilemmas: Theoretical Issues and Research Findings* (Oxford: Pergamon Press) pp. 267–287.

Yamagishi, Toshio, N. Jin and Toko Kiyonari (1999), 'Bounded Generalized Reciprocity: In-Group Boasting and In-Group Favoritism,' *Advances in Group Processes* 16:161–197.

3. Anti-utilitarianism and the gift-paradigm
Alain Caillé

I intend to give a sketchy presentation of the academic work accomplished by an interdisciplinary review in social science, *La Revue du MAUSS*, The Review of the Anti-utilitarian Movement in Social Science (see www.revuedumauss.com and www. journaldumauss.net). This review was founded in 1981 by economists and sociologists as a reaction to the overwhelming development and imperialism of what has been called the 'Economic model' in the social sciences. In the 1960s, and especially with the Chicago School and the work of Gary Becker (or effectively Hayek but in another form), economists began to believe that their Rational Action (or Choice) Theory was fit to explain not only what is happening on the market and through monetary exchanges, but any kind of social behavior: learning, wedding, love, crime etc. And, what is more surprising, the other social sciences, starting with sociology, at this time largely agreed with this contention. In fact, this enlargement of the traditional scope of economic science has been the prelude and the starting point to neo-liberalism which is nowadays triumphing in academic economic science as well as in the real world.

What can oppose, on a theoretical level, this victory of the economic model? 1) One can show that the vision of man as *homo œconomicus*, which underlies this economic model, is a crystallization and a condensation of a broader and more ancient anthropology and philosophy: utilitarianism. 2) And what objections are there to this utilitarian vision? Our main intellectual resource can be found, I believe, in the discovery made in 1923–24 by the French anthropologist Marcel Mauss (the nephew and intellectual heir of Emile Durkheim) that primitive societies do not rely upon contract and commercial exchange but on the gift, or, more precisely, the triple obligation to give, take and return.

In this chapter I explain how utilitarianism and gift can be defined. The conclusion is that economics and sociology should not think of themselves as separate sciences but as parts of a general social science which we have to build together.

UTILITARIANISM

A doctrine is frequently understood in quite different ways. This is the reason why, for instance, Marx may have been reputed at times to be Hegelian or as Spinozist, Bergsonian or Husserlian etc. Yet in the case of utilitarianism, this diversity of possible interpretations is somewhat astounding.

In Germany, France or Italy, until quite recently, almost nobody was interested in utilitarianism any more. It was held to be an empty and outdated doctrine. Histories of philosophy, of sociology and economics hardly mentioned it. Only sometimes they reminded their readers of the existence of a Jeremy Bentham – thought of as the father of utilitarianism and a poor philosopher as well – and of his main book, *Principles of Morals and Legislation* (1789). If they were to go into details, they added the names of his alleged precursors – the Scottish moralists, Frances Hutcheson, David Hume and Adam Smith; or, on the continent, Helvetius, Maupertuis or Beccaria – and at least one important and famous heir, John Stuart Mill, supposed to have given the utilitarian doctrine its most synthetic formulation in *Utilitarianism* (1861).

This deep lack of interest in utilitarianism is amazing if we remember that the main theoretical and political debates of the 19th century developed within its realm and around it. Just three examples: first, Nietzsche, when he was Paul Rhée's friend, was an utilitarian, before he became a radical anti-utilitarian, mocking and stigmatizing the calculating and utilitarian 'last man' and only looking for his own happiness. Second, it was in order to oppose the utilitarian sociology of Herbert Spencer – the most popular in the occidental world around the 1880s – that Émile Durkheim created the French School of Sociology and *L'Année sociologique*. Third, French 19th-century socialism, which culminated with Jean Jaurès, developed an ambivalent relationship to Bentham's utilitarianism. He agreed with it based on his materialistic rationalism but tried to surpass it by giving altruism a bigger importance than egoism. The same is in some sense true for Marxism as well.

Egoism? Altruism? Here we reach the puzzling core of the debate. For most economists and sociologists, utilitarianism is this doctrine which asserts first that actors are, or should be supposed to be, mere individuals seeking nothing else but their own happiness or self-interest. Second, that this is good and legitimate for there is no other possible rational goal. Third, that this rational goal is to be pursued rationally, *i.e.* through maximizing their pleasures (or their utility, or their preferences) and minimizing their pains (or their disutility). Understood in this way, utilitarianism is what one of his best connoisseurs, Élie Halévy, called 'une dogmatique de l'égoïsme' and more than the anticipation of what is called today the 'economic model in the social sciences' (Philippe Van Parijs) or, more generally, rational-actor theory. It simply is the general theory of the *homo oeconomicus*. This is how Talcott Parsons or Alvin Gouldner still understood utilitarianism in *The Structure of Social Action* (1937) or in *The Coming Crisis of Western Sociology* (1970). For them, as for Durkheim or Max Weber, sociology must be thought of as anti-utilitarian, *i.e.* a theoretical discourse recognizing the reality and the importance of interested calculations, but refusing to admit that the whole of social action could or should be reduced to instrumental rationality.

But what makes things difficult is that the mainstream Anglo-Saxon moral philosophy, from J.S. Mill to John Rawls, via H. Sidgwick, G. Moore or J.C. Harsanyi, has developed in the wake of utilitarianism but in giving much less importance to the postulate of rational egoism than to the utilitarian principle of justice formulated by Bentham: what brings the largest amount of pleasure to the greatest number. The conclusion can be easily guessed: if I intend to be (or look) just and morally irreproachable, I may have to sacrifice my self-interest for the sake of general happiness. Utilitarianism which seemed to be a 'dogmatique de l'égoïsme' suddenly turns into a plea for altruism. Or even for sacrifice. This is precisely why John Rawls tried to formulate principles of justice other than the utilitarian ones which might prevent urging the sacrifice of individual freedom for the sake of the greatest number's interest. Did he succeed, one might ask? This is another story.

Egoism? Altruism? Is *Homo oeconomicus* necessarily self-interested? Not always, answers Gary Becker, the herald of rational-actor theory. Some of the individual's satisfaction implies maximizing the satisfaction of others. They might be called altruistic egoists. Here we begin to understand that the discussion of the true nature of utilitarianism is full of enigmas and mysteries. Lacking space to explore them, I will just state five thesis:

1. Utilitarianism can be defined by the paradoxical and probably impossible combination of two assertions, one positive and the other normative. The positive one (about what *is*) holds actors to be self interested and rationally calculating individuals. The normative one (about what *ought to* be) says that it is just what permits to obtain the greatest possible happiness for the largest number.
2. Theories which advocate that the conciliation of the greatest possible happiness with individual self-interest is obtained through contract and free market can be held to be utilitarian *largo sensu*. Those, like Bentham's theory of legislation, which believe that it is possible only through the action of a rational legislator who manipulates desires through rewards and punishments – realizing what É. Halévy called an artificial harmonization of interests – can be said to be utilitarian *stricto sensu*.
3. If the word 'utilitarianism' is recent the two basic principles of utilitarianism (about the *is* and the *ought to*), are as old as European philosophy (not to speak of the Chinese, for example The Legist School) whose history can be read as an ever renewed struggle between utilitarian and anti-utilitarian formulations.
4. Utilitarianism is a theory of practical rationality, viewed as instrumental rationality, enlarged to the whole of moral and political philosophy. Economic theory can be seen as the crystallization of the positive dimension of utilitarianism.
5. The critic of utilitarianism and of rational-actor theory can only succeed if it takes seriously the discovery by Marcel Mauss of the central place of gift in social relations.

GIFT

Since 1923–24, with the publication in *L'Année sociologique* of *L' Essai sur le don (The Gift)* by Marcel Mauss – Durkheim's nephew and intellectual heir – enquiries on the practices of ceremonial gift have been central in the work of ethnologists. But it would be a great mistake to believe that gift practices are relevant only for primitive societies and have disappeared in ours. The obligation to give – or, better, the triple obligation to give, take and return – which embodies the basic social rule in at least a certain amount of primitive and archaic societies, as Mauss shows, is just the concrete face of the principle of reciprocity. This principle of reciprocity has been erected by Claude Lévi-Strauss as the basic anthropological principle and set by Karl Polanyi in sharp contrast with market and redistribution. If economic sociology is to thrive it will necessarily be through asking, for each case of economic practice today, which role the logics of market, redistributive hierarchy or reciprocal gift respectively play. Beyond the special case of economic sociology, one can argue that the theory of gift relation is indispensable to general sociological theory.

   Mauss' essential discovery is that in what one can call the first society (this generalization is mine: Mauss is more cautious) the social bond is not built on the basis of contract, barter or market exchange, but through obeying the obligation of rivalry through displayed generosity. Primitive gift indeed has nothing to do with Christian charity. Pervaded with aggression and ambivalence, it is an agonistic gift. It is not through economizing but in spending and even dilapidating or in accepting to lose his most precious goods that one can make his name grow and acquire prestige. This discovery represents of course a huge challenge to the central postulates of economic theory and of rational-actor theory, since it shows that '*homo oeconomicus* is not before but after us', as Mauss writes. He entirely lacks the naturality which economists attribute to him. The goods which are so given, taken and returned (counter-given) generally have no utilitarian value at all. They are valued only as symbols of the social relation they allow to create and feed through activating the unending circulation of a debt, which can be inverted but never liquidated. Gifts are symbols, and they are reciprocal. The gifts which circulate are not only positive ones, benefits, but as well negative ones, misdeeds, insults, injuries, retaliations or bewitchings. The most famous illustrations of this type of gift are the *potlatch* of the Kwakiutl Indians (Canada's northwest coast) and the *kula* of the Trobrianders.

What remains today of this primitive universe of the gift apart from Christmas or birthday gifts? Apparently not a great many things, and anyway our conception of gift has been altered and reshaped by 2,000 years of Christianity (all great religions moreover must be construed as the results of a universalistic transformation of the primary system of archaic gift). Yet, if one looks closer, it appears that a large amount of goods and services still circulate through the gift principle. Since Titmus' *The Gift Relationship*, the best-known illustration is the case of blood givers. Jacques T. Godbout shows that the genuine specificity of modern gift is that it can become a gift to strangers. More generally, it is possible to hypothesize that the obligation to give remains the fundamental rule of 'primary sociality', *i.e.* of the face-to-face relationships. And even in the sphere of 'secondary sociality' – impersonal on principle; the sociality of Market, State or Science, ruled by impersonal laws – the obligation to give, receive and reciprocate still matters. It is subordinated to market and hierarchy but its role is often nonetheless decisive.

The connection between Mauss's discovery of the gift and the new economic sociology is clearly visible. As Mark Granovetter explains, the key to the understanding of social action must not be looked for in an overarching holistic rule nor in individual rationality, but in the networks or, more precisely, in the trust which the participants to the network share. All this is true, but it must be added that networks are created by gifts and that it is through the renewal of those gifts that networks are nourished. Network relationships are gift relationships (the first large network study was the *kula ring* described by B. Malinowski).

But we can go a step further. A possible and even obligatory step if we believe the M.A.U.S.S. group and the *Revue du MAUSS* (founded by Alain Caillé, Serge Latouche and J.T. Godbout among others). This group advances the idea that the specificity of sociology, as compared to economics, lies in an anti-utilitarian way of thinking shared by Durkheim, Weber, Marx or even Pareto. This principled anti-utilitarianism, however, can make full sense only on the basis of Mauss's discovery of the gift and in taking seriously what Caillé calls the paradigm of the gift. What Mauss shows, through his enquiry on archaic gift, is that social action is not only shaped by the individual and rational self-interest stressed by rational-actor theory but also by a primary logic of sympathy (called *aimance* by Caillé), and that this tension between self-interest and sympathy is crossed by another tension between obligation and freedom. The obligation to give is a paradoxical obligation to be free and to oblige others to be free too. Social bond is constructed starting neither from rational interest nor from an overarching and eternal law. It can be correctly construed on neither an individualistic nor a holistic paradigm. It is built through a logic of alliance and association. Maussian gift is a political gift. It was long thought and enacted through religion. Today, the democratic ideal represents its most advanced form.

BIBLIOGRAPHY

In an article like this one, which tries to synthetize 2,500 years of philosophical, economic or sociological thought, there might be hundreds or thousands references. Rather than multiply useless and arbitrary references I limit myself to indicating a very few, specific to the point of view I develop here.

Caillé Alain, (2000) *Anthropologie du don. Le tiers paradigme*, Desclée de Brouwer Paris.
Caillé, Alain, Christian Lazzeri, Michel Senellart (eds) (2001) *Histoire raisonnée de la philosophie morale et politique. Le bonheur et l'utile*, La Découverte, Paris.
Godbout, Jacques T. (with Alain Caillé) (2000[1998]), *The World of the Gift*, Mac Gill-Queen's University Press, University Press, Montreal, Kingston, London, Ithaca.
Élie, Halévy (1995) *La formation du radicalisme philosophique* (1905), 3 vol. PUF, Paris.
Mauss, Marcel (1950[1923–24]) 'Essai sur le don', in *Sociologie et Anthropologie*, PUF, Paris. English translation (1990) *The Gift* (with an introduction by Mary Douglas), Routledge, London.
Schumpeter, Joseph (1954) *History of Economic Analysis*, Allen & Unwin, and Oxford University Press.

4.   Business ethics
Russell G. Pearce and Brendan M. Wilson

The fundamental question of business ethics is how people should behave when they are in the context of business. As scholars have grappled with this question, business ethics has emerged as a specialized normative discipline. Despite the proliferation of courses, books and publications on business ethics, and even the adoption of corporate social responsibility policies by businesses themselves, commentators have argued that business ethics has provided 'little practical guidance to business managers' and that the field itself is 'in a quandary' and risks 'a decline in relevance' (Mayer 2001; see also Rollert 2010[1]).

In this chapter, we divide the approaches to business ethics into three categories: profit maximization, social duty, and ordinary ethics. We review the arguments for each, including the range of perspectives that fall within the category of social duty. Next, we suggest that all of these approaches have proven ineffective in promoting ethical business conduct because they rely on an autonomous understanding of self-interest and a false dichotomy between economic and ethical conduct. Instead, we offer a conception of business ethics that recognizes the relational dimension of self-interest and identifies mutual benefit as the goal of business conduct. We suggest that recent developments, such as the MBA Oath Movement and the popularity of Clayton Christensen's essay 'How Will You Measure Your Life?', indicate the potential appeal of an ethic of mutual benefit (Anderson & Escher 2010; see also Christensen 2010; Askar 2010).

THE THREE APPROACHES TO BUSINESS ETHICS

Profit Maximization

Probably the dominant approach to business ethics among business leaders is Profit Maximization. Proponents of this view assert that profit maximization without deception and within the bounds of the law is the only ethic appropriate for business. They argue that profit maximization is the only strategy consistent with promoting efficient markets and that efficient markets represent the highest societal good. The prominent economist Milton Friedman, for example, asserts that:

> there is one and only one social responsibility of business – to use its resources and engages in activities designed to increase its profits so long as it stays within the rules of the game, which is to say, engages in open and free competition, without deception or fraud. (Friedman 1970, p. 35)

In fulfillment of this social responsibility, Friedman asserts that businesses and those who work in them have a duty to 'make as much money as possible while conforming to

[the] basic rules of the society, both those embodied in law and those embodied in ethical custom' (p. 35). Indeed, he explains that seeking social goals other than profit maximization harms society by undermining efficient markets.

While the ethic of profit maximization would apply to all businesses and all business actors, business ethics scholars have primarily considered it in the context of corporations. Like Friedman, they have argued that the corporation's basic obligation to maximize profit is a matter both of social utility and of obligation to stockholders. Commentators have described this approach as 'stockholder theory.' They assert that the goal of stockholders is to maximize profit and that the corporation cannot seek any other goal without violating its obligations to the stockholders (Hasnas 1998; see also Bowie 2002, pp. 2–3; Parker 1998, pp. 24–25). They also emphasize methods for ensuring that firms comply with law and avoid 'fraud or deception' (Friedman 1970, p. 35). In this regard, profit maximization provides business persons with a relatively simple ethical objective – making profits and complying with the law.

Rakesh Khurana has described how the ethic of profit maximization has become dominant in business schools (Khurana 2007, pp. 303–66). Khurana, while critical of the approach, observes that the focus on profit maximization has helped to restore 'necessary balance to a corporate governance system that had tilted too far in favor of managers' (Khurana 2007, p. 363).

Social Duty

Although the ethic of profix maximization has become dominant in business schools today (Khurana 2007, pp. 303–66), Rakesh Khurana explains that 'a rhetoric of social duty that framed business education as possessing a higher aim than mere "moneymaking"' shaped the 'invention of the business school' in the late nineteenth and early twentieth centuries (Khurana 2007, pp. 91, 100–22; see also Cortina 2008, pp. 69–70). Today, the concept of social duty underlies a range of related approaches to business ethics, including stakeholder theory, contractarian theory, and corporate social responsibility. These concepts seek to explain why businesses and business people have ethical obligations to individuals and communities beyond profit maximization. While these approaches are somewhat distinct, they share a commitment to a social duty that extends to stakeholders other than investors.

Stakeholder theory takes its name from this perspective. It asserts that business people have responsibilities to the businesses' range of stakeholders, including colleagues, creditors, customers, suppliers, employees, investors, and communities (Friedman & Miles 2006, pp. 1–14; see also Bowie 2002, pp. 19–35). A business not only maximizes profit but also coordinates stakeholder interests. The goal of an ethical business person is thus to seek the optimal balance among stakeholders (Friedman & Miles 2006, pp. 1–2; see also Bowie 2002, pp. 21–22). Only some stakeholders, such as investors, seek to maximize the businesses' profits. Employees are likely to want rewarding salaries, customers lower prices, and communities conduct that does not harm – and actually benefits – the community. Stakeholder theorists assume that these stakeholders cannot participate in management of the business and that therefore managers must represent the interests of stakeholders in making decisions for the business.

Commentators have offered a variety of justifications for stakeholder approaches. These diverse arguments include reliance on a Kantian principle of treating all people as ends in themselves, a Rawlsian 'veil of ignorance' to establish that 'fair contracting' requires consideration of stakeholder interests, or a view that a corporation exists as a nexus of contracts (Freeman and Evans 1990; see also Cortina 2008, pp. 74–78).

One variation of stakeholder theory is contractarian theory. Contractarian approaches perspectives posit an implicit contract between the members of society and businesses in which the members of society grant businesses the right to exist in return for certain specified benefits. Thomas Donaldson and Thomas Dunfee, two of the prominent supporters of contractarian theory, have identified two terms in this social contract: a social welfare term and a justice term. The social welfare term recognizes that members of society will be willing to authorize the existence of businesses only if they gain by doing so. This implies that businesses must benefit members of society as consumers, as employees, and as members of society. The justice term recognizes that members of society will be willing to authorize the existence of businesses only if businesses agree to remain within the bounds of the general canons of justice.

Commentators have debated the specific content of these terms. At minimum, they require that businesses avoid fraud and deception, show respect for workers as human beings, and avoid practices that systematically worsen the situation of a given group in society.

Donaldson and Dunfee's Integrative Social Contracts Theory (ISCT) posits that business leaders should consider the customs and mores of a particular community to discover viable ethical norms for business activity within that community, subject to certain ethical hyper-norms that are applicable to business activity conducted in every community. ISCT recognizes that communities are places where ethical reflection occurs and ethical norms are generated, and that implicit contracts occur among members of such communities that guide ethical behavior. The ethical obligations of businesses and business leaders are based upon two levels of consent: first, to a theoretical 'macrosocial' contract appealing to all national contractors, and second, to real 'microsocial' contacts by members of numerous localized communities. By considering both these macrosocial and microsocial contracts, ISCT enables business leaders to take account of the ethical expectations and shared understandings of the participants in the business transaction and thereby make appropriate ethical decisions (Donaldson and Dunfee 1994; see also Dunfee 1991).

Another variation of stakeholder theory is corporate social responsibility (CSR), a rather broad concept that encompasses a wide range of corporate practices and policies. In general, CSR represents an attempt by businesses to pursue ethical practices not as a matter of conformity with legal mandates, but as recognition that ethical behavior is good for society, and in turn good for business (Mullerat 2005, p. 4). CSR is a voluntary initiative that attempts to place corporations as pioneers of ethical procedures and practices, rather than as followers that can be thought of as being constrained by morality in their pursuit of profit (Roselle 2005, p. 117). CSR encourages executives to become moral entrepreneurs who seek to discover how they can transform the market they operate in for the better, and further the needs and interest of those they serve and employ (their stakeholders). Given that every entrepreneur does not operate in the same market, nor can claim mastery of the same skills, CSR avoids asking every business to abide by the same set of rules and procedures, or to pursue the same substantive objectives.

Examples of organizational polices that exhibit the ethos of CSR are those that '[encourage] a precautionary approach to environmental challenges' (Prandi & Lozano 2005, p.188), '[foster] corporate cultures that promote the adherence to human rights (e.g., suitability reporting, and using corporate culture based concepts . . . in deciding corporate accountability)' (Karlsson & Granström 2011, p.297), or '[demand] honesty in communications with employees . . . limited only by legal and competitive constraints' (Brennan 2011, p.313). Although such polices span considerations of human rights, the environment, and corporate transparency, all exhibit a universal tendency to go above and beyond the letter of the law in promoting their respective social objective.

Adherents of CSR debate whether it represents long-term profit maximization or an independent ethical commitment. Those who view CSR as maximizing long-term profit assert that pursuit of social responsibility often simultaneously increases profits. They rely on various empirical studies (Aupperle & Hatfield 1985; see also Siegel & Vitaliano 2007) with the editor of a major textbook on CSR going so far as to claim, 'everyone recognizes today that CSR is also good for business' (Mullerat 2005, p.5). On the other hand, many advocates of CSR view it as an ethical perspective that is sometimes in tension with profit maximization. They propose striking a 'balance' between social responsibility and the maximization of profits, thus reinforcing, at least conceptually, a distinction between the two objectives (Roselle 2005, p.117).

Ordinary Ethics

Some commentators have rejected the effort to develop a separate field of business ethics. They argue instead that an ethical person in business need only rely on ordinary ethics. Peter Drucker, a prominent exponent of this view, asserts that 'there is only one ethics, one set of rules of morality, one code, that of individual behavior in which the same rules apply to everyone alike' (Drucker 1981, p.19).

Of course, not all those who endorse ordinary ethics for business conduct would agree on how to apply ordinary ethics to any particular situation. Some, for example, assert a religiously grounded ethic, while others rely on moral philosophy (see O'Brien and Paeth 2007; Drucker 1981). Drucker offers two specific applications to business conduct. First, he suggests that business leaders exercise 'Ethics of Prudence,' which requires them not only to act ethically but also to avoid even the appearance of unethical behavior (p.27). Second, Drucker proposes an ethic of mutual obligations, and not rights, between interdependent individuals. (p.32). He envisions the development of an understanding, similar to Confucian ethics, that particular obligations are appropriate to particular relationships (pp.35–36).

ASSESSING THE THREE APPROACHES TO BUSINESS ETHICS

Each of these approaches has strengths and weaknesses as a guide to ethical decision-making in business.

Comparative Assessment

Profit maximization offers the clearest guidance: to maximize profits within the bounds of the law. While determination of how to maximize profits and observe the law is not always simple, identifying and balancing the interests of stakeholders, or even applying ordinary ethics, is a far less bounded and more complex inquiry.

Profit maximization also accords with legal concepts of a fiduciary obligation to investors, such as shareholders. To the extent that social duty or ordinary ethics interfere with profit maximization, they would arguably contravene these duties unless, as some proponents of corporate social responsibility argue, these approaches promote long-term profit maximization.

On the other hand, many people in business or among the public do not consider profit maximization as the full measure of ethical obligation. They would find social duty or ordinary ethics preferable approaches to the ethics of business actors. Although social duty derives from business people's special ethical obligations by virtue of their role, ordinary ethics does not. Both social duty and ordinary ethics require trust that business decision-makers are capable of pursuing those goals, and not only the pursuit of profit. In contrast, advocates of profit maximization reject the possibility that business people are capable of reliably identifying and pursuing ethical objectives other than profit maximization.

Last, both profit maximization and social duty are on their own terms part of a field of 'business ethics.' That is, they apply particular ethical and policy approaches to prescribe ethical conduct in business. Ordinary ethics, on the other hand, suggests that business does not require any study of ethical conduct more specialized than that for ethics generally. Drucker's examples of ordinary ethics, however, illustrate a weakness of this approach. Both of Drucker's particular applications of ordinary ethics begin to resemble the field of business ethics in terms of constructing conduct appropriate to business role (the Ethics of Prudence) or to business conduct (prescribed obligations for business relationships). Indeed, Drucker's rejection of business ethics as a field is in significant part semantic in that all the approaches to business ethics represent applications of general ethical theory to the particular context of business.

Theoretical Critique

While each of the three approaches differ significantly, they share theoretical weaknesses. Both profit maximization and social duty rely on the false dichotomy between ethics and economics. Luigino Bruni and Robert Sugden describe the economic assumptions underlying these approaches. The dominant approaches build on Adam Smith's famous observation that it is:

> not from the benevolence of the butcher, the brewer, the baker, that we expect our dinner, but from their regard to their own self interest. We address ourselves, not to their humanity but to their self-love, and never talk to them of their own necessities but of their advantage. (Smith 1937, p. 14)

Market theory assumes that in 'well-functioning markets . . . the relationship between trading partners is that of separate individuals, each pursuing his own interests within the constraints of the law of contract' (Bruni & Sugden 2008, p. 36). With this view, the market functions best when people in business pursue self-interest and self-interest exists independent of the altruism found in 'truly social or communal relationships' (Bruni & Sugden 2008, p. 36).[2] Accordingly, the dominant economic theories view the market as a 'morally free zone, a zone in which the constraints of morality would have no place' (Gauthier 1986, p. 84).

In recent years, economists, such as Bruni and Sugden, as well as Amartya Sen and Stefano Zamagni, have demonstrated that the dichotomy between business conduct and morality fails on both descriptive and normative grounds. Sen has explained that '[t]hat the jettisoning of all motivations and valuations other than the extremely narrow one of self-interest is hard to justify on the grounds of predictive usefulness, and it also seems to have rather dubious empirical support' (Sen1987, p. 89; see also Zamagni 2008; Sacco et al 2006).

Bruni and Sugden offer a number of examples where profit maximization fails to explain economic conduct, such as where economic actors are willing to take actions that benefit others, as well as themselves, even if they do not obtain the maximum return in the particular transaction. They describe an economic transaction as '*both* a mutually beneficial exchange, in which neither partner makes a sacrifice for the benefit of the other, *and* a genuinely social interaction, carrying moral value by virtue of this social content' (Bruni & Sugden 2008, p. 41). Indeed, they suggest that markets are only viable where people 'are ready to work jointly with others for mutual benefit' (Bruni & Sugden 2008, p. 57; see also Sacco et al 2006, pp. 724–726).

This emphasis on relationships highlights how conventional economic theory assumes an autonomous, as opposed to a relational, self. Russell Pearce and Eli Wald describe autonomous self-interest as the 'understanding of people and organizations as atomistic actors who seek to maximize their own atomistic good.' The autonomous measure of self-interest excludes consideration of consequences to others (Pearce et al 2013). The analysis of Bruni, Sen, Sugden, and Zamagni, in contrast, describes an actor that exists only in the context of relationships. Relational self-interest views all participants in the market as 'inter-connected' – they cannot maximize their own good in isolation. Businesses and business leaders promote their own interests only when they take into account the consequences to all parties to a transaction, including the community.

Both the relational nature of self-interest and the understanding of economic behavior as social conduct highlights weaknesses in the three approaches to business ethics. Profit maximization, grounded in the autonomous self-interest of the individual business person or business organization, fails to provide both an adequate description of business behavior and a persuasive theory of business ethics. Social duty presents a more complicated picture. The very notion that social duty exists in contrast to profit maximization itself rests on the unpersuasive dichotomy between economics and ethics. Given this problematic foundation, the failure of advocates of social duty to develop a consensus perspective on the basis for social duty – or to develop arguments that are persuasive to business persons who understand themselves as autonomously self-interested – is not surprising. A social duty independent of self-interest would have no appeal to such business persons. Moreover, while social duty theories recognize that business conduct implicates a variety of relationships, they fail to conceive of these relationships as reciprocal. Rather they view these relationships as grounded in agreements that are only 'implied' or 'theoretical.' They locate ethical responsibility in the autonomous decisions of business actors. Nonetheless, the relational character of social duty does facilitate helpful insights consistent with the work of Bruni, Sen, Sugden, and Zamagni, such as that branch of corporate social responsibility that explores the intersection of ethical business conduct and long run profit maximization.

The defects in the ordinary ethics approach are less obvious. On its face, the ordinary ethics approach accords with Bruni and Sugden's description of an economic exchange as a social relationship with moral implications. Unfortunately, ordinary ethics commentators also focus on the ethical implications of the autonomous decisions of the business person or entity and not on the development of an ethic of mutual benefit through reciprocal relationships in which that person or entity participates. For example, although Drucker uses the relational language of interconnected actors, his approach remains focused on the participants in the relationship from their individual perspective. He uses the relationship as a source of obligations for autonomous individuals, not the location for a dynamic and reciprocal relationship. In addition, by focusing only on obligations – and not interests or rights – Drucker ignores a key dimension of the mutually beneficial exchanges that are the hallmark of market transactions.

NEW DIRECTIONS FOR BUSINESS ETHICS

The insights of Bruni, Sen, Sugden, and Zamagni provide the foundation for a new approach to business ethics that focuses on mutual benefit and relational self-interest. This approach makes the identification and pursuit of business ethics a central, rather than marginal, concern for business persons, by making ethics an intrinsic dimension of the business transactions that mutually benefit and enrich the parties to those transactions. It also provides a framework for considering the institutional arrangements that encourage ethical business behavior. For example, Pearce, Wald and Vonnegut-Gabovitch argue that command and control regulations tend to assume and promote autonomous self-interest, while outcome based regulations, in encouraging dialogue within organizations and between organizations and the government, promote relational self-interest.

This approach offers the potential for greater effectiveness than the three existing approaches. Profit maximization offers no ethical content beyond autonomous self-interest and to the extent that social duty and ordinary ethics ask business persons to behave ethically they are asking people with an autonomous perspective to do something that makes no sense to them. Relational self-interest and the ethic of mutual benefit speak in the language of self-interest that business people understand. Moreover, the idea of relationality – that promoting one's own interests requires consideration of mutual benefit with others – is one that will also appeal to business people, many of whom understand that they achieve success precisely because they are able to develop relationships of mutual benefit (Shestack 2011, pp. 121–122).

Two recent developments evidence a growing appetite for this approach. In 2009, graduates of Harvard Business School devised an MBA oath that embodies notions of relational self-interest and mutual benefit, without using that specific language. Since then, it has gained the support of hundreds of business schools and thousands of signatories throughout the world, indicating that the oath movement has struck a responsive chord in the business community. Similarly, in the spring of 2010, the Harvard graduating class invited Professor Clayton Christensen to speak to them about how to live a meaningful life as a business person (Christensen 2010). Christensen described his life experience in terms of relationships both in business and in the other parts of his life. With regard to business, he described management in terms of relational self interest and mutual benefit: 'Management . . . offers . . . ways to help others learn and grow, take responsibility and be recognized for achievement, and contribute to the success of a team.'[3] Christensen's talk went viral. After the Harvard Business Review invited him to submit it for publication, it became 'one of the most popular articles [the *Harvard Business Review* has] ever run' (Askar 2010). Both of these developments illustrate the resonance of the notions of relational self-interest and mutual benefit within the business community and suggest a way for business ethics to regain its relevance.

NOTES

1. In his short essay, he notes that if you 'survey the syllabi from MBA programs across the country, you will soon discover that there is no agreement, broad or otherwise, on what passes for 'business ethics.' There are many reasons for this, but the most obvious may be that, as opposed to students at law and medical schools, MBAs do not have a canon of professional ethics they must learn and be bound by if they wish to practice business.
2. Commentators disagree on the extent to which Smith fully embraced this dichotomy. Compare Bruni and Sugden with N.T. Philipson and Adam Smith: *An Enlightened Life* (2010, New Haven, Ct.: Yale University Press, Emma Rothschild, *Economic Sentiments: Adam Smith, Condorcet, and the Enlightenment* (2002, Harvard University Press).
3. Christensen's commitment to relational self-interest and mutual benefit was not complete. He did not recognize the potential for realizing those goals in 'buying, selling, and investing in companies' (Christensen, p. 2).

BIBLIOGRAPHY

Anderson, Max and Peter Escher (2010), *The MBA Oath: Setting a Higher Standard for Business Leaders*, USA: Penguin Group.

Askar, Jamshid Ghazi (2010), 'Life advice from Utah native, Harvard business professor Clayton Christensen an online hit', *Desert News*, available at http://goo.gl/tlfxn (last accessed 10 November 2012).

Aupperle, K., A. Carroll and J. Hatfield (1985), 'An Empirical Examination of the Relationship Between Corporate Social Responsibility and Profitability', *Academy of Management Journal*, **28**(2), 446–463.

Bowie, Norman E. (2002), *The Blackwell Guide to Business Ethics*, Malden, Mass: Blackwell.

Brennan, Daniel (2011), 'Corporate Responsibility and Corporate Governance: The OECD Guidelines For Multinational Enterprises', in Mullerat, Ramon (ed.) (2005), *Corporate social Responsibility: the corporate governance of the 21st century* (1st ed), Alphen aan den Rijn: Kluwer Law International, pp. 275–284.

Bruni Luigino and Robert Sugden (2008), 'Fraternity: why the market need not to be a morally free zone', *Economics and Philosophy*, 24, pp. 35–64.

Christensen, Clayton M. (2010), 'How Will You Measure Your Life?', *Harvard Business Review*, July–August, 1–7.

Cortina, Adela (2008), 'Corporate Social Responsibility and Business Ethics', in Jesus Conill, Christoph Luetge and Tatjana Schonwalder-Kuntze (eds), *Corporate citizenship, contractarianism and ethical theory: on philosophical foundations of business ethics*, Farnham, England: Ashgate, pp. 69–78.

Donaldson, Thomas and Thomas W. Dunfee (1994), 'Toward a Unified Conception of Business Ethics: Integrative Social Contracts Theory', *Academy of Management Review*, **19**, 252–284.

Donaldson, Thomas and Thomas W. Dunfee (1999), 'A Social Contracts Approach to Business Ethics', in Thoms Donaldson and Patricia Hogue Werhane (eds) (2008), *Ethical issues in business: a philosophical approach* (8th ed), Upper Saddle River, N.J.: Pearson/Prentice Hall, pp. 448–453.

Donaldson, Thomas and Patricia Hogue Werhane (eds) (2008), *Ethical issues in business: a philosophical approach* (8th ed), Upper Saddle River, N.J.: Pearson/Prentice Hall.

Drucker, Peter F. (1981), 'What is "Business Ethics"?', *The Public Interest: National Affairs*, **63** (Spring), pp. 18–36.

Dunfee, Thomas W. (1991), 'Business Ethics and Extant Social Contracts', *Business Ethics Quarterly*, **1**(1), pp. 23–51.

Freeman, R. Edward (2007) 'Managing for Stakeholders', in Thomas Donaldson and Patricia Hogue Werhane (eds) (2008), *Ethical issues in business: a philosophical approach* (8th ed), Upper Saddle River, N.J.: Pearson/Prentice Hall, pp. 39–50.

Freeman, R. Edward and William Evans (1990), 'Corporate Governance: A Stakeholder Interpretation', *Journal of Behavioral Economics*, **19**, p. 337.

Friedman, Milton, (1970), 'The Social Responsibility of Business Is to Increase Its Profits', in Thomas Donaldson and Patricia Hogue Werhane (eds) (2008), *Ethical issues in business: a philosophical approach* (8th ed), Upper Saddle River, N.J.: Pearson/Prentice Hall, pp. 34–39.

Friedman, Andrew L. and Samantha Miles (2006), *Stakeholders: theory and practice*, Oxford: Oxford University Press.

Gauthier, David (1986), *Morals by Agreement*, Oxford: Oxford University Press.

Hasnas, John (1998), 'The Normative Theories of Business Ethics: A Guide for the Perplexed', *Business Ethics Quarterly* **8**:19, January.

Heath, Joseph (2009), 'The Uses and Abuses of Agency Theory', *Business Ethics Quarterly*, **19**:4 October.

Karlsson, Michael & Max Granström (2011), 'Business and Human Rights: The Recent Initiatives of the UN', in Ramon Mullerat (ed.) (2005), *Corporate social responsibility: the corporate governance of the 21st century* (1st ed), Alphen aan den Rijn: Kluwer Law International, pp. 285–306.

Khurana, Rakesh (2007), *From Higher Aims to Hired Hands: The Social Transformation of American Business Schools and the Unfulfilled Promise of Management as a Profession*, Princeton University Press, Princeton, NJ.

Kolm, Serge-Christophe and Jean Merder Ythier (eds) (2006), *Handbook of the Economics of Giving, Altruism and Reciprocity, Volume 1: Foundations*, Amsterdam: Elsevier.

Mayer, Do (2001), 'Community, Business Ethics, and Global Capitalism', *American Business Law Journal*, Winter, 216.

Mullerat, Ramon (2005), 'The Global Responsibility of Business', in *Corporate Social Responsibility: The Corporate Governance of the 21st Century*, pp. 3–30.

Mullerat, Ramon (ed.) (2005), *Corporate social responsibility: the corporate governance of the 21st century* (1st ed), Alphen aan den Rijn: Kluwer Law International.

O'Brien, Thomas and Scott Paeth (eds) (2006), *Religious Perspectives on Business Ethics: An Anthology*, Wisconsin: Sheed & Ward, Franklin.

Parker, Martin (1998), *Ethics & Organizations* (1st ed), London: Sage.

Pearce, Russell G., Eli Wald & Zachary Vonnegut-Gabovitch (2013), 'Business Culture as an Obstacle to Financial Reform: The Importance of the Cultural Dimension of Addressing the Causes and Consequences of the Great Recession', *Fordham Journal of Financial and Corporate Law*, **19** (forthcoming 2013).

Prandi, Maria and Joseph M. Lozano (2005), 'Corporate Social Responsibility and Human Rights', in Ramon Mullerat (ed.) (2005), *Corporate social responsibility: the corporate governance of the 21st century* (1st ed), Alphen aan den Rijn: Kluwer Law International, pp. 183–204.

Prandi, Maria and Josep M. Lozano (2011), 'Corporate Social Responsibility and Human Rights', in Ramon Mullerat (ed.) (2005), *Corporate social responsibility: the corporate governance of the 21st century* (1st ed), Alphen aan den Rijn: Kluwer Law International, pp. 209–228.

Rollert John Paul (2010), 'Going Beyond Business Ethics as Castor Oil', available at http://goo.gl/e5Va7 (last accessed 10 November 2012).

Roselle, James (2005), 'The Triple Bottom Line: Building Shareholder Value', in Ramon Mullerat (ed.) (2005), *Corporate social responsibility: the corporate governance of the 21st century* (1st ed), Alphen aan den Rijn: Kluwer Law International, pp. 113–139.

Sacco, Pier Luigi, Paolo Vanin and Stefano Zamagni (2006), 'The Economics of Human Relationships', in Kolm, Serge-Christophe and Jean Merder Ythier (eds) (2006), *Handbook of the Economics of Giving, Altruism and Reciprocity, Volume 1: Foundations*, Amsterdam: Elsevier, pp. 696–726.

Sancho, Jesús, Christoph Luetge and Tatjana Kuntze (eds) (2008), *Corporate citizenship, contractarianism and ethical theory: on philosophical foundations of business ethics*, Farnham, UK: Ashgate.

Sen, Amartya (1987), *On Ethics and Economics*, Malden, Mass.: Blackwell Publishing.

Shestack, J. Jerome (2011), 'Corporate Social Responsibility in a Changing Corporate World', in Ramon Mullerat (ed.) (2005), *Corporate social responsibility: the corporate governance of the 21st century* (1st ed), Alphen aan den Rijn: Kluwer Law International, pp. 113–126.

Siegel, D. and D. Vitaliano (2007), 'An Empirical Analysis of the Strategic Use of Corporate Social Responsibility,' *Journal of Economics and Management Strategy*, **16**(3), 773–792.

Smith, Adam (1937), 'An Inquiry into the Nature and Causes of the Wealth of Nations', New York: Modern Library.

Zamagni, Stefano (2008), 'Comparing Capitalistic and Cooperative Firms on the Ground of Humanistic Management', *1st IESE Conference*, 'Humanizing the Firm & Management Profession', Barcelona, IESE Business School, June 30–July 2, 2008, available at SSRN: http://ssrn.com/abstract=1295314 (last accessed 10 November 2012).

5. Capitalism
Nicolò Bellanca[1]

MARKET ECONOMY OR CAPITALISM?

The modern economic system is commonly classified as a 'market economy'. This means that the allocation of resources is the outcome of individual decisions taken by producers and consumers. Producers and consumers answer to public signals such as prices which work automatically as they are the outcome of aggregated individual buying and selling decisions.

Hence, on the market, anyone plans or rules; the coordinating mechanism is decentralized and voluntary. Prices give incentives which bring individuals to choose behaviours which are advantageous for them and, with some other condition, efficient. 'The assumption is that society, in spite of frictions, dis-equilibria and evident inequalities can be interpreted as an equalitarian system in which each subject is rewarded according to its merits' (Graziani 1981, 9). Those which disappear are the asymmetries of power: 'an economic transition is a solved political problem. Economic science gained the title of queen of social sciences by choosing as an object political problems which were *already solved*' (Lerner 1972, 259).

Marx opposed himself to this conception by distinguishing the organizational forms of the economic system through the criteria of the property of the means of production. He started from a common traditional interpretation (e.g. Sweezy 1942), a system called 'simple mercantile production', as a yardstick in which inequalities do not exist: each subject is at the same time worker and owner of all the goods he uses in the production process; moreover, in the division of labour, everyone has to offer that part of goods he produces which he doesn't use for his own consumption in order to have the goods he needs. 'Capitalism' is an ideal type system which Marx conceives as opposed to the latter and which is characterized by: the division of labour and the means of production; private property of the means of production; the legal freedom of the worker, which sells on the market its own working capacity; the generalization of production and the exchange of goods. Power asymmetries are embedded in the system as it is made by three agents: pure workers, owners of the means of production, and owners of natural resources. While workers take part to the production process to gain a wage that they will use for consumption, and the owners of natural resources tend to enhance their revenues to buy luxury goods, the aim of capitalists is the maximum expansion in time of the value of their capital: they are pushed to do so both by the competition with the other capitalists and by the fact that their social position depends on the amount of money they control. The means through which they are able to reach this objective is profit maximization, the difference in the value of the goods sold and the value of the production means used. Marx suggests also a third ideal type system called 'socialist', which, despite keeping the separation between work and the property of the means of production, starts reducing the asymmetries of power. Such a system collectivizes property by taking it to a particular group of subjects. Moreover it solves the problem of what and how much to produce through a public authority which plans and manages economic production activities, admitting that individuals will have the possibility to choose only on the consumption side (Napoleoni 1967). It is thus the kind of ownership system, as a peculiar feature of the economic systems, which has to be modified in the transition, pacific or revolutionary, from one system to another. This main idea has historically limited the understanding of the features and processes of contemporary capitalism such as state ownership of many enterprises and industrial sectors, the diffusion of private property, the public companies, the control of banks on productive enterprises, and the role of financial markets in the process of allocating the control of production. The other bigger limit of Marxist theory relies on the research of a *primum movens* of the economic system, identified in the capacity of giving a value to human labor. More than recalling the incongruence of the theory of labor's value, our objective is to underline the epistemological approach used to look for the *causa causantes* from which comes the 'true' genetic explanation of capitalism. How much do the limits just recalled influence the entire approach of Marx? To answer, we have to recall three powerful and still-existing reasons. According to Marx, capitalism generates a specific historical process of economic alienation (Petry 1915; Rubin 1928). As any action is, in the ideal typical system, mediated by the market, goods are not considered for what they are (value of use), but for their value (exchange value). Thus the attribution to the relations among people of the typical features of the relations among things ('reification'), or the attribution to the relations among things of typical features of the relations among people ('feticism') is realized. Some social relations appear as relations among things, as when the capacity to answer the needs from individual works is expressed by the terms of trade of the goods produced by those works; some social laws show themselves as natural laws, as when producers operate according to market indexes which are not under their control; other social relations appear as the nexus between a thing and the thing itself, as when money generates other money, loosing any trace of its origin; at last, the productive forces of the labour appear as productive forces of the capital, since in the labour process the former depend on the latter and vice-versa (Vercelli 1973). The estrangement of inter-subjective relations causes a serious and systematic opacity in scientific knowledge of capitalism: superficial forms do not coincide with the forms through which this system auto-reproduces itself. Social reality has two levels: the phenomenological one, of the dense thickness of alienation, and the structural one, which accomplishes the deepest power asymmetries. Social agents are immediately aware only of the first level, while the objective of the social science and political practice is to demystify the 'market economy', revealing the conflicting reasons of capitalism.

A second crucial contribution of Marx puts at the centre of his analysis the auto-reproductive feature of capitalism. The autonomization of money, which historically starts with the minting of coins, represents the first reversal from means to ends. When goods are mediated by money, every human objective looks reachable only through money itself; for this reason, money from the mean becomes an end which imposes itself on all other things. Now purposes, usually meant as 'final causes' of action, become effects which are the result of doing the procedures required by the mean. 'Acting' (*praxis*), as the choice of ends, is substituted by 'doing' (*téchne*), as production of results functional to the enhancement of the mean itself. This overthrow among means and ends which comes from ancient Greece (Sohn-Rethel 1972), is being replaced, with capitalism, by the absence of distinction between the two. We are in the presence of a circular coincidence of assumptions and results, of initial premises and terminal effects. As Hannah Arendt points out:

> we call automatic all process of spontaneous movement which are out of reach of human will and deliberated interferences. In an automated production the distinction between operation and product, as the bigger importance of the product on the operation (which is only the mean to produce the end), has no more sense and is exceeded. [. . .] Designing the objects for the operational capacity of the machine, instead of designing machines for the production of objects, could reverse the relationship between means and ends, assuming that these categories will still have a meaning. [. . .] As things are, describing machines in terms of means and ends is like asking nature whether it produces the seed for the tree or the tree for the seed. (Arendt 1958, pp. 107, 198)

This is the transition from self-regulated social systems to social systems which reproduce themselves or are autopoietic. As long as we stop the exchange between goods and money, we have to take into account the labour process: this exchange doesn't produce its effects by itself. We can exchange an unlimited number of times, aspire to unlimited gains, but each exchange can only involve the volume of goods which has been or will be produced. We are in a self-regulated system, that doesn't reproduce itself, though. In order to get to the latter is needed a process in which – thanks to the circular coincidence between premises and results – there are no limits to growth, which effects its own reproduction. According to Marx this happened when the emphasis was put on the production of money and not on its circulation, on accumulating capital rather than on the monetary gain. The last contribution from Marx which we are recalling concerns the analysis of the relation owner-not worker and worker-not owner in capitalism: while in pre-capitalistic societies the command of the former was *external* to the labour processes, now it is inside it. This has a great importance. It is in fact how the labour process works – its technical and productive organization – which reproduces the nexus between 'the one who appropriates' and 'the one who is expropriated'. In order for it to happen, it is necessary to completely submit the worker, separating him also from the *subjective* condition of his work. Any specific ability, professional preparation, or capacity of comprehending and governing the interconnections of the production cycle of a certain good (or of its important part) are being subtracted to the producer. The worker's job is divided into the most elementary movements that do not require any specific learning to be completed, while the whole coordination of the specialized fragmented operations is up to the technical-scientific direction of the labour process. Thus the passage from the *social* division of labour (the social distribution of tasks, jobs and specializations) to the *technical* or fragmented or 'manufacturing' division of labour (which divides the tasks in a factory or in an office) is realized. In the labour process, the technical division divides handwork from intellectual work, and, more generally, the executive tasks from the tasks of creating and thinking. This thus separates the 'powers of the minds' of cooperative work from the great mass of producers, centralizing them in the hands of capitalists and their functionaries.

Moreover fragmenting each task makes more complex the entire production hierarchy. In this analysis of Marx, due principally to the Althusserian school (see La Grassa 1980, 1996), capitalists not only have the juridical-economical ownership of the labour process, as it happens in the traditional interpretation; they also *own* it, which gives them the possibility to use it to reproduce the social relation.

Summing up, the discussion of the peculiarity of the capitalistic system compared to the market economy can't, according to us, put aside at least three features of Marx's thought: economic estrangement, the self-reproduction of the system and the separation between command and execution in the labour process.

MOVING TO A DEFINITION OF CAPITALISM

Among the attempts of conceptualizing capitalism after two and a half centuries from the first 'industrial revolution' we will focus on those by Manuel Castells and Samuel Bowles.[2] According to Castells (1996, 2000), 'capitalism' is a social system in which the economic surplus is taken by who retains the control of the economic organizations and the objective is profit maximization, while in 'statalism' the surplus goes to who has the power in the State apparatus and the objective is power maximization. These two categories bifurcate themselves in 'industrialism', a growth model in which the principal factors of productivity are the quantitative increment of productive factors (work, capital and natural resources) or in 'informationalism', a growth model in which the biggest factor of productivity is the capacity of optimizing the combination of production factors on the basis of knowledge and information. By combining systems and models – 'industrialist capitalism', 'industrial statalism', 'informational capitalism' – Castells interprets the evolutionary phases of the modern economy.

Bowles (2004) draws upon the neo-institutionalist theory of property rights (Groosman and Hart 1986; Hart and Moore 1990). To benefit from specialization and economies of scale, economic activities become social instead of individual. Conflicts of interest between participants are settled by contracts – as binding mechanisms – which are necessarily incomplete. In fact, contracts can't specify what each part has to do in each possible circumstance, as: (i) not all occurrences can be foreseen, (ii) there is not an optimal action for all (iii) there cannot necessarily be certainty, due to the opportunism and limited rationality of the agents, that the contract terms will be honoured. The peculiarity of 'capitalism', as Bowles says, is about solving the incompleteness of contracts through the enterprise as main form of economic organization.

Power in the enterprise manifests itself when someone decides the asset of a resource when not directly defined by a contract. The implementation of power occurs when, among a group of technological and interdependent subjects and capitals, everyone tends to reduce its effort, being aware that they will still receive benefits from the others' results. With the aim of fighting that common damage, it's convenient to incentivize someone to follow the management and innovation of the entire economic process. The given incentives consist of the 'residual claim to income', so that, after the contractual terms are fulfilled, s/he can never be excluded by the economic process; and in the 'residual claim to control', for which s/he can exclude whoever eludes his orders. That institutional and fundamental gear of capitalism is also identified, besides Marx, by Coase and Simon: as, according to Marx, the worker stipulates an incomplete contract in which s/he assumes her/his duty of compliance for a given number of hours; according to Coase and Simon the capitalist is the one who imposes a contract in which the worker exchanges the power of the goals of his activity for the wage (Bowles 2004, 268–269). In brief, for Bowles capitalism is an economic system in which, considering the constitutive incompleteness of the contracts, the capitalist-manager imposes, within the enterprise, those decisions that, according to him, maximize the net income that he takes for himself.

The theoretical schemes by Castells and Bowles capture some important aspects. Though, Castells drops one of Marx's crucial knots: that only in capitalism two 'reality levels', one phenomenical and the other structural, unravel almost on parallel lines. Bowles, on the other hand, reclaims the idea of control within the working process, but, just like Castells, he drops the other two crucial aspects that, in the reconstruction here suggested, connote the Marxian theory of capitalism: the autopoietic nature of the system and the economical estrangement. We suggest, in brief, a definition that gathers and generalizes the Marxian one. 'Capitalism', as an ideal type, is a self-expansive social system that destroys all the forms of human relations based on personal constraints, turning them into transactions (of buy-and-sell trading, but also about relational or legal exchange) among subjects endowed with contractual freedom. The *universal transaction* is thus the way capitalism shows up: it does not include only goods, capital and work; it leads to the involvement of nature goods and the most unique aspects of everyone, from personal pride to poetry, from erotic affection to religious prayer. In this system people build relations as they are owners of things: from this, it seems that things themselves have the ability to set up connections. The reification of relationships among people and the personification of things is, together with that of transaction, a universal dimension of capitalism. Under such a phenomenical level, in which all the subjects seem formally equal and are equally alienated, there is, rooted in the productive processes, a structure of asymmetrical links among who, step by step, controls the *critical resource* – without whom the others have a reduced or any value – and who obeys (Emerson 1963; Rajan and Zingales 1998).

Therefore, the specific feature of capitalism stays in the 'double level' of the reproduction of society: that of everyone's equality, as exchangers and in front of alienation, and that of everyone's inequality, towards the current critical resource, in terms of being producer of goods and services to exchange. Historically, the critical resource has changed several times. A usual and not far-fetched manner of classifying those changes consists in involving all of them under the term 'capital': starting with physical capital (that makes private property of production means critical), through monetary and financial capital (that makes decisive the access to purchasing power), to technological and organizational capital (that gives importance to innovation processes), to human capital (that enhances competences, abilities and knowledge as features that make the difference), to social capital (for which the quality of inter-subjective connections creates a competitive advantage). The change of the critical resource entails, or can entail:

> the passage from a total helplessness situation (besides the union and politic response) of those who didn't owe the esosomatic tools of production, to a situation in which the endosomatic tools (productive knowledge first) give the worker a market power [. . . That] worsens the position of the capital owners towards those workers endowed with productive knowledge, and among these it improves the one of those who owes a knowledge that is requested by the market, though not very reproducible nor transferable. (Becattini 1999, 68–69)

If we accept this comfortable taxonomy, we are probably legitimized to still name the major part of modern societies, in the several versions they assume, 'capitalisms'.

Whatever is the chosen label, what really counts is that, while the definition of 'market economy' appears strongly ideological and a-problematic, the historically qualified concept of 'capitalism' points to an autoreproductive economic system with no limits, featured by universal transactions and alienation, as well as the control of critical resources within the material and cognitive conditions of production.

CAPITALISM BEYOND CAPITALISM

Relying on the previous definition of capitalism, it is necessary to distinguish three main angles from which this economic system can be expanded: that of 'capital-less market', that of 'ownerless capital', and that of 'ownerless enterprises'. There are several arguments claiming those changes, though it is not necessary to face them all here. It is enough to reason on the evolutionary (or involutionary) possibilities of a historically fading system. The first angle suggests that, while the market is a regulation mechanism, capitalism is a type of economic society. The former can still exist without the latter. Universal alienation starts, in capitalism, not simply because of trading goods, but because they implement interpersonal relationships. On its own, that mainly happens because only in capitalism is the market charged with the function to allocate (also) the social consideration (Hirschman 1977): the amount of money, thanks to the universality of transactions, coincides with the level of success, of others' consensus and of power. The construction of subjective identity, solely relying on everyone's ability to obtain money on markets, generates the inversion between person and thing that Marx names economic alienation. To eradicate alienation it is necessary, then, to loosen the link between money and virtue, revenue and prestige, goods possession and individual fulfilment.

> The possibility, that capital achieves, of reducing the working time needed to produce basic means, can be used to change the relationship between time that people spend in production and time that people dedicate to self-care. [. . .] It is not a matter of going out from capitalism to get into another thing, but a matter of enlarging as widely as possible the difference between society and capitalism, of extending thus the non identification zone of man towards the reversed subjectivity. (Napoleoni 1986, 215–16)

From consumption, to working, to politics, to interpersonal relations behaviours, today there are several social pushes in this direction (La Valle 2004). According to the answers to these questions the relevant forms of social and solidarity economy affirm themselves.

On the ownerless capital side, let's start by mentioning copartnership. For example, the workers' involvement in productivity, the risk and the company profits, can be realized through the dual governance model that separates surveillance from management. The trade union takes part in the surveillance board and, according to the strategic goals sharing the enterprise, it agrees to bond the dynamic of workers' income to that of the production of wealth, agreeing to transfer a certain part of the retribution into shares. John Roemer (1994) suggests a more radical approach, introducing two types of currencies in capitalism: the ordinary one would be used for trading goods, while the purchase of property rights in corporations would be possible through the use of *coupons*. Exchanging *coupons* with euros, or using euros to purchase shares in a corporation would be illegal. Companies (only) would trade their shares for *coupons*; then, they could convert *coupons* into euros in a public bank, to purchase capital goods. The term of trade between euros and *coupons* would be defined by the central bank, who would aim the investments in specific directions. The companies would compete to keep the value of the *coupons*, because they could gain more capital in this way. The value of the economy expressed in *coupons* would initially be divided into equal parts for each adult citizen. On reaching their 18th birthday, everyone would receive her/his quota. It could be spent to buy shares that would provide bigger or smaller dividends and the right to vote in assemblies, or placed in some investment fund. Shares would not be tradable among people, nor they would be inheritable: in this way, the different earnings in the stock exchange during the whole life would not be accumulated in time. One interesting point of this reform consists in keeping the 'market economy' and the capitalistic sphere separated: the two exchange circuits, the money and the *coupon* ones, would prevent the summing of power asymmetries and the use of an advantage in one sphere to gain more advantage in the other. This is an extension of the non-profit idea: Roemer's corporations, as non-profit entities, can't distribute dividends which must be reinvested in the activity.

But not every sector of the economy is made to be organized in the competitive way that Roemer suggests: this is the case of commons, the set of gifts that we inherit or create collectively. They include air and water, habitat and ecosystems, languages and cultures, science and technology, political and legal systems, social infrastructures, and way more. One suggestion, by Peter Barnes (2006), starts from the statement that, in capitalism, commons are either collected into the hands of minorities, that use them to maximize profits, or managed by the public sector, which, besides great deficiencies, is almost never able to make a single persons pay for the social costs of their use. It is, despite this, necessary to create, when 'windows of opportunities' open up in the power relations among groups, a 'common sector' that comes alongside the enterprise sector. In that sector, the commons property would be assigned to trusts that are bonded to administrate them, first focusing on the interests of future generations. The common goods would thus be 'proprietized', not privatized or statalized. Whether they are scarce or threatened, their use should be limited and, thanks to the prices required for their utilization, the trust would generate a revenue to be shared among citizens, ensuring a minimum income and reducing the capitalistic tendency to inequalities. When, on the other hand, they are illimitate, such as culture and the internet, the trust intends to give, at the lowest possible price, the biggest benefit to the largest number of people, further improving equality and well-being for everyone. In both cases the 'common sector' of the economy would proceed with a logic that is opposed to the capitalistic sector. The three reforms (dual governance, Roemer and Barnes), besides details and the examination of their conditions of applicability, all seek the introduction of diarchy and counterbalance among the opposed powers in capitalism: in the enterprise's strategies, in the allocation of money, in the management of economic goods. They point out the way the 'chromosome set' of capitalism, besides the change depending on time and places, can be modified by collective action, up to alter its basic features such as the illimitate push to accumulation and the universality of the mercantile transactions.

There is still something to add about the last feature that may be the hardest to be modified: the control *within* the working process. This is the perspective that we have been calling 'ownerless enterprise'. Can the existing hierarchy in the workplace be relieved or even eliminated? The function of authority is structured at three levels: (a) the definition of goals, (b) the action and (c) the control. Traditionally, the one who holds the hierarchical authority merges the three moments. But we can imagine that (a) and (c) are managed by collective subjects: in several organizational contexts, the formulation of a strategic planning, as well as monitoring, work well under 'peer-to-peer' pressure. Concerning the monitoring activity, in the traditional structure of the capitalistic firm, the result of a working team is better than the one single workers would obtain by themselves. Although, due to the difficulty of measuring the contribution that each of them would give to the collective results, in the end expedience wins: everyone feels less bonded to the commitment, all wages being equal, thinking that the others will work. It is necessary thus to have a central inspector, who decides who deserves to be employed and who needs to be fired. This organizational mode, nevertheless, is not unavoidable. Imagine stipulating a contract with the entire team, for which its members are paid as much as when the team reaches an equivalent productive level to the one potentially obtained with no one acting as a free rider: in those circumstances, monitoring would be useless and the hierarchical structure of the company would be relieved (Holmström 1982). An alternative mechanism contemplates:

> the concession from a public body (or from a private grant-making foundation) of a fund, on condition that the company provides on its own an optimal cofinancing, and that is withdrawn otherwise. That would operate exactly as dissuading everyone from acting as free riders, because the lack of each contribution would probably be decisive for the loss of the contribution. (Sacconi 2002, 268)

The biggest difficulty concerns (b): when it is necessary to decide and realize, can the hierarchy be actually reduced? Generally, the criteria a democratic company refers to consists in maximizing the number of people that are able to effectively participate to the formulation and the accomplishment of relevant decisions; minimizing the number of positions of authority; charging, for all or almost all of these positions of authority, individuals who are freely elected from the members of organizational units that contain the relative positions as coordination centres; making everyone responsible for the other members of the organization; offering the biggest number of people the possibility of being trained with the purpose of giving them a chance to occupy a wide range of positions of authority, and to introduce themselves as eligible candidates to several types of charges; making the number of individuals who compete for occupying the authority positions wider than the positions themselves, and letting them freely compete among them to obtain the collective mandate; and making a statement, when taking decisions, that the subjects cannot achieve any advantage without considering privations (negative externalities) for other subjects, inside or outside the company. According to Luciano Gallino (2007), to whom we owe the criteria just pointed out, the analysis of the technical and economic possibility of a democratic enterprise, thus not capitalistic, has just seen its birth.

NOTES

1. All quotations have been translated by the author.
2. We don't report on the several elaborations of the concept of capitalism; we just limit it to a few telegraphic recalls. In classic German sociology, Werner Sombart (1902–16) defines capitalism as pre-eminence of profit pursuit and as economic rationalism, while Max Weber (1919–20) enriches the analysis by proving that the peculiar institutional constructions – city, state, law – strengthen the market economy, which still maintains the central position (Collins 1980, Trigilia 1988). The Austrian school of the economic theory, with Eugen Böhm-Bawerk (1887), denies that capitalism is a category of historical differentiation and relates it to the mere use of the so-called indirect or prolonged time methods of production. Moreover, within the Austrian context, Joseph Schumpeter (1911) argues rather that capitalism is specific for the incessant dynamism that gives it the individualistic innovative initiative of entrepreneurs, and for the social screening of investment projects by financial banks. According to the neo-Marxists of the beginning of the 20th century, as Rudolf Hilferding (1910), or of the second part of that century, as Paul Sweezy (1942) the strategic projects of integration between enterprise and finance appear increasingly important, together with the imperialistic processes of direct and indirect control of countries in which capitalism is less developed. With the historic French school of Annales the notion of capitalism is radically reformulated: according to Fernand Braudel (1967–79, 1977), capitalism is that superior level of the economic system in which large amounts of financial, commercial and productive capitals operate: a level that, instead of being submitted to market and technology, tends to dominate both. At last, according to the Heideggerian Emanuele Severino (1993), capitalism is a mere intermediate historical passage. It is still located in a pre-technological and thus humanistic horizon: the capitalist uses the technique as a tool to obtain profit, alienating himself and the workers. But, since pursuing the goal of capital growth requires technical availability, it's the technique itself that becomes crucial, and it has no other goal but its own generic empowerment. Therefore, man is no longer a subject that capitalism alienates, but rather a product of technological alienation that establishes itself as a subject and the man as its own appendix.

REFERENCES

Arendt, H. (1958), *The Human Condition*, Chicago: University of Chicago.

Barnes, P. (2006), *Capitalism 3.0*, San Francisco: Berrett-Koehler Publishers.

Becattini, G. (1999), 'Un'utopia per il mercato: il capitalismo dal volto umano', vol. LV, *Il Ponte*, 3: 54–73.

Böhm-Bawerk, E. von (2006[1889]), *The Positive Theory of Capital*, New York: Cosimo Inc.

Bowles, S. (2004), *Microeconomics. Behavior, institutions, and evolution*, Princeton: Princeton University Press.

Braudel, F. (1992[1967–79]), *Civilization and Capitalism*, 3 vols, Los Angeles: University of California Press, 1992.

Braudel, F. (1977), *La Dynamique du Capitalisme*, Paris: Arthaud.

Castells, M. (2000), *End of Millennium*, Oxford: Blackwell.

Castells, M. (2002[1996]), *The Rise of Network Society*, Oxford: Blackwell.

Collins, R. (1980), 'Weber's last theory of capitalism: a systematization', *American Sociological Review*, vol. XLV, December: 925–942.

Emerson, R. (1963), 'Power dependence relations', *American sociological review*, 27: 31–41.

Gallino, L. (2007), *Tecnologia e democrazia*, Torino: Einaudi.

Graziani, A. (1981), *Macroeconomia*, 3rd ed., Napoli: Edizioni Scientifiche Italiane.

Grossman, S. and O. Hart (1986), 'The costs and benefits of ownership: a theory of vertical and lateral integration', *Journal of Political Economy*, **94**(4), 691–719.

Hart, O. and J. Moore (1990), 'Property rights and the nature of the firm', *Journal of Political Economy*, **98**(6), 1119–1158.

Hilferding, R. (1910), *Finance Capital*, London: Routledge & Kegan Paul, 1981.

Hirschman, A.O. (1977), *The Passions and the Interests*, Princeton: Princeton University Press.

Holmström B. (1982), 'Moral hazards in teams', *Bell Journal of Economics*, **13**(2), 324–340.

La Grassa, G. (1980), *Il valore come astrazione del lavoro*, Bari: Dedalo.

La Grassa, G. (1996), *Lezioni sul capitalismo*, Bologna: Clueb.

La Valle D. (2004), *Economia di mercato senza società di mercato*, Bologna: Il Mulino.

Lerner, A.P. (1972), 'The economics and politics of consumer sovereignty', *American economic review*, **62**(1/2), 258–266.

Marx, K. (1993[1857–58]), *Grundrisse: Foundations of the Critique of Political Economy*, London: Penguin.

Napoleoni, C. (1967), *Economia politica*, Firenze: La Nuova Italia.
Napoleoni, C. (1992[1986]), 'Critica ai critici', reprinted in Napoleoni, C., *Dalla scienza all'utopia*, Torino: Bollati Boringhieri.
Petry, F. (1915), *Der soziale Gehalt der Marxschen Werttheorie*, Jena.
Rajan, R. and L. Zingales (1998), 'Power in a theory of the firm', *Quarterly Journal of Economics*, 112: 387–432.
Roemer, J.E. (1994), *A Future for Socialism*, Boston: Harvard University Press.
Rubin, I.I. (1972[1928]), *Essays on Marx's Theory of Value*, Detroit: Black & Red.
Sacconi, L. (2002), 'Impresa non profit: efficienza, ideologia e codice etico', in F. Cafaggi (ed.), *Modelli di governo, riforma dello stato sociale e ruolo del terzo settore*, Bologna: Il Mulino.
Schumpeter, J.A. (1982[1911]), *The Theory of Economic Development*, New York: Transaction Publishers.
Severino, E. (1993), *Il declino del capitalismo*, Milano: Rizzoli.
Sohn-Rethel, A. (1972), *Intellectual and Manual Labour*, London: Macmillan, 1983.
Sombart, W. (1902–16), *Der moderne Kapitalismus*. München und Leipzig: Duncker & Humblot.
Sweezy, P.M. (1942), *La teoria dello sviluppo capitalistico*, London: Dobson.
Trigilia, C. (2002[1998]), *Economic Sociology: State, Market, and Society in Modern Capitalism*, London: Wiley-Blackwell.
Vercelli, A. (1973), *Teoria della struttura economica capitalistica*, Torino: Fondazione L. Einaudi.
Weber, M. (2007[1919–20]), *General Economic History*, New York: Cosimo Classics.

6. Catholic social teaching
Helen Alford

Just as new academic disciplines started forming in the 19th century, such as sociology, anthropology and psychology, so the Catholic Church began developing a specific body of thought in relation to the social, economic and political changes taking place at that time, even though it had antecedents in moral philosophy and theology for centuries before this. The scale of the social upheavals created by industrialisation, as well as the development of new socio-economic theories such as those of Marx, were changing the cultural presuppositions held by many and presented new situations that called for critical ethical evaluation and practical responses on the part of the Church. Not surprisingly, the first signs of this reaction often emerged among educated lay people directly in contact with these developments, such as Frédéric Ozanam (1813–1853) and Armand de Melun (1807–1877) in France, but in some countries priests were among the first to respond, such as Adolf Kolping (1813–1865) in Germany and Luigi Taparelli d'Azeglio (1793–1862) in Italy. One of the first really influential ecclesiastical voices raised around 1850 was that of the Bishop of Mainz, Wilhelm Emmanuel von Ketteler (1811–1877), whose *Die Arbeiterfrage und das Christentum* (1864) is often regarded as a precursor to the later papal social teaching.

Although any of the bishops, as official teachers within the Catholic Church, can contribute to this corpus of teaching, it has been especially associated with documents on social questions produced by the Popes, as the various collations of documents on social teaching indicate (O'Brien and Shannon 1992; but see Berthouzoz and Papini 1995 as an alternative), not least because most scholars locate its beginning with a papal document called an 'encyclical' published in 1891 (while a minority, such as Schuck (1991), argue that Catholic Social Teaching (CST) begins earlier, they still see it beginning on a papal initiative).

After having to absorb the shocks of the French Revolution and, from 1870 onwards, the loss of the Papal States, the Papacy gradually became better able to confront the challenges that modern thought and practice presented to social, economic and political life. Thus it was that in 1891 Pope Leo XIII launched what becomes known as CST with the encyclical *Rerum Novarum*, meaning 'Of New Things'. Its author had been sensitised to the problems of industrialisation during his mandate as nuncio in Belgium, the first country in mainland Europe to industrialise extensively.

Rerum novarum sets the tone for later social teaching; a consideration of key social issues in the light of the Church's moral teaching and in relation to competing positions (in this case, laissez-faire, socialism and communism). Central to Leo's concern is the condition of working people, and, in particular, their right to organise to defend themselves (though Leo favours, where possible, unions of employers and workers, rather than of workers alone, since he does not accept any fundamental antagonism between social classes) and the need for workers to be able to acquire property, primarily to provide the security needed to found a family. Leo's vision of society is somewhat paternalist for current sensibilities – he explicitly enjoins different duties on employers and workers, for instance – but the most powerful message of the encyclical is his concern for the vulnerable worker. When it was published, *Rerum novarum* caused a sensation, since an institution that, at least since the French Revolution, had been seen as conservative, and supportive of a return to the *ancien regime*, had now taken a clear position in defence of working people.

After *Rerum novarum*, the corpus of CST was developed by subsequent papal documents. The next major one was *Quadragesimo Anno*, published in 1931 as a celebration of the 40th anniversary of *Rerum novarum*. Much of the encyclical deals with the weaknesses in liberalism, demonstrated especially by the effects of the Wall Street Crash, proposing a 'reconstruction of the social order'. It is in this context that Pius introduced the principle of 'subsidiarity' into the corpus of Catholic social teaching. This holds that it is 'gravely wrong' to take control away from people regarding 'what they can accomplish by their own initiative and industry' and to give this control to a higher authority; higher authorities should offer 'help [latin: *subsidium*, hence the word 'subsidiarity'] to the members of the body social, and never destroy or absorb them' (*Quadragesimo Anno*, n. 79) The basic idea is that larger socio-political structures need to support smaller groups, including families, in running their lives. This principle would later be incorporated into the 1992 Treaty on European Union (Maastricht Treaty). Pius laid out a blueprint for 'corporatism', a way of organising society through free, intermediate bodies of workers and employers (developing initial ideas in this line found in *Rerum novarum*) that promote their industry, thus avoiding both the extremes of *laissez-faire* and its opposite, state control. He provided a thinly-veiled critique of the misuse of corporatism that Mussolini had made in Fascist Italy. His successor, Pius XII, produced no encyclical; instead, he favoured the use of many addresses, especially radio messages, as a means of developing CST. John XXIII produced two major social encyclicals, *Mater et Magister* in 1961 and *Pacem in Terris* in 1963. The first followed the lead of Pius XI by rereading *Rerum novarum* in the context of the early 1960s. The primacy of personal initiative in economic affairs was strongly affirmed, while the increasing possibilities for people to relate to each other (what John XXIII called 'socialisation') was seen as fundamentally positive. Particular attention was given to the determination of just wages and aid for development. The second, *Pacem in Terris*, dealt especially with human rights, and their correlative duties, and the relation between authority and conscience, but above all with the relations between states and the question of nuclear conflict and the need for disarmament. Many of these themes appeared again, with added authority, in the document of the Second Vatican Council, 1962–1965, on the Church in the Modern World, *Gaudium et spes*, along with the addition of special chapters on the need to foster marriage and the family and on the role of culture.

In 1967, Pope Paul VI published *Populorum Progressio*, a document which subsequently came to be seen as a parallel foundation for CST to *Rerum novarum*, giving the concept of development an equivalent place in the social teaching to that of work and the defence of workers. It took the most explicitly global position of CST thus far, with concern for the poor being seen just as much in terms of providing the proper conditions for poorer nations to develop as for the poor within a given national community. It was shortly followed by *Octagesima adveniens*, another official document in the series celebrating *Rerum novarum*, this time on its 80th anniversary (as the name of the document indicates) in 1971. Here we find stronger emphasis on the problems of urbanisation and the need for the protection of the environment, both connected with a healthy approach to development. Here too the Pope encouraged the local churches to reflect on the specific issues that they must face in the light of the universal social teaching proposed by the Popes. It is along this line of thinking that the US bishops produced their 1986 document *Economic Justice for All*.

John Paul II issued three social encyclicals, the first and third of which are especially relevant to economics, philanthropy and social enterprise. *Laborem Exercens* (LE), as the title suggests, focuses on human work, fittingly on another of the anniversaries of *Rerum novarum*. One of the key ideas in LE is that work has two 'dimensions': one 'objective' and the other 'subjective'. The objective dimension we all know well; it concerns the product or service that is produced through a person's work, and which, like all objective outcomes, can be measured and monitored. The subjective dimension, however, is not so easily recognised in business; it concerns the effect of work on the person him or herself. Especially where work is boring and monotonous, or where the dignity of a working person is not recognised, this effect can be quite negative (as, indeed, Adam Smith recognised in the last volume of *The Wealth of Nations*). Concepts like human or social capital could be linked to the subjective dimension of work, as could the wider idea of 'intangibles'. Another important pair of terms discussed in the encyclical is that of the direct and indirect employer. While he re-iterated the classic duties of the direct employer, John Paul II developed a new approach to the responsibilities of other 'stakeholders' with regard to employees, especially the state, regarding them as 'indirect employers'.

The second encyclical, *Sollicitudo rei socialis*, issued in 1988 for the 20th anniversary of the encyclical *Populorum progressio*, presented a more pessimistic view of the prospects for international development than its predecessor. Again, the approach is quite analytical and some very helpful concepts are introduced into CST. For instance, the Pope contrasted the tragedy of underdevelopment with a parallel in the rich countries that he calls 'superdevelopment'. This term indicates a situation where people define themselves by what they consume or own, to the extent that any genuine meaning to their lives may be lost. They end up bereft of different, but no less basic, goods for human flourishing than those suffering from underdevelopment. Another key concept is that of 'structures of sin'; these result from the accumulated effects of individual sins that create consolidated social, economic and political structures that are difficult to change and block the path of true development. In this regard, special mention is made of the split of the world into two blocs (lead by the USSR and the US), and the way this skewed the action of various actors with regard to development. The central chapter is a consideration of 'authentic human development', clearly focusing the development agenda on human development rather than economic growth. It is of some note that a major seminar took place at the UN on this encyclical shortly after its publication, and that the first Human Development Report, with its fundamental Human Development Index which soon began to replace growth in GDP as the main measure of development, was issued in 1990.

The third encyclical, *Centesimus annus*, coming out on the 100th anniversary of *Rerum novarum* and two years after the fall of the Berlin Wall, is one of the most significant documents of the CST thus far for economics and business. Opening as the previous celebratory encyclicals do with a re-reading of *Rerum novarum*, it then focused on the 'new things' of today's society, with an analysis of the collapse of communism or real socialism as its main focus. The underlying problem in communism is 'anthropological' (*Centesimus annus*, n. 13), since the good of the person is subordinated to that of the wider society, personal freedom is of no account, and the human person is reduced to 'a series of social relationships'. Existence is only on the material level, with no recognition of a spiritual or transcendent dimension to the human person. In the chapter 'The Year 1989' a detailed analysis of the causes of the fall of communism is given, with the 'decisive factor' identified as 'the violation of the rights of workers' (*Centesimus annus*, n. 23). John Paul II, in his encyclical *Centesimus annus* also mentions another key cause: 'the inefficiency of the economic system, which is not to be considered simply as a technical problem, but rather a consequence of the violation of the human rights to private initiative, to ownership of property and to freedom in the economic sector' (*Centesimus annus*, n. 24). The longest of the six chapters of the encyclical, Chapter 4, returns to one of the key issues of *Rerum novarum*, private property and the universal destination of material goods. Private property is 'fundamental for the autonomy and development of the person' but its use 'while marked by freedom, is subordinated to [its] original destination as created goods' (*Centesimus annus*, n. 30). This teaching is based fundamentally on the source of property: it is God's gift to humanity as a whole in creation. At the end of the 20th century, human sources of wealth (created through work) are more important than land or other more classical forms of property. This means that there are now new ways for people to be excluded from owning property, where people 'have no way of entering the network of knowledge and intercommunication which would enable them to see their qualities appreciated and utilized' (*Centesimus annus*, n. 33). Most people in this situation are to be found in 'Third World' countries, although the elderly and the young as well as women in developed countries can also find themselves in this position.

Market mechanisms are given a qualified welcome, since for 'solvent' needs they are 'the most efficient instrument for utilizing resources and effectively responding to needs' (*Centesimus annus*, n. 34). Since, however, many human needs 'find no place on the market', the key basis for a just social order is a 'society of free work, of enterprise and participation . . . not directed against the market' but where the market is 'appropriately controlled by the forces of society and by the state, so as to guarantee that the basic needs of the whole of society are satisfied' (*Centesimus annus*, n. 35). Profit is 'legitimate' and an 'indication that a business is functioning well', but it 'is not the only indicator': 'It is possible for the financial accounts to be in order, and yet for the people – who make up the firm's most valuable asset – to be humiliated and their dignity offended' (*Centesimus annus*, n. 35). Not surprisingly, such a situation, over time, will also have negative economic effects. John Paul then gives a definition of the purpose of business, which harks back to *Mater et magistra*: 'the purpose of the business is not simply to make a profit, but is to be found in its very existence as a community of persons who in various ways are endeavouring to satisfy their basic needs' (*Centesimus annus*, n. 35). Linked to this affirmation is the statement that 'it is unacceptable to say that the defeat of "Real Socialism" leaves capitalism as the only model of economic organization' (*Centesimus annus*, n. 35). The questions of the indebtedness of poor countries, the growth of consumerism –

meaning life where consumption is an end in itself – and the ecological crisis, referred not only to natural ecology, but also to 'human ecology' and 'social ecology' (*Centesimus annus*, nn. 38, 39) all indicate that we suffer from an 'ethical and cultural system' where 'production and consumption of goods become the centre of social life and society's only value' (*Centesimus annus*, n. 39). There is a danger of an 'idolatry of the market', against which the encyclical defends, for instance, the action of the state in the preservation of common goods, and where alienation, meaning 'a reversal of means and ends', remains a major problem (*Centesimus annus*, n. 40).

The pontiff poses the question: 'can it perhaps be said that . . . capitalism should be the goal of the countries now making efforts to rebuild their economy and society? Is this the model which ought to be proposed to the countries of the Third World which are searching for the path to true economic progress?' He gives a qualified yes, distinguishing the understanding of capitalism that can be accepted from that which cannot:

> If by 'capitalism' is meant an economic system which recognizes the fundamental and positive role of business, the market, private property and the resulting responsibility for the means of production, as well as free human creativity in the economic sector, then the answer is certainly in the affirmative, even though it would perhaps be more appropriate to speak of a 'business economy', 'market economy' or simply 'free economy'. But if by 'capitalism' is meant a system in which freedom in the economic sector is not circumscribed within a strong juridical framework which places it at the service of human freedom in its totality, and which sees it as a particular aspect of that freedom, the core of which is ethical and religious, then the reply is certainly negative. (*Centesimus annus*, n. 42)

Apart from his three encyclicals, John Paul is also responsible for the *Compendium of the Social Doctrine of the Church*, compiled by the Pontifical Council of Justice and Peace and published in 2004. The historical development of CST that we have charted so far is complemented by the Compendium, in that it aims to provide a general synthesis of CST up to that time (since then, another social encyclical has been produced). The Compendium starts with a chapter on God's love for humanity; Chapter 2 outlines how, driven by this love, and in response to it, the Church carries forward its social mission. The third chapter focuses on the nature of the human person and human rights, the understanding of which is fundamental to the whole corpus of CST. Human dignity is based in CST on the biblical revelation that the human person is made 'in the image of God' (Genesis, 1:27) and is capable of a relationship with God which flows over into relationships with others. The relational dimension of each human being is the foundation of social life, though it is damaged by the effects of human sin. Various aspects of the human person are also treated in this chapter: the unity of the material and spiritual aspects of the human being; the openness to transcendence (relationship with God) and the uniqueness of each person; human freedom, which in CST is inevitably linked to truth and natural law, as well as the equality of all people in dignity. CST recognises that the development of the idea and legal application of human rights is helpful for upholding the dignity of the human person.

Following on from the consideration of the human person and human dignity, the other fundamental principles of CST are presented in Chapter 4, starting with the principle of the common good. This is the shared social and physical value that human beings hold together, starting with the gift of the earth and of human society, and including all that human communities develop together, including infrastructure, education systems and the growth of all the members of society in a shared way of life. Closely related to this principle is that of the universal destination of goods. The idea here is that, fundamentally, the goods of the earth are given to all human beings, but that due to human weakness and sin, the sharing of all goods in common leads to economic collapse and social ruin. Systems of private property are therefore needed, since their owners have the incentive to make effective use of their resources, they care for and maintain of them, and clarity regarding who owns what, other things being equal, tends to prevent social disorder. However, private property remains a means to an end: the creation of sufficient goods to promote the good of all. Hence, while CST strongly supports institutions of private property, it attacks any theory of absolute property rights and supports just systems of taxation and other legitimate forms of economic redistribution towards the end of providing access for all to the goods of the earth. The principle of subsidiarity has already been mentioned above, and is closely linked to that of participation. The last major principle presented is that of solidarity, which is also presented as a moral virtue, that is, 'the firm and persevering determination to commit oneself to the common good' (*Compendium of the Social Doctrine of the Church*, n. 193).

Various elements in the chapters that follow, including those on the family, human work, economic life, and the political community are relevant to economics, philanthropy and reciprocity. Here we can note three among the most important:

1. The family is the fundamental social unit, a microcosm of society as a whole in which each member is valued as a person. Furthermore, the 'economy (*'oiko-nomia'*, household management) was born from domestic work' (*Compendium of the Social Doctrine of the Church*, n. 248), and in many parts of the world remains a central economic unit. The balance between work and family life is a complex one, but central for society.
2. Economic activity is to serve human beings and social progress, not the other way around. In this way, 'the economy . . . can be transformed into [a] place [. . .] of salvation and sanctification' (*Compendium of the Social Doctrine of the Church*, n. 326). Profit-making businesses need to orient their profit-making activities towards the common good, as part of the 'social ecology' of society (*Compendium of the Social Doctrine of the Church*, n. 340). Civil society organizations are a crucial part of creating an environment in which this kind of attitude towards economic gain is present, for they 'unite efficiency in production with solidarity' (*Compendium of the Social Doctrine of the Church*, n. 356).
3. The political community is oriented towards the service of civil society, as 'the sum of relationships and resources, cultural and associative, that are relatively independent from the political sphere and the economic sector' (*Compendium of the Social Doctrine of the Church*, n. 417). The understanding of this relationship differs radically from individualistic social theories that tend to recognise only the individual and the State. Since human beings develop in community with each other, primarily through their work, and the promotion of the full development of the human person is the goal of politics and the economy, it follows that politics is at the service of the human person in his and her relationships with others.

The most recent social encyclical produced by Pope Benedict XVI in 2009, *Caritas in veritate*, included some new emphases that are less prominent in previous social teaching. It is the second encyclical, after *Sollicitudo rei socialis*, in the series of celebrations of *Populorum progressio* and includes a re-reading of that encyclical in the light of later developments. It emphasises love as the driving force and motivation behind all action for development, in a way that builds on and complements action based on justice. It also recognises more clearly than in the past the breakdown of 'binary models', such as production of wealth vs distribution of wealth, or market vs state, and gives a number of reasons for this. Economies now work on a global scale, while political systems are still largely nation-state based. This means that a two-stage logic in terms of producing wealth and then distributing it is no longer possible; profits and financial flows move around the world and are not necessarily taxed at the point of their production, providing resources for the provision of necessary services. Production and distribution need to be seen in an integrated way, which is the basic reason for the development of the idea and practice of 'corporate social responsibility'. Similarly, markets need to be 'pluralist', with an 'ecology' of business types and 'hybrid forms of commercial behaviour' that sees mutual influence between civil society organisations, business and the organs of the state (*Caritas in veritate*, n. 38). In some ways, this represents a deepening of the idea of 'business' down to its more fundamental core; business involves marshalling resources towards the satisfaction of human needs and the creation of value through innovation. It may involve making a profit, or it may not; it does involve sustainability in terms of the inflow and outflow of resources. Another way in which binary models are breaking down is through the recognition that love, in the sense of gratuitousness, gift and fraternity, is increasingly finding its place in the world of business, as part of building a 'civil economy'. Cooperatives and the Economy of Communion are given as examples of this. The encyclical ends with a long chapter on technology and its role in promoting true human development.

REFERENCES

Benedict XVI (2009), *Caritas in veritate*, Rome, Libreria Editrice Vaticana.

Berthouzoz, Roger O.P. and Roberto Papini (1995), *Ethique, économie et dévéloppement: L'enseignment des évêques des cinq continents (1891–1991)*, Paris, Le Cerf.

Centesimus annus in David O'Brien and Thomas A. Shannon (1992), *Catholic Social Thought: The Documentary Heritage*, New York, Orbis.

Laborem Exercens in David O'Brien and Thomas A. Shannon (1992), *Catholic Social Thought: The Documentary Heritage*, New York, Orbis.

Mater et Magister in David O'Brien and Thomas A. Shannon (1992), *Catholic Social Thought: The Documentary Heritage*, New York, Orbis.

O'Brien, David J. and Thomas A. Shannon (1992), *Catholic Social Thought: The Documentary Heritage*, New York, Orbis.

Octagesima Adveniens in David O'Brien and Thomas A. Shannon (1992), *Catholic Social Thought: The Documentary Heritage*, New York, Orbis.

Pacem in Terris in David O'Brien and Thomas A. Shannon (1992), *Catholic Social Thought: The Documentary Heritage*, New York, Orbis.

Pontifical Council of Justice and Peace (2004), *Compendium of the Social Doctrine of the Church*, Rome, Libreria Editrice Vaticana.

Populorum Progressio in David O'Brien and Thomas A. Shannon (1992), *Catholic Social Thought: The Documentary Heritage*, New York, Orbis.

Quadragesimo Anno in David O'Brien and Thomas A. Shannon (1992), *Catholic Social Thought: The Documentary Heritage*, New York, Orbis.

Rerum Novarum in David O'Brien and Thomas A. Shannon (1992), *Catholic Social Thought: The Documentary Heritage*, New York, Orbis.

Schuck, Michael (1991), *That They May Be One: The Social Teaching of the Papal Encyclicals 1740–1989*, Washington DC, Georgetown University Press.

Sollicitudo Rei Socialis in David O'Brien and Thomas A. Shannon (1992), *Catholic Social Thought: The Documentary Heritage*, New York, Orbis.

7. Catholic social thought
Albino Barrera

This chapter examines the theological and anthropological foundations of Catholic social thought and then describes its contributions to the fields of philanthropy, social entrepreneurship, and reciprocity. It concludes by briefly assessing the practical problems associated with implementing its proposals.

THEOLOGICAL AND ANTHROPOLOGICAL FOUNDATIONS

Catholic social thought is a subdivision of moral theology, that is, the study of proper human conduct based on faith and reason. Faith is founded on Revelation: God's initiative of self-disclosing the divine interior life which culminates in the life, death, and resurrection of Jesus Christ. In contrast to the Reformation belief in *sola scriptura*, Catholics hold that Revelation is comprised of two major pillars – Sacred Scripture and tradition – served by the teaching office of the Church. The Old and the New Testament are accorded a privileged position because of their inspired nature. Christians believe that God is the principal author of Sacred Scripture, and it is the Holy Spirit that guarantees the integrity of these writings. Revelation requires faith since its claims are not dependent on empirical validation nor are they subject to empirical verification. They are accepted on the basis of God's word alone.

Tradition, the supporting pillar of Revelation, is that which receives, records, preserves, and transmits that which have been self-revealed by God. Examples of what are included in tradition are the teachings of Augustine, Aquinas, and the Magisterium, that is, the college of bishops in communion with the pope. Thus, the scope of Catholic social thought (CST) is extensive and includes the Old and New Testament, the Patristic Fathers, the Scholastic Doctors, and the papal and episcopal social documents of the last century from Leo XIII's *Rerum novarum* (1891) to Benedict XVI's *Caritas in veritate* (2009).

CST is also founded on human reason. Human beings are created in the image and likeness of God. Because of their God-given reason, they are capable of knowing and understanding the nature of God's divine order. Morality is intelligible. Consequently, CST is not merely deontological (because of the need to conform to the will of God), but it is also teleological. People pursue that which is good because of their self-understanding. They know who they are as persons and who they are as a human community, created and sustained by divine providence. Furthermore, despite their wounded nature, they are nevertheless capable of exercising the divine gift of authentic freedom. Humans are able to choose that which is good and right. They are capable of moral choices that ennoble life. Thus, faith and reason mutually reinforce one another.

Such optimistic anthropology complements CST's sanguine view of and active engagement with the larger culture. All creation, including the material world, is good because of the infinite wisdom and goodness of the Creator. Thus, far from withdrawing and isolating itself from the world, CST situates itself in the heart of the larger world and dialogues with it. Defending the dignity and life of the human person and the order of divine creation is not merely an option for the Catholic Church, it is in fact a grave obligation. This accounts for why the Church is vigorously involved in rectifying social problems. This also explains why CST is neither a completed nor a closed set of teachings. It is a living tradition that continues to grow.

Over the centuries, this active tradition has accumulated a rich store of theological and philosophical tools for dealing with social problems. Despite its wide range of materials, CST's salient teachings are evident in the following key social principles. The principle of human dignity stems from the human person's creation in the image and likeness of God, redemption in Jesus Christ, and filial divine adoption. Because of this human dignity, the principle of integral human development calls for balanced personal growth – body, mind, and spirit. The principle of the common good affirms that the human person can flourish only within community. The good of the individual and the good of the community, while distinct from one another, are inseparable.

The universal destination of the goods of the earth notes that creation is a divine gift meant to benefit all, regardless of how titles of ownership are assigned. The principle of subsidiarity calls on higher bodies (e.g., government) not to do what lower bodies or individuals are able to do for themselves. However, these higher bodies are obligated to step in and provide assistance once lower bodies are no longer able to function on behalf of the common good. The principle of solidarity elicits a genuine and active concern for others because we see in them a fellow child of God, a brother or a sister. As part of solidarity, the principle of preferential option for the poor calls for according even greater solicitude for those with the greatest need. The principle of relative equality asserts that while there are legitimate inequalities in society, such inequalities must be kept within reasonable bounds that protect the common good. The principle of stewardship is an appeal for due care and the prudent use of the divine gift of the earth and our personal endowments.

Modern Catholic social documents are predominantly concerned with political economy. Consequently, the tradition has much to contribute to the study of philanthropy, reciprocity, and social enterprise. Given the severe space limitation, readers are referred to the references at the end of this chapter for more thorough expositions of CST.

THE ECONOMICS AND THEOLOGY OF RECIPROCITY

The Old Testament has an impressive array of social safety nets, such as interest-free loans; debt remission after seven years; slave release after six years; gleaning privileges for aliens, widows, and orphans; a tri-annual tithe for the poor; shared feasts to which the landless and the needy were invited; the return of ancestral land to their original owners; land and kin redemption in which relatives were obligated to buy back family land or kin sold into slavery; and Sabbath fallow years when the poor got to keep whatever grew on land that was supposed to be left idle every seven years. These norms were meant to assist those who had fallen on hard times to recover their status as independent landholding families.

Many of these norms were longstanding practices that were then codified in law as the nation Israel was formed from approximately 1300 B.C. onwards. Directly relevant for this handbook is the belief of most scripture scholars that these community norms arose out of pragmatic self-interest. Life was extremely uncertain and fraught with danger in a nomadic or agricultural setting. Disease, drought, the predation of roving bandits, war, and crop failures were common. Given such precarious subsistence living, the best use of what little surplus one may be able to produce at the moment is 'to bank' or 'to invest' it by helping distressed neighbors. Not only does this build goodwill, but it also ensures that one is able to ask for others' help in return at some point in the future. Thus, their common practice of mutual assistance was, in fact, a rational economic strategy of mutual survival. At the heart of it is the principle of reciprocity.

An operative reciprocity is also evident in many of the motive clauses appended to numerous Old Testament statutes. These motive clauses were straightforward in reminding the Chosen People to be generous and solicitous of the poor because God was merely asking them to extend to others the same favors that they themselves had received from God in their own moment of need (e.g., Dt 15:12–18; Lev 25:35–38).

Such reciprocity is reflected in the New Testament as well, as in the case of the synagogue leaders interceding with Jesus on behalf of the Roman centurion whose servant boy was dying (Lk 7:1–10). Recall, too, the account of the neighbor who had to badger a friend for a loaf of bread because of a late-night guest (Lk 11:5–8). Even more impressive is the example of some early Christians who held things in common – giving according to what they had and simply taking according to what they needed (Acts 4:32–35). Similarly, in his collection for the poor in Jerusalem, Paul reminds the various churches to give from their plenty, so that in their own need, they too could in turn receive help from other churches (2 Cor 8:13–15). Such spirit of reciprocity can still be found in the medieval ages as we see in the account of Bruni and Zamagni (2007).

PHILANTHROPY

Almsgiving and generosity are constitutive of biblical teachings. These are central precepts in all three Abrahamic faiths: Judaism, Christianity, and Islam. In addition to the aforesaid pragmatic and theological reasons animating the practice of reciprocity, the Chosen People and the disciples of Christ were obligated to be openhanded in giving to the distressed because the poor are beloved by God. Furthermore, such generosity is the means by which humans actualize God's gift of conditional prosperity for all. There is supposed to be no poor in their midst, if people would only heed God's economic norms (Dt. 15:4).

Among the Patristic Fathers, hoarded wealth is viewed as 'theft from the poor' (Phan 1984). For Aquinas, it is a duty to use whatever is superfluous in one's income or wealth for the benefit of the poor. John XXIII builds on this insight to note that superfluity is measured not on the basis of what is needed to maintain one's station in social life, but on the relative unmet needs of one's neighbor. In the modern social documents, the principle of solidarity calls on higher bodies and individuals to step in and to assist lower bodies or individuals who are no longer able to function on their own for the common good. No one can claim to have reached integral human development or the common good if one's neighbor, whom one could help, wallows in destitution. After all, while integral human development is a path that every individual has to take, it is a journey that can only be completed together. Integral human development is the self-actualization of the whole person and of every person.

In the final analysis, the opening lines of the Second Vatican Council's social document *Gaudium et spes* eloquently and succinctly state a simple but profound theological rationale for generosity:

> The joys and the hopes, the grief and the anxieties of the men and women of this age, especially those who are poor or in any way afflicted, these are the joys and hopes, the grief and anxieties of the followers of Christ. Indeed, nothing genuinely human fails to raise an echo in their hearts. (Vatican Council II 1965)

Christians reach out to those in need with generosity, not out of fear of punishment or in anticipation of a reward, but because they see and love Christ in the needy, the hungry, the naked, and the sick (Mt 25:31–46).

SOCIAL ENTERPRISE

Corporate social responsibility and social entrepreneurship may be contemporary terms, but their spirit has always been very much part of the Catholic social tradition. For example, consider once again the Old Testament's economic ordinances. The economic cost of these admonitions is enormous: debt forgiveness, foregone interest, foregone crops, tithes, and many others. Note that the burden of such social safety net for the distressed falls entirely on members of the community with the necessary property or productive capacity. After all, they are the ones who have the surplus to lend and to tithe or the land with which to let people glean. Note the following two features of Old Testament economic life.

First, unlike Jesus, the Old Testament does not call on the Chosen People to divest themselves of property. Radical voluntary poverty was not part of their Sinai Covenant. In fact, the writers of the Old Testament took great care to describe how the conquered lands were carefully allotted to the various tribes based on the productivity of the soil and the size of the families (e.g., Num 26:52–56; 33:54). Clearly, the goal was to ensure that families were able to earn an independent livelihood. Second, ordinances such as interest-free loans, debt remission, and gleaning are clearly contrary to the modern neo-classical paradigm of profit-maximization. Putting these two observations together gives us an appreciation for the *via media* of Proverbs 30:8, that is, 'give me neither poverty nor riches; feed me with the food that I need.' This is the ideal of economic life. Note that this, too, is the underlying and unspoken rule of contemporary social enterprises: They have to operate in the black, but only that they might be self-sustaining in their efforts to achieve larger social goals.

In the New Testament, Paul is one who exemplifies such an ideal. Even though he was entitled to receive material support from the churches, he nonetheless labors manually to support himself so that he might be able to preach the Gospel (the social goal) while not being a burden on anybody else (self-sustaining feature).

In the modern social documents, we recognize the same principle at work. Consider the seminal encyclical *Rerum novarum* (Leo XIII 1891). It affirms the right to private property ownership and thereby validates the claim of capitalists to their profits. However, the document goes further, noting that the right to private property ownership has attendant just-use obligations, that is, these properties must be used to benefit all. There is a distinction between ownership and usufruct. Moreover, it also means that it is stewardship rather than a proprietary attitude that should animate property owners. Thus, the neo-classical maxim of profit-maximization has no place in this tradition. In all this, however, there is a hard realism and balance to the modern Catholic social documents. We see this on so many occasions. *Quadragesimo anno* (Pius XI 1931) calls on employers to provide living wages to workers, but it is also acknowledges that business survival and, consequently, continued employment take precedence in the event of a trade-off. *Populorum progressio* (Paul VI 1967) sees the urgent need for land reform, but it calls for caution in the speed of implementation, lest greater harm be inflicted on the poor. *Laborem exercens* (John Paul II 1981) teaches that the subjective dimension of work (the fact that the worker is a human person and with dependents, to boot) should take priority, but at the same time it affirms the importance of the objective dimension of work that ensures the continued viability of the business enterprise. *Centesimus annus* (John Paul II 1991) affirms the value of profits and entrepreneurship, but only that they might contribute to the common good.

All this is to bring home the point that social entrepreneurship and its underlying mechanism of using business tools and practices to achieve larger social goals are not alien to the Catholic social tradition. This should not come as a surprise because of its longstanding and foundational belief that the goods of the earth and economic activity are merely instrumental and not ends in themselves. The end is friendship with God (Gen 1:1–31).

PROBLEMS AND CONTROVERSIES IN ECONOMICS

Philanthropy, reciprocity, and social enterprise work well in theory, but not always in practice. Take the case of reciprocity. For this to work, at least one of two conditions must be satisfied. First, members of the community are people of high character. They are virtuous and can be taken at their word. They are self-policing and voluntarily give others their due. Second, there are iron-clad community mechanisms for enforcing reciprocity either through moral suasion (e.g., appeal to people's sense of honor or public shaming) or through formal law.

The most significant hurdle to reciprocity is enforcement. By its nature, reciprocity entails exchanging goods, services, or good will across different time periods. This means that there is an incentive for earlier beneficiaries to 'cheat' and not to return the favors or benefits previously received to their counterparts at a later date, especially when the latter are in need. Thus, one or both of the above conditions are needed in order to make reciprocity work. For example, microfinancing is viable largely because loans are guaranteed through the shared liability of neighbors, friends, or relatives. Similarly, rotating savings and credit associations (ROSCAs) succeed because early beneficiaries continue paying into the pool even after they have drawn on their allotted benefits. In both cases, the incentive to welch on one's agreement is great, but people do not do so, either because of their virtue or because of the informal enforcement mechanisms. Losing face in one's community, the risk of being ostracized, and the threat of not being able to secure future help from others are effective deterrents to wholesale cheating.

The economics of this is encapsulated in the prisoner's dilemma and the assurance game in which the best solution requires the cooperation of all parties. In an iterated game, people learn and adjust their behavior accordingly. Thus, as people see a high compliance rate, they too have the incentive to conform to the solution that provides an optimum result for all members of the group. Of course, there will always be the incentive to free ride over others' compliance.

All these aforesaid formal and informal mechanisms of enforcement fall apart as the circle of exchange expands and as transactions become increasingly impersonal, anonymous, or one-time. Furthermore, a much larger marketplace provides a much larger pool of potential counterparties for future trades. Moral suasion does not work in such a marketplace. Thus, while reciprocity might work in small local communities (e.g., buying from the neighborhood grocer on credit), it quickly falls apart as we move from the local to the national and the global because free-riding becomes much easier.

A necessary condition for reciprocity to work in a large setting is public education. Unless individual market participants internalize virtuous conduct, we will be back to the prisoner's dilemma and reciprocity will not work. Good examples of such well-informed, self-policing, virtuous conduct are consumers who voluntarily support Fair Trade products and the carbon offset programs at great personal cost. There is evidence in Sacred Scripture that free-ridership might have been a problem in the early Church. Recall the Pauline criticism of those who refused to work (2 Thess 3:6–12). In the final analysis, reciprocity is about justice and the self-respect that comes with knowing that one has been fair and has not taken advantage of others. Reciprocity is thus important for personal fulfillment.

The economics of philanthropy and social enterprise also poses significant hurdles. Take the simple case of social enterprises. Their profit-income statement must necessarily be in the black if they are to be self-sustaining entities not dependent on donations. They can continue doing good and pursuing larger societal goals, but only if they are able to pay their way through and finance their own operations. This is what distinguishes social entrepreneurship from many other non-governmental organizations that are dependent on a continuous stream of donations. For social entrepreneurs, a key issue is knowing how much of the accounting profit-surplus has to be retained in order to build up the entity's further development, growth, and competitiveness.

Or, take the case of Catholic social thought's two desiderata of full employment at a living wage. Such a dual goal entails a massive transfer of resources that may even exceed the individual firm's or the entire community's surplus (Barrera 2001, 305–313). Furthermore, such requisite transfers might be so huge as to require confiscatory tax rates. This destroys private initiative and devolves into a downward spiral in which fewer incentives for private economic activity mean less job creation, and even larger requisite transfers from those who are able to produce surplus. In the end, nothing will be produced and everyone loses out. In other words, we cannot focus on distribution alone. Equally and perhaps even more important is the need to ensure that individual firms remain viable business entities, that individuals have the incentives to do what they ought to be doing on their own (principle of subsidiarity), and that the community gives them the opportunity to do so. The implosion of the heavily centralized and regimented Soviet economies at the end of the 20th century is ample warning on how the pursuit of larger social goals is sustainable only if we are attentive to the requirements of smoothly operating markets. At the same time, the 2008 global financial meltdown and the Great Recession it precipitated also remind us that unfettered smoothly operating markets require extra-market oversight.

In these aforesaid cases, observe that both philanthropy and social enterprises must necessarily still operate within the bounds of economic realities if they are to be self-sustaining and not dependent on external donations. To be sure, economics is not the primary consideration. *Populorum progressio* (Paul VI 1967) long ago argued passion-ately that authentic development is not principally an economic phenomenon; it is a moral phenomenon. Nevertheless, economics also matters and, in many cases, it matters enormously. As *Gaudium et spes* (Vatican Council II 1965:#36) notes, God endowed temporal realities (e.g., economic life) with their particular requirements and unique modes of operation as part of the divine order of creation. In other words, it is futile to go against the workings of the natural order.

MOVING AHEAD

As we have seen in the preceding sections, we face formidable hurdles to making the economics of reciprocity, philanthropy, and social enterprises work. Their theology and philosophy are widely understood and appreciated. But the economics of their practical implementation has so many gray areas as to require much prudential judgment. In fact, it is extremely difficult to enforce them in the external forum of the law. It is very likely that they can be effectively implemented at minimal transaction cost only in the internal forum, that is, in every person's heart and mind. In addition, people should have the conceptual tools to be able to make their prudential judgment intelligently. Herein lies another contribution of CST.

The delicate economics behind reciprocity, philanthropy, and social enterprise only goes to underscore one important feature of Catholic social thought – its realistic bal-anced approach. When used together within a single framework, Catholic social princi-ples balance each other and ensure that individual principles are not abused or misused beyond their intended ends. Thus, note that CST's political economy calls for balance: free market operations with extra-market oversight; the private sector and the govern-ment as both legitimate agents of development and necessary partners; the common good and the individual good as necessary conditions to each other; simultaneous mat-erial and spiritual development; private property ownership and its concomitant just-use obligation; efficiency and equity as macroeconomic goals.

In sum, Catholic social thought has two significant contributions. First, it provides theological and philosophical justification for reciprocity, philanthropy, and social entrepreneurship. Second, CST's social principles and overarching framework provide conceptual tools for dealing with the problems and clashing claims spawned by the economics of these social practices that are laudable but extremely difficult to implement and sustain in practice.

BIBLIOGRAPHY

Barrera, Albino (2001) *Modern Catholic Social Documents and Political Economy*, Washington, DC: Georgetown University Press.
Benedict XVI (2005) *Caritas in Veritate*, Boston: Daughters of St. Paul.
Bruni, Luigino and Stefano Zamagni (2007) *Civil Economy: Efficiency, Equity, Public Happiness*, Bern: Peter Lang.
Catholic Bishops' Conference of England and Wales (1996) *The Common Good and the Catholic Church's Social Teaching*, London.
Finn, Daniel (ed.) (2010) *True Wealth of Nations: Catholic Social Thought and Economic Life*, Oxford University Press.
John Paul II (1981) *Laborem Exercens*, Boston: Daughters of St. Paul.
John Paul II (1991) *Centesimus Annus*, Boston: Daughters of St. Paul.
Leo XIII (1891) *Rerum Novarum*, Boston: Daughters of St. Paul.
National Conference of Catholic Bishops (1986) *Economic Justice for All (Pastoral Letter on Catholic Social Teaching and the US Economy)*, Washington DC: National Conference of Catholic Bishops.
Paul VI (1967) *Populorum Progressio*, Boston: Daughters of St. Paul.
Phan, Peter (1984) *Social Thought. Message of the Fathers of the Church*, Wilmington, Delaware: Michael Glazier.
Pius XI (1931) *Quadragesimo Anno*, Boston: Daughters of St. Paul.
Pontifical Council for Justice and Peace (2004) *Compendium of the Social Doctrine of the Church*, Vatican.
Vatican Council II (1965) *Gaudium et Spes*, Boston: Daughters of St. Paul.

8. Cooperative enterprise
Derek C. Jones and Panu Kalmi*

INTRODUCTION

In this brief introduction to economics research on cooperatives, we first provide definitions and then some examples of the incidence of different types of cooperatives around
the world. Concerning research, we note that the theoretical literature on cooperatives
and particularly worker cooperatives has been comparatively well developed following the seminal contributions of Ward (1958) and Vanek (1970), although subsequent
empirical work has shown that often theory was insufficiently informed by empirical
regularities observed in actually existing worker cooperatives. For other types of cooperatives, there is no unifying theoretical framework, and most of these cooperatives
have received attention in the literature far below what one might have expected based
on their economic significance. However, much of this literature has been empirically
and institutionally oriented. In the final section we discuss some recent themes in recent
research and emphasize ways in which the availability of new datasets may contain
significant promise for research on cooperatives.

TYPES OF COOPERATIVES AND COOPERATIVE INCIDENCE

For our purposes the essential features of cooperatives are given by enterprises that
have the following characteristics: 1) ownership is not determined solely by investment
in shares, but owners have another transaction relationship with the enterprise (as
employees, suppliers, or customers); 2) voting rights are not determined in relation to
capital ownership but are divided equally among members.[1] As such this definition de-
emphasizes other Rochdale principles including open membership, limited interest on
capital, religious neutrality, cash trading and the promotion of education (Bonner 1961).
　Diverse forms of cooperatives exist. Hansmann (1996) and Birchall (1997) amongst
others provide good descriptions of cooperatives around the globe.[2] Empirically, the
most important forms of primary cooperatives, both in the US and elsewhere, appear
to be cooperatives in the agricultural sector (mainly in food production), in banking
and finance (in the form of credit unions and cooperative banks), in insurance (either
mutual or cooperative form), and in retailing, where cooperatives are either retailer- or
consumer-owned (the latter is fairly uncommon in the US but is very popular in some
European countries). Cooperatives are economically significant actors all around the
globe. According to the International Cooperative Alliance, the combined membership
in cooperatives is over 1 billion people (see http://2012.coop/en/ica/cooperative-facts-
figures, last accessed November 2012). In some countries cooperatives represent a most
significant form of economic organization. Thus, in New Zealand, it has been estimated
that the turnover of cooperatives and mutuals amounts to more than 20 percent of GDP

(see http://nz.coop/understanding-co-ops-in-new-zealand/, last accessed November 2012), while in Iran the Fifth National Development plan calls for the cooperative sector to soon account for 25 percent of GDP (Ministry of Cooperatives, Iran 2010).

Moreover some cooperative forms, including cooperative banks, have been found to be of growing importance in their sectors (Fonteyne 2007). For example, around 91 million inhabitants of the US (about 44 percent of the economically active population) were members of credit unions in 2007 (WOCCU 2011), representing a substantial growth from 1996 when the membership totaled around 70 million (Emmons and Schmid 1999). In France, cooperative financial institutions have more than 50 percent market share of deposits and they have almost 20 million members or almost one-third of total population.[3, 4] Another example is in Singapore where the NTUC group has about 2 million policy holders (representing about 40 percent of the population, see http://www.income.com.sg/aboutus/factsheet.asp, last accessed November 2012). However, the importance of cooperatives does not derive solely from their economic significance, but also because of their democratic governance and their perceived ability to address market failures (see, e.g., Kalmi 2007). In part reflecting their social objectives, associations of cooperatives are a prominent feature of the cooperative landscape.

While a wide variety of firms can be listed under the cooperative umbrella, the form that has proved to be of particular interest to economists is the producer or worker cooperative. In such firms the position of the worker is crucial so that membership is restricted to worker-members in the business who effectively own and control the firm. One of the best known examples today of worker cooperatives is the Mondragon cooperatives (see http://www.mondragon-corporation.com/ENG.aspx, last accessed November 2012) though there are other prominent examples in Italy and France.[5] Cases of producer cooperatives that have attracted attention in the past include the US plywood co-ops (Craig and Pencavel 1992) and producer cooperatives (PCs) in the former Soviet-type economies (e.g. for the case of Poland, Jones 1993).

KEY ISSUES

Since the bulk of the economics literature has investigated issues surrounding worker cooperatives, our focus is on that body of work. Most studies have been theoretically focused, and empirical literature has followed with a considerable lag. However, this has not been the case in the study of other cooperatives, for example those within development economics. In that field, empirical observations have motivated theoretical models, but a unifying theoretical framework has been lacking.

Issues Concerning Worker Cooperatives

Much of the economics literature on worker cooperatives has followed the pioneering work of Ward (1958) and later Vanek (1970) where worker cooperatives are positioned within a standard microeconomic (comparative static) framework and it is argued they maximize income per member.[6] Subsequent theoretical literature has either extended directly from these assumptions or has examined the consequences of deviations from these standard assumptions and the ways that worker cooperatives respond to changes in the economic environment. Most empirical literature has tested predictions arising from that theoretical framework and Bonin, Jones and Putterman (1993) and Dow (2003) provide useful surveys of that literature, while Ben-Ner (1988a) is an interesting early attempt to provide stylized facts on worker co-ops.

One set of issues concerns the *comparative scarcity of worker cooperatives*. Why, apparently, are such firms rare (compared to conventional investor-owned firms)? In turn this leads to examination of issues relating to formation, survival, and life cycle. One might also include the many studies that examine issues of the incidence of cooperatives.

Most investigations of producer cooperatives have a micro focus and proceed by examining a set of such firms within one country. See for example studies of the entry and exit of French worker-co-ops (Perotin 2006). This is also the case for studies of firm survival. Such studies tend to refute the prediction that producer co-ops, will have lower survival rates (e.g. Perotin 2006). At the same time, beginning with the work of the Webbs (e.g. Potter 1891) and continuing with formal economic modeling by, amongst others, Ben-Ner (1988b) researchers have analyzed the tendency of particular types of cooperatives (notably producer cooperatives) to transform themselves into organizations within which control rights are vested in a small number of worker-members. A related theoretical literature investigates the question of which conventionally-owned firms are apt to be bought by their employees (e.g. Ben-Ner and Jones 1995).

A second area of inquiry revolves around issues of *employment and output*. For worker cooperatives a vast body of theoretical work was triggered by a seminal paper by Ward (1958). By assuming that worker-members maximized their per capita income (rather than total profits, as in a capitalist firm), a key finding emerging from this early model is that, relative to a capitalist twin, the producer cooperative will tend to have smaller employment, a negatively sloped supply curve and that labor will be inefficiently allocated within an economy of producer cooperatives. Most subsequent theoretical work overturned the pessimistic conclusions that resulted from this simple Ward model and little or no empirical support was found for these key propositions. Thus Craig and Pencavel (1995) find that, after a fall in output price, whereas the investor-owned plywood firm adjusts by cutting employment and hours worked, the cooperatives responded by changing worker's earnings but maintaining stable employment. Nor has any empirical evidence been found of short run inefficiencies or of perverse supply curves.

A third area of investigation is *investment and finance*. The way in which capital requirements are financed and the resulting structure of ownership of the firm's assets are matters that have attracted the interest of many students of cooperatives. The issues are particularly interesting in cooperatives since assets may be owned by members individually or collectively as well as by non-member financiers. The non-transferability of ownership rights in many cooperatives has led some theorists to argue that some cooperatives, notably worker cooperatives, will face persistent underinvestment. However empirical support for such predictions is weak (e.g. Jones and Backus 1977), a finding that many find unsurprising since many real world cooperatives have implemented specific institutional design to ameliorate potential problems that pure theorists have identified.

A fourth and final area is the matter of the role of *incentives and performance* in firms that are cooperatives or within which there is some degree of employee ownership. One issue of especial interest to theorists is whether employee ownership and/or cooperation will lead to employees supplying efficient effort. For example, will democratic firms suffer from shirking by employees? For both types of organization a vast empirical literature has emerged to examine not only the links between employee ownership and firm performance but also the roles of employee involvement in decision-making. To date the bulk of the evidence rejects the hypothesis that employees in firms with employee ownership supply lower levels of effort. Following Jones and Backus (1977) a commonly favored approach to test this and similar hypotheses has been to augment a standard production function by a vector of ownership and participation variables. The key result is that the null hypothesis that the various forms of participation taken together do not affect productivity is rejected.

Other Types of Cooperatives

The fact that worker cooperatives have received most of the attention in the economics literature (disproportionately so compared to the size of this sector) continues a pattern observed in the economics literature of cooperatives since the early 20th Century (Kalmi 2007). More recently, financial cooperatives have begun to be studied and there are attempts to model their specific characteristics such as whether members may have diverging preferences depending on whether they are net savers or net borrowers. Also, the composition of the membership is likely to influence the setting of interest rates, as demonstrated in theoretical models by (e.g. Taylor 1971; Smith et al 1981). More recently, Emmons and Schmid (2002) have extended this framework into a situation where cooperative banks can also distribute dividends. However, very little empirical work has been undertaken to date in this field. There is also a large empirical literature that uses data from cooperative banks, with much of this literature testing more general propositions using samples of cooperative banks. Fonteyne (2007) is an excellent guide to much of the literature. Studies of interest that focus on issues of more specific cooperative issues include Angelini, Di Salvo and Ferri (1998), who find that cooperative banks provide better access to credit for small firms, and Hesse and Cihak (2007), who find that cooperative banks are more stable than commercial banks. There is also literature analyzing the determinants of membership rates in financial cooperatives including Emmons and Schmid (1999) and Jones et al (2009), the latter attempting to explore the role of various motivations (in particular monetary versus social) in the membership decision.

There is a surprising dearth of research concerning consumer cooperatives, with Ireland and Law (1983) constituting a notable exception, and, more recently, Marini and Zevi (2011). In contrast, research on farmer producer cooperatives has proven to be an enduring topic of interest in the field of agricultural economics in journals such as the *American Journal of Agricultural Economics* (see e.g. Sexton 1986; Torgerson et al 1998).

Perhaps the most lively area within the field of cooperatives is that of development economics. Much of this research is motivated by the rise of microfinance and other grass-roots economic initiatives. In recent years, the research on cooperatives that has found its way into major economics journals has often come from development economics (e.g. Banerjee et al 1994; Pitt and Khandker 1998).

Finally, there is literature that attempts to provide more general approaches to cooperatives. Hansmann (1996) presents an elaborate theory on optimal ownership structures, building especially upon the argument that different ownership structures have different implications for collective decision-making costs. Jones and Kalmi (2009) use the ICA Global 300 (see www.global300.coop, last accessed November 2012) dataset on the largest cooperatives in the world and find that cooperative incidence is very strongly and positively related to the level of interpersonal trust in a society. They determine that trust is a much more robust predictor of cooperatives than is the case in large listed firms, although there is some evidence that the presence of large listed firms is also higher in the presence of higher trust.

RECENT WORK AND FUTURE DIRECTIONS

Commenting on the literature on worker cooperatives up to the early 1990s, Bonin et al (1993) noted that the literature had been theory-led and that empirical literature had lagged significantly behind. At the same time, it was apparent that theory building had often ignored many well-known stylized facts. Also, most of that early literature on labor-managed firms (worker co-ops) used a comparative static framework that appears somewhat dated by current standards (e.g. Vanek 1970). By contrast some of the leading figures in contract theory have developed models that are based on more modern approaches (e.g. Rey and Tirole 2007). While such models are still in their infancy and have not been subject to empirical testing, potentially large dividends will accompany better modeling that is grounded in stylized facts.

Early empirical studies often contained results that contradicted the most basic propositions of the early theory. Reflecting the general rise in the of esteem of applied work in economics, in part because of improved access to data and the broader availability of more powerful statistical software, empirical research on cooperatives has made great strides in the last thirty years or so. However, it is also clear that much remains to be done. Before many research questions can be addressed it is also clear that much more and better data are needed. And while much progress in assembling improved data sets continues to be made, it is also apparent that empirical research in particular will continue to suffer because of the demanding requirements imposed by the challenges posed by robust empirical design.

These points can perhaps be best illustrated by considering work on questions at the *macro* level – for example, work which aims to understand the reasons for the varying importance of cooperatives across time and space as well as the impact of these phenomena on macro variables such as employment adjustment. In this respect most useful beginnings have been made by the ICA and its recent efforts to provide systematic data on the top 300 co-ops around the world. One example of the potential that such macro data have to offer is the paper by Jones and Kalmi (2009) that was discussed earlier. Equally such work is necessarily still in its infancy since the available data are typically restricted in important ways, including the span of years or the less-than-comprehensive way in which the universe of co-ops or employee-owned firms is covered. In turn these deficiencies often reflect the historical ways that data have been collected by national authorities (such as census data), with a continuing failure to, for example, distinguish alternative organizational forms such as co-ops from conventional firms.[7]

It is also the case that better *micro* data is needed. Again the traditional ways that government agencies collect data is often quite limited – there is a tendency to give only cursory attention to what goes on inside the 'black-box' that is the firm. Consequently there is little on-going and systematic data collection on phenomena such as the presence and extent of member ownership and control within cooperatives. In this context it is unsurprising that many firm-level studies have suffered from several important shortcomings. For example, many studies operate with samples of convenience rather than samples that are representative of the underlying populations. Often the range of key variables that are able to be measured is limited – thus studies of cooperatives may omit measures of other potentially important variables, such as the extent of employee involvement. And when key variables are measured sometimes this is done so in an oversimplified way – for example a dummy variable for a producer cooperative, which ignores differences among producer cooperatives in critical respects such as the extent of worker membership. However, we are also seeing research on cooperatives that uses empirical approaches that are close to the frontier of current applied work; for example the work of Pencavel et al (2006) that creatively combines and matches organization-level with individual-level data. In the field of banking, there is already a relatively active research program comparing the performance of cooperative banks with that of other ownership structures (e.g. Altunbas et al 2001; Iannotta et al 2007; Ferri et al 2011). The emergence of better micro data is also allowing some of the classic issues surrounding worker cooperatives to be studied more rigorously than in the past. Thus Arando et al (2011a) use new micro data to study the comparative efficiency of stores with differing ownership types within the Ersoki retail chain in Spain.

Apart from these empirical issues, there are also theoretical issues that are underdeveloped in current economics research. One glaring example is the role of cooperative networks in the growth and survival cooperatives. All types of cooperatives are often organized into federations. Among the services these federations provide are collaboration in marketing, raising public awareness of cooperatives, economic cross-insurance, training, liquidity management in the case of financial cooperatives, wholesale operations in the case of cooperative stores, and so on. These networks have a regional character (e.g. Mondragon cooperatives in Spain, Antigonish movement in Nova Scotia, Maharahstra cooperatives in India, Emilia-Romagna cooperatives in Italy). Despite the fact that the importance of such networks has been recognized in the cooperative literature from its early dawn, economists, in contrast to sociologists (e.g. Halary 2006), have not paid much attention to it. Moves in that direction include Joshi and Smith (2008) and Arando et al (2011a).

A second promising research field is the relationship between cooperatives and social capital. While much of the literature emphasizes how cooperatives can contribute to the building of social capital (e.g. Borgen 2001), there is much less literature that looks into social capital as a prerequisite of meaningful cooperatives or as a motivator to participate in cooperatives (e.g. Jones and Kalmi 2009). This research can potentially give important insights into whether it is the narrower, 'bonding' type of social capital that is associated with the rise and sustainability of cooperatives, or the more general, inter-group 'bridging' social capital that matters. It is also possible that the determinants of local cooperative formation and successful operations of large cooperative networks require different types of social capital. The importance of social capital can also give indications for general development plans for cooperatives in developing countries; for instance, it suggests that centralized attempts to promote cooperative either by large donor aid infusions or government decrees may not be appropriate.

Another promising research strategy is the use of econometric case studies to shed new light on crucial issues. This approach has been successfully applied in studying the links between wages and training in cooperative banks in Finland (Jones et al 2012). It is also being used in on-going investigations of the Mondragon cooperatives including studies of the Eroski retail chain (e.g. Arando et al 2011b).

Finally it is worth pointing out that core features of cooperatives may have served to stimulate the surge of literature in some related research fields. One such area is corporate social responsibility. The link between social responsibility and cooperative principles is often clear in both theoretical and empirical (e.g. Desjardins 2011) work. Also, arguably the growth of the field of social entrepreneurship has cooperative roots (e.g. Spear 2006).

NOTES

* The paper has benefitted from comments by Saul Estrin and Avner Ben-Ner.
1. Ben-Ner and Jones (1995) investigate the roles of variation in control and return rights among diverse enterprises, including some cooperatives.
2. The first cooperatives appear to have been established in the eighteenth century. Early utopian writers, notably Robert Owen, who saw cooperative communities as alternatives to competitive and individualistic capitalism, were a major stimulus to the establishment of these first cooperatives. Equally, practical necessities, such as the need to obtain unadulterated foods, played major roles in the formation of early co-ops such as the flour mills at Woolwich in the 1760s and the famous Rochdale store in 1844. Subsequently while the development of the coop movement continued to be inspired by the writings and actions of individuals such as Fourier, Blanc, and Buchez, pragmatic considerations have always played prominent roles in the evolution of cooperatives.
3. This information comes from the European Association of Cooperative Banks (EACB) (www.eurocoop-banks.coop, last accessed November 2012), augmented with information from Caisse D'Epargne (which is a cooperative banking group not affiliated with EACB) www.caisse-epargne.fr (last accessed November 2012).
4. For comparison, the number of trade union members in France in 2005 was 3.2 million and in the US around 17 million (Blanchflower, 2007).
5. As such cooperatives are distinguished from most employee owned firms and firms with other financial incentives such as profit sharing and other forms of 'shared capitalism' (Kruse, Freeman and Blasi, 2011). In the vast majority of instances of employee ownership, and unlike in cooperatives, voting rights reflect ownership of capital which are not equal either amongst employees or between employee and non-employee owners. In firms with employee ownership, capital owners sometimes do introduce arrangements that enable employees to have enhanced involvement in decision-making. While this often happens, it is also rarely to such a degree that firms with employee ownership and worker cooperatives are aligned in this respect. Instances in which this has happened, such as the Eroski retail chain in Spain (Arando et al. 2011b) or in some British consumer cooperatives where employee directors are present (Jones, 1987) are the exception rather than the rule.
6. Note that the main institutional impetus for the emergence of this theoretical literature was the Yugoslav firm during the Tito era.
7. In some countries it does appear that some standard data sets do allow cooperatives to distinguished (e.g. Spain.) This does not appear to be the case in the US although tax returns do allow employee owned firms to be separated from conventional firms.

BIBLIOGRAPHY

Altunbas, Yener, Lynne Evans and Philip Molyneux (2001) 'Bank Ownership and Efficiency,' *Journal of Money, Credit and Banking* 33(4): 926–954.

Angelini, P., R. Di Salvo and G. Ferri (1998) 'Availability and Cost of Credit for Small Businesses: Customer Relationships and Credit Cooperatives,' *Journal of Banking and Finance* 25 (6–8): 925–954.

Arando, Saioa, Fred Freundlich, Monica Gago, Derek C. Jones and Takao Kato (2011a) 'Assessing Mondragon: Stability and Institutional Adaptation in the face of Globalization,' Chapter 9 in *Employee Ownership and Shared Capitalism: New Directions in Research*, edited by Ed. Carberry. Published by the Labor and Employment Relations Association and distributed by ILR Press/Cornell University Press.

Arando, Saioa, Monica Gago, Derek C. Jones and Takao Kato (2011b) 'Productive Efficiency and Job Satisfaction in the Mondragon Cooperatives: Evidence from an Econometric case study,' IZA DP # 5711.

Banerjee, Abhijit V., Timothy Besley and Timothy Guinnane (1994) 'Thy Neighbor's Keeper: The Design of Credit Cooperatives with a Theory and A Test,' *Quarterly Journal of Economics* 109(2): 491–515.

Bénabou, Roland and Jean Tirole (2010) 'Individual and Corporate Social Responsibility,' *Economica* 77(305): 1–19.

Ben-Ner, Avner (1988a) 'Comparative Empirical Observations on Worker-Owned and Capitalist Firms,' *International Journal of Industrial Organization* 6(March): 7–31.

Ben-Ner, Avner (1988b) 'The Life Cycle of Worker-Owned Firms in Market Economies: A Theoretical Analysis,' *Journal of Economic Behavior and Organization* 10(October): 287–313.

Ben-Ner, Avner and Byoung Jones (1996) 'Employee Buyout in a Bargaining Game with Asymmetric Information,' *American Economic Review* 86(3): 502–523.

Ben-Ner, Avner and Derek C. Jones (1995) 'Employee Participation, Ownership, and Productivity: A Theoretical Framework,' *Industrial Relations* 34(4): 532–554.

Birchall, Johnston (1997) *The International Cooperative Movement*, Manchester: Manchester University Press.

Blanchflower, David G. (2007) 'International Patterns in Union Membership,' *British Journal of Industrial Relations* 45(1): 1–28.

Bonin, John P., Derek C. Jones and Louis Putterman (1993) 'Theoretical and Empirical Studies of Producer Cooperatives: Will Ever the Twain Meet?' *Journal of Economic Literature* 31(3): 1290–1320.

Bonner, Arnold (1961) *British Cooperation*, Manchester: Cooperative Union.

Borgen, Svein Ole (2001) 'Identification as a Trust Generating Mechanism in Cooperatives,' *Annals of Public and Cooperative Economics* 72(2): 209–228.

Burdin, Gabriel and Andres Dean (2009) 'New evidence on wages and employment in worker cooperatives compared with capitalist firms,' *Journal of Comparative Economics* 37(4): 517–533.

Craig, Ben and John Pencavel (1992) 'The Behavior of Worker Cooperatives: The Plywood companies of the Pacific North West,' *American Economic Review* 82(5): 1083–1105.

Craig, Ben and John Pencavel (1995) 'Participation and Productivity: A Comparison of Worker Cooperatives and Conventional Firms in the Plywood Industry,' *Brookings Papers on Economic Activity Microeconomics* 1995:121–160.

Desjardins (2011) 'Social and Cooperative Responsibility Report', available at http://www.desjardins.com/en/a_propos/publications/bilans_sociaux/rapport-sociale-2011.pdf (last accessed November 2012).

Dow, Gregory K. (2003) *Governing the Firm: Workers Control in Theory and Practice*, Cambridge, UK: Cambridge University Press.

Emmons, William R. and Frank A. Schmid (1999) 'Credit Unions and the Common Bond,' *Review, Federal Reserve Bank of St. Louis*, September/October, pp. 41–64.

Emmons, William R. and Frank A. Schmid (2002) 'Pricing and Dividend Policies in Open Credit Cooperatives,' *Journal of Institutional and Theoretical Economics* 158(2): 234–255.

Ferri, Giovanni, Panu Kalmi and Eeva Kerola (2011) 'Organizational Structure and Performance in European Banks: a Reassessment,' unpublished manuscript, University of Bari and Aalto University.

Fonteyne, Wim (2007) 'Cooperative Banks in Europe: Policy Issues,' IMF Working Paper 159/07.

Halary, Isabelle (2006) 'Cooperatives in Globalization: The Advantages of Networking,' in Panu Kalmi and Mark Klinedinst (eds) *Participation in the Age of Globalization and Information* (*Advances in the Economic Analysis of Participatory and Labor-Managed Firms*, vol. 9), Amsterdam: Elsevier.

Hansmann, Henry (1996) *The Ownership of Enterprise*, Cambridge, MA: Belknap.

Hesse, Heiko and Martin Cihak (2007) 'Cooperative Banks and Financial Stability,' IMF Working Paper, WP/07/02.

Iannotta, Giuliano, Giacomo Nocera and Andrea Sironi (2007) 'Ownership Structure, Risk and Performance in the European Banking Industry,' *Journal of Banking and Finance* 31(1): 2127–2149.

Ireland, Norman J. and Peter J. Law (1983) 'A Cournot-Nash Model of the Consumer Cooperative,' *Southern Economic Journal* 49(3): 706–716.

Jones, Derek C. (1987) 'The Productivity Effects of Worker Directors and Worker Financial Participation in the Firm: The case of British Retail Cooperatives,' *Industrial and Labor Relations Review* 41(1): 79–92.

Jones, Derek C. (1993) 'The Effects of Worker Participation on Productivity in Command Economies: Evidence for the Case of Polish Producer Cooperatives,' *Managerial and Decision Economics* 14(5): 475–485.

Jones, Derek C. and David Backus (1977) 'British Producer Cooperatives in the Footwear Industry: An empirical examination of the theory of Financing,' *Economic Journal* 87: 488–510.

Jones, Derek C. and Panu Kalmi (2009) 'Trust, Inequality and the Size of the Cooperative Sector: Cross-country Evidence,' *Annals of Public and Cooperative Economics* 80(2): 165–195.

Jones, Derek C., Iiro Jussila and Panu Kalmi (2009) 'What Determines Membership in Cooperatives? A New Framework and Evidence from Banks,' Hamilton College Working Paper 09–09, Hamilton College, Department of Economics, Clinton NY.

Jones, Derek C., Panu Kalmi (2009) 'Trust, Inequality and the Size of the Co-operative Sector: Cross-country Evidence', *Annals of Public and Co-operative Economics* 80(2): 165–95.

Jones, Derek C., Panu Kalmi and Antti Kauhanen (2012) 'The Effects of Training on Performance and Incomes: Econometric Evidence from Finnish Cooperative Banks,' *Oxford Economic Papers* 64(1): 151–175.

Joshi, Sumit and Stephen C. Smith (2008) 'Endogenous Formation of Co-ops and Cooperative Leagues,' *Journal of Economic Behavior and Organization* 68(1): 217–233.

Kalmi, Panu (2007) 'The Disappearance of Cooperatives from Economics Textbooks,' *Cambridge Journal of Economics* 31(4): 625–647.

Kruse, D.L, R.B. Freeman and J.R. Blasi (eds) (2011) *Shared Capitalism at Work: Employee Ownership, Profit and Gain Sharing, and Broad-based Stock Options*, Chicago, IL and Cambridge, MA: University of Chicago Press and NBER.

Marini, Marco and Alberto Zevi (2011) '"Just one of us": Consumer Cooperatives and Welfare in Mixed Oligopoly,' *Journal of Economics*, 104: 239–264.

Ministry of Cooperatives, Iran (2010) 'Cooperative Movement in Iran,' Tehran, Iran.

Pencavel, John, Luigi Pistaferri and Fabiano Schivardi (2006) 'Wages, Employment and Capital in Worker-Owned and Capitalist Firms,' *Industrial and Labor Relations Review* 60(1): 23–44.

Perotin, Virginie (2006) 'Entry, Exit and the Business Cycle: Are Cooperatives Different?' *Journal of Comparative Economics* 34(2): 295–316.

Pitt, M. and S. Khandker (1998) 'The Impact of Group-Based Credit Programs on Poor Households in Bangladesh: Does the Gender of Participants Matter?' *Journal of Political Economy* 106(5): 958–996.

Potter, Beatrice (1891) *Cooperative Movement in Great Britain*, London: Swan Sonnenschein and Co.

Rey, Patrick and Jean Tirole (2007) 'Financing and Access in Cooperatives,' *International Journal of Industrial Organization* 25(5): 1061–1088.

Sexton, Richard J. (1986) 'The Formation of Cooperatives: A Game Theoretic Approach with Implications for Cooperative Finance, Decision Making and Stability,' *American Journal of Agricultural Economics* 68(2): 214–225.

Smith, Donald J., Thomas F. Cargill and Robert E. Meyer (1981) 'An Economic Theory of a Credit Union,' *Journal of Finance* 36(2): 519–528.

Spear, Roger (2006) 'Social Entrepreneurship: A Different Model?' *International Journal of Social Economics*, 33(5/6): 399–410.

Taylor, Ryland (1971) 'The Credit Union as a Cooperative Institution,' *Review of Social Economy* 29(2): 207–217.

Torgerson, R.E., B.J. Reynolds and T.W. Gray (1998) 'Evolution of Cooperative Thought, Theory, and Purpose,' *Journal of Cooperatives* 13: 1–20.

Vanek, Jaroslav (1970) *The General Theory of Labor-Managed Market Economies*, Ithaca: Cornell University Press.

Ward, Benjamin (1958) 'The Firm in Illyria: Market Syndicalism,' *The American Economic Review* 48(4): 566–589.

WOCCU (2011) 'Member Statistics,' Madison, WI: World Council of Credit Unions, available at www.woccu.org (last accessed November 2012).

9. Cooperative entrepreneurship
Stefano Zamagni

INTRODUCTION

All economists, from the period of civil humanism in the 15th century up until Adam Smith, Alfred Marshall and Joseph Schumpeter have been unanimous on the point that the entrepreneurial function is essential for the existence of the market economy. (A command economy can manage without entrepreneurs, since astute politicians and industrious functionaries are enough.) Who is this entrepreneur, a term used for the first time in 1730 by the Irish economist Richard Cantillon? There are three fundamental characteristics that distinguish this figure from others: i) propensity to risk; ii) capacity to innovate; iii) *ars combinatoria* (art of combining elements together). Let's focus on the last one. Like the conductor of an orchestra, the entrepreneur needs to know the capacities, strengths, weaknesses and, above all, the motivational structure of his/her collaborators so as to organise the productive process so that it integrates individual human actions into a harmonious and effective whole. When the entrepreneur is not up to this task, the enterprise becomes a place of more or less intense conflict, which reduces results to suboptimal levels and can even lead to failure. It is important to remember that this is an art, not a technique that can be learnt from an instruction manual.

These three attributes are present in various ways, and to varying degrees, in the entrepreneurs of the real world. There are some who are successful and others who are not. This depends on a variety of factors, not only at the personal level. For example, there are cultures that facilitate entrepreneurship and its approach to risk. These cultures are based on the idea of development and integral human development. There are also systems that, more than others, favour the *ars combinatoria* in enterprises: for instance, it is almost impossible to create real harmony within the business if there are large and pressing inequalities in the distribution of wealth and income in the economy. What is important to keep in mind is that all three of these elements have to coexist in one way or another and to some degree or another, within the entrepreneurial function.

Why is it so important, above all in this day and age, to insist on the *ars combinatoria*? Every time people carry out different interdependent tasks, as part of the division of labour, the problem of coordination arises. Interdependence can be twofold: *technological* or *strategic*. In the first case, the characteristics of the production process itself fix the way in which coordination takes place. The typical example would be the assembly line, and the Fordist system in general. Today, however, the reality is different, and is dominated by the other kind of interdependence. Strategic interdependence depends to a large extent on the expectations that each person has regarding the intentions and the behaviour of others. In these cases, coordination is based on the *meeting of minds*, to use the expression of the American economist, and Nobel prize winner, Thomas Schelling.

What can be said about the final end towards which the entrepreneur does what she does? The common answer is: the goal of an enterprise is to maximise profit. But this is not correct, because, as the real situation tells us, enterprise can have many different goals. Maximising profit is ideal-typical of a capitalistic enterprise (for-profit enterprise), which then proceeds to distribute the profit created among the suppliers of capital in proportion to their share of the overall investment. This is the dominant, but not the only, form of enterprise in the market economy.

The goal could also be to maximise the net income that the enterprise distributes among its members according to the work that each has put it. This is the situation of enterprises that are producer cooperatives. Furthermore, the goal can also be to maximise the social utility associated with production. This is the situation of social enterprises and social cooperatives. The point that needs underlining is that it is not the goal that is pursued that defines entrepreneurial activity, but the three attributes outlined above. The goal to be pursued should be left to the free choice of the persons involved, which in its turn depends on their motivational structure; there are entrepreneurs who are moved only by extrinsic motives – i.e. profit – and entrepreneurs who are guided by intrinsic motives, for whom profit or net annual income are means for achieving a goal of a social nature.

In substance, enterprise is the *genus* that includes several *species* within itself: capitalistic, social, civil, cooperative, public. An authentically liberal economic system, that is, respectful of the reasons behind the exercise of liberty, can neither therefore favour or discourage, on fiscal or legal grounds, one or other model of enterprise.

Organisations that do not pursue profit as their only primary goal are certainly not new. In reality, a glance at history shows that the normal ways of carrying forward the economy or of enterprise were for reasons not only, and not primarily, economic: arsenals for prosecuting wars; abbeys for giving praise to God; Francisan banks (the *Monti di Pietà*) to confront poverty in the Italian cities of the 14th and 15th centuries. Even the activity of merchants was profoundly interwoven with the civil, political and, above all, religious life of the time, so that what moved them to engage in trade was much more complex than the simple maximisation of profit. In more modern times, the cooperative movement has been, and still is, an important experience of enterprise that is not capitalistic, since what moves people to engage in this form of enterprise is not profit but mutual help through which the needs of the members are satisfied. In cooperatives, the non-capitalistic nature is not limited to a different reason for joining or to a different (non-profit) goal, but is also expressed in a form of governance that is democratic and pluralist (the principle 'one man one vote' is very different from the principle in the capitalistic businesses where one votes in accord with the capital held by a particular shareholder, or 'one share, one vote').

Over the last three centuries the Western economic system has to some extent 'emancipated' itself from these religious and symbolic presuppositions, and enterprises have become ever more focused on the maximisation of profit as their goal, thus creating the capitalistic system. But even in the capitalistic economy, however, it remains true that the majority of enterprises (in Italy, for instance, by far the largest number of enterprises would be in this group) are still driven by various different objectives, not only by profit, despite the fact that many continue to think that the maximisation of profit remains the only business objective. When they operate in the market, their action continues to be a mixture of motivations and elements that are social, community-focused, political and not only the search for individual profit.

ON THE EMERGENCE OF COOPERATION

Historically, cooperatives came into being after capitalist enterprises and began to expand, in various modes and at different paces, in all the advanced economies. Cooperatives, therefore, are the unexpected fruit of industrial civilisation that ripened during the 'Belle époque'. Two main interpretations of this historical fact have been suggested. One explains the spreading of the cooperative movement as a response to some 'failures' of the capitalist form of enterprise. The other explanation, instead, considers the diffusion of the cooperative movement as crowning the aspirations of those who see labour as the opportunity for self-fulfilment and not just as a mere factor of production. This is the interpretation suggested by the great liberal thinker John Stuart Mill when he added the following passage to the third edition of his *Principles of Political Economy*, published in 1852:

> The form of association, however, which if mankind continues to improve, must be expected in the end, to predominate is not that which can exist between a capitalist as chief and work-people without a voice in the management, but the association of the labourers themselves on terms of equality, collectively owning the capital with which they carry on their operations and working under managers elected and removable by themselves, (p. 772)

A similar line of thought was taken by Alfred Marshall when in his essay *Cooperation* (1889) he wrote that in a cooperative:

> the worker does not produce for others but for himself, which unleashes an enormous capacity for diligent, high-quality work that capitalism suppresses. There is one ruined product in the history of the world, so much greater in importance than all the others that it can truly be called the 'wasted product' – the best working capacities of most of the labouring classes. (p. 130)

The two interpretations obviously carry different practical consequences. The first relegates cooperatives to a niche, useful and effective to be sure, but always an exception to the rule. On close inspection, the reasoning behind this interpretation is the same as that of those who want the market to compensate for government failures and non-profit organisations to compensate for market failures. This interpretation, albeit with significant differences of shading and nuance from author to author, fundamentally guides a whole school of thought starting from the pioneering work of Benjamin Ward (1958). The second interpretation sees the cooperative as the form of enterprise to which the capitalist firm will ultimately converge as the path of development proceeds. Indeed, the main reason for this is that ownership of the means of production is not the sole relevant factor characterising economic organisation. Much more important today is the question of control – knowing who in the final instance controls the process of production.

It can be conjectured that the 21st century will be marked by a dialectical confrontation between the two principal modes of control within the enterprise: by capital and by labour. That is, the confrontation will no longer turn so much on the nature of ownership, which will certainly remain largely private. Rather, it will involve the question of who ultimately controls the enterprise: the providers of capital, as in the business corporation, or the suppliers of labour, as in labour cooperatives. Milgrom and Roberts (1990), although from a different perspective, also see the question of control as central: 'The crucial characteristic of differentiation of the enterprise is not the model of ownership of its equity, but the substitution of centralized authority in the place of the relatively infinite negotiations that characterize market transactions' (p. 72). On a similar line of thought one finds Hansmann (1996) when he writes: 'Freedom of enterprise is an essential characteristic of the most advanced market economies. Capitalism, by contrast, is contingent. It is simply that particular form of ownership of patrons that most often, but not always, proves to be efficient based on available technology.' Which is to say that whereas the market economy is a *genus*, capitalism is just one of its *species*.

COMPARING CAPITALIST AND COOPERATIVE FIRMS

The principal yardstick adopted in the literature in the post-war period to gauge the relative performance of the two types of enterprise is efficiency. The reason behind this choice is that since in a market economy only efficient firms can pass the test of 'survival of the fittest', determining which form of business is more efficient is tantamount to predicting the long-term success of one type or the other.

How did this methodological choice translate into practice? The answer starts from the observation that a firm is basically a coalition of persons who supply the inputs required for production and then sell the obtained output in the market. As the relationships between these persons and the firm are governed by inherently incomplete contracts, it follows that one of these economic agents must be assigned the role to control productive activity. The only possible candidates for this role are the suppliers of capital and the suppliers of labour (for the sake of simplicity, we ignore other persons, such as suppliers of raw materials and consumers). Needless to say whoever has the control, it is a fact that authority always entails the risk of abuse of power. Indeed, the person in control can impose costs or grant benefits to the other members of the coalition, who can do little to mitigate the impact. Indeed, this is so because within the firm – unlike what happens within the market – no short-term negotiations between controller and controlled are possible. As Dow (2003) correctly notes, the Coase theorem does not apply within the firm. Only in extreme cases of grave abuse of power will the other members exercise the 'exit' option. Starting from this frame of reference, economists look for the causal factors that explain the differential capacity for ultimate control of the providers of capital and of labour. The winner, the one that will eventually prevail in the market, is the type of enterprise that is more efficient in the exercise of control.

The pioneering work of Ward (1958) can be taken as a sort of prototype of this line of reasoning. Ward attributes the different performance of the two types of firm to the difference in their objective function. His model makes two basic assumptions: that market and technological conditions (expressed by a standard neoclassical production function) are the same for both firms; and that the objective function of the capitalist firm is to maximise total profit while that of the co-op is to maximise net earnings per unit of labour (or per member, if all the workers are also members of the cooperative). The results that Ward derives from his model are the notorious 'perversities' of which so much has been made. First, the co-op's short-term supply curve has a negative slope; that is, if the price rises the volume of output falls, and with it the amount of labour employed. Second, the co-op's response to changes in market parameters – input prices and the form of the production function – runs counter to the conventional laws of microeconomic theory. Whence the accusation levied to cooperatives of being a 'minor' form of enterprise.

The model of Furobotn and Pejovich (1970) adds a further perverse result, namely the purported 'underinvestment' (hence, undercapitalisation) of co-ops. These authors show that whenever the time horizon of the median member (i.e. his remaining time within the co-op) is shorter than the economic horizon of the investment (the time during which it generates positive returns), the democratic governance based upon the 'one head, one vote' principle will produce a sub-optimal investment strategy. It follows that cooperatives are inescapably condemned to smallness, hence irrelevance. The explanation of this perverse result is simple enough. If the members' assembly is composed by a majority of 'old' people, i.e. people close to their retirement age, these will not likely vote in favour of long-run investment plans, in spite of their profitability. This is not the case with the shareholders of a capitalist firm. If she/he decides to leave the company, she/he can always hope that the selling price of her/his shares will embody, proportionally, the present value of the net future benefits of the investment under consideration.

What, actually, underlies these 'perverse' results? Essentially, an epistemological error. In this literature, the capitalist firm is examined in the framework of a supposedly perfectly competitive market, which precludes any sort of market failure. The analysis of the cooperative enterprise, by contrast, is conducted under the assumption that there is no market for members' rights. In fact, if such a market, were to exist a member who has decided to leave the co-op could gain the present value of future earnings by selling his/her position to a new interested member or to the co-op itself. Schlicht and Weizsacher (1977) were the first to show the perfect equivalence between the capitalist stock market and the market for co-op members' rights. Assuming the existence of a membership market, the phenomenon of underinvestment simply disappears. The point is that the members' rights market does for co-ops what the labour market does for capitalist firms.

The question arises: is the membership rights market compatible with the nature of the cooperative enterprise? The answer is certainly affirmative: as long as the enterprise is controlled by those who provide labour, the identity of the co-op is safeguarded, not threatened. The question concerning the practical feasibility of such a market is a different one. It is certainly true that there are several obstacles to its practical implementation. Dreze (1993) and Bowles and Gintis (1993) have pinpointed the capital constraint on worker members (lack of personal wealth and various forms of credit rationing) as the main cause of the *practical* difficulty of creating a members' rights market. However, such a consideration has nothing to do with the 'perversities' mentioned above since they touch exclusively the theoretical level.

The truth is that the comparison of the two types of enterprise is not carried on an equal footing, in the sense that the co-op is never allowed the same degree of freedom as the capitalist firm. For example, why should the latter's putative objective be to maximise total profit and not – as, for symmetry, it should be – profit per unit of capital? As Paul Samuelson (1957) clearly anticipated, in a perfectly competitive environment where equal conditions prevail, 'it doesn't matter who hires whom': an economy in which workers rent machinery (say, under leasing contracts) and one in which capitalists 'rent' workers through labour contracts will yield exactly the same results in terms of efficiency. Three decades later this conclusion was demonstrated in formal terms by Dreze (1989).

A different line of analysis – represented by such scholars as Hart and Moore (1996), Kremer (1997), and Bacchiega and De Fraja (1999) – traces the cause of the relative inefficiency of cooperatives to the heterogeneity of members' preferences. In their contribution, Hart and Moore observe that under the democratic governance rule typical of the cooperative, the winning option (an investment project, say) is the one favoured by the median member, while its cost is sustained by all members equally. Consequently, the more the mean distribution of members' preferences diverges from the median, the greater the risk of inefficiency for the cooperative with respect to its capitalist twin. In other words, whenever the cooperative's general assembly is fragmented among different groups of members characterised by heterogeneous preferences, it is clear that unlike the capitalist firm, with its 'one share, one vote' principle, the cooperative inevitably risks the tyranny of majority, whence decisional paralysis or the *de facto* transfer of control to the managers. In one case we have inefficiency; in the other, the giving up of the cooperative identity.

Kremer (1997) obtains partially similar results in a model in which members pay in a fixed amount to constitute the co-op's capital. The assembly of members adopts a wage policy depending on volume of output. If the skill (or effort) of the median member is lower than the mean of the efforts of all members, this policy will redistribute income from the more to the less productive members. At the same time the more productive members cannot leave the co-op, on pain of losing their initial payment. This explains the relatively flat earnings curve of cooperative as against capitalist enterprises and highlights inefficient wage policy as an alleged impediment to growth. Where is the flaw in this argument? It is in the unstated, and quite unjustified, assumption that the motivations of the agent who elects to join a cooperative are exactly the same as those of the agent who decides to invest in the equity of a capitalist firm. That this is not so in reality is abundantly confirmed by the empirical evidence and is common knowledge nowadays. For instance, as Borzaga (2001) observes, all we need do is to include in the agent's utility function a parameter to reflect the preference for fairness to completely or at least partly undo the results of Hart and Moore or Kremer.

Particularly useful to clarify the point just raised is the essay by Bacchiega and De Fraja (1999). In a comparative setting that focuses on the constitutional design of the firm, typified by the procedures for making decisions at the general assembly, the authors posit that technological possibilities, prices, and utility functions are all the same. The agent's utility function is of the following type: $U_i = U(c_i, E, w_i)$, where c_i denotes the consumption good of the *i-th* agent, E is a local public good, and w_i is the usual stochastic variable. In a world of complete contracts the choice of the firm's institutional set-up would be perfectly indifferent: in any case one would get the first-best solution, the one that maximises the sum of individual utilities. With incomplete contracts, however, the authors show that organising common action to achieve the production target in a cooperative leads to underinvestment, hence to an inefficient outcome. The reason, basically, is that the member of the cooperative has a rational incentive to contribute less than the shareholder of the capitalist firm to the common action.[1]

The intuition is that any common action always implies the production of some local public good, which raises the problem of free-riding. The members of the cooperative although knowing they will derive a low benefit *ex-post* from an insufficient production of public good are not stimulated to contribute to it *ex-ante*. Not so in the capitalist firm where a minority of shareholders with a majority of shares can always take decisions against the majority of members. This means that shareholders are motivated to invest more in their company so as to 'buy the power to make decisions'. This incentive overcomes in general the problem of free-riding, which exists, *per se* also in capitalist enterprises. It is worth stressing that what makes the difference between the two types of enterprise is the asymmetrical holding of capital among the shareholders of the capitalist firm. Where the shareholders do hold the same number of shares they would behave like the members of a co-op.

WHY EFFICIENCY IS NOT THE CORRECT TEST-BED

What is wrong with this way of comparing the two types of enterprise? Simply, that the behaviour of the agents in the two types of firms is not accorded the same treatment. Why should the cooperative worker's utility function be the same as the capitalist shareholder's? Isn't it true, rather, that the very choice of joining a cooperative instead of a capitalist firm postulates what Schumpeter called a 'pre-analytical' judgement, a value judgement involving in particular personal autonomy? How can one miss the fact that working in a company as a subordinate is quite a different thing from working in a firm that you yourself control? So while it is perfectly legitimate to posit the shareholder's utility function as the one indicated in the previous paragraph, that of the co-op worker cannot fail to include, as an *additional* argument, the enjoyment of the relational good associated to cooperative action (Bruni and Zamagni, 2007): $U_i = U(C_i, E, R_i, w_i)$, with $R_i = 0$ if the agent decides to become shareholder in a capitalist firm and $R_i > 0$ if she/he decides to join a co-op as worker member.

Indeed, the consumption of R_i is capable of countering free-riding, and considerably more so than is 'buying the power to make decisions'. The extensive literature on the theory of organisations, in fact, teaches us that the relationship between an individual and an enterprise does not consist solely in the economic exchange. It also includes a sense of belonging that expresses people's fundamental need for identity, engendering a psychological exchange involving such intangible but real objects as loyalty, mutual trust, a sense of fairness (Rousseau, 1995). No one can fail to see that in analysing the decision whether to join a cooperative these relational incentives cannot be ignored. If the only incentives considered in comparing the two types of enterprise are material incentives, then the ultimate judgement handed down on the cooperative – inefficiency – is inevitable from the start.

Also the neo-institutional and transactional approach associated above all with Oliver Williamson and Henry Hansmann utilises efficiency as the only test-bed to compare cooperative and capitalistic firms. Their work explains the existence of different types of enterprise as depending on the differing ability of the various classes of stakeholders to minimise the total sum of the costs of contract (those due to ex-ante market power, ex-post market power and informational asymmetries) and the costs of exercising ownership rights (those of controlling managers, making collective decisions, and risk-taking). It is the differing ability of the different classes of stakeholders to perform efficiently that determines whether the enterprise 'should' be structured in the capitalist or the cooperative form.

As long as the members' quotas or retained earnings are sufficient to guarantee expansion, cooperative governance raises no problems. But when venture capital has to be raised from outside, the prospective investors – fearing abuse of power by the worker members who exercise ultimate control – will not invest as much as is needed for growth. This is why there are so few cooperatives in capital-intense industries, or where the members are 'too poor' to endow the enterprise with the required capital, or when the necessary capital goods are hard to lease. The capitalist firm's difficulties are analogous, but symmetric. How to motivate employees to supply information and exert optimal effort? The employee is unlikely to disclose his/her real ability to perform his/her assigned tasks, fearing that those exercising control gain a unilateral advantage. Moreover, while the capitalist firm requires employees to make a specific investment in human capital, it offers no guarantee on the duration of the labour contract. This gives workers an incentive not to overdo specialisation, in order to avoid the lock-in effect. So we can see why the cooperative form will be successful whenever, for technological reasons, workers have to make a large, investment in a specific skill and where tacit rather than codified knowledge is a strategic factor in the enterprise's development.

So according to the neo-institutional approach the outcome of the comparison between capitalist and cooperative firm is not a foregone conclusion – that is, the result is not already implicit in the premises. This itself is major progress. However, some relevant shortcomings should be noted. The first – basically minor – limitation is that the standard of efficiency is applied to the individual firm in isolation. This excludes from the efficiency calculus both the externalities involved in the firm's operation and the strategic complementarities between firms. Now while this neglect does not produce major problems as far as the capitalist firm is concerned, for cooperatives it does. Notoriously, in fact, cooperative enterprises form a system – the so-called 'intercooperativism' – characterised by a series of relational agreements and contracts among the cooperatives themselves whose practical effect is to cut transaction costs. Leaving this factor out of Hansmann's algorithm affects considerably the efficiency ranking.

A second and certainly more serious limitation involves the very significance and suitability of efficiency as the only basis for comparison. First of all, the concept of efficiency – as it is used in economics – is not a primitive notion, as it derives from Bentham's utilitarian principle, which is neither an economic principle – it is a moral principle – nor the only possible criterion against which to assess efficiency. Therefore, efficiency is not a neutral evaluation yardstick and it is certainly not an objective criterion which can be applied in order to enable the market to work at its best. It must be recalled that market economies existed well before utilitarian moral philosophy began to enter the economic discourse at the beginning of the 19th century.

A second reason indicates why the notion of efficiency is inadequate for the purpose at hand. It is because it does not take into account the various social externalities of economic activities, whether positive or negative. To recall, two are the categories of externalities to be considered: technical and pecuniary. Whereas economic theory has extensively dealt with the former – from Pigou to Coase – it has irresponsibly forgotten the latter. (Pecuniary externalities are the unintended consequences of price shifts.) Let us take as an example a common scenario in which the aim of efficiency is opposed to that of liberty. If positive liberty has to be sacrificed in the name of efficiency, what will guarantee the sustainability of the market over time? It is true that, within a short-term perspective, this issue can be cast aside. However, such a short-term perspective would soon acquire pathological connotations, since the market cannot exist for long without liberty. What must be always borne in mind is that economic progress is the result of the interplay between elements which do not necessarily belong to the sphere of efficiency. Emile Durkheim was correct in arguing that the values of a society are not mere elements to be inserted in economic calculation, as society has the ability to 'force' or persuade its members to act in a way which neutralises the prescriptions arising from such calculations.

It might be of interest to recall what Adam Smith wrote in *The Wealth of Nations* on the consequences of the discovery of America and the passage of the Cape of Good Hope – 'The two greatest and most important events recorded in the history of mankind' (Smith, 1950[1776], vol. 2, p. 141). Dealing with the effects of these events, Smith remarked:

> What benefits or what misfortunes to mankind may hereafter result from those great events, no human wisdom can foresee. By uniting, in some measure, the most distant parts of the world . . . their general tendency would seem to be beneficial. To the native, however, both of the East and West Indies, all the commercial benefits which can have resulted from those events have been sunk and lost in the dreadful misfortunes which they have occasioned . . . At the particular time when these discoveries were made, the superiority of force happened to be so great in the side of the Europeans, that *they were enabled to commit with impunity every sort of injustice in those remote countries.* Hereafter, perhaps, the natives of those countries may grow stronger, or those of Europe may grow weaker and the inhabitants of all the different quarters of the world may arrive at that equality of courage and force which . . . can alone overawe the injustice of independent nations into some sort of respect for the rights of one another. But nothing seems more likely to establish this equality of force than the mutual communication of knowledge and of all sorts of improvements which an extensive commerce from all countries to all countries naturally, or rather necessarily, carries along with it. (Ibid. p. 141; italics added)

I consider this passage a remarkable anticipation of the argument according to which we need a more balanced (and wise) approach when we have to compare different institutional types of enterprises.

CHALLENGES FACING PRESENT-DAY COOPERATIVE ENTREPRENEURSHIP

In the light of the above, what organisational arrangements should a cooperative adopt if it wants to win today's competitive challenge? This is not a banal question, since the organisation of a firm is never neutral vis-à-vis its identity and its goals. Those who believe that management science is based on objective principles, which are always true, and therefore that its practical recommendations are neutral with respect to the type of enterprise one is considering, should remember that when engineer F.W. Taylor published his famous *Principles of Scientific Management* in 1911, giving origin to the modern scientific organisation of work, he had in mind one specific type of enterprise: a capitalistic business where capital controls labour and whose ultimate aim is long run maximisation.

Chester Barnard, in his well-known text on business organisation published in 1938, uses an anecdote to clarify this issue. A gentleman starts his journey to reach a certain destination, but at a certain point the road ahead of him is blocked by a huge rock which he cannot remove on his own. If the group of people who are shortly going to come to that location need to reach the same destination, they will try to cooperate, creating an 'organisation' adequate to reaching that common end. If, on the contrary, the people arriving there do not share that same objective (because, for example, they are just taking a walk), they could be persuaded to help move the rock if our gentleman offers them, with an agreement, some kind of reward. In both cases the result is the same (the rock is moved away from the road), but the organisations created to achieve it differ significantly.

What features should the governance of a cooperative exhibit? In the renowned Mintzberg scheme, non-profit subjects such as cooperatives fall within the category of 'ideological organisations'; that is to say they are based on strong ideals. The life of such subjects evolves in three phases: birth and first childhood, where enthusiasm and a powerful initial drive are the engine; the consolidation phase, where rationalisation of the organisational design prevails; and the third phase, with two possible outcomes: widespread contamination of the society or involution in which the 'ideological organisation' is subordinated to the surrounding environment. This is the final outcome hypothesised by Di Maggio and Powell (1983) in their famous essay when they talk about organisational isomorphism: in the long run, an organisation initially moved by strong ideals tends – either by coercion or by mimesis – to converge on the capitalistic form of enterprise. To avoid the trap of organisational isomorphism, the cooperative enterprise has to adopt a governance inspired by the *democratic stakeholding* principle. Why is it so?

To answer, it is useful to consider that acting in association always involves a common action, i.e. an action which in order to be carried out needs the intentional participation of two or more subjects. It is the difference in talent and individual preferences that gives associated actions the status of common actions. It is a fact that our modern societies constitute a world densely inhabited by common actions. Common actions have three identifying characteristics. First, they cannot be completed without everybody who takes part being conscious of what is being done. The simple meeting or gathering of a group of individuals is not enough. Second, each participant maintains the 'ownership', hence the responsibility over what he/she does. This is precisely what differentiates common actions from collective actions. In the latter, in fact, the individual with his/her own identity disappears together with personal responsibility for the action. The third distinctive element is the unification of the efforts of the participants in order to achieve the same goal. The interaction of multiple subjects within a given context is not yet common action if those subjects pursue different or conflicting goals.

There are different kinds of common action, depending on the object of communality. In fact, the latter may concern either the means or the ends of the action. In the first case, we have a capitalistic enterprise and the form of intersubjectivity is, typically, that of a contract. As we know, the parties to a contract work together at its implementation, although each party pursues different, often opposing, ends, as in sales agreements between a seller and a buyer or employment contracts. On the contrary, when communality is declined around the ends, it results in a cooperative. There is a difference between a situation where it is agreed that everyone pursues his/her own end (as in capitalistic enterprises) and a situation where there is a common end to be shared. It is the same difference between a common good and a (local) public good. In the first case, the individual benefit deriving from it cannot be separated from the benefit that others enjoy from it too. In other words, individual interest is served *together* with others' interests, not *against* them, as with private good, or *apart from them*, as with a public good. In brief, while public is opposed to private, common is opposed to 'own'. Common is what is neither *only* your own, nor what is indistinctly *everyone's*.

What is the economically significant consequence of this distinction? When the 'common' dimension of an action is limited to the means, the problem to be solved is one of *coordination* of the actions of many subjects. On the other hand, when the 'common' dimension of an action goes beyond the means, then the problem to be solved is how to create *cooperation*. In more formal terms, a coordination problem arises from the strategic interdependence of a plurality of subjects; a cooperation problem, instead, arises from the axiological interdependence of those subjects. Which means that while in cooperation intersubjectivity is value, in coordination it is circumstance. In addition, in coordination the modality is determined by the characteristics of the production process. The typical example is the assembly line: hierarchy and an adequate system of incentives (or sanctions) suffice. In cooperation, by contrast, the conduct of each and every member of the organisation also depends on the expectations that he/she has with regard to the intentions and motivation of the other members. Thomas Schelling (1960) coined a nice expression in this regard: cooperation is a 'meeting of minds'.

The important implication of the above is that for a cooperative firm 'psychological coherence' (as H. Schlicht (1998) calls it) between the stated end and what is actually done is a prerequisite for its very survival. This is not the case with the capitalistic enterprises, whose management does not need to know the motivations and state of mind of the work force. It is enough for it that the actual conduct of work force be in line with the coordination plan. Here is the first challenge: how to design the organisational model of the cooperative so as to let the dispositions of all the participants come to the surface while also acknowledging the value of their intrinsic motivations.

This is not an easy task, and all the more so since there cannot be a general solution, valid for all cooperatives. However, a solution needs to be found, if one wants to avoid decline. What can be said, in general, is that *democratic stakeholding* is the way to go. The key is to provide all those having a relationship with the cooperative with the actual (not virtual) possibility of taking part in some way in the decision-making process. It is useful to point out that transparent communication (giving correct and true information) is not enough; nor will consultation for concertation suffice. The need is to include all those operating in the organisation in its decision-making process. This is the only way for cooperatives to protect themselves from the self-referentiality to which they are subjected. While the management of a capitalistic enterprise must answer to the shareholders, the management of a cooperative enjoys greater discretion, hence the risk of self-referentiality, which can be warded off thanks to multi-stakeholding. The organisation of a cooperative must therefore find a safe route to sail between the Scylla of traditional corporatist models (such as the well-known *keirestu* model) according to which governance should be based *only* on shared values rooted in a common history, and the Charybdis of realistic critics who, proceeding from the anthropological postulate of *homo oeconomicus*, believe that the only thing to do is to improve the incentive schemes and try to make the contracts more and more complete. In both cases, quite clearly, the doom of cooperative would be sealed.

In fact, the knowledge of the motivational structure of a subject deciding to join a cooperative is essential in order to forecast its performance. Amartya Sen was among the first to demonstrate how and to what extent what he calls 'sympathy' – meaning the importance that a member assigns in his/her own objective function to the utility of the other members – impacts the performance of the cooperative. This is because at the basis of the decision to join a cooperative there isn't only an economic reason, but also the need to affirm one's freedom (in a positive sense) and a strong preference for the fairness principle. Hence, if a subject with these preferences chooses to join a cooperative, he (she) cannot but react negatively in the face of repeated violations of democratic stakeholding.

A FINAL REMARK: THE COOPERATIVE AS GENERATOR OF CIVIC CULTURE

A central characteristic of the social capital of a country is the specificity of the cultural matrix moulding its public ethos. It is well known that modern economic development, rather than being the result of the action of more effective incentives or of more adequate institutional systems, is the result of the creation of a new culture. Indeed, the idea that in the economy efficient incentives or institutions produce positive results regardless of the mainstream culture is unfounded, since what makes the difference is not incentives *per se*, but the way in which economic agents perceive and react to them. And the different reactions depend precisely on the specificity of the cultural matrix, which is itself connoted by traditions, social rules of behaviour, by religion, conceived as a set of organised beliefs. A telling confirmation of this is the industrial revolution itself. The industrial revolution took place in England in a time (the 18th century) when economic institutions and incentives were basically those of the previous centuries. For example, the opportunities for profit granted by the conversion of commons into private land – an opportunity that had been available for centuries – started to be exploited only when the entrepreneurial spirit of capitalism began to spread, consequent to a radical cultural transformation associated with the thought of Hobbes, Mandeville and Bentham. An interesting and detailed report of these developments is G. Clark's work (2007). Another authoritative confirmation is the well-known work by the economic historian Avner Grief on the communities of medieval merchants in the Maghreb and the Mediterranean, where he shows, in great detail, that the comparative success of Genoese merchants is to be attributed, above all, to a dominant culture whose symbolic codes and rules of behaviour favoured economic cooperation and, consequently, trade thanks to the reduction of transaction costs.

It is now a well-established fact that values and dispositions such as the propensity to risk, the granting of loans, the attitude towards work, the willingness to trust others, and so on, are closely bound up with the dominant culture in a given space-time context. Capitalism, like any other model of social order, needs a variety of cultural inputs and a well-structured code of ethics, which it was not able to generate itself, although it no doubt helped to modify its characteristics over time, in order to continue to reproduce itself. One of the greatest lessons of biology is that life develops best when there is diversity; our societies do best when we allow the greatest diversity possible among organisations to exist within them.

I would like to conclude with an image borrowed from Charles Baudelaire's famous novel *Fiori del male*. I refer to the image of the albatross: a bird which has very wide wings and short and thin legs, disproportionate compared to its wingspan. When it catches an up draught, the albatross flies agile and majestic, effortlessly. But as soon as it touches the ground it becomes clumsy, awkward and incapable, without the aid of the wind, to spread its wings and fly again. The more it moves its huge wings, the clumsier it seems: it can only hop forward ridiculously. Cooperative enterprise is like the albatross: when it flies high it earns consensus and admiration; when it touches ground, and does not spread its wings to the wind, it reveals its powerlessness, because 'on the ground' people clash and divide over petty things. The suggestion is therefore to spur those who with bravery and intelligence dedicate themselves to the study of cooperatives always to seek out the up draughts. This is why, now more than ever, the cooperative world needs conscious thinking thought, that is to say a thought capable of tracing the route to follow. Calculating thought, although necessary, is clearly not sufficient.

NOTE

1. Observe that while in the Furobotn-Pejovich model the co-op's underinvestment is due to the divergence between the time horizon of the median member and the economic horizon of the investment project, here the same result comes from the specific form of the agents' objective function.

REFERENCES

Bacchiega, A. and G. De Fraja (1999) 'Constitutional design and investment in cooperatives and investor-owned enterprises', Department of Economics, University of York.
Barnard, C. (1938) *The Functions of the Executive*, Cambridge (MA), Harvard University Press.
Borzaga, C. (2005) 'Dalla cooperazione mutualistica alla cooperazione per la produzione di beni di interesse collettivo', in E. Mazzoli and S. Zamagni (eds.), *Verso una nuova teoria economica della cooperazione*, Bologna, Il Mulino.
Bowles, S. and H. Gintis (1993) 'A political and economic case for the democratic enterprise', *Economics and Philosophy*, 9, 75–100.
Bruni L. and S. Zamagni (2007) *Civil Economy*, Oxford, Peter Lang.
Clark, G. (2007) *Farewell to Alms*, Princeton, Princeton University Press.
Di Maggio P.J. and W.W. Powell (1983) 'The Iran Cage Revisited', *American Sociological Review*, 48, 147–160.
Dow, G. (2003) *Governing the firm*, Cambridge, Cambridge University Press.
Dreze, J. (1989) *Labour management, contracts and capital markets: a general equilibrium approach*, Oxford, Blackwell.
Dreze, J. (1993) 'Self-management and economic theory', in P. Bardhan and J. Roemer (eds) *Market Socialism: the Current Debate*, Oxford, Oxford University Press.
Furobotn E. and S. Pejovich (1970) 'Property right and the behaviour of the firm in a socialist state', *Zeitschrift für National ökonomie*, 30, 431–454.
Grief, A. (2006) *Institutions and the Path to the Modern Economy*, Cambridge, Cambridge University Press.
Hansmann, H. (1996) *The ownership of enterprise*, Cambridge (MA), Harvard University Press.
Hart O. and J. Moore (1996) 'The governance of exchanges: members' cooperatives versus outside ownership', *Oxford Review of Economic Policy*, 12, 53–69.
Kremer, M. (1997) 'Why are worker cooperatives so rare?', NBER WP 6118.
Marshall, A. (1889) 'Cooperation', Speech at the XXI Cooperative Congress, Ipswich, reprinted in A.C. Pigou (ed.) (1925) *Memorials of Alfred Marshall*, London, Macmillan.
Milgrom, P. and J. Roberts (1990) 'The economics of modern manufacturing: technology, strategy, and organizations', *American Economic Review*, 80, 511–528.
Mill, J.S. (1987[1852]) *Principles of Political Economy*, Rist. A. Kelley, Fairfield, NJ.
Mintzberg, H. (1994) *The Rise and Fall of Strategic Planning*, London, Prentice Hall.

Rousseau, D. (1995) *Psychological contracts in organizations*, Sage, Thousand Oaks (CA).

Samuelson, P.A. (1957) 'Wages and interest: a modern dissection of Marxian economic models', *American Economic Review*, 67, 884–912.

Schelling, T. (1960) *The Strategy of Conflict*, Cambridge (MA), Harvard University Press.

Schlicht, E. (1998) 'Consistency in organizations', IZA DP, February.

Schlicht, E. (2003) 'Consistency in organizations', IZA DP 718, February.

Schlicht, E. and C. Weizsacker (1977) 'Risk financing in labour managed economies', *Zeitschrift für die gesanite staatsswissenchraft*, 133, 53–66.

Sen, A. (1970) 'The Impossibility of a Paretian Liberal', *Journal of Political Economy*, 72.

Smith, A. (1950[1776]), *The Wealth of Nations*, E. Cannan (ed.), London, Meuthen, 6th ed.

Taylor, F.W. (1911) *Principles of Scientific Management*, New York, Harper and Bros.

Ward, B. (1958) 'The firm in Illyria: market syndicalism', *American Economic Review*, 48, 566–589.

Zamagni, S. (2005) *Verso una nuova teoria economica della cooperazione*, Bologne, Il Mulino.

Zamagni, S. and V. Zamagni (2010) *Cooperative Enterprise*, Cheltenham, Edward Elgar.

10. Do dictator games measure altruism?
Daniel John Zizzo*

INTRODUCTION

As communism once haunted Europe according to the *Communist Manifesto*, so does the dictator game haunt the hallways, if not of Europe, of the standard consensus in behavioral and experimental research as developed in the last 20 years or so. Grand claims on the significance of this game for altruism and for the relevance of a wide array of social factors in studying dictator games have been made and developed in what has been a successful cottage industry of academic research in economics; at least, successful in terms of its ability in getting published (e.g., for recent *Econometrica* and *European Economic Review* examples, see Andreoni and Berheim, 2009, and Servatka, 2009, respectively).

This chapter considers briefly whether dictator games are a good tool to measure altruism. The answer is negative: behavior in dictator games is seriously confounded by what I shall label experimenter demand effects (Zizzo, 2010). The following section briefly defines dictator games and reviews some of its purported enduring appeal. The last section criticizes dictator games as a measure of altruism and concludes by considering whether a role for dictator games can still be found that may be of relevance for the economics of philanthropy.

THE APPEAL OF DICTATOR GAMES

Dictator games were originally thought of as an elegant way to identify the altruistic component of behavior in the most standard ultimatum games. In the standard ultimatum game (Güth et al, 1982; Camerer, 2003), a first mover receives an amount of money (say, x dollars) and needs to decide how much to offer to give to a second mover (say, y dollars), with him or her retaining the rest ($x - y$ dollars). The second mover then decides whether to accept the offer, in which case he or she gets y and the proposer gets $x - y$, or not, in which case neither player gets anything. Different motivations (e.g., not only altruism but also envy and fear of envy) can underlie behavior in ultimatum games, and, in an attempt to identify the role of altruistic preferences by decomposing a key aspect of it, the dictator game was born (Forsythe et al, 1994). In the dictator game, the first mover (the 'dictator') decides again how much money to give the receiver (x) but this time the split he or she decides gets implemented automatically, without the second mover being able to decide whether to accept it or not. As such, any giving *should* only be attributable to altruism – or so is the usual claim. More recently, the dictator game has been used in combination with trust game settings to putatively identify the role of altruism in those games.

The dictator game has been immensely popular as a way of measuring altruism and to study social factors affecting pro-social behavior (see, e.g., Engel, 2011 and Camerer,

2003). There are three reasons for this. First, it is a deceptively simple game, and economists like simple things because they give the promise of the greatest interpretability, even when, as will be shown in the next section, the promise is not fulfilled. Second, it provides seemingly very good value for money: the very reason the terminology 'dictator game' is a misnomer, for it is not really a game but an individual choice problem also implies that it is possible to collect a lot of independent observations for comparatively little money. Third, seemingly intriguing results can be obtained comparatively easily, and academic journals like to publish statistically significant results. Fourth, once the literature got kick-started for all of these reasons, it has been a case in which everyone keeps producing dictator game experiments because everyone else has, and has produced papers to show for it. None of these is a good reason to keep investing limited time and resources on dictator game experiments if dictator games cannot deliver a good measurement of altruism or other such pro-social motivations. And, as discussed next, it turns out they do not.

DO DICTATOR GAMES WORK?

In coming to the experimental laboratory, or answering questions to the experimenter in the field, a subject needs to make sense of the decision environment to identify what he or she is expected to do. Problems of experimental control arising from this can be classified under the label of experimenter demand effects (EDE) (Zizzo, 2010) and have, at least in part, been previously analyzed in the psychological literature (e.g., Orne, 1962, and Rosnow and Rosenthal, 1997). They come into two guises. *Purely cognitive* EDE derive from the cognitive dimension of identifying the task at hand and behaving accordingly, by employing cues about what constitutes behavior that is appropriate to the task. *In addition* to the cognitive dimension, *social* EDE reflect the perceived social pressure that the experimenter, as an authority, explicitly or implicitly puts on a subject through instructions and cues; in the light of this, the subject forms beliefs about the experimental objectives and his or her actions can be played out in the direction most congruent to such objectives.

Now imagine that you come to the lab and you are given a random amount of money and asked to consider giving some to a random stranger. This is an unfamiliar environment (as Smith, 2010, p.9 puts it in describing this situation, 'the Gods must be crazy!') with an inbuilt obvious cognitive demand to give some money and to follow whatever other cue can be read by the decision environment. This is precisely what happens. Significant amounts of money are given to strangers in a way that is rarely done in the real world (Schram, 2005; Bardsley, 2008), and dictator games are sensitive to cues – whatever they are – in a way that other more natural economic settings are not, such as changes in deservingness (e.g., Ruffle, 1998), the availability of a picture of the recipient (Burnham, 2003), other information provided on the recipients (Branas Garza, 2006) and awareness of observation (Haley and Fessler, 2005). Behavior changes dramatically as a result: e.g., only around 10 percent of the subjects gave money in treatments by Hoffman et al (1994, 1996) and Koch and Normann (2008), but over 95 percent did so in a treatment by Aguiar et al (2008) and Branas Garza (2006). By their unusual nature, dictator games are typically done only once, although within-treatment manipulations are sometimes made (as in Andreoni and Miller, 2002) which lead to further questions as this may, e.g., induce more behavior which is more consistent or cue-sensitive across tasks (as discussed in Zizzo, 2010).

Direct evidence for the impact of EDE on dictator game behavior has come in experimental work by List (2007), Bardsley (2008) and Zizzo and Fleming (2011). For example, Zizzo and Fleming (2011) find that behavior in a dictator game is connected to a standard questionnaire measure of sensitivity to social pressure (Stöber, 2001). They also find that, when a dictator game and a symmetrical back to back money burning game in which the first mover can simply destroy money of the second mover are played, there is a *positive* rather than negative relationship between giving and destroying, which is not compatible with a preference based explanation of giving but is predicted by an experimenter demand explanation.

There has been a recent attempt to reconfigure the objective of dictator game experiments as one aimed to identify social norms (Guala and Mittone, 2010) rather than measuring altruism or social preferences. However, this objective would predict actions that work in the same direction as the EDE confound, and, as the identified social norms would normally be claimed to generalize beyond the dictator game environment, it is not a satisfactory solution for reinterpreting dictator game results.

Overall, one can forgive Oechssler (2010, p. 66) for recently imploring, 'please, not another dictator game!' And yet there may be still some scope for *some* experiments employing dictator games. Obviously, if the focus of the experiment is to look at experimenter demand and associated vertical social pressure, and the sensitivity of subjects to it, the dictator game can be a suitable game. In the context of the economics of philanthropy, if the focus of the experiment is to look at how social pressure (e.g., by the means of phone calls to ask for charitable giving) practically affects giving, it may be possible to use the experimenter demand effect as a way to mirror in the lab what is otherwise possible in the real world. This may be considered an example of what Zizzo (2010) labels the magnifying glass argument against EDE: an EDE would be a tool used in the same way in which a scientist may use a magnifying glass or a microscope; specifically, to better, if artificially, identify effects of comparable social pressure on inducing greater charitable giving which otherwise may not be observable. Fong and Luttmer (2011) and Reinstein and Reiner (2011) provide examples of dictator game experiments that may receive some justification in this way.

NOTE

*   In writing this chapter, I have benefited from discussions on dictator games with participants to presentations in Erfurt, Heidelberg, Jena, Munich and the XIV Summer School on Economics and Philosophy at the University of the Basque Country, San Sebastian. This paper also benefits from an ongoing collaboration with Piers Fleming, which has been funded by the Nuffield Foundation and by the University of East Anglia. The usual disclaimer applies.

REFERENCES

Aguiar, F., Branas-Garza, P. and Millar, L.M. (2008), 'Moral distance in dictator games', *Judgment and Decision Making*, **3**, 344–354.

Andreoni, J. and Miller, J. (2002), 'Giving according to GARP: An experimental test of the consistency of preferences for altruism', *Econometrica*, **70**, 737–753.

Andreoni, J. and Bernheim, B.D. (2009), 'Social image and the 50–50 norm: A theoretical and experimental analysis of audience effects', *Econometrica*, **77**, 1607–1636.

Bardsley, N. (2008), 'Dictator game giving: Altruism or artefact?' *Experimental Economics*, **11**, 122–133.

Branas-Garza, P. (2006), 'Poverty in dictator games: Awakening solidarity', *Journal of Economic Behavior and Organization*, **60**, 306–320.

Burnham, T.C. (2003), 'Engineering altruism: A theoretical and experimental investigation of anonymity and gift giving', *Journal of Economic Behavior and Organization*, **50**, 133–144.

Camerer, C.F. (2003), *Behavioral game theory: Experiments in Strategic Interaction*. Princeton: Princeton University Press.

Engel, C. (2011), 'Dictator games: A meta study', *Experimental Economics*, **4**, 583–610.

Fong, C.M. and Luttmer, E.F.P. (2011), 'Do fairness and race matter in generosity? Evidence from a nationally representative charity experiment', *Journal of Public Economics*, **95**, 372–394.

Forsythe, R., Horowitz, J.L., Savin, N.E. and Sefton, M. (1994), 'Fairness in simple bargaining experiments', *Games and Economic Behavior*, **6**, 347–369.

Guala, F. and Mittone, L., (2010), 'Paradigmatic experiments: The dictator game', *Journal of Socio-Economics*, **39**, 578–584.

Güth, W., Schmittberger, R. and Schwarze, B. (1982), 'An experimental analysis of ultimatum bargaining', *Journal of Economic Behavior and Organization*, **3**, 367–388.

Haley, K.J. and Fessler, D.M.T. (2005), 'Nobody's watching? Subtle cues affecting generosity in an anonymous economic game', *Evolution and Human Behavior*, **26**, 245–256.

Hoffman, E., McCabe, K., Shachat, K. and Smith, V.L. (1994), 'Preferences, property rights, and anonymity in bargaining games', *Games and Economic Behavior*, **7**, 346–380.

Hoffman, E., McCabe, K.A. and Smith, V.L. (1996), 'On expectations and the monetary stakes in ultimatum games', *International Journal of Game Theory*, **25**, 289–302.

Koch, A. and Normann, H.-T. (2008), 'Giving in dictator games: Regard for others or regard by others?', *Southern Economic Journal*, **75**, 223–231.

List, J.A. (2007), 'On the interpretation of giving in dictator games', *Journal of Political Economy*, **115**, 482–493.

Oechssler, J. (2010), 'Searching beyond the lamppost: Let's focus on economically relevant questions', *Journal of Economic Behavior and Organization*, **73**, 65–67.

Orne, M.T. (1962), 'On the social psychology of the psychological experiment: With particular reference to demand characteristics and their implications', *American Psychologist*, **17**, 776–783.

Reinstein, D. and Riener, G. (2011), 'Reputation and influence in charitable giving: An experiment', *Theory and Decision*, **72**, 221–243.

Rosnow, R.L. and Rosenthal, R. (1997), *People Studying People: Artifacts and Ethics in Behavioral Research*, New York: Freeman.

Ruffle, B. (1998), 'More is better but fair is fair: Tipping in dictator and ultimatum games', *Games and Economic Behavior*, **23**, 247–265.

Schram, A. (2005), 'Artificiality: The tension between internal and external validity in economic experiments', *Journal of Economic Methodology*, **12**, 225–237.

Servatka, M. (2009), 'Separating reputation, social influence, and identification effects in a dictator game', *European Economic Review*, **53**, 197–209.

Smith, V.L. (2010), 'Theory and experiments: What are the questions?', *Journal of Economic Behavior and Organization*, **73**, 3–15.

Stöber, J. (2001), 'The social desirability scale-17 (SDS17): convergent validity, discriminant validity, and relationship with age', *European Journal of Psychological Assessment*, **17**, 222–232.

Zizzo, D.J. (2010), 'Experimenter demand effects in economic experiments', *Experimental Economics*, **13**, 75–98.

Zizzo, D.J. and Fleming, P. (2011), 'Can experimental measures of sensitivity to social pressure predict public good contribution?', *Economics Letters*, **111**, 239–242.

11. Economy of communion
Lorna Gold

OVERVIEW

The Economy of Communion (EOC) is a Christian socio-economic movement advocating and practising equality and redistribution. The term was first coined by Chiara Lubich, founder of the Focolare Movement, during a trip to visit members of the Movement in Sao Paolo, Brazil, in May 1991. It provides private business owners with a practical way to use their resources to help people in need and support the development of a value-based economic culture. Since it started in 1991, around 750 businesses from around the world have become involved in the project, voluntarily sharing their profits in three parts: one for those in need, one for the promotion of a 'culture of giving' and a third for re-investment in the business. The majority of the businesses involved are small and medium sized enterprises in the services sector. The majority of the businesses are located in Europe and South America. Others are dispersed across the world. As well as involving individual businesses, the project has also resulted in the creation of nine business parks across the world[1] where the dominant economic ethic is based around the values and principles of communion. Although strictly speaking the EOC refers to the specific project linked to the Focolare, as the project has grown and the theoretical basis has been deepened, it has become recognised as a potential business model, aspects of which could be replicated by other communities.

PHILOSOPHICAL AND SPIRITUAL ROOTS

Whilst the EOC started in 1991, the origins of the socio-economic movement date back to the start of the Focolare Movement[2] in Northern Italy in the 1940s. This movement was founded by Chiara Lubich (born Silvia Lubich), an Italian Catholic activist who has been described as one of the most influential Catholic women of her generation. She was born in Trento on 22 January 1923 during the Fascist period in Italy. As a result of his socialist leanings, her father lost his job and the Lubich family spent Silvia's early years in poverty. In 1943 Silvia consecrated her life to God in chastity and poverty and changed her name to Clare in honour of Clare of Assisi. She did not feel called to enter a convent, however, and instead founded the lay communities of the Focolare, the aim of which is to build unity between peoples in accordance with Jesus' last testament: 'Father, may they all be one' (John 17:21). Lubich led the Focolare until her death at the age of 85 in 2008.[3] During her life, the movement grew globally to around 140,000 members and branched out into promoting unity in many different areas, in particular, ecumenism and inter-religious dialogue. Lubich enjoyed the favour of many popes, in particular Pope John Paul II, who gave final approval to the statutes of the movement in 1991. In her later years, Lubich received many awards and honorary degrees for her work in various fields[4] although the movement also has its vocal detractors, many of who are ex-members.[5] In particular, they criticise the movement, alongside other lay Catholic movements, for its alleged underhand methods and secretive structures. There is also criticism that the Focolare promotes a fundamentalist strand of Catholicism, though this is disputable.

It is from the Focolare movement that the socio-economic reality of the EOC emerged. In the midst of the suffering of the Second World War, Chiara Lubich and her companions had a profound mystical experience. It was an experience which altered their deepest perceptions of reality (Zambonini, 1991, p. 45) and understanding of the immanence of God's presence in human existence (Cerini, 2009). She called this profound experience/belief in the love of God the 'inspiring spark' (ibid, p. 11). It challenged her perspective on every aspect of human life, including economic and social realities. It was an experience which could be regarded as religious, but it also gave rise to powerful socio-economic ideas which form the spiritual and cultural foundations of the EOC.

Providence

Trust in God's providence was a defining feature of this early experience of the Focolare movement. The roots of the term 'providence' can be traced back to classical Greek and Latin thought. In the Bible, particularly in the Old Testament,[6] it signifies that God, the Creator, did not merely decree what should be, and then 'retire to heaven' to watch what inevitably must come to pass in the created universe. Rather, in infinite wisdom and power, God mysteriously governs all circumstances, making all things work together to accomplish the divine will. Whereas the Old Testament emphasises providence as God's blessing of the good and punishment of the wicked, the New Testament, emphasises the mercy of God, who makes the sun rise and set on everyone. Many texts from the early days of the Focolare underline the revival of a profound belief in providence.[7]

Such belief in God's providence has continued throughout the history of the Focolare and still remains a key point in understanding the relationship between economic affairs and spirituality. Within the movement as a whole and in the individual Focolare houses, providence (in the form of unexpected, timely gifts and donations) is even calculated formally as a part of the overall budget. Calculations and decisions regarding future developments are made on the basis of such unexpected (yet expected) resources arriving. Necessary resources not arriving signifies that a given development is not in God's will. In this way, Focolare institutions have evolved without accumulating debt.

Communion of Goods

Another key socio-economic phenomenon which can be traced back to the early history of the Focolare which has informed the development of its economic vision is the 'communion of goods'. The early Focolare community placed great focus on putting into practice words from Scripture, taking a sentence at a time. Living in this way generated a profound sharing, or communion of material and spiritual goods. Lubich highlighted a connection between material giving and living the gospel. They regarded their commitment to the gospel not only a form of spiritual edification, but also a means of emancipation for the poor, leading individuals to 'review' their relationship with the various institutions and to make concrete changes in how they live. The 'heart of the [social] problem', in Lubich's view, was the desire to claim possessions for one's self as opposed to feeling connected to others as a family. The distribution of wealth is perceived as an economic matter, but the question of being brothers and sisters is regarded as a spiritual one.[8] The gospel offered a means of bridging this divide and bringing about a peaceful social revolution that would achieve greater equality through the charity that imbued people's hearts. In this way the 'evangelical poverty' that traditional spiritualities considered a form of asceticism took on a new function within the Focolare. It was not an end in itself but a means of serving other people and creating greater equality. Reaching this equality became the main aim of the first Focolare community in Trent.

Since the 1940s, the practice of the communion of goods has been a cornerstone of Focolare communities all over the world. Those living in the Focolare houses share everything that they possess, including their salaries and any inheritance. Those living in their families make a commitment of spiritual detachment from worldly goods, but live in accordance with their state in life. They share any surplus goods with the community, enabling a dynamic exchange of goods within communities, where the ultimate goal remains 'No one in need'. Over the years, through a range of social projects, the communion of goods has been expanded to incorporate development projects financed by members of the Focolare across the world.

GOALS OF THE EOC

The EOC emerged in 1991, as a consequence of the desire to make this ideal of communion within the Focolare work on an increasingly global scale. As the Focolare grew and developed, it became an international movement. Since the late 1970s, the number of members of the Focolare grew disproportionately within the poorest communities of Latin America, Asia and Africa, as did many other religious groups (Gutierrez, 1984; Slater, 1985). For many of these groups, such as the Christian Base Communities of Brazil, religious affiliation was also seen as a means of emancipation from poverty (Wirth, 1987). During this same period, Pope Paul VI launched his Encyclical on the 'Development of Peoples' in which he drew attention to the desperate inequalities throughout the world and the Christian challenge of responding to these. While this internationalisation gave rise to many initiatives to attend to the needs of people linked to the Focolare throughout the world, by the early 1990s there were increasing strains on the capacity of the movement to create equality *within the movement* on a global scale.[9] In particular, the fall of the communist block in 1989 revealed entire Focolare communities numbering several thousand behind the Iron Curtain who were in desperate need of basic food and shelter.

In May 1991, Lubich visited the Focolare communities in Brazil. While she was there, she saw for herself the extent of the inequality that is so apparent in the city of Sao Paulo and its surrounding areas. The scale of the poverty caused her to reflect on what action the Focolare was taking in order to alleviate the problem. In a sense, her visit was an opportunity for everyone in the Focolare community in Brazil to reflect on how they were attending to the needs of the poor, who also numbered amongst members of the community. She visited some of the projects run by the Focolare to see for herself the work being done. She became all too aware that the efforts of the Focolare were just one drop in the ocean faced with the scale of the poverty in a city like Sao Paulo. She asked herself whether the Focolare, as a group, could make a greater contribution to resolving this entrenched social and economic inequality.

In Lubich's view, it was no longer enough to sit back and watch as the economy created ever greater inequalities. The principles of the Focolare spirituality had to be extended into the realm of business and industry. The communion of goods practised by individual Focolare members certainly contributed to greater equality, but the scope of this communion had to be recognised and the root causes of the inequality on a structural level had to be addressed. Lubich suggested that the Focolare in Brazil was perhaps being called to start to live the communion of goods in a 'superior way', what would later be called the EOC. The thinking behind the EOC is clear in a speech that she gave in Araceli on 30 May 1991:

> This is the novelty: in the Movement we have always practiced the communion of goods; the focolarini do it in a complete way, because they give everything; volunteers give what is superfluous, families also share out their surplus among themselves. Now we would like to propose a communion of goods which is at a superior level, that is, to give rise to businesses and industries here around the Mariapolis,[10] which would be run by our people, who would put all the profits in common for the poor, having kept what is necessary to keep the business running. With these profits we will live the reality of the first Christians in the twentieth century: they brought all that they had to the feet of the apostles and distributed it to the poor, so that there was no one in need, there were no poor.[11]

What was new about this communion of goods, therefore, was that it would involve the participation of legally constituted commercial enterprises and not just individuals, who would choose to share what they regarded as superfluous or to proceed with social projects aimed at providing welfare for the poor. People were encouraged to start enterprises that would generate profits to be shared for predetermined aims. The EOC hence aimed to make the communion of goods productive, generating new wealth from the existing communion between the people of the movement.

At the same time, the businesses themselves would create a new space in which the ethos of the Focolare could be extended. Through creating businesses run by people who lived out the Focolare ideals, the actual causes of inequality would be addressed in a radical way. It was a simple, but extremely challenging proposal. Although the communion of goods can work as a powerful strategy of wealth redistribution at a local scale, it had obvious limitations in the context of the inequalities seemingly endemic within a globalised economy. The communion of goods said nothing about the nature of work and how value is created and distributed within an industrial (or post-industrial) society. In a sense, the practice of communion of goods is a kind of *post hoc* redistribution that may have a profound spiritual meaning, but does not have a direct impact on the public economy. It emerged during the Second World War, at a time when normal peacetime means of producing and sustaining wealth had been suspended. In the context of the economic imbalances within countries such as Brazil, the communion of goods did little to address the root causes of inequality. In a sense, the Focolare, like other civil society organisations in Latin America, was picking up the pieces left by both an economic system that tolerated on inequality and a government which was unable to cope with the rising social 'fall out' from economic crisis (Green, 1996).

KEY EOC CONCEPTS

EOC Businesses

The first key concept underpinning the EOC is the creation of private businesses which are run in accordance with the EOC business principles. All EOC businesses are private entities and are not formally linked to the Focolare. They can take on a range of juridical forms, depending on local jurisdiction. Most are limited companies, though some are sole traders and others are cooperatives.

Two types of business are associated with the EOC. The first are 'new businesses' which have the EOC as their founding principles and main motivation. Many of these businesses refer to the EOC in their company statutes and generally are owned and managed by a number of people who share the ethos of the EOC. From the outset, their principal objective is to contribute to the creation of a new economic culture through the business. In many cases, since the new businesses are starting from scratch they are able to make choices which benefit the EOC, such as where to locate. The second type of businesses could be termed 'reformed' businesses. These are businesses which either pre-date the EOC project or whose owners subsequently wish to participate in the project. In this case, the businesses are often well established and make reforms to bring them into line with the EOC principles, as far as is possible. The circumstances of the businesses vary greatly, meaning that they often have less flexibility to make changes. Nonetheless, these businesses are a critical part of the project as they often bring a greater business knowledge and maturity to the project as a whole.

The current phase of development of the EOC could be termed one of consolidation. The growth rate began to slow down in 1996 and since then the number of businesses participating in the project seems to have leveled off around the 750 mark. The geographical distribution of the businesses throughout the world correlates closely with the diffusion of the Focolare movement. The first concentration is in Brazil, with 84 businesses. The second such concentration is in Western Europe, and in particular Italy, with 242 businesses and Germany, with 53 businesses. There are also relatively high concentrations of EOC ventures in Argentina, the former Yugoslavia and in the USA. There are several regions with few or no EOC ventures. The most noticeable absence is Africa, north and south of the Sahara. In North Africa there is only one EOC business (in Egypt). In the whole of Africa south of the Sahara there are 11 businesses in total. In part, this absence could be the result of lack of communication between the Focolare communities in African countries and the Focolare Centre. The more likely explanation, however, relates to the inability of those who would like to participate in the EOC to generate adequate funds to start businesses. Likewise, there are few EOC ventures in former Soviet countries.

Business Guidelines

All of the businesses, regardless of whether they are new or pre-existing, agree voluntarily to a number of guidelines for businesses which were drawn up in the early stages of the project (Gold, 2010, p. 169). These guidelines are generic pointers to areas of business life which need to be addressed in order to achieve a culture of communion within the workplace. They cover every aspect from environmental considerations, to ethics and taxation. They encourage the business leadership to run the businesses as far as possible along egalitarian lines, in accordance with the Focolare ethos of communion.

Profits Shared in Three Parts

The second concept relates to the sub-division of profits from the businesses in three parts. The main principle that underpins the EOC is that of increasing equality through making the communion of goods productive. People linked to the Focolare were encouraged to set up businesses as a means of increasing the overall amount of resources available to help those in the community who were in desperate need of food, clothing and shelter. The novelty of the project was initially seen as the division of the profits of the businesses into three parts (Lubich, 2001). One part was to be given to the poor, one kept for re-investment in the firm and the third part for creation of educational structures to promote the 'culture of giving'.

Business Parks

A final key concept is the creation of business parks which fully operate according to the principles of the EOC. The rationale for the creation of business parks is three-fold.

Firstly, the creation of a physical space where all business actively share the same economic culture creates the space for new norms in business practice to develop. The businesses create a kind of demonstration effect which has the potential to have multiplier effects beyond the business part itself. The second rationale is that the physical proximity of the businesses creates the potential for synergies to develop across the different businesses. Businesses can also pool their resources to share services. Finally, the creation of a business park enables a larger number of people to become involved in the EOC through becoming shareholders in the holding company.

Six business parks have so far been established and a further three are under construction. All of the business parks are relatively small enterprises, involving between five and 10 businesses. The first business park to be established in 1991 was Spartaco, in the outskirts of Vargem Grande Paulista near Sao Paolo in Brazil. Spartaco currently has five businesses incorporated into the park with three additional businesses located nearby, but linked to the park. It is managed by a holding company, Espri.[12]

AN ECONOMIC ETHIC OF COMMUNION

It is possible to discern certain principles that form the cultural matrix against which all other dimensions of human life, including the economic, have to be measured. The application of communion within the sphere of business gives rise to new concepts and principles that shape economic choices. It is interesting that, unlike certain fundamentalist forms of Christianity, the EOC vision does not reject the capitalist system per se but, rather, it represents both a radical critique of the unsustainable dimensions of the current capitalist system, and a positive vision of the place of wealth and business. The EOC conveys signs of an economic rationality framed by important religious principles that drives a new form of capitalism, much along the lines described by Max Weber in his 'economic ethic of a religion'.[13] These can be seen in many spheres of economic activity:

- Work: Because people are *co-creators* with God, their creative capacity has to be developed, advanced. Work is a source of personal fulfilment and service, and plays an important function in building the community. It also entails sacrifice, which can be united to the sacrifice of Christ. Work represents the principal Will of God.
- Trade, finance and industry: Christians and people of good will ought to actively seek to apply appropriate the means of production to be used to good ends, such as the redistribution of wealth to the poor. Debt is generally avoided within the institutional structures of the Focolare Movement, and is strongly discouraged for all members of the movement. Abandonment to God's will also means trusting his ability to intervene in the practical circumstances of life, as well as in having the material resources to carry out that will. Nevertheless, certain forms of low interest micro-finance are valued and alternative financing structures have been promoted.
- Wealth and possessions: in general there is a positive view toward wealth, with people expected to maintain a living standard and level of security appropriate to their function in society. Possessions, however, are generally put at the disposal of the common good. Poverty has value, both positive and negative. On the one hand, the involuntary surrender deprivation of essential basic needs is an injustice that must be addressed. On the other, it is a virtue, an essential prerequisite to spiritual fulfilment. Material attachments can form an obstacle to one's relationship with God and neighbour. The voluntary deprivation of surplus resources is encouraged through the communion of goods. This encourages simple living and the avoidance of clutter. Trusting in providence means that God will accompany people on their journey, using circumstances to reveal the divine will.
- Relations with other economic actors: the market retains its basic function as the most efficient form of exchange in an open economy. This, however, is set within the wider framework of the market as a 'meeting place' between two or more ethical subjects – a place of fraternal relationships. The highest function of economic interaction is social, the normative aim of every economic encounter being communion. Within the EOC, economic activity serves to build up the human community.
- Economic change and technological development: as stewards of God's creation, protection of the environment is an essential part of personal and corporate economic activity. Progress and technology derive from the innate creativity of the human person, made in God's image.
- Relation to those without economic resources: those without economic resources are regarded as *brothers and sisters*. The redistribution of wealth ought to occur from the grass roots upwards, as well as from the top down. Sharing is a practical sign of love for Christ and for neighbour. The practice of a communion of goods, drawing inspiration from the first Christians, is a key part of building the mystical body.

CONCLUSION

The EOC is an example of how a religious movement can extend its philosophical prin-ciples and ideas into the sphere of economic activity. Through the EOC, the ideals of the Focolare Movement, and in particular Chiara Lubich, have been applied within the busi-ness sphere, giving rise to new businesses which seek to operate along principles of 'com-munion'. This includes bringing about changes within the governance and operations of the businesses as well as sharing profits in three parts. Since the EOC started in 1991, the practical results of the EOC have been modest, with around 750 small and medium busi-nesses participating in the project throughout the world. Whilst this is a relatively small number of businesses, there is scope for greater application of the principles underpin-ning the EOC particularly amongst business owners seeking to apply a Christian ethos in their business life.

FURTHER READING

The two texts which provide the most comprehensive overview of the EOC are L. Gold (2010) *New Financial Horizons: The Emergence of an EOC*, New City Press, New York and L. Bruni (ed.) (2002) The *EOC: Towards a Multi-Dimensional Economic Culture*, New City Press, New York. The former provides a historical and philosophical analy-sis of the project. The latter is a collection of essays on various aspects of the project. Other works providing an outline of the EOC include L. Gold (2006) 'The Focolare Movement's economic ethic', *Markets and Morality* Spring; L. Bruni and A.J. Uelmen (2006) 'Religious Values and Corporate Decision Making: The EOC Project', *Fordham Journal of Corporate and Financial Law*, 11: 645–680 and L. Bruni (2008) 'EOC: When a Charism Changes Even the Economy', *Nuova Umanitá* 30(177). For a good overview of the spiritual and philosophical underpinnings of the EOC see Amelia J. Uelmen (2010) 'Caritas in veritate and Lubich: Human Development from the vantage point of Unity', *Theological Studies*, 71: 29–45. Bruni is a key proponent of the project and writes extensively on matters related to economics, happiness and altruism – all key themes within the EOC. For a good overview see L. Bruni (2008) *Reciprocity, Altruism and Civil Society: In Praise of Heterogenity*, Routledge, London.

NOTES

1. These are listed on the Official EOC website: www.edc-online.org (last accessed November 2012).
2. The Focolare Movement is an international ecumenical movement founded by Italian Chiara Lubich during the Second World War. The aim of the movement is to contribute towards peace and unity through the practical living of the Gospel. The main structures of the Focolare are lay communities of six to eight individuals who take vows of poverty, chastity and obedience and live together as the focal point for the wider community. The majority of Focolare members, however, do not live in communities but have live the spirit of the movement in their daily lives and participate in meetings and events. The Focolare Global Centre is in Rocca di Papa just outside Rome. The leadership of the movement is formed by an elected Council and Assembly. See www.focolare.org (last accessed November 2012).
3. The leadership and governance of the Focolare is set out in the General Statutes of the movement, available from www.focolare.org (last accessed November 2012).

4   For example the 1977 Templeton Price and 1996 UNESCO Peace Education Prize.
5   See Urquart, G. (1999) *The Pope's Armada*, Prometheus Books. See also blogspot, www.thepope-sarmada.com (last accessed November 2012).
6.   See, for example, Daniel 4: 32, 35; Psalm 139: 7–18; Isaiah 41: 21–31.
7.   Many of the original sources such as personal letters have since been lost or destroyed. Edited versions of the remaining original sources from 1943–54 have been published in C. Lubich, *Essential Writings: Spirituality, Dialogue, Culture* (New York, London: New City Press, 2006).
8.   C. Lubich, 'Letter to the Focolare communities in Italy' *Gen* 6: (1968 [1944]): 1.
9.   This concern for the poor within the movement is clear in the inaugural talk that Lubich gave on the 29 May 1991 in Araceli, Brazil, in which she launched the idea of the EOC.
10.   Permanent Focolare community.
11.   Chiara Lubich's address to the Focolare Community in Araceli, Brazil, 30 May 1991, page 13.
12.   See www.espri.com.br (last accessed November 2012) for more details.
13.   See Weber (1958) for more on the concept of an economic ethic of a religion.

BIBLIOGRAPHY

Araujo, V. (1994a) 'The challenge of giving' *New City* April, pp. 72–4.
Bruni, L. (ed.) (1999) *Economia di Comunione: per una nuova dimensione nell'economia* (Rome: Città Nuova).
Bruni, L. and Pelligra, V. (eds) (2002) *Economia come impegno civile: relazionalitá, ben-essere ed Economia di Comunione* (Rome: Città Nuova).
Cerini, M (2009) *God who is Love in the Experience and Thought of the Focolare Movement* (New York: New City Press).
Gallagher, J. (1997) *Lubich: A Woman's Work* (London: Fontana).
Gold, L. (1996) 'The EOS in Brazil', unpublished M.A. dissertation, University of Glasgow.
Gold, L. (2010) *New Financial Horizons – The Evolution of the EOC* (New City Press, New York).
Gold, L. (2003) 'The Focolare Movement's economic ethic' *Markets and Morality* Spring.
Green, D. (1996) 'Latin America: neo-liberal failure and the search for alternatives' *Third World Quarterly* 17 (1): 109–122.
Guella, G. and Basso, O. (1984) *The communion of goods and work guidelines* Part 1 (internal Focolare document, Focolare Centre, Rome).
Guella, G. and Basso, O. (1985) *The communion of goods and work guidelines* Part 2 (internal Focolare document, Focolare Centre, Rome).
Gutierrez, G. (1984) *We drink from our own wells: the spiritual journey of a people* (London: SCM Press).
Lubich, C. (2001) *L'Economia di comunione: storia e profezia* (Rome: Città Nuova).
Marshall, G. (1982) *In search of the spirit of capitalism* (London: Hutchinson).
Movimento Umanità Nuova (1984) *Il lavoro e l'economia oggi nella visione cristiana* Conference proceedings (Rome: Città Nuova).
Slater, D. (1985) *New social movements and the state in Latin America* (Amsterdam: Centro de Estudios y documentacion).
Sorgi, T. (1991) Un modello diverso *Città Nuova* n.15/16: 36–39.
Weber, M. (1958[1904–45]) *The Protestant ethic and the spirit of capitalism* Trans. Talcott Parsons (New York: Scribners).
Weil, S. (1951) *Waiting for God* (New York: Harper Colphorn).
Wirth, J.D. (ed.) (1987) *State and society in Brazil: continuity and change 1970–1984* (Boulder and London: Westview).
Zambonini, F. (1991) *Lubich: l'avventura dell'unitá* (Cuneo: Paoline).

12. Egotism: making sense of social preferences
Elias L. Khalil[1]

WHAT IS THE QUESTION?

The term 'egotism' or 'egoism' is common in the philosophical literature, where the main issues are whether it is a descriptive or a normative position, i.e., how it is related to actual decision making, and how it is related to morality (e.g., Gauthier, 1970). This issue does not arise in the standard economics literature. The economics literature, insofar as it is based on the weak axiom of revealed preferences, regards all actions as egotistical. This is the case because actions are aimed, by definition, to advance the objective function of the self or the actor's ego. So, the term 'egotism' is no different from 'self-interest' – i.e., it would be redundant to employ it in standard economics.

Further, the philosophical and psychological literature defines egotism as ego-centricism, narcissism, or self-aggrandizement. The egotistical agents give excessive importance to their own ego – which may include demanding others to respect and admire them. Actually, Adam Smith reserved his harshest words when he discussed self-aggrandizement—which he regarded as stemming from a weakness in one's character (Khalil, 1996). Again, the economics literature, insofar as it focuses on rational choice, is blindfolded with regard to the issue of self-aggrandizement or the demand for what can be called maligned or distorted 'symbolic utility' (see Khalil, 2000). Given the focus on analyzing egotism in relation to rational choice, this chapter does not directly discuss egotism in the sense of self-aggrandizement.

Like 'self-interest', the term 'egotism' suggests a divide between the self (ego) and the non-self, i.e., the other. While such a divide is useful, it is insufficient to shed light on the varieties and nuances of egotism and, correspondingly, to make sense of the diverse usages of the term 'social preferences.' One important divide is whether an action is optimal or suboptimal. In order to allow for optimal/suboptimal divide, we have to consider seriously the rational choice approach *and* simultaneously reject one of its major tenets, the weak axiom of revealed preference. The rational choice approach is necessary in order to identify what is rational, while the rejection of the weak axiom of revealed preference is necessary in order to admit the possibility that agents act in an irrational manner (i.e., suboptimal) on some occasions.

This chapter defines an egotistical act as the act that fails to carry out what the actor has *ex ante* decided to be the rational choice. This failure largely arises from succumbing to temptations. And there are diverse kinds of temptations, following diverse types of actions, as Table 12.1 below enumerates. This chapter provides an informal discussion of the diverse actions and the consequent diverse variety of egotism, but it does not discuss a host of actions that are motivated by dark emotions ranging from envy, schadenfreude, spite, to hate. Such emotions/actions are not, in the first place, the product of succumbing to temptations, where the intention of the actor is to promote wellbeing. Rather, the intention behind these dark emotions is to annihilate wellbeing altogether. The choice of healthy emotions, as opposed to dark ones, does not involve substitution in response to incentives and, hence, such a choice is orthogonal to rational choice theory, as detailed elsewhere (Khalil, 2011).

In addition to the self/other-self divide and the rational/irrational divide, there are other important distinctions relevant to understanding the varieties and nuances of egotism. The most important is a three-way distinction among the types of action under focus:

1. Is the action aimed simply at the enhancement of wellbeing (interest) – such as sharing one's resource between the self and the other? In this context, egotism could either be the excessive (i.e., suboptimal) denial of the interest of the other (selfishness) or could be the excessive denial of the interest of the self (miserliness).[2] It could also be the excessive tolerance of the consumption of the other (pampering) or the excessive tolerance of the consumption of the self (indulgence).
2. Is the action aimed at preserving obligatory commitment – defined as obeying the requirement not to cheat others, e.g. by delivering a promised good, or the requirement not to cheat one's future self, e.g. by refraining from over-eating or smoking? In this context, egotism could either be the negation of one's commitment to the other (opportunism or dishonesty) or could be the negation of the commitment to the future self (recklessness). It could also be excessively strict adherence to rules of honesty towards the other or self (Puritanism).
3. Is the action aimed at preserving a goal commitment – defined as pursuing with tenacity either the ambitious goal of the group, such as taking part in nationalist causes, or the ambitious goal of the self, such as the pursuit of a career as a carpenter? In this context, egotism could either be the negation of the pursued group goal (defeatism) or could be the negation of the pursued personal goal (lethargy). It could also be excessive single-mindedness in pursuing the goal (pride) – of either the other or the self.

However, what is the justification of the proposed three-way distinction, i.e., the distinction between interest and commitment, on one hand, and the distinction between obligatory commitment and goal commitment, on the other? The much touted delineation, advanced by the social preference literature, between self-regarding preferences and other-regarding preferences cannot act as the crane upon which to move the proposed three-way distinction. As should be made clear from this chapter, the three-way distinction is of great importance, if not of greater importance than the self/other divide, to make sense of the variety of egotism.

SEN: THE COMMITMENT/INTEREST DIVIDE

In his famous essay, 'Rational Fools,' Amartya Sen (1982[1977]) faults rational choice theory for failing, at first approximation, to capture the phenomenon of commitment or ethical rules. Sen is emphatic that commitment is antithetical to interest – as in the case when agents do not break their commitments even when the net payoff of opportunism is clearly positive. Sen argued that economic theory should be reformulated so that it can avoid portraying agents as 'fools': agents in the real world do not substitute commitment with interest. Such a position, called here the 'multiple-self' approach, regards interest and commitment as arising from irreconcilable selves, where commitment cannot be reduced to interest.

The relation between interest and morality (i.e., commitment) has occupied the attention of philosophers going back to ancient Greece. The commitment/interest relation promises to continue to be at the core of criticism leveled at the rational choice approach. It is pivotal to chart the issues involved in such criticisms, where Sen's essay is one example, in order to make sense of the proposed three-way distinction and, correspondingly, the variety of egotism.

Critics of rational choice theory point out that the theory reduces commitment or ethical rules to interest – every choice involves the same primitives of costs and benefits. Such reduction takes three different forms. First, they generally treat commitment as a device to restrain temptations and impulses in order for the agent to act non-myopically, i.e., to perform what is regarded as the optimum action. Second, agents may continue to cooperate even when defection pays because of a belief that the other agent is, with some probability, irrational, i.e., ready to retaliate even when it is not in his or her interest (Kreps et al, 1982). Third, if these two explanations do not work, and as a last maneuver, rational choice theorists tinker with the utility function and suppose that agents have a taste for commitment, i.e., commitment is similar to the tastes for tomatoes or clothes. Consequently, agents are ready to sacrifice pecuniary benefit from opportunism because they are maximizing a function that includes the taste for pride, self-respect, or other symbolic emotions associated with commitment.

For Sen, however, commitment cannot be reduced to interest because it flows from a source, viz., moral and ethical principles, that is ultimately independent of interest. So, the agent acts according to commitment because it is the principled way to act. For Sen, there is a non-bridgeable gap between commitment and preferences and, to wit, calls commitment 'counterpreferential choice' (*ibid.*, p. 93).

When Sen calls commitment 'counterpreferential choice,' Sen has in mind the commitment to pay back one's debt or deliver the promised service, when defection could not be punished. Thus, the actor's action definitely lowers the utility of the actor. If a decision is determined by utility only, the actor should renege according to standard theory. But often individuals do pay their debts and fulfill their commitments to the apparent detriment of their interest. Sen argues that such counterpreferential actions must be motivated, in the Kantian sense, by duty and, hence, cannot be reduced to arguments in the standard objective (utility) function that is inhabited by ordinary preferences.

To illustrate his point, Sen introduces Richard Dudgeon, the protagonist of Bernard Shaw's play, *The Devil's Disciple* (see Khalil, 1999). Richard exemplifies, for Sen, why commitment is counter-preferential choice. Richard, a sympathizer of the American revolutionaries against the British crown, chooses to sacrifice his own life rather than reveal his true identity to his captors, the British army. The British army is actually seeking the apprehension of another man, Reverend Anderson. When Judith, Reverend Anderson's wife, interprets the motive of Richard as arising from sympathy for Reverend Anderson or from love for her, Richard rejects this explanation: his readiness to sacrifice his life does not arise from preferences (utility); rather it arises from commitment. As Richard answers Judith:

What I did last night, I did in cold blood, caring not half so much for your husband, or for you as I do for myself. I had no motive and no interest: all I can tell you is that when it came to the point whether I would take my neck out of the noose and put another man's into it, I could not do it. (Quoted in Sen, 1982, pp. 93–94)

For Sen, standard rationality theorists would not understand Richard's statement – acting out of commitment rather than acting out of sympathy (understood as preferences or interest). The man that inhabits the world of standard rationality theory is rather a 'rational fool' in the sense that he or she is an automaton where all motives can be reduced to utility and, hence, easily adjudicated. He or she would have no appreciation of difficult decisions, viz., when interest and commitment clash.

For Sen, the recent findings of experimental economics should not be surprising. The findings consist of documenting in laboratory experiments that participants cooperate in finite games – when they should defect according to the prediction of subgame perfect Nash equilibrium. A whole literature has risen, advancing the notion of 'social preferences,' which reasons that agents are motivated by the welfare of others (altruism) or by a sense of duty (commitment) (see Gintis et al, 2005; Fehr & Gächter, 2000a, 2000b). However, is the term 'social preferences' a concept similar to 'self-interest' – i.e., supposed to denote a particular type of preferences – or is it a catch-all phrase that includes any preference from which others benefit? The social preference literature is generally unclear on this question: is commitment simply about utility/sympathy and, hence, part of preferences – as is the case with altruism – or is commitment outside the utility function à la Sen?

The celebrated model of Ernst Fehr and Klaus Schmidt (1999; see Khalil, 2009a) illustrates a counter-intuitive result that arises directly from treating utility and commitment as lying along a continuum, i.e., as symmetrical elements that make up the utility function. Fehr and Schmidt want to model 'inequity aversion' – a discomfort that stems from the violation of one's commitment to be fair. In their model, a person's utility is increasing in income and decreasing in inequality between the agent under focus and, say, a neighbor. Let us suppose that the person under focus gains extra income above the neighbor's. The person consequently gains utility that usually offsets the inequity aversion – assuming that the utility function is monotonic. So, inequity aversion amounts to a price, no different from other prices such as labor toil and trouble. So, if rich people feel unfair about inequity arising from extra income, such a 'disutility' is easily washed away by the utility gained from extra income.

Thus, the model of Fehr/Schmidt is no different from the standard neoclassical model: the commitment to fairness is substituted at the margin, i.e., bought and sold like any other preference. This model confirms the adage 'every man has his price.' So, when bribe-taking rises with the rise of the benefit, we can supposedly state that the benefit must offset the cost of taking a bribe, ranging from expected punishment, the negotiation of the bribe, and the feeling of shame. This amounts to treating shame as an ordinary cost, similar to the cost of expected punishment or the transaction cost of negotiating the bribe. But such a result is counter-intuitive: Agents generally do not consider shame an ordinary price, i.e., it cannot be lumped with other costs such as punishment, the toil and trouble of labor, and so on. This is the case because, agents do not resort to self-deception to hide their usual toil and trouble, but they often resort to self-deception to avoid the cognitive dissonance afforded by shame. If shame is an ordinary price, agents should take pride in bribe-taking – as they take pride when they collect their wage after an honest day's work.

Shame, as well as self-deception to avoid shame, is basically anomalous in standard rational theory of choice. The anomalies of shame and self-deception highlight why Sen's point is important: it is imperative, given that shame is a non-ordinary price, to distinguish interest (utility) from commitment.

Amitai Etzioni (1986) also advances a similar multiple-self view, the distinction between interest and commitment. Etzioni calls interest 'pleasure utility,' while calls commitment 'moral 'utility' – where the latter 'utility' is in scare-quotes to stress that it differs from 'pleasure utility.' Etzioni does not provide a model of how to distinguish the two kinds of utility, but he provides the philosophical justification: the agent is better conceived of as constituted by two irreconcilable selves: one seeks pleasure while the other seeks moral identity.

A CRITIQUE OF SEN: SENTIMENTAL FOOLS

Sen's multiple-self approach drives a deep or irreconcilable divide between commitment and interest. While it helps us avoid the anomalies facing standard theory, the multiple-self approach invites another set of problems. How can the moral self (commitment) be glued back to the utilitarian self (interest)?

This failing of the multiple-self approach shows itself in different forms. It presupposes an anti-naturalist research program: how do we explain the origin of moral principles and moral action, if they are totally independent of interest? Sen, who appeals to Shaw's *The Devil's Disciple*, has, ironically, misunderstood the play (see Khalil, 1999): Shaw's play is actually critical of Richard, Sen's 'hero'. For Shaw, Richard is a misguided idealist who fails to employ the basic tenet of cost–benefit calculation. The act of self-sacrifice, and many of the actions of similarly-minded Puritans of New England, exemplifies utter stubbornness or stupidity, according to Shaw. Shaw calls the Puritans, who are ready to commit themselves to commitment irrespective of circumstances, 'sentimental fools.' In Shaw's play, Richard could easily have saved the Reverend's life without having to die in his place. So, the commitment to principle, once disconnected from interest (i.e., for Richard to use a cheaper method to save the Reverend's life), can lead to irrational actions: the unnecessary sacrifice of the life of Richard. So, once Sen and Etzioni build an iron wall between interest and commitment, they cannot, at first approximation, show when the pursuit of commitment is recommended and when it amounts to sentimental foolishness.

Put differently, the multiple-self approach fails to provide the theoretical tools to make links between interest and commitment (ethics) because of the iron wall. For instance, Adam Smith (1976) maintains a distinction between interest and commitment – but he does not set up an iron wall between them. The view adopted in this chapter follows Smith's line: while commitment arises from interest, commitment cannot be treated as a good that lies along a continuum with interest. While this chapter cannot review Smith's theory of the interest/commitment link, it can briefly recount two links. First, concerning the virtue of prudence, Smith regarded it as connected to self-interest. While self-interest is about utility, prudence amounts to the commitment to follow a path that advances self-interest. So, while commitment (prudence) is not the same as self-interest, it arises from self-interest. Second, Smith (1976, pp.156–161) explains self-imposed rules to avoid cheating on the basis of interest. For Smith, agents erect the self-imposed rules to check self-serving biases (Babcock & Loewenstein, 1997). Agents who want to cheat and indulge often do so after manufacturing rationalizations. And, to avoid such rationalization, which injures one's interest in the long-term, the non-myopic self sets up 'general rules' of conduct to prevent self-deception, as detailed elsewhere (Khalil, 2009b).

We have seen that, in light of shame, the phenomenon of commitment challenges the standard theory of choice. Still, the multiple-self approach fails to distinguish between two radically different kinds of commitment (Khalil, 1999). The first kind, which we may call 'obligatory commitment,' involves making a promise to keep one's word: if an agent promises to deliver a good or a service of certain quality, but finds it more profitable to renege, they negate *obligatory* commitment. Such a negation goes under different names, e.g., 'loafing,' 'free-riding,' 'opportunism,' and, if the reneging was pre-planned, 'deception' and 'connivance.' The second kind, which we may call 'goal commitment,' involves the tenacious pursuit of a goal such as a career as a carpenter, violinist, a poet, or an automobile mechanic. It also includes the pursuit of an ideological conviction that involves the shaping of one's society after a particular image or, as in the case of nationalism and team spirit, the protection of one's community against diverse challenges. While obligatory commitment has a legal binding, goal commitment is a matter of finding meaning in life through the single-minded pursuit of a goal with zealousness, steadfastness, and stubbornness.

If so, does 'moral "utility"' consist of obligatory or goal commitment? Do both kinds of commitment involve, following Sen's framework, counterpreferential choice? How does goal commitment, which may involve collective action and develop into nationalism and ethnic identity (Akerlof & Kranton, 2000), relate to obligatory commitment? Do actions which are motivated by collective and personal identity relate more to pleasure utility or to moral 'utility'? Ultimately, how do the two kinds of commitment relate to each other and, in turn, relate to ordinary interest (wellbeing)?

The supposed *deep* interest/commitment divide, underpinning the multiple-self approach, fails, on one hand, to capture the two kinds of commitment or the two kinds of morality. On the other hand, it fails to explain how each kind of commitment is related to interest. A better classification, proposed in the following section, is a three-way distinction: interest, obligatory commitment, and goal commitment. The proposed three-way distinction promises, first, to respect the difference between the two commitments and, second, to show that the interest/commitment divide is not deep – in fact, interest and commitment are organically intertwined.

Further, the proposed three-way distinction can salvage the term 'social preferences.' The term, by stressing the usual self/other divide at first approximation, has been used to denote both altruism, based on sympathy or utility, with commitment such as honesty and trust. Given that the beneficiary of both altruism and commitment is usually the 'other,' as opposed to the 'self,' the social preferences literature has largely treated altruism and commitment as lying along the same continuum. This leads to conceptual confusions and impasse. Confusion also arises when the action of a third party to enforce fairness is treated as a kind of altruism – since the third party is evidently receiving nothing – as Ernst Fehr and Simon Gächter (2002) suggest. Such third-party enforcement of contracts or norms, even when voluntary, is trying to enforce rules of fairness, which ultimately can be traced to self-interest – i.e., has no connection to altruism that is understood as charity.

So, to make sense of 'social preferences,' we need, besides the self/other distinction, the three-way distinction of the type of action. Then we can delineate among different kinds of optimal action and, correspondingly, define egotism as the set of actions that deviate from rational actions.

THE THREE-WAY DISTINCTION AMONG THE TYPES OF ACTION

We need to distinguish interest (wellbeing) from, first, obligatory commitment and, second, from goal commitment. This three-way distinction seeks the middle ground: it avoids reducing commitment to utility (interest) à la standard theory of rational choice and, simultaneously, it avoids constructing an iron wall between commitment and utility à la Sen's multiple-self approach. The three-way distinction allows us to conceive commitment as, on one hand, springing from interest and, on the other hand, not an element of the ordinary utility function (see Khalil, 2000). Obligatory commitments, such as abstinence from over-eating and cheating others, are obviously based on interest. Goal commitments, such as the pursuit of a career or the support of a national aspiration, are also based on interest. But neither commitment should be placed side-by-side the interests that gave them origin.

Concerning the link between interest and obligatory commitment, the agent may judge on a particular occasion that it is advantageous to abstain from stealing or over-eating simply because the penalty exceeds the reward. If so, why would agents ever resort to obligatory commitment or rules of conduct, supposed to apply to every case? There is, at least apparently, a deadweight loss associated with rule-governed action. It is obvious that one rule cannot fit all occasions. It is better to exercise calculations of cost and benefit in each case. When agents impose on themselves obligatory commitments, they cannot, at first look, be optimal since they prevent the agents from stealing, over-eating, or under-saving, when it is advantageous to steal and indulge.

There are many ways to solve the anomaly of obligatory commitments, other than Sen's problematic multiple-self view, i.e., the setting up of an iron wall between interest and commitment. One way to solve the anomaly is to postulate that agents adopt obligatory commitments or internal rules of conduct, precisely to rule out advantageous incidents of indulgence or stealing, because of some long-view consideration of interest. For instance, agents may reason that if they allow themselves to cheat or indulge when it is advantageous, it might encourage them to cheat or indulge even when it is disadvantageous. And if the cost of disadvantageous consumption exceeds the benefit arising from advantageous consumption, agents, at least according to this view, erect obligatory commitments to stop themselves from cheating or indulging even on these occasions when it is advantageous to do so. So, obligatory commitments need not spring from principles that are radically separate from utility.

Once we view obligatory commitments as, at first approximation, based on interest, it becomes easier to explain the phenomenon of 'precommitment.' The most famous illustration of precommitment is the story of Ulysses and the Sirens (Elster, 2000) – and less glamorous illustrations include self-imposed saving-schemes and checking oneself into a fat farm in order to lose weight. Obligatory commitments amount to the first line of defense to protect non-myopic interest. And if this line fails as a result of weakness of will, agents usually resort to external rules (precommitments) such as setting up a police to punish them if they cheat or indulge. In this light, while obligatory commitments are similar to 'cheap talk,' precommitments are 'enforceable talk' where defection is either impossible, as in the case of Ulysses, or invites credible and weighty punishment that prevents the defection. If one accepts that precommitments are based on interest, obligatory commitments, which are soft constraints, can also be shown to be based on interest.

Concerning the link between interest and goal commitments, goal commitments can also be squarely based on interest. When an agent pursues with tenacity a career, or tries to construct a project with stubbornness, obviously the agent is pursuing his or her interest. But tenacity or firmness are problematic for standard theory of choice. As Jonathan Baron (2008, ch. 12) shows, when the agent is tenacious in his or her pursuit, he or she is inflexible, i.e., does not make substitutes at the margin in response to incentives. The agent rather pursues one single good, while ignoring almost all other goods. Such inflexibility can be explained away by eccentric preferences: such excessive fondness for one goal. But following George Stigler and Gary Becker (1977), the appeal to preferences as an explanation amounts to undermining the assumption of stable preferences.

A better strategy is to explain goal commitment by appealing to the nature of tenacity in relation to ability (Khalil, 1997). Stated briefly, one may be unsure about one's ability to produce a commodity, and the only way to gain such knowledge is to try to produce the commodity. But the attempt usually enhances one's ability and, hence, the agent may set up a still higher goal to find out if he or she can achieve it. This amounts to tenacity, and as detailed elsewhere, tenacity stems from ambitious action that might be the core of what differentiates entrepreneurial action from mundane optimization (Khalil, 2008).

The role of tenacity with regard to action might be at the core of what sets the two kinds of commitment apart (Khalil, 2010). Obligatory commitment does not involve tenacity: when the agent promises to deliver a service, the only obstacle is opportunism, i.e., the temptation to enhance self-benefit if it pays to renege. In contrast, goal commitment, by definition, involves tenacity: When the agent promises to pursue a career, such as becoming a pianist or an automobile mechanic, the only obstacle is weariness or the disappearance of tenacity. If the agent decides to quit a goal, it cannot be judged as reneging or suboptimal because the promise to undertake a goal, to start with, is subject to whether one can sustain the pain of tenacity. To quit a goal does not amount to opportunism. Friends may even urge one to quit a goal after seeing him or her failing many times, and rather urge him or her to attain 'peace of mind.'

Put differently, when one pursues a career or an ideology with zeal, the commitment is voluntary. The agent can 'call it quits' at any time. The quitting might be judged as betrayal if the agent did not try hard enough. Otherwise, it might be a wise decision. In contrast, when one reneges on a promise because of opportunism, it amounts to fraud.

A TAXONOMY OF EGOTISM

We can only make sense of the varieties of egotism by analyzing the anatomy of human action *per se* – and to do so, we have to use the rational choice approach. But this approach is applied in a non-conventional fashion in three different ways. First, it allows for agents to behave suboptimally, i.e., succumb to temptations in general, which amounts to violating the weak axiom of revealed preference. Second, it recognizes that actions arising from dark emotions – ranging from envy, schadenfreude, hate, and vengeance – are not about suboptimal actions. These dark emotions are rather about the destruction of utility altogether, and not simply deviation from optimality, and, hence, cannot be discussed here insofar as egotistical acts are defined as suboptimal actions (see Khalil, 2011). Third, while it takes the three-way distinction seriously, it does not build an iron wall between interest and commitment à la Sen's multiple-self approach.

Table 12.1 provides a panoramic view of human action *per se*, resulting from the integration of four distinctions: i) the three-way distinction among types of action; ii) the self/other divide; iii) the optimal/suboptimal divide; and iv) is the suboptimal action involves over- or under-consumption of the good under focus. The variety of egotism, as enumerated in columns 3 and 4, are acts that the agent *ex ante* judges to be suboptimal.

In Table 12.1, the rows specify the type of action under focus: whether it is interest, obligatory commitment, or goal commitment. Column 1 specifies the actions when the beneficiary is the self. Column 2 classifies the actions when the beneficiary is the other – who could be another person or the group with which the actor identifies. Columns 1 and 2 use terms that express optimal or reasonable actions. In contrast, columns 3 and 4 are also about, respectively, the self/other divide, but employ terms that connote actions that are suboptimal. These suboptimal actions represent (non-exhaustively) the varieties of egotism, which can only be possibly captured if we abandon the weak axiom of revealed preferences. Otherwise, the term 'egotism' would be redundant in the theoretical apparatus of rational choice theory, as stated at the outset.

It is proposed here that there are two flavors of suboptimal action, as expressed in

Table 12.1   Taxonomy of action

	1. Self (Optimal)	2. Other (Optimal)	3. Egotism vis-à-vis the Self (suboptimal)	4. Egotism vis-à-vis the Other (suboptimal)
Interest (wellbeing)	Self-interest	Altruism	Miserliness Indulgence	Selfishness Pampering
Obligatory Commitment	Prudence	Duty; Honesty; Justice; Cooperation in social dilemma	Puritanism Recklessness	Meanness Opportunism
Goal Commitment	Tenacity; Ambition; Entrepreneur-ship	Team Spirit; Loyalty; Nationalism	Lethargy Obsession	Cringe Pride

each box of columns 3 and 4: when the agent errs on the side of under-consumption as opposed to erring on the side of over-consumption of the good under focus. So, in the boxes related to columns 3 and 4, the first row represents actions where the agent errs on the side of under-consumption, while the second row represents actions where the agent errs on the side of over-consumption.

When the beneficiary is the self and the action is optimal (column 1), the action is called 'self-interest' if it consists of simple interest as when one purchases X automobile rather than Y. But it is called 'prudence' if the action stems from obligatory commitment as when one abstains, as a matter of rule-bounded choice, from the consumption of tobacco or from over-eating. And it is called 'tenacity,' 'ambition,' or 'entrepreneurship' when it arises from goal commitment as when one undertakes, as part of a single-minded strategy, a series of actions to become a teacher, a painter, or a clothes designer.

When the beneficiary is the other and the action is optimal (column 2), the action is named 'altruism' if it consists of simple interest as when one donates resources to a charity such as supporting children with AIDS in a foreign country. But it is called 'duty,' 'honesty,' 'justice,' or 'cooperation in social dilemma' if it arises from obligatory commitment as when one abstains, as a matter of rule-bounded choice, from shirking one's responsibility, deceiving others, failing to act with fairness, or defecting in the prisoner's dilemma and the production of public goods. And it is called 'team spirit,' 'loyalty,' or 'nationalism' when it stems from goal commitment as when one undertakes, in a single-minded manner, a series of actions to advance the interest of one's group after a particular vision or ideology.

When the beneficiary is the self and the action is suboptimal (column 3), the action is called 'miserliness,' in the case of interest, if the agent errs on the side of under-consumption, while it is dubbed 'indulgence' if the agent errs on the side of over-consumption. In popular usage, indulgence is seen as egotistical. In contrast, miserliness, which may take the form of anorexia, is not usually seen as a form of egotism.

In addition, the action is called 'Puritanism,' in the case of obligatory commitment, if the agent errs on the side of under-consumption, while dubbed 'recklessness' if the agent errs on the side of over-consumption as in the case of over-eating at the expense of future self. While there is a rule-bounded behavior on how one should take care of the self, one is supposed to be flexible in emergency circumstances – and hence would be a Puritan if he or she fails to account for such circumstances. In popular usage, it seems that only recklessness is categorized as egotistical, ignoring the possibility that Puritanism can also be a form of egotism – at least as Bernard Shaw's play suggests with respect to Richard's sentimental foolishness.

Further, the action is called 'lethargy,' in case of goal commitment, if the agent errs on the side of under-consumption, while dubbed 'obsession' if the agent errs on the side of over-consumption. If one is excessively obsessed, one acts with stubbornness and, hence, does not know when to quit a goal. Lethargy or indolence is egotistical in the sense of forming dependency on others (family or the state) for support. It is obvious, at least in popular usage, that obsession is egotistical, while it is less obvious that lethargy can also be a form of egotism.

When the beneficiary is the other and the action is suboptimal (column 4), the action is called 'selfishness,' in the case of interest, if the agent errs on the side of under-consumption by the other, while it is dubbed 'pampering' if the agent errs on the side of over-consumption by showering goods on the other. In popular usage, it seems that only selfishness is perceived as egotistical, ignoring the possibility that the pampering of others actually can involve egotistical motives – as in the case when the donor is acting in an ego-centric manner (Khalil, 2004).

But the action is called 'meanness' in the case of obligatory commitment, if the agent errs on the side of under-consumption at the expense of others, while dubbed 'opportunism' if the agent errs on the side of over-consumption at the expense of others. While there is a rule-bounded behavior on how one should take care of the other, one is supposed to act with suppleness in emergency circumstances. An agent is supposed to suspend honesty or fairness, and hence the agent would be regarded as a mean person if he fails to take into consideration such cases. In popular usage, it seems that only opportunism, but not meanness, is seen as a form of egotism.

Further, the action is called 'cringe,' in case of goal commitment, if the agent errs on the side of under-consumption, while dubbed 'pride' if the agent errs on the side of over-consumption. Cringe or shying away from a challenge is seen as egotistical in the sense of acting as a coward when one abandons the commitment to the group goal when the challenge becomes hard. In contrast, one is very proud of national or ethnic identity in the sense of clinging to it despite mounting challenges to such identity. More clearly, at least in popular usage, pride or smugness about one's group is egotistical, ignoring the possibility that cringe is also a form of egotism.

CONCLUSION

This chapter shows that we cannot understand the phenomenon of egotism without understanding human action *per se*. And this understanding is possible only if we adopt the rational choice approach, at least to a first approximation. But for such an approach to be non-trivial, we have to allow for the possibility of suboptimal action, i.e., abandon the weak axiom of revealed preference. Abandoning the strict application of the weak axiom should not undermine, in general, the predictive power of the rational choice approach.

This chapter provides taxonomy along four distinctions:

1. **The Three-Way Distinction Among the Types of Action:** is action motivated to satisfy ordinary interest (wellbeing), to abide by rule-bounded behavior concerning obligatory commitment, or to meet the requirement of single-minded pursuits stemming from goal commitment?
2. **The Self/Other Divide:** who is the beneficiary of the action – the actor (self) or the other (another self or group of persons)?
3. **Optimal/Suboptimal Distinction:** is the action optimal or suboptimal – given who is the beneficiary?
4. **Over-and Under-Consumption Distinction:** if the action is suboptimal, does the agent err on the side of excessive consumption or on the side of deficient consumption of the good under focus?

Given these four axes, this chapter locates 12 different varieties of egotism. Some of these identified phenomena – such as miserliness or Puritanism – are not usually regarded as forms of egotism. But other phenomena – such as selfishness, indulgence, and pride – are readily recognized as different kinds of egotism. What matters, though, is how these different kinds of suboptimal actions are connected. The proposed framework affords a coherent way to connect these kinds of behavior and the varieties of egotism, ultimately connected to the rational choice approach. This should allow us to see some phenomena, such as miserliness and Puritanism, as having sister-like relationships with explicitly egoistic phenomena such as indulgence and opportunism.

NOTES

1. This chapter benefitted greatly from the comments of Richard Posner, Birendra Rai, Steven Gardner, Ian McDonald, and an anonymous referee. The usual caveat applies.
2. Miserliness is a kind of egotism: the miser self is involved in self-denial basically out of anxiety about the future. John Maynard Keynes (1937) traced the deficiency of aggregate demand, and hence the macro instability of the market, to such anxiety. The issue of when such anxiety translates into mob behavior through contagion, as a result of animal spirits, is another matter. What matters is that the primitive, i.e., the anxiety that prompts miserliness is directly related to the Allais Paradox (the Certainty Effect) – where agents are motivated by irrational fear: the fear of regretting in the future the choices they are making currently, where such choices are *ante* rational. Such fear makes agents choose options with certainty that cannot be justified by their normal taste for risk aversion. The succumbing to anxiety, which prompts miserliness, is similar to succumbing to the Certainty Effect – both are about succumbing to temptations, i.e., choosing suboptimal outcomes.

REFERENCES

Akerlof, George A. and Rachel Kranton (2000) 'Economics and Identity.' *Quarterly Journal of Economics*, August.
Babcock, Linda and George Loewenstein (1997) 'Explaining Bargaining Impasse: The Role of Self-Serving Biases.' *Journal of Economic Perspectives*, Winter, 11(1): 109–26.
Baron, Jonathan (2008) *Thinking and Deciding*, 4th ed. Cambridge: Cambridge University Press.
Elster, Jon (2000) *Ulysses Unbound: Studies in Rationality, Precommitment, and Constraints.* Cambridge: Cambridge University Press.
Etzioni, Amitai (1986) 'The Case for a Multiple-Preference Conception.' *Economics and Philosophy*, October, 2(2): 159–183.
Fehr, Ernst and Klaus M. Schmidt (1999) 'A Theory of Fairness, Competition, and Cooperation.' *Quarterly Journal of Economics*, August, 114(3): 817–868.
Fehr, Ernst and Simon Gächter (2000a). 'Cooperation and Punishment in Public Goods Experiments.' *American Economic Review*, September, 90(4): 980–994.
Fehr, Ernst and Simon Gächter (2000b). 'Do Incentive Contracts Crowd Out Voluntary Cooperation?' Working Paper no. 34, Institute for Empirical Research, University of Zürich.
Fehr, Ernst and Simon Gächter (2002) 'Altruistic Punishment in Humans.' *Nature*, January, 415: 137–140.
Gauthier, David (1970) *Morality and Rational Self-Interest*. Englewood Cliffs: Prentice-Hall.
Gintis, Herbert, Samuel Bowles, Robert Boyd, and Ernst Fehr (eds) (2005) *Moral Sentiments and Material Interests: The Foundations of Cooperation in Economic Life.* Cambridge, MA: MIT Press.
Keynes, John Maynard (1937) 'The General Theory of Employment.' *Quarterly Journal of Economics*, February, 52(1): 209–223.
Khalil, Elias L. (1996) 'Respect, Admiration, Aggrandizement: Adam Smith as Economic Psychologist.' *Journal of Economic Psychology*, September, 17(5): 555–577.
Khalil, Elias L. (1997) 'Buridan's Ass, Uncertainty, Risk, and Self-Competition: A Theory of Entrepreneurship.' *Kyklos*, 50(2): 147–163.
Khalil, Elias L. (1999) 'Sentimental Fools: A Critique of Amartya Sen's Notion of Commitment.' *Journal of Economic Behavior and Organization*, December, 40(4): 373–386.

Khalil, Elias L. (2000) 'Symbolic Products: Prestige, Pride and Identity Goods.' *Theory and Decision*, August, 49(1): 53–77.

Khalil, Elias L. (2004) 'What is Altruism?' *Journal of Economic Psychology*, February, 25(1): 97–123.

Khalil, Elias L. (2008) 'Action, Entrepreneurship and Evolution,' in Michel Weber and Will Desmond (eds), *Handbook of Whiteheadian Process Thought*, 2 vols. Frankfurt/ Lancaster: Ontos/Verlag, vol. 1, pp. 145–160.

Khalil, Elias L. (2009a) 'Self-Deceit and Self-Serving Bias: Adam Smith on "General Rules".' *Journal of Institutional Economics*, August, 5(2): 251–258.

Khalil, Elias L. (2009b) 'Introduction: A Taste for Every Season,' in Elias L. Khalil (ed.) *New Behavioural Economics*, 3 vols. 'The International Library of Critical Writings in Economics,' series editor: Mark Blaug. Cheltenham, UK: Edward Elgar, pp. ix–xxii.

Khalil, Elias L. (2010) 'The Bayesian Fallacy: Distinguishing Internal Motivations and Religious Beliefs from Other Beliefs.' *Journal of Economic Behavior and Organization*, August, 75(2): 268–280 (doi: 10.1016/j.jebo.2010.04.004).

Khalil, Elias L. (2011) 'The Mirror Neuron Paradox: How Far is *Understanding* from *Mimicking*?' *Journal of Economic Behavior and Organization*, January, 77(1): 86–96 (available at http://dx.doi.org/10.1016/j.jebo.2009.12.005).

Kreps, David M., Paul Milgrom, John Roberts and Robert Wilson (1982) 'Rational Cooperation in the Finitely Repeated Prisoners' Dilemma.' *Journal of Economic Theory*, 27: 245–252.

Sen, Amartya K. (1982[1977]) Rational Fools: A Critique of the Behavioral Foundations of Economic Theory,' in *Choice, Welfare and Measurement*. Oxford: Basil Blackwell, 1982, Ch. 4 (reprinted from *Philosophy & Public Affairs*, 6(4): 317–344).

Smith, Adam (1976) *The Theory of Moral Sentiments*, editors: D.D. Raphael and A.L. Macfie. Oxford: Oxford University Press.

Stigler, George J. and Gary S. Becker (1977) '*DE Gustibus Non Est Disputandum*.' *American Economic Review*, March, 67(1): 76–90.

13. Ethical finance: an introduction
Leonardo Becchetti

The term ethical finance is used to define a new vintage of financial intermediation pioneers whose activity is oriented toward the pursuit of some variously defined common goods and not toward the unique goal of profit maximization. It is seen by some as a provocation and by others as an oxymoron. A provocation because it seems to imply that all the finance which is outside the newly defined 'ethical' one is non ethical. An oxymoron because, for some, finance and ethics are two terms which are incompatible.

A third preferred interpretation is that the traditional financial system pursues fundamental social and ethical goals in a market economy but the new 'ethical finance' actors (ethical investment funds, ethical banks, social microfinance institutions) have shifted further the frontier by discovering new ways to pursue the goal of creating economic value in a socially and environmentally sustainable way.

With regard to the traditional financial system what has to be acknowledged is the importance of the role of traditional financial intermediaries for the economic system. Insurance companies pool resources and diversify risk thereby increasing the wellbeing of risk averse individuals. Banks pool savings and allocate them to the most profitable destinations, provide liquidity services by assuming liquid liabilities against (partially) illiquid assets. Non banking financial intermediaries transform asset duration and diversify risk cross-sectionally and intertemporally (Bhattacharya and Takor, 1993).

Against these undoubtedly socially desirable consequences of the action of traditional financial intermediaries we are well aware that many limits and degenerations exist.

First, the recent global financial crisis and many financial scandals documented that information asymmetries among different actors, combined with the increasing complexity of many financial activities, are such that self interested agents may destroy the organizations in which they operate generating serious negative externalities on the real economy. Furthermore, profit maximization in absence of a transparent and perfectly functioning mechanisms to monitor risk may lead financial intermediaries to take excessive risk (diverting them away from the traditional lending activity, especially to small borrowers) at the expense of the same shareholders. Second, creating a sophisticated system of rules and regulators is not enough since the latter tend to be captured by regulated institutions. Third, even under its correct functioning, the traditional banking system seems unable to lend to poor borrowers who do not have collateral to pledge. The paradoxical consequence is that, if this is the case, financial intermediaries cannot perform their main role, that is, matching individuals with productive ideas with those with financial resources needed to finance them. As evidenced by recent growth theories this task which promotes inclusion and equal opportunities is crucial to ensure that economic growth reaches its full potential. If at the origin of the capitalistic system inequality played an important role since large individual savings were essential to finance the initial capital accumulation, at the current state of affairs in which savings accumulation and financial resources are more than abundant at world level, access to them from the unbankable becomes essential to economic development (Galor and Moav, 2004). If we paradoxically figure out a community in which half of the population has money but no productive ideas and the other half productive ideas but no money, the creation of economic value is zero without traditional banks and equal to its full potential with banks which are able to lend to uncollateralized borrowers.

In what follows we briefly sketch characteristics and the literature debate on the three forms of ethical finance.

ETHICAL INVESTMENT FUNDS

Ethical investment funds are investment funds which try to promote corporate social responsibility with *shareholder advocacy* and *screening*.

For shareholder advocacy we refer to the presentation of resolutions on social and environmental issues at shareholder meetings. For ethical screening we intend the activity of those investment funds which voluntarily introduce an additional constraint in their portfolio management consisting in the exclusion of those stocks which do not pass minimum acceptable standards of corporate social responsibility. Seen from another perspective, through these funds 'socially and environmentally concerned' investors 'vote' with their savings for those corporations which are at vanguard in reconciling creation of economic value with social and environmental sustainability.

The Social Investment Forum (2007) report claims that socially responsible investments involve around 11 percent of assets under professional management in the US with a 324 percent growth (from $639 billion to $2.71 trillion) between 1995 and 2007, much stronger than that of all professionally managed assets (260 percent) in the same period. Sensitivity of shareholders for Corporate Social Responsibility (CSR) seems to have grown in the last years if we look at support for resolutions on social and environmental issues rising from 9.8 percent in 2005 to 15.4 percent in 2007.

Theoretical and empirical literature has recently focused mainly on the consequences of screening on socially responsible investing. From a theoretical point of view screening implies the incorporation of an additional (zero investment) constraint on a subset of the universe of the investable stocks. As such it may have the effect of making the risk-return efficient frontier steeper, that is, minimum variance portfolios on the modified frontier have higher variance for socially responsible investors vis à vis those of standard investors for each return level.

Actually, theoretical models demonstrate that the diversification loss is negligible if the subset of investable stocks is large enough or, in other terms, excluded stocks do not co-vary negatively and in a significant amount with stocks in the ethically managed portfolio. In reality other two additional costs need to be added to the above mentioned one for socially responsible investors. First, socially responsible investors need an additional source of information (on CSR ratings of listed securities) which is costly. Second, they may suffer additional costs in case of transition of stocks held in the portfolio from the CSR (investable) to the excluded subset. In this last case the cost depends on disinvestment rules and on the length of the window within which the stock has to be sold.

Many empirical contributions have investigated in practice whether these three sources of costs have penalized performance of socially responsible versus standard investors.

Bauer, Koedijk and Otten (2002) document mixed findings when they compare active strategies of the two types of funds, even though they identify a learning process which gradually improves the performance of ethical investment fund managers. Geczy, Stambaugh and Levin (2005) evaluate the specific cost of ethical fund management an document that it depends on the share of socially responsible investment, views about asset pricing models (socially responsible funds are less able to offer exposure to size and value factors than to the standard Capital Asset Pricing Model (CAPM) factor and stock manager ability).

Harjoto and Jo (2009) document that CSR is only positively associated with firm value in well-governed companies (i.e., companies with low values in the G-Index, a shareholder friendly board structure, etc.). Barnea and Rubin (2010) provide an explanation for it by warning that firm managers may try to over-invest in CSR for private benefits if this improves their reputation as good global citizens. By finding a negative correlation between managerial ownership and CSR investment they conclude that managers overinvest in CSR when they do not bear the cost of it.

In the same direction Fisman, Heal and Nair (2006) using data on CSR from the Kindleberger, Linder and Domini (KLD) database find in general a negative relation between CSR and firm value. However, they show that the presence of outside blockholders with board representation and a stronger competition on product markets both lead to a more positive relationship between CSR and profitability. Ammann, Oesch, and Schmid (2010) show that a CSR index based on data provided by Governance Metrics International (GMI) has a significantly positive effect on firm value.

Overall, what emerges from this literature is that 'ethical' portfolios tend to have lower return but also lower risk (Becchetti and Ciciretti, 2009). This implies that they generally do not underperform in terms of risk adjusted returns. Roughly speaking, what seems to emerge is that there is neither a disadvantage nor an advantage in being ethical in terms of financial performance even though not being ethical entails some risk. The two main interpretations for this higher risk are that CSR firms minimize transaction costs with stakeholders and that non CSR investors may be 'less patient' and more oriented at short term returns therefore trading more and making non CSR stock dynamics more volatile.

ETHICAL BANKS

The banking industry may be seen as a complex ecosystem which includes very large transnational banks, merchant banks, commercial banks and various forms of cooperative banks. For a while, before the global financial crisis, theoretical thinking has endangered banking biodiversity stressing the importance of economies of scale in the industry and arguing that all banks had to conform strictly to profit maximization. Furthermore, since risk and returns tend to be positively correlated, profit maximizing financial intermediaries however tend to assume too much risk to increase profits especially when the complexity of new financial instruments makes it difficult to understand how much risk they have taken. The global financial crisis had documented that regulatory authorities have not been strong enough to prevent that complexity of new financial systems and informational asymmetries among self interested managers, shareholders and young skilled traders could bring these institutions to financial collapse with dramatic contagion effects on globally integrated real and financial markets. Given that cooperative banks have also performed well during the financial crises, in some countries being almost immune from its consequences, the pressure against banking biodiversity seems to have phased down.

Many scholars now warn against the risk of banks too big to fail, acknowledge the importance of banks doing the traditional lending job and acknowledge that cooperative banks have mechanisms which allowed them to accumulate equity capital across time making them more apt to face new capital requirements.

Ethical banks are aimed at enriching this biodiversity. Their main specificity is in the use of a socio-environmental screening, in addition to the traditional screening procedure looking at borrower's credit worthiness, with the goal of directing their financial resources toward those investment projects which perform better in creating economic value in socially and environmentally responsible way. In practice this implies investing in preferred sectors such as renewable energy, social and cooperative firms, not for profit institutions and microfinance (Becchetti and Garcia, 2011; Becchetti, Garcia and Trovato, 2011).

The sections which follow will try to explain what is modern microfinance and what it has to do with ethical finance.

MICROFINANCE

With the term microfinance we define those financial institutions which succeed in providing access to credit to the so called 'unbankable', that is, to poor borrowers devoid of assets which can be used as collateral. Modern microfinance creates a series of mechanisms (group lending with joint liability, individual lending with progressive instalments, notional collateral) which try to solve this problem (Armendáriz de Aghion and Morduch, 2010).

We prefer the term microfinance to that of microcredit since small financial intermediaries which promote access to credit for the poor do not limit their supply to bank loans but generally offer formal or informal insurance mechanisms, provide liquidity services and manage small savings. Even though there are many ways of providing financial resources to the poor which date far back in time (the origin of the Raffaisen Bank, ROSCAs, tontines, etc.), modern microfinance is generally thought to coincide with the creation of the Grameen Bank in 1983 by Mohammad Yunus. Since then the multiplication of microfinance institutions has been impressive. The Grameen Bank has now more than 8 million borrowers while, according to the *Microcredit Summit Campaign*, there were around 10,000 microfinance programs in the world at the end of 2009 serving approximately 155 million borrowers of which 82 million were in straight poverty conditions. The growth is expected to continue since the market potential is considered to be around 1.5 million clients.

The Theoretical Challenge of Microfinance

The success of microfinance institutions challenges the standard banking theory in which formal guarantees are fundamental for lenders to prevent opportunistic behavior of borrowers and to reduce negative consequences when they default. The main surprise documented by microfinance is its incredibly low share of nonperforming loans in absence of such formal guarantees.[1] It is always difficult to get aggregate data about microfinance due to the fragmentation of this industry were a few big players face a multiplicity of very small organizations. However one of the most reputed sources of evidence – the *Micro Banking Bulletin* (http://www.themix.org/microbanking-bulletin/ microbanking-bulletin, last accessed November 2012) which created a panel of 1,019 MFIs from different continents – documents that the average sample loan loss rate was 1 percent in 2005.

To understand this paradox in more depth we must remember that the standard incentive theory predicts that, under asymmetric information between borrowers and lenders, lending activity is plagued by three well-known pathologies respectively related to ex ante project selection, interim verification of borrower's effort and ex post verification of project results. The three pathologies are *adverse selection* (under mean preserving spread distribution of project revenues which implies positive correlation of projects' risk and return, higher lending rates select more risky borrowers), *moral hazard* (with hidden action and imperfect monitoring the borrower may save on effort with negative effects on project success) and *strategic default* (with ex post hidden information about the outcome of the project the borrower may have interest to falsely declare default not to reimburse the debt). In this line of thought collateral is fundamental to prevent borrowers from taking actions against the interest of the bank. As a consequence lenders generally refuse loans to uncollateralized borrowers.

Microfinance has three main devices to overcome the problem (group lending with joint liability, progressive individual loans and notional collateral) and several theoretical contributions in the literature explain how (see, among others, Armendáriz de Aghion and Gollier, 2000; Banerjee and Duflo, 2010; Gangopadhyay, Ghatak and Lensink, 2005; Ghatak, 2000; Laffont and N'Guessan, 2000; Chowdhury, 2005; Conning, 1999, 2005; Laffont and Rey, 2003; Stiglitz, 1990; Ghatak and Guinnane, 1999).

To grasp the essential of how group lending may work consider the following simple benchmark situation borrowed and adapted from Prescott (1997) with two types of agents (lenders and borrowers). Each risk neutral lender has $1/m$, $m > 1$, unit of the investment good and can choose between: i) a safe, low-return investment technology which transforms x units of the investment good into Rx units of the good, receiving for it an interest rate of $R-1$ percent; and ii) a risky indivisible investment (I) which requires one unit of the investment good whose expected return is $E(Y) = pX + (1 - p)f > R$, with X and f being respectively the value of output in good and bad state and $p \in (0,1)$.

Lenders can choose between: i) individual lending with liquidation; ii) individual lending with monitoring; and iii) group lending.

Individual lending with liquidation

We define F as the total cost (interest plus principal) repaid by the borrower to the bank with $f < F < X$. The financial intermediary has the following zero profit condition $R = pF + (1 - p)0 - K_S$, where K_S are its screening costs. Under the low output value of the project both the borrower and the MFI obtain 0 since the output is liquidated and retains no value for the lender. Rearranging we have the following equilibrium total cost of the loan $F_{NM} = (R + K_S)/p$ which is invariant in the project value in the good state of nature, but depends on the probability of the occurrence of such state (p), and the following utility for the borrower $U_{NM} = pX - R - K_S$.

Individual lending with monitoring

The second case is different since the MFI monitors the borrower and gets the low output value f in the bad state of affairs. The new MFI zero profit condition is $R = pF + (1 - p)f - K - K_S$ in which (K) is the cost of monitoring. The equilibrium total payment of the borrower which satisfies the zero profit condition, is $F_M = [R + K + K_S - (1 - p)f]/p$, while the borrower's utility is $U_M = pX + (1 - p)F - R - K - K_S$.

Group lending

To understand the potential benefits of group lending with joint liability, consider the following third scheme in which the MFI gives the loan to a group of two borrowers jointly responsible for each other so that each of them has to repay a fraction η of the debt of her groupmate in case the latter defaults. Assume for simplicity that $\eta = 1$. In this case the total amount to be repaid to the MFI by the group is $2F$ and the expected value of the joint project becomes $p^2 2X + 2p(1-p)(X + f) + (1-p)^2 2f$. The equilibrium total repayment of the group which satisfies the lender zero profit constraint is $F_{GL} = \frac{R + K_S}{p^2 + 2p(1 - p)}$, while it is easy to check that the groupmate utility is $U_{GL} = pX + (1 - p)f - R - K_S - K_G - (1-p)^2 f$.

Note that the crucial condition for the joint liability to reduce bank risk is that the output of a single borrower in the group is enough to repay to total group debt or $X + f \geqslant 2F$.

Comparison among the three cases

The comparison among the three cases highlights two fundamental points.

1. First, group lending definitely reduces bank risk since the probability of default for any single project drops from $(1 - p)$ to $(1 - p)^2$.
2. Second, it however has non univocal effects on borrowers' welfare.

Intuitively this is because, on the one side, the reduced risk of the bank may be transferred on the borrower if, as in this simple model example, the bank is not for profit. On the other side, though, group lending poses an extra burden on the borrower which has the joint liability and therefore an extra payment when she is successful and her groupmate is not.

In more detail, the combination of these two effects is such that, while the total cost of lending is higher under individual lending with monitoring than under group lending $(F_M > F_{GL})$, borrower's utility under group lending is higher only if MFI monitoring costs are higher than the sum of liquidation costs plus borrowers' monitoring costs under group lending – that is, $U_{GL} > U_M$ iff $(1 - p)^2 f + K_G < K$.

Similar results can be found when comparing group lending with individual lending with the liquidation scheme. In this case $U_{GL} > U_{NM}$ iif $K_G + (1 - p)^2 f < (1 - p)f$. This implies that group lending yields higher utility for the borrower only if her costs (monitoring and liquidation costs) are inferior to liquidation costs of individual lending without monitoring.

What does Microfinance have to do with Ethical Finance?

There are at least two rationales for including microfinance in our broad definition of ethical finance. The first, mentioned at the beginning, is that microfinance devices a solution to lend to uncollateralized poor, thereby playing a crucial role in the promotion of equal opportunities intended as conditions under which individual achievements are in the best case independent from initial conditions (wealth, talent, human relationships). To understand the second, consider that a well-known empirical phenomenon in microfinance is the trade-off between profitability and outreach. The more MFIs lend to the poor, the lower the loan size and the higher the weight of the fixed costs. As a consequence, the equilibrium total payment needed to satisfy the zero profit condition can become unsustainably high.

Imagine however that the microfinance institution may ask to benevolent providers of financial resources to accept an opportunity cost R' below R in exchange of the satisfaction of allowing credit access to the poor. In such case the MFI zero profit condition turns into: $2R' = [p^2 + 2p(1 - p)]2F + (1 - p)^2 2R' - 2K_s - (1 + \pi)2R'(1 - p)^2$ and the total borrower repayment required to satisfy the MFI zero profit conditions falls to $F_{GL'} = \frac{R' + K_s + \pi R'(1 - p)^2}{p^2 + 2p(1 - p)}$ thereby improving borrowers' welfare.

While purely self-interested individuals with standard preferences would refuse the deal, individuals with social preferences (inequity aversion, warm glow, altruism, etc.)[2] would accept it. This is what happens in microfinance markets in which microfinance investment vehicles collect financial resources with bond issues from socially responsible investors and channel them into MFIs. The role of social investors is actually more complex than just that of providing cheap equity capital which profit maximizing investors would not invest since some of them also play an important 'tutoring' role by transferring bank knowledge and helping to shape governance (Conning and Morduch, 2011).

Departures from the Base Benchmark

By modifying the simple assumptions of the base group lending model it is possible to provide some interesting insights on characteristics of microfinance. First of all, it is clear that group lending with joint liability displaces its main positive effects in terms of reduction of risk for the bank when group projects are negatively correlated (that is, the case in which one project is successful and the other not and therefore the joint liability applies). This implies that, if we remove the assumption of uncorrelated projects in the group, we find that diversification benefits of group lending are reduced when there is a common shock which may hit all projects.

To develop this point consider the following definition of conditional probabilities by Armendáriz de Aghion (1999):

$$\alpha = \text{pr}(Y_i = X | Y_j = X), \ (1 - \alpha) = \text{pr}(Y_i = F | Y_j = X), \ \beta = \text{pr}(Y_i = X | Y_j = F), \ 1 - \beta = \text{pr}(Y_i = F | Y_j = F)$$

where i and j are the two groupmates. Based on that we may rewrite:

$$p^2 = \alpha p, (1 - p)^2 = (1 - p)(1 - \beta), p(1 - p) = (1 - p)\beta \text{ or } p(1 - \alpha).$$

This implies that project returns are uncorrelated if $\alpha = p = \beta$, positively correlated if $\alpha > p > \beta$, negatively correlated if $\alpha < p < \beta$.

Under this framework the equilibrium total cost of debt for the borrower which satisfies the MFI's zero profit condition becomes $F = \frac{R + K_s}{p\alpha + 2(1 - p)\beta}$. From this condition it is clear that positive project correlation reduces the probability area in which at least one of the two projects is successful, that is, the area in which the joint liability may generate its positive effects in terms of reduction of non repayment risk for the MFI. By considering this, it is remarkable that microfinance has been successful in areas such as Bangladesh in which the high likelihood of natural catastrophes generating common shocks reduces room for risk diversification.

The most important departures from the benchmark model are however related to various forms of asymmetric information and to the effects of microfinance and group lending on the three pathologies of adverse selection, moral hazard and strategic default.

On the first problem, it has been shown that group lending with joint liability may be a solution to adverse selection since it fosters assortative matching. The simple reasoning beyond this result is that groupmates prefer to create groups with borrowers with the lowest possible probability of default in order to reduce the expected cost of the joint liability. As a consequence, even though the MFI does not know borrowers' quality it may expect a virtuous selection of group members. Consider however that assortative matching may never be perfect. If only bad quality borrowers are left on the pool and they strictly prefer to borrow, they nonetheless form groups with other low quality members even though their repayment capacity is low.

The introduction of moral hazard further complicates the picture. Imagine in our benchmark model that the probability of success is not endogenous and depends on borrower's effort (as for instance in Ghatak and Guinnane, 1999). Effort has a cost and the borrower optimal effort will depend on it and on the total cost of the loan which is an implicit tax on borrower's success under limited liability. It is possible to show in this case that group lending may generate more effort than individual lending if borrowers cooperate (and may verify without costs each other behavior) since, under group lending, borrowers coordinated effort has not only a positive effect on the individual groupmate probability of success but also a negative effect on the probability of paying the joint liability penalty. The situation becomes more complex in the non cooperative case in which the cost of effort is crucial to define borders between high or low effort Nash equilibria.

Finally, it is important to conclude that the role of group lending and, above all, joint liability, in microfinance must not be overemphasized. The benchmark model described here has been modified in many directions in order to reduce the negative effects of the extra burden that the joint liability poses on borrowers. In many cases cosigning is used as an alternative to group lending. In others individual lending is preferred and the incentive to repay in absence of formal guarantees is created with progressive loan installments which stop in case of default at a given repayment round. Another solution to make individual lending feasible is the use of notional collateral. Even when the collateral has no market value for the bank, the latter may still avoid borrower's opportunistic behavior (i.e. strategic default) if the collateral has value for the borrower (i.e.

a used car for a taxi driver or any other kind of borrower investment good which still works but has low replacement value).

EMPIRICAL EVIDENCE ON MICROFINANCE

The big *querelle* between Junus and Compartamos is a good starting point to look at microfinance from an empirical perspective. Cull et al (2009) discuss the two models as two alternative locations on the trade-off between maximizing shareholders or borrowers wellbeing. If borrowers are preferred, real lending rates will be moderate, but equity capital will be more difficult to raise and socially responsible investors are requested come in support. If shareholders are preferred, lending rates can be extremely high but stock market IPOs may easily convey equity financing. The extreme heterogeneity of MFIs around the world is prompting the demand for some forms of industry rating which may help to bridge the informational gap between financiers and MFIs by matching socially responsible and profit maximizing actors with their proper counterpart.

The success of microfinance in low income countries prompted the emergence of similar experiences in high income countries which faced increasing levels of inequality and new marginalities in the last decades. The scenario however is very different since the 'raw material' of microfinance, that is, poor uncollateralized borrowers with high entrepreneurial potential is scarce. To understand it, it is enough to consider that while in some Sub-Saharan African countries 90 percent of the population may not have access to traditional banks the proportion is reversed in high income countries. The problem in the latter is more related to small segments of marginalized which require care and psychological guidance before credit. The most successful MF experiences in high income countries are therefore those working with immigrant communities which are both rich in entrepreneurial capacity and relational ties, a crucial ingredient to produce substitutes (cosigning, group lending) of traditional individual guarantees in microfinance.

NOTES

1. Becchetti and Conzo (2011) document a self-reinforcing effect of microfinance which contributes to explain its performance. With a field experiment they show that the MFI's loan concession increases borrowers' trustworthiness in the local communities thereby increasing their potential payoffs in business activities.
2. For a reference to this literature see among others, the seminal papers of Fehr and Schmidt (1999) and Andreoni (1990).

REFERENCES

Ammann, Manuel, David Oesch and Markus M. Schmid (2010) 'Corporate Governance and Firm Value: International Evidence', November 3, available at SSRN: http://ssrn.com/abstract=1692222 or http://dx.doi.org/10.2139/ssrn.1692222 (last accessed November 2012).
Andreoni, J. (1990) 'Impure Altruism and Donations to Public Goods: A Theory of Warm-Glow Giving', *Economic Journal*, 100, 464–77.
Armendáriz de Aghion, B. (1999) 'On the design of credit agreement with peer monitoring', *Journal of Development Economics*, 60, 79–104.

Armendáriz de Aghion, B. and C. Gollier (2000) 'Peer Group Formation in an Adverse Selection Model,' *The Economic Journal*, 110, 632–644.

Armendáriz de Aghion, B. and J. Morduch (2010) *The economics of microfinance*, MIT press, Cambridge Massachusetts.

Banerjee, A. and E. Duflo (2010) 'Giving Credit Where it is Due', *Journal of Economic Perspectives*, 34, 61–79.

Barnea, Amir and Amir Rubin (2010) 'Corporate Social Responsibility as a Conflict between Shareholders', *Journal of Business Ethics*, 97, 71–86.

Bauer, R., Koedijk K.C.G. and R. Otten (2002) 'International evidence on ethical mutual fund performance and investment style', CEPR Discussion Paper 3452.

Becchetti, L. and R. Ciciretti (2009) 'Corporate Social Responsibility And Stock Market Performance', *Applied Financial Economics*, 19(16), 1283–1293.

Becchetti, L. and P. Conzo (2011) 'Creditworthiness as a signal of trustworthiness', *Journal of Public economics*, 95, 3–4, 265–278.

Becchetti, L. and M. Garcia (2011) 'Informal collateral and default risk: do "Grameen-like" banks work in high-income countries?', *Applied Financial Economics*, 21, 13, 931–947.

Becchetti, L., M.Garcia and G. Trovato (2011) 'Credit rationing and credit view: empirical evidence from loan data', *Journal of Money Credit and Banking*, 43, 6, 1217–1245.

Bhattacharya, S. and A. Thakor (1993) 'Contemporary Banking Theory', *Journal of Financial Intermediation*, 3, 2–50.

Chowdhury, P.R. (2005) 'Group-Lending: Sequential Financing, Lender Monitoring and Joint Liability', *Journal of Development Economics*, 77, 415–439.

Conning, J. (1999) 'Outreach, Sustainability and Leverage in Monitored and Peer-Monitored Lending', *Journal of Development Economics*, 60, 51–77.

Conning, J. (2005) 'Monitoring by Delegates or by Peers? Joint Liability Loans under Moral Hazard', paper presented at the international conference 'Does Microfinance Work?', Groningen, The Netherlands, 1–2 July 2005.

Conning, J., and J. Morduch (2011) 'Microfinance and Social Investment', mimeo.

Cull, Robert, Asli Demirguc-Kunt and Jonathan Morduch (2009) 'Microfinance Meets the Market', *Journal of Economic Perspectives*, 23(1), 167–192.

Fehr, E. and K.M. Schmidt (1999) 'A Theory of Fairness, Competition and Co-operation', *Quarterly Journal of Economics*, 114, 817–868.

Fisman, R., Heal, G. and V. Nair (2006) 'Corporate social responsibility: Doing well by doing good?', Working Paper, Columbia University.

Galor, O. and O. Moav (2004) 'From physical to human capital accumulation: inequality in the process of development', *Review of Economic Studies*, 71(4), 1001–1026.

Gangopadhyay, S., M. Ghatak and R. Lensink (2005) 'Joint liability lending and the peer selection effect', *Economic Journal*, 115, 506, 1005–1015.

Geczy, C.C., Stambaugh, R.F. D. and Levin (2005) 'Investing in Socially Responsible Mutual Funds', SSRN Working Paper.

Ghatak, M. and T. Guinnane (1999) 'The economics of lending with joint liability: theory and practice', *Journal of Development Economics*, 60, 195–228.

Ghatak, M. (2000) 'Screening by the Company you Keep: Joint Liability Lending and the Peer Selection Effect', *The Economic Journal*, 110, 601–631.

Harjoto, M.A. and H. Jo (2009) 'Why do firms engage in corporate social responsibility?', Working Paper, Santa Clara University.

Laffont, J. and T. N'Guessan (2000) 'Group Lending with Adverse Selection', *European Economic Review*, 44, 773–784.

Laffont, J. and P. Rey (2003) *Moral Hazard, Collusion and Group Lending*, IDEI, University of Toulouse.

Prescott, E.S. (1997) 'Group lending and financial intermediation: an example', *Federal Reserve of Bank Richmond Economic Quarterly*, 83, 23–48.

Social Investment Forum (2007) *SRI trends report 2007*, Boston, MA: Author.

Stiglitz, J.E. (1990) 'Peer Monitoring in Credit Markets,' *World Bank Economic Review*, 4, 351–366.

Townsend, R. and K. Ueda (2001) 'Transitional growth financial deepening', IMF working paper 01 no 108.

14. Fair trade
Leonardo Becchetti

FAIR TRADE AND ITS ROLE: INTRODUCTORY REMARKS

Fair trade is a trade creation initiative, originated by importing organizations in Europe and the US, whose goal is to promote capacity building, inclusion and equal opportunities for marginalized agricultural and textile producers in poor income countries. A leading characteristic of the fair trade initiative is the strict definition of criteria required for producers' organizations in order to have access to the fair trade value chain.

With regard to the above mentioned criteria the International Fair Trade Association (IFAT, the umbrella gathering fair trade producer cooperatives and associations, export marketing companies, importers, retailers, national and regional fair trade networks and fair trade support organizations) defines that, when choosing which products to import, fair trade organizations have to be consistent with the following rules:

- *Creating opportunities for economically disadvantaged producers:* fair trade is a strategy for poverty alleviation and sustainable development. Its purpose is to create opportunities for producers who have been economically disadvantaged or marginalized by the conventional trading system.
- *Transparency and accountability*: fair trade involves transparent management and commercial relations to deal fairly and respectfully with trading partners.
- *Capacity building*: fair trade is a means to develop producers' independence. fair trade relationships provide continuity, during which producers and their marketing organizations can improve their management skills and their access to new markets.
- *Promoting Fair Trade*: fair trade organizations raise awareness of fair trade and the possibility of greater justice in world trade. They provide their customers with information about the organization, the products, and in what conditions they are made. They use honest advertising and marketing techniques and aim for the highest standards in product quality and packing.
- *Payment of a fair price*: a fair price in the regional or local context is one that has been agreed through dialogue and participation. It covers not only the costs of production but enables production which is socially just and environmentally sound. It provides fair pay to the producers and takes into account the principle of equal pay for equal work by women and men. Fair traders ensure prompt payment to their partners and, whenever possible, help producers with access to pre-harvest or pre-production financing.
- *Gender equity*: fair trade means that women's work is properly valued and rewarded. Women are always paid for their contribution to the production process and are empowered in their organizations.

- *Working conditions*: fair trade means a safe and healthy working environment for producers. The participation of children (if any) does not adversely affect their well-being, security, educational requirements and need for play and conforms to the UN Convention on the Rights of the Child as well as the law and norms in the local context.
- *Child labour*: fair trade organizations respect the UN Convention on the Rights of the Child, as well as local laws and social norms in order to ensure that the participation of children in production processes of fairly traded articles (if any) does not adversely affect their well-being, security, educational requirements and need for play. Organizations working directly with informally organized producers disclose the involvement of children in production.
- *The environment*: fair trade actively encourages better environmental practices and the application of responsible methods of production.
- *Trade relations*: fair trade organizations trade with concern for the social, economic and environmental well-being of marginalized small producers and do not maximize profit at their expense. They maintain long-term relationships based on solidarity, trust and mutual respect that contribute to the promotion and growth of fair trade. Whenever possible producers are assisted with access to pre-harvest or pre-production advance payment.

In practice, such criteria include: i) an anti-cyclical mark-up on prices that incorporates a floor which prevents them from falling below a certain threshold; ii) anticipated financing schemes; iii) export services provided through a long term relationship between FT importers and producers; iv) direct investment in local public goods (health, education) through the contribution provided to the local producers' association (Moore, 2004).

From these features it is clear that what we mean here for fair trade need not be confused with the use of the same 'fair trade' concept in the more recent trade literature, indicating 'arguments that relate to certain conditions under which trade, and the production of traded goods, should minimally take place' (Maseland & De Vaal, 2002). In this sense the term is used for dealing with issues related to duties, controls and dumping practices in international trade. For a similar use of the term see also Bahadur & Mendoza, 2002; Bhagwati, 1996; Stiglitz, 2002; Suranovic, 2002).

Consumer consensus on FT has grown significantly especially in Europe. In the period 2003–2007, net sales in this area grew by 40 percent per year and FT products conquered significant market shares (49 percent of bananas in Switzerland, around 20 percent and 3.3 percent of ground coffee in the US and in the UK, respectively, according to the FT importers' association).

Fair trade has recently gained support of several institutions. Among them the EU Commission, in a communication to the European Parliament on May 2009, declared that:

> Fair Trade has played a pioneering role in illuminating issues of responsibility and solidarity, which has impacted other operators and prompted the emergence of other sustainability regimes. Trade-related private sustainability initiatives use various social or environmental auditing standards, which have grown in number and market share.

FAO has recently acknowledged that fair trade is an effective mechanism to increase value added for marginalized farmers launching pilot program to inform farmers about fair trade opportunities. More specifically, investigating the banana market Liu (2009) concludes that the FT choice:

> is the one that yields the highest FOB prices and export/retail price ratio, above conventional and even organic bananas. Also, Fairtrade gives producers more stability and visibility through the system of guaranteed minimum price and premium. Another advantage of (the Fairtrade standard is that it does not raise much the costs of production. For small-scale growers seeking to improve their incomes Fairtrade certification seems to be the most profitable option provided they can meet FLO's requirements.

Overall, fair trade may be seen as one of the most well-known examples of bottom-up action of socially concerned consumers who 'vote with their wallet' by purchasing a product which is a bundle of physical and ethical characteristics. Since in most cases fair trade products have a higher price than their non fair trade correspondents, it is clear that those buying them reveal non standard consumer behavior where the negative price differential must be more than compensated for by the satisfaction of some forms of social preferences (i.e. inequity aversion, warm glow, altruism, etc.).[1] In the same way fair trade retailers are often not-for-profit entities which reveal on their side that 'solidarity spirits' may be as effective as 'animal spirits' to promote entrepreneurial activity. In this sense fair trade is a natural (non laboratory) experiment proving that both anthropological and corporate reductionist perspectives are wrong.

THE FAIR TRADE LITERATURE

The fair trade literature has taken three main directions. On the theoretical side a first debate revolves around the price 'heresy'. The following section will discuss whether the non market clearing intermediate price fixed by FT importers can be defended on efficiency grounds. In a theoretical section (pp. 148–9) we will abstract from this judgment and take the existence of fair trade as given in order to analyze its contagion effects in oligopolistic competition. The question we pose is what happens in terms of industrial economics when newcomers start retailing 'public goods' (Besley and Ghatak, 2007) and conquer small market shares satisfying social preferences of 'concerned' consumers. The main literature result here is that, under reasonable parametric conditions, the not for profit newcomer triggers (partial) imitation of profit maximizing incumbents thereby providing a theoretical rationale for the widely observed phenomenon of corporate social responsibility. In the specific case of fair trade this kind of model explains why large multinationals such as Nestlè, Starbucks, Sainsbury and many others have started producing, distributing and retailing fair trade products.

Last but not least, since the ethical component of the fair trade product is not an experience good (i.e. consumers cannot bridge the informational asymmetry by purchasing and tasting the product), the empirical literature has tried to ascertain with impact studies whether fair trade goals are actually achieved in the real practice. In the penultimate section we will discuss the main findings and methodological issues related to this literature.

THE THEORETICAL DEBATE

Economists generally manifested two main objections about fair trade. The first is related to the fact that prices should be market clearing while distributive concerns should be addressed with standard tax or redistributive policies. Fair trade seems to conflict with this approach since one of its main features, the fair trade price, is clearly a non market clearing price and, as such, it is expected to provide distorted signals to producers leading them to oversupply. A second related concern is well expressed by LeClair (2002) who argues that, in a static labor supply framework, we may remain on the same indifference curve of the primary product worker/producer if we replace the fair trade purchase with the purchase of a standard product at market prices plus a subsidy which is lower than the price premium. In other terms LeClair argues that the combination of market plus charity is more efficient than its 'bundle' in the fair trade product.

The first critique is valid only in the static partial equilibrium framework and provided that there is no imbalance of bargaining power between demand and supply. If the last condition is not met, the same textbook economics tells us that, even in the static case, in the presence of monopsony, the price determined by market forces is below the perfect competition price and a higher minimum price rule may restore the competitive equilibrium. A second argument is that the fair trade may actually be conceived as a *general purpose innovation* creating a new variety of products. In this perspective the FT price is the intermediate price of a new product variety and not a distortion of the traditional product price. Since, the 'downstream price distortion' generated by the fair trade rule is the innovation which creates additional demand on the final product, such 'distortion' (a different partition of value between producers and importers in the value chain) can be justifiable as far as it meets consumer ethical tastes (or as far as consumers are willing to pay for it).

On the second critique it must be considered that the alternative 'standard purchase+charity' pattern of action does not produce the same potential benefits that fair trade does. This is because charity does not generate contagion effects on profit maximizing competitors of fair trade (see section on pp. 148–9) and has no 'antitrust effects'; that is, it does not modify the imbalance in bargaining power between primary producers and monopsonistic intermediaries along the value chain. Finally, it does not generate a multipurpose innovation introducing a whole new range of products which combine physical and ethical features and satisfy tastes for variety of 'ethically concerned' consumers.

Following this point Reinstein and Song (2008) devise a contract-theoretic model in which they document how altruistic consumption is compatible with rational and informed behavior and helps to solve the farmer underinvestment problem under asymmetric information in a competitive setting, while Poret and Chambolle (2007) add further theoretical evidence about potential efficiency gains from FT through product differentiation. Finally, Maseland and De Vaal (2002) examine the fair trade issue from the perspective of standard international trade models documenting cases under which fair trade is a first best over the two alternatives of free trade and protectionism.

Contagion Effects of Fair Trade: Corporate Social Responsibility as a New Competitive Dimension

To understand how fair trade may trigger ethical imitation, consider the following simple 'contagion model'. A monopolist incumbent sells a standard good to consumers with inelastic unit demand distributed along the typical unit segment of horizontal differentiation models (D'Aspremont et al, 1979; Dasgupta & Maskin, 1986; Economides, 1984). The incumbent maximizes profits and its activity consists of transforming commodities purchased from primary producers in the South of the world at a subsistence price (w) and selling the final product at the price P_A to consumers.

The unit segment has a special significance in the model since it measures ethical and not geographical location for both producers and consumers. More specifically, it measures on the supply side the premium paid above the subsistence price to South producers. Consider now the entry of a fair trader which locates at the extreme right of the segment by being a zero profit producer which transfers everything to the South by setting its price $P_B = w + s$ (s is the transfer and, for simplicity, all other production costs are assumed to be equal to zero). By locating at an any intermediate distance (a) between the two extremes of the unit segment a producer decides to transfer a share a[0,1] of the fair trade entrant premium.[2]

Let us assume that consumer utility functions decrease in the product price and in the distance between their location and that of the producer (that is, in the distance between their ethical stance and that incorporated in the product). The distance is a disutility only when consumers move to the right since being less ethical than the product they buy implies no ethical costs for them. If consumers' psychological costs of buying something below their ethical standard are f times the ethical distance, consumer welfare (Wc) may be written as:

$$Wc = R_p - P_i - f(x-a) \text{ if } x - a \geqslant 0 \text{ or } Wc = R_p - P_i \text{ if } x - a < 0$$

with (P_i) being i-th (i = A,B) seller product price, (R_p) the maximum price consumers are willing to pay in case of zero costs of ethical distance and x consumer location on the unit segment.

The main result of this kind of model is that, under reasonable parametric conditions related to the marginal benefits and costs of imitation, the profit maximizing incumbent finds it optimal to move right and therefore becomes more socially responsible to react to FT's entry. Imitation is necessarily partial and well corresponds to what we observe in the reality where imitators adopt FT rules for a few products of their wide product range. An interesting result of these models is that, if we consider a domestic benevolent planner concerned with North consumers surplus, socially optimal locations produce less transfers toward the South than privately optimal ones. In this sense, the duopolistic competition between a standard producer and a fair trader generates more benefits for South producers than domestic benevolent planners and therefore compensates underrepresentation of the interests of the former and lack of global governance.

Many extensions of this approach may be conceived. Asymmetric information on the ethical properties of the products complicate the picture. The main issue is whether reputational concerns are strong enough to prevent producers from cheating on social responsibility. The situation becomes even more complex if we consider that, as it really occurs in FT, third actors such as labeling entities enter the market to solve informational asymmetries. Another interesting extension of the base model is represented by the introduction of a law of motion for consumer ethical tastes. The rationale for it is that we reasonably expect that consumer sensitivity to social and environmental responsibility is influenced by the duration of their fair trade consumption habits with the latter being, in turn, highly influenced by fair trade promotion and educational campaigns (as documented empirically by Becchetti and Rosati, 2007). In this dynamic setting it is possible to show that FT existence is necessary to trigger imitation since, in absence of fair traders, the profit maximizing incumbent, even when perfectly informed about consumers' ethical tastes, has no interest in stimulating them.

THE EMPIRICAL LITERATURE

Several impact studies have tried to verify whether fair trade maintains its promises. Many of them are interesting case studies (Bacon, 2005; Pariente, 2000; Castro, 2001; Nelson and Galvez, 2000; Ronchi, 2006) which however cannot answer the main question on whether economic and social conditions of fair trade affiliated improve vis-à-vis those of non affiliated. A few papers try to do so by looking at the impact of affiliation years on various performance indicators (Ruben, 2008). The main problem in all these papers, which examine the impact of a 'treatment' (such as fair trade affiliation) started before the beginning of the inquiry, is in the impossibility of running a randomized experiment in which selection bias can be excluded by random placement of experiment participants to the treatment or control sample.

Even considering this limit, it is important to take the challenge. The obsession of randomization may in fact exclude from empirical research the impact analysis on the whole range of ongoing programs and organizations existing before an experiment is devised, that is, the most important part of economic life.

The empirical literature on fair trade tries to solve the issue by creating situations as close as possible to the counterfactual. It selects in the control sample non FT affiliated farmers doing the same activity in the same area, uses all sort of techniques (propensity score matching, instrumental variables) or it further reduces heterogeneity between treatment and control samples by restricting the analysis to affiliated producers only and looking at the impact of affiliation years on younger and older affiliated producers.

The main findings seem to support the capacity building hypothesis documenting that in most cases income per capita significantly increases with affiliation years, even though the effect on productivity in equilibrium is not always significant since FT affiliated tend to increase worked hours (Becchetti et al, 2012).

One of the dimensions in which the impact of fair trade is less trivial both from a theoretical and empirical point of view is child labor. From IFAT criteria we do not find an explicit ban of child labor products even though it is said that child labor must:

> respect the UN Convention on the Rights of the Child, as well as local laws and social norms in order to ensure that the participation of children in production processes of fairly traded articles (if any) does not adversely affect their well-being, security, educational requirements and need for play.

In essence Fair Trade adopts the pragmatist and not the abolitionist approach according to which banning child labor does not improve the situation if economic conditions for child schooling are not created in parallel. According to the well-known 'luxury axiom', benevolent parents send their children to school whenever they overcome a minimum income threshold below which child schooling is a luxury good they cannot afford (Basu and Van, 1998). Fair trade aims to tackle the problem of child labor/schooling in this way by creating conditions which raise parental income and reduce parental vulnerability to income shocks, which are a well known determinant of school dropout.

The question however is not simple since, in the most favorable cases in which children work in the FT affiliated parental activity, the price premium effect generates (beyond a positive income effect) a substitution effect which actually increases the opportunity cost of sending children to school. Empirical results from impact studies indicate however that the effect of fair trade affiliation is generally positive (Becchetti et al, 2012; Becchetti et al. 2011) and at most not significant (Becchetti and Costantino, 2006).

The main problem which this literature is still unable to solve is that of measuring fair trade externalities. In spite of a few descriptive findings on the effects of fair trade affiliation on producers' bargaining power on the other trade channels, we have no final answer on whether the effects described above have to be attributed entirely to an improvement of affiliated producers or also in part to a negative externality on non affiliated producers.

CONCLUSIONS

The fair trade debate is still in its infancy. On the theoretical side, provided that the introduction of fair trade products definitely improves the well-being of concerned consumers satisfying their taste for variety, it remains to be seen how much the distortion critiques of static models can be rejected due to the potential fair trade benefits seen in a dynamic perspective. The balance is in favor of the second if fair trade affiliation actually promotes inclusion and its capacity building mechanisms work. It does not if it perpetuates mechanisms of dependence from 'benevolent' foreign consumers reinforcing patterns of de-specialization. Empirical evidence on the productivity improvements and child schooling effects seems to document that the positive side is robust even though each project is a story in itself and it is not possible to draw aggregate conclusions given that rigorous empirical analyses have been run on a very limited number of FT projects.

What can be definitely concluded is that the rise of FT has been a bottom-up answer to the lack of global governance and to the misrepresentation of the interests of the poorest in the global integrated economy. Its rise has generated interesting phenomena for economists transforming social responsibility into a competitive dimension and helping us to understand the potential welfare enhancing effects of a society with more bottom-up participation in which the vicarious action of concerned consumers and importers may help to address market failures and compensate for missing global governance.

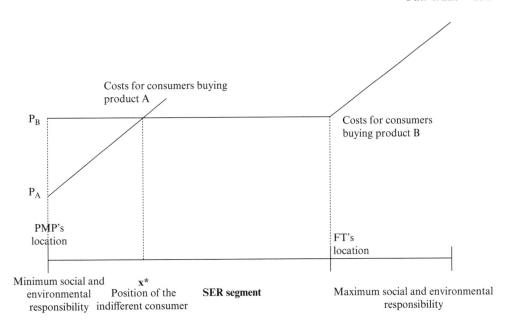

Costs for consumers buying product A

P_B

Costs for consumers buying product B

P_A

PMP's location

FT's location

Minimum social and environmental responsibility

x*
Position of the indifferent consumer

SER segment

Maximum social and environmental responsibility

Notes: PMP (profit maximizing producer); FT (fair trader).
A move to the left along the segment implies choosing a product below one's own ethical standards (and therefore is costly) while a move to right implies choosing a product above one's own SER standards (and therefore does not yield added psychological benefits or costs for the buyer).

Figure 14.1   The social and environmentally responsible (SER) product differentiation and the asymmetric costs of SER distance

NOTES

1. For a reference to this literature see, among others, the seminal papers of Fehr and Schmidt (1999) and Andreoni (1990).
2. Due to the heterogeneity of competitors the closest reference for this kind of model in industrial organization is the mixed duopoly literature (Cremer et al, 1991). Note however that in this case: i) the not-for-profit producer is a private and not a public enterprise; ii) the welfare problem is more complex involving in partially opposite directions consumers in the North and commodity producers in the South; and iii) the main concern of not for profit producers is welfare in the South and not product quality in the North. These distinctive features derive from the observed specific characteristics of fair trade competition and make the model a hybrid between horizontal and vertical product differentiation. A possible analogy is with situations in which producers add to the product 'quality' features on which consumers have heterogeneous views (i.e. the introduction of a giant TV screen in a restaurant).

REFERENCES

Andreoni, J. (1990). 'Impure Altruism and Donations to Public Goods: A Theory of Warm-Glow Giving', *Economic Journal* 100, 464–77.
Bacon, C. (2005). 'Confronting the Coffee Crisis: Can Fair Trade, Organic, and Specialty Coffees Reduce Small-Scale Farmer Vulnerability in Northern Nicaragua?', *World Development* 33(3), 497–511.
Bahadur, C. and Mendoza, R. (2002). 'Toward Free and Fair Trade: A Global Public Good Perspective', *Challenge* 45, 21–62.

Basu, K. and Van, P.H. (1998). 'The Economics of Child Labor', *American Economic Review* 88, 412–427.

Becchetti, L. and Costantino, M. (2006). 'Fair Trade on marginalised producers: an impact analysis on Kenyan farmers', *World Development* 36(5), 823–842.

Becchetti, L. and Rosati, F. (2007). 'Globalisation and the death of distance in social preferences and inequity aversion: empirical evidence from a pilot study on fair trade consumers', *The World Economy*, 30(5), 807–830.

Becchetti, L. and Huybrechts B. (2008). 'The dynamics of Fair Trade as a mixed-form market', *Journal of Business Ethics*, 81(4), 733–750.

Becchetti, L., Conzo, P. and Gianfreda, G. (2009). 'Market access, organic farming and productivity: the determinants of creation of economic value on a sample of Fair Trade affiliated Thai farmers', *Australian Journal of Agricultural Resource and Economics*, 56, 117–40.

Becchetti L., Giallonardo L., and Tessitore M.E. (2010). 'A CSR product differentiation model with asymmetric information', *Rivista Italiana degli Economisti* 15(2), 209–236.

Becchetti, L. Castriota S. and Solferino N. (2011). 'Development Projects And Life Satisfaction: An Impact Study On Fair Trade Handicraft Producers', *Journal of Happiness Studies*, DOI: 10.1007/s10902–009–9179–9.

Becchetti, L., Conzo, P. and Gianfreda, G. (2012). 'Market access, organic farming and productivity: the determinants of creation of economic value on a sample of Fair Trade affiliated Thai farmers', *Australian Journal of Agricultural Resource and Economics*, 56(81), 117–140.

Besley, T. and Ghatak M. (2007). 'Retailing Public Goods: The Economics of Corporate Social Responsibility' (with Tim Besley), *Journal of Public Economics* 91(9), 1645–1663.

Bhagwati, J. and Hudec, Robert E. (1996). 'Fair Trade and Harmonization: Prerequisites for Free Trade?', Volume 1 of *Economic Analysis: Introduction*, Cambridge and London: MIT Press.

Castro, J.E. (2001) *Impact assessment of Oxfam's fair trade activities. The case of Productores de miel Flor de Campanilla*. Oxford: Oxfam.

Cremer, H., Marchand, M. and Thisse, J. (1991). 'Mixed Oligopoly with Differentiated Products', *International Journal of Industrial Organization* 9, 43–53.

Dasgupta, P. and Maskin, E. (1986). 'The Existence of Equilibrium in Discontinuous Economic Games, I: theory; II: applications', *Review of Economic Studies*, 53, 1–41.

D'Aspremont, C., Gabsewicz, J.J. and Thisse, J.-F. (1979). 'On Hotelling's Stability in Competition', *Econometrica*, 47, 1045–1075.

Economides, N. (1984). 'The Principle of Minimum Differentiation Revisited', *European Economic Review* 24(3), 345–368.

Fehr, E. and Schmidt, K.M. (1999). 'A Theory of Fairness, Competition and Co-operation', *Quarterly Journal of Economics* 114, 817–868.

LeClair, M.S. (2002). 'Fighting the tide: Alternative trade organizations in the era of global free trade', *World Development* 30(7), 1099–1122.

Liu, P. (2009). 'Certification in the value chain for fresh fruits. The example of banana industry', FAO commodity studies n.4, FAO.

Maseland, R. and De Vaal, A. (2002). 'How Fair is Fair Trade?', *De Economist* 150(3), 251–272.

Moore, G. (2004). 'The Fair Trade Movement: parameters, issues and future research', *Journal of Business Ethics* 53(1–2), 73–86.

Nelson, V. and Galvez, M. (2000). *Social Impact of Ethical and Conventional Cocoa Trading on Forest-Dependent People in Ecuador*. University of Greenwich.

Pariente, W. (2000). *The impact of fair trade on a coffee cooperative in Costa Rica. A producers behaviour approach*. Université Paris I Panthéon Sorbonne, No 1161–98.

Poret, S. and Chambolle, C. (2007). 'Fair Trade labeling: inside or outside supermarkets?', *Journal of Agricultural & Food Industrial Organization* 5, 1–22.

Reinstein, David and Joon Song (2008). 'Efficient Consumer Altruism and Fair Trade', Economics Discussion Papers 651, University of Essex.

Ronchi, L. (2006). '"Fairtrade" and Market Failures in Agricultural Commodity Markets', World Bank Policy Research Working Paper 4011, Washington: IBRD.

Ruben, R. (2008). *The impact of fair trade*. Wageningen Academic Publishers, Wageningen.

Stiglitz, J. (2002). *Globalization and Its Discontents*. New York: Norton.

Suranovic, S. (2002). 'International labour and environmental standards agreements: is this fair trade?', *World Economy*, 25(2), 231–245.

15. Fraternity

Adrian Pabst

INTRODUCTION: ETYMOLOGY AND MEANINGS

The word 'fraternity' derives from the Latin word '*frater*' or brother. Broadly speaking, 'fraternity' refers to some group or association that is constituted by a sense of brotherhood, governed by the ties of friendship and bound together by the mutual aid among its members. In contrast with solidarity, which is impersonal and refers to an abstract community based on identity, fraternity is inter-personal and emphasises the diversity between equals based on differentiation (Bruni and Zamagni 2004). As such, it depends on the principle of reciprocity linked to mutual obligations. Fraternity so configured is like an 'artificial family' that differentiates itself from other social or civic arrangements on account of a distinct ethos that is binding upon its members (Le Bras 1940–41; Michaud-Quantin 1970; Black 2003).

Far from being confined to the fellowship of small groups, fraternities are part of a wider set of reciprocal relationships in the realm of civil society that are marked by a shared sense of mutual assistance (Bruni and Sugden 2008). Fraternity – as a communal intentionality and also as set of institutions and practices – can embed the economic and the political in the social. Thus, the practice of fraternity can give rise to a genuine commonwealth whose bonds of reciprocity are not based on blood ties or professional links (e.g. Le Roy Ladurie 1982).

Linked to this is the Christian idea of a universal body of believers and of charity for all in need, an idea that translates into parishes and guilds organised as 'confraternities'. In short, the idea and reality of a fraternity blends the civic with the religious, a fusion wherein the secular is *not* a separate, discrete space that is synonymous with the fallen world of 'pure nature', sinfulness, evil and violence. Much rather, the *saeculum* is a temporality that for catholic orthodox Christianity is ultimately structured by the liturgical cycle of praise and thanksgiving: it mediates the supernatural Good in God, offering intimations of peace and human perfectibility first fully revealed in the Incarnation and Resurrection of Jesus Christ. By contrast, the dominant traditions of modernity instituted the secular as the primary locus of society that restricts the remit of the sacred and redefines religion in terms of abstract belief to which people give asset based on their private consciousness – rather than the communal practice of a shared, embodied faith. As such, the notion of fraternity has roots in Greco-Roman Antiquity, whose models of association were transformed by patristic and medieval Christianity that sought to overcome the opposition between the secular and the religious on which much of modernity rests.

HISTORICAL ORIGINS AND EVOLUTION

Broadly speaking, the tendency to create groups and associations, which are separate from the blood ties of family and kinship and also distinct from the bonds of citizenship and nationhood, seems to be coextensive with the formation and evolution of human societies and cultures. In many tribal societies, it was particularly young men who formed such arrangements. More specifically in Europe, fraternities in ancient Greece ranged from male drinking clubs and other social structures via cultic groups and burial societies to associations that were variously more cultural or more economic. Similarly, the Roman Empire featured *collegia*, which were 'also called *corpora*, *sodalitia* [. . . and] went back "earlier than recorded history", being mentioned in the Twelve Tables as an imitation of a Greek model' (Black 2003: 3 [the indented quote is from Duff 1938: 103]).

As Antony Black has argued, in Antiquity there was no clear, constitutionally enshrined independence of fraternities. The emergence of political clubs in the late Roman Republic under the consulate of Cicero and then Caesar led to strict control and even suppression of the colleges (cf. *Corpus Iuris Civilis*, in Krüger and Mommsen 2010). Augustus protected friendly societies for religious and other non-political purposes (e.g. burial societies and other examples of mutual aid). The distinction between 'licit' and 'illicit' fraternities originated at the same time and inaugurated a tradition that exists to this date, notably subordinating fraternal arrangements to political authority and common law (Duff 1938, esp. 107–117). This involved an official licensing system, state powers to dissolve fraternities and their exclusion from politics (Black 2003: 4).

However, the unfolding of Christendom in late Antiquity and the Middle Ages changed all this. Building on the legacy of Hellenic Judaism, the Church offered a free 'space' between the citizen and the state in a break with the pagan Roman collusion of *civitas*, *imperium* and *sacerdotium*. From the outset, the idea of the Church as a universal brotherhood found institutional expression in the universal episcopate, transnational monastic networks and local parishes organised as confraternities (Michaud-Quantin 1970). First of all, the Church transformed the Roman-law *collegia* in a political direction by introducing election and consent (Black 1997). On account of greater participation beyond citizenship, class or colour, ecclesial arrangements were arguably far more democratic than associations in ancient Greece. In turn, early Christian congregations gradually gave rise to a whole host of corporate bodies, which flourished in particular after the twelfth century. These included cathedrals, monastic chapters and the new order of friars – electing superiors, managing property communally and subjecting major decisions to communal consent (Tierney 1955, 1982; Black 2003).

Second, the development of canon and civil law saw the fusion of Roman and Germanic principles with Christian notions of justice and charity. In this complex process, new forms of association and corporation emerged and blossomed, whether the conciliarist movement within the Church or corporate guild-like bodies. Over time, the latter acquired a distinct legal personality (irreducible to the individual or the state – or indeed both), their own constitutional structure and their formal incorporation into civic polities. As Black remarks, '[l]ike cities themselves and parliaments, they had formal constitutions, established procedures, could issue regulations, and their members were formally equal in decision-making rights' (Black 2003: xxii).

As such, medieval (con-)fraternities crossed the false, double divide of the political and the economic as well as the social and the religious. For they were themselves part of civil society broadly conceived – embedding the polity and the economy in relations of reciprocity, mutuality, brotherhood and friendship. What distinguished medieval fraternities from both ancient and modern ones was their constitutional status and political role. Thus, in late Antiquity and particularly in the Middle Ages, the notion of fraternity covered a wide spectrum of meanings – from organisations such as craft-guilds via associations like religious confraternities to secret societies (e.g. Freemasonry). Fundamental differences notwithstanding, all these examples have a number of key features in common: they constitute groups that are bound together by ties of friendship and ritual, offering and providing mutual support to members according to the principle and practice of reciprocal duty that ensures both equality and diversity (Zamagni 2009).

Modern fraternities, by contrast, have tended to be less tightly-knit, more private and more specialised. In this way, they shift the emphasis away from mutual duties and reciprocal responsibilities of brotherhood and friendship towards a narrower focus on common interest and members' formal entitlements. Instead of upholding the autonomy of civil society, such fraternities risk being complicit with the modern state. In the name of legal impartiality and meritocratic criteria, the modern state subjugates the self-governing organisations that mediate between individuals, families and the sovereign centre (Pabst 2010a).

This is exemplified by the French Revolution, which abolished all the intermediary institutions of civil society and recreated them under the absolute authority of central state law. Indeed, the '*Loi Le Chapelier*' of 1791 banned guilds and fraternities (or *compagnonnage*) defended by figures such as Montesquieu. The law was followed by a decree of 18 August 1792, which dissolved all types of congregations, both of the clergy and of the laity, including universities, faculties and learned societies. Taken together, the law and the decree eliminated the right to strike and they instituted free enterprise as the fundamental mode of association or corporation. That is why the revolutionaries did not put an end to the power of privilege, whether in the form of patronal clubs or monopolistic arrangements that were in league with the central state. From the outset, the bureaucratic statism of the French Revolution was complicit with cartel capitalism (Pabst 2010b).

Since the time of the French Revolution, the meaning of the term 'fraternity' has changed radically compared with late Antiquity or the Middle Ages. It is true that fraternity remains associated with more reciprocal and mutual notions: first, moral obligations rather than constitutional-legal rights; second, informal ties rather than formal rules; third, trust and gift-exchange rather than contract, central state 'policing' and enforcement; fourth, an overlapping network of corporate associations rather than the dialectical oscillation between the individual and the collective. However, according to Mona Ozouf (1997), two main modern meanings can be distinguished: one that derives from liberty and equality and is ultimately subordinate to them. The other flows from Christian notions of brotherhood and reciprocity and thus provides a basis for both free societies and equal citizens. Thus, modernity encompasses at least two senses of fraternity: 'one, that followed liberty and equality, was the object of a free pact; the other preceded liberty and equality as the mark on its work of the divine craftsman' (Ozouf 1997: 1996–97). In part, this distinction underpins the difference between a more 'organicist' and a more 'atomistic' liberalism, with the latter dominant in much of modern political and economic thought.

KEY THINKERS AND SEMINAL TEXTS IN ANTIQUITY AND THE MIDDLE AGES

Contrary to much of pre-Socratic thinking on the priority of the universe over the self or the city, both Plato and Aristotle viewed families and fraternities as the most primary locus of life in society that in some way mirrors the cosmic whole. The polity is the principal locus of association that actualises the potential of the soul, the household and relations of friendship (*The Republic*, book VIII; *Politics*, book I (Plato 1937a)). Based on his metaphysics of participation, Plato argued that justice in politics is about the right ordering of relations in accordance with the Good or 'author of all things' (Plato 1937a: 508E, 511B, 516B), which endows all things with goodness (Pabst 2012). As such, both practical, manual and theoretical, contemplative activities and professions are complementary in perfecting the republic, as illustrated by the prominence of the philosopher-king and the craftsman. In addition to laws and virtues (Plato 1937b: book X), Plato's political philosophy blends metaphysical principles with doxological practices (praise of the divine) that translate into bonds of friendship and other forms of fraternal association (Planinc 1991; Pickstock 2001, 2002).

Similarly, Aristotle's idea of an associative polity reflects his ethics of virtue. Understood as the middle way between extremes, virtue mediates competitive and potentially conflictual relations, directing them away from mutually diminishing vice towards standards of excellence and the common good in which all can share. Just as courage is the middle way between recklessness and cowardice, so too justice charts an alternative course between selfishness and altruism. By linking citizens to one another in terms of mutual rights and reciprocal duties, justice is the 'bond of men in states' (Plato 1937b: I, 2, 1253ª37–38) and the ordering principle in political societies. Since friendship involves the shared pursuit of truth and also the promotion of one another's honourable and righteous aims, fraternities are central to the blossoming of the *polis*.

Cicero viewed friendship as the primary mode of human association that gives rise to the practice of politics. Like Plato and Aristotle, he also accentuated the natural sociability of man: in his *De Officiis* (*On Duties*), it is said that '[. . .] the bond of human community and association [. . .] is reason and speech, which [. . .] reconcile men to one another and join them in a kind of natural partnership (*naturali quadam societate*)' (*De Officiis*, book I, chap. xvi (Cicero 1991)). In this manner, cities and commonwealths reflect a wider cosmic order in which reciprocal ties are mutually augmenting. The principle that underpins the creation of public realms (*res publica*) is itself 'a kind of natural coming-together (*congregatio*) of men' (*De Republica*, book I, chap. xxv (Cicero 1928)). Crucially, Cicero linked the bonds of friendship to the 'will of the people' and common consent that are at the heart of the *res publica*. Thus, it is bonds of fraternal, corporate association that bind together the rights and shared interests of cities and commonwealths (*De Republica* I, xxv (Cicero 1928)).

Augustine and Aquinas transformed the Greco-Roman legacy by fusing it with Christian principles of justice and charity. In addition to notions of friendship and virtue, they developed the biblical and patristic idea of an impersonal Good that fashions the *cosmos* out of chaos in the direction of a supernatural good in God that infuses nature and directs humans to their proper ends – praising the divine and perfecting the fallen world. Augustine extended Ciceronian notions of popular will by emphasising democratic virtues of consent and peace (*De Civitate Dei*, book XIX (Augustine 1998)). This position was diametrically opposed to the ancient, aristocratic virtue of *agon* (or violent contest), which Machiavelli would later retrieve. Similarly, the Bishop of Hippo broadened and deepened the scope of fraternity by linking association to the universal brotherhood in the Church.

Crucially, the polity is not a human artifice that regulates the violent 'state of nature' (as for most theorists of social contractualism). Rather, for Augustine (as for Aquinas) it reflects in some partial and imperfect way the divinely created universe: the body politic represents both God's punishment and God's remedy for sin (*remedium peccatorum*), while the ecclesial body embodies the peace and reconciliation revealed in Jesus Christ. Within the universal brotherhood of the Church, fraternal relations are connected with the supernatural virtues of faith, hope and charity that translate into practices of reciprocal giving and mutual aid. In the Middle Ages, this was exemplified by the radical continuity between the liturgy, processions and the associative ties of guilds, universities as well as other intermediary institutions (Bossy 1983). Insofar as it upholds the dignity of each person and the autonomy of corporate bodies, the ecclesial body transforms the earthly city in accordance with the City of God.

Aquinas and other high medieval theologians accentuated the profound links between the ideal of friendship and charity, on the one hand, and the reality of life in society, on the other hand. Just as manual, material work mirrors in some sense the creative work of God (*Summa Theologiae* I*ᵃ*–II*ᵃᵉ* q.95 a.1 resp. (Aquinas 1964–75)), so too fraternal relations translate into practices of mutual help. Unlike pre-Christian Antiquity, the Middle Ages viewed the activity of craftsmen and peasants in terms of vocation and sanctifying works (*Summa Theologiae* I*ᵃ* q.96 a.3 (Aquinas 1964–75)). In a clear difference with later feudal arrangements, the Church supported the development of new orders of friars who combined theological study with agriculture and handicraft.

Rather than viewing theoretical and practical work as separate, medieval thinking stressed the importance of creative perfectibility, honourable practices, excellent products and the proper treatment of workers. As such, fraternity was indissociable from notions of justice, profession, *officium* (lit. duty), each with its own sense of dignity. Thus, Aquinas rejected the practice of usury and argued for just prices and fair wages: 'just purchases, sale and suchlike, without which men cannot live together', as 'derived from natural law' (*Summa Theologiae* I*ᵃ*–II*ᵃᵉ* q.95 a.4 (Aquinas 1964–75)). While defending individual property as 'necessary for human life' for the purposes of social order and individual industriousness (*Summa Theologiae* I*ᵃ*–II*ᵃᵉ* q.66 a.2 concl.), Aquinas also championed the communal sharing of land and other assets as a way of mitigating the will of the individual and the sovereign (e.g. *De Regno*, book I, chap. VI, XI–XIV (Aquinas 2002)).

As the historian Otto Gierke documented, craft-guilds embodied in some measure the universal brotherhood of the Church in the particular fraternal relations of its members. Guilds mediated between families, households and the state: they 'embraced the whole man', represented 'for its members a miniature commonwealth (*Gemeinwesen in*

Kleinen)' and 'united its members with one another like brothers' (Gierke 1868: 359, 383, 387, quoted in Black 2003: 12). Likewise, guilds sought to uphold standards of excellence and honourable practices. They 'made the colleagues have, in relation to one another, an earnest brotherly love for duty' (Gierke 1868: 387, quoted in Black 2003: 13), if necessary by means of punishment and exclusion based on an ethos that combined extensive rights with strict duties and moral codes. Frequently organised as confraternities that were variously more or less religious, craft-guilds participated in the life of the polity based on their own distinct 'legal personality'. Thus, the late Middle Ages saw the development of a new theology of work (Hughes 2007) that blended notions of contract with practices of fraternal gift-exchange – a vision that Renaissance figures such as Coluccio Salutati, Leonardo Bruni, Pico della Mirandola and Marsilio Ficino further developed in different directions (Bruni and Zamagni 2004).

For example, Francesco Patrizi of Siena spoke of 'social or civil friendship (*socialis seu civilis amicitia*)' as the moral pillar of the state. Such friendship is the least specific and most diffuse form of fraternity, based as it is primarily on individual advantage (*utilitas*), but it may 'as days go by through use and customs become more abundant (*accumulator*), until advantage is mostly set aside and gracious benevolence and friendship remain' (*On the Kingdom*, quoted in Black 2003: 97). Following the medieval fusion of contract with gift, Patrizi and other Renaissance thinkers viewed fraternity as a sentiment and virtue that underpins the whole of civic life, including political and economic relations. As Black documents, '[b]y sharing a market-place and other civic facilities, citizens can achieve "a wonderful charity", a "common friendship" among themselves' (Black 2003: 97). As such, neither the polity nor the economy was separated from the intermediary institutions of civil society and the fraternal bonds of mutual benevolence that were themselves inscribed in a liturgically ordered cycle.

EARLY AND LATER MODERN IDEAS

While there is no single break in the history of the idea of fraternity, the work of William of Ockham and Marsilius of Padua deviates markedly from ancient, patristic and high medieval thinking. Both Ockham and Padua introduced three new elements: first, the rupture between general sociability and political association; second, the artificial character of the body politic; third, the absolute (unconstrained) character of political authority vis-à-vis the corporate bodies of civil society (Pabst 2010a). There can be little doubt that Machiavelli's vision of politics marks a fundamental rupture compared with late Antiquity and the Middle Ages. The key point is that there simply was no secular, neo-pagan default model of city states, eschewing clerical control in favour of an unrestrained economic and political power. As John Milbank has argued:

> recent research (for example, by Augustine Thompson OP) utterly belies this: the earlier Italian republics were not founded on pagan models, but were more like 'confraternities of confraternities'; citizenship was liturgically linked to baptism (as the free-standing baptisteries of Italian cities still attest today) and participation in local church and civic life (often astonishingly and directly democratic in character) were so complexly interwoven as to be inseparable. Suspicion of the Pope and even of the clergy does not here amount to 'secularity' [. . .]. Moreover, the emergence of a more pagan republicanism with Machiavelli coincided with an evolution of the

city-states towards princedoms and local imperialism. (Milbank 2004: 218; the reference is to Thompson 2005)

Another critical juncture occurred with the influential Jesuit Francisco Suárez (1548–1616), who eschewed the shared patristic and medieval Neo-Platonist idea of a universal brotherhood governed by fraternal bonds in favour of a modern formalistic account of popular unity. For Suárez, the people constitute a 'single mystical body' (*unum corpus mysticum*). That body is a purely human unity that is prior to the *ecclesia*, the universal Church founded upon the Body of Christ. Contrary to Aquinas's distinction between the church as *corpus mysticum* and the state as 'body politic', Suárez's conception of the population as a 'single mystical body' replaces the patristic and medieval primacy of the ecclesial community over the state with the early modern supremacy of the state over the people (e.g. *De Legibus, Ac Deo Legislatore*, Book III, chap. ii, para. 3 (Suárez 1856–87)). Though Suárez rejects the divine right of kings, he emphasises absolute state sovereignty and the primacy of the governing king over the church. This provides the conceptual basis for the sacralisation of the state and the subordination of civic institutions to political power (Pabst 2012).

In the later seventeenth century, Johannes Althusius sought to recover the earlier Neo-Platonist vision of a universal brotherhood and mutual and reciprocal ties of fraternity. He spoke of civil society as the primary form of association that is based on family and friendship, embedding both the body politic and the economy. As Carl Friedrich wrote:

> [b]eginning with the family [. . .] Althusius suggested that on successive levels of political community those who live together in order and harmony [. . .] are united by a pact, expressed or implied, to share things in pursuit of common interests and utility. The village was for him a federal union of families, as was the guild; the town a union of guilds, the province a union of towns and villages; the kingdom or state a union of such provinces; and the empire a union of such states and free cities. (Friedrich 1964, p. ix)

In this manner, Althusius combined the Catholic Christian principles of subsidiarity and solidarity with the Greco-Roman emphasis on association governed by reciprocal ties of brotherhood and friendship.

With the invention of 'political economy' in the eighteenth century, much of liberalism shifts the emphasis away from notions of fraternity to the idea of instrumental utility. Linked to this is a greater accentuation of the 'free' market and the strong state at the expense of civil society and its intermediary institutions. As Luigino Bruni and Robert Sugden have shown (Bruni and Sugden 2008), the difference between Adam Smith's 'political economy' and Antonio Genovesi's 'civil economy' encapsulates these developments. Smith views market relations predominantly in terms of self-interest subject to the law of contract, thereby separating the pursuit of profit from the practice of gift-exchange (cf. Pabst 2011). Connected with this is Smith's critique of guilds and other intermediary institutions, which he blames for price-fixing and other anti-commercial practices: 'people of the same trade seldom meet together, even for merriment and diversion, but the conversation ends in a conspiracy against the public, or in some contrivance to raise prices [. . .]' (Smith 1991, Book I, chap. x, para. 2, p. 117). Smith judged guilds not to defend the excellence of products or the equality of their members but rather as privileged corporations that promote monopoly.

Thus, Smith tended to equate the competitive market with a morally neutral space that is free from the constraints of moral and civic virtues, which govern the 'thick ties' of family, friends and associations (Bruni and Zamagni 2004). As such, he viewed market relationships as distinct from the bonds of civil society. That is why Smith's political economy stands half-way between the model of 'civil economy', on the one hand, and the model of 'commercial society', on the other hand – an idea that can be traced to Locke and Hobbes (Macpherson 1962) and also Mandeville who in different ways privileged purely instrumental relationships over above non-instrumental relationships of fraternity.

By contrast, Genovesi rejects the separation of self-interest from notions of sympathy and instead argues for wider reciprocal relationships in civil society that are marked by shared intentions for mutual aid: 'for Genovesi, there is no fundamental distinction between market relationships and those of other domains of civil society. This conception of economics is expressed in the name Genovesi tries to give to the discipline: *civil economy*' (Bruni and Sugden 2008: 46 [orig. ital.]). Crucially, the form and content of such reciprocal relationship is that of fraternity. For Genovesi, fraternity binds together interpersonal, particular dimension of 'friendship' with the universal outlook of 'brotherhood' – a form of unity and equality in diversity that is expressed by the principle of reciprocity (Zamagni 2009). Fraternal relations are connected with common membership in groups (such as guilds, religious communities or the body politic) that embed instrumental relations within non-instrumental relations. This idea was recovered by various thinkers and movements in the nineteenth century but marginalised in much of the twentieth century by the convergence of political and economic liberalism, which coincided with the collusion of the strong state and the unbridled 'free market'.

CONTEMPORARY DEBATES AND POLICY ISSUES

Since the collapse of state communism and the ongoing crisis of 'free-market' capitalism, both academic research and public policy-making have been concerned with alternative economic models (cf. Pabst and Scazzieri 2012) and also transformations of the welfare state away from state paternalism or private contract delivery towards civic participation and community-organising. Whilst it has provided some much-needed minimum standards, statist-managerial welfare subsidises the affluent middle classes and undermines (traditional or new) networks of mutual assistance and reciprocal help amongst workers and within local economies (Beito 2000). One reason is that the late nineteenth- and twentieth-century centralised welfare state risks trapping the poor in dependency while simultaneously redistributing income to middle-income groups. Moreover, the neo-liberal 'structural reforms' of the 1980s and 1990s that rationalise welfare compensate the failures of capitalism by promoting freely-choosing reflexive and risk-taking individuals who are removed from the relational constraints of nature, family and tradition.

Today, by contrast, there is a renewed emphasis on the principles of reciprocity and mutuality, which translates into policies that incentivise the creation of mutualised banks, local credit unions, and community-based investment trusts. Beyond redistributive policies, alternatives to the centralised bureaucratic state and the unfettered 'free market' include asset-based welfare and decentralised models that foster human relationships of communal care and mutual help – rather than state paternalism or private contract delivery (Bruni and Zamagni 2004). For example, there is a compelling case for a system that combines universal entitlement with localised and personalised provision, e.g. by fostering and extending grassroots' initiatives like 'Get Together' or 'Southwark Circle' in London that blend individual, group and state action. Both initiatives reject old schemes such as 'befriending' or uniform benefits in favour of citizens' activity and community-organizing supported by local council – instead of being determined by central target and standards.

Crucially, the 'civil economy' model differs from both statist and free-market welfare in that it focuses on human relationships of mutuality and reciprocity (rather than formal rights and entitlements or monetarised market relations). Citizens join welfare schemes like social care as active members who shape the service they become part of rather than being reduced to merely passive recipients of a 'one-size-fits-all' top-down model. Southwark Circle works on the principle that people's knowledge of their neighbourhood, community and locality is key to designing the provision and delivery of welfare. Services are delivered involving civic participation, social enterprise (e.g. the company Participle) and the local council. This can be linked to 'time banks' where voluntary work by members of the community can lead to certain entitlements that reward their contribution (e.g. by reducing their local tax).

A new dimension of fraternity appears in the emerging information network society. Non-interested forms of cooperation, which are linked to the practice of fraternal gift-exchange, are fundamental to the operation of new communities such as Wikipedia and widely used tools like open-source software programs, among many other initiatives.

By contrast, state paternalism or private contract delivery cost more to deliver less, and they lock people either into demoralising dependency on the state or financially unaffordable dependency on outsourced, private contractors. The reason why civic participation and mutualism costs less and delivers more is because it cuts out the 'middle man' – the growing layers of gate-keepers such as managers, social workers and bureaucrats who assess people's eligibility and enforce centrally determined standards and targets instead of providing services that assist genuine individual needs and foster human relationships.

The vision of civic participation and mutualism is inextricably linked to the decentralisation of the state in accordance with the twin Catholic Christian principles of solidarity and subsidiarity (action at the most appropriate level to protect and promote human dignity and flourishing). A genuine alternative to the prevailing options eschews both conservative paternalism and liberal *laissez-faire* in favour of something like an organic pluralism and a radical communitarian virtue ethics that blends a hierarchy of values with an equality of participation in the common good.

BIBLIOGRAPHY

Aquinas (1964–75), *Summa Theologiae*, ed. T. Gilby and P. Meagher, New York: McGraw-Hill.
Aquinas (2002), *De Regno* (*On Kingship*), in *Aquinas: Political Writings*, ed. and tr. R. W. Dyson, Cambridge: Cambridge University Press, pp. 5–52.
Augustine (1998), *De Civitate Dei* (*On the City of God*), ed. and tr. R. W. Dyson, Cambridge: Cambridge University Press.

Beito, David T. (2000), *From Mutual Aid to the Welfare State. Fraternal Societies, 1890–1967*, Chapel Hill, NC: The University of North Carolina Press.

Black, Antony (1997), 'Christianity and Republicanism from St. Cyprian to Rousseau', *American Political Science Review* **91**: 647–56.

Black, Antony (2003), *Guild & State. European Political Thought from the Twelfth Century to the Present*, with a new introduction, London: Transaction Publishers (orig. pub. 1984).

Bossy, John (1983), 'The Mass as a Social Institution', *Past & Present* **100**: 29–61.

Bruni, Luigino and Sugden, Robert (2008), 'Fraternity: Why the Market Need Not Be a Morally Free Zone', *Economics and Philosophy* **24**(1): 35–64.

Bruni, Luigino and Zamagni, Stefano (2004), *Economia civile. Efficienza, equità, felicità pubblica*, Bologna: Il Mulino; trans. *Civil Economy: Efficiency, Equity, Public Happiness*, Bern: Peter Lang, 2007.

Cicero (1928), *De Re Publica, De Legibus*, tr. Clinton Walker Keyes, Cambridge, MA: Harvard University Press.

Cicero (1991), *De Officiis (On Duties)*, ed. M. T. Griffin and E. M. Atkins, Cambridge: Cambridge University Press.

Duff, Patrick W. (1938), *Personality in Roman Private Law*, Cambridge: Cambridge University Press.

Friedrich, Carl (1964), 'Preface', in *The Politics of Johannes Althusius*, abridged trans., London: Eyre and Spottiswoode.

Gierke, Otto von (1868), *Das deutsche Genossenschaftsrecht*, Vol. 1, Berlin: Weidmann.

Hughes, John (2007), *The End of Work: Theological Critiques of Capitalism*, Oxford: Wiley-Blackwell.

Krüger, Peter and Mommsen, Theodor (2010) (eds), *Corpus Iuris Civilis*, reprint, New Jersey, NJ: Lawbook Exchange (orig. pub. 1895).

Le Bras, Gabriel (1940–41), 'Les confréries chrétiennes: problèmes et propositions', *Revue Historique du Droit Français et Étranger* **4**(19–20): 310–363.

Le Roy Ladurie, Emmanuel (1982), *Montaillou, village occitan de 1294 à 1324*, Paris: Gallimard (orig. pub. 1975).

Macpherson, C.B. (1962), *The political theory of possessive individualism: Hobbes to Locke*, Oxford: Clarendon.

Michaud-Quantin, Pierre (1970), *Universitas: expressions du mouvement communautaire dans le moyen âge latin*, Paris: Vrin.

Milbank, John (2004), 'The Gift of Ruling: Secularization and Political Authority', *New Blackfriars* **85**(996): 212–238.

Ozouf, Mona (1997), 'Liberté, égalité, fraternité', in Pierre Nora (ed.), *Les Lieux de Mémoire*, Paris: Gallimard, Vol. 3, pp. 4353–4389; trans. Pierre Nora (ed.), *Realms of Memory*, New York: Columbia University Press, pp. 1996–1998 (abridged translation).

Pabst, Adrian (2010a), 'Sovereignty in Question: Theology, Democracy and Capitalism', *Modern Theology* **26**(4): 570–602.

Pabst, Adrian (2010b), 'The Crisis of Capitalist Democracy', *Telos* **152**: 44–67.

Pabst, Adrian (2011), 'From Civil to Political Economy: Adam Smith's Theological Debt', in Paul Oslington (ed.), *Adam Smith as Theologian*, London: Routledge, pp. 106–124.

Pabst, Adrian (2012), *Metaphysics: The Creation of Hierarchy*, Grand Rapids, MI: Eerdmans.

Pabst, Adrian and Scazzieri, Roberto (2012), 'The Political Economy of Civil Society', *Constitutional Political Economy* **24**: 337–356.

Pickstock, Catherine (2001), 'Justice and Prudence: Principles of Order in the Platonic City', *Telos* **119**: 3–17.

Pickstock, Catherine (2002), 'The Problem of Reported Speech: Friendship and Philosophy in Plato's Lysis and Symposium', *Telos* **123**: 35–64.

Planinc, Zdravko (1991), *Plato's Political Philosophy: Prudence in the* Republic *and the* Laws, Columbia: University of Missouri Press.

Plato (1937a), *The Republic*, in *The Dialogues of Plato*. tr. B. Jowett, New York: Random House, Vol. I, pp. 589–879.

Plato (1937b), *Laws*, in *The Dialogues of Plato*. tr. B. Jowett, New York: Random House, Vol. II, pp. 405–703.

Smith, Adam (1991), *An Inquiry into the Nature and Causes of the Wealth of Nations*, intro. D. D. Raphael, London: Random House.

Suárez, Francisco (1856–1887), in *Franciscus Suarez. Opera omnia*, ed. Michel André, Paris: Vivès, Vol. IV.

Thompson, Augustine (2005), *Cities of God: The Religion of the Italian Communes, 1125–1325*, University Park, PA: The Pennsylvania State University Press.

Tierney, Brian (1955), *Foundations of Conciliar Theory: The Contribution of the Medieval Canonists from Gratian to the Great Schism*, Cambridge: Cambridge University Press.

Tierney, Brian (1982), *Religion, Law, and the Growth of Constitutional Thought 1150–1650*, Cambridge: Cambridge University Press.

Zamagni, Stefano (2009), 'Europe and the Idea of a Civil Economy', in Luk Bouckaert and Jochanan Eynikel (eds), *Imagine Europe. The Search for European Identity and Spirituality*, Antwerpen-Apeldoorn: Garant, pp. 13–24.

16. From arts patronage to cultural philanthropy: collaborating with granting foundations
Elisa Bortoluzzi Dubach and Pier Luigi Sacco

PREMISE

Miguel de Unamuno y Yugo, a great thinker and rector of the University of Salamanca, once wrote: 'Only by aiming for the unattainable can the attainable be achieved. Only if one's goal is impossible can the possible be achieved.' The choice of this particular quotation as an *incipit* for this chapter is not incidental. Foundations and nonprofit associations worldwide put themselves on the line each and every day as they strive to support, manage and promote cultural and social activities whose goals are to change the lives of those who may benefit from them. Although the purposes and funding methods quite often differ – from subsidies to grants, from capital expenditures to microloans – what these bodies all have in common is an unassailable determination and passion for giving both time and themselves to achieve pro-social goals.

It is to all these realities that this chapter is dedicated, its aim being to stimulate dialogue and allow anyone who so wishes to discover the fascinating world of foundations, to explore their strategies and practices, and thus provide a simplified description of their decision-making and operational logic to the advantage of aspiring grant-seekers. This chapter has therefore to be taken as a short guide to successful application to grant-making foundations for the cultural practitioners.

FROM ARTS PATRONAGE TO INSTITUTIONAL PHILANTHROPY

In order to understand the role of foundations in the contemporary context, it is necessary to provide a sketchy account of the relationship between the cultural and economic spheres in a historical perspective. In the pre-industrial economy, cultural production was typically not a source of economic value, but was rather absorbing resources generated in other fields of activity, such as landlord rent collecting, banking, or commerce. The reason was that the forms of cultural production that prevailed in the pre-industrial context were not structured in ways that could ensure profitability in an organized way. The size of potential cultural markets was very limited in that very few people could afford to buy cultural artifacts, and also because most of them would be unique copies (such as in the case of artworks), or could be produced in a very limited amount of copies (such as in the case of pre-Gutenberg books) or would require hiring entire groups of performers (such as in the case of music, theatre, or dance, i.e. all forms of live performance). Even when (slow) technological progress allowed some early form of mechanized production, such as in the case of post-Gutenberg book publishing, the cost of creative products remained substantial enough to prevent most of the population to be able to buy them. In the pre-industrial phase, therefore, cultural production was basically ensured by patronage, i.e. by the generosity of commissioners, be they in charge of a public office or not, who decided to invest resources in covering the living and production expenses of cultural producers for their own entertainment and that of their acquaintances. As a consequence, with a few exceptions (such as, for instance, the art shown in cathedrals and churches and the music played in functions), only a very limited audience could actually access cultural goods and experiences.

A major discontinuity was provoked by the advent of the bourgeois revolutions, which, under the influence of the French Encyclopedia, identified in a more generalized access to culture and science one of the key components of a new concept of citizenship. As a consequence, with the birth of the modern nation states, private patronage was partially substituted by 'public' patronage under the form of state cultural policies, financed by public taxes and pursued in the interest of the community.

At the turn of the 19th century and throughout the 20th century, a stream of technological innovations finally made space for truly inclusive cultural mass markets, which progressively addressed larger and larger audiences by developing new media such as cinema, radio, television, photography, and recorded music, while at the same time substantially reducing the cost of printed books and magazines (Sassoon 2006). Thus, on the one side there were now sectors which could make profits on private markets (publishing, music, movies, and so on) but on the other side there were others that could not survive without external subsidies because of their peculiar structure and their inability/unwillingness to incorporate technological progress (most of the visual and performing arts, heritage, etc). This situation has essentially carried over until today, and defines the context in which we can analyze and understand the role of private foundations.

One could think that, with the advent of public cultural policies and with the expansion of cultural markets, there should be no need or use for private support to cultural production. But in fact, this is far from reality. Both public policies and private markets cannot possibly support all possible forms and instances of cultural production, although for different reasons. This means that there are potentially many instances of cultural production that could not be realized, in that they fail to match both the objectives and interests of the public policy makers and the conditions for market success, or simply of market feasibility. Therefore, private patrons could still be motivated to support cultural production if, by doing so, they are ensuring the viability of forms of cultural and creative expression that would not find support otherwise and thus could not be produced. This is particularly true for those forms of cultural expression that are experimental or controversial, and which initially do not meet the tastes of large audiences or the criteria of public commissioning, but that nevertheless could prove in time to be truly original and interesting forms which would play a role in the historical development of a specific discipline. Moreover, the role of private patrons can be substantial in ensuring that certain forms of cultural expressions, whether innovative or not, become accessible to the inhabitants of certain regions, or to certain categories of audience that would not be adequately served otherwise. Or, again, private patrons could be interested in pursuing a cultural project or initiative of their own, and to link this endeavor to specific circumstances (the commemoration of a beloved one that passed away, the promotion of certain religious or philosophical beliefs, or simply the patron's personal prestige or visibility). Patronage in the context of advanced socio-economic settings thus takes the form of philanthropy, i.e. of the promotion of specific ideals of human advancement and development, which can be in turn supported and encouraged in many ways (e.g. by means of specific fiscal privileges) insofar as they meet the public interest in specific and objective terms (Schervish 2007). At the same time, philanthropy can be regarded as an expression of the creativity and far-sightedness of private citizens who explore new ways to pursue the public interest (Anheier and Leat 2006) and do this by employing their own financial means – in this sense, philanthropy may be seen as a sort of social entrepreneurship which is not mediated by the market, but that nonetheless contributes at its own risk to the search for innovative, welfare-improving initiatives.

Thus, there are many reasons why private patronage still finds a role (and possibly a relevant one, especially in periods of financial crisis, such as the present one, that cut down public resources) even in an advanced socio-economic context where both public action and private markets are well developed. This does not mean, of course, that one should think of private patronage as an *alternative* to public cultural policies, but only as a complement. In fact, whereas public policies are pursuing the public interest, private patronage is and cannot be but the expression of private inclinations, aims and tastes, and thus private patrons must maintain their full autonomy in making their choices – a possibility that would be at least partially precluded if one intended private patronage as a surrogate for public policies. At the same time, however, modern forms of private support to initiatives of general interest cannot be entirely subsumed under the familiar categories of patronage, as we will explain in more detail below, in that they are strictly regulated and may establish complex links with actual governance structures and may engage in public–private partnerships, whereas the classical patronage model pertains to a self-referential private activity, pursuing its own aims in a totally independent and unregulated way.

Granting foundations are the organizational structures through which these sophisticated forms of private support to the public interest can find their role in contemporary cultural arenas (for example see Whitaker 1974). The foundation is endowed with its own resources, and is constrained to use them according to the will and orientations set forth by the founder. At the same time, foundations can participate in more complex projects, carry out partnerships with other subjects, including public ones, and can both provide grants to support external cultural projects and produce their own projects. A sound analysis of the dynamics of cultural supply thus cannot simply do without a careful consideration of the role and potential of granting foundations.

PHILANTHROPY AND SOCIAL CHALLENGES

What is the social context in which foundations operate? If philanthropy can be seen as a form of non-market mediated entrepreneurship, it is not surprising that it is subject to competitive pressures, which grow stronger with the unfolding of the social and economic development process and provide new challenges for the economy as a whole (Lomax et al 2010). And these challenges entail not only the functioning of the economy and of the society, but also our very models of well-being and quality of life.

This aspect becomes particularly evident when we consider what can be defined as one of the key issues of contemporary economy and society: Sustainability. Over the last 10 years, sustainability has evolved from being an abstract and somewhat exotic concept, fairly unknown to the general public, into a concrete, pressing need, intensely perceived by all as a vital aspect of everyday life and, moreover, as a major constraint on the living conditions of the future generations – and this does not concern environmental issues only, that is to say, those dealing with natural non-renewable assets, but increasingly issues related to the cultural heritage, namely, human made, non-renewable assets. The public at large is now being asked to come to terms with such major issues as the conservation of cultural assets in countries struck by natural catastrophes, or in those where wars are being waged.

As a consequence of this, new public attitudes have developed:

- interest in the conservation of the natural and built environment has grown considerably;
- education and continuing education have become crucial factors for professional success vs. failure, and for successful vs. unsuccessful social integration of individuals;
- the distribution of wealth and the differences in individual and social levels of well-being have become the focus of discussion at every political and economic level.

These are, ultimately, the challenges that define the entrepreneurial and competitive context within which philanthropy operates as an engine of social change. Such challenges are deeply woven into state-of-the-art conceptions of governance, and therefore define an important aspect of public/private partnerships, which can be subject to further evolution in the future in ways that can only be partially anticipated at the moment.

THE ROLE OF FOUNDATIONS WITHIN THE INTERNATIONAL CONTEXT

That foundations, in light of the profound changes currently underway, increasingly represent a driver of socio-economic advancement and change, is indirectly but eloquently demonstrated by a simple fact: the number of foundations with a liberal legislative orientation has substantially grown in European countries, where the facilitation of private commitment for purposes of general interest has caused an exponential response by the civil society (think of Germany, where foundations have increased fourfold in the last 30 years). Likewise, in many countries in the European Community, the presence of major foundations, with substantial assets amounting to over 5 billion Euros, has also grown (examples include Cariplo Foundation, the Robert Bosch Foundation, the Calouste Gulbenkian Foundation, to name just a few). And especially for foundations of such a remarkable dimension, networking coordination cooperation at a national and sometimes even at an international level become a matter of substantial interest in order to ensure an efficient allocation of resources and to exploit potential synergies. To this emerging tendency, a parallel one corresponds as to the formation of consortiums among grant-seekers themselves, thereby enhancing the level of social organization of the philanthropic field.

On the other hand, the *modus operandi* of the granting foundations has also changed profoundly. Over the last 10 years, a great effort has been made to professionalize the work of the granting foundations:

- Studies are currently underway on the theme of the harmonization of laws for the promulgation of the 'European Foundation Statute'.[1] Irrespective of whether these efforts will actually lead to a concrete set of rules, the very fact that a discussion is ongoing is already a big step ahead.
- States themselves are working hard on the rules inherent to the right to reduce the complexity of the legal procedures required to set up and govern foundations. The experiences of countries with an extremely liberal law such as Switzerland, but also Germany, and the consequence of this choice on philanthropic growth have provided compelling evidence about the need to rethink regulation of the field.[2]
- Very important documentation centers have been established, and have become the driving force for an increasing number of studies and initiatives on the subject (e.g. the European Foundation Center in Brussels).[3]
- The number of university studies devoted to the subject of foundations has grown considerably (e.g. the CSI-Centre for Social Investment of the University of Heidelberg).[4]
- There has been a rise in the number of trade associations whose aim is not only to promote an exchange of experiences, but also to give birth to joint initiatives between foundations.[5]
- Codes for good governance for the granting foundations have been developed, which delve deeply into crucial issues for the interaction between foundations and civil society, as well as for the governance of the foundations themselves, and their communication with grant-seekers.
- The operational instruments that make up the foundations' toolbox have evolved greatly. Planning instruments, auditing, databases, websites, and the communication of foundations have all undergone changes that we could go so far as to call epic. A glance at the websites of the larger foundations will give the viewer an immediate, pictorial impression of the efforts underway. Among other things, the larger foundations also make great use of advanced IT platforms and of social media.[6]
- The level of accessibility, and of the direct involvement of the grant-seekers, is increasing considerably. In the foundation websites, the interface functions with the non-profit world are improving on a daily basis.

Lastly, by analyzing the complex world of culturally proactive granting foundations, although the extreme individualization of intents and activities is an ineluctable value, it is nonetheless evident that a twofold way of understanding the role of the foundation is becoming crystallized: that is, a traditional one, which we believe is essential precisely at a time when the world economy – and that of the single countries – is so fragile; and an entrepreneurial one, where the philanthropist entrepreneur truly acts as a manager who sets up the foundation and transfers into its management all the skill and expertise he or she has built up in the company, with the clear aim of taking on a proactive role in putting forward models for the solution of problems that are not meant to mitigate the situation from within, but rather to resolve it completely.

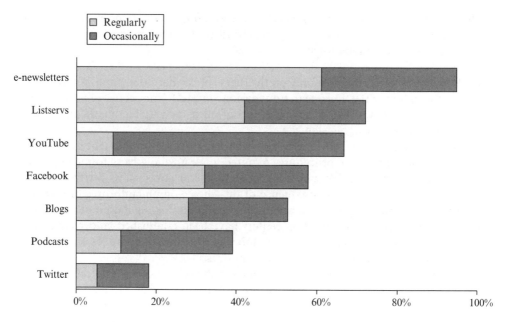

Note: Figures based on the responses of 73 members of the Foundation Center's Grantmaker Leadership Panel.

Source: The Foundation Center, September 2010.

Figure 16.1   Use of social media/Web 2.0 services by foundation leaders

This latter type of foundation tends to stimulate self-sustainability and the organizational efficiency of the beneficiaries, which are increasingly being supported by training initiatives and by specific consultancies, so as to make available to them not only resources, but also know-how.

Within such a complex scenario, it becomes more and more essential for the potential grant-seekers, be they cultural institutions or single cultural operators, to deeply connect with this world, so as to try to understand better just what granting foundations are and how they operate.

WHAT EXACTLY DO WE MEAN BY GRANTING FOUNDATIONS?

The term 'granting foundation' refers to those foundations (i.e. nonprofit bodies) that use their own assets for cultural aims, social purposes, and so on – declared by a 'founder' from the inception – carrying out such aims through the granting of contributions to projects promoted by other institutions, which are generally nonprofit.

This is not, as already pointed out above, arts patronage in the traditional sense of the term. The patron is a private individual who donates freely, without an agreed return, reporting only to him- or herself (or possibly also to other family members) as regards the money invested. Unlike a foundation, which has a statute to adhere to, he or she is not subject to any sort of constraint. It is not even a matter of sponsoring, because this latter form of private contribution presumes the existence of a company as the actor that makes financial resources, services and/or know-how available, in exchange for a measurable advantage in terms of visibility, reputation and corporate image, with the goal of implementing its own strategic objectives, which are often of a business nature.

Unlike the foundations (for which the grant-seeker's project and its quality are at the very heart of each venture) as the realization of the project matches the accomplishment of the statutory aims of the foundation itself, for the sponsoring company the decision as to whether or not to support a person, institution or project depends on the chance to achieve the company's pre-set goals (which will typically be functional to profit-making) with greater efficiency, rapidity and at a lower cost as compared to what could be attained by means of other marketing and communication instruments (Bortoluzzi Dubach 2009, p. 12).

Then, whereas for a granting foundation there will be an intrinsic motivation (see for example Pink 2009) to support a specific project in view of its nature, aims, and cultural value, in the case of a sponsoring company the motivation is generally instrumental to goals which do not refer to cultural quality or values.

GRANT-MAKING FOUNDATIONS: A PRACTICAL GUIDE

How Does One Choose the 'Right' Foundation to Put Forward a Project?

In order to identify the partner or foundation most suited to one's own needs and projects, it is best to proceed in a targeted and systematic way. The so-called 'funnel' method may be an effective way of operating: we begin with a selection that is as broad and exhaustive as possible, taking into account the highest number possible of potential financers, and gradually, by exclusion, we determine which one will be the ideal partner.

For a first screening phase, it is worth considering several criteria:

- the aim of the foundation and its areas of activity: if the project is in line with the foundation's goals, and if the reference groups targeted by the project and the estimated impact are in turn coherent with the grant-maker's focus of interest, then the foundation will be well disposed to assessing the application.
- The territorial sphere: once the match between the project and the foundation's goals has been assessed, it will be helpful to identify the correspondence between the project's regional sphere and the foundation's own zone of operations. Indeed, foundations often focus their activity in one region, or are keen to preserve or develop certain types of relations across the territory.
- Considerations of a financial nature are an important selection criterion for the foundation: if the project is broad in scope and calls for a substantial amount of financing, then the number of institutions that can actually finance it will drop, and the number of potential contacts that will have to be activated to succeed eventually will have to increase.
- A personal relations network: an in-depth knowledge of the founder's personality

and history will foster a better understanding of the foundation's mission; a painstaking analysis of his or her environment and personal relations network will make it possible to formulate the kinds of requests that correspond best to his or her desires and expectations. The same can be said for the various members of the foundation's administrative board and for any other relevant internal bodies.

- Lastly, the activity of the competitors: checking whether and where similar projects are being carried out – with special attention to the project's target environment or to closely related ones – and who provided the financial support are often the quickest and most efficient ways to detect the ideal partner (Pink and Drive 2009, p. 49).

Structural Difficulties in Performing Research and in Addressing Foundations

At first sight, the market for foundations is not very accessible; the search for information can prove to be rather demanding, and may call for a great deal of time and effort. Certain obstacles and barriers need to be overcome:

- The market for foundations is not a particularly transparent one and it is also hard to assess, and this means that the search for relevant information may prove laborious and time-consuming, and not necessarily successful. But one should not be put off by this. In situations such as these, the most important aspect is the mindset: the solution is to 'be positive', and not give up. There are no obstacles that cannot be overcome. The secret is a mix of commitment, respect for what one is doing, tenacity, untiring optimism and what is known as a 'nose' for things . . . While you can learn to be optimistic, a 'nose' must be cultivated.
- Granting foundations must stick to the goals laid down by the founder. They can only respond to the changed conditions of the socio-economic context to a certain extent. The more the definition of the foundation's goal is broadly formulated, the greater, of course, is the room for maneuver of those in charge.
- One serious obstacle may well be the duration of the decision-making processes. Depending on the size of the foundation, a few weeks may pass before the application is even assessed. It is important not to feel disappointed if an answer does not arrive immediately. Rather, it is useful to consider beforehand whether or not the timing of the project and that of the foundation are indeed compatible.
- From a practical point of view, anyone with decision-making powers within an institution has a more or less structured opinion from the very outset about what is positive, less positive or totally negative for the organization (see for example Katz 2005, pp. 123–131). They think they know why some things cannot be changed, and what must be done to produce change. It is difficult to challenge these beliefs, and this has to be kept in mind throughout the interaction with the grant-maker.
- Previous failures in fundraising activities and efforts may condition the interaction with the grant-maker in a substantial way, and may foster critical attitudes that should be kept under control, avoiding unwarranted negative generalizations as a

defensive form of maintaining one's perception of self-efficacy (Bortoluzzi Dubach 20011, p. 71).

How Do We Go About Collecting Information Efficiently?

A few reference principles are useful for the sake of efficient gathering of information:

- being systematic, and cultivating an analytical mentality and common sense pragmatism in the collection and processing of information represent a fair starting point;
- creativity can help you find information even where it is not so apparent or simple;
- lastly, a person has to be willing to personally take on the responsibility for a task, something that is often underestimated at first.

For this purpose it may well be helpful to:

- surf the internet in depth, visiting the websites of the foundations, the trade associations, the specialized databases, and cross-referencing all of the collected information;
- closely examine the specialized trade publications and carefully read any related articles, including those published in the national and local press;
- read market surveys and specialist publications;
- pay special attention to developments and trends;
- analyze similar projects.

Analyzing in depth and with a fair attitude the projects put forward by the competitors can also be very stimulating. These remarks are all the more true in the light of the current trends of increasing professional standards in fundraising activities, which make competition fiercer and which cause a corresponding upgrading of the expectations of the grant-makers in terms of the documentation and motivation supporting a specific project. As a consequence, the very number of relevant sources to be searched and to stay updated about grows considerably, and often requires multi-language skills and an in-depth knowledge of different social and cultural contexts. It is reasonable to expect that this trend will further progress in the future, and therefore one should be prepared either to achieve high specific skills on the search and documentation phase, or to invest in their acquisition on the market in the case of larger organizations or of long-term projects. Very often, to the contrary, the strategic importance of this crucial phase is overlooked, with the consequence of jeopardizing the project's sustainability from the very beginning.

Who Can Provide the Necessary Information?

A precious source, besides those previously cited, is personal exchange, namely, getting in direct contact with people who have had a specific experience.

A successful conduct in this respect means being able to optimize the choice of who to contact: the right references might be persons who, at the same time, play an active role in a foundation and are very familiar with the project, or else they are:

- specialized editorial staff, officials and executives (e.g. municipal and provincial administrators whose job is to deal with cultural issues);
- consultants who work for foundations and specifically deal with fundraising;
- fundraising and sponsoring specialists;
- people in charge of trade associations;
- university professors who have good teaching and professional experience about sponsoring and fundraising.

A good network is built over a relatively long period of time; it calls for a sense of fulfillment in contacting others and for a true interest in human relationships. It requires flair, creativity, skill at using new technologies, also with a view to exploiting the opportunities offered by the social media.

Key Information on Foundations

Thanks to the screening process discussed above, at this point several potential foundations will have been singled out, with which it might be fruitful to start a dialogue. The more you know about the people you will be facing, the greater the chances of success.

The following aspects should be securely mastered when engaging in a meeting with a grant-maker:

- the foundation's goal;
- the foundation's guidelines and policies;
- thematic and geographical key points;
- limitations of action and scope (e.g. nationality, etc.).

Another significant element which needs to be examined is the way the foundation is organized, that is to say, its structure:

- foundation board (chairperson and names of the people involved);
- administration;
- collaborators or people in charge of projects.

A professional and meticulous analysis of the foundation's nature and history is crucially important for a better understanding of its policies; a thorough intelligence of its environment and relations network allows for drawing up applications that closely match the foundation's aims and are then consequently perceived as the 'right' projects to support. The same can be said of the members of the foundation's board of administration and all its internal bodies. It is important to be aware of the decision-making processes and the educational and work-related backgrounds of those involved, just as it is to have accurate information about their personal relations networks. Similarly, it is important to find out beforehand whether direct or indirect contacts with the foundation already exist, of what nature, with what level of reliability, and so on (Bortoluzzi Dubach 2011, p. 72).

Financial Resources

Another important aspect is of course the one inherent to financial resources:

- capital of the foundation (when accessible), yearly volume of costs, mean amount of contributions paid out;
- type of contributions paid out (i.e. cash, know-how, services);
- methods (i.e. subsidies, microcredit, venture capital, etc.).

Checking whether or not the foundation grants to a given beneficiary are repeated in time can be a significant criterion of choice as far as long-term projects are concerned, and an audit of the foundation's financial resources is no doubt one of the best ways to safeguard oneself as a grant-seeker.

Methods Used by Foundations to Grant Contributions

Before starting, it is also important to understand what is required by the foundation as regards the call for funding applications, what the deadlines are, and the amount of time that is needed to process the requests, regardless of whether this is to be presented in digital or paper form, or by means of specific application forms.

Lastly, it is useful to put oneself in the shoes of the potential partner and ask: 'which factors might help to persuade the foundation to collaborate with our institution?' In concrete terms, this calls for studying the foundation's documents carefully, visiting its website (if it has one), checking deadlines so as not to be late and, lastly, all the various formalities required, including the accurate completion of any application forms according to the guidelines provided, if any.

Only at this point will it be right and appropriate to go ahead with the proper grant-seeking activity.

How to Draft an Application for Funding

Drafting a good application means, first of all, fulfilling several criteria which are indispensable for its preparation:

- *Choosing the 'right language'*: cultural operators often forget that in their field practitioners typically make use of a specialized language, which professionals outside the field cannot be expected to be conversant with. To be concise and convincing, avoiding terminology that is incomprehensible to the reader, write in an accurate, meaningful way, and avoid rhetoric. These are all elements that convey clarity, an ability to get organized and to be concise – in other words, expertise.
- *The length of the application*: the length of an application varies depending on the complexity, the costs, the goals of the project for which funding is being required, as well as the amount of money needed. For a small project, a simple text of just

a couple of pages might suffice. For a more ambitious project, a whole dossier accompanied by a covering letter will be necessary. Crucially important when deciding which of the two formats is best are common sense, experience and, most of all, the indications laid down by the foundation itself.

- *Presentation/appearance*: form is substance: depending on the environment and the sum of money for which an application is being made, the quality of the presentation can express and stress one's artistic background, social commitment, artistic/qualitative level, etc., and may, in a nutshell, demonstrate the applicant's credibility, ability, and reliability. On the other hand, a good application must be legible and inviting, it must be capable of capturing the reader's attention and conveying not just facts but emotions as well (Bortoluzzi Dubach 2011, p. 150).

In general, applicants tend to regard form filling activities as a loss, i.e. as a waste of time, energy, and resources they would willingly skip if they could. But, especially in the cultural field, conscientious application preparation may also be very important for the applicant, in terms of clarifying its aims, learning how to communicate the project effectively, reflecting on overlooked organizational or financial aspects, and so on. At the same time, if the previous activity of documentation and research has been conducted properly, the applicant will have a sense of what references, or catch phrases, or what style will be likely to be most effective for that particular grant-maker. If the application has been drafted reluctantly and unwillingly, this will creep out sooner or later and will negatively influence the evaluators. Thus, the application phase should be considered as a form of training and learning. The more this happens, the more effective the application preparation process will become through time.

How Does an Idea Become a Project and a Project an Effective Claim for Funds?

A professional application implies that the idea was previously sketched out and refined, and accompanied by all of the appropriate sources of information that are relevant for the decision maker, including a dedicated business plan.

The document to be sent to the foundations will then be drafted according to a grid that will include information concerning the topics listed below (Bortoluzzi Dubach 2011, pp. 151–165).

Grant-seeker's organization

The foundation expects to receive detailed information concerning the beneficiary, in order to be able to verify the professional skills and competence of those involved in the management of the project; the foundation needs to ascertain whether – both as a result of prior experience and of the operational size, of the track record and of the reputation of the beneficiary – the proposal put forward is likely to be carried out properly within the allotted time. The key elements in one's career, experience and training can help to convince the reader of the grant-seeker's competence. Also, the presence of a patronage committee may be useful in convincing the foundation of the importance of the initiative.

Likewise, well-known and competent figures who endorse an initiative are in most cases an added value, not just because of their fame, but above all because of their contacts and the relational networks they usually have behind them. Yet, this is not a sufficient element to bring to the attention of the granting foundation a project whose profile does not fully match the other requirements laid down.

The project and its goals

The project's contents are at the heart of the reader's interest. Very briefly, it is all a question of convincing the evaluator that:

- the objectives formulated are realistic and compatible with those of the foundation;
- the project has potential as such, and as an instrument to accomplish the foundation's goals;
- it is innovative;
- it is interesting to well-targeted audiences;
- the quality of the project is guaranteed and suitable;
- a social and possibly a media impact can be expected;
- the project communication is carried out professionally.

Budget and financial planning

A well-structured budget and an accurate financial plan are key elements for a well-posed claim for a contribution. These are also the cornerstones for carrying out any initiative, whatever its nature.

As regards the budget, a minimal reference scheme is the following:

- Costs for planning and for the project
  + implementation costs
  + costs for audit and final costs
- own accruals;
- accruals from other partners;
  + a reserve for unbudgeted costs
  = claim for financing.

In drafting the budget, it is important to specify overall costs, defining them in detail, explaining and justifying each item, including in the list the costs for one's own work, listing expenses for any consultants as an integral part of the plan, including the costs for audit, and calculating and setting aside a reasonable reserve.

Financing plan

The financing plan is also very important as it will tell us how much money we can expect from the foundation, whether the contribution will be in a single installment or recurrent, which additional sources of financing have been requested and which contributions have already been made.

The foundation will also check which other partners are involved in the financing. In this regard, the coexistence between sponsors and foundations can at times be delicate, especially if the sponsor has declared business interests.

Return

Generally speaking, foundations do not ask for financial or other sorts of material returns, although they may ask to receive feedback in terms of some pre-defined performance indicator (e.g. in terms of audience, media coverage, etc.); see below. Quite often, though, an acknowledgment in the project's documentation or at the place of operation of the project is enough.

Results audit

A most important component of a project's statement is the pre-definition of the criteria that will be used to assess it, as well as the parameters and the instruments used to monitor it in order to measure its success (Constantine and Braverman 2004). If easily measurable indicators exist, ones that are suitable to the nature of the project, it is advisable to state them from the very beginning. This will certainly be positively received, in that commitment to measurable indicators signals the receiver's disposition to act effectively, and its self-confidence to be able to do so.

The granting foundation will give substantial emphasis to the clarity and integrity with which such commitments are expressed. Moreover, evaluators have generally developed a long experience in this field, and are able to discriminate truly professional statements in this respect from opportunistic, instrumental ones.

How best to conclude the document

The concluding paragraph of an application usually contains words of acknowledgement. This is also an opportunity for the person drafting the project to explain why he or she specifically chose to apply to that particular granting foundation.

The enclosures will vary depending on the type of application, from copies of the program, to information on previous projects, from accomplishments made up to the present time, to mentions in the press. The documentation may be on paper or in digital format, but the enclosures can also be objects if they have to do with the contents of the project (for example, a CD in the case of an orchestra). In this case as well, the more complex and ambitious a project, the more articulate and detailed the enclosures should be.

CREATING VALUE FOR ALL: GRANT-MAKING, GRANT-SEEKING AND THE PRO-SOCIAL DIMENSION OF CULTURE

Cultural organizations know all too well that both public funding and private financing through the market pose several constraints on their range of sustainable activities. On the one hand, projects that receive public funding must often have to comply with the state of the public opinion on a number of key issues, the moment of the political-economic cycle at which the request is being made, the nature of the incumbent political coalition at the relevant administrative level, and the level and quality of personal relationships. On the other hand, funding through the market entails considerable entrepreneurial risks and severely constrains the nature of the projects that can be carried out. Too challenging or experimental projects are likely to be turned down by audiences which are unaccustomed to them, and a long phase of selective exposure may be needed before a certain form of cultural expression can become popular or simply widely accepted by the non-expert public opinion. Applying to foundations is probably the best channel to have one's own project evaluated at its face value, i.e. in terms of quality of the cultural contents, project design, social relevance of aims, and so on. Therefore, foundations perform a considerable role in contemporary cultural supply systems. The capacity to encourage private actors to launch their own foundations and to support cultural initiatives coherently with pro-social attitudes and beliefs is therefore a major issue, especially so in times of diminishing public resources and increased competition for access to the available ones. Countries that are effective in fostering these social dynamics are likely to benefit considerably, in ways that create value for all of the involved stakeholders: the grant-receiver, of course, but also the grant-maker, which finds meaningful and socially useful ways to employ its resources; the public administration, which is relieved of part of the financial burden from the support of worthy cultural projects; the audiences, which may benefit from a wider and qualitatively richer menu of possibilities (Davenport 2000).

Therefore promoting more effective practices of grant-seeking (Ostrower 2004) is not only a way of improving the chances of specific organizations to get funding; it is also, and most importantly, a way of enhancing the professionalism and credibility of beneficiaries in ways that are likely to further encourage more private subjects to become in turn grant-makers as a response to positive evidence of good practices and of effective use of allocated funds. It would be wrong, therefore, to confine best practices of effective grant-seeking in the specific domain of practical advice. Effective grant-making guidelines have to be also the subject of scholarly research, in order to develop more and more compelling protocols that become part of the conventional wisdom. It is also in this spirit that in the present chapter we have been carefully pinning down the main bullet points of each single aspect of a successful grant-seeking application.

In order to progress further in this direction, interdisciplinary research is called for. For instance, getting fresh insight from the psychology of reasoning, the psychology of organizations, and social psychology in terms of the key elements that make applications successful both from the vantage point of the grant-maker (see Schervish and Havens 2001) and of the grant-seeker would be most welcome and useful. Also, some systematic research on comparative evaluations of alternative national systems (see for example Anheier 2001), and their legal and allocative implications in terms of the grant-making practices of foundations would be of great help not only for practitioners but also for public policy makers. Furthermore, additional research is needed in terms of elaboration, monitoring and validation of performance indicators for grant-making institutions (see for example Bertelsmann Foundation 2001), depending on the nature of the project, on its size and complexity, on the grant-maker's aims, and so on.

A final aspect to be considered is that, as we have already noted, not all countries pay the same attention or provide the same positive conditions for the development of grant-making foundations. Behind the few leaders in the field, other countries are lagging, most often because the social and economic advantages from fostering the development of the sector have been poorly understood or misevaluated. Comparative research would be useful, as well as dissemination of carefully packaged evidence and information aimed at national decision makers.

In the near future, then, an interesting research and policy agenda is opening up, and should receive due attention from all of the involved parties. There is reason to believe that it will be taken increasingly seriously. And, for once, this is good news for everybody.

NOTES

1. See http://europa.eu/legislation_summaries/institutional_affairs/institutions_bodies_and_agencies/l33315_it.htm (last accessed May 2011).
2. Cf. http://www.efc.be/Legal/Pages/FoundationLaw.aspx (last accessed May 2011).
3. Cf. http://www.efc.be (last accessed May 2011).
4. Cf. http://www.csi.uni-heidelberg.de (last accessed May 2011).
5. Cf. The Donors and Foundations' Networks in Europe (DAFNE) http://www.efc.be/Networking/Pages/Dafne.aspx (last accessed May 2011).
6. Cf. http://foundationcenter.org/gainknowledge/research/pdf/social_media.pdf (last accessed May 2011).

REFERENCES

Anheier, H.K., 'Foundations in Europe. A Comparative Perespective'. In: A. Schlueter, V. Then, and P. Walkenhorst, (eds), *Foundations in Europe. Society, Management and Law*, Bertelsmann Foundation, Guetersloh, 2001, pp. 35–38.
Anheier, H.K. and D. Leat (eds), *Creative Philanthropy*, Routledge, London, 2006.
Bertelsmann Foundation, 'Striving for Philanthropic Success. Effectiveness and Evaluation in Foundations'. International Foundation Symposium 2000, Bertelsmann Foundation Publisher, Gütersloh, 2001.
Bortoluzzi Dubach, E., *Lavorare con le fondazioni. Guida operativa*, Franco Angeli Publisher, Milan, 2009.
Bortoluzzi Dubach, E., Stiftungen-Der Leitfaden für Gesuchsteller, Huber Frauenfeld Publisher, 2 revised and expanded edition, 2011.
Bortoluzzi Dubach, E. and C. Degen, 'Fördern macht Schule'. *Förderstiftungen, Sponsoren und geldsuchende Stiftungen schaffen Synergien für die gemeinnützige Sache*, proceedings of the proFonds Convention held in Basel in 2007.
Constantine, N.A. and M.T. Braverman, 'Appraising evidence on program effectiveness.' In: M.T. Braverman, N.A. Constantine and J.K. Slater (eds), *Foundations and Evaluation: Contexts and Practices for Effective Philanthropy*, Jossey-Bass, San Francisco, 2004, pp. 236–258.
Davenport, K., 'Corporate Citizenship, A Stakeholder Approach for Defining Corporate Social Performance and Identifying Measures for Assessing It'. *Business & Society*, 39(2), 2000, pp. 210–219.
Katz, S.N., 'What Does it Mean to Say that the Philanthropy is "Effective"? The Philanthropist's New Clothes', *Proceedings of the American Philosophical Society*, 149, 2005, pp. 123–131.
Lomax, P., Brookes, M. and L. de Las Casas, *The business of philanthropy. Building the philanthropy advice market*. New Philanthropy Capital, London, 2010.
Pink, D.H., *Drive. The Surprising Truth About What Motivates Us*, Riverhead, New York, 2009.
Sassoon, D., *The Culture of the Europeans. 1800 to the Present*, HarperPress, London, 2006.
Schervish, P.G., 'The Moral Biography of Wealth: Philosophical Reflections on the Foundations of Philanthropy', *Nonprofit and Voluntary Sector Quarterly* 36, 2007, pp. 356–372.
Schervish, P.G. and J.J. Havens, 'The Mind of the Millionaire. Findings from a National Survey on Wealth with Responsibility'. In: E. Tempel (ed.), *New Direction for Philanthropic Fundraising*, n. 32, Wiley, New York, 2004.
Stiftung, Bertelsmann, 'Striving for Philanthropic Success. Effectiveness und Evaluation in Foundations'. International Foundation Symposium 2000, Bertelsmann Foundation Publishers, Gütersloh, 2001.
Whitaker, B., *The Foundations: An Anatomy of Philanthropy and Society*, Eyre Methuen, London, 1974.

17. Gifts and gratuitousness
Serge-Christophe Kolm

GIVING AND EMPATHY

Your mirror-neurons make you enjoy other people's satisfaction and feel sadness for other people's pain or sadness. This empathy goes along with a propensity (you feel it as an inducement) to give to others and help them for an altruistic motive or reason, and to praise and value people who give to and help others. Since you like to be praised (and hence to be praiseworthy), this also induces you to give and help. This judgment by most others then crystallizes into a social norm, which just says that it is advisable, good, and sometimes required to give, and is also a moral norm. This is particularly important concerning other people's pain and the corresponding compassion and desire to relieve. Neuro-imagery also shows that people are gratified not only by what they have and by what other needy people receive, but also by their choosing a transfer from them to the other, by their being responsible for it (see below). Moreover, your mirror-neurons also tend to induce you to imitate other givers or helpers.

Gift-giving, in the most general understanding, is an action which is costly or painful in any sense for the giver or helper, and is made to favour the receiver in any sense.

The first experience of a human life is receiving gifts and help from the care of a mother who also 'gives' birth and life to begin with. Receiving such care is also most often the last experience of a life. All through life, the most basic relations with others in a normal society consist of gifts within the family or between friends.

However, empathy in such cases is particularly high because the individuals are related by relations of affection, liking, friendship or love, the relation is lasting or recurrent, and the relation, sentiments, attention and gifts are reciprocal.

Yet, gifts motivated by sentiments of compassion or pity are also important, even in modern societies not in traumatic situations such as national disasters or wars (such charitable transfers commonly amount to a few percent of GNP, up to 5 percent in the Netherlands).

Moreover, benefits from large public goods and services or catering for basic needs are often provided to beneficiaries free of charge, hence as gifts, even though they are financed by taxpayers (or by forced contributions to 'social insurance') in the end.

On the whole, therefore, a large amount of goods, help and services are received free, gratuitously. This clearly tends to make an intrinsically much better relation to society than the two other modes of transfer, grasping or taking by force, and 'exchange' in its most standard meaning (retained here) of jointly agreed upon conditional exchange between self-interested transactors.

Logically, the first and most basic gift to others is not to harm them in any way, which constitutes a free and peaceful society.

ACTIONS AND SENTIMENTS, GIVING AND ALTRUISM

Our direct evidence or impression is that an agent's action is a consequence of her intention, which is a consequence of her motives including reason, sentiments (and emotions) and of her information. This evidence comes from a large number of life experiences of ourselves and of other people whom we observe, listen to or learn about and whom we think we 'understand', plus some inherited information. The neural inscription of this causal chain is not yet well known, however. In fact, neurological experimental evidence sometimes suggests different relations. For instance, rather than giving being the consequence of an intention to give which results from altruism of some kind (sympathy, compassion, pity, liking, love, or moral, social or rational duty), altruism would sometimes appear as the set of the conceptions of the corresponding giving, helping or favoring. Then, giving would be the primary reality (including as a potentiality) and altruism a secondary, constructed reality. Nevertheless, our direct psychological information is very rich and cannot be bypassed for understanding the world. This holds in particular for giving and all its possible motives and types.

RECIPROCITY AND MUTUALLY INDUCED GIFTS

The same mirror-neurons are activated by the consideration of the same aspects (action, part, intention, emotion, sensation, etc.) of all individuals. Hence the shared notion that people can have the same or similar characteristics. Moreover, an allocative judgment or choice of any kind is rational (in the most basic and standard sense of the term) if some reason is given for it. This reason refers to a set of characteristics of the beneficiary (or liable) person. If some other person has the same set of these characteristics deemed relevant, then rationality implies that she should receive (or yield) the same items. This is 'equal treatment of equals' and is the basis of the notions of social equality and comparative justice.

Applied to a gift from one person to another, this tends prima facie to value a 'return-gift' in the reverse direction of approximately the same value. Such a set of related gifts is called 'reciprocity' by social science, for which it is a central and has been a primary concept (Morelly, Adam Smith, Hobhouse, Mauss, etc.). These two related gifts can also depend, in nature and amount, on the specificities of the participants (such as means of the giver or needs of the receiver). There can also be a longer sequence of such gifts in a more steady reciprocal relationship – a particularly important social bond. Since such transfers are genuine gifts, this reciprocity is something completely different from 'sequential exchange' in which each voluntary transfer to the other is made in order to receive later from the other, between two self-interested agents. However, a gift can be made in order to benefit from a genuine return-gift from the other person (this is a 'half-reciprocity' originated by an agent who 'exploits the return-gift' and the reciprocitarian reaction of the other). Moreover, the relationship of reciprocity extends into 'generalized reciprocity' including 'extended reciprocity' in which the return-gift is provided to a third person, 'general reciprocity' in which each person considers that she receives from and gives to society as a whole or the set of the others, perhaps the 'generalized other' (G.H. Mead) (for a more or less extended society), and 'reverse reciprocity', a tendency to give to givers even when one is not an initial receiver (discussed, for instance, by René Descartes and Adam Smith).

A society is held together by its network and loops of reciprocities of all kinds (one ingredient of this social glue is that people are correspondingly morally 'indebted' towards those who have helped them). In a free and peaceful society, people mostly voluntarily respect others and their property, abstain from using violence and systematic fraud towards them, and provide them with the various menial helpings necessary to the smooth working of a society. They commonly would not do it if they were not so respected and aided themselves. A family is a bundle of reciprocities of acts, attitudes and, to begin with, affects and sentiments (one tends to like he who likes oneself). No organization could function without various reciprocal supports between its members and between them and the group (cooperation, loyalty, fair matching of pay and work). This reciprocal respect for others and their property is also necessary for the working of exchanges and markets (minimizing theft and fraud – exclusive reliance on violence or force in defence and punishment would be too costly and often not sufficiently possible). Hence, these opposites of gift-giving rest on widespread gift-giving of some type in the first place. Reciprocity permits a society to rest importantly and durably on gift-giving relationships because, in it, people who give also receive.

JOINT GIVING AND PUBLIC TRANSFERS: THE LOGICAL PARADOXES OF CHARITY

The Paradox of Joint Private and Public Transfers

The generality of empathy and of the resulting altruism entails that one person's welfare is valued by several – indeed, many – others. This tends to be accompanied by several gifts, from various persons, to the same person. This situation of 'joint giving' has a particular intricate logic. Prima facie, a higher gift to alleviate some need permits (and thus tends to induce) other givers to give less. A receiver's welfare (e.g. income, wealth, happiness or reduced pain) is a classical 'public good' for all the people who care for it. A giver cannot be excluded from enjoying an improvement in this welfare: this is a 'non-excludable' public good, hence one which cannot be marketed. The potential givers are too numerous and dispersed to be able to spontaneously agree between them about their various gifts. This is a case of large public good, the provision of which is a standard function of the public sector (and use of tax revenues). The situation is particularly important for the alleviation of poverty by transfers benefiting 'the poor' (which can to some extent be seen as an aggregate of the poor people) from other people, for providing 'income' or 'wealth', consumption, education, health care, means of working, etc. At any rate, distributive transfers are also a basic function of the public sector. Actually, the alleviation of poverty is often one of the main issues and duties of societies, and transfers to the poor are provided jointly by the private gifts and by the public sector, in large amounts. Assume non-poor individual i gives (voluntarily from the definition of the term) the amount g_i to the poor (directly or through charitable organizations), and denote as t_i her 'distributive tax', that is, the amount of the taxes she pays which the public sector redistributes to the poor.

$c_i = g_i + t_i$ is her 'contribution' to the alleviation of poverty. Her choice to give g_i allocates her wealth and that of the poor between them. The public sector's choice of t_i has the same effect. If this individual a priori wants to transfer the amount g_i^* as a gift to the poor but now is taxed for t_i, she now wants to give $g_i = g_i^* - t_i$ only (if $t_i \leqslant g_i^*$). As a result, a higher tax t_i is exactly compensated by a lower gift g_i, the public sector is unable to make an effective transfer, and public transfers cannot be explained. This does not occur if $t_i > g_i^*$. Then, individual i reduces her gift to 0 and finds the distributive policy excessive. In this case, private gifts cannot be explained. However, there generally is a joint presence of private gifts and distributive policies and $g_i > 0$ for many individuals i with $t_i > 0$.

'Warm-Glows' and Their Contradictions

This might be explained if individuals have some preference about their gifts g_i *per se*, i.e., not or not only because of their effect on the poor's wealth. Individual i may like a larger g_i because (or also because) this gift makes her praiseworthy or praised (this has been called a 'warm-glow' motive for giving (Andreoni)). However, this explanation entails a number of contradictions and has to be considered more in detail. First, this giver cannot be praised or praiseworthy as an altruist because altruism implies an altruistic motivation and sentiment (hence a preference for lower poverty) and this is not the 'warm-glow' motive (she may in addition be altruistic by valuing the poor's welfare, but this leads to the previous situation in so far as it entails some gift). However, the gift may induce valuing the giver because it is a sacrifice of hers which benefits the poor. Nevertheless, this 'sacrifice warm-glow' relates again to the poor's welfare and to the distribution of wealth between the individual and the poor, as simple benevolence does, with the same effect. Formally, this is seen by the fact that this effect of the gift g_i also holds for the tax t_i. What this effect actually values is their sum, the 'contribution' $c_i = g_i + t_i$, and g_i and t_i are perfect substitutes for this effect, as they are for contributing to the poor's wealth or welfare. What makes a difference between g_i and t_i and may induce some effective 'warm-glow' effect is *responsibility*: individual i is a priori responsible for her gift g_i and not for the tax t_i she has to pay. The actuality of this effect happens to be proven by neuro-imagery experiments. Consider a transfer from some person to the poor (to a free food stand). Brain imagery shows that, when the person likes this fact, her reward center is particularly excited when this transfer is a voluntary gift from her, rather than being forced (as a tax is) (Burghart *et al.* 2007).

Moreover, 'warm-glow' effects in general, which rest on the noted contradiction, are also bound to rest on immoral sentiments such as vanity, vainglory, or sentiments of superiority towards the receiver or, by comparison, co-givers. An optimal fiscal policy that 'respects citizens' preferences' may have to discard the effects of such immoral or irrational sentiments for moral or political reasons. However, responsibility warm-glow, which is responsible for non-crowd out, is concerned with gift g_i per se alone and not with t_i, and hence discarding it has no direct effect on this choice of the distribution tax t_i. By contrast, sacrifice warm-glow is concerned with contribution $c_i = g_i + t_i$ and hence discarding its effect leads a priori to choosing a lower t_i. This tends to induce the individual's choice (with her actual motives) of a higher gift g_i and finally to lesser crowd-out. Hence a logical paradox with, however, a basic morality: discarding a warm-glow sentiment that favors giving and transfers leads to higher gifts in the end, but the higher individual aid results from discarding an immoral sentiment.

'External Preferences' for Lower Contributions

The comparisons between gifts or contributions also have another effect on gifts, albeit one with a seemingly contradictory influence. Indeed, it turns out that a person's *gift* is *boosted* if other people prefer her *contribution* to be *lower*. Such a preference may be due to comparative sentiments comparing with other givers or with norms, such as envy, jealousy, or sentiments of inferiority or superiority. Indeed, if optimum fiscal policy respects individuals' preferences and sentiments and if other people prefer individual *i*'s contribution $c_i = g_i + t_i$ to be lower, this tends to induce tax t_i to be lower and this, in turn, tends to induce individual *i* to augment her gift g_i for compensation (a 'crowd-in' effect), from both altruism and sacrifice warm-glow motives. Such 'external preferences' on gifts alone have no such effects. This opposes the case of 'warm-glows', which have an effect when they bear on gifts ('responsibility') and none when they bear on contributions ('sacrifice'). On the whole, gift g_i tends to be higher and not crowded out by distributive taxation if individual *i* wishes it to be higher (by the 'responsibility warm-glow' effect) or if other individuals prefer individual *i*'s contribution c_i to be lower (thanks to *i*'s altruism or sacrifice warm-glow and a democratic and respectful fiscal policy). Finally, discarding such external preferences, because they result from immoral sentiments (when this is the case) or because they are nosy externalities, in the optimum respectful fiscal policy leads to higher taxes, and hence tends to induce lower gifts and higher crowd out. This again opposes the effects of moral or political warm-glow laundering.

Large Societies

Apart from these particular 'external preferences' about others' contributions, working out the conditions for gifts not being 'crowded out' by distribution taxes chosen in a democracy (respecting individuals' preferences and in particular their altruism) shows that if there is a large number of people and at least one actual gift g_i, then almost all the non-poor should think that the poor have enough ('almost all' means except perhaps for a vanishing fraction of them when their number becomes large). Now, the large number and the existence of gifts are the case, and this vanishing of concern for poverty is not the case. This seems to be a basic paradox. One possible explanation is the presence of norms of giving, which are moral norms and can be raised by moralities or be also social norms (including for instance traditions and social habits) – a criterion of distinction is that failure to obey a norm induces shame for a social norm and guilt for a moral norm.

In a standard society, both the non-poor and the poor are numerous. If there is at least one gift and one fiscal transfer, almost all the non-poor's altruism happens to have to be concerned with the *relative* variation of the poor's wealth and their preference about their gift, and their choice of it should be independent of the poor's wealth. Then, the just, equal, non-vanishing concern for all needy is not possible. Concern for an average or representative needy is possible but hardly moral ('when you have seen one, you have seen all') (see Kolm, 2010).

Praise Warm-glows

If a gift is valued, this is ultimately, whatever the social and psychological influences, because of its effect on the receiver's welfare. A warm-glow can then result from the gift, the giving and the giver being praised for this reason (praise, approval, non-blame, non-reproach, . . .). The praiser can be any (benevolent) altruist valuing the receiver's welfare in 'altruism warm-glows'. This can be the giver herself if she is also such an altruist (self praise) or someone else (external praise). Then the giver is not praised for being an altruist (which she may or may not be), but for giving. Gratitude has a similar effect. Several effects can act jointly. The praisers may be more or less imagined by the giver (e.g., some others may have praised her if they knew about the gift). The resulting gift or its crowd out depend on the praiser's altruism-benevolence, on their praise reaction, and on the giver's sensitivity to praise. An important parameter is the way in which the giver 'aggregates' the praises of several (possibly many) praisers. She may be sensitive to some average praise or to some additive form with an effect of the number of praisers. Self and average altruism warm-glows have similar effects. They entail crowd out in large populations. Non-crowd out with additive praise altruism warm-glows requires sufficiently high sensitivities to praises of sufficiently many praisers, or relative altruism.

Cooperative Charity

The above described giving and taxing behaviors are non-cooperative. However, the joint giving may also be cooperative in various possible ways, and this may explain the observed gifts.

Motives for giving to fight poverty refer sometimes to some moral reasoning or theory more or less elaborate. Three types of them can apply to all public goods: implicit agreement; lateral reciprocity or fair matching; and reasonings of the 'Kantian' family. On the contrary, the motive of putative reciprocity is specific to giving (irrespective of the public good issue). These reasonings tend to induce giving or contributing, and to arouse other people's praise for such behavior. These effects can a priori be described as kinds of 'warm-glows' in the structure of preferences or utility functions, but only after the modeling of the corresponding theory. Then, these propensities can be mitigated by the effects of g_i or c_i on the giver's self-interest.

An implicit agreement between the non-poor for giving or contributing belongs to the theoretical family of social contracts (Rousseau and Hume are clear about the public good nature of social contracts – for Rousseau each party contributes and benefits from all others' contributions). There may be some psychic moral cost of shirking (total or partial free riding), including the effects of other people's judgments, compared with the material advantage taking others' reaction into account. Lateral reciprocity or matching is reciprocity with co-givers or contributors (not the usual meaning of the term reciprocity as providing a standard return-gift), that is: given that they give or contribute, then so do I; given that they provide their fair share, I provide mine. The coordination between the participants is realized either by a public enforcement of these gifts (they are no longer voluntary in a formal sense but everybody voluntarily abides by this constraint, which thus is not binding, because others' contributions are then guaranteed), or by a sequential dynamics (people may give at time t because they have seen others giving at time $t - 1$, and this may in particular support a steady state). Reasons of the Kantian family include folk-Kantianism ('I give because what if nobody gives' – the most common magical 'reason' given for voting in large elections), or ideas closer to Kant's ('follow the rule that you want everybody to follow'). Kantian conducts raise a problem of consistency: each individual may assume that the others act or follow rules different from those they actually choose, notably if they also have the same Kantian reasoning and conduct, because an individual's preferred 'general rule' depends on her own preferences (Kant did not see this because he actually considered very crude rules only, such as lie or do not lie, help or do not help; specific contributions to a public good would be different). Moreover, the outcomes of both fair moral matching and Kantian conducts may a priori not be Pareto efficient (some other sets of gifts may satisfy everybody more) – they are for 'consistent rules' belonging to a particular set only.

Helping because one wants to be helped when one needs it is an explicit example given by Kant of a universal rule and of a reason to want it. The more specific motive of *putative reciprocity* is also common and leads to giving without the public good problem. This is: 'I help them because they would have helped me if our situations were reversed, or I would have been helped by others if I needed it, or they would have helped others if they could' (respectively direct, extended and reverse reciprocity, applied hypothetically). This choice of one's behavior given that of the others can be described by the maximization of one's utility function and a model of the interaction. However, there are two types of genuine reciprocity (Kolm 2008). In *balance* (or *matching*) *reciprocity*, each gift tends to establish some kind of balance with the other. This leads to a warm-glow structure. In *liking reciprocity*, by contrast, one comes to like the benevolent person who gives to oneself (or to others) and to give to her because one likes her. Then the reasoning is simply a cause of altruism. An actual return gift of a putative balance reciprocity is no longer a contribution to a public good. It is a personal (two by two) relation with the receiver. The number of givers is irrelevant. The induced propensity to give need not vanish if the altruism does (however, if the object of reciprocity is considered to be the gift relative to the need of the receiver, the return gift may depend on the receiver's means and therefore on other people's gifts to her).

Finally, cooperation resulting from repeated or sequential giving meets obstacles that prevent it. Giving less or not at all in order to punish another giver who failed to give at the expected level first punishes the poor still more; it also punishes all the other altruistic co-givers, and, with the large number of givers, at any rate the actions of a relatively 'small' giver are not even noticed by other people.

Rebate and Matching-Grant Neutrality or Dual Effects (Cost or Benefit)

In many instances, philanthropy is subsidized by tax exemptions or rebates, or encouraged by matching grants. The basic thing about these policies is that, a priori, they have no effect, if all is considered by the analysis and the agents, including with all kinds of warm-glows, external preferences, etc. Notably, the financing of the cost of these policies should not be forgotten. Other things equal, they are financed by taxes. This product could have been directly provided to the poor, that is, what the poor receive from taxes is diminished by this amount. Their income is in this way diminished by the matching grant they receive. Or it is diminished by the rebate or subsidy received by the giver, and the gift minus the rebate is both the cost for the giver and the *final* receipt of the poor for which the giver's choice is responsible. Hence, in all cases, when the giver chooses her gift by balancing the cost for her and the benefit for the poor, both are equal, and this amount is also what the giver or other people may directly value as her gift or as a part of her contribution.

Of course, if grants, rebates or subsidies are financed, in total or in part, from outside this system, and one forgets about their cost, or if the givers suffer from 'gift illusion' and forget about this financing and its effects, other results obtain, with generally increases in the gifts. Then, such a given amount generally enriches the receivers more when it is used for financing matching grants, rebates or subsidies increasing with the gift. In these cases, the cost for the giver differs from the corresponding benefit for the receivers, actually or as they are perceived. This raises, for concerns about a gift or a contribution, the problem of whether what matters is the giver's actual sacrifice, or the increase in the poor's benefit due to her action, or both, or some combination of both. This choice may more or less differ according to whether the issue is the gift g_i or the contribution c_i. It may also depend on who evaluates (the giver herself or someone else – relevant in particular for induced warm-glows, such as by praise). The results may also depend on the hypotheses about the origin of the funds (possibly part exogenous and part endogenous, etc.). They include the determination of the optimum subsidy or matching-grant schedules.

Conclusion

Fighting incapacitating poverty, perhaps the first duty of society, requires, first of all, the organization of the necessary transfers. This is done by both public and private actions. Their interaction reveals a number of crucial phenomena, necessary distinctions, and surprising and often paradoxical important results which had often escaped previous attention and explain some puzzling facts or raise new questions.

This is the case, for instance, of: external preferences; the distinction between sacrifice and responsibility warm-glows and external preferences; the fact that, for warm-glows, one is ineffective and the other contradictory; the reverse and doubly contrarian effect of external preferences (preferring a lower sacrifice – contribution – induces a higher gift, and preferences about gifts have no effect); gifts in large numbers of givers implying that almost all the non-poor think that the poor have enough; nevertheless large numbers often favoring non-crowd out of gifts (as observed) but with warm-glows not based on altruism; the necessity and immorality of relative (logarithmic) altruism; the shameful necessity of practically caring about an average or a representative poor; the necessity of explaining norms of giving; the powerlessness of fully informed grants-in-aid and tax rebates. Various types and reasons for implicit cooperation have been noted, notably lateral reciprocities or matching gifts, folk Kantianism and implicit agreement (with, again, sometimes a favorable effect of large numbers of givers), plus putative reciprocity.

As a result, the facts and possibilities of fighting poverty depend very much on the social, political, institutional and mental structures of the society in question. For instance, crowd out of private gifts by public policy is lower in the US than in most other societies, notably in those with some 'welfare state' ('aid is what we pay taxes for'), and the rationales seem to be based more on charity and warm-glows, whereas some sense of solidarity or justice may be more influential in more homogeneous nations. The characteristics of the various modes of transfers are socially important. Even when they manifest cooperation for producing a public good, public transfers have their shortcomings with the imperfections of the political system, bureaucracy or anonymity. More direct aid also has its shortcomings, however. Altruism is oriented towards the receivers' needs, but its effects are crowded out. Efficient motives rest, for instance, on warm-glows for which the poor's welfare is only a means to a self-serving objective – the worst Kantian sin – and which have the noted irrationality and immoralities. At any rate, giving is an inegalitarian relationship. Charity is sometimes condescending. Not uncommonly, it jeopardizes the dignity of the assisted person. Giving may demand or arouse gratitude when the transfer may just be a very partial correction of an unjust wealth distribution. Deontic actions are possible explanations, with or without a warm-glow, for acting dutifully. Kant-like rationality intends to make the individual choice coincide with the social requirement and could refer to altruistic judgment about 'the result one can want', but it has the noted shortcomings. Actually social norms are important but have to be explained.

At any rate, giving is also the best of worlds when it uses liberty to remedy unjust inequalities thanks to a spirit of solidarity both towards receivers and between givers.

NON-ALTRUISTIC GIFTS

Giving and its motives exhibit, in fact, a bewildering variety of forms, reasons and functions. Sacrificing one's interest (up to one's life) on behalf of other persons (or a cause) is a breach of self-centeredness which is a strong action, sometimes a dramatic one, and is bound to arouse powerful emotions. For this reason, gifts are used to show, express and prove various types of social sentiments, relations, commitments and statuses – love, liking, attachment, gratitude, devotion and service or protection, inferiority or superiority, etc. – and to mark social events such as an encounter, an agreement or a relationship. The same strength permits using gifts to harm the receiver, for instance to humiliate her (perhaps suggesting that she is unable to take care of herself and of her relatives). Moreover, a number of gifts have further effects which benefit the giver, and, hence, they can actually be motivated by self-interest. For instance, one may give in order to receive a return gift (direct or reverse), to initiate or maintain a sequential exchange, to provide or suggest information about one's means, wealth and character, to elicit gratitude, approval, praise, acclaim or admiration, to benefit from material, social or political advantages that these judgments may entail, etc. Some gifts may also be simple individual or social habits (without much intent).

GRATUITOUSNESS

Scope

Considering gratuitousness implies an interest for application in social systems, an important part of which is geared by its opposite: prices, exchanges and markets. This is the case of many societies, notably for the economy of modernity. Free access is normally particularly favorable to the quality of the relations between individuals and their society. Kant finds that there are two kinds of things, those that have a price and those that have a dignity. Items can be provided for free by any agent, individuals or any institution – governments at all levels, firms, institutions set up more or less specifically for this purpose, etc. Gratuitousness permits providing 'to each according to her needs' as she sees them. It also permits favoring some consumption deemed particularly valuable by society (vicarious goods). The goods most appropriate to be provided for free include the satisfaction of basic needs, safety, health care, education, access to places and services providing the amenities of nature and culture, etc. (life, reduced pain, human assets and their quality, culture and nature have a particular 'dignity'). However, items provided for free, using resources including labor, have eventually to be financed. This is and can be achieved in various ways: beneficiaries' voluntary restraint, individuals' gifts directly or through institutions (e.g. charities, special purpose organizations, etc.), taxes of various kinds, compulsory 'contributions' to various public goods or social insurance schemes, etc.

Prices and Efficiency

Consumption obtained for free, on demand, or at a reduced price with price rebates is a priori likely to be produced in excessive amount relative to other goods. The result is overall economic inefficiency and social waste. Classical economic efficiency of decentralized decisions requires that the user pays a price which reflects the cost. By the quantities she so buys, she 'reveals' her relative desires or needs for the various goods, thus directing production. This role of the price system in a market economy is in fact the central 'theorem' of economics. There are qualifications to this wastefulness of gratuitousness, however. If someone is aided by a transfer in income, that is, general purchasing power, she 'reveals' her preferences by the way in which she chooses to spend it. In other situations, a good may have to be provided whatever its price, for instance if it saves the consumer's life; then it can be provided for free. Moreover, a good can be provided for free but in a given amount, in a quantity chosen by the supplier alone. If there is in addition a free market for this good, on which the consumer can sell her endowment or buy extra amounts of it, and she does so, this transfer is equivalent to an income transfer: the proceeds of the sale or the cost saved can be used to buy other goods. If the given amount is all the user's consumption of this good (she cannot buy more or sell this commodity), this can be justified by a lack of information from the customer about some risk or some virtue of this consumption. This is the case of 'vicarious goods', which can concern health, education, culture, or consumption that may present some danger for the consumer or for other people.

Markets and Egoism

Market exchanges are usually between self-interested agents. In particular, the efficiency theorem recalled above rests on assuming this motive, hence on a regrettably selfish mankind. The success of the market system may even justify, favor and encourage this behavior and motive. However, this refers to behavior in markets only. The same individuals may be altruistic in their family or in charity, and seek market profit for these purposes. All that is required is that, when they exchange, they do not value the other party's interest also. This is what the economist and clergyman Philip Wicksteed (1906, 1933) labeled *non-tuism*, rather than egoism. Moreover, market exchange also requires that people do not steal others' property and its efficiency also requires that they do not cheat in the transaction. These behaviors are maintained by self-defence, rules and laws, but they are sufficient at a reasonable cost only if they are in fact sufficiently voluntary, as is often the case. This is a case of gift-giving, more or less according to a norm of conduct and often in a relation of reciprocity. In addition, the efficiency of markets is often jeopardized by 'market failures' due to questions of information, or of impossibility or cost of exclusion from the benefit of some good or just of writing or implementing contracts. The 'failure' is due to the interaction between these facts and the self-interested motives. A number of remedies to these situations are provided by actions differently motivated and which are types of gifts – often reciprocities.

Economics and Human Nature

Since economics has mainly studied markets, it is natural that it relied on models of self-interested agents. However, economists have not forgotten altruism and gifts, as they have often been accused of. Actually, all great economists have studied this topic, sometimes in separate volumes. Walras, Pareto, John Stuart Mill, Edgeworth, Wicksteed and Marshall should be mentioned. The 'founding father', Adam Smith, presently best known for his intuition of the economic efficiency of self-interested exchanges in the *Wealth of Nations*, was, in his time, more famous for his first book about society, *The Theory of Moral Sentiments*, concerned with general empathy, impartiality and giving. Reading *The Theory of Moral Sentiments* in its second French translation is advised, because, there, it is corrected and completed by eight *Letters on Sympathy* written by the translator, Sophie de Condorcet. She reproaches Adam Smith on several counts, the two most important being that his topic is explaining moral sentiments from empathy but he does not explain empathy, and he forgets the intervention of reason when empathy induces actions of giving and helping or even the propensity to such actions in sympathy. De Condorcet explains empathy from a theory of sensations. A cause of pain would arouse two sensations of pain. A specific one, focussed on the cause, and a more general one, unfocussed and milder. Different specific pains similar in nature and intensity induce the same general sensation. Remembering pain or observing it in some other person arouses the general sensation only. Pleasure and happiness give rise to a similar structure although with lower intensities. With our present-day information, the most tempting way to make sense of de Condorcet dual theory is to relate it to effects of the mirror-neurons.

CONSEQUENCES

Giving and receiving for free constitute modes of transfers endowed with particular virtues. They often result from, manifest or accompany praiseworthy pro-social virtues of the givers (generosity, altruism, compassion, etc.). They imply, for the receiver, a social relation of particular quality, often including consideration, respect, benevolence or care towards her. They often permit the satisfaction of unforeseen needs. They may underline the specific 'dignity' of the item transferred, its being immune from debasing profit-seeking 'merchandization' (for items of culture, nature, or manifesting a relation or an attitude of particular intrinsic value).

Giving naturally exists, in contrast to its opposite: exchange. For instance, there are gifts in animal societies (even non-instinctual gifts – i.e. not in 'social insects' societies), whereas standard exchange or barter does not seem to exist in animals (although there are cases of reciprocity and of sequential exchanges). However, in market societies the standard mode of transfer between agents beyond family and close friends consists of exchanges which lack most of the noted intrinsic value of gifts and gratuitousness, and the corresponding motives, attitudes and social relations tend to pervade the whole of social relations.

Hence, giving and gratuitousness should be more or less protected and favored by motivations, moralities, education and institutions.

REFERENCES

Burghart, D.R., W.T. Harbaugh and U. Mayr (2007) 'Neural responses to taxation and voluntary giving reveal motives for charitable donation', *Science* 316(5831): 1622–1625.

Condorcet, Sophie de Grouchy de (1994[1793]) *Lettres sur la sympathie*, edited by J.-P. de Lagrave, L'Etincelle, éditeur: Montréal, Paris.

Kolm, S.-Ch. (2008) *Reciprocity (An Economics of Social Relations)*. Cambridge University Press: Cambridge, UK.

Kolm, S.-Ch. (2010) *On the Public Good of Fighting Poverty. Paradoxes of Solidarity*. EHESS, Paris.

Kolm, S.-Ch. and J. Mercier Ythier (eds) (2005) *Handbook of the Economics of Giving, Altruism and Reciprocity*. Elsevier, North-Holland: Amsterdam, Netherlands.

Rizzolatti, G. and C. Sinigaglia (2008) *Les Neurones miroirs*, Odile Jacob: Paris.

Smith, A. (1778[1759]) Year 6 of the Republic. *Théorie des Sentimens (sic) Moraux*. Translated from A. Smith, *The Theory of Moral Sentiments*, by Sophie de Grouchy de Condorcet. With *8 Lettres sur la Sympathie*, volume II. F. Buisson: Paris.

Wicksteed, P. (1906) 'Review of professor V. Pareto manuale di Economia Politica', *Economic Journal* 16, 553–557.

Wicksteed, P. (1933) *The Common Sense of Political Economy*, Robbins Edn: London.

18. Humanistic management
Cristian R. Loza Adaui and André Habisch

INTRODUCTION

The adjective 'humanistic' derives from Humanism. Literature about humanism tackles this concept in two main senses. In a wider sense humanism is understood as a kind of *Weltanschauung* stressing the dignity and worth of human beings and the search of good for them. Humanism in this wider sense has been proposed with different nuances and a variety of approaches throughout history, sometimes stressing the rational capacity of man and rejecting transcendent realities (Huxley, 1957, 1961) and sometimes embracing religion and transcendent values (Maritain, 1936). In this wider sense humanism includes diverse approaches ranging from: the *homo mensura* definition given by Protagoras: 'man is the measure of all things', to the multiple *post-humanistic* or even *anti-humanistic* approaches developed in the late 20th century which were built over the failures of past humanist experiments. The structuralism of authors such as Michel Foucault, Claude Lévi-Strauss, Jacques Lacan and Louis Althusser might be perceived in that perspective. Other post-humanistic approaches reflect contemporary concerns about global climate change and the unpredictable influences of technology and biotechnology on human nature (Hayles, 1999; Sloterdijk, 1999; Badmington, 2000) or question anthropocentrism and the role of men in society (Regan & Singer, 1989).

In a more narrow sense, humanism refers to an intellectual movement born within the Italian renaissance of the 15th century, which offered a renewed attention to the classical cultures and in particular to its study: the *studia humanitatis*, which refers to the study of classical disciplines as grammar, rhetoric, poetry and moral philosophy (Davies, 2008).

The origin of the word humanism and the meaning it has today refers to the German term '*Humanismus*' used by the theologian and philosopher F.I. Niethammer (1808) in his book *The Dispute between Philanthropinism and Humanism in the Educational Theory of our Time (Der Streit des Philantropinismus und des Humanismus in der Theorie des Erziehungsunterricht unserer Zeit)*. Niethammer describes as humanistic the 'reformed education system inspired by the romantic hellenism of Winckelmann and Goethe' (Davies, 2008, p. 2).

Throughout history humanism, including its diverse developments and propositions, influenced the way of thinking and acting of people in society. Management considered in a broader sense as a discipline aimed at the effective administration of enterprises, has always been influenced by traditions of cultural thought. Thus, in a certain sense, management has always been a potential playing field for humanism. However, direct references to humanistic management can be traced back only to the last decades.

DISMAL SCIENCE? TOWARDS THE PROGRAM OF HUMANISTIC MANAGEMENT

Finding fault with Thomas Malthus' population theory, Victorian historian Thomas Carlyle qualified economics as 'the dismal science'. Primarily focussing on scarcity as a basic human condition, economists (and in their tradition management scholars) systematically base their analysis on the limits of human rationality, on unintended side effects and on organizational constraints. Moreover, with the strong focus on profit orientation and the 'instrumentalization' of man as a 'human resource' they seem to mistake the instrument–goal ratio. However, it has to be seen that even with this apparently 'inhumane' methodical approach economic analysis clearly follows a (sometimes hidden) humanistic programme. That becomes especially obvious in the literature on economic systems. Most scholars would agree that the overall goal of collective economic activity is to overcome scarcity, fight poverty and illiteracy and allow human beings to live a life in dignity according to their value convictions. Building the institutional framework of a market economy and creating competitive business organizations within that context are therefore expressions of civility and thrive towards humanization.

The disputed question is whether labour is a mere – and sometimes necessarily inhumanly structured – instrument of achieving this ethically qualified goal; or whether (and to what extend) the overall humanistic goal should also structure the economic activities and labour relations as such, which are in themselves an expression of the human nature of man. Particular cultural traditions like the civil economy in Italy (Bruni and Zamagni, 2007), the Lutheran professional Ethics, the Catholic Social Teaching tradition of the late 19th and early 20th centuries, the social market economy of the Freiburg School of Economics (W. Eucken being the son of the philosopher and Nobel Prize laureate Rudolph Eucken) and many others stress the later. However, they have rarely been able to spell out the implications on an organizational and managerial level. This concretization has to be a basic subject of any form of management, which calls itself 'humanistic'. Such a new paradigm will not be limited to niche issues like corporate responsibility, communication, corporate citizenship, social entrepreneurship or even human resource management but rather embrace all managerial disciplines including its most important tools like strategy, accounting, operations, organization, etc. It will have to account for the human factor of economic success in a systematic way spelling out the paradigm shift even in the development of innovative tools and techniques.

HUMAN BEINGS IN MANAGEMENT HISTORY

During the still rather short history of management theory a reference to human beings was central, but not all managerial models could be named humanistic. In the following we present the principal management approaches from the 20th century, categorizing them according to their underlying conceptualization of the human person.

Productivity-centred Approaches

At the beginning of the 20th century Frederick Taylor, an American engineer, who aimed to find the most efficient way to complete jobs, proposed the *Principles of Scientific Management* (1964 [1911]). Applying the scientific method to improve productivity Taylor, for example, suggested breaking a job into a series of simplified jobs. Following that line Henry Gantt in his books *Work, Wages and Profits* (1913) and in *Organizing for Work* (1919) made use of scientific methods to increase workers' efficiency. Gantt introduced the incentive system for workers and foremen: workers were paid a bonus if the job was completed before established deadlines. Foremen were paid for each worker who made the deadline and received additional bonuses if all workers under their direction were able to do so. Contemporarily to Gantt, the German-American psychologist Hugo Münsterberg published his book *Psychology and Industrial Efficiency* (1913). He applied psychology to the study of working people and was able to identify problems such as monotony, attention and fatigue, including their physical and social consequences on workers. Henry Fayol, the pioneer of the General Administrative Theory, focussed on the activities of managers. In his book *Administration Industrialle et Generalle* (Fayol 1916) he proposed forecasting, planning, organizing, commanding, coordinating and monitoring as the five functions of management and identified another 14 principles for management which could be taught in schools and universities.

Following the transformative power of industrialization during the first decades of the 20th century the attention of management scholars was oriented more towards efficiency and productivity than towards workers an their labour conditions, conceiving men and women in a mechanistic way (Melé, 2003, p.77). Scholars like Gantt, Taylor and Fayol were engineers and their approaches were certainly linked to that academic background. They perceived the managerial task as a 'fight against nature' with 'labour' being an important factor of production. However, recent historical research on Taylor's scientific management tries to threaten the widespread notion of an underlying negative image of human nature. Wagner-Tsukamoto (2008) reconstructs Taylor's portrayal of managers as naturally good and heartily cooperative persons, uncovering conceptual misunderstandings on the Taylorian image of human nature and reopening the research agenda on this topic.

Psychological Approaches

The Hawthorne studies, conducted at the Western Electric Company from 1924 through 1932 were designed to examine the effects of physical working conditions on employee's productivity and fatigue. This marks the beginning of a behavioural approach towards humans in management. Fritz Roethlisberger was the lead researcher in the Hawthorne project and the first to publish the findings, which were reprinted in a more comprehensive edition as *Management and the Worker* (Roethlisberger & Dickson, 1939). One of the researchers of these studies was Elton Mayo; he and his colleagues were concerned about the scientific vision of man, which saw human beings as self-interested optimizers and exclusively extrinsically motivated. On the contrary Mayo accounted for the psychosocial complexity of human beings and accepted the multiplicity of individual needs, desires and goals (Mayo, 1933). But he was also aware of the crucial role that membership in different social groups and human relations in organizations played in business and society. In his book *The Social Problems of an Industrial Civilization*, written in 1945 but first published in 1949 he states:

> Humanity is not adequately described as a horde of individuals, each actuated by self-interest, each fighting his neighbour for the scarce material of survival . . . For all of us the feeling of security and certainty derives from membership of a group. If this is lost, no monetary gain, no job guarantee, can be sufficient compensation. (Mayo, 1949, pp. 51, 67: for an overview see Bruce, 2006)

The psychologist Abraham Maslow, who is remembered as the founder of the humanistic psychology, developed a theory of human motivation, presenting a hierarchy of needs, which can be applied to deal with employee motivation. Maslow assumes that the basic inner nature of human beings was good and that unsatisfied human needs motivate behaviour. For Maslow needs can be presented in a hierarchy, he identified five different levels: psychological needs, safety needs, belongingness and love needs, esteem needs and self-actualization needs (Maslow, 1943). One consequence of that concept is that non-pecuniary factors could also serve as ('intrinsic') motivational instrument for an employee. Thus managers have to develop positive relationships with workers in order to comprehend their motivational needs. Maslow used also the term meta-motivation to clarify why some self actualized people are sometimes driven by innate forces that lead them to go beyond their basics needs to reach their full potential. In his own words meta-motivated people 'are dedicated people, devoted to some tasks "outside themselves", some vocation, or duty, or beloved job' (Maslow, 1971, p. 301)

The reflection on self-actualization of men was also a part of Douglas McGregor approach to human beings, in his book titled *The Human Side of Enterprise* (McGregor, 2008 [1960]), he developed the Theory X and Theory Y. Theory X presented people who have to be supervised closely because they have little ambition, dislike work and avoid responsibility. Theory Y describes people who can exercise self-direction, accept responsibility and consider work as natural. Many scholars and especially managers interpreted McGregor's theories directly as managerial advices; however, E. Schein, a colleague of his at the MIT, argues that 'there is nothing in this theory [Theory X and Theory Y] that says a manager should behave in any particular manner, only that how he or she behaves is driven by deep cognitive assumptions that may not be very changeable in adulthood' (Schein, 2011, p. 157).

Work-Satisfaction-Centred Approaches

Mary Parker Follett recognizes that organizations could be viewed from a perspective of individual and group behaviour. She argued that organizations should be focused on a group ethic rather than on individualism and emphasized employee participation, autonomy and the building of cross-functional teams. Managers should search the coordination of group efforts and view workers as partners.

According to D. Melé one of the first humanistic management approaches can be attributed to Mary Parker Follett. For her 'there were no psychological, ethical or economic problems, but human problems and these cover aspects which could be psychological, ethical, economic and whatever' (Melé, 2003, p. 79). Her holistic approach to human condition permits her to understand the dynamics of power within groups (Melé & Rosanas, 2003).

Another humanist and management scholar was Chester Barnard, who argued that organizations were social systems, which required human cooperation in order to achieve success. One of Barnard's frequent citations directly considers the inquiry into human nature as an indispensable prerequisite of the study of organizations:

> I have found it impossible to go far in the study of organizations or of behaviour of people in relation to them without being confronted with a few questions which can be simply stated. For example: 'What is an individual?' 'What is a person?' 'To what extent do people have power of choice or free will?' The temptation is to avoid such difficult questions, leaving them to philosophers and scientists who still debate them after centuries. It quickly appears, however, that even if we avoid answering such questions definitely, we cannot avoid them. (Barnard, 1938, p. 8)

Organizational-Culture Approaches

According to D. Melé (2003) also organizational culture literature is ingrained by humanism, in particular the works of scholars as Pettigrew (1979), Deal and Kennedy (1982), Peters and Waterman (1982) and Schein (1984; 1985; 1990). According to Schein organizational culture can be defined as:

> the pattern of basic assumptions that a given group has invented, discovered, or developed in learning to cope with its problems of external adaptation and internal integration, and that have worked well enough to be considered valid, and, therefore, to be though to new members as the correct way to perceive, think, and feel in relation to those problems. (Schein, 1984, p. 3)

These basic assumptions can also be expressed as beliefs and as values. According to Sathe (1983, p. 7) beliefs are 'basic assumptions about the world and how it works'; in difference to beliefs, values express a kind of duty, an 'ought to' (Sathe, 1983 p. 7).

Since these foundational studies, organizational culture has developed itself as a research focus relating organizational culture with many other management variables ranging from motivation to ethical behaviour. Melé considers these approaches as an expression of humanism because they enlarge and enrich the study of organizations including not only motivations and needs but paying particular attention to other elements present in culture. In his words:

> if culture is part of human life and organizational cultures have such an influence on the behaviour of its members, there is no doubt that considering organizational culture is a better way to understand the human condition than considering only human needs. (Melé, 2003, p. 82)

Peter Drucker on Human Management

Peter Drucker insisted recurrently in the centrality of human beings for management. In his own words:

> No part of the productive resources of industry operates at lower efficiency than the human resources. The few enterprises that have been able to tap this unused reservoir of human

ability and attitude have achieved spectacular increases in productivity in the great majority of enterprises – so that the management of men should be the first foremost concern of operating managements, rather than the management of things and techniques on which attention has been focused so far. (Drucker, 1950, p. 158 as quoted by Stein, 2010 p. 102)

Moreover, Drucker reflects the formative responsibility of management for the corporate culture:

A manager develops people. Through the way he manages he makes it easy or difficult for them to develop themselves. He directs people or misdirects them. He brings out what is in them or he stifles them. He strengthens their integrity or he corrupts them. He trains them to stand upright and strong or he deforms them. (Drucker, 1955, p. 298)

In other words:

Management is about human beings. Its task is to make people capable of joint performance, to take their strengths effective and their weaknesses irrelevant. This is what organization is about, and it is the reasons that management is the critical, determining factor. (Drucker, 1990, p. 221)

In these sense Drucker is to be considered as a pioneer of humanistic management although he never used this expression.

CONTEMPORARY TENDENCIES

Even in contemporary management literature there are always more elements with a background of humanism finding their way into the mainstream of management and management research. Melé (2009, p. 136) presents four transitions:

1. 'from rigid job design towards searching a better fit between persons and organizational structures';
2. 'from organizations in which each person is just a cog of the business machine to organizations in which people are put first, with a greater degree of involvement, commitment, and participation';
3. 'from perceiving firms as a net of contracts to considering business as a self-governing community of people'; and
4. 'from a management aligned to maximization of shareholder value to management by values'.

To be sure, these developments as such are not enough to speak already about humanism in management. Probably the most intensively discussed feature in the context of humanism is the dichotomy individual – community. According to Morden, 'humanists' believe that mankind should seek to satisfy both individual needs and the needs of the community at the same time' (Morden, 2004, p. 190). This idea of community is recurrent discussion among humanist and had brought some scholars to identify humanism as a feature of the management styles of some geographical areas were community represents an important social feature. In that sense Lessem and Neubauer (1994) stress the importance of cultural roots and consider the best examples for humanistic management

styles to be those born in regions were family business and strong regionalized coopera-
tional traditions flourish.

European humanistic management as presented by Lessem and Neubauer (1994, p. 41) is
the result of a transition from family businesses to socio-economic networks, where managers became a kind of social architect evolving from the mere patriarchal manager they used
to be in the past. The study of Lessem and Neubauer focussing on European management
styles can be well complemented with the findings from a recent publication edited by the
members of the Humanistic Management Network. They present the inputs of 19 companies from all over the world in different industries and even with different ownership structures and sizes in order to 'explore the principles of humanistic management and examine
its theoretical merits by assessing its practical feasibility' (von Kimakowitz et al, 2011, p. 2).

The members of the Humanistic Management Network understand the main goal
of management as: 'the promotion of human flourishing through economic activities
that are life-conductive and add value to society at large' (von Kimakowitz et al 2011,
pp. 4–5). Their proposal of a humanistic view on the business organizations is presented
according to five different features:

1. Business strategies in which 'shared value-creation processes are theoretically and
    practically imperative; a balance between multiple stakeholders and between short
    and long-term interests is essential' (Pirson et al, 2011, p. 318).
2. Governance mechanisms focused more on strategic support for corporate leaders
    than controlling manager's opportunistic behaviour (Pirson et al, 2011, p. 319).
3. Organizational structures are 'extremely decentralized and focus on self-governance',
    thus supporting the development of human capabilities and focus on effectiveness
    (Pirson et al, 2011, p. 320).
4. Transformational leadership styles 'based on moral values, oriented to inspire fol-
    lowers, stimulate them intellectually, and engage them emotionally with organiza-
    tional tasks' (Pirson et al, 2011, p. 321).
5. Organizational cultures that 'allow constant organic change and evolution', 'open
    and participative not only within but also outside the organization'; cultures 'capable
    to create organizational identities based on inter-human relations (relationally) and
    inclusive of a larger group (communal) (. . .) aimed to promote human flourishing
    within, but also outside, the organization' (Pirson et al, 2011, pp. 321–322).

Another approach of humanistic management stresses the importance of community for
realizing personal values. They consider firms fundamentally as communities of persons
(Bruni, 2009, Mion and Loza Adaui, 2011, Melé, 2011) and consider the relation of
humanism and business and economics in different religious and cultural traditions, for
example the work of Vittal (2004) on Indian management and more recently Grassl and
Habisch (2011) within the Christian Social Tradition.

LIMITS AND FUTURE RESEARCH

The history of market economy and business organizations reminds us that moral
calls for ethics and humanism have periodically also been contra-productive for their

followers. Only some quick points should indicate a necessary discussion on limits and frameworks for humanistic management:

- Important aspects of humanism are human rights and economic freedom. This has to be pointed out to avoid any tendency towards self-sufficiency, in-group biases, intolerance or even totalitarianism.
- Humanistic goals have still to be implemented in a competitive market economy. Thus, from a business perspective professionalism is an important aspect, here. Mutual inspiration between goals of humanism on the one hand and professional tools or techniques on the other should invigorate management education (Gagliardi & Czarniawska, 2006; Arenas, 2006).
- Secular developments redefining the concept of man should also resonate in humanistic management. For example family relationships (including division of labour among genders, parent–child relations etc.) have undergone dramatic transformations recently. This should also be reflected in organizational research where work–life arrangements for both parents and increasing responsibility towards elder parents should invigorate humanistic business solutions.
- Economic relations and empirical evidences should also instruct humanistic thinking and start a dialogue of mutual learning. For example a complete neglect of the role of incentives for organizing effective cooperation may threaten humanistic goals and ultimately promote cynicism and moral apathy. Humanism may serve as 'heuristics'; meanwhile economics plays the role of restriction analysis.

In order to promote managerial goals humanistic research and education in business should avoid any normative bias. It is neither the task of the humanist philosopher to 'domesticate' the dismal science of economics or management nor the role of the manager or economist to destroy seemingly utopian ideals of the humanist; rather, both should engage in a cooperative search for better organizational and strategic solutions for the pressing challenges of the 21st century.

REFERENCES

Arenas, D. (2006), 'Problematizing and enlarging the notion of humanistic education', in P. Gagliardi and B. Czarniawska (eds), *Management Education and Humanities*. Cheltenham: Edward Elgar, pp. 113–134.
Badmington, N. (ed) (2000), *Posthumanism*, Hampshire: Palgrave Macmillan.
Barnard, C.I. (1938), *The Functions of the Executive*, Cambridge, MA: Harvard University Press.
Bruce, K. (2006), 'Henry S. Dennison, Elton Mayo, and Human Relations historiography', *Management & Organizational History*, 1 (2), 177–199.
Bruni, L. (2009), *L'impresa civile: Una via italiana all'economia di mercato*, Milano: EGEA.
Bruni, L. and S. Zamagni (2007), *Civil Economy: Efficiency, Equity, Public Happiness*, Bern: Peter Lang.
Davies, T. (2008), *Humanism*, London & New York: Routledge.
Deal, T.E. and A.A. Kennedy (1982), *Corporate cultures: The rites and rituals of organizational life*, Massachusetts: Addison-Wesley.
Drucker, P. (1950) *The New Society: The Anatomy of Industrial Order*, New York: Harper & Brothers, reprinted in Drucker, P.F. (2003), *The new society: anatomy of industrial order*, New Brunswick (USA) and London (UK): Transaction Publishers.
Drucker, P. (1990), *The new realities*, London: Mandarin.
Fayol, H. (1916), *Administration industrielle et générale: prévoyance, organisation, commandement, coordination, contrôle*, Paris: H. Dunod et E. Pinat.

Gagliardi, P. and B. Czarniawska (eds) (2006), *Management Education and Humanities*, Cheltenham: Edward Elgar.

Gantt, H.L. (1913), *Work, wages, and profits*, New York: The Engineering Magazine Co.

Gantt, H.L. (1919), *Organizing for work*, New York: Harcourt, Brace and Howe.

Grassl, W. and A. Habisch (2011), 'Ethics and Economics: Towards a New Humanistic Synthesis for Business', *Journal of Business Ethics*, 99 (1), 37–49.

Hayles, N. (1999), *How we became posthuman: virtual bodies in cybernetics, literature, and informatics*, Chicago: University of Chicago Press.

Huxley, J. (1957), *Religion without revelation*, New York: Harpers.

Huxley, J. (ed.) (1961), *The Humanist Frame*, New York: Harper & Brothers.

von Kimakowitz, E., Pirson, M., Dierksmeier, C., Spitzeck, H. and W. Amann (2011), 'Introducing this book and humanistic management', in von Kimakowitz, E., Pirson, M., Spitzeck, H., Dirksmeier, C. and W. Amann (eds) (2011), *Humanistic Management in Practice*, Chippenham: Palgrave Macmillan, pp. 1–12.

Lessem, R. and F.-F. Neubauer (1994), *European management systems: towards unity out of cultural diversity*, London: McGraw-Hill.

Maritain, J. (1936), *Humanisme integral: problemes temporels et spirituels d'une nouvelle chrétienté*, Paris: Fernand Aubier. (Two translations: *True humanism*, Tr. M.R. Adamson. London: Bles, 1938; *Integral Humanism: Temporal and Spiritual Problems of a New Christendom*. Tr. Joseph W. Evans, New York: Charles Scribner's Sons, 1968.)

Maslow, A. (1943), 'A Theory of Human Motivation', *Psychological Review*, 50 (4), 370–396.

Maslow, A. (1971), *Farther Reaches the Human Nature*, New York: McGraw-Hill.

Mayo, E. (1933), *The Human Problems of an Industrial Civilization*, London: Macmillan.

Mayo, E. (1949), *The Social Problems of an Industrial Civilization*, Cambridge, MA: Harvard University Press.

McGregor, D. (1960), *The Human Side of Enterprise*, in McGregor, D. (2008) *The Human Side of Enterprise: Annotated Edition* Reprint and Updated, New York: McGraw-Hill Professional.

Melé, D. (2003), 'The Challenge of Humanistic Management', *Journal of Business Ethics*, 44 (1), 77–88.

Melé, D. (2009), 'Current trends in humanism and business', in Spitzeck, H., Pirson, M., Amann, W., Khan, S. and E. von Kimakowitz (eds) *Humanism in Business*, Cambridge, UK: Cambridge University Press, pp. 123–140.

Melé, D. (2011), 'The Firm as a "Community of Persons": A Pillar of Humanistic Business Ethos', *Journal of Business Ethics*, available at: http://dx.doi.org/10.1007/s10551-011-1051-2 (accessed 15 October 2011).

Melé, D. and J.M. Rosanas (2003), 'Power, freedom and authority in management: Mary Parket Follett's "Power-with"', *Philosophy of Management*, 3 (2), 35–46.

Mion, G. and C. Loza Adaui (2011), *Verso il metaprofit: gratuità e profitto nella gestione d'impresa*, Siena: Cantagalli.

Morden, T. (2004), *Principles of management*, Aldershot, UK: Ashgate.

Münsterberg, H. (1913), *Psychology and Industrial Efficiency*, Cambridge, MA: The Riverside Press.

Niethammer, F.I. (1808), *Der Streit des Philanthropinismus und Humanismus in der Theorie des Erziehungs-Unterrichts unsrer Zeit*, Jena: F. Frommann.

Peters, T. and R. Waterman (1982), *In search of excellence: lessons from America's best-run companies*, New York: Harper & Row.

Pettigrew, A.M. (1979), 'On Studying Organizational Cultures', *Administrative Science Quarterly*, 24 (4), 570–581.

Pirson, M., von Kimakowitz, E., Dierksmeier, C., Spitzeck, H. and W. Amann (2011), 'Concluding remarks', in von Kimakowitz, E., Pirson, M., Spitzeck, H., C. Dierksmeier and W. Amann (eds), *Humanistic Management in Practice*, Chippenham: Palgrave Macmillan, pp. 307–324.

Regan, T. and P. Singer (1989), *Animal rights and human obligations*, Englewood Cliffs, NJ: Prentice-Hall.

Roethlisberger, F.J. and W.J. Dickson (1939), *Management and the worker: an account of a research program conducted by the Western Electric Company, Hawthorne Works, Chicago*, Cambridge, MA: Harvard University Press.

Sathe, V. (1983), 'Implication of Corporate Culture: A Manager Guide for Action', *Organizational Dynamics*, 12(Autumn), 5–23.

Schein, E. (1984), 'Coming to a new awareness of organizational culture', *Sloan Management Review*, 25 (2), 3–16.

Schein, E. (1985), *Organizational culture and leadership*, San Francisco: Jossey-Bass.

Schein, E. (1990), 'Organizational culture', *American Psychologist*, 45 (2), 109–119.

Schein, E. (2011) 'Douglas McGregor: Theoretician, moral philosopher or behaviourist?: An analysis of the interconnections between assumptions, values and behaviour', *Journal of Management History*, 17 (2), 156–164.

Sloterdijk, P. (1999) *Regeln für den Menschenpark: ein Antwortschreiben zu Heideggers Brief über den Humanismus*, Frankfurt am Main: Suhrkamp.

Stein, G. (2010), *Managing People and Organizations: Peter Drucker's Legacy*, Bingley, UK: Emerald.

Taylor, F.W. (1964 [1911]), *The Principles of Scientific Management*, in F.W. Taylor (ed.), *Scientific Management*. London: Harper & Row.

Vittal, N. (2004), 'Human values in Indian Management', in A. Das Gupta (ed.) *Human Values in Management*. Aldershot, UK: Ashgate, pp. 193–203.

Wagner-Tsukamoto, S. (2008), 'Scientific Management revisited. Did Taylorism fail because of a too positive image of human nature?', *Journal of Management History*, 14 (4), 348–372.

19. Identity
John B. Davis

INTRODUCTION: ECONOMICS AND IDENTITY

The concept of identity has begun to be employed only relatively recently in economics, and accordingly still lacks a standard meaning and established set of applications in the subject. However, in its most influential initial uses by Amartya Sen (1999) and George Akerlof and Rachel Kranton (2000) it has been developed largely in terms of the concept of social identity (though in quite different ways). Social identity as understood in social psychology (see Brown, 2000), where the concept was influentially developed by Erik Erikson in connection with his idea of an identity crisis (Erikson, 1950), concerns individuals' 'identification with' social groups of which they are members. There are different ways of understanding the idea of 'identification with,' with both more psychological and sociological types of interpretations, but generally it means that individuals treat the characteristics of the social group with which they identify as their own individual characteristics, for example, as when people think of themselves as individuals having a certain nationality, gender, or religion. Akerlof and Kranton, then, adopt this sort of understanding when they rewrite the standard utility function representation of the individual to include a vector of self-images which people are said to have in virtue of their having corresponding characteristics associated with certain social groups. Sen employs the same idea that social group characteristics and social identities are applied to individuals and influence how they think of themselves, but in contrast he also argues that individuals deliberate over whether to embrace these assignments.

Understanding the concept of identity primarily in terms of social identity, however, creates a problem in that it leaves unexplained 'who' it is that identifies with social groups (Kirman and Teschl, 2004). Since social identity is understood in terms of the idea of 'identification with' others, it follows that we also need to be able to say what the individual's identity is 'apart from' others. Indeed, if the concept of identity is only explained in terms of the concept of social identity, then since individuals have many social identities, they must fragment across their many social identities, and have no distinct unitary identities as individuals. This is inconsistent with referring to them as individuals. Philosophers consequently address the idea that individuals are distinct unitary beings by focusing on the concept of personal identity (Noonan, 2003). Though there are many issues that this leads them to investigate within this framework, in general the concept of personal identity is understood to concern characteristics that make a person distinct from others, perhaps enduringly so. Nonetheless, this is not incompatible with an individual having a collection of social identities, and indeed one way in which an individual could be said to have a distinct personal identity would be to say that the individual is made up of a unique combination of different social identities. In any case, given that people can have multiple social identities, and given that economists treat people as individuals having social identities, it seems incumbent upon them to explain how their view of the individual relates social identity to personal identity (Davis, 2003).

Another issue that economics' employment of the concept of social identity brings up concerns the behavioral implications of individuals having social identities and moreover of having multiple social identities. This is particularly important to the topic of philanthropy, reciprocity, and social enterprise – all ways in which people are other-regarding and orient towards others – since not only can people's orientation towards others be understood as a reflection of their identification with them, but differences between the ways people have of orienting towards others can be understood in terms of the different kinds of social identities people have. Note, then, that when social psychologists investigate people's different kinds of social identities, they generally distinguish between '(i) those that derive from interpersonal relationships and inter-dependence with specific others and (ii) those that derive from membership in larger, more impersonal collectives or social categories' (Brewer and Gardner, 1996; Brewer 2001). This can be understood to mean that individuals have social identities that are 'identifications of the self *as* a certain kind of person' – a role-based social identity – and they also have social identities involving 'identifications of the self *with* a group or category as a whole' – a collective social identity (Thoits and Virshup, 1997, p. 106). Thus broadly speaking people's social identities can be classified as being relational or categorical. They are relational when a person occupies a position in a 'relational web' (kinship, friendship, patron-client, team member, etc.), and socially identifies with another person or set of people to whom they are connected in this relational setting in a specific kind of way. They are categorical in regard to their 'sharing some categorical attribute' with other like people (race, ethnicity, gender, age, disability, language, class, nationality, sexual orientation, etc.) when a person socially identifies with another person as representative of that shared category (Brubaker and Cooper, 2000, pp. 15ff). One way, then, in which philanthropy, reciprocity, and social enterprise can be investigated in economics is by asking how individuals' behavior and orientation towards others varies according to whether they identify socially with them in a relational or categorical way. This perspective links up with the previous question of how personal identity and social identity are connected, since an orientation 'towards' others – a matter of social identity – presupposes the individual having such an orientation – a matter of personal identity. The following section consequently looks more closely at how individuals' orientation towards others can be understood in overall identity terms when we differentiate between the different kinds of social identities individuals have, focusing specifically on the concept of reciprocity and the different ways in which it can be explained.

IDENTITY AND RECIPROCITY

Economics chiefly explains an individual's orientation towards others in terms of the idea of other-regarding or social preferences, framing this in terms of standard instrumental rationality theory in which individuals act in order to maximize utility. On this view, when individuals act on their social preferences, they gain utility when others are better off. However, this analysis is limited in what it can explain about the nature of reciprocity, since it implies that reciprocity is always conditional in nature in that a person only reciprocates the actions of others when in expectation of a private utility payoff. That is, by relying on standard rationality theory it leaves out all non-instrumentally rational reciprocal behavior which, as Luigino Bruni puts it, is unconditional in nature and not motivated by an expectation of a private payoff (Bruni, 2008). In such cases, the individual unilaterally reciprocates the action of another – a type of action which is ordinarily associated with altruism. Proponents of standard rationality theory generally deny such actions are rational, and reject the entire idea that people can be non-instrumentally rational, but this requires that they re-interpret and reformulate the testimony many people commonly express regarding this sort of 'selfless' behavior, in order to fit it into the standard view. Debates, however, over whether this is a reasonable strategy and about what rationality involves can be interminable, and so here the different ways in which reciprocity can be understood are tied to the different ways in which people have social identities to see what this can tell us. Specifically, it will be argued that categorical social identities can generally be better explained in terms of instrumentally rational reciprocity behavior, while relational social identities often (but not always) need to be explained in terms of a non-instrumentally rational kind of behavior.

Consider, then, the nature of the social distance between people involved in the two types of social identities, and also note that when people identify with a social group, they are actually identifying with other individuals in that social group through their membership in it. Here the idea of social distance may be taken to refer to degree of familiarity one has with a person with whom one identifies. Though there are many ways of explaining the idea of familiarity, one important aspect of it is the extent to which a person actually sees, has contact with, or personally interacts with another person. At one extreme, then, there are people with whom an individual identifies who they never see, have contact with, or interact with; at the other extreme, there are people whom a person regularly sees, has contact with, and interacts with. Thus taking identification with social groups to be a proxy for identification with individuals in those social groups, we can distinguish between categorical and relational social identities according to whether this involves close or distant contact. In the case of categorical social identities, clearly social distance is great and contact limited; in the case of relational social identities there is less social distance and much more contact. For example, if one is of a certain nationality – a categorical social identity – there are usually millions of individuals with whom one identifies who one has never met nor ever will and who one only knows in the most abstract, representative sort of way. Alternatively, if one occupies a particular role or position in a family, community organization, business, or social network – a relational social identity – there are not very many people with whom one identifies, and for those with whom one identifies one has specific types of relationships which are understood in terms of regular as well as quite specific forms of interaction that one has with them.

Relational social identities, then, tend to be tied to established, customary, institutionalized, and rule-driven types of interaction between people. We need to understand people relationally when we see them in this capacity, and understand them in terms of social structures. Categorical social identities, in contrast, tend to be individualizing in the sense that each person having a given identity is equally and in the same way a member of the set of all people having that social identity. They are in part social statistical artifacts and in part social organizational in nature. But because they apply homogeneously, there is generally nothing in the way in which people have categorical social identities that distinguishes one individual from the next, whereas people who share relational social identities are heterogeneous and distinguished from one another according to the ways in which they have them, reflecting their different positions and roles in the associated social groups on which these identities depend. This difference thus points to an important difference between the kinds of behavior people exhibit in connection with these different kinds of social identity. In the case of relational identities, the fact that people occupy positions and roles means that their behavior is considerably more circumscribed by what they ought to do in those contexts in comparison with what is implied by their having categorical social identities. They also know what they ought to do according to what their circumstances dictate, and thus rely to an important degree on a non-instrumental rationality. This may also be true in important ways with respect to categorical social identities, in that a sense of obligation applies there also to membership in large social groups, though given the less structured way in which this sort of social identity operates, more space remains for instrumentally rational decision-making.

This all accordingly allows us to distinguish different kinds of reciprocity, or at least a spectrum of forms of reciprocity associated with a spectrum of social identities. What Robert Trivers (1971) originally labeled 'reciprocal altruism' then gets placed at the end of the spectrum where instrumental rationality theory best applies, and what Bruni (2008) contrasts as a unilateral altruism best applies where rationality is non-instrumental or deontological in nature (meaning in particular that it reflects a sense of obligation). Somewhere along this spectrum one would also want to include conceptions of reciprocity such as the much debated 'strong reciprocity' concept (e.g., Gintis, 2000; Fehr et al, 2002). At the same time, we may draw a general conclusion about the economics of reciprocity and identity. That is, what we find when we look at the different forms of social identity is that how we understand rationality depends upon how rationality is endogenous to individuals' social circumstances. That is, what counts as rational is not something we can determine in and of itself, axiomatically, and apart from how we understand the identity of individuals, especially in connection with their social identity side.

This then returns us to the question of how individuals with different social identities also have personal identities associated with 'who' it is that has those different social identities. The discussion above tells us that relational and categorical social identities mean different things to individuals, implying that they contribute to personal identity differently. Though there are many ways this issue can be approached, one view is that individuals' personal identities depend on how they use their relational social identities to organize and interpret their categorical social identities (Davis, 2011, 201ff). That is, their closer connections to others in their positions and roles are a key to their approach to their more distant connections to others in large social groups. This makes personal identity first and foremost relational in nature. To show how such a view might be developed, two different recent accounts of personal identity treated as relational in nature, both of which emphasize social identity and reciprocity, are the subject of the next section.

TWO VIEWS OF PERSONAL IDENTITY AS RELATIONAL IN NATURE

Michael Bacharach (2006) develops a game-theoretic conception of the single individual as a being who possesses multiple selves which function together as a team. When individuals are faced with a choice of action, Bacharach argues that rather than seeing the person asking, 'what should *I* do?' we ought to see the person's multiple selves asking, 'what should *we* do?' On his view, an individual's multiple selves are simply all the person's social identities, so that we have a sub-personal self for each social identity we have. This is central to Bacharach's account of why the personal identity of the individual can be understood as a team, because having a social identity (he primarily means categorical social identity) is akin to having membership in a team. Thus, just as one's many social identity selves each identify with the teams/social groups to which they belong, so they also have the same capacity to identify with the team made up of the single person to which they belong. This makes the individual's personal identity explicitly relational in nature in that what makes the individual a single distinct person is the relations they have to others through their identification with them in social groups. For comparison, it is a different kind of view from one that says individuals may act on team preferences (Sugden, 2000) – a kind of social preference – since these views attribute such preferences to a unitary individual rather than make the individual itself a team.

Another view of personal identity as relational in nature derives from collective intentionality theory (e.g, Searle, 1995; Gilbert, 1989; Tuomela and Miller, 1988). Collective intentionality theory examines the behavior of individuals when their intentions are formed in social settings and expressed in first person plural 'we' language rather than in first person singular 'I' language. An important difference between 'we' intentions and 'I' intentions concerns their conditions of success. To successfully express an 'I' intention, a person needs to use language correctly to communicate that intention. In the case of 'we' intentions, however, not only must this be true, but those to whom this is expressed must agree with the content of the intention since the 'we' binds them as well to what has been said (Davis, 2002). Thus, a person fails to successfully express a 'we' intention about something if those to whom it applies reject what has been said. Individuals, of course, regularly express 'we' intentions, as shown by the cross-language nature of this form of speech. Thus at least a part of what is involved in being an individual is a matter of being embedded in relationships to others where collective intentions operate. Note, then, when individuals express 'we' intentions, they make what others want part of what they want, so that their own identities are partially relational in nature. At the same time, they do so in a non-instrumentally rational way, since in the expression of a 'we' intention one is (deontologically) obliged to put things in a way to which others will agree for that 'we' intention to be successful, quite apart from one's preferences. The choice to express a 'we' intention could be understood in an instrumentally rational manner, but the actual expression of it must be non-instrumentally rational.

For both Bacharach and collective intentionality theory, then, individuals' personal identities can be understood to have a relational character. However, the degree of this relationality is not same, as reflected in the different kinds of social identities involved. Bacharach is largely though not exclusively concerned with categorical social identities which typically involve considerable social distance between individuals and those with whom they identify. Collective intentionality theory, at least as developed around the logic of success conditions for 'we' intentions, makes a person's contact with others central, and accordingly puts more emphasis on relational social identity. We may consequently distinguish between these two ways of talking about personal identity as relational according to the different kinds of reciprocity associated with these different kinds of social identity. Bacharach's view better fits instrumentally rational or conditional reciprocity, while collective intentionality theory better fits non-instrumentally rational or unilateral reciprocity. More could be said about this basic distinction, but for comparative purposes, the following section turns to what this might tell us about the implicit view of personal identity in the standard *Homo economicus* view of the individual.

THE PERSONAL IDENTITY OF *HOMO ECONOMICUS*

Though standard economics does not employ the concept of personal identity, it is fair to say that it identifies individuals with their utility functions or as collections of well-ordered preferences defined in terms of a set of axiomatic assumptions ascribed to those preferences. However, much experimental research has cast doubt on whether these assumptions have a sound empirical basis (see Starmer, 2000). If these assumptions do not hold, or if they require significant revision, then it becomes unclear whether they can still support a unique monotonic utility function which would represent individuals' personal identities. In addition to this problem, there is an even more serious problem with the utility function representation of individuals' personal identities. Individuals' preferences are also always assumed to be their *own* preferences and not someone else's. Indeed, two people could have identical preferences, but on the standard view would be two different people because those preferences in each case would still be their own. This means, then, that the definition of the individual as a single distinct being is circular, because it makes individuals' identities depend on having their own preferences. Having an 'own' set of preferences accordingly does not distinguish and identify an individual, but rather counts as a formal procedure for mapping given preference ranking information into a choice space for whoever or whatever is to be called an 'individual' (person, firm, nation, neural process, etc.) to which those preferences belong. As Gerhard Debreu aptly put it, 'an axiomatized theory has a mathematical form that is completely separated from its economic content' (Debreu, 1986, p. 1265).

The utility function conception of the individual, then, fails as an account of an individual's personal identity. Since the circularity problem is at the root of this, it makes sense to ask how one would go about explaining personal identity in a way that avoids this problem. That would involve describing the individual in a manner that does not presuppose the individual, that is, in terms of characteristics that do not refer to or imply the individual, as in the case of having an own set of preferences. There are different ways in which this can be done (see Davis, 2011), but one element that can profitably be drawn upon is patterns of relationships between people, as in the two relational views of identity set out above. The basic idea is that patterns of relationships between people can individualize particular persons if they occupy distinct locations in these patterns. The advantage of this approach is that reference to 'patterns of relationships between people' does not presuppose any particular individuals who might be identified by those patterns, and thus potentially makes it possible to pick them out as individuals in a non-circular way. Explaining individuals' personal identities in this way would then also make it possible to investigate how individuals' personal identities could be seen to evolve over time as individuals' social relationships change. This allows for a variety of views of what individual personal identity involves alternative to the standard *Homo economicus* conception, and as the discussion here has argued provides additional foundations for explaining behavior in connection with such phenomena as reciprocity.

REFERENCES

Akerlof, George and Rachel Kranton (2000) 'Economics and Identity,' *Quarterly Journal of Economics* 115: 715–753.

Bacharach, Michael (2006) *Beyond Individual Choice: Teams and Frames in Game Theory*, in N. Gold and R. Sugden (eds)., Princeton: Princeton University Press.

Brewer, Marilyn (2001) 'The Many Faces of Social Identity: Implications for Political Psychology,' *Political Psychology* 22: 115–125.

Brewer, Marilyn and Wendy Gardner (1996) 'Who Is This "We"? Levels of Collective Identity and Self-Representations,' *Journal of Personal and Social Psychology* 71 (1): 83–93.

Brown, Rupert (2000) 'Social identity theory: past achievements, current problems and future challenges,' *European Journal of Social Psychology*, 30: 745–778.

Brubaker, Rogers and Frederick Cooper (2000) 'Beyond "identity",' *Theory and Society* 29: 1–47.

Bruni Luigino (2008) *Reciprocity, Altruism and the Civil Society*, London: Routledge.

Davis, John (2002) 'Collective Intentionality and the Agency-Structure Model,' in E. Fullbrook, (ed.) *Intersubjectivity in Economics in Economics: Agents and Structures*, London: Routledge, pp. 11–27.

Davis, John (2003) *The Theory of the Individual in Economics: Identity and Value*, London: Routledge.

Davis, John (2011) *Individuals and Identity in Economics*, Cambridge: Cambridge University Press.

Debreu, Gerard (1986) 'Theoretical Models: Mathematical Form and Economic Content,' *Econometrica* 54 (6): 1259–1270.

Erikson, Erik (1950) *Childhood and Society*, New York: Norton.

Fehr, Ernst, Urs Fischbacher, and Simon Gächter (2002) 'Strong Reciprocity, Human Cooperation and the Enforcement of Social Norms,' *Human Nature* 13: 1–25.

Gilbert, Margaret (1989) *On Social Facts*, London: Routledge.

Gintis, Herbert (2000) 'Strong Reciprocity and Human Sociality,' *Journal of Theoretical Biology* 206:169–179.

Kirman, Alan and Miriam Teschl (2004) 'On the Emergence of Economic Identity,' *Revue de Philosophie économique* 9 (1): 59–86.

Noonan, Harold (2003) *Personal Identity*, Second Edition, London: Routledge.

Searle, John (1995) *The Construction of Social Reality*, New York: Free Press.

Sen, Amartya (1999) *Reason before Identity*, New Delhi: Oxford University Press.

Starmer, Chris (2000) 'Developments in Non-Expected Utility Theory: The Hunt for a Descriptive Theory of Choice under Risk,' *Journal of Economic Literature* 38: 332–382.

Sugden, Robert (2000) 'Team Preferences,' *Economics and Philosophy* 16: 175–204.

Thoits, Peggy and Lauren Virshup (1997) 'Me's and We's: Forms and Functions of Social Identities,' in R. Ashmore and L. Jussim (eds) *Self and Identity: Fundamental Issues*, Oxford: Oxford University Press, pp. 106–133.

Trivers, Robert L. (1971) 'The Evolution of Reciprocal Altruism,' *Quarterly Review of Biology* 46: 35–57.

Tuomela, Raimo and Kaarlo Miller (1988) 'We-intentions,' *Philosophical Studies* 53: 367–389.

20. Law and religion
Amelia J. Uelmen

INTRODUCTION: LAW, RELIGION AND SOCIAL ENTERPRISE

Businesses which are not publicly traded, such as closely-held and family owned enterprise and cooperatives, and which take numerous forms across the international spectrum, generally face no legal obstacles to the influence of cultural drivers beyond the spheres of economic and business judgment. In contrast, publicly traded corporations in the United States have faced a series of legal constraints. This chapter on the intersecting sets of law, religion and social enterprise considers the topic from three angles. First, in the realm of publicly traded companies, to what extent would legal regimes allow space for the consideration of cultural drivers beyond economic and business concerns – such as religion? Second, what insights might the theory and experience of religiously inspired and informed social enterprise bring to the perceived legal constraints of publicly traded corporations? Third, as a descriptive matter, how do religiously-inspired and religiously-informed social enterprises interact with existing legal regimes? The chapter concludes by noting a few areas for further research and discussion.

OPENING A SPACE BEYOND 'SHAREHOLDER PRIMACY' AND 'PROFIT-MAXIMIZATION'

At certain points in the history of US corporate law, the principles 'shareholder primacy' and 'profit-maximization' seem to have crowded out space for other cultural drivers, such as religion, to inform the goals and policies of publicly traded enterprise.

In a 1919 case from United States, the Dodge brothers, two of the original shareholders in the Ford Motor Company, brought a suit claiming that Ford's plan to withhold a special dividend ought to be enjoined as inimical to the best interests of the company and its shareholders. As Ford testified: 'My ambition is to employ still more men, to spread the benefits of this industrial system to the greatest possible number, to help them build up their lives and their homes. To do this we are putting the greatest share of our profits back in the business.' Further, Ford thought that the company's profits should be shared with the public by reducing the price of the company's product. (*Dodge*, p. 684)

The court's response emphasized what then become the principles of 'shareholder primacy' and 'profit-maximization':

> A business corporation is organized and carried on primarily for the profit of the stockholders. The powers of the directors are to be employed for that end. The discretion of directors is to be exercised in the choice of means to attain that end, and does not extend to a change in the end itself, to the reduction of profits, or to the non-distribution of profits among stockholders in order to devote them to other purposes.

Thus, under *Dodge v. Ford*, 'it is not within the lawful powers of a board of directors to shape and conduct the affairs of a corporation for the merely incidental benefit of shareholders and for the primary purpose of benefiting others.' (*Dodge*, p. 684) Or as economist Milton Friedman famously put it several years later, 'The social responsibility of business is to increase its profits.' (Friedman, p. 32; see also Bainbridge 1993)

In the 1930s the important debate between Berle and Dodd probed the duties of corporate managers and directors beyond shareholders to other groups. (Wells p. 79) Beginning with the 1953 New Jersey case of *A.P. Smith v. Barlow*, later cases have confirmed that corporations may make transfers to charity as an expression of their 'enlightened self interest.' (Wells pp. 103–104)

Current principles of corporate governance generally acknowledge that a corporation's long-range profitability depends on careful analysis of how the corporation's actions and decisions impact a variety of stakeholders both within and external to the company. As Eisenberg explains: '[t]he corporation is a social actor. It benefits from the social climate. It is now widely accepted that the corporation should at least consider the social impact of its activities, so as to be aware of the social costs those activities entail.' (Eisenberg p. 19)

Legal constraints are also read narrowly in light of an expansive interpretation of the 'business judgment rule' in which directors are given wide latitude to pursue determined goals. (Velasco p. 828–830) Further, many United States jurisdictions have adopted 'nonshareholder constituency statutes' that explicitly permit directors to consider how their decisions might affect the interests of nonshareholders.

As the American Law Institute (ALI) Principles of Corporate Governance note:

> The modern corporation by its nature creates interdependencies with a variety of groups with whom the corporation has legitimate concerns, such as employees, customers, suppliers, and members of the communities in which the corporation operates. The long-term profitability of the corporation generally depends on meeting the fair expectations of such groups.' (§ 2.01 cmt. f; see also Mitchell 2001, p. 69)

In fact, in a later interview, even Friedman conceded that charitable activity may ultimately contribute to corporate profit-maximization. (Johnson p. 14)

Further, the ALI Principles explain:

> the ethical considerations reasonably regarded as appropriate to the responsible conduct of the business necessarily include ethical responsibilities that may be owed to persons other than shareholders with whom the corporation has a legitimate concern, such as employees, customers, suppliers, and members of the communities within which the corporation operates. (ALI § 2.01 cmt. h)

Recent scholarship has also posed formidable alternatives to the 'shareholder primacy' principle. For example, Mitchell proposes a model which recasts the board of directors 'as a mediating body among the different corporate constituent groups'. (Mitchell 1992) With their 'team production theory' of corporate governance, Blair and Stout challenge shareholder primacy as an error of legal analysis: 'the board of directors is already charged not with maximizing shareholder value, but with the balancing of competing demands of "team members" [managers, stockholders, employees].' (Wells, p. 137) Similarly, Dallas proposes a model for a 'relational board' in which the board 'assist[s] the corporation in forging relationships with various stakeholders and others in its social environment.' (Dallas, p. 3)

Further, 'amoral' views of business, particularly the perception that making money is the only and ultimate achievement, contradict common business experience, in which corporate decisions are based on the fact that profit is only one indication of a healthy business. Sophisticated business planning and legal counseling recognize that the health of a business is much more complex than raw profit margins. As a comment to an ALI Principle explains: 'Short-term profits may properly be subordinated to recognition that responsible maintenance of [interdependencies on various relationships] is likely to contribute to long-term corporate profit and shareholder gain. The corporation's business may be conducted accordingly.' (§ 2.01 cmt. f)

Businesses must, and do, consider the impact of their decisions on each of the relationships on which they depend: whether internally, in the form of employee relations, safety and morale; or externally, in the form of customer relations, product quality and relations with the public and the government. Even if such decisions are grounded in the desire to avoid bad publicity, government fines, or litigation, such decisions nevertheless reflect the essence of the nature of a corporate entity as a social being that relies on a network of social relationships for its life, health and growth. (Solomon, 1992a, 1992b)

Thus the development of United States corporate law over the course of the twentieth century points toward a space for the expression of cultural drivers which allows a corporation to orient itself toward goals beyond profit-maximization, and which can shape how a corporation relates to persons other than shareholders.

However, important questions still remain. For example, Fisch articulates concerns about the lack of transparency in the decision-making process. Shifting the responsibility for deciding which projects are worthy of funding into the hands of corporate decision-makers in effect 'both hide[s] the decision-making process from shareholders in particular and the public more generally, and [creates] a system of social spending which is profoundly undemocratic.' (Fisch, p. 1094) Kahn agrees: 'The absence of substantive regulation, in combination with the absence of a disclosure requirement, has meant that corporate senior executives have had a blank check to make corporate charitable contributions independent of both business objectives and shareholder preferences.' (Kahn, p. 586)

According to scholars in this line, if individual investors would like to contribute to the alleviation of poverty, that is certainly their prerogative – but generally the current structures of large publicly held corporations are not well equipped to handle such complex commitments in an open and democratic way. The laws of transparency and accountability which form the foundations of US corporate laws, and which facilitate the public's participation in the market are premised on the assumption that market relationships are anonymous, and should therefore be free of personal and possibly partial interests or commitments.

Given the dynamics of the stock market, practical obstacles also include the extent to which short-term measures of profit remain the powerful incentive and practical driver for corporate decision-making. In addition, most individual investors have neither the time nor the inclination to work through the layers of information they would need to consider in order to push publicly traded companies to consider factors beyond the profit-maximization principle.

RELIGION AS A CULTURAL DRIVER FOR SOCIAL ENTERPRISE

As mentioned above, businesses which are not publicly traded have for the most part enjoyed the freedom to integrate other cultural influences as a guide or inspiration for a socially-oriented approach to enterprise. This section offers a few notes on the extent to which religion has served as a cultural driver for social enterprise, and the perspective that such intersection offers regarding the legal concerns discussed above.

Whether or not religion functions as a cultural driver for social enterprise is largely shaped by historical and cultural conditions. (Gold, pp. 31–36) Discussions often recognize that religious traditions are one of many potential cultural drivers toward ethical and social orientations for business enterprises. (McMahon)

As a survey of corporate social responsibility in various European countries indicates, the influence of religion on business life depends on each country's unique historical interaction with religion. In some countries, a tendency to privatize religious values and perspectives can limit religion's direct impact on social enterprise. In France, for example, where the role of the Catholic Church in economic activities is discreet, its influence is weak; while at the same time, probably at the root of a general attitude of mistrust toward business and money. (Habisch et al, p. 99) By contrast, German faith-based associations such as the BKU Association of Catholic Entrepreneurs and Austrian 'Sozialwort' projects have brought the dialogue between religion and social enterprise to the public stage. (Habisch et al, pp. 115, 126) Similarly, in Italy, Catholic culture has been a major driver pushing toward social activism. (Habisch et al, p. 279) In the United States, religious influence on business culture and ethics has 'waxed and waned' over time. (Knouse et al, p. 95)

With a given culture, how religion impacts the social role of business can be the subject of tension and controversy, and can also shift over time. (see Weber) As Zamagni explains, the Catholic tradition's reflection on economic life spans the complexities and tensions of two millennia, both contributing to the economic institutions that later serve the 'full flowering of the spirit of capitalism,' and at the same time, essentially rejecting 'the very mind-set of capitalism.' (Zamagni) Similarly, Resnicoff notes that Jewish law authorities do not agree on the question of how, as a matter of Jewish law, a corporation is to be perceived. (Symposium, p. 690)

In the United States one could also note the variety of currents and historical shifts within the 'Social Gospel' movement – the response of US Protestantism to the challenges of an increasingly industrialized nation. While Evangelical currents pushed for strong government intervention on social issues throughout the nineteenth century, in the twentieth century they shifted toward more private and voluntary efforts to address poverty. (Anglim, p. 554)

The empirical work regarding the influence of religion on perspectives and decisions regarding social enterprise is still tentative. The results of one large cross-country sample indicated that religious individuals show some tendency to hold broader conceptions of the social responsibilities of business than non-religious individuals, but also admitted the need for further research to understand distinctions across religious groups, and across areas of corporate social responsibility. (Brammer et al)

Stabile posits that religious perspectives offer the potential for a fundamental shift in the 'anthropological' grounding of our conception of the corporation. A 'religious view of the person' leads to 'a recognition of a communion of beings' which in turn suggests a set of values that is different and broader than merely allowing individuals the freedom to pursue their individual self-interest. (Stabile p. 863) Within this anthropological shift, religiously informed perspectives can facilitate a broader inquiry into what is owed to other constituencies. (Stabile p. 873) 'At a minimum, a notion of communion justifies imposing meaningful limits on that autonomy for the benefit of the whole.' (Stabile p. 866) Applications of this anthropological vision lead to radical critiques of both shareholder primacy and profit-maximization principles.

Using Fuller's two principles of human association, Mitchell describes the distinction between organizations bound by shared commitment and common goals, typically marked by a stronger sense of community; and organizations bound by 'the legal principle' – formal rules which set out the rights and duties of members, typically more formalistic and procedural in operation. (Mitchell 2001, p. 79) Mitchell describes how the 'tendency of corporate law over the past century has been consistently and markedly to replace any sense of common purpose with a very individualized concept of competing legal rights and duties.' Within this vision, 'the corporation is really nothing more than a collection of individuals pursuing their self-interest and bound together by a set of loose contractually based rules – a free market within a shield of limited liability.' (Mitchell 2001, p. 81)

When a religious perspective which recognizes, in Stabile's turn of the phrase, a 'communion of beings' is brought to bear on what would otherwise be perceived as anonymous social structures, these principles of human association may be brought together, highlighting the potential for shared human commitment in an organization in which people would otherwise see themselves as bound only by more formalistic contractual duties and obligations. As Naughton describes, within a religiously-grounded vision, the corporation has the potential to be 'a community of work where members are in the pursuit of goods in common that build real communions, where its authenticity of developing itself is premised on serving those outside it.' (Naughton, p. 34)

Further, within a religious framework, one might also imagine solutions to problem of participants in publicly held corporations distancing themselves from the human consequences of their business decisions and externalizing their social costs. Mitchell explains the dilemma of how to get managers to consider the corporation's long-term interests when they themselves may not personally benefit from a long range perspective.

> Good behavior *is* good business, but the rewards of good behavior lie largely in the long run. And who knows quite how long that is? In the short run (from which we have more confidence we will profit) bad or at least indifferent may be better. The structure of American corporate law encourages most managers to focus on the short term.' (Mitchell 2001, p. 52)

A religious commitment to the common good provides one path to travel toward a longer-range perspective.

Religious perspectives can also help to loosen the grip of the profit-maximization principle. In response to philosophical questions regarding the moral meaning of the accumulation of wealth, (Mitchell 2001, p. 85) religious traditions offer a way to contextualize the accumulation of wealth. While appreciating the purpose of wealth and the importance of wealth creation, they also acknowledge the limitations of current market structures and what has been termed the 'social mortgage' on prosperity. (John Paul II, p. 35, see also Alford et al 2006, p. x)

Within this framework, while profits can serve as a means to an end – a 'foundational' or 'instrumental' good, how profits are ultimately used is also subject to the question of how they promote the more 'excellent' goods of human flourishing. (Alford and Naughton 2001, p. 68) As one company whose principles are informed by a religious framework explained, profits are like food – not the purpose of life, but essential to maintaining health and strength, ultimately for the service of the common good. (Alford and Naughton 2001, p. 44; see also Alford et al 2006, pp. 298–326)

HOW RELIGIOUSLY INFORMED SOCIAL ENTERPRISE INTERACTS WITH LEGAL STRUCTURES

Religiously inspired and informed social enterprise projects which are not publicly traded generally do not face legal restraints regarding the integration of religious values into the management and operation of their business. Nonetheless, they do interact with existing legal regimes. This section considers some of the elements and insights that religiously informed social enterprise might bring to discussions of corporate law.

When religiously informed social enterprise operates in a cultural terrain of corruption and evasion, religious values offer one incentive to operate with transparent compliance to existing legal and regulatory regimes. Gold describes how a religiously-inspired project for social enterprise, the 'Economy of Communion,' informed participants' attitudes toward taxation and other regulatory requirements, even against the backdrop of business cultures plagued by widespread evasion or corruption. Participants experienced 'a heightened sense of responsibility toward fulfilling their legal obligations as a first step toward other aims.' (Gold, p. 155) One participant in the project described the shift:

> It is a big effort, but inside you feel you are doing right. It is not that you feel you are better than the others but let's say that I am doing my part . . . Before I was living a different kind of life and trying to evade the tax man was normal for me. There was this change in mentality. (Gold, p. 152)

Second, corporate reform movements have long been plagued by the extent to which social *desiderata* do not always translate neatly into the language of the law. As Stone put it, the 'thou shalt not' prohibitions and the specification of minimum standards seem to lend themselves to legal enforcement better than 'thou shalts,' and 'exhortations to realize one's fullest potential.' The law, it seems, is too rigid an instrument to push beyond the enforcement of 'acceptable minimums.' (Stone, p. 101)

Might these patterns shift when religiously inspired and informed social enterprise begins to see legal standards and relationships through the lens of what tends to foster respect for the integrity of other persons and to nourish a 'communion of beings?' Might aspects of safety indications expressed in tort standards or other areas of product regulation be welcomed as a tool and a measuring rod to reach the goal of increased respect for the human communion, rather than an interference with 'rational' profit-maximization?

(Symposium, p.679) Through this lens, aspects of the more aspirational 'thou shalts' may be received as a helpful guide rather than oppressive impediments to autonomy.

Third, religiously informed social enterprise has served as one of the prompts to think creatively about corporate legal structures so as to accommodate the aspirations of religiously grounded goals for business life. As Pope Benedict XVI explained in his 2009 analysis of how Catholic social teaching applies to economic life, the emergence of a 'broad intermediate area' between profit-based companies and non-profit organizations:

> It is made up of traditional companies which nonetheless subscribe to social aid agreements in support of underdeveloped countries, charitable foundations associated with individual companies, groups of companies oriented towards social welfare, and the diversified world of the so-called 'civil economy' and the 'economy of communion'. (Benedict XVI, n.46)

Benedict submits that the development is new in the sense that it does not exclude profit, 'but instead considers it a means for achieving human and social ends.' His analysis expresses the hope that these hybrid structures will find 'suitable juridical and fiscal structure in every country.' Benedict notes two specific benefits of these forms of business life: first, 'they steer the system towards a clearer and more complete assumption of duties on the part of economic subjects;' and second, 'the very plurality of institutional forms of business gives rise to a market which is not only more civilized but also more competitive.' (Benedict XVI, n.46)

Hybrid forms include Low-Profit Limited Liability Companies (L3Cs) in the United States, and Community Interest Companies (CICs) in the United Kingdom. (Sertial, pp.280–290)

REMAINING QUESTIONS AND CONTROVERSIES

While some of the intersecting sets of this topic – particularly law and social enterprise, and religion and social enterprise – have been the subject of in-depth study, research on the more complex interactions of law, religion and social enterprise is a relatively new venture. How the relatively new religiously inspired 'hybrids' are navigating their relationship with law and legal structures is a particularly fertile area for empirical and theoretical research. Cultural research on the questions of integrity and intentions is also an important and relatively open field.

From economic and legal perspectives, it would be interesting to consider the extent to which integration of religious perspectives might threaten or impede the integrity of current business structures. Similarly, religious communities are currently facing the question of whether integration of religious beliefs and communities lead to their being manipulated for commercial purposes, thus threatening their authenticity and integrity. And in all aspects of the interdisciplinary research, the crucial move from abstract theoretical principles to practical implementation remains a question of paramount importance. As Sargent notes: 'A broad frame of reference exists, but translation of the abstract theological and moral principles' into 'legal theory and specific recommendations for legal reform' has only just begun. (Sargent, p.592)

BIBLIOGRAPHY

A.P. Smith v. Barlow, 98 A.2d 581, 586 (N.J. 1953).

Alford, Helen and Michael J. Naughton (2001), *Managing as if Faith Mattered*, Notre Dame, IN: University of Notre Dame Press.

Alford, Helen, Charles M.A. Clark, S.A. Cortright and Michael J. Naughton (2006), *Rediscovering Abundance*, Notre Dame, IN: University of Notre Dame Press.

Anglim, Christopher Thomas (2009), *Encyclopedia of Religion and the Law in America* (2d ed) Amenia, NY: Grey House Publishing.

Bainbridge, Stephen M. (1993), 'In Defense of the Shareholder Wealth Maximization Norm: A Reply to Professor Green,' *Washington & Lee Law Review*, **50**, 1423–1448, 1423–1428.

Bainbridge, Stephen M. (2003), 'Director Primacy: the Means and Ends of Corporate Governance,' *Northwestern University Law Review*, **97**, 547–606, 576.

Benedict XVI, Pope (2009), *Caritas in veritate*.

Blair, Margaret M. and Lynn A. Stout (1999), 'Team Production in Business Organizations: An Introduction,' *Journal of Corporation Law*, **24**, 743–750.

Blair, Margaret M., and Lynn A. Stout (1999), 'A Team Production Theory of Corporate Law,' *Virginia Law Review*, **85**, 247–328.

Brammer, S., Geoffrey Williams and John Zinkin (2007), 'Religion and Attitudes Toward Corporate Social Responsibility in a Large Cross-Country Sample,' *Journal of Business Ethics*, **71**, 229–243.

Dallas, Lynne L. (1996), 'The Relational Board: Three Theories of Corporate Boards of Directors,' *Journal of Corporation Law*, **22**, 1–26, 3.

Dodge v. Ford Motor Co., 170 N.W. 668 (Michigan 1919).

Eisenberg, Melvin Aaron (1998), 'Corporate Conduct That Does Not Maximize Shareholder Gain: Legal Conduct, Ethical Conduct, The Penumbra Effect, Reciprocity, The Prisoner's Dilemma, Sheep's Clothing, Social Conduct, and Disclosure,' *Stetson Law Review*, **28**, 1–26, 19.

Finn, Daniel K. (ed.) (2010), *The True Wealth of Nations*, New York: Oxford University Press.

Fisch, Jill E. (1997), 'Questioning Philanthropy from a Corporate Governance Perspective,' *New York Law School Law Review*, **41**, 1091–1106, 1094.

Friedman, Milton, (1970), 'Social Responsibility of Business', *New York Times Magazine*, September 13, 122–126.

Gold, Lorna (2010), *New Financial Horizons: The Emergence of an Economy of Communion*, Hyde Park, NY: New City Press.

Habisch, André, Jan Jonker, Martina Wegner, and René Schmidpeter (eds) (2005), *Corporate Social Responsibility Across Europe*, Berlin: Springer.

John Paul II, Pope (1991), *Centesimus Annus*.

Johnson, Willa (1989), 'Freedom and Philanthropy: An Interview with Milton Friedman,' *Business & Society Review*, Spring 11–18, 14.

Kahn, Faith Stevelman (1997), 'Pandora's Box: Managerial Discretion and the Problem of Corporate Philanthropy', *University of California Law Review*, **44**, 579–676, 586.

Knouse, Stephen B., Vanessa D. Hill and J. Brooke Hamilton (2007), 'Curves in the high road: a historical analysis of the development of American business codes of ethics,' *Journal of Management History*, **13** (1), 94–107.

McMahon, Thomas F. (1985), 'The Contribution of Religious Traditions to Business Ethics,' *Journal of Business Ethics*, **4**, 341–349.

Mitchell, Lawrence E. (1992), 'A Critical Look at Corporate Governance,' *Vanderbilt Law Review*, **45**, 1263–1318, 1272.

Mitchell, Lawrence E. (2001), *Corporate Irresponsibility: America's Newest Export*, New Haven: Yale University Press.

Naughton, Michael J. (2006), 'The Corporation as a Community of Work: Understanding the Firm within the Catholic Social Tradition,' *Ave Maria Law Review*, **4**, 33–75.

Sargent, Mark (2004), 'Competing Visions of the Corporation in Catholic Social Thought,' *Journal of Catholic Social Thought*, **1**, 561–594, 592.

Sertial, Heather (2012), 'Hybrid Entities: Distributing Profits with a Purpose,' *Fordham Journal of Corporate and Financial Law*, **17**, 261–298.

Smith, D. Gordon (1998), 'The Shareholder Primacy Norm,' *Journal of Corporation Law*, **23**, 277–324.

Solomon, Robert C. (1992a), *Ethics and Excellence: Cooperation and Integrity in Business*, New York, NY: Oxford University Press, p. 146.

Solomon, Robert C. (1992b), 'Corporate Roles, Personal Virtues: An Aristotelian Approach to Business Ethics,' *Business Ethics Quarterly*, **2**, 317–339, 322.

Stabile, Susan J. (2004), 'Using Religion to Promote Corporate Responsibility,' *Wake Forest Law Review*, **39**, 839–901.
Stone, Christopher D. (1975), *Where the Law Ends: The Social Control of Corporate Behavior*, Illinois: Waveland Press.
Symposium (2006), 'Religious Values and Corporate Decision Making,' *Fordham Journal of Corporate and Financial Law*, **11**, 537–695.
Uelmen, Amelia J. (1998), 'Can a Religious Person be a Big Firm Litigator,' *Fordham Urban Law Journal* **26**, 1069–1110.
Velasco, Julian (2004), 'Structural Bias and the Need for Substantive Review,' *Washington University Law Quarterly*, **82**, 821–917.
Weber, Max (1958 [1905]), *The Protestant Ethics and the Spirit of Capitalism*, New York: Charles Scribner's Sons (Talcott Parson's translation, 1958).
Wells, C.A. Harwell (2002–2003), 'The Cycles of Corporate Social Responsibility: An Historical Retrospective for the Twenty-first Century,' *University of Kansas Law Review*, **51**, 77–140.
Zamagni, Stefano (2010), 'Catholic Social Thought, Civil Economy, and the Spirit of Capitalism,' in Finn, Daniel K. (ed), *The True Wealth of Nations*, New York: Oxford University Press.

21. Liberalism
Adrian Pabst

INTRODUCTION: COMPETING ACCOUNTS OF LIBERALISM

Until the global economic crisis struck in 2008, liberalism was the dominant ideology of our time and undoubtedly the most influential political philosophy of the last 300 years or so. Its origins, evolution and meaning are deeply contested by liberal and non-liberal thinkers alike. Many contemporary historians and political philosophers claim that liberal thought first emerged in the late sixteenth or early seventeenth century and evolved into a distinct philosophical tradition during the Age of Enlightenment (e.g. Mesnard 1969; Kelly 2005, Paul et al 2007). Thus, key liberal figures such as John Locke (1632–1704), Jean-Jacques Rousseau (1712–1778) and Immanuel Kant (1724–1804) opposed what they viewed as the unholy alliance between the Church, absolutist monarchs and the feudal capitalism of the landed gentry. They defended alternative ideas such as freedom of religion, tolerance, constitutional rule, individual property and free trade. These antecedents were important, but – so the dominant narrative goes – liberalism's evolution as an ideology and political movement only took off following the impact of the American and the French Revolution. Thereafter the liberal tradition was instrumental in the 'three waves of democratization' (Huntington 1991). The first wave saw liberal governments triumph in much of Europe and the Americas in the nineteenth and the early twentieth centuries. The second wave after 1945 rolled back some of the authoritarian regimes of the interwar period and also coincided with de-colonisation, while the third wave after 1974 overthrew the military dictatorships of Southern Europe and Latin America and later the Communist regimes of the eastern bloc. Based on the fundamental principles of liberty and the equal rights of all, most advocates of liberalism defend political freedom, economic opportunity, social emancipation and equality before the law (e.g. Gray 1995, 2004).

However, recent genealogical accounts suggest that the roots of liberalism go back to the late Middle Ages and the early modern age (Manent 1987; Dupré 1993). As a variety of theologians, philosophers and political theorists have argued (e.g. Milbank 1990; de Muralt 2002; Coleman 1999), notions such as individual subjective rights, popular sovereignty and national autonomy can be traced to shifts within theology, politics and law that were pioneered by key figures like John Duns Scotus (c1265/66–1308), William of Ockham (c1248/49–1349) and Francisco Suárez (1548–1617). Thus, core liberal principles are unintelligible without reference to late medieval and modern theological debates and ecclesial-political transformations. Similarly, modern categories such as the rule of the 'one' or the 'many' (associated with the political 'right' and 'left' since the French Revolution) and ideas like individual self-determination or the general will ultimately rest on nominalist and voluntarist theories that originated in the late Middle Ages (Pabst, 2010a). Even the values of liberality (e.g. fair detention and trial, presumption of innocence, *habeas corpus*, etc.) that liberalism purports to uphold were in reality the product of infusing Roman and Germanic law with Christian notions of justice and charity that liberals took over but did not invent (Milbank 2006). As such, the liberal claim to universal validity seems to be a secularised version of religious claims to universal truth.

These two rival accounts of the origins and meaning of liberalism show just how contested the liberal tradition is. This chapter discusses both liberal and non-liberal perspectives on liberalism. It begins by suggesting that there is no single essence that defines all visions of liberalism. Rather, one can identify four 'family resemblances' that characterise seemingly incompatible variants of liberal thinking. The second section outlines the main ideas of key early modern liberal thinkers, including Locke, Rousseau, Kant and J.S. Mill. The third section turns to alternative genealogies that trace the roots to the late Middle Ages and highlight profound continuities between Scotus, Ockham, Suárez, Machiavelli and Hobbes and contemporary liberal thinking (e.g. John Rawls). The final section explores recent debates, notably on social and economic liberalism as well as the much disputed notion of neo-liberalism.

LIBERALISM: ETYMOLOGY AND 'FAMILY RESEMBLANCES'

Liberalism derives from the Latin word *liber*, which means 'free'. Originally referring to the education worthy of a free person in Antiquity (*studia liberalia*), the notion of the 'liberal arts' described the study of the seven classical subjects (*artes liberales*) at Roman and medieval universities, the *Trivium* (grammar, logic, rhetoric) and the *Quadrivium* (arithmetic, geometry, music and astronomy) – as opposed to the *artes illiberales* that were for economic not scientific purposes. Politically speaking, the term 'liberal' referred to the status of 'free' citizens and peasants (as opposed to slaves or serfs). Much later, the term 'liberal' entered the political lexicon in connection with rival political traditions (e.g. Whigs and Tories in eighteenth-century Britain). In the late eighteenth century and early nineteenth century, 'liberalism' was used as a term of abuse for 'godless utilitarians' like Jeremy Bentham before it acquired positive connotations following the work of J.S. Mill and others.

This etymological origin has led many political thinkers to claim that liberalism is primarily concerned with the principle of liberty (e.g. J.S. Mill and Isaiah Berlin). However, fellow liberals view other values as equally if not more fundamental to the tradition of liberalism, whether justice (e.g. John Rawls) or equality (e.g. Ronald Dworkin). What this fundamental disagreement suggests is that there is no such thing as 'liberalism'. The liberal myth according to which both classical and modern liberalism emerged from the Dark Ages and rescued the Greco-Roman legacy of free inquiry and free speech is historically and conceptually untenable. This myth rests on liberalism's claim to universalism, which has led numerous liberal thinkers partially to distort and ultimately to falsify the history of their own thinking (Manent 1987; Gray 1989; Losurdo 2011). While there are elements and traits which are distinctly liberal, liberalism does not have a core essence (Gray 2000). Since there is no single defining characteristic, it is more accurate to speak of 'family resemblances' (Ludwig Wittgenstein) – features that can be found in all the strands but are not reducible to a sole element. The liberal tradition has four such 'family resemblances': universalism, individualism, egalitarianism and meliorism.

First, liberalism's claim to universalism consists in the argument that liberal values have universal authority, which in turn rests on ideas of moral unity, universal criteria of judgement (e.g. Kant) and legitimate rule. Linked to this is the notion that the liberal system of government and liberal societies are universal because they maximise liberty, both individually and collectively. Second, liberalism's commitment to individualism is grounded in the moral primacy of each individual person over any collectivity – whether communities, groups or nations (e.g. Dumont 1983). As such, institutions are only justified insofar as they promote individual rather than collective well-being. The fundamental reason given by liberals is that the ultimate repository of both rights and values is the individual, not groups or associations.

Third, liberalism's defence of egalitarianism refers to the idea that all human beings have the same standing. The principle of equality recognises the equal moral status of all mankind, which limits the exercise of power and authority – a core liberal conviction. Fourth, meliorism describes liberalism's pursuit of progress, which is founded upon the view that progress is good and that things are improvable. As such, the liberal tradition sees itself as a historical philosophy of progress. What underpins this perspective is the idea of human imperfection and fallibilism that requires constant correction and improvement.

The concept of 'family resemblances' captures the paradox that the various strands of liberalism do not share a single essence but are nevertheless related through a series of common features. However, it is also the case that there are some modern or contemporary liberals who do not agree with all four 'family resemblances'. For example, John Rawls and Joseph Raz reject the claim to universalism, except for the application of the principle of justice. Likewise, liberal figures such as Immanuel Kant or J.S. Mill tend to speak of general or collective well-being rather than simply individual interest or entitlements. However, it is equally correct to suggest that (elements of) the four 'family resemblances' are constitutive of a specifically liberal outlook that has its roots in late medieval nominalism and voluntarism (de Muralt 2002). Thus, one can identify a series of shared features that define liberalism as a distinct political philosophy.

KEY LIBERAL THINKERS AND SEMINAL TEXTS

Common to all the classical liberal thinkers such as Locke, Rousseau, Kant and J.S.Mill is the idea that in the state of nature, human beings are primarily individuals who should be thought of in abstraction from any individuating characteristics or mutual relations. As 'bare individuals', they are bearers of rights and endowed with a free will. For example, John Locke – in the *Second Treatise of Government* – writes that humans are naturally in:

> a State of perfect Freedom to order their Actions [. . .] as they think fit [. . .] without asking leave, or depending on the Will of any other Man (Locke 1960 [1689]: 287). Similarly, J.S.Mill suggests that the burden of proof is supposed to be on those who are against liberty; who contend for any restriction or prohibition [. . .]. The *a priori* assumption is in favour of freedom (Robson 1963–69, vol. 21: 262).

Taken together, rights and free will enable individuals to contract with each other – whether for largely economic aims (Locke) or predominantly political purposes

(Rousseau and Kant). As such, the social order is a human artifice, a conception that contrasts sharply with the ancient idea that man is a 'political animal' (Aristotle) and cognate notions in the thought of the Church Fathers and Doctors. Likewise, the modern emphasis on competing wills and their summation into one common, powerful collective will (e.g. Rousseau's *volonté générale*) is at odds with ancient, patristic and medieval ideas that man has a natural desire the supernatural good, which acts as an overarching *telos*.

Linked to individual subjective rights and the free will is the liberal notion of the social contract. Locke fuses contractualism with a consent theory of political association (rather than a coercion theory, as in Hobbes). For Locke, only the recognition of an equal moral status of all mankind can provide a proper foundation for political (but not civil) society and a non-absolutist outlook of government. In the second volume of his *Two Treatises of Government*, he argues that in the state of nature that precedes axiologically (and not historically) the body politic, men enjoy the same basic rights to life, liberty and land (or property). Locke's non-absolutism consists in the argument that political authority is – and always must be – subordinate to the moral norm of the natural equality of right. This basic moral norm imposes constraints on the nature and reach of sovereign power.

In *An Essay Concerning Human Understanding*, he attempts to account for this normativity by referring to natural law without however embracing a theological conception that views the law of nature in terms of a supernatural gift. Instead, he turns to notions like impartiality and consent or endorsement. Such and similar notions shift the emphasis from patristic and medieval theories of mutual duties to the idea of entitlements and obligations that are variously more individual (the person) or more collective (the state). Crucially, Locke treats individuality as an *a priori* given which is coextensive with the existence of all things: 'All Things, that exist, being particulars [. . .]' (Locke 2008: 409). This ontological claim begs the question, which is why he links ontological atomism to a politics of self-possession, arguing that mankind's freedom ultimately consists in being individual self-proprietors. Property is the central concept that links natural freedom to an artificially established social order based on the individual ability to work and trade.

Rousseau shares Locke's attack on the classical notion of human beings as naturally social. In his *Discourse on the Origin of Inequality*, he suggests – like Locke – that society is essentially an invention and that the state of nature precedes both civil and political society. Two issues arise from Rousseau's early work. First, what, if any, is the historicity of the state of nature? Second, which comes first, the representing state or represented civil society? By contrast with Locke, Rousseau argues that self-preservation or self-interest is only one of two principles that are constitutive of mankind. The other principle is pity or empathy, 'an innate repugnance to see his fellow suffer' (Masters and Kelly, Vol. II: 36). And unlike all other creatures, humans are born free and endowed with reason. It is the development of this faculty that marks the transition from the state of nature to civilisation, a stage in which mankind is capable of moral goodness, which Rousseau describes in *The Social Contract*, one of his main works. Chapter one commences with Rousseau's famous dictum: 'Man is born free, and everywhere he is in bondage' (Masters and Kelly 1994: 131). Since there are variants of the social contract that effectively enslave people, it is the task of legitimate government to preserve the equality of its citizens and promote the formation of their character.

Here Rousseau's concept of the general will (*volonté générale*) is key. It seeks to blend the exercise of personal freedom with the promotion of collective well-being that can differ from individual self-interest. Far from being contradictory, Rousseau's brand of liberalism attempts to link morally legitimate rule to the public good in which all citizens can share. Thus, proper sovereign power defends the good of society that overrides individual interests or needs. That is why the general will is no amalgamation of individuals wills but rather an abstraction from private interest in favour of the common public good:

> There is often a great deal of difference between the will of all and the general will. The latter looks only to the common interest; the former considers private interest and is only a sum of private wills. But take away from these same wills the pluses and minuses that cancel each other out, and the remaining sum of the differences is the general will. (Masters and Kelly 1994, Vol. IV: 146)

(Arguably, Rousseau's account of the social contract was a half-successful attempt to make civic corporatism the vehicle for individual liberty.)

Immanuel Kant and J.S. Mill develop the liberal tradition in different directions, but both share some of the fundamental tenets such as naturally given freedom and society as a human artifice. For Kant, the authority and normativity of laws by which both individuals and governments are bound is not based on an express or tacit contract but rather on a hypothetical agreement to which reasonable men would give their assent. Such assent rests on a nominalist abstraction from interpersonal, mutual agreement and also on a voluntarist grounding of reason in the 'good will' (Kant 1996). This, coupled with the categorical imperative and the separation of moral or political justification from any substantive conception of the good, leads Kant in the *Critique of Pure Reason* to posit a general foundation for all moral norms that is removed from actual personal character and the pursuit of virtuous behaviour (Kant 2000).

John Rawls, the most influential contemporary liberal philosopher, develops this theory by linking democratic debate to the inter-subjectivity of communication in the public sphere, which is the practical correlate of Kant's transcendental conditions for agreeing the norms of social rules. For Rawls we can make judgements about what is fair by way of the 'veil of ignorance' – a state in which we abstract from the specificities of people and contexts (Rawls 1971). But unlike Kant, Rawls eschews a metaphysical system in favour of a liberalism that is 'concrete, political and practicable' (Rawls 1985). Given 'the fact of pluralism', there can be no 'overlapping consensus' among individuals with incommensurate beliefs and values other than that of political liberalism (Rawls 1993). Such political – not metaphysical – liberalism is based on a theory of justice that corresponds to the quotidian experience extending beyond well-ordered liberal societies to all 'decent peoples' (Rawls 1999).

J.S. Mill's utilitarianism goes beyond Kant's procedural formalism by arguing that equality before the law is necessary but not sufficient in order to achieve genuine social justice. What is required is a thicker conception of political, economic and social equality that involves the redistribution of resources – not just the recognition of rights or the enforcement of the law (Robson 1963–69, vol. IV). Against his father James Mill and

Jeremy Bentham (who was a friend of the Mill family), J.S. Mill re-oriented utilitarianism from the idea of 'the greatest happiness of the greatest number' towards the pursuit of individual liberty. For only maximal individual autonomy leads to collective happiness. In *On Liberty*, he is adamant that public opinion and social conformism – not the law – are the biggest obstacles to individual liberty. As such, the emphasis shifts from utility to notions of higher and lower pleasure (Robson 1963–69, vol. XVIII).

However, the main focus of liberalism – whether the Lockean, Kantian-Rawlsian or Millian strands – is the equal concern and respect of all individuals *qua* individuals, a political philosophy with a universal outlook that purports to deliver progress. In short, the classical liberal tradition features many distinct strands that are nevertheless united by a number of shared 'family resemblances' that distinguish liberalism from other political theories and practices.

ALTERNATIVE GENEALOGIES OF LIBERALISM

In order to assess liberalism's claims, it is necessary to consider a number of alternative genealogies of the liberal tradition that are linked to different visions and narratives (e.g. Levine 1995). First of all, liberals have not simply failed to live up to their ideals, which is true for the advocates of all ideologies and political movements. In the case of liberalism, there is a more fundamental problem to do with the hagiography of its own tradition (Losurdo 2011). The internal contradictions of liberalism are not confined to a discrepancy between ideals and reality or theory and practice but extend to its core claims – defending freedom, autonomy and self-government while at the same time failing to universalise these principles. Prominent examples include the liberal John C. Calhoun, who combined the promotion of individual and state rights with an explicit apology of slavery, an argument that can be traced all the way back to Locke. Even when liberals began to champion the abolition of slavery, they proceeded to exclude former slaves in more subtle ways, e.g. as indentured labour. Likewise, a number of liberal economists – beginning with Adam Smith – sought to restrict the power of labour to form associations and self-organise by demonising trading and other guilds. Smith wrongly claimed that they would always and everywhere engage in price-fixing and other anti-competitive measures. Coupled with the Whig Protestant project of imperialism, the liberal pursuit of certain forms of exploitation at home and abroad led to the defence of pauperism in Britain and famine in Ireland.

A second genealogical corrective can be found in the work of contemporary philosophers and theologians. First of all, the liberal abstraction from any individuating characteristics or mutual relations draws on Duns Scotus' univocity of being whereby all things are 'bare beings' rather than things in relations to other things and their shared source in being itself. As such, liberalism rests on an ontology of univocally existing beings that are stripped of all metaphysical positioning to other beings and common being (Aquinas' Neo-Platonist *ens commune*). This ontology is the ultimate philosophical foundation for liberal individualism (de Muralt 2002; Pabst 2012). Second, linked to this is William of Ockham's twin claim that will is the ultimate principle of being (voluntarism) and that universals are merely mental concepts or names (nominalism). Ockham's nominalist and voluntarist theology is of special significance for the genesis of modern politics in general and liberalism in particular because it establishes the primacy of the individual over the universal and posits a radical separation between the infinite eternal and the finite temporal 'realm'. That, in turn, provides the foundation for state supremacy vis-à-vis the church and all other institutions within the temporal-spatial realm of the *saeculum* (Coleman 1999; Pabst 2010a).

Third, it was Marsilius of Padua who developed and radicalised the absolutism of Ockham's 'secular politics' (Coleman) by attacking the political role of the papacy. Like Scotus and Ockham, Marsilius separated the supernatural being and goodness of God from the natural univocal existence and falleness of nature and all beings therein, a dualism that is partly indebted to Aristotle's separation of the Prime Mover from the sublunary world and marks a break with the Christian Neo-Platonism vision of the supernatural Good in God that brings everything out of nothing into being (Pabst 2007; Pabst 2012). On these counts, Scotus, Ockham and Marsilius can be described as proto-liberal (de Muralt 2002). Fourth, liberalism inverts the primacy of the good over evil (e.g. evil defined by St. Augustine as *privatio boni*) and instead assumes the greater reality of evil vis-à-vis goodness. This inversion goes back to Ockham's denial of universal good-ness in particular beings and Machiavelli's consecration of evil as politically more real than the good. That, in turn, translates into a vision of the city that, contrary to Plato and Aristotle, is not governed by a hierarchy of goods and ends but instead by a compe-tition for survival and power. In Machiavelli's *The Prince* (esp. Skinner and Price 1990, chap. IX), it is the exercise of violence and the use of fear that regulate civic life, not the pursuit of peace or the practice of virtuous behaviour (Manent 1987).

Fifth, by equating the latter with the aristocracy and the former with the populace, Machiavelli is the first modern political thinker to champion a centrally ruled 'popular democracy' that privileges the 'honesty' of the many over above the 'virtue' of the 'few'. This inaugurates a dialectic between the executive power of the 'one' and the sovereign power of the 'many' that characterises the political thought of Hobbes, Locke and later liberal thinkers (Pabst 2010a). Atomistic liberalism, as 'organicist' liberals such as Constant and Tocqueville observed, subordinates the intellect to a tyranny of mere opinion, given that nature does not reflect universal truths. Therefore all opinions are in the end equally valid, in which case one opinion must somehow prevail – typically supported by a monopoly of power. That is why many liberals lay claim to exclusive universality and progress, dismissing all other ideologies and political movements as particularist and retrograde.

Sixth:

> under liberalism, since only what is generally represented is publicly valid, the spectacle of rep-resenting always dominates the supposedly represented people, ensuring that what they think is always already just what they are represented as thinking. Thus Tocqueville noted that in America, the freest society on earth, there is least of all public debate, and most of all tyranny of general mass opinion. (Milbank 2004: 222; the reference is to de Toqueville 1969: 232)

Paradoxically, liberal tyranny unfolds in the name of liberty. Absent any substan-tive ends or goods, the only standard that liberalism recognises is a regulated logic of competition. This is not unlike the ancient *agon*, though according to formalised procedures. Connected with this is the fact that liberals purport to provide diversity of choice, giving rise to a utopia that Michael Oakeshott poignantly called 'the blank sheet of infinite possibility' (Oakeshott 1991: 9; cf. Gray 2007). Yet at the same time, it is really an imposed, even coercive, consensus in order to ensure that no choice other than liberalism can ever be legitimately and effectively exercised. As such, the notion of illiberal liberalism is not wholly unwarranted. These alternative, non-liberal narratives and genealogies show just how historically contingent and theologically-philosophically peculiar the liberal tradition is – a stark contrast with the purported universal normativity of liberalism.

RECENT AND CURRENT DEBATES

Since Adam Smith, liberals have debated the extent and limits of the market in relation to the state. The last 250 years seem to have witnessed a cyclical evolution from Smith's 'progressive liberalism' via the economic liberalism of *laissez-faire* capitalism to the social liberalism of the welfare state and (back) to the free-market economics associated with neo-liberalism. However, such and similar narratives need to be corrected and supplemented in a number of ways. First of all, liberalism comes fully into being in the eighteenth century with the invention of the science of 'political economy' (Foucault 2004). Coupled with Machiavelli's science of 'politics' that elevates evil over goodness, political economy redefines the nature of power by suggesting that the sovereign can rule more by ruling less. Instead of trying to 'police' every aspect of their subjects' lives, governments can paradoxically exercise greater control by extending the operation of the market. The market balancing of supply and demand is seen as both natural and anarchic, constantly requiring state regulation and intervention – not least in relation to labour supply for the purposes of war. That is why Foucault described the liberal state-cum-market as 'biopolitical', applying political power to all aspects of human life (Pabst 2010a).

Second, Adam Smith argued for state intervention in the market and an important role for government in the economy. Moreover, he viewed the market as natural and morally neutral: production and trade based on self-interest are sundered from mutual sympathy and concern for the personal well-being of fellow 'economic actors' such as our 'butcher, brewer or baker'. As such, Smith's political economy breaks with the tradition of civil economy that fuses moral and civic virtues with self-interest and market activity (Bruni and Zamagni 2004). Crucially, Smith's dismissal of trading and other guilds represents a thinly veiled attack on the autonomy of civil society and all the intermediary institutions that mediate between the central state, the 'free' market and the individual.

Third, nineteenth-century *laissez-faire* capitalism combines the 'free' market with the strong state. For example, the creation of an unlimited market in human labour, land and money in Britain in the 1830s coincided with an unprecedented expansion of state power in terms of the collecting of statistics, of policing and of promotion of scientific education, civic sanitation and national transportation (Polanyi 1944). Likewise, post-1945 statist welfare that is run centrally based on uniform standards and targets is subservient to capitalism because it compensates for market failure but does not change the fundamental relation between capital owners and wage labourers. As such, much of economic and political liberalism combines market atomism with elements of state collectivism (Gray 1998; Pabst 2010b). This has reinforced the modern 'disembedding' of the economic sphere from the social order and a re-embedding of the social in the economic.

Luigi Sturzo said as much when he wrote that:

> [l]iberalism meant the liberation from such a past, but it tended to disorganize society, resolving it in the individual; so that afterwards to reorganize that society it had recourse theoretically to the system of an omnipotent state, and practically accentuated the defense of the bourgeoisie as the ruling class, identifying the economic interests of such a class with those of the nation as a whole: whence the strong and decisive socialistic reaction. (Sturzo 1947: 13)

Here one can suggest that both conservatism and socialism are trying to resolve the *aporia* of liberalism – which comes first, the representing state or the represented civil society? Since most conservative and socialist thinkers view state, market and civil society as disconnected from one other, their critique of liberalism remains wedded to an essentially liberal paradigm. Thus, conservative and socialist alternatives to liberalism are really an aporetic extension of liberalism, not a break with it. Unless an alternative political economy replaces the unholy alliance of social and economic liberalism, the liberal tradition will by default remain the hegemonic ideology and political philosophy of the modern age.

BIBLIOGRAPHY

Bruni, Luigino and Stefano Zamagni (2004), *Economia civile. Efficienza, equità, felicità pubblica*, Bologna: Il Mulino; trans. *Civil Economy: Efficiency, Equity, Public Happiness*, Bern: Peter Lang, 2007.

Burns, Edward M. (1948), 'The Liberalism of Machiavelli', *Antioch Review* 8(3): 21–30.

Coleman, Janet (1999), 'Ockham's right reason and the genesis of the political as "absolutist"', *History of Political Thought* XX: 35–64.

de Muralt, André (2002), *L'unité de la philosophie politique. De Scot, Occam et Suárez au libéralisme contemporain*, Paris: Vrin.

de Tocqueville, Alexis (1969 [1830–35]), *Democracy in America*, trans. G. Lawrence, New York: Doubleday.

Dumont, Louis (1983), *Essais sur l'individualisme. Une perspective anthropologique sur l'idéologie moderne*, Paris: Seuil.

Dupré, Louis (1993), *Passage to Modernity. An essay in the hermeneutics of nature and culture*, New Haven, CT: Yale University Press.

Dupré, Louis (2004), *The Enlightenment & the Intellectual Foundations of Modern Culture*, New Haven, CT: Yale University Press.

Foucault, Michel (2004), *Naissance de la biopolitique: Cours au Collège de France, 1978–1979*, Paris: Seuil, 2004; trans. *The birth of biopolitics: lectures at the Collège de France*, tr. Graham Burchell, New York: Palgrave, 2008.

Gray, John (1989), *Liberalism. Essays in Political Philosophy*, London: Routledge.

Gray, John (1995), *Enlightenment's Wake. Politics and Culture at the Close of the Modern Age*, London: Routledge.

Gray, John (1998), *False Dawn. The Delusions of Global Capitalism*, London: Granta.

Gray, John (2000), *Two Faces of Liberalism*, Cambridge: Polity Press.

Gray, John (2004), *Heresies: Against Progress and Other Illusions*, London: Granta.

Gray, John (2007), *Black Mass. Apocalyptic Religion and the Death of Utopia*, London: Allen Lane.

Huntington, Samuel P. (1991), *Democratization in the Late Twentieth Century*, Norman, OK: University of Oklahoma Press.

Kant, Immanuel (1996 [1785]), *Groundwork of the Metaphysics of Morals*, tr. and ed. Mary Gregor, Cambridge: Cambridge University Press.

Kant, Immanuel (2000 [1781]), *Critique of Pure Reason*. ed. P. Guyer and A.W. Wood, Cambridge: Cambridge University Press.

Kelly, Paul (2005), *Liberalism*, Cambridge: Polity Press.

Levine, Donald N. (1995), *Visions of the Sociological Tradition*, Chicago, IL: University of Chicago Press.

Locke, John (1970 [1689]), *Two Treatises of Government*, ed. Peter Laslett, Cambridge: Cambridge University Press.

Locke, John (2008 [1690]), *An Essay Concerning Human Understanding*, ed. P. H. Nidditch and intro. Pauline Phemister, Oxford: Oxford University Press.
Losurdo, Domenico (2011), *Liberalism: A Counter-History*, tr. Gregory Elliott, London: Verso.
Manent, Pierre (1987), *Histoire intellectuelle du libéralisme. Dix leçons*, Paris: Calmann-Lévy; trans. *An Intellectual History of Liberalism*, tr. Jerrold Seigel, Princeton: Princeton University Press, 1996.
Masters, Roger and Christopher Kelly (eds) (1990–1997), *Collected Writings of Rousseau*, Hanover: University Press of New England.
Mesnard, Pierre (1969), *L'essor de la philosophie politique au XVIᵉ siècle*, 3rd ed., Paris: Vrin.
Milbank, John (1990), *Theology and Social Theory. Beyond secular reason*, Oxford: Blackwell.
Milbank, John (2004), 'The Gift of Ruling: Secularization and Political Authority', *New Blackfriars* 85(996): 212–238.
Milbank, John (2006), 'Liberality versus Liberalism', *Telos* No. 134 (Spring): 6–21.
Oakeshott, Michael J. (1991), *Rationalism in Politics and Other Essays*, Indianapolis, IN: Liberty Fund.
Pabst, Adrian (2007), 'The Primacy of Relation over Substance and the Recovery of a Theological Metaphysics', *American Catholic Philosophical Quarterly* 81(4): 553–578.
Pabst, Adrian (2010a), 'Sovereignty in Question: Theology, Democracy and Capitalism', *Modern Theology* 26(4): 570–602.
Pabst, Adrian (2010b), 'The Crisis of Capitalist Democracy', *Telos* 152: 44–67.
Pabst, Adrian (2012), *Metaphysics: The Creation of Hierarchy*, Grand Rapids, MI: W.B. Eerdmans.
Paul, Ellen Frankel, Fred D. Miller Jr. and Jeffrey Paul (eds) (2007), *Liberalism: Old and New*, Cambridge: Cambridge University Press.
Polanyi, Karl (1944), *The Great Transformation. The Political and Economic Origins of Our Time*, Boston: Beacon Press.
Rawls, John (1971), *A Theory of Justice*, Cambridge, MA: Harvard University Press.
Rawls, John (1985), 'Justice as Fairness: Political not Metaphysical (1985)', in John Rawls, *Collected Papers*, ed. Samuel Freeman, Cambridge, MA: Harvard University Press, pp. 388–414.
Rawls, John (1993), *Political Liberalism*, New York: Columbia University Press.
Rawls, John (1993), *The Law of Peoples with 'The Idea of Public Reason Revisited'*, Cambridge, MA: Harvard University Press.
Robson, J.M. (ed.) (1963–69), *Collected Works of John Stuart Mill*, Toronto: University of Toronto Press.
Skinner, Quentin and Russell Price (eds) (1990), *The Prince*, Cambridge: Cambridge University Press.
Sturzo, Luigi (1947), 'The Philosophic Background of Christian Democracy', *The Review of Politics* 9(1): 3–15.

22. Microfinance
Antonio Andreoni[1]

INTRODUCTION

Many historical moments and contexts have witnessed the emergence of microfinance practices, that is, of specific financial techniques designed for providing the unbanked poor with access to credit, saving, insurance and other complementary non-financial services. Different institutional formats and innovative financial techniques have been locally experimented with to reduce information asymmetries, transaction costs and lack of collaterals, all factors which are extremely severe especially when we come to the poorest. In fact, being unbanked is only one of the many interdependent forms of exclusion the poor suffer. Financial, economic, and social exclusion interact in a circular and cumulative process which triggers multiple poverty traps (Myrdal, 1958).

Throughout the last 30 years, thanks to institutions like Grameen Bank, BRAC (Bangladesh Rural Advancement Committee) and ASA (Association for Social Advancement) in Bangladesh, Bank Rakyat in Indonesia, BancoSol in Bolivia, modern microfinance has become a global movement reaching around 190 million clients worldwide (Reed 2011). During the 1980s and 1990s, the increasing number of microclients and their high repayment performances convinced the majority that microfinance was a 'revolution' in the global fight to poverty as well as in development thinking (Yunus and Jolis 1999; Ledgerwood 1999). Under the flag of the win–win proposition (Morduch 2000), microfinance promised to reduce poverty in a sustainable way: a promise which attracted massive investment from the aid industry, multilateral organizations and private donors.

However, during the last decade, observers have been increasingly recognizing that the picture is much more complex and that not all promises can be delivered, for everyone and everywhere. In particular, recent impact studies have shown how after 30 years we still lack any solid evidence that microfinance is able to significantly improve the lives of the poorest. Moreover, the idea that microfinance can contribute to development dynamics, that is, processes of structural change and technological learning, has been critically questioned. Other overlapping lines of research have been enriching our understanding of microfinance. On the one hand, theoretical studies drawing from behavioural economics have clarified the difficulties encountered by the poor in the saving process and, secondly, explained the working of micro-credit techniques such as joint liability, weekly repayment schedules, and dynamic incentives. On the other hand, researchers and practitioners have allied in disentangling the multiple transformations occurring in the microfinance sector such as: a shift from mainly group lending methodologies to individual credit schemes; an increasing provision of multiple financial services by different actors operating at various levels; finally, a commercialization process and, as a result, an increasing demand for regulation, new forms of subsidies, higher operational efficiency and broader technological innovations (Armendáriz and Labie, 2011).

The following sections offer a roadmap around the extremely rich literature on microfinance. The first section proposes a historical-analytical journey around the different institutional formats and financial techniques developed in the microfinance sector. Two sections on the main debated issues and current trends in the microfinance sector follow. The last section concludes by positioning microfinance in the broader context of development, in particular questioning microfinance as an enabling institution for poverty reduction and broader development.

FINANCIAL EXCLUSION, ASYMMETRIC INFORMATION AND RELATIONAL CREDIT

Between 2 and 3 billion people are today unbanked or under-banked, while gaps in financial access across and within countries remain stark (Demirguc-Kunt et al, 2007). Why do traditional banks fail to provide the poorer with access to financial services? According to the principle of diminishing marginal returns to capital, money should naturally reach poor entrepreneurs as they have higher marginal returns to capital. In an attempt to explain this puzzle, scale economies, asymmetric information, transaction costs, lack of collaterals and different levels of risk have been brought into the picture. Firstly, by removing the assumption of concavity of production functions and by allowing for people being endowed with different levels of complementary inputs we find that, in fact, the poorer generally show lower marginal returns to capital. Moreover, being exposed, as the poorer are, to riskier environments negatively affects their returns. These two elements make the poorer less attractive for banks (Armendáriz and Morduch 2010).

Secondly, relationships among borrowers and lenders are characterized by asymmetric information. Specifically, lenders cannot distinguish between more or less risky borrowers and, thus, they cannot calibrate interest rates accordingly. As a result of the fact that safer clients will face relatively higher interest rates, only riskier borrowers will remain in the market, which would be a case of *adverse selection* (Stiglitz and Weiss 1981). Two other typical principal–agent problems result from the fact that the lender lacks information about the efforts clients are making for honouring their credits – i.e. *ex ante moral hazard* – as well as about clients' intentions to repay their loans or, eventually, voluntary default – i.e. *ex post moral hazard*. These problems are particularly severe for the poorer: on the one hand, because they cannot compensate asymmetric information by offering collaterals; on the other hand, because banks find it more difficult to collect information about the poorer – i.e. *high transaction costs* (Karlan and Morduch 2009).

Throughout centuries and across countries, there are many examples testifying that these problems can be mitigated by specific institutional formats and financial techniques tailored to the poor. Rotating savings and credit associations (ROSCAs) are the oldest and most universal informal mechanisms through which the poor accumulate small amounts in a structured way and have access to large lump sums (Rutherford 2000). The mechanism is very simple, although quite rigid. Individuals embedded in the same social context constitute groups and agree to meet regularly. At each meeting a common amount of money is collected and allocated to one member of the group. For each member, this 'saving through' mechanism introduces a 'commitment to save' in a regular way and it mitigates the 'household conflict motive' (Gugerty 2007; Anderson et al 2009; Collins et al 2009). Moreover, asymmetric information problems are minimized by peer selection and peer monitoring among group members (Banerjee and Newman 1994).

For group members being able to save different amounts in time and to access lump sums only when in need – e.g. emergencies, life-cycle events, micro investments – ROSCAs very often mutate in accumulating savings and credit associations (ASCAs). These more structured institutional formats permit their members to be in different moments in time borrowers and lenders, according to their needs and capacities. Based on the same principles of ASCAs, the first credit cooperatives appeared in Germany in the nineteenth century. They quickly evolved in different institutional formats such as credit unions, mutual loan guarantee societies and saving banks in all continental Europe, Japan, Canada, and America, in this last case with the *Morris Plan Banks* and the 'Franklin codicil' programme (Yenawine 2010). In Germany the Credit Cooperatives such as *Raiffeisen* were mostly concentrated in the rural areas, while the cooperatives such as *Schulze*, which in Italy came to be known as Popular Banks, operated in urban areas (Prinz 2002; Zamagni and Zamagni 2010; Guinnane 2011).

Long before them, during the fifteenth century, in Italy the *Montes Pietatis* introduced refined financial techniques and individual lending methodologies for micro economic actors and less advantaged people (Hicks 1969; Bruni and Zamagni 2007).

These institutional formats and 'relational credit' practices are very effective for many reasons (Andreoni and Pelligra 2009). Firstly the fact that financial interactions are embedded in a dense network of interpersonal relationships minimizes adverse selection, moral hazard and enforcement problems. As a result, even those more marginalized people in the community who have no collateral can access credit. Moreover, their small savings can be collected and channelled in more productive 'small tech/small capital' activities. Secondly, ROSCAs as well as more structured ASCAs maintain a high level of proximity between credits and savings, so the same person can be a borrower and a lender at different and, sometimes, the same moment in time (Collins et al 2009). Finally, financial activities are functionally linked to productive activities. In particular, financial products and services are designed according to the specific needs and features of the borrowers' micro and small enterprises. For example, cooperatives such as *Raiffeisen* developed specific financial products which better responded to the specific needs of agricultural activities, namely long-term loans; while popular banks working with artisans and merchants offered small and short-term loans because in these activities the financial turnover is faster and there is a continuous need of working capital.

THE MICROFINANCE FORMULA

The roots of the modern microfinance movement can be found in the late 1970s. Since then, many stories of microfinance pioneers like Muhammad Yunus[2] and his Grameen Bank have spread worldwide (Yunus and Jolis 1999; Rutherford 2009). During the 1980s, the microfinance formula was increasingly welcomed by the international development community mainly focused on poverty reduction and the implementation of bottom-up strategies (Sen 1999; Chang 2010a). By learning from the past, the first innovations adopted by modern microfinance institutions were group lending schemes based on various mechanisms of joint liability and short term repayment schedules.

Three main models can be identified. First, in the *classic Grameen* scheme, each borrower is part of a 'group' of five women which, in turn, is part of a 'centre'. Loans are assigned in a sequential and individual way to the members of the group, while various mechanisms of compulsory saving work at the centre level. Although there is no joint liability among group members, the sequential lending scheme entails that initially only some members in the group will access credits (typically two women), while the others (the remaining three) will do so provided that previous borrowers in the group are repaying their loans regularly. At each lending round, if one borrower runs into repayment difficulties the provision of subsequent loans to the members of the group is interrupted. The *solidarity group* methodology, initially introduced by ACCION and adopted by BRAC, is based on the idea that a group can provide a bank with a form of 'social collateral'. Each member of the group, from three to nine borrowers, is jointly responsible for the repayment of the group loan. The third scheme, the *village bank*, was initially adopted among the others by FINCA, Pro Muyer and SANASA. A village bank works very similarly to the accumulating savings and credit associations described above. However, here, the initial fund is provided by an external microfinance institution which leaves the village community as soon as the village bank repays the initial fund and is able to self sustain the credit and saving processes (Montgomery 1996).

The functioning of these institutional formats and financial techniques has captured the attention of many economic theorists (Stiglitz 1990; Besley and Coate 1995; Ghatak and Guinnane 1999; Armendáriz and Morduch 2010). The fundamental explanation these models provide is that lending techniques allow microfinance institutions to overcome information problems by creating a strong incentive for peer selection, peer monitoring and contracts enforcement. The fact that group members are embedded in a dense network of multiple interpersonal relationships allows them to collect information among each other in a daily base, at a low cost. Interestingly, it has been argued that not only does social capital foster repayment under group lending schemes but also, given certain circumstances, microfinance institutions can enable processes of social capital building (Dasgupta and Serageldin 2000; Andreoni and Pelligra 2009; Feigenberg et al 2010).

As for the working of group lending, case studies as well as an increasing number of laboratory and field experiments (Widick 1999; Ahlin and Townsend 2007; Karlan 2007; Cull et al. 2007) have been providing mixed results. The latter are biased by various methodological difficulties that researchers encounter in isolating causal links and disentangling complex interpersonal dynamics (see Armendáriz and Morduch 2010 for a review). Notwithstanding, these empirical works have suggested that group lending schemes can have unexpected outcomes. For example they can trigger free riding behaviours (Fischer 2008) as well as degeneracy in various forms of excessive and inefficient peer pressure (Montgomery 1996; Rai and Sjostrom 2004). Among the set of limits affecting group lending, the following have been stressed. First, microfinance institutions run the risk that group members collude and voluntarily default. Second, if group members are not physically proximate, information will be dispersed and, thus, the peer monitoring will be less effective and eventually too costly to be supported by group members (Andreoni et al 2013). Other costs and tensions arise from the fact that borrowers are required to attend very frequent meetings and, secondly, as a result of the rigidities that sequential lending or group loans imply (Madajewicz 2005). All these limits and hidden costs can transform a virtuous mechanism of mutual support into an extremely dangerous mechanism of marginalization of the less capable or poorest in the group.

In order to overcome some of these limits, group lending practices have been refined and made more flexible. Microfinance institutions worldwide have been increasingly relying on dynamic incentives, progressive lending, public and frequent repayments, symbolic collaterals, moral guarantors, cross-reporting and, in some cases, microcredit scoring techniques based on the information stored in credit bureaus (Armendáriz and Morduch 2010; Andreoni 2011). Some institutions like the Grameen Bank have integrated individual loan packages into their traditional group lending schemes – i.e. the *Grameen Generalized System* – while other microfinance institutions have started to adopt individual lending techniques. These latter overcome problems of asymmetric information, contract enforcement and lack of collaterals by making defaults very disadvantageous for individual clients. Specifically, dynamic incentives provide borrowers with the possibility of receiving a certain benefit in the future – e.g. larger loans, other complementary financial or non financial services – in exchange for a certain repayment behaviour in the present (Karlan and Morduch 2009).[3] The most recent statistics report that of the 890 microfinance programmes surveyed in the *MicroBanking Bulletin*, 277 adopt individual lending. A comparative analysis shows that microfinance institutions relying on individual lending schemes tend to serve better-off clients and fewer women, although they are more sustainable and charge lower interest rates and fees (Armendáriz and Morduch 2010, 138).

The adoption of individual lending techniques by a certain number of institutions has triggered a process of diversification in the microfinance sector, whose identity has long been connected to group lending. The plain movement 'from microcredit to microfinance' represents another focal transformation of the sector. If during the 1980s institutions like the Grameen Bank were mainly concerned about providing microcredit for the poorest, they have been increasingly realizing that also savings, insurances, money transfer services and other non financial services were equally important (Collins et al 2009). Few institutions like BRAC deliver an integrated package of complementary non financial services such as education, vocational training, business planning, marketing and access to markets.

In the last decade, some of these transformations have been increasingly generating tensions and contradictions. In particular, with the explosion and massive promotion of a commercial model, the microfinance movement has been experiencing a profound process of mission drift which has culminated in the renowned case of Compartamos in Mexico (Copestake 2007; Hulme and Arun, 2007; Armendáriz and Labie 2011). As Muhammad Yunus observed:

> Microcredit should be about helping the poor to get out of poverty by protecting them from the moneylenders, not creating new ones. [. . .] When socially responsible investors and the general public learn what is going on at Compartamos there will very likely be a backlash against microfinance. (See Daley-Harris 2007, 29–30).

MICROFINANCE IN CONTEXT: TRADE-OFFS, INNOVATIONS AND REGULATION

The commercial microfinance model was launched in the wake of a new vision clearly stated in the *Pink Book* (2004, 1), the CGAP guidelines for microfinance institutions: 'microfinance can pay for itself, and must do so if it is to reach very large numbers of people. Unless microfinance providers charge enough to cover their costs, they will always be limited by scarce and uncertain supply of subsidies from donors and governments'. Thus, the fundamental rationale behind the commercial model is that microfinance can be a *win–win* strategy for poverty reduction and that the achievement of a certain financial performance is a precondition for a sustainable expansion of the social performance (Rhyne 1998; Morduch 1999). To become financially self sustainable, not simply operationally self sufficient, microfinance institutions must also aim to reach a critical mass of clients (Balkenhol 2007). This would allow them to benefit from economies of scale and, thus, to reduce the high unit costs associated to microfinancial transactions, especially in the case of individual lending schemes (Hulme and Arun 2007).

However, the development process envisioned by the supporters of the commercial model implies a series of trade-offs between social and financial performances. For example, although increasing financial performance can align with expanding the breadth of the outreach, it is difficult to reconcile profitability with higher social impact and increasing depth of the outreach. This is the reason behind the shift we observe in the sector from 'banks for the poorest' to 'banks for the less poor among the poor' (Mosley and Hulme 1998). If decisions taken by microfinance institutions about their interest rates, the provision of complementary services and the targeting of clients are framed into a 'growth-first strategy', microfinance institutions will very likely experience a process of *mission drift*. As analytically demonstrated (Copestake 2007, 1725), this happens 'when their goals and preferences for the future subconsciously change in response to actual performance outcomes rather than being a fixed point against which performance can be guided and assessed'. Thus, year after year the obsessive attempt to pursue sustainability affects the set of strategic policies and attitudes adopted by microfinance institutions.

In particular, the possibility of using certain levers such as increasing interest rates does not stimulate the accomplishment of a more fundamental goal, namely increasing operational efficiency by innovating financial techniques and services tailored to the poor. As Balkenhol (2007) among others has claimed, being financially self sufficient does not imply that a microfinance institution is operating at the maximum possible level of operational efficiency. Financial sustainability may result from the lack of competition in the microfinance sector and, thus, the possibility of applying higher interest rates.[4] For this reason, instead of blindly pursuing financial sustainability at the cost of social performance, the central problem to tackle is 'how much innovation and increasing efficiency can modify the nature of the trade-offs and increase the range of possible options' (Simanowitz 2007, 63).

Innovations can operate at different levels, and involve multiple actors. Three lines of research have been investigated: technological and institutional innovations, smart subsidies and regulation. Firstly, documented case studies have shown how those microfinance institutions which are increasingly adopting new technologies such as smart phones, remote transaction systems, automated teller machines have been able to bring transaction costs down. Moreover, in countries like India and Brazil, the use of pre-existing postal networks for providing microfinance services has been demonstrated to be an effective solution for increasing efficiency, reducing operational costs and fostering public–private partnerships (Claessens 2006; Helms 2006).

Secondly, in spite of the strong emphasis for sustainability the sector is still heavily subsidized. This is a quite paradoxical situation as microfinance institutions emerged in the wake of disenchantment with state-led development banks (von Pischke et al 1984; Armendáriz and Morduch 2010). Recently, scholars have been arguing for new forms of subsidies – i.e. smart subsidies – which can strategically help the sector in developing best practices and overcoming some trade-offs (Morduch 2007). Moreover, it has been shown how in a different socio-economic context, such as areas with different population density, different levels of sustainability are reachable (Balkenhol 2007). Thus, public actors can selectively intervene by supporting efficient microfinance institutions which are generating positive externalities, although are not fully sustainable, by increasing the level of competition or reducing the oversupply of microfinance services if necessary, by providing a series of complementary measures which have been demonstrated to make credits for micro and small enterprises more effective (Andreoni et al 2013).

Finally, with the increasing shift from microcredit to microfinance, regulation is becoming extremely important, especially for deposit-taking institutions. Data from a recent empirical work (Cull et al 2009a) show that those microfinance institutions which are subjected to more supervisions face higher costs and tend to target less-cost segments of the population – i.e. low depth of the outreach. However, costs are counterbalanced by the fact that more regulated institutions can directly collect deposits and, thus, can access a cheaper and more stable source of capital.

QUO VADIS MICROFINANCE? THE PROMISE AND THE ILLUSION

Today's microfinance is at the same time the result and one of the main drivers of the New Millennium Development Goals Agenda. To what extents do microfinance institutions are delivering their promises? Is it illusionary to think that microfinance can actually drive economic development? Answers to these questions are still very mixed and not definitive. A recent paper by Roodman and Morduch (2009), attempts a critical assessment of the most-noted econometric studies on the impact of microcredit on households (Pitt and Khandker 1998; Khandker 2005). They found that after 30 years 'we have little solid evidence that [microfinance] improves the lives of clients in measurable ways', although at the same time on these bases it is not possible to 'conclude that microcredit harms' (Roodman and Morduch 2009:3–4). Several studies adopting randomized control trials techniques (RCTs) (Karlan and Zinman 2009; Banerjee et al 2009) have been also performed in different countries with the aim of overcoming various selection biases in the assessment of the microfinance impact.[5] The main concern in these studies is to capture how microfinance institutions are 'making a difference'. Problems however arise from the fact that microfinance institutions do not target and lend to the random poor. For example, lending in a particularly disadvantaged context where clients cannot benefit from complementary inputs can provide downward biased results (and vice versa). This is why control areas have to be factored in the analysis.

Other studies have focused on decrypting how the poor manage their money and, thus, how the provision of financial services can reduce their vulnerability and morbidity. Among them, a recent study (Collins et al 2009) presents systemic information on the financial practices of the poor, their 'portfolios'. By collecting more than 250 financial diaries in three selected contexts in Latin America, Africa and South Asia this impressive research provides important and unexpected insights. Firstly, living on a small, irregular and uncertain income makes the inter-temporal management of resources extremely important. Thus, having access to credit, savings and micro insurances can avoid vicious circles or allow the escape from poverty traps. Surprisingly, financial diaries also report that the poor 'can even borrow to have something to save' (Collins et al 2009, 23), and are sometimes willing to pay for saving in security or even paying a high interest rate on very short duration loans.

However, more critical contributions have shown how the same financial tools, especially when misused, can trigger over-indebtedness and various forms of unsustainable consumption (Dichter and Harper, 2007; Roy 2010; Karim 2011). From a more systemic perspective, finally, it has been observed that many informal microenterprises do not undergo processes of scaling up and technological learning. Thus, their impact on a country's development process is very modest, and sometimes even counterproductive (Bateman 2010; Chang 2010a).

Microfinance is today at a turning point. After a long time in which it was perceived as a panacea, recent critical voices are revitalizing the debate, suggesting new possible trajectories, envisioning new worlds of possibilities. In this view, the millenarian history of alternative financial practices seems to offer important insights for reinventing the future of microfinance.

NOTES

1. The author is grateful to Hassan Akram, Leonardo Becchetti, Ha-Joon Chang, Shailaja Fennell, Vittorio Pelligra, Roberto Scazzieri and Stefano Zamagni for comments and critics. The usual disclaimer applies.
2. Yunus' intellectual background is not well known. During his studies at Vanderbilt University he was greatly influenced by Nicholas Georgescu Roegen and exposed, among others, to his work on the economics of peasant communities (Georgescu Roegen 1976).
3. In this sense, they work as various conditional cash transfer programmes where the cash is transferred under the condition that certain goals such as school attendance are achieved (Hanlon et al 2010).
4. A global survey has recently reported that after adjusting for inflation, interest rates in the microfinance sector range from 13 to 25 per cent (Cull et al, 2009b). However, there are also alarming cases such as the one of Compartamos that applied interest rates above 100 per cent at its peak.
5. For an in depth review of randomized control trials and other impact studies based on non randomized approaches see Armendáriz and Morduch 2010, Chapter 9. For a critical perspective on the use of these methodologies see Woolcock 2009.

REFERENCES

Ahlin, Christian and Robert Townsend (2007), 'Using Repayment Data to Test Across Models of Joint Liability Lending', *Economic Journal*, 117 (517), F11–F51.

Anderson, Siwan, Jean-Marie Baland and Karl Ove Moene (2009), 'Enforcement in informal saving groups', *Journal of Development Economics*, 90 (1), 14–23.

Andreoni, Antonio (2011), 'The Technology of Microcredit. State of the art and prospects of development in Italy', *Bancaria*, 2, 56–70.

Andreoni, Antonio and Vittorio Pelligra (2009), *Microfinanza. Dare credito alle relazioni*, Bologna: Il Mulino.

Andreoni, Antonio, Marco Sassatelli and Giulia Vichi (2013), *Nuovi Bisogni Finanziari: La Risposta del Microcredito in Italia*, Bologna: Il Mulino.

Armendáriz, Beatriz and Jonathan Morduch (2010), *The Economics of Microfinance*, Cambridge, MA, USA and London, UK: MIT Press.

Armendáriz, Beatriz and Marc Labie (eds) (2011), *The Handbook of Microfinance*, London, UK: World Scientific Publishing.

Balkenhol, Bernard (ed.) (2007), *Microfinance and Public Policy. Outreach, Performance and Efficiency*, Basingstoke, UK and New York, USA: Palgrave Macmillan.

Banerjee, Abhijit and Andrew Newman (1994), 'Poverty, incentives, and development', *American Economic Review Papers and Proceedings*, 84 (2) (May), 211–215.

Banerjee, Abhijit, Esther Duflo, Rachel Glennerster and Cynthia Kinnan (2009), 'The miracle of microfinance? Evidence from a randomized evaluation', MIT Department of Economics and Abdul Latif Jameel Poverty Action Lab Working Paper.

Bateman, Milford (2010), *Why doesn't microfinance work? The destructive rise of local neoliberalism*, London, UK and New York, USA: Zed Books.

Besley, Timothy and Stephen Coate (1995), 'Group lending, repayment incentives and social collateral', *Journal of Development Economics*, 46 (1), 1–18.

Bruni, Luigino and Stefano Zamagni (2007), *Civil Economy. Efficiency, Equity and Public Happiness*, Bern: Peter Lang.

CGAP (2004), Building Inclusive Financial Systems. Donor Guidelines on Good Practice in Microfinance, Washington, D.C.: CGAP.

Chang, Ha-Joon (2010a), *23 Things They Don't Tell You About Capitalism*, London: Allen Lane.

Chang, Ha-Joon (2010b), '*Hamlet* without the Prince of Denmark: How development has disappeared from today's development discourse', in Sharukh Rafi Khan and Jens Christiansen (eds), *Towards New Developmentalism. Market as means rather than master*, Abingdon, Canada and New York, USA: Routledge.

Claessens, Stijn (2006), 'Access to Financial Services. A Review of the Issue and Public Policies Objectives', *World Bank Research Observer*, 21 (2), 207–240.

Collins Daryl, Jonathan Morduch, Stuart Rutherford and Orlanda Ruthven (2009), *Portfolios of the Poor: How the World's Poor Live on $2 a Day*, Princeton: Princeton University Press.

Copestake, James (2007), 'Mainstreaming Microfinance: Social Performance Management or Mission Drift?', *World Development*, 35 (10), 1721–1738.

Cull Robert, Asli Demirguc-Kunt and Jonathan Moduch (2007), 'Financial performance and outreach: a global analysis of leading microbanks', *Economic Journal*, 117 (517), F107–F133.

Cull Robert, Asli Demirguc-Kunt and Jonathan Moduch (2009a), 'Microfinance meets the market', *Journal of Economic Perspectives*, 23 (1), 167–192.

Cull Robert, Asli Demirguc-Kunt and Jonathan Moduch (2009b), 'Does regulatory supervision curtail microfinance profitability and outreach?', World Bank Policy Research Working Paper, Washington, D.C.: World Bank.

Cull Robert, Asli Demirguc-Kunt and Jonathan Moduch (2009c), 'Microfinance Trade-Offs: Regulation, Competition and Financing', in Armendáriz, Beatriz and Marc Labie (eds), *The Handbook of Microfinance*, London, UK: World Scientific Publishing, pp. 141–157.

Daley-Harris, Sam (2007), *State of the Microcredit Summit Campaign Report 2007*, Washington, DC, USA: Microcredit Summit Campaign.

Dasgupta, Partha and Ismail Serageldin (2000), *Social Capital: A multifaceted perspective*, Washington, DC, USA: World Bank.

Demirguc-Kunt, Asli, Thurston Beck and Patrick Honohan (2007), 'Finance for all? Policies and pitfalls in expanding access', World Bank Policy Research Report, Washington, D.C.: World Bank.

Dichter, Thomas and Malcolm Harper (eds) (2007), *What's Wrong with Microfinance?*, Bourton on Dunsmore, UK: Practical Action.

Feigenberg Benjamin, Erica M. Field and Rohini Pande (2010), 'Building Social Capital Through Microfinance', CID Working paper 209, October, Harvard University.

Fischer, Greg (2008), 'Contract structure, risk sharing and investment choice', Institute for Financial Management and Research Centre for Micro Finance, Working Paper 24.

Georgescu-Roegen, Nicholas (1976), *Energy and Economic Myths*, New York: Pergamon Press.

Ghatak, Maitreesh and Timothy Guinnane (1999), 'Group lending, local information and peer selection', *Journal of Development Economics*, 60 (1), (October), 195–228.

Gugerty, Mary Kay (2007), 'You can't save alone: Commitment in rotating savings and credit associations', *Economic Development and Cultural Change*, 55, 251–282.

Guinnane, Timothy (2011), 'The Early German Credit Cooperatives and Microfinance Organizations Today: Similarities and Differences', in Armendáriz, Beatriz and Marc Labie (eds), *The Handbook of Microfinance*, London, UK: World Scientific Publishing, pp. 59–75.

Hanlon Joseph, Armando Barrientos and David Hulme (2010), *Just Give Money to the Poor: The Development Revolution from the Global South*, Sterling, VA, USA: Kumarian Press.

Helms, Brian (2006), *Access for All. Building Inclusive Financial Systems*, Washington, D.C.: CGAP.

Hicks, John (1969), *A Theory of Economic History*, Oxford: Clarendon Press.

Hulme, David and Thankom Arun (eds) (2009), *Microfinance. A reader*, Abingdon, Canada and New York, USA: Routledge.

Karim, Lamia (2011), *Microfinance and its Discontents: Women in Debt in Bangladesh*, Minnesota, USA: University of Minnesota Press.

Karlan, Dean (2007), 'Social Connections and Group Banking', *Economic Journal*, 117 (517), F52–F84.

Karlan, Dean and Jonathan Morduch (2009), 'Access to Finance', in Dani Rodrik and Mark Rosenzweig (eds), *Handbook of Development Economics*, Amsterdam: Elsevier, pp. 4703–4784.

Karlan, Dean and Jonathan Zinman (2009), 'Expanding credit access: Using randomized supply decisions to estimate the impacts', *Review of Financial Studies*, 23 (1), 433–464.

Khandker, Shahidur (2005), 'Micro-finance and Poverty: Evidence Using Panel Data from Bangladesh', *World Bank Economic Review*, 19, 263–286.

Ledgerwood, Joanna (1999), *Microfinance Handbook. An Institutional and Financial Perspective*, Washington D.C.: World Bank.

Madajewicz, Malgosia (2005), 'Can microcredit reduce poverty? The effect of the loan contract on loan size', in Patrick Bolton and Howard Rosenthal (eds), *Credit Markets for the Poor*, New York: Russell Sage.

Montgomery, Richard (1996), 'Disciplining or protecting the poor? Avoiding the social costs of peer pressure in micro-credit schemes', *Journal of International Development*, 8 (2), (March-April), 289–305.

Morduch, Jonathan (1999), 'The microfinance promise', *Journal of Economic Literature*, 37 (December), 1569–1614.

Morduch, Jonathan (2000), 'The microfinance schism', *World Development*, 28 (4), 617–629.

Morduch, Jonathan (2007), 'Smart Subsidies', in Bernard Balkenhol (ed.), *Microfinance and Public Policy. Outreach, Performance and Efficiency*, Basingstoke, UK and New York, USA: Palgrave Macmillan.

Mosley, Paul and David Hulme (1998), 'Microenterprise Finance: Is there a Conflict between Growth and Poverty-alleviation', *World Development*, 26 (5), 783–790.

Myrdal, Gunnar (1958), *Economic Theory and Underdeveloped Regions*, London: Duckworth.

Pischke von, J.D., Dale Adams and Gordon Donald (eds) (1984), *Rural Financial Markets in Developing Countries: Their Use and Abuse*, Baltimore: World Bank and John Hopkins University.

Pitt, Mark and Shahidur Khandker (1998), 'The Impact of Group-Based Credit Programs on Poor Households in Bangladesh: Does the Gender of Participants Matter?', *The Journal of Political Economy*, 106 (5), 958–996.

Prinz, Michael (2002), 'German rural cooperatives, Friedrich-Wilhelm Raiffeisen and the organization of trust: 1850–1914', Typescript, Germany: Universitate Bielefeld.

Rai, Ashok and Tomas Sjostrom (2004), 'Is Grameen lending efficient? Repayment incentives and insurance in village economies', *Review of Economic Studies*, 71 (1), (January), 217–234.

Reed, Larry (2011), 'State of the Microcredit Summit Campaign Report 2011', Washington, DC, USA: Microcredit Summit Campaign.

Rhyne, Elisabeth (1998), 'The yin and yang of microfinance: Reaching the poor and sustainability', *The MicroBanking Bulletin*, 2, (July), 6–8.

Roodman, David and Jonathan Morduch (2009), 'The impact of Microcredit on the Poor in Bangladesh: Revisiting the Evidence', Centre for Global Development Working Paper 174.

Roy, Ananya (2010), *Poverty Capital: Microfinance and the Making of Development*, Abingdon, Canada and New York, USA: Routledge.

Rutherford, Stuart (2000), *The Poor and Their Money*, New Delhi: Oxford University Press.

Rutherford, Stuart (2009), *The Pledge. ASA, Peasant Politics, and Microfinance in the Development of Bangladesh*, USA: Oxford University Press.

Sen, Amartya (1999), *Development as Freedom*, Oxford: Oxford University Press.

Simanowitz, Anton (2007), 'Achieving Poverty Outreach, Impact and Sustainability: Managing Trade-offs in Microfinance', in Bernard Balkenhol (ed.), *Microfinance and Public Policy. Outreach, Performance and Efficiency*, Basingstoke, UK and New York, USA: Palgrave Macmillan.

Stiglitz Joseph E. and Andrew Weiss (1981), 'Credit markets with imperfect information', *American Economic Review*, 71, 393–410.

Stiglitz, Joseph (1990), 'Peer monitoring and credit markets', *World Bank Economic Review*, 4 (3), 351–366.

Widick, Richard (1999), 'Can Social Cohesion be Harnessed to Repair Market Failures? Evidence from Group Lending in Guatemala', *Economic Journal*, 109 (457), 463–475.

Woolcock, Michael (2009), 'Toward a Plurality of methods in project evaluation: a contextualized approach to understand impact trajectories and efficacy', *Journal of Development Effectiveness*, 1 (1), 1–14.

Yenawine, Bruce H. (2010), *Benjamin Franklin and the Invention of Microfinance*, London: Pickering and Chatto.

Yunus, Muhammad with Alain Jolis (1999), *Banker to the Poor: Micro-Lending and the Battle against World Poverty*, New York, USA: Public Affairs.

Yunus, Muhammad (2008), *Creating a World Without Poverty: Social Business and the Future of Capitalism*, New York, USA: Public Affairs.

Zamagni Stefano and Vera Zamagni (2010), *Cooperative Enterprise: Facing the Challenge of Globalization*, Cheltenham, UK and Northampton, USA: Edward Elgar.

23. Mutualism
Vera Negri Zamagni

MEANING OF THE WORD

Mutualism or mutuality has at least three meanings. At the highest level, it is a doctrine according to which individual and collective wellbeing can be obtained only by common action. It is the operational content of the third principle of modern societies – fraternity – which prevents the first principle – liberty – from undermining the second principle – equality. Mutuality can be seen as the sense of common citizenship that leads people to limit their liberty and accept a certain amount of basic equality conditions among citizens (Halsey, 1978). Mutualism provides the long run stability and cohesion of modern societies, helping to overcome the 'collective goods' problem specified by the rational choice theorists. The word seems to have being used in the 1820s more or less at the same time by Charles Fourier in France, John Gray in Britain and some of the American friendly societies and was often employed by the non-Marxist socialists like Proudhon and the American Clarence Lee Swartz, author of a famous book on mutualism (Swartz, 1927), in which he writes in favour of private property and against communism. For this reason, often mutualism was advocated by the so-called 'libertarian left', but not only by this school of thought, and does contain a more or less extended critique of capitalism as an economic system that does not embody either equality or fraternity, a critique that does not prevent mutualists when they form an enterprise from staying in the market and competing with capitalists.

At the middle level, mutuality refers to a way of solving the 'agency problem' faced by all complex organizations. Given that in any business there are multiple stakeholders, the basic choice faced by an enterprise concerns the selection of the stakeholder(s) which should have priority in the distribution of benefits. In capitalist enterprises, they are the investors-owners and the maximization of their dividends can run against the wellbeing of the labour force, the clients and the suppliers, and even against the long run sustainability of the enterprise. In mutual organizations, the members, be they customers or workers, are given priority as members, though they are also owners. So that 'mutuality may be redefined not as customer ownership but as stakeholder ownership by any of those who are beneficiaries *other than* a separate group of investors' (Birchall, 2001, p. 4). Ideally, mutual organizations should cut down their agency costs precisely because they do not have a separate group of investors with different aims, but in practice other problems arise: asymmetric information, pressure from capitalist competitors, discriminatory legislation, individualistic propensity of managers to improve their remuneration. Economic theory could well deal with these problems, but the predominance of the capitalist form of enterprise has dwarfed the cultivation of a line of research dealing with the problems of mutual organizations.

Finally, there is a third level of the meaning of the word, which has to do with real business: how mutuals were born, how they operate, where they are particularly strong, the conditions under which they can be competitive, their managerial cultures, the extent of their identity preservation, the participation of members and the like. In this chapter, I will mostly develop this third level, with special reference to the origin of mutuals and to their actual presence in today's world.

HISTORY

'Mutual' organizations or societies are to be found all over the world, in advanced as well as in developing countries, and have a long history dating back to ancient times. They arise as voluntary organizations of people, who decide to satisfy common needs with a direct production of services, practising self-help and avoiding intermediaries. This is done for several reasons: a) to shape services in direct contact with recipients (voice rule); b) to distribute the surplus benefits derived from production to the recipients of the services themselves rather than to owners of capital; c) to run the organization by democratic rules.

The precursors of the modern form of mutuals can be found in China, Egypt, Greece and in the Roman Empire, mostly among categories of workers in the construction trade, but also among artisans. In ancient Rome, for instance, the 'collegia opificum' were fundamentally trade associations, but also offered additional services, like the provision for a burial. It was however in the Middle Ages that mutual organizations became diffuse as charitable brotherhoods, or confraternities, connected with guilds. Beside worship practices, these societies provided a number of welfare interventions in favour of their poorest members in cases of illness, for widows and orphans and for old age. Guilds themselves were active in ensuring the welfare of their members and in practising the spirit of solidarity, friendship and peace, with attention to feasting, ceremonies and charitable interventions.

In some Italian cities there were additional specialized forms of mutual organizations, like the dowry fund of Bologna (created in 1583 and still in existence today), which functioned according to an insurance scheme: parents, relatives, friends of a newly born girl opened up a deposit with the fund in her name, into which they were regularly paying a contribution, capitalized by the fund, for the purpose of paying a dowry when the girl would marry. If this did not happen, the money deposited increased the capitalization of the fund to the benefit of the other depositors (Carboni, 2000). Occasionally, the deposit with the fund could also be opened in the name of a boy, with the aim of helping him to set up his own firm after getting a university degree. The Pawn banks (Monti di Pietà) must also be remembered (the first created in Perugia in 1462 by Franciscan monks), being a hybrid between a charitable and a self-help institution.

Later on in other places associations were formed according to the principle of mutual assistance, such as that for mill workers in 1663 in the Netherlands and the 'British Amicable Society for Perpetual Insurance Office' in 1706 in the UK. A special kind of mutual organization was the *tontine*, the creation of which is credited to the Italian financier Lorenzo De Tonti, who developed the first example in France in 1653. There are various versions of it, but basically a small group of people agrees to pool a fixed yearly contribution into the fund, which pays an annuity and grants loans to members on a rotation basis, ending the life of the fund when all have enjoyed the loan. Governments were sometimes using a version of the tontine for war purposes, when they could not use other means and today it is still widespread in community villages of Africa as ROSCA (Rotating Savings and Credit Association).

But the full fledged period for mutual organizations started with the birth of friendly societies (also called friendlies, mutual aid societies or benevolent societies), which developed when guilds and brotherhoods started to decline at the end of the 18th century, both in Great Britain and in the Continent of Europe (some decades later), but also in the USA, where the development of these associations was especially dynamic, as Alexis De Tocqueville noted in his famous book written in the 1830s, *Democracy in America* (Beito, 1997). The first friendly societies took the form of small local clubs of workers with a common profession, who paid a regular fee in exchange for support if they became ill or disabled and for their old age, and also in exchange for the services of sociability and conviviality supplied by their club (Clark, 2002). Most of these associations paid for doctors' services, burial expenses, annuities to widows and educational expenses for orphans. Sometimes they also built old-age homes or offered unemployment benefits and supported maternity leave. The way these organizations kept their budgets in order was not always solid, so governments had to intervene with appropriate legislation up until they took upon themselves most of the welfare roles of the friendly societies (Cross, 1974). Apart from the friendly societies, mutuals devoted to protecting against fire, hail and cattle mortality were born, especially in the countryside.

We have however to stress that friendly societies were not the only form of mutuals born out of the very deep mutualistic root of European civilization. In the 19th century three different but related groups of associations were formed, having mutuality as a base: 1) one group consisted of *cooperative enterprises*, often created by members of friendly societies, competing with capitalist corporations in various sectors of the economy different from insurance (see Chapter 8 in this handbook); 2) a second group was made up of *fraternities* such as the Freemasons, the Lions, the Rotary and tens of others devoted to common cultural, religious, sporting and charitable activities, in addition to denominated *charities* in the Anglo-Saxon world; 3) the third group is the one which maintained the original welfaristic approach, developing into proper *mutual insurance companies* (dealing with property and life risks) and *mutual benefit societies* (protecting their members against the social risks), plus in a few places into financial institutions called *building societies*, devoted to financing the purchase of a house (Harris and Bridgen, 2007).

This last type of mutual organization refers to those still called mutuals today; they share with all the 'social' enterprises the aim of meeting the needs of their members in a context of solidarity and democratic governance. But, unlike cooperatives, whose capital is represented by shares, the funds of mutuals are owned and managed jointly and indivisibly. To join a mutual, the future member must pay for the services provided by the mutual, rather than buy a share in the capital. The new member is not, therefore, subject to initial membership costs. On the other hand, members do not have any property rights over the capital. Consequently, departure from the mutual has no effect on the capital, which will continue to serve the remaining members.

DEVELOPMENTS OF MUTUALS AFTER THE WELFARE STATE AND CURRENT SITUATION

In the 20th century mutuals had to cope with a number of serious challenges. Mutual insurance societies had to withstand the tough competition of for profit companies active in the same fields. Their advantage relies precisely on the solidaristic principle, which allows them to have a better quality to price ratio than their competitors, because they care for the services to their members rather than for the maximization of profits for their shareholders. They have a high financial solidity, because their investments are less risky and more ethical and also because they are not subject to take-over bids. As mutuals, they are not quoted in the stock exchange and so they do not suffer from the great volatility of that market. However, over time hybrids have developed, namely insurance businesses incorporated as joint stock companies, but owned by cooperatives often active in different fields. Hybrids can be effective when there is a common value system between co-ops and their controlled joint stock companies, something that does not always happen. Their financial solidity allows them to pursue long term investment aims. The disadvantage of mutuals generally stems from the limited access to external capitals, which is exactly the reason why a number of cooperatives decided to make their insurance company as a joint stock company. Also, other problems arise from their size – either too small to be economically efficient or too large to keep effective control in the hands of members – and from the generalization of individualism in our advanced societies that leads to an increasing lack of understanding both of the advantages of mutual societies and of the correct way to manage them.

The presence of mutual insurance societies in Europe is substantial: in 2008 more than two thirds of all insurers in Europe belong to the mutual sector, reaching 25 percent of all the insurance premiums paid (mutual insurance companies are smaller on average than the for profit ones). They have an association – AMICE (Association of Mutual Insurers and Insurance Cooperatives in Europe) – with more than 100 direct members. But in some countries their presence is much more substantial: in France and Germany mutuals account for around 40 per cent of the market. The market share at the world level is only slightly below the European share, 24 per cent, with Japan at 38 per cent, USA and Canada at 30 per cent. There is also a world organization – ICMIF (International Cooperative and Mutual Insurance Federation) – which was initially established by ICA (International Cooperative Alliance) in 1922, but became independent in 1972. With only five members at the beginning, ICMIF in 2010 reached 210, one third in Europe, one third in the Americas and one third in the rest of the world. These 210 members represent directly 600 organizations, and indirectly 2,700 (through their national mutual trade organizations), including joint stock companies controlled by cooperatives or mutuals.

A special reference must be made to the building societies, not least because they are a demonstration of the problems arising in the management of mutuals in the present world. The origin of building societies dates back to late 18th-century Birmingham, a city that was rapidly growing and hosted clubs and societies for cooperation. The first building society was founded by Richard Ketley in 1775 with the payment of a monthly subscription from members into a fund used to finance the building of new popular houses for members. Such societies rapidly multiplied, but each one dissolved with the actual delivery of the house. It was in the 1840s that permanent building societies were formed, on a rolling basis. Soon there were hundreds of building societies in Britain, which were legislated by government in a successive series of Acts, giving rise to amalgamation and strengthening of some of these mutuals (Cleary, 1976). Building societies developed also in Australia, New Zealand and Ireland on the British model. In the USA the savings and loans associations played a similar role, while in Austria and Germany some banks became specialists in mortgages and loans to the construction industry, but not all of them were mutuals (often they were savings banks). In the 1980s with the liberalization of financial markets, many of these building societies became de-specialized banks and the tendency to de-mutualize them appeared, led by managers who saw this working in their interest (increased salaries). The first to de-mutualize in Britain was Abbey National in 1989, which was soon bought by Banco Santander, together with other de-mutualized building societies. In 1997 Northern Rock de-mutualized, adopting after that a highly speculative stance, which brought it to bankruptcy in 2008; it was bailed out by the British government, which came to control it and in 2011 decided to privatize it. Less than 50 mutual building societies are left in Britain today with 18 million members, while in Ireland they have practically disappeared.

As for the mutual benefit societies, they had to measure themselves with the State monopoly of welfare in many European countries, but they reacted creatively. In some countries (Germany, Belgium, the Netherlands, Czech Republic, Slovakia) mutuals run the compulsory health insurance and therefore cover from 80 to 100 per cent of the population; in others (notably France), they provide complementary insurance against sickness or old age; in others still (UK and the Nordic countries) they represent an alternative to the National Health System for those who want quicker services or higher pensions. All in all, 230 million people are in Europe covered by a mutual benefit society as against 69 million in Asia, while elsewhere the presence of these societies is marginal. Their association – AIM (Association Internationale de la Mutualité) – was set up in 1950 in Geneva and moved to Brussels in 1997; members of AIM are the national federations of mutual benefit societies. The estimate of employment in Europe in this sector exceeds 350,000 (Chaves and Monzón Campos, 2007). It must be underlined that mutual benefit societies rely on principles which are very different from their commercial insurance competitors: fees are paid according to the member's income and not according to age or risk. Bad risks are not rejected, and therefore there is a cross-subsidization between bad and good risks and between rich and poor, as there is in publicly funded schemes, but it is present to a much lesser degree in for profit companies.

In spite of this significant presence of mutuals in Europe, the effort to get a European statute for mutual societies has not achieved any result at the time of writing (April 2011). The European Commission even withdrew the proposal from its agenda in 2006. In 2008 another proposal was put forward jointly by AIM and AMICE, but it is still pending. What is underlined by the associations in their analysis of the situation is the discrimination they suffer as a result of not having a statute suited to their needs, which basically are an absence of share capital, involvement of members in the governance of the company, collective solidarity, and cross-border operations. This is more necessary in the presence of the introduction of a new European-based solvency system (Solvency II), which increases the pressure for regrouping of mutuals. In absence of such a legal instrument, de-mutualization would become a necessity at the very time when more and more governments delegate tasks of social protection to the private sector. Mutuals, as private companies which do not seek profit as their main aim and 'can offer a useful tool in executing public tasks within a private framework, without losing on accessibility, solidarity and social responsibility', as the 2008 document recites, but they must be permitted to work properly, if they are to successfully face the new challenges.

As a final comment, it must be underlined that mutuals are better suited to face the demand of personal services in post-industrial societies, where standardization is no longer the rule and new social needs are arising. Their link with civil society, their democratic management that allows the emergence of innovative demands and solutions and the correct treatment of asymmetric information typical of the sector, and the inbuilt social responsibility of the enterprise, which gives mutuals a better financial solidity and a more ethical propensity to investment, are all elements that should guarantee the continuous presence of this time-honoured type of economic activity also in the future.

REFERENCES

Beito, D.T. (1997), 'This Enormous Army: The Mutual Aid Tradition of American Fraternal Societies before the Twentieth Century', *Social Philosophy and Policy*, 14: 20–38.
Birchall, J. (ed.) (2001), *The New Mutualism in Public Policy*, London: Routledge.
Carboni, M. (2000), 'Un approccio previdenziale al problema dotale nella Bologna del tardo Cinquecento', in Zamagni V. (ed.), *Povertà e innovazioni istituzionali in Italia dal medioevo ad oggi*, Bologna: Il Mulino: 247–58.
Chaves, R. and Monzón Campos, J.L. (2007), *The Social Economy in the European Union*, CIRIEC Report to the European Economic and Social Committee, no. CESE/COMM/05/2005.
Clark, P. (2002), *British Clubs and Societies 1580–1800: the Origins of an Associational World*, Oxford: Oxford University Press.
Cleary, E.J. (1976), *The Building Society Movement*, London: Elek Books.
Cross, M. (ed.) (1974), *The Workingman in the 19th Century*, Toronto: Oxford University Press.
Halsey, A. (1978), *Change in British Society*, Oxford: Oxford University Press.
Harris, B. and Bridgen, P. (eds) (2007), *Charity and Mutual Aid in Europe and North America since 1800*, New York: Routledge.
Swartz, C.L. (1927), *What is Mutualism?*, New York: Vanguard Press.

24. Pecuniary externalities and fairness
Albino Barrera

This chapter briefly describes the nature of pecuniary externalities, examines the case for mitigating them, and then evaluates the practical requirements and difficulties of dealing effectively with this economic phenomenon.

THE NATURE OF PECUNIARY EXTERNALITIES

Externalities are unintended effects that impact bystanders. In economic terms, externalities arise when the market price does not include the full cost of the ensuing consequences of an economic choice. There are two kinds of externalities that are relevant for our study: technical and pecuniary externalities.

Pollution is the most famous example of a technical externality. In an unregulated market, factories have no incentive to employ expensive cleaner technologies and processes because they can operate at a much cheaper cost and maximize their profits by dumping their waste into the air or the water for free. Their cost of production (and therefore their selling price) does not include the cost of cleaning up the air or the water. In effect, these polluting factories pass on part of their production cost to the people downwind or downstream who will incur higher health or clean-up costs, or both. There is a disparity between the private cost of these factories and the true social cost incurred by the entire community, and as a result, there will be an overproduction of the factories' goods. A remedy for this anomaly is for the community to tax the offending firms. In effect, they are forced to internalize the true cost of their production.

Pollution is an instance of what is called a technical externality. The unintended consequences arise because of missing protocols or mechanisms that equalize the private and social cost or benefit of economic activities. Technical externalities are considered a market failure because, left unattended, they hinder the community from reaching its optimum economic efficiency. Consequently, governments actively rectify such externalities, as in the case of carbon taxes and caps on greenhouse gas emissions.

In contrast to technical externalities, very little attention is devoted to pecuniary externalities, much less to its deleterious effects. The market is much touted for its ability to allocate scarce resources to their most valued uses, and in the most cost-efficient manner at that. The market supplies the right goods and services of the right kind and quality, in the right quantity, at the right time, in the right place, at the right price, and with the right production methods and inputs. What makes this even more impressive is that the market accomplishes all this by seamlessly orchestrating the activities, transactions, and decisions of innumerable individuals, households, businesses, non-profit organizations, and governments. In the end, consumers get the goods and services they want, while societal resources are put to their most valued uses. This, in a nutshell, is economic efficiency, also known as allocative efficiency.

The key to the market's remarkable allocative ability is its price system. Market price conveys an enormous amount of information to widely dispersed economic agents simultaneously. Market participants watch price movements and adjust their economic behavior and decisions accordingly. For example, a rise in oil prices is a signal for drivers to curtail their driving or to switch to cars with better gas mileage. Households will improve the heat and cooling insulation of their homes. Businesses will seek engineering efficiencies that minimize their energy cost. Oil prospectors will redouble their exploration efforts or develop new technologies that can recover more oil from the ground. For green-energy proponents, it means that more expensive alternative energy sources will become commercially viable. In other words, market price has an allocative dimension because it provides the necessary incentives for economic agents to use their resources in the most efficient manner. And the market does this ceaselessly because market prices keep changing. As empirical proof, note the collapse of the centralized Soviet economies toward the end of the last century due to their lack of a fully functioning price system.

Unfortunately, there is a mirror image to the allocative function of market price – it also distributes incomes and wealth across the economy. After all, it is market price that sets the exchange value of goods, services, and resources. It is price that determines the market value of skills, jobs, land, houses, savings, etc., indeed, of all assets and liabilities. It is also price that determines people's purchasing power in the marketplace. In other words, market price has a distributive dimension to it.

Market price changes are a de facto redistribution of burdens and benefits across the community. Thus, cheaper goods and services from international trade are a boon and an increase in the real incomes of consumers, but they come at the expense of manufacturing or service jobs in the developed countries that are outsourced to cheaper overseas sites. The entry of Wal-Mart or mega-stores in a particular area brings a much wider selection of goods to local consumers, and at a much lower price, but it also drives out of business small neighborhood mom-and-pop stores. An aging population drives up the price for healthcare and pharmaceuticals, even for the younger and healthier members of the community. The emergence of the Chinese and Indian middle class in the wake of globalization means higher oil and commodity prices for the US and the EU, and more expensive food for developing countries. These are all examples of unintended consequences of shifting market prices – pecuniary externalities. And since price changes are by their nature redistributions of burdens and benefits across market participants, there will always be relative winners and losers, despite the neo-classical claim that trade is not a zero-sum phenomenon. Even the Stolper-Samuelson theorem of the Hecksher Ohlin model of international trade shows that there will be changes in the relative position of all participants in a market exchange.

Theorists and policymakers are keen on rectifying technical externalities such as pollution, but they devote less attention or energy to addressing pecuniary externalities. We can only surmise that this difference in interest may be due to these externalities' differential impact on economic efficiency. On the one hand, technical externalities are an impediment to allocative efficiency because they distort the true social price and thereby prevent society from putting its resources to their most valued uses. Consequently, they must be corrected for the sake of economic efficiency (besides the intrinsic value of a pristine ecology in the case of pollution). On the other hand, pecuniary externalities are the very means by which the market achieves allocative efficiency. After all, it is price changes that compel market participants to constantly adjust their economic decisions and behavior in line with what society requires. Thus, from a strictly economic viewpoint, there is less reason and urgency to ameliorate pecuniary externalities. That would be akin to throwing sand in the gearbox, thereby slowing down, or worse, even impairing market operations.

THE CASE FOR RECTIFYING DELETERIOUS PECUNIARY EXTERNALITIES

Is there a moral or economic case that can be made for mitigating the more severe instances of pecuniary externalities? To begin with, let us examine two arguments against such action. First is the legal axiom 'to the consenting, no injury is done.' Economic agents are assumed to be rational and act in their own best interest. They will not pursue and consummate economic transactions that are not in their own best interest. Consequently, some would argue that there are no residual obligations, economic or moral, once the terms of contracts are fulfilled. Pecuniary externalities are simply a fact of economic life that comes with participating in the marketplace. People are well aware of this risk, and yet still choose to participate in market exchange. Hence, some argue that given the voluntary and fully informed nature of market participation, there are no obligations to relieve dire instances of pecuniary externalities.

A second argument is that of contributory negligence. Since people know that pecuniary externalities are an unavoidable feature of market operations, they should have prepared themselves for it. For example, manufacturing workers should have constantly upgraded their skill set. Businesses should have continuously innovated and diversified into new ventures as their comparative advantage changed. Households should have built up their financial and human resources to ride out market volatility. Retirees should have saved assiduously during their peak earning years. In other words, market participants could have taken measures to insure themselves against the chance and contingencies of the marketplace. Thus, some would argue that the failure to prepare for these adverse pecuniary externalities constitutes contributory negligence on the part of market participants who suddenly find themselves harmed or disadvantaged in the wake of normal market operations.

There are strong counter-arguments that can be made against these objections. First, market participation is not truly voluntary because few people can survive on their own as a Robinson Crusoe. Specialization and division of labor are not modern phenomena. They applied just as well in an ancient, nomadic economy. Thus, chores were divided among family members or tribes as a matter of mutual survival. With division of labor comes the need to exchange. Thus, market exchange is not merely an option for the vast majority of people. It is a necessity. Consequently, we cannot use the axiom 'to the consenting, no injury is done.'

Second, while it is true that market participants could have insured themselves against grievous pecuniary externalities, such insurance is well beyond the finances or the capabilities of most people. Moreover, pecuniary externalities come in many forms, such as the loss of a job, higher prices, lower earnings, obsolete or redundant skills, geographic dislocation, and many others. Only the well-off have the necessary resources to prepare for many of these simultaneously. To be sure, it is contingent on individuals to prepare themselves for such market developments, but as we will see in the next section, the key question is knowing what is reasonable to expect from ordinary market participants.

Third, there is a moral duty to prevent harm. One cannot stand idly on the sidelines when one possesses the resources and the ability to assist those who are in distress. This obligation is part of natural law and what it is to be a human person. This duty is not dependent on a social contract or on belief in God. Human decency alone requires it.

Fourth, mitigating pernicious pecuniary externalities is a matter of corrective justice. We can arguably claim that beneficiaries in the marketplace do not pay the full price for their gains. For example, consumers who reap the windfall of cheaper goods from abroad do not share in the cost of having to move displaced manufacturing workers to another industry. The price they pay for their cheaper imports does not include the cost of retraining laid-off domestic workers. Thus, consumers' private cost (the market price of imports) does not reflect the social cost of international trade. In other words, the benefits consumers reap from international trade are underpriced. The benefits enjoyed are widespread and public (the consumers), but the costs are borne privately (by displaced workers). This is a case of benefitting at the expense of others.

Fifth, given the difficulty of correctly anticipating and preparing for all possible ruinous pecuniary externalities, it would seem that the logical and fair approach is to pool risks as a community. Such risk-sharing has been an effective response to uncertainty, as in the case of health, auto, and home insurance. It is akin to Rawls' 'veil of ignorance.' Since people do not know what lies ahead, they would be more inclined to agree to community rules that provide aid to the distressed and the disadvantaged, in case they find themselves in such a position.

Finally, in a knowledge economy in which human capital is the source of value creation, it is in the interest of all to ensure that no one is marginalized from participating meaningfully in the economy. By mitigating the most burdensome pecuniary externalities, communities can ensure that people are able to recover from distress and keep up with a fast evolving knowledge-based economy. In this way, the community preserves its most valuable 'resource' – its human capital. Consequently, long-term economic efficiency is a function of equity in the short term. The knowledge economy has brought about a convergence in the requirements of both the allocative and distributive dimensions of market prices. It is in the community's own economic self-interest to rectify the market's most deleterious unintended consequences.

THE PRACTICAL DIFFICULTIES OF ATTENDING TO SEVERE PECUNIARY EXTERNALITIES

There are strong moral and economic arguments that justify extra-market intervention in alleviating some of the more harmful unintended consequences of market operations. Not surprisingly, even the most capitalist economies, such as the United States, have social safety nets that address the most injurious pecuniary externalities. For example, note its unemployment insurance and trade adjustment assistance programs. Note the manifold programs that aid the elderly with rising drug costs and the poor with their heating oil, rent, and medical care. Even pharmaceutical firms provide access to lifesaving medicines to those who are unable to pay the full cost of these drugs. Indeed, there are strong economic and moral reasons to attend to the more problematic pecuniary externalities.

Unfortunately, implementing this in practice is extremely difficult. Consider the following examples. First, we have to identify the threshold of what constitutes a serious setback as to warrant assistance. We cannot blithely intervene in the marketplace because it distorts prices, imposes unnecessary costs, and often inflicts even more harm and onerous unintended consequences. The key is to identify those specific instances of acute pecuniary externalities that merit assistance. Thus, the first problem is defining what constitutes severe distress. Economic rights may be helpful by providing a concrete way of identifying and measuring this all-important threshold.

Second, assuming we have a political consensus on the threshold that triggers assistance, we have to define the scope and duration of such remedial action. What should we put in the basket of goods or services that will be provided to assist those disadvantaged by normal market operations? For how long do we provide such assistance? To get an idea of the difficulty of getting public consensus on these questions, recall the bitter recriminations surrounding the US government bailout of General Motors, American International Group (AIG), Fannie Mae, Freddie Mac, and the banking industry during the 2008 sub-prime fiasco.

Third, related to the second question is the problem of moral hazard. There is a real danger of breeding dependency. There is a point to the earlier argument made that market participants ought to take the necessary precautions against well-known market volatility and disequilibria. While it is true that we cannot prepare fully for all possible market contingencies, nonetheless, there are certain minimum steps that market participants can take, such as, continuing innovation, ongoing education and skill development, and prudential saving for a rainy day. In other words, harmful pecuniary externalities are not purely exogenous events. There is an endogenous component to them because economic agents are able to mitigate, on their own, some of the unintended dire consequences of market operations.

The difficulty with this is that the ability to insure against such foreseen pecuniary externalities varies across individuals depending on their sociohistorical location and personal circumstances. This poses at least two problems for policymakers: how to design assistance programs that are able to discriminate recipients' efforts at helping themselves, and how to differentiate the endogenous from the exogenous dimensions of a detrimental pecuniary externality, ex post.

Fourth, who gets to pay the cost of mitigating troublesome pecuniary externalities? Who are properly the addressees of this moral obligation? Beneficiaries of pecuniary externalities immediately come to mind. After all, they reaped the benefits. Unfortunately, this is not a straightforward issue. Making these beneficiaries pay for the cost of their windfall gains would be defensible if the pecuniary gains were, in fact, completely exogenous, a genuine windfall. However, in reality, there is also an endogenous element to this. Beneficiaries gain partly because of their past investments, decisions, and discipline. Sociohistorical location is not purely accidental. Many create opportunities for themselves and profit handsomely when conditions fall into place. Thus, this creates both practical and conceptual problems for policymakers. If designed or implemented poorly, income or wealth transfers through taxes and subsidies can be unjust and destroy altogether the community's creative productive capacity.

This is just a sampling of some of the practical and conceptual difficulties of attending to the most harmful after-effects of market operations. Extra-market interventions are difficult to design because they have to achieve a delicate balance. Set up the wrong incentives by being overly paternalistic, and people will free-ride, thereby destroying private initiative. Be timid in providing assistance, and large segments of the population will be effectively marginalized, thereby setting the economy on a much lower growth trajectory. At the end of the day, the question is not about whether we should mitigate adverse pecuniary externalities. Even the most capitalist nations see an economic and moral need to do so. Rather, the questions are in which instances to provide assistance, what to provide, by how much, for how long, and how to provide and pay for such assistance. These questions are prudential in nature because they vary according to the context of the time and place and the available resources. There is constant need for adjustment and political conversation. Note, for example, the EU's hard look at its generous welfare programs in the wake of global competition and its burgeoning fiscal deficits.

Many of these policy questions are empirical in nature. Nonetheless, in the final analysis, the most critical determinant is the evaluator's worldview. Many will subscribe to John Rawls' lexical rule of ensuring that inequalities are permitted only to the extent that the most disadvantaged benefit. Others will embrace Ronald Dworkin's egalitarianism or A.K. Sen's call for securing people's 'functionings and capabilities.' Some will adopt Henry Shue's 'moral floor' beneath which no one will be allowed to sink. Still others will prefer Milton Friedman's and Robert Nozick's less intrusive standards that call for more expansive individual economic freedoms. What constitutes fairness in dealing with grievous pecuniary externalities though depends on the decision-makers' philosophical commitments.

LOOKING AHEAD

The need to attend to the market's hurtful unintended consequences will only get more urgent in light of global economic integration. Globalization has accelerated economic life and has increasingly turned the world into a single workshop. Ever more of inter-personal and inter-national relations are mediated through the marketplace. This means that just as there will be impressive beneficial pecuniary externalities (e.g., the emergence of Chinese, Indian, and Brazilian middle classes), there will also be pernicious pecuniary externalities (e.g., industrial decline, decay, and unemployment in the developed countries). These disequilibria will come with ever greater speed, potency, and frequency. The dotcom and housing bubbles of the 2000s, the 2008 Great Recession, and the 2009 euro crisis demonstrate just how interdependent we have all become. Events from halfway around the globe can have dire local consequences.

As a first step to addressing the market's ruinous unintended consequences, peoples and nations have to talk about their understanding of (1) their obligations for their own integral human development and (2) their duty for the well-being of their neighbors who may be in distress.

BIBLIOGRAPHY

Barrera, Albino (2005). *Economic Compulsion and Christian Ethics*. Cambridge University Press.

Barrera, Albino (2011). *Market Complicity and Christian Ethics*. Cambridge University Press.

Feinberg, Joel (1970). 'Collective Responsibility' in *Doing and Deserving: Essays in the Theory of Responsibility*. Princeton: Princeton University Press.

Feinberg, Joel (1984). *Harm to Others: The Moral Limits of the Criminal Law*. New York and Oxford: Oxford University Press.

Hausman, Daniel (1992). 'When Jack and Jill Make a Deal,' in *Economic Rights*. Edited by Ellen Frankel Paul, Fred Miller, Jr., and Jeffrey Paul. New York: Cambridge University Press and Bowling Green, OH: Social Philosophy and Policy Foundation.

Jonas, Hans (1984) *The Imperative of Responsibility: In Search for an Ethics for the Technological Age*. Translated by Hans Jonas and David Herr. Chicago: University of Chicago Press.

Pogge, Thomas (2005). 'Severe Poverty as a Violation of Negative Duties,' *Ethics and International Affairs*, 19:55–83.

Rawls, John (1971). *A Theory of Justice*. Cambridge, MA: Harvard.

Shue, Henry (1980). *Basic Rights: Subsistence, Affluence, and U.S. Foreign Policy*. Princeton, NJ: Princeton University Press.

25. Philanthropy beyond the sectoral approach
Ricardo Abramovay

INTRODUCTION

There are two basic dimensions to the study of philanthropy. The first emphasizes the impressive magnitude of charitable donations, whether in money, property or time. There are 11 million American citizens engaged in the non-profit sector through their participation in 2 million tax-exempt organizations (Teegarden et al, 2011:7). Their 15 billion hours of work would correspond to 279 billion, if they were converted into salaries (Wing et al, 2010). At the end of 2010, the 100 million American foundations held assets amounting to US$ 569 billion (Stuckler et al, 2011:3). Internationally, the sector handles no less than US$ 2 trillion a year and employs 45 million workers, if volunteers are included; that is 4.5 percent of all the economically active individuals in the world. If the sector were a country on its own, it would be the world's fifth largest economy (Salamon, 2009).

It would be a mistake, however, to examine philanthropy from a sector-based perspective alone, as if it were a kind of segment apart from social life, albeit a highly important one. Charitable acts, donations motivated by conviction or compassion, local organizations set up for the sole purpose of opposing unjust situations, have been inherent to all social organization throughout history (Ambrose, 2005). The classic works of Mauss, Malinowski and Polanyiare are just a few of the innumerable examples that demonstrate the decisive role of donations in maintaining social cohesion. Far removed from the idea of heartfelt gratitude that philanthropy evokes at first thought, Mauss (1990:31), for example, studies archaic societies on the basis of the reciprocity of gifts and donations that create a constructive set of obligations establishing a form of order whereby the objects are never completely separated from the men who exchange them. In the same way, Malinowski (1984) shows how the Kula personalizes the ties between individuals that are nominally distant from one another, with no kinship relationship, but associated through the obligations it implies. Polanyi uses Malinowski's example and counterpoises that reciprocity to the social logic that emerges from the generalization of mercantile relations, in what he does not hesitate to refer to as a Satanic mill. In doing so, he reaffirms an opposition – that is decisive in all classical social thinking from Marx and Weber to Mauss, Malinowski and Tonnies – between, on the one hand, social structures warmly supported by donations, personalized obligations and status, and on the other, those that supposedly merely respect the cold order of goods, contracts, and blind impersonal bonds among their components.

The work of Carrier (1995) and, from the mid-1980s on, the so-called new economic sociology (Smelser and Swedberg, 1994) rails against this separation of market and donations, work and home, economy and society, all unduly transformed into hostile worlds (Zelizer, 2005). 'The pure gift and the pure commodity, like the pure gift relationship and the pure commodity relationship, are polar terms that define a continuum along which one can place existing transactions and relationships' (Carrier, 1995:189). The new economic sociology was to insist on the embeddedness (Granovetter, 1985) of the economy in a social world in which the very market itself could be interpreted on the basis of requirements of a moral nature (Fourcade and Healy, 2007).

In that light, it is indeed crucial to understand philanthropy as a specific sector but without losing sight of the fact that sharing, giving without any mercantile counterpart being involved, and spending time for the explicit purpose of achieving goals that are socially valuable (and not individually instrumental) have been, and still are important aspects of the creation of wealth, not only in ancient societies but, increasingly, in our own times as well. The best examples of that are free software and Wikipedia (Benkler, 2006), but they also include the efforts of big corporations to incorporate the diffuse contribution of public cooperation among their innovations (Lessig, 2008). Furthermore, the donation of time (and often money and property) by means of these new and increasingly widespread modes of cooperation is not conducted in a sphere apart from private business, but is to be found at the very heart of the dynamics of contemporary innovation (Benkler, 2011; Slavin, 2011).

The importance of non-state organizations is on the increase. They are not to be confused, however, with private companies as they are explicitly directed towards achieving public goals (Salamon, 2002). Often they are associated to big corporations or stem from the use of the fortunes of their main shareholders, as the recent appearance of the term philanthrocapitalism (Bishop and Green, 2009) shows; or they may be derived from organizations designed to enhance the role of the owners of great fortunes in formulating solutions to global problems (Hudson Institute and The Center for Global Prosperity, 2010; Yach et al, 2010). Actually such use of great fortunes to promote the most varied kinds of public causes (from education to founding libraries, from the museums and orchestras, to providing protection for refugees, combating unemployment, or the defense of ethnic minorities) has been going, in the United States at least, since as far back as the 17th century (Bremmer, 1988). In spite of the fascinating richness of the information available on that, this chapter is not about the history of philanthropy. It concentrates on gaining an understanding of philanthropy by addressing three central questions.

The first is one usually formulated by economists: what could explain the fact of private entities employing their time, money or property to satisfy the public interest? In that sense the challenge is to face what many economists refer to as the paradox of corporate philanthropy (Andreoni et al, 1996; Godfrey, 2005; Kulscar et al, 2011).

Two other important questions emerge from the spheres of sociology and social sciences: what are their principle organizational forms (DiMaggio and Anheier, 1990; Galaskiewicz and Burt, 1991), and why do their control and governance mechanisms resemble those of the private sector so closely, seeing that philanthropic organizations are not designed to make profits (Porter and Kramer, 1999; Constantine and Braverman, 2004)? This question is not only important in studying philanthropic initiatives rooted in corporations or the great fortunes of their shareholders but also in enabling an understanding of the way in which even the most nonconformist civil society organizations adopt professionalized forms of intervention and subject themselves to governance styles highly typical of the corporate world.

Apart from the aspects of its motivation and governance structure, philanthropy is studied in light of the social principles that explain it and the political power that underlies it. Domhoff (2009: 956), for example, insists on the 'relevance of class-based organizational networks for understanding the role of many nonprofit organizations'. His five case studies illustrate a variety of situations. Sometimes philanthropic organizations help to reinforce grassroots social groups. On other occasions however there may be 'ultraconservative members of the corporate community who help finance nonprofit right-wing organizations that try to overturn any gains that are made by liberal–labor and progressive activists during times of upheaval' (Domhoff, 2009:956). Stuckler et al (2011), following a similar line, show that the links between public health foundations and private food and pharmaceutical corporations encourage us to view them more in the light of their strictly private interests than that of the universal causes in whose name they act. It is not unusual for beneficiary foundations to extol a reduction in government's role in elaborating public policies in the name of expanding personal responsibility and the consumer's supposed freedom of choice; and that in problematic areas like the use of tobacco and the consumption of soft drinks, alcoholic beverages and medicines (Rampton and Stauber, 2010; McKoy et al, 2009). At the same time, the bottom-up initiatives dedicated to promoting emancipating causes and that do not depend on corporate funding for support are of fundamental importance and highly emblematic of the current scene.

The following three items will present social science's more important responses to the three questions.

OVERCOMING THE PARADOX

The attitude of two biggest names in 20th-century economics to what is known today as 'corporate philanthropy' is emblematic. In 1970 Milton Friedman declared that the idea of the socio-environmental responsibility of companies was nothing but 'pure and unadulterated socialism'. To him, corporate philanthropy was an absolute contradiction in terms. The task of a corporate director is to run the business in accordance with the interests of those that entrusted him with the job, namely, the shareholders. Obviously, as an individual, he could have other responsibilities to his church, his family or his community. In these latter situations he is the master of his own resources and can act in regard to them as he sees fit. As the administrator of a company, however, he is the agent of those that placed on his shoulders the responsibility for making their assets yield good returns, and, accordingly, his mission is to obtain the greatest possible gains for the shareholders.

Friedrich Von Hayek (Hayek, 1945) uses a different argument but comes to the same conclusion. Imagining that companies and corporate structures are capable of dedicating themselves to social causes presupposes that they possess a certain kind of knowledge that they do not in fact possess at all. In a decentralized economy, the appropriate knowledge needed for decision-making by the social actors involved is always fragmented into millions of tiny separated units. It is exactly the practical experience of each individual that offers him the best ways of carrying out whatever he is dedicated to doing. Socio-environmental causes have no part in that particular knowledge, precisely because they involve a farseeing vision of the social world that is entirely incompatible with the information available to the individual producer.

Such skepticism about corporate responsibility is far from being a mere intellectual relic; it can be readily found in the contemporary literature. Henderson (2004), for example, argues that companies are vehicles for innovation and they have no need to worry about questions of public interest. Proponents of the Agency Theory (Jensen, 2002) and of running companies strictly according to the shareholders' interests frontally contest the idea that a company could have multiple objectives because, in their view, it is an economic organization whose performance can only be measured by the profits it brings in (Sundaram and Inken, 2004).

Fortunately, within the field of economics and management sciences, there are several fairly solid explanations to be found for a phenomenon that only began to emerge at the beginning of the 1970s when Friedman first railed against it: corporate socio-environmental responsibility. Three of them deserve special attention.

The first is well expressed in the term 'warm-glow giving' that Andreoni (2007) coined to describe this model of altruism that can be explained by the satisfaction it provides to those that practice it. From the corporate point of view, philanthropy can be an important element in risk reduction and, as such, contribute to an improved performance of the company's shares by enhancing its moral capital (Godfrey, 2005). An empirical corroboration of that idea appears in the work of Kulscar et al (2011), who alleges that, 'the higher the contribution to charitable giving of a firm, the less product failure it will suffer.' In that light, philanthropy is entirely explicable in terms of conventional economics, that is to say, it fosters the interests of those that carry it out.

A second line of explanation diverges from the idea that self-interest is the necessary and sufficient reason for explaining human conduct. The work of Amartya Sen (1987) attempts to refute what is one of the most solid pillars of economic science and show that altruism, consideration for others, can also be a strong motivator of social action. The refutation appears in the very title of a collection organized by Zamagni (1995). The Economics of Altruism, is one of the pillars of a research program that is being organized around the idea of a civil economy (Bruni and Zamagni, 2007; Bruni and Sugden, 2008). From the ethical angle, the idea of justice – fundamental to legitimizing philanthropic actions – does not accept that all of an individual's objectives are exclusively related to his own well-being (Sen, 2009:287). In the same way, Margolis and Walsh (2003:282) show that corporate responses to social problems cannot be viewed exclusively in the light of the instrumental benefits they provide to shareholders. Incorporated legal entities also have moral obligations regarding the unjust situations they create, or from which they benefit directly or indirectly.

The third area of explanations for corporate philanthropy, within the sphere of economics and management sciences, concerns the relationship of a private company and the set of social actors with which it has dealings or on which it depends. The work of Porter and Kramer (2006) shows that consumer well-being, ecosystem resilience and the social consequences of private sector activities cannot be treated as the unforeseen or undesired consequences of what corporations do. That means that specific concern with socio-environmental issues must be integrated into business strategies (Porter and Kramer, 2011) in such a way that creating value becomes a process shared by different social actors and not strictly limited to the financial interests of the corporations. It is essential to move beyond the conventional trade-offs that typify the relations between business and society (Freeman et al, 2004).

It is based on this double nature of contemporary philanthropy – the increasing embodiment by the private sector of socio-environmental objectives, which, up until a few years ago were not part of their mission and, at the same time, the functioning of philanthropic entities on the basis of organizational forms that are typical of companies – that their governance will be examined in the next item.

SMUDGING THE BOUNDARIES

Andrew Carnegie, in *The Gospel of Wealth*, states that the life of an economically suc-cessful man should consist of two parts: the accumulation of wealth followed by its dis-tribution. While it is true that concern for transparency in the use of resources has been present in American foundations throughout their history (and the same can be said of the European ones), up until recently there was a clear separation of business activities and any charitable acts that were the expression of the proprietor's personal inclinations. The main organizational feature of corporate philanthropy consists of overcoming that division in two basic ways.

Firstly, with the widespread demand for corporate socio-environmental responsibility, several of the themes that are dear to philanthropic organizations have become incorpo-rated to the logic of business. Authors Porter and Kramer (2011:66) cited above, show that 'the competitiveness of a company and the health of the communities around it are closely intertwined.' The expansion of the Grameen Bank and its recent association with Danone to complete the so-called 'base of the pyramid' corresponds to 'the rise of social enterprise, low-profit corporate forms, and the idea that social venture capital is a valid alternative way to fund nonprofit organizations' (Teegarden et al, 2011:20). The Brazilian venture capital fund Guardiam combines private capital and philanthropic donations with the specific aim of contributing to the sustainable development of the Amazon.[1] Those are just a few examples of how the very legitimacy of the private sector is increasingly dependent on the direct results of the relations between economy and society. The distance separating human action and human design, so dear to the think-ing of (Hayek, 1967), has, at least in part, been overcome: global consultants McKinsey (2008:12), for example, warn companies about new sources of risk, insofar as they may be held responsible for problems that lie far beyond the immediate outreach of the activi-ties they perform, as for example, in the case of obesity and the foodstuffs industry. One example of the corporate world's reaction to such pressure is the North American ini-tiative 'Benefit Corporation', a group of companies that deliberately sets out to use the power of business to solve social and environmental problems.

Just as important in guiding private corporate management strategies as any of those changes (obviously still merely incipient and largely fragmentary) are the changes in governance taking place in the philanthropic sector itself. In the latter half of the 20th century, organizations coordinating philanthropic activities began to appear all over the world. Furthermore, philanthropy began to be guided by goals that were more typical of an organization engaged in professionalizing itself and started adopting corporate modes of management (OECD, 2003). The more they grew in importance, the more the organizations incorporated effectiveness and performance measures (Salamon, 2002). McKinsey (2008) neatly expresses that transition when he states that contemporary philanthropy is 'moving from check-writing to leadership, collaboration, and global efforts'. There is an interesting contrast between the current global nature of philanthropy and the situation twenty years ago described by DiMaggio and Anheier (1990), who found that 'non profitness has little to do with transnational affairs'. The global nature of corporate philanthropy is now visible in the networks and alliances that are formed among companies, and, even more so, by the fact that according to McKinsey (2008) 58 percent of companies collaborate with other companies in this particular field of action. Organizations are being formed that seek out international expertise and authentic learning networks are being established among philanthropic organizations (Ambrose, 2005:4).

However promising this gradual suppression of the boundaries between private business and public socio-environmental aspirations may be, it would nevertheless be delusive to ignore the contradictions and the conflicts of interests and visions that underlie contemporary philanthropy. That is what will be examined next.

POWER, INTERESTS AND COMMUNITIES

There is an important body of critical literature on corporate philanthropy. On the one hand it questions the interests and visions of the world that this drawing closer of business and socio-environmental causes contains. On the other hand, it is important to underscore that public and non-state actions directed at socio-environmental problems are far from being limited to what organizations directly linked to the big corporations do. Even if philanthropy is studied in a sector-based perspective, it clearly goes way beyond the actions unfurled by private company shareholders.

There are actually two schools of critical thought regarding corporate philanthropy. The first holds that sporadic, local actions undertaken by charitable organizations to meet certain social needs actually undermine the political potential for revolt and transformation inherent to unjust situations. In that sense Nickel and Eikenberry (2009:975) do not hesitate to speak openly of 'marketized philanthropy' that 'creates the appearance of giving back, but is based in tacking away'. In the same vein, Žižek (2004) calls on us to: 'Consider how we relate to capitalist profiteering: It is fine IF it is counteracted with charitable activities – first you amass billions, then you return (part of) them to the needy.' Domhoff (2009:966) is in clear alignment with the same position when he states that charitable giving 'makes further social change very difficult, because activists and the staffs of community organizations walk a tightrope between organizing for social change and delivering social services'. The second type of criticism is directed at the potential conflict of interests between private foundations and public causes. Stuckler et al (2011) study the composition of the activities portfolios of the five largest American philanthropic organizations: the Bill and Melina Gates Foundation, the Ford Foundation, the J. Paul Getty Trust, the W. K. Kellog Foundation and the Robert Wood Johnson Foundation. Those five organizations hold more than 10 percent of all the assets held by the 100,000 private foundations in America. In the case of the Bill and Melina Gates Foundation, Stuckler et al (2011:4) show that their assets are strongly concentrated in the food and pharmaceutical industries, in companies like McDonald's, Coca-Cola, Johnson & Johnson, Schering-Plough, Merck, and others. The example of the Foundation's interests in Coca-Cola is emblematic. Soft drinks are mainly responsible for the rapid spread of obesity and diabetes in the developing countries. Even though 'non-communicable diseases constitute more than half of all deaths in low- and middle-income countries', only 3 percent of the Bill and Melina Gates Foundation's resources are dedicated to those problems. Stuckler et al (2011) have identified similar conflicts of interest in the other four major American foundations they study. The examples cited by Rampton and Stauber (2010), showing the direct connection between American medical associations and the medicines industry, illustrate the same point.

It would be a mistake, however, on the basis of these conflicts of interests, to underestimate the transforming capacity of philanthropic actions or to view corporate philanthropy as merely an extension of the strictly private interests of the companies unfolding them. As Domhoff (2009) himself readily admits, in the contemporary world, nongovernmental organizations play a fundamental role in variety of social movements, and very often those roles are supported by the resources of some of the biggest corporate foundations. Gunnar Myrdal's (1996) important book on race relations in the United States, for example, was written with the support of the Carnegie Foundation. The Ford Foundation, in turn, financed a series of groups that played an important part in the struggle against the dictatorship that installed itself in Brazil in 1964.

Similarly, there is a vigorous movement in course to extend the power self-organizing capacity of different communities independently of the allocation of any philanthropic resources. Edgar Cahn (2004) is at the origin of an international voluntary movement based on the idea of reciprocity. The principle underlying his 'Time Banks' (that now exist in 22 countries on all six continents) is that for 'every hour you spend doing something for someone in your community, you earn one Time Dollar. Then you have a Time Dollar to spend on having someone do something for you'. David Boyle defines the basic co-production principles that underlie the idea, which he does not hesitate to call the new philanthropy: 'no more giving by wealthy, no more *noblesse oblige* and grateful recipients. Instead, it means reciprocal agreements with neighborhoods or traditional welfare groups that – if they are not exactly based on the market – they do certainly imply contracts and agreements.' The Hureai kippu are a 'Japanese community currency created in 1995 by the Sawayaka Welfare Foundation so that people could earn credits helping seniors in their community' (Wikipedia). Interestingly, the old people seem to prefer the services of those that are paid in that way to those of professionals that are paid in cash.

The network information society allows bottom-up grass-root organizations created by their users or by a group of volunteers to take on unprecedented, massive dimensions. The 21st century is witnessing the emergence of forms of collective action that are no longer based on price systems or on practices typical of companies or groups of companies. A new public sphere is being fashioned, not to be confused with the market or with public or private organizational hierarchies but, nevertheless, exercising a considerable influence over both. The 'Penguin' of Yochai Benkler's (2011) book symbolizes this direct, voluntary and gratuitous form of human cooperation whereby the main source of gratification lies in feeling that the relations among people are fair, stimulate their intelligence, value their participation, widen their knowledge, base their support on communication, and open up spaces for the joint solution of problems. The expression 'crowdsourcing' synthesizes the most important aspect of this emerging production model. The term itself conjures up the idea that cooperative work performed in a network, that is, by the 'crowd', is a decisive source of prosperity and the 'crowd' endeavors to use collective intelligence not only in addressing problems but also to improve the quality of the goods and services offer.

CONCLUSION

However professionalized and specialized philanthropy may have become in the contemporary world, it is crucial to recognize that relations of reciprocity traverse the body of social organization as a whole, and they are not merely an archaic and traditional feature that the markets and the domination of the big corporations are going to overcome. Quite the contrary; the examples presented here show that today, the rigid separation between private interests and public causes is increasingly losing ground. Obviously the process is still only incipient, but social organization, cooperation among individuals and the new means available to reinforce them are all decisive elements in keeping up the pressure on corporations and they represent an immense potential (not necessarily guaranteed) for philanthropy to become a formative element of our very idea of justice.

NOTE

1.   See http://www.guardiam.com/index2_pt.html (accessed June 26, 2011).

REFERENCES

Ambrose, Nathalie (2005) *Global Philanthropy*. Council of Foundations (http://www.cof.org/files/Documents/Family_Foundations/Family-and-Global-Philanthropy/Overview-of-Global-Philanthropy-COF.pdf, accessed June 26, 2011).
Andreoni, J., W. W. Gale and Scholz, J. K. (1996) 'Charitable Contributions of Time and Money' (http://www.altruists.org/static/files/Charitable%20Contributions%20of%20Time%20and%20Money%20%28James%20Andreoni%29.pdf, accessed June 26, 2011).
Andreoni, J. (2007) *Charitable Giving*. Prepared for the New Palgrave Dictionary of Economics, 2nd Edition (http://econ.ucsd.edu/~jandreon/WorkingPapers/Palgrave%20on%20Charitable%20Giving.pdf, accessed June 26, 2011).
Benkler, Y. (2006) *The wealth of networks: how social production transforms markets and freedom*. New Haven, CT, Yale University Press.
Benkler, Y. (2011) *The Penguin and the Leviathan*. New York, NY, USA, Crow Business.
Bishop, M. and Green, M. (2009) *Philanthrocapitalism. How Giving Can Save the World*. New York, Berlin, London, Bloomsbury Press.
Boiley, D. (w/d) The New Philanthropy. New Economics Foundation (http://www.timebanks.org/documents/NewPhilanthropywcover.pdf, accessed June 26, 2011).
Bremmer, R. H. (1988) *American Philanthropy*. Chicago, IL, USA, The University of Chicago Press.
Bruni, L. and Zamagni, S. (2007) *Civil Economy – Efficiency, Equity, Public Happiness*. Oxford, UK, Peter Lang.
Bruni, L. and Sugden, R. (2008) 'Fraternity: Why the Market Need Not Be a Morally Free Zone?' *Economics and Philosophy*, 24:35–64.
Cahn, E. S. (2004) *No More Throw-Away People. The Co-Production Imperative*. Washington, DC, USA, Essential Books.

Carnegie, A. (1998[1889]) *The Gospel of Wealth*. Bedford, MA, Applewood Books.

Carrier, J. G. (1995) *Gifts and Commodities: Exchange and Western Capitalism Since 1700*. London, UK, Routledge.

Constantine, N.A. and M. T. Braverman, (2004) 'Appraising evidence on program effectiveness'. In M.T. Braverman, N. A. Constantine and & J.K. Slater (eds), *Foundations and evaluation: Contexts and practices for effective philanthropy*. San Francisco, CA, USA, Jossey-Bass, pp. 236–258.

DiMaggio, P. J. and Anheier, H. K. (1990) 'The Sociology of Nonprofit Organizations and Sectors'. *Annual Review of Sociology*, **16**:137–159.

Domhoff, G. W. (2009) 'The Power Elite and Their Challengers: The Role of Nonprofits in American Social Conflict'. *American Behavioral Scientist* 52: 955–973.

Fourcade, M. and Healy, K. (2007) 'Moral Views of Market Society'. *Annual Review of Sociology* 33:285–311.

Freeman, E. R., A. Wicks and Parmar, B. (2004) 'Stakeholder Theory and the Corporate Objective Revisited'. Organization Science 15 (3):364–369.

Friedman, M. (1970) 'The Social Responsibility of Business is to Increase Profits'. *New York Times Magazine*, September, 13: 32–33, 122, 124, 126.

Fureai Kippu. Wikipedia (http://en.wikipedia.org/wiki/Fureai_kippu, accessed June 26, 2011).

Galaskiewicz, J. and Burt, R. S. (1991) 'Interorganization Contagion in Corporate Philanthropy'. *Administrative Science Quarterly* 36:88–105.

Godfrey, P. C. (2005) 'The Relationship Between Corporate Philanthropy and Shareholder Wealth: A Risk Management Perspective'. *Academy of Management Review* 30 (4):777–798.

Granovetter, M. (1985) 'Economic Action and Social Structure – The Problem of Embeddedness.' *American Journal of Sociology* 91:481–510.

Hayek, F. A. (1945) 'The Use of Knowledge in Society'. *American Economic Review* 35 (4):519–530.

Hayek, F. A. (1967) *Studies in Philosophy, Politics and Economics*. Chicago, IL, USA, Chicago University Press, pp. 96–105.

Henderson, D. (2004) *The Role of Business in the Modern World Progress, Pressures and Prospects for the Market Economy*. Institute of Economic Affairs of Australia (http://cei.org/gencon/026,04305.cfm, accessed May 25, 2007).

Hudson Institute and The Center for Global Prosperity (2010) *The Index of Global Philanthropy and Remittances 2010* (http://www.hudson.org/files/pdf_upload/Index_of_Global_Philanthropy_and_Remittances_2010.pdf, accessed June 26, 2011).

Jensen, M. (2002) 'Value maximization, stakeholder theory, and the corporate objective function.' Business Ethics Quarterly 12:235–256.

Kulcsar, B. A., Fosfuri, A. and Giarratana, M. S. (2011) 'The Link Between Corporate Philanthropy and Product Failure'. Paper presented at the DIME-DRUID ACADEMY Winter Conference 2011 on Comwell Rebild Bakker, Aalborg, Denmark, January 20 – 22.

Lessig, L. (2008) *Remix. Making Art and Commerce Thrive in the Hybrid Economy*. New York, NY, USA, The Penguin Press.

Malinowski, B. (1984) *Argonauts of the Western Pacific*. Illinois, USA, Prospect Heights.

Margolis, J. D. and Walsh, J. P. (2003) 'Misery Loves Companies: Rethinking Social Initiatives by Business'. *Administrative Science Quarterly* 48:268–305.

Mauss, M. (1990) *The Gift: The Form and Reason for Exchange in Archaic Societies*. New York, NY, USA. W.W. Norton Inc.

McCoy, D., Kembhavi, G., Patel, J. and Luintel, A. (2009) 'The Bill & Melinda Gates Foundation's grant-making programme for global health' *Lancet* 373(9675):1645–1653.

McKinsey (2008) Business's Social Contract: Insights from CEOs on achieving efficient philanthropy (http://www.thecalgaryfoundation.org/documents/SocialContract.pdf, accessed June 26, 2011).

Myrdal, G. (1996) *An American Dilemma: The Negro Problem and Modern Democracy*. New Jersey, NY, USA, Transaction Publishers.

Nickel, P. M and Eikenberry, A. M. (2009) 'A Critique of the Discourse of Marketized Philanthropy'. *American Behavioral Scientist* 52(7): 974–989.

OECD (2003) Philanthropic Foundations and Development Co-operation. Off-Print of the DAC Journal 2003, Volume 4, No. 3 (http://www.oecd.org/dataoecd/23/4/22272860.pdf, accessed June 26, 2011).

Polanyi, K. (1984) *The Great Transformation: The Political and Economic Origins of Our Time*. Boston, MA, USA, Beacon Press.

Porter, M. and Kramer, M. (1999) 'Philanthropy's New Agenda: Creating Value'. *Harvard Business Review* Nov/Dec: 212–130.

Porter, M. and Kramer, M. (2006) 'Strategy and Society – The Link between Competitive Advantage and Corporate Social Responsibility'. *Harvard Business Review* December: 1–14.

Porter, M. and Kramer, M. (2011) 'Creating Shared Value. How to reinvent capitalism – and unleash a wave of innovation and growth'. *Harvard Business Review* January/February: 62–77.

Rampton, S. and Stauber, J. (2002) *Trust us, We're Experts*. New York, N. Y. USA, Penguin Putnam Inc.
Salamon, L. (2002) Summary of 'The Resilient Sector: The State of Nonprofit America' in L. Salamon (ed.), *The State of Nonprofit America*. Brookings Institution Press. Washington, D.C.. Published in collaboration with the Aspen Institute.
Salamon, L. (2009) 'The Future of Civil Society', in UBS (ed.) *UBS Philanthropy Services. Viewpoints 2009. Balancing Creativity and Control*. UBS, Zurich, Switzerland.
Sen, A. (1987) *On Ethics and Economics*. Malden, MA, USA, Blackwell Publishing.
Sen, A. (2009) *The Idea of Justice*. Cambridge, MA, USA, The Belknap Press of Harvard University Press.
Slavin, T. (2011) 'Business working together to drive innovation'. *The Guardian* (http://www.guardian.co.uk/sustainable-business/companies-punished-greener-products, accessed June 24, 2011).
Smelser, N. J. and Swedberg, R. (1994) *The Handbook of Economic Sociology*. Princeton, NY, USA, Princeton University Press, Russell Sage Foundation.
Stuckler, D., Basu, S. and McKee, M. (2011) 'Global Health Philanthropy and Institutional Relationships: How Should Conflicts of Interest Be Addressed'? *PLoS Medicine* 8 (4), 1–10.
Sundaram, A. and Inken, A. (2004) 'The Corporate Objective Revisited'. Organization Science 15 (3): 350–363.
Teegarden, P. H.; Hinden, D. R. and Sturm, P. (2011) *The Nonprofit Organizational Culture Guide. Revealing the Hidden Truths that Impact Performance*. San Francisco, CA, USA: Jossey Bass.
Wing, K. T., Roeger, K. L. and Pollak, T. H. (2010) *The Nonprofit Sector in Brief. Public Charities, Giving, and Volunteering*. The Urban Institute (http://www.urban.org/uploadedpdf/412209-nonprof-public-charities.pdf, accessed June 26, 2011).
Yach, D., Feldman, Z. A., Bradley, D. G. and Khan, M. (2010) 'Can the Food Industry Help Tackle the Growing Global Burden of Undernutrition?' *American Journal of Public Health* 3–8, http://www.foodpolitics.com/wp-content/uploads/Point.pdf, accessed November 28, 2012.
Zamagni, S. (ed.) (1995) *The economics of altruism*. Cheltenham UK, Edward Elgar.
Zelizer, V. A. (2005) *The Purchase of Intimacy*. Princeton, NY, USA. Princeton University Press.
Žižek, S. (2004) 'Passion: Regular or Decaf?' *In These Times* (http://www.inthesetimes.com/article/146/passion_regular_or_decaf/, accessed June 26, 2011).

26. Poverty
Andrea Brandolini[1]

In September 2000, world leaders committed their nations to reduce extreme poverty and set the Millennium Development Goals. The first goal is to halve the proportion of the world's people whose income is less than one dollar a day by 2015, relative to 1990. In June 2010, the European Union (EU) adopted the Europe 2020 strategy aimed at achieving smart, sustainable and inclusive growth. One of the five headline targets used to assess progress in meeting this objective is the reduction by at least 20 million by 2020 of the number of people at risk of poverty and social exclusion. The latter comprise all individuals who live in households either with low income, or severely materially deprived, or with adults working less than 20 per cent of their total work potential. In November 2011, the United States (US) Census Bureau released the supplemental poverty measure, which significantly departs from the existing official poverty measure in adopting a broader reference unit, a different resource concept, and a quasi-relative rather than absolute poverty threshold (Short 2011). The new measure is meant to provide an additional macroeconomic statistic integrating but not replacing the official poverty measure, developed in the early 1960s and still used in legislation to define eligibility conditions and funding allocation of certain welfare programmes.

These three examples indicate how a growing political concern for poverty has come to explicitly inform policy objectives, although the extent to which this concern has translated into concrete policy actions is open to debate. They also illustrate the wide range of measures that are used to frame these objectives, even in comparable socio-economic contexts like the US and the EU. In terms of Sen's (1976) classical distinction of the main problems in poverty measurement, differences relate more to the 'identification' of the poor than to their 'aggregation' into an index of poverty.

Identifying who is poor requires characterising the relevant variable(s) according to which the poverty status is evaluated, and fixing a threshold below which a person is classified as poor; the aggregation step implies constructing an index that summarises the available information. These problems are separately examined in the following sections. Before that, the next section briefly defines the welfare unit and the reference unit. The final section concludes.

WELFARE UNITS AND REFERENCE UNITS

The welfare unit is the subject of the poverty assessment. It is usually the person or the household: in the former case the welfare indicator is counted as many times as there are persons in the household, while in the latter it is counted only once. The reference unit denotes the level at which the variable used in the poverty assessment is aggregated. It may be the household, the inner family, the tax unit, or the individual. The broader the definition of the unit, the more measured inequality tends to decrease, since the dispersion across individuals is abated by the aggregation and supposedly egalitarian distribution among all members of the unit. The impact on measured poverty is however ambiguous and depends on the composition of the unit. According to Johnson and Webb (1989), the British poverty headcount ratio in 1983 falls from 11.1 to 8.1 per cent by moving from family units to households. An important innovation of the US supplemental poverty measure is to focus on households instead of families or unrelated individuals.

FOCAL VARIABLES

Sen (1992: 20) observes that:

> the relative advantages and disadvantages that people have, compared with each other, can be judged in terms of many different variables, e.g. their respective incomes, wealths, utilities, resources, liberties, rights, quality of life, and so on. The plurality of variables on which we can possibly focus (the *focal variables*) to evaluate interpersonal inequality makes it necessary to face, at a very elementary level, a hard decision regarding the perspective to be adopted.

Income and consumption expenditure are the two variables traditionally analysed in poverty evaluation. Both variables are used in the estimation of world poverty carried out at the World Bank, with expenditure-based estimates more common for developing countries: for instance, Chen and Ravallion (2010: 1591) report using consumption surveys for all countries in the Middle East and North Africa, in South Asia and in Sub-Saharan Africa, although income surveys are generally used in Latin America. Consumption is often preferred to income on practical grounds, because it is smoothed over time and less affected by seasonal fluctuations, especially in agrarian economies. Conceptually, many regard consumption as a better proxy of well-being than current income, either because the goods and services actually consumed are the argument of the utility function or because consumption has a closer link to lifetime resources. However, focusing on the commodities actually purchased (expenditure) rather than the means available to purchase them (income) makes the assessment of living standards dependent on personal purchasing choices and preferences. Also the simple link between consumption and permanent income becomes weaker after extending the baseline inter-temporal consumer's optimisation problem to allow for heterogeneity in life-spans, inherited wealth, labour earnings uncertainty, and so forth. In the real world, capital markets are imperfect and many persons face borrowing constraints that render their actual living conditions strictly dependent on current available resources: 'the promise of resources in the future may do little to pay the bills today', as put by Deaton and Grosh (2000: 93).

On the other hand, it is true that income fails to represent the full amount of resources on which individuals can rely to cope with the needs of everyday life and to face unexpected events: individuals may have earnings below the poverty threshold and still reach a decent standard of living thanks to their past savings, or to the possibility to borrow (Brandolini et al 2010). This points to the importance of considering both income and wealth in the assessment of poverty. Haveman and Wolff (2004: 145) suggest defining 'asset poverty' as the condition in which wealth is insufficient 'to sustain a basic needs level of consumption during temporary hard times'. The concept of asset poverty entails a finer partition of the population: it separates the income-poor who also lack sufficient wealth to keep them at the poverty line for a given time period from the income-poor who instead have such a buffer; it identifies those individuals who are not poor but would fall into poverty should they suffer a sudden drop of earnings, due to their insufficient asset holdings. Alternatively, one could construct the 'income-net worth' measure proposed by Weisbrod and Hansen (1968). In this measure, the annual net revenue from assets and liabilities is replaced with the annuity value of net wealth, that is the constant (discounted) flow of income that the stock of net worth could generate over a period of T years, where T is typically taken to coincide with the person's life expectancy under the assumption that no wealth is left at death. This measure is an elegant way of combining income and net worth, but imposes much structure on the measurement and has wide implications for the age structure of poverty: a higher wealth at older ages and a shorter annuity horizon contribute to raise the indicator of economic welfare of the elderly as compared to younger persons, who typically have longer time horizons and fewer accumulated assets.

Considering income and wealth together is a simple example of multidimensional evaluation of poverty, which is facilitated by their using the same monetary metric. The recognition of the limits of income and expenditure in assessing living standards has stimulated the exploration of other dimensions of well-being. A long research tradition measures economic hardship as the lack of socially perceived necessities (e.g. Townsend 1979; Nolan and Whelan 2011). Building on this tradition, the Eurostat indicator of severe material deprivation adopted in the Europe 2020 strategy assumes that living conditions are constrained by a lack of resources whenever persons cannot afford four or more of the following nine items: to pay rent or utility bills, to keep the home adequately warm, to face unexpected expenses, to eat an adequate meal every second day, a week's holiday away from home, a car, a washing machine, a colour TV, and a telephone. As seen, the Europe 2020 strategy goes even further in applying a multivariate approach, as it identifies the risk of poverty or social exclusion with the failure to achieve a minimum standard in at least one of three distinct dimensions: income, material living conditions, and work intensity.

A more radical shift towards multidimensionality underlies Sen's 'capability approach', which is based on '. . . a view of living as a combination of various 'doings and beings', with quality of life to be assessed in terms of the capability to achieve valuable functionings' (1993: 31). Functionings are the things that persons value in life, and range from elementary ones, such as being well-nourished and escaping avoidable illnesses, to more complex ones, such as being able to take part in the life of the community; the alternative combinations of functionings that persons can achieve determine their capabilities to function. The operationalisation of the capability approach raises numerous problems that have been the object of extensive research (e.g. Alkire 2002; Robeyns 2006; Chiappero-Martinetti and Moroni 2007; Brandolini and D'Alessio 2009). Nevertheless, the approach growingly informs policy-oriented analyses, such as the official reports on poverty and wealth released in Germany since 2001 (Arndt and Volkert 2011).

Even when income or expenditure is taken to be the focal variable, there is ample leeway for choosing the exact definition. The EU statistics typically consider monetary disposable income, that is the sum of wages, salaries and earnings from self-employment, cash receipts from property and private pension schemes, public transfer payments (pensions, family allowances, unemployment and welfare benefits) less income taxes and social security contributions. In the United States, official poverty statistics are traditionally based on gross before-tax cash income, and it is only in the new supplemental poverty measure that income is taken after taxes and net of out-of-pocket medical expenses and work-related expenses. All these definitions leave out items that may be important for living standards, such as the imputed rent on owner-occupied dwellings (Frick and Grabka 2003), the imputed value of public in-kind benefits for education, health care and housing (Smeeding et al 1993; Paulus et al 2010), or indirect taxes.

Moreover, income and expenditure may be adjusted for the size and the composition of the reference unit in order to account for the economies of scale generated by cohabitation and for the different needs of its members (for instance, due to age). This is generally accomplished by using an equivalence scale. Eurostat recommends the use of the modified OECD scale, which assigns value 1 to the first adult, 0.5 to any other person aged 14 or older, and 0.3 to each child younger than 14. Atkinson, Rainwater and Smeeding (1995) adjust household income by diving it by the square root of the household size. Both scales are an example of parametric scales defined, somewhat arbitrarily, by researchers; alternative scales are derived from econometric studies of consumption behaviour, expert judgements about basic needs, people's subjective perceptions of what represents an adequate income, and the differential tax-and-benefit treatment of different types of families. Whatever the underlying method of calculation, each equivalence scale entails specific ratios between the needs of households of different composition, so that varying the scale used in the estimation may significantly affect the size and the composition of the poverty population (Buhmann et al 1988; Coulter et al 1992). Atkinson (1992) derives dominance conditions that would allow reaching qualitative conclusions in a poverty comparison (before and after a certain policy, over time, between countries) without adopting a specific equivalence scale but only agreeing on how different types of family should be ranked by needs.

Equivalence scales are an effective way of dealing simultaneously with two dimensions, income and needs. Within the capability approach, they lead to derive 'functionings-equivalent incomes', that is incomes adjusted for differences in the capacity to function, as in the case of disabled people analysed by Kuklys (2005). However, the implicit monetisation of these important capability differences should not be seen to imply that an appropriate money transfer can compensate for every disadvantage.

POVERTY THRESHOLDS

The line dividing the poor from the non poor can be drawn on the basis of various criteria: absolute, relative, subjective, or policy-based. With an absolute standard, a person is classified as poor if his or her income falls short of the level required to purchase a basket of basic goods and services. An absolute poverty threshold is usually derived by estimating the cost of a food basket that meets minimum or adequate nutritional requirements and then allowing for other necessities (clothing, housing, transports, etc.). This threshold is then updated over time only for price changes. Historically, absolute standards have characterised early poverty studies, such as those by Rowntree (1901) in the United Kingdom or the Parliamentary Enquiry into Poverty in Italy (Cao- Pinna 1953). Nowadays, two significant examples of an absolute standard are the one-dollar-a-day poverty line used by international organisations and the US official poverty line. The former, which provides the basis of the first Millennium Development Goal, was originally developed for the World Bank in 1990 by averaging out the standards adopted in the poorest countries on the basis of a survey of 33 national poverty lines for the 1970s and 1980s (Ravallion et al 2009). The latter was calculated in the early 1960s by Orshansky (1965) by estimating the minimum cost of a subsistence food budget and multiplying the result by three, the inverse of the food budget share in total expenditure. The threshold varies by family size and composition and by the householder's age and is updated every year by the change in the consumer price index.

The problem with fixing an absolute standard stems from the difficulty of finding objective criteria: needs vary widely across people, reflecting also the variety of circumstances in which they live; experts hold discordant views, like for instance nutritionists about minimum dietary requirements (Livi-Bacci 1991). Moreover, necessities are inevitably socially determined, as well exemplified by tea, which Rowntree (1901) included among necessities, despite its little nutrient value, because it is deep-rooted in British habits. Eventually, the possibility of deriving a purely absolute standard is undermined by the recognition that 'every estimate of necessaries must be relative to a given place and time', as put by Marshall (1890: 70). The main practical shortcoming of an absolute standard is that it is totally unresponsive to changes in living conditions: when real income grows, the gap between the mean income and the poverty threshold is hence bound to widen. This is the case with the US official poverty line, which has fallen, for a family of four, from about half of the median in 1959 to below 30 per cent in 2010 (Blank 2008).

On the contrary, a relative standard is fully sensitive to progress in living conditions, as it takes the resources enjoyed by a typical member of the society as the reference for identifying the poverty status. A certain income or consumption level might warrant physical subsistence, but may be inadequate for the full participation in the life of an advanced society. The lack of a phone does not prevent people from living a decent life, but may limit the chances of a job-seeker of finding an occupation or hamper the social activities of a disabled old person. The conversion of this idea into a specific poverty threshold is however not straightforward. What is a 'typical' situation? How far from it should someone be in order to be classified as poor? In practice, as first suggested by Townsend (1962) and Fuchs (1965), the solution has been to set the poverty line at some fraction of the mean or median income – the most intuitive proxy of a society's typical standard of living. The value of this fraction is inevitably arbitrary, a consideration that '. . . casts doubt on the meaning of the cardinal poverty levels obtained at specific cutoffs and leads to a consideration of the robustness of results to changes in the cutoff' (Foster 1998: 337). Indeed, while the EU poverty target takes the line at 60 per cent of a country's median equivalised income, the Eurostat website provides statistics for other six cutoffs: 40, 50 and 70 per cent of the median, and 40, 50 and 60 per cent of the mean.

While the income elasticity of an absolute poverty line is nil, that of a relative line is one by construction, so that real income growth is fully accounted for. However, such a relative standard may lead to the counterintuitive result that poverty goes down during recessions if the mean or median income, hence the poverty line, falls. The new US supplemental measure limits this drawback by taking a five-year moving average of relevant expenditure levels as the poverty cutoff. Alternatively, one might construct a hybrid threshold by taking a weighted geometric average of a relative line z_r and an absolute line z_a, $z_\rho = z_r^\rho z_a^{1-\rho}$, where ρ measures the income elasticity of the poverty line (Foster 1998). A way to pin down the value of ρ is to equate it with the elasticity of the subjective evaluation of the income necessary to make ends meet as measured in public opinion polls: according to Kilpatrick's (1973) estimates on US data for the period 1957–1971, ρ would be around 0.6, meaning that the poverty line rises by about 0.6 per cent for any percentage point increase of per capita income.

In the same vein, Atkinson (1998) has proposed using the weighted geometric average to construct the thresholds for monitoring poverty in the EU, with z_a and z_r now representing the national line and the line calculated for the EU as a whole, respectively. If the poverty line is regarded as the minimum level of resources that a European citizen should have in order to fully participate in the community's life, this hybrid threshold would blend the national and EU-wide standards, and ρ would represent a political parameter capturing the pace of the convergence towards seeing the EU as a social entity: the higher ρ, the more important the common European reference would be.

All poverty thresholds described so far are defined by experts or analysts. Poverty thresholds could also be recovered from the analysis of people's judgements, either explicit (as collected in surveys) or implicit (as embedded in the rules of welfare schemes). As seen, public opinion polls gather information on the level of income that people regard as the minimum necessary for subsistence or for a decent life without luxuries. Controlling for family types, this self-perceived necessary income is generally found to be positively correlated with the respondent's actual income. In order to transform these individual norms into a social standard, the 'Leyden approach' proposes setting the poverty threshold at the level where necessary and actual incomes approximately coincide, under the assumption that people who earn an income close to the level that they consider necessary have a better understanding of its value than people who earn much less or much more (e.g. Goedhart et al 1977). On the other hand, social pensions and income support schemes are based on eligibility rules that identify the income levels below which the society feels no one should fall. These socially-determined minimum income levels provide a natural reference against which the effectiveness of public policies can be judged. Their value, however, likely reflects other policy objectives, beyond poverty reduction, as well as budget constraints: the extent of poverty comes to depend on the generosity of legislators, and paradoxically, measured poverty can increase as a consequence of a rise in the minimum standards of public assistance.

The criteria used to define the poverty thresholds have been illustrated by taking income as the reference variable, but they could be equally applied to other focal variables. For instance, schooling deprivation could be defined with respect to an absolute standard (the number of years necessary to achieve some minimum level of education), a relative standard (some fraction of the median number of years spent in school by the whole population), or a policy-based standard (the years of compulsory education). Note, however, that the conceptual distinction between an absolute and a relative standard may appear less neat than previously discussed, when different dimensions are taken into consideration. As argued by Sen, '. . . absolute deprivation in terms of a person's capabilities relates to relative deprivation in terms of commodities, incomes and resources' (1983: 153).

POVERTY INDICES

The last problem in poverty measurement is the choice of the index summarising the available information. The most common and intuitive statistic is the proportion of the poor in the total population, that is the headcount ratio $H = q/n$, with q and n denoting the number of people in poverty and in the whole population, respectively. H ignores the depth of poverty, or how far the poor are from the poverty line. The poverty gap, or deficit, D is the sum of all their shortfalls from the poverty line z: $D = \sum_{i=1,\ldots,q}(z - y_i) = q(z - \mu_q)$, where μ_q is the average of the focal variable y across the poor. D is a measure of the total transfer that, ceteris paribus, would allow eradicating poverty. The normalised poverty gap obtained by dividing D by qz, $I = (1/q)\sum_{i=1,\ldots,q}(z - y_i)/z = 1 - \mu_q/z$, is the average shortfall of the poor, which measures the severity of poverty.

Whereas H is insensitive to the severity of poverty, I does not depend on the number of poor people. More generally, both H and I do not account for the distribution among the poor: both indices would not change, should a transfer take place from a richer to a poorer person among the poor. Sen (1976) hence proposed the adoption of the Pigou-Dalton transfer principle for poverty measurement, which would entail lower poverty after the previous progressive transfer, and derived the index $S = H[I + (1 - I)G_q]$, where G_q is the Gini index among the poor. Following Sen's lead, Foster, Greer and Thorbecke (1984, 2010) characterised the class of poverty indices $FGT = (1/n)\sum_{i=1,\ldots,q}[(z - y_i)/z]^\alpha$, which are generally sensitive to transfers among the poor. The parameter α captures the degree of poverty aversion: the higher α, the higher is the weight assigned to the poorest poor. FGT includes H ($\alpha = 0$) and HI ($\alpha = 1$).

The measurement of poverty in a multidimensional space can take two different routes. If the different dimensions are collapsed into a composite indicator of well-being, the univariate indices discussed so far can be straightforwardly applied to this well-being variable. (This variable may have its own metric or may use a monetary metric, if all dimensions are transformed into income equivalents by means of an equivalence scale.) Alternatively, poverty can be measured using a multidimensional index that does not entail the aggregation of the dimensions at the individual level. When it is additively separable across persons, a multidimensional index implicitly defines an individual well-being indicator: this aggregation function reflects, however, the social evaluator's judgement, not individuals' utilities. With a multidimensional index there is a separate poverty threshold for each dimension instead of the single threshold applied with a composite well-being indicator.

Tsui (2002) and Bourguignon and Chakravarty (2003) characterise families of multidimensional poverty indices that differ for the way in which they embody the Pigou-Dalton transfer principle. An index that generalises the FGT univariate index to two dimensions is: $BC = (1/n)\sum_{i=1,\ldots,n}[\sum_{j=1,2}w_j[\max(1 - y_{ij}/z_j,0)]^\theta]^{\alpha/\theta}$, where $\theta \geq 1$, $\alpha > 0$, and w_j and z_j are the weight and the poverty threshold for dimension j. The extent of poverty as measured by BC depends on the interaction of three elements: the degree of concavity α is common to the FGT univariate index; the parameter θ, which governs the degree of substitution between the dimensions, and the weights w_j, which capture the importance of either dimension in the poverty assessment, are new to the multidimensional case.

Atkinson (2003) observed that the empirical literature on multidimensional deprivation has largely concentrated on counting deprivations, rather than taking a weighted mean of shortfalls from the poverty line as in the *BC* index. By shifting the emphasis to the importance of multiple deprivations, Atkinson (2003) proposed the bivariate deprivation indicator $A = 2^{-\kappa}(H_1 + H_2) + (1 - 2^{1-\kappa})H_{12}$, where $\kappa \geq 0$, H_j is the headcount ratio for dimension j and H_{12} is the proportion of those deprived in both dimensions. (This expression differs from Atkinson's original formula for dividing through by 2^κ.) When κ equals 0, the index A counts as poor all people with at least one deprivation ('union principle'), irrespective of the number of multiple failures. The weight on multiple deprivations gradually increases as κ rises: at the limit, A coincides with H_{12} and classifies as poor only those who are deprived in both dimensions ('intersection principle').

The two approaches are merged by Alkire and Foster (2011), who developed a measure which uses the counting approach to identify the poor and a multivariate generalisation of the *FGT* index to account for the depth of poverty. For d equally-weighted dimensions, they propose the index $AF = (1/nd) \sum_{i=1,...,q(k)} \sum_{j=1,...,d} [\max(1 - y_{ij}/z_j, 0)]^\alpha$. The number of poor persons $q(k)$ depends inversely on the number of deprivations k, comprised between 1 and d, that a person must experience to be classified as poor: the union principle applies for $k = 1$ and the intersection principle for $k = d$. When $\alpha = 0$, *AF* equals the headcount ratio multiplied by the average proportion of deprivations experienced by the poor.

CONCLUDING REMARKS

Political concerns have sometimes been a potent stimulus for research on poverty. On the other hand, the work of social scientists has contributed to refining theoretical approaches and analytical tools, to improving data quality and empirical estimation, and ultimately to reshaping the political debate. The measurement of multidimensional poverty is a thriving research area which has benefitted from this reciprocal influence of policy and research. The challenge is to translate the great progress in our measurement capacity into more effective policies to combat poverty and social exclusion.

NOTE

1. The views expressed here are solely those of the author and do not necessarily reflect those of the Bank of Italy.

REFERENCES

Alkire, Sabina (2002). *Valuing Freedoms: Sen's Capability Approach and Poverty Reduction*. Oxford: Oxford University Press.

Alkire, Sabina, and James Foster (2011). 'Counting and multidimensional poverty measurement'. *Journal of Public Economics* 95 (7–8): 476–487.

Arndt, Christian, and Jürgen Volkert (2011). 'The Capability Approach: A Framework for Official German Poverty and Wealth Reports'. *Journal of Human Development and Capabilities* 12 (3): 311–337.

Atkinson, Anthony B. (1992). 'Measuring Poverty and Differences in Family Composition'. *Economica* 59 (233): 1–16.

Atkinson, Anthony B. (1998). *Poverty in Europe*. Oxford: Basil Blackwell.

Atkinson, Anthony B. (2003). 'Multidimensional Deprivation: Contrasting Social Welfare and Counting Approaches'. *Journal of Economic Inequality* 1 (1): 51–65.

Atkinson, Anthony B., Lee Rainwater and Timothy M. Smeeding (1995). *Income Distribution in OECD Countries: The Evidence from the Luxembourg Income Study (LIS)*. Paris: Organisation for Economic Co-operation and Development.

Blank, Rebecca M. (2008). 'How to Improve Poverty Measurement in the United States'. *Journal of Policy Analysis and Management* 27 (2): 233–254.

Bourguignon, François and Satya R. Chakravarty (2003). 'The Measurement of Multidimensional Poverty'. *Journal of Economic Inequality* 1 (1): 25–49.

Brandolini, Andrea and Giovanni D'Alessio (2009). 'Measuring Well-Being in the Functioning Space'. In E. Chiappero Martinetti (ed.), *Debating Global Society: Reach and Limits of the Capability Approach*: 91–156. Milano: Fondazione Giangiacomo Feltrinelli.

Brandolini, Andrea, Silvia Magri and Timothy M. Smeeding (2010). 'Asset-Based Measurement of Poverty'. *Journal of Policy Analysis and Management* 29 (2): 267–284.

Buhmann, Brigitte, Lee Rainwater, Guenther Schmaus and Timothy M. Smeeding (1988). 'Equivalence Scales, Well-Being, Inequality, and Poverty: Sensitivity Estimates Across Ten Countries Using the Luxembourg Income Study (LIS) Database'. *Review of Income and Wealth* 34 (2): 115–142.

Cao-Pinna, Maria (1953). 'Le classi povere'. In *Atti della Commissione parlamentare di inchiesta sulla miseria in Italia e sui mezzi per combatterla. Vol. II: Indagini tecniche. Condizioni di vita delle classi misere*. Roma: Camera dei Deputati.

Chen, Shaohua and Martin Ravallion (2010). 'The Developing World is Poorer than We Thought, But No Less Successful in the Fight Against Poverty'. *Quarterly Journal of Economics* 125 (4): 1577–1625.

Chiappero-Martinetti, Enrica and Stefano Moroni (2007). 'An analytical framework for conceptualizing poverty and re-examining the capability approach'. *Journal of Socio-Economics* 36 (3): 360–375.

Coulter, Fiona A. E., Frank A. Cowell and Stephen P. Jenkins (1992). 'Equivalence Scale Relativities and the Extent of Inequality and Poverty'. *Economic Journal* 102 (414): 1067–1082.

Deaton, Angus, and Margaret Grosh (2000). 'Consumption'. In Margaret Grosh and Paul Glewwe (eds), *Designing household survey questionnaires for developing countries. Lessons from 15 years of the Living Standards Measurement Study*, vol. 1: 91–133. Washington, DC: World Bank.

Foster, James E. (1998). 'Absolute versus Relative Poverty'. *American Economic Review Papers and Proceedings* 88 (2): 335–341.

Foster, James, Joel Greer and Erik Thorbecke (1984). 'A class of decomposable poverty measures'. *Econometrica* 52 (3): 761–766.

Foster, James, Joel Greer and Erik Thorbecke (2010). 'The Foster–Greer–Thorbecke (FGT) poverty measures: 25 years later'. *Journal of Economic Inequality* 8 (4): 491–524.

Frick, Joachim R. and Markus M. Grabka (2003). 'Imputed rent and income inequality: A decomposition analysis for Great Britain, West Germany and the U.S.'. *Review of Income and Wealth* 49 (4): 513–537.

Fuchs, Victor R. (1965). 'Toward a theory of Poverty'. In Victor R. Fuchs (ed.), *The Concept of Poverty*. Washington, DC: The Chamber of Commerce of the United States.

Goedhart, Theo, Victor Halberstadt, Arie Kapteyn and Bernard van Praag (1977). 'The Poverty Line: Concept and Measurement'. *Journal of Human Resources* 12 (4): 503–520.

Haveman, Robert and Edward N. Wolff (2004). 'The concept and measurement of asset poverty: Levels, trends and composition for the U.S., 1983–2001'. *Journal of Economic Inequality* 2 (2): 145–169.

Johnson, Paul and Steven Webb (1989). 'Counting People with Low Incomes: the Impact of Recent Changes in Official Statistics'. *Fiscal Studies* 10 (4): 66–82.

Kilpatrick, Robert W. (1973). 'The Income Elasticity of the Poverty Line'. *Review of Economics and Statistics* 55 (3): 327–332.

Kuklys, Wiebke (2005). *Amartya Sen's Capability Approach. Theoretical Insights and Empirical Applications*. Berlin: Springer.

Livi-Bacci, Massimo (1991). *Population and Nutrition: An Essay on European Demographic History*. Cambridge: Cambridge University Press.

Marshall, Alfred (1890). *Principles of Economics*. London, Macmillan and Co.

Nolan, Brian and Christopher T. Whelan (2011). *Poverty and Deprivation in Europe*. Oxford: Oxford University Press.

Orshansky, Mollie (1965). 'Counting the Poor: Another Look at the Poverty Profile'. *Social Security Bulletin* 28: 3–29.

Paulus, Alari, Holly Sutherland and Panos Tsakloglou (2010). 'The Distributional Impact of In-Kind Public Benefits in European Countries'. *Journal of Policy Analysis and Management* 29 (2): 243–266.

Ravallion, Martin, Shaohua Chen and Prem Sangraula (2009). 'Dollar a Day Revisited'. *World Bank Economic Review* 23 (2): 163–184.
Robeyns, Ingrid (2006). 'The Capability Approach in Practice'. *Journal of Political Philosophy* 14 (3): 351–376.
Rowntree, B. Seebohm (1901). *Poverty: A Study of Town Life*. London: Macmillan.
Short, Kathleen (2011). 'The Research Supplemental Poverty Measure: 2010'. US Census Bureau, Current Population Reports, P60–241. Washington DC: US Government Printing Office.
Sen, Amartya K. (1976). 'Poverty: An Ordinal Approach to Measurement'. *Econometrica* 44 (2): 219–231.
Sen, Amartya K. (1983). 'Poor, Relatively Speaking'. *Oxford Economic Papers* 35 (2): 153–169.
Sen, Amartya K. (1992). *Inequality Reexamined*. Oxford: Clarendon Press.
Sen, Amartya K. (1993). 'Capability and Well-Being'. In Martha C. Nussbaum and Amartya K. Sen (eds), *The Quality of Life*: 30–53. Oxford: Clarendon Press.
Smeeding, Timothy M., Peter Saunders, John Coder, Stephen P. Jenkins, Johan Fritzell, Aldi J. M. Hagenaars, A. Richard Hauser and Michael Wolfson (1993). 'Poverty, inequality and family living standards impacts across seven nations: The effect of non-cash subsidies for health, education and housing'. *Review of Income and Wealth* 39 (3): 229–256.
Townsend, Peter (1962). 'The Meaning of Poverty'. *British Journal of Sociology* 13 (3): 210–227.
Townsend, Peter (1979). *Poverty in the United Kingdom: A Survey of Household Resources and Standards of Living*. Harmondsworth: Penguin.
Tsui, Kai-yuen (2002). 'Multidimensional poverty indices'. *Social Choice and Welfare* 19 (1): 69–93.
Weisbrod, Burton A. and W. Lee Hansen (1968). 'An income-net worth approach to measuring economic welfare'. *American Economic Review* 58 (5): 1315–1329.

27. Prizes and awards
Bruno S. Frey and Susanne Neckermann

PRIZES AND AWARDS EXIST EVERYWHERE

Orders, medals, decorations, titles and other honours can be found everywhere in society. Prizes and awards exist in monarchies as well as in republics.[1] Even in the United States, a country that separated from the British monarchy and explicitly chose the republic as a form of governance, the president and Congress bestow medals such as the Congressional Gold Medal created in 1776, the Presidential Medal of Freedom created in 1945, or the Presidential Citizens Medal, created in 1969. In the military sector, purple hearts and bronze and silver stars are handed out quite liberally, and at an increasing rate (Cowen 2000: 93). In communist countries, such as the former Soviet Union or the German Democratic Republic, a flood of orders, medals and titles (such as 'Hero of the Soviet Union' or 'Hero of Socialist Labour') was distributed. This flood of awards is also typical for dictatorships.

In the arts, culture, sports and the media. Prominent examples are the Academy Awards (Oscars), the Emmy award for outstanding achievement in television in the United States, the Grammy award for artistic significance in the field of recording, or the Booker Prize and the Pulitzer Prize in literature. Arts institutions, such as museums, bestow titles, such as benefactor or patron, upon their supporters. In chess, there are International Masters (IM) and Great Masters (GM). Athletes get the honour of being 'Sports Personality of the Year', and are admitted into one of the many Halls of Fame. Religious organizations such as the Catholic Church award the titles Canon or Monsignore, and beatify and canonize distinguished persons.

Academia has an elaborate and extensive system of awards. Universities hand out the titles honorary doctor and senator, while professional associations award an enormous number of medals, the most important one probably being the Fields Medal in mathematics. And then, of course, there are the Nobel Prizes. Many prestigious fellowships exist in academies of science (e.g. Fellow of the Royal Society FRS, founded in 1660; Fellow of the American Academy of Arts and Sciences, founded in 1780; Fellow of the Royal Society of Edinburgh FRSE, founded in 1783; or Fellow of the Academy of Social Sciences in Australia FASSA). Moreover, there is a very complicated system of titles (not always connected to functions), such as that of lecturer, reader, assistant professor, associate professor with or without tenure, full professor, named professor, university professor, distinguished professor etc. And then there is the flood of best paper awards handed out at conferences and by journals (Coupé 2003).

Somewhat surprisingly, titles and awards are also very important in the corporate sector. Managers like to be vice-president, senior vice-president, or first senior vice-president. Firms also commend their own employees for being 'Salesman of the Month' or 'Employee of the Week'; there seems no limit to the ingenuity of inventing new awards. The media support this activity by regularly choosing a 'Manager of the

Month', 'Manager of the Year' or even 'Manager of the Century'. Organizations, such as the World Economic Forum, appoint people to the position of 'Global Leader of Tomorrow' (1,200 people), and 'Young Global Leaders' (1,111 people below the age of 40).

THE LITERATURE ON AWARDS

There is a large literature on specific awards, in particular on orders, decorations and medals. It is historically oriented and mainly devoted to presenting legal rules and regulations.[2] Particular awards have been analysed in the context of arts and culture, such as the Academy Awards (Oscars) in film, the Booker Prize in literature, and the Eurovision Song Contest (Ginsburgh and van Ours 2003; Ginsburgh 2003), or the International Queen Elisabeth Prize in piano competition (Glejser and Heyndels 2001).

There is only a small literature by economists.[3] Forerunners are Hansen and Weisbrod (1972), Besley (2005), Frey (2005), and Brennan and Pettit (2004) more generally on esteem. A few isolated works discuss awards as incentives, e.g. Gavrila et al (2005), Neckermann and Kosfeld (2011). For the case of corporations, Frey and Neckermann (2008) study the channels via which awards motivate and investigate the differences to monetary rewards. Malmendier and Tate (2005) as well as Neckermann, Cueni and Frey (2010) find that awards significantly affect the subsequent behaviour of winners. Markham et al (2002), Asch (1990), and Neckermann and Frey (2007) and Frey and Neckermann (2008) show that award systems have a systematic incentive effect on performance in the corporate sector, and that managers rightly take awards seriously as incentive instruments.

CHARACTERISTICS OF PRIZES AND AWARDS

The typical features of prizes and awards are best understood when they are contrasted to monetary compensation:

- The material costs of awards, consisting of a certificate or a small trophy, are typically low for the donors, but the value to the recipients may be very high. To some extent this also applies to prizes where, despite their name, the monetary value is often low.
- Accepting an award establishes a special relationship. The recipient owes some measure of loyalty to the donor. This is not the case when a particular task is carried out in exchange for monetary compensation.
- Prizes and awards tend to be handed out for a vaguely defined achievement. In these cases, they are more adequate incentive instruments than monetary payments.
- Prizes and awards are less likely to crowd out the intrinsic motivation of their recipients than monetary compensation because when they are conferred the donor commends the recipients for their performance.

- Prizes and awards are not taxed, while monetary income is. Due to taxes falling on the giver and the recipient, there typically is a considerable wedge between the sum of money the donor has to spend and the net sum the recipient receives.

These are substantial differences making it worthwhile to analyse awards as a separate phenomenon from monetary compensation.

THE IMPORTANCE OF HONOURS

Data limitations make it difficult to empirically measure the importance of prizes and awards in modern societies. The best source providing information on the awards received by the most important personalities is the *International Who's Who (IWW)*, covering individuals from 212 countries (Neal 2006) who were asked to indicate the prizes and awards they received. This data source provides information on the number and kinds of awards each person received as well as on person-specific characteristics such as nationality, job, age, and international mobility. A sub-sample of 82 countries was selected according to the availability of the basic country specific variables necessary for the statistical analysis. For these 82 countries a random sample of 50 people per country was chosen. We collected the following information with respect to awards when available: source of the award (country of origin, foreign country, or international); award giving institution (state, private organizations, non-profit organizations, university, media) and category in which the prize was awarded (social welfare, military, science, culture/art, sport, media, business, religion). This information allows us to construct the number of awards received per person.

On the basis of this evidence, the following five results can be put forward.

1. Prizes and awards are important not only in monarchies: in the past, awards have mainly consisted of state orders, honours and decorations and have been closely connected to monarchies. In Spain, for example, the Golden Fleece (founded in 1430) is the most important and best-known Order, but there is also the Order of Carlos III, of Santiago, of Isabella the Catholic and the Laureate Cross of Saint Ferdinand.

   Among the countries with the highest number of awards, seven are republics (the Anglo-Saxon countries Canada, Australia – we count them as republics – and New Zealand; and the European countries Poland, Hungary, Switzerland and Finland) and only two are monarchies (the United Kingdom and Spain). Americans living in the United States receive a considerable number of awards, more than French and Italian citizens. The data indicate that today awards are no longer linked to monarchies. Indeed, staunch republics such as France, the United States and Switzerland are at the top of the list of the 82 countries in our sample.

2. Awards are not only a military matter: judging from pictures appearing in the press of soldiers and officers having their chests covered with orders, decorations and medals, it may be concluded that most awards are received by the military. However, our data suggest that awards are not mainly a military affair.

   Of the 82 countries in the sample, 49 countries contain individuals from the military sector in their sample of individuals drawn from the *IWW*. Averaged over these 49 countries, these people receive 11 per cent of the total number of awards. If one includes the remaining countries in the calculation, assuming that these exhibit zero awards per person in the military sector, this figure falls to 7 per cent. But in a few countries awards do focus on the military. In Uganda, Paraguay, and Venezuela, for example, one third to almost one half of all awards are given to people in the army. However, these countries are the exception rather than the rule. When considering domestic government awards only, the share of awards going to persons in the military sector is larger (15 per cent or 9 per cent depending on whether countries without military personnel in the sample are included in the calculation). However, this share is still far from being dominant.

3. There are many awards in academia: academia has an elaborate and extensive system of professional associations awarding a great number of medals. Nobel Prizes are certainly the most visible. There are many prestigious fellowships in academies of science. Moreover, there is a complicated system of titles (not always connected to functions), such as that of lecturer, reader, assistant professor, associate professor with or without tenure, full professor, named professor, university professor, distinguished professor etc. Honorary doctorates are another form of highly valued awards in academia.

    Almost one quarter of all awards are given to individuals in academia. Switzerland and Belgium lead with a share of two thirds of all awards going to individuals in academia. In Turkey the academic sector is also a major recipient. There are five additional countries in which half or more of the awards go into this sector (Netherlands, Germany, Australia, and Nigeria).

    The 10 top countries according to the average number of awards received include the United States, and several other countries whose university system count among the leading ones: Belgium, Switzerland, Japan, France and Australia. But some other countries give much weight to bestowing academics with awards though their universities are not considered to be among the best ones (Venezuela, Lithuania, Poland and Argentina).

4. There are many prizes and awards in the business sector: prizes and awards, including titles, are very important in business. Consider, for example, Federal Express, which confers a host of honours to individuals as well as to teams. These include the 'Circle of Excellence Award' that is presented monthly to the best-performing FedEx station, and the 'Golden Falcon' that is awarded to employees who go beyond the call of duty to serve their customers. Honourees of the latter award receive a golden uniform pin, a congratulatory phone call from a senior executive and 10 shares of stock.

Across all 82 countries in our sample, the 11 countries with the highest number of business awards per individual comprise a broad variety of countries in terms of GDP per capita. The top 10 include some wealthy countries such as Canada, Singapore, the United States, Saudi Arabia, Sweden or Switzerland, but also some developing countries such as the Philippines and Turkey. In some countries such as Canada, Venezuela, Israel or Luxemburg business-people included in *IWW* on average indicate to have received quite a number of awards (between four and five). China's business people listed in

IWW receive a substantial number of awards, more than even the respective US business people.

Awards going to individuals active in business are of little importance in many countries, such as Spain or Italy, but are central in some of the economically most successful countries of the world, such as Singapore, the United States, China or Israel with between 9 and 15 per cent of all awards. This picture is likely to change in the future. An increasing number of countries may well adopt the practice of honouring business people with awards, thus imitating the economically particularly successful countries.

PRIZES AND AWARDS PLAY AN IMPORTANT ROLE

The statistics presented allow some interesting and unexpected insights. Awards are widely used in modern society and are not solely a remnant of monarchy; they are predominantly used in the civilian sector and are not mainly a military affair; and they are important in academia as well as in business. Prizes and awards present a multitude of incentive instruments such as feedback, information and social recognition.

Honours are a relevant phenomenon deserving the attention of psychologists and economists, as well as other disciplines. Prizes and awards cannot be equated with monetary compensation. The academic study of awards is only at its beginning, especially in economics. However, it has already become clear that it deals with an important phenomenon. It allows us to see motivation in a broader context than has been considered so far, ranging from the extremes of extrinsic monetary compensation to intrinsic motivation, with honours as extrinsic, but non-material incentives inbetween.

NOTES

1. An incomplete but extensive list of types of official awards is given in the article 'List of Prizes, Medals, and Awards' in wikipedia (http://en.wikipedia.org, last accessed August 2007). See also Werlich (1974) and the House of Commons (2004).
2. Examples are Risk (1972) or Galloway (2002).
3. There is a considerable literature on awards in sociology, e.g. Bourdieu (1979) or Braudy (1986). This literature address awards and distinctions in general, but does not analyse particular types of awards but fails to provide a theoretical analysis in a comparative perspective, and does not offer any empirically testable propositions.

BIBLIOGRAPHY

Asch, Beth J. (1990), 'Do Incentives Matter? The Case of Navy Recruiters'. *Industrial and Labor Relations Review*, 43(3), S89–106.
Besley, Timothy (2005), 'Notes on honours', Mimeo, London School of Economics.
Bourdieu, Pierre (1979), *La Distinction. Critique sociale du jugement*. Les editions de minuit, Paris.
Braudy, Leo (1986), *The Frenzy of Renown: Fame and its History*. Oxford University Press, New York.
Brennan, Geoffrey and Pettit, Philip (2004), 'Esteem, Identifiability and the Internet'. *Analyse und Kritik*, 26(1), 139–157.
Coupé, Tom (2003), 'An analysis of the best paper prizes of economics journals', Working Paper, Université Libre de Bruxelles.
Cowen, Tyler (2000), *What price fame?* Harvard University Press, Cambridge, Mass.

Cueni, Reto, Neckermann, Susanne and Frey, Bruno S. (2008), 'Of Awards in Companies: Managers' Views on Awards as Incentives'. Mimeo, University of Zurich, Switzerland.

Frey, Bruno S. (2005), 'Knight Fever. Towards an Economics of Awards', IEW Working Paper, Institute for Empirical Research in Economics, University of Zurich.

Frey, Bruno S. (2006), 'Giving and Receiving Awards'. *Perspectives on Psychological Science*, 1, 377–388.

Frey, Bruno S. and Neckermann, Susanne (2008), 'Awards: A View From Psychological Economics'. *Journal of Psychology*, 216, 198–208.

Galloway, Peter (2002), *The Order of St Michael and St George*. Third Millennium Publishing, London.

Gavrila, C., Caulkins, J. P., Feichtinger, G., Tragler, G. and Hartl, R. F. (2005), 'Managing the Reputation of an Award to Motivate Performance'. *Mathematical Methods of Operations Research*, 61 1, 1–22.

Ginsburgh, Victor A. (2003), 'Awards, Success and Aesthetic Quality in the Arts'. *Journal of Economic Perspectives*, 17(2), 99–111.

Ginsburgh, Victor A. and van Ours, Jan C. (2003), 'Expert Opinion and Compensation: Evidence from a Musical Competition'. *American Economic Review*, 93(1), 289–296.

Glejser, Herbert and Heyndels, Bruno (2001), 'The Ranking of Finalists in the Queen Elisabeth International Music Competition'. *Journal of Cultural Economics*, 25(2), 109–129.

Hansen, J. Lee and Weisbrod, Burton (1972), 'Toward a General Theory of Awards, or, Do Economists Need a Hall of Fame?' *The Journal of Political Economy*, 80(2), 422–431.

House of Commons, Select Committee on Public Administration (2004), 'A Matter of Honour: Reforming the Honours System'. Fifth Report of Session 2003–04, vol. 1. Stationary Office, London.

Kosfeld, Michael and Susanne Neckermann (2011), 'Getting More Work for Nothing? Symbolic Awards and Worker Performance'. *American Economic Journal: Microeconomics* (3): 1–16.

Malmendier, Ulrike and Tate, Geoffrey (2005), 'Superstar CEOs', mimeo, University of Stanford, University of Pennsylvania.

Markham, Steven E., Dow, Scott, K. and McKee, Gail H. (2002), 'Recognizing Good Attendance: A Longitudinal, Quasi-Experimental Field Study'. *Personnel Psychology*, 55(3), 639–660.

Neal, Alison (ed.) (2006), *The International Who's Who*. Routledge, London.

Neckermann, Susanne, Cueni, Reto and Frey, Bruno S. (2010), 'Awards at Work', Working Paper No. 411. Zurich: Department of Economics, University of Zurich.

Neckermann, Susanne and Frey, Bruno S. (2007), 'Awards as Incentives', IEW Working Paper, Institute For Empirical Research in Economics, University of Zurich, Switzerland.

Phillips, Sir Hayden (2004), 'Review of the honours system'. Cabinet Office, London.

Risk, James C. (1972), *The History of the Order of the Bath and its Insignia*. Spink and Son, London.

Werlich, Robert (1974), *Orders and Decorations of All Nations, Ancient and Modern, Civil and Military*. Quaker Press, Washington DC.

28. Rationality
Shaun P. Hargreaves Heap

INTRODUCTION

People usually think that they act for a reason. The dominant model in economics of individual rationality in this sense holds that people act so as to satisfy best their preferences. This is an instrumental model of rationality: reason is cast in the role of selecting the best means to an end, the satisfaction of preferences.

The model is also sometimes known as the 'rational choice' or 'utility maximisation' model. Nothing deep should be read into 'utility' here. A 'utility' function is simply the device for representing people's preferences mathematically. The best outcome for that person receives the highest ('utility') number, the next best outcome gets the next highest number, and so on, until the least favoured one has the lowest number. As a result when one acts so as to satisfy best one's preferences, it is the equivalent of selecting the outcome from those available with the highest 'utility' number.[1]

The rational choice model is usefully quiet about the character of people's preferences. The preferences themselves can be selfish, altruistic, honourable, admirable, spiteful, etc. All that is required is that they yield a preference ordering over outcomes (otherwise it makes no sense to say that people act so as to satisfy best the preferences). In the next section I sketch how preferences can be specified in ways that produce philanthropic behaviour and reciprocity.

In section on page 281, I turn to some of the difficulties with the rational choice model that help explain why other models of rationality remain attractive. The difficulties come in two forms. First, the accounts of reciprocation, in particular, within this model seem to depend rather too heavily, in the manner of a *deus ex machina* begging questions about their origins, on the introduction of things like 'norms' or 'groups' or 'teams'. Second there is some troubling evidence on how we behave which is difficult to reconcile with the consequentialism of the model. Conclusion section follows.

I end this section by noting that the rational choice model is sometimes presented without the accompanying psychological account of behaviour in terms of preference satisfaction. It is set out in terms of a series of constraints on people's actual choices (e.g. that these choices should exhibit transitivity, completeness, etc.). These requirements form the axioms of rational choice and it can be shown that when an individual's actions satisfy them, it is 'as if' they had preferences which could be represented by a utility function and they acted so as to maximise their utility/expected utility (e.g. see Green, 1971).

It is sometimes claimed that the axiomatic version is to be preferred to the explicitly psychological one because it deals only in observable behaviour and does not require a commitment to any account of what goes in people's heads. This is not especially appealing because it is not obvious why these axioms should characterise 'rational' behaviour unless one also holds some account of the underlying rational psychology; and given the formal equivalence between the two approaches, the most plausible explanation of why the axioms constitute rationality involve appeals to the instrumental conception of reason. Indeed, it is often argued (e.g. Davidson, 1980) that the point of the axioms is not to undo the need for a psychology of choice; rather they give substance to what an instrumental psychology is. In addition, in this instance, the purported grounds for dispensing with the psychology (dealing only in observables) is very likely to disappear when considering philanthropic and reciprocating behaviours because these behaviours are often distinguished not only by their physical properties (which can be defined independently of what is going on in people's minds) but also by their symbolic ones, what they mean (which cannot).

PREFERENCES FOR PHILANTHROPY AND RECIPROCATING BEHAVIOUR

Most people plausibly have preferences that are self interested in some degree, but not always exclusively so. They can also have 'other regarding' ones, sometimes called 'social preferences'. As a result, they often do not act in a straightforwardly selfish way. Their actions in these circumstances are, in part, dependent on the strength of the 'other regarding' preferences and the terms of the current trade-off with the self interested ones, sensitive to the interests of others. Further, when these 'other regarding' preferences are 'nice' rather than 'spiteful' (that is, the person positively values the welfare of others), this sensitivity will produce behaviour which is broadly understood as 'kind' to others. There are a variety of such 'other regarding' preferences that might produce such 'kind' behaviours (e.g. 'altruistic' or Utilitarian ones), but there is one that is particularly relevant to specifically 'philanthropic' behaviour: an aversion to inequality (see Fehr and Schmidt, 1999). This is because philanthropy is often associated not just with gifts, broadly understood, to others but specifically with gifts from those who are 'rich' to those who are 'poor' (and not the other way round).

I will illustrate how a preference for equality in this sense can account for non-selfish behaviour using the example of what is, under an assumption of selfishness, a prisoner's dilemma. Table 28.1 reproduces the dilemma when each person's preferences are (selfishly) only concerned with the dollars that he or she receives through their action and each prefers more dollars to less. In this case the $ value becomes an index of each person's utility pay-off and defect is the best action for each person (whatever they expect the other person to do).

When people play this game in experiments, however, anything between 30 per cent and 70 per cent of people don't defect, but cooperate (see Dawes and Thaler, 1988; Clark

Table 28.1   Prisoner's dilemma

		Person B	
		Cooperate	Defect
Person A	Cooperate	$3,$3	$0,$4
	Defect	$4,$0	$1,$1

Table 28.2   Assurance game

		Person B	
		Cooperate	Defect
Person A	Cooperate	3,3	−2,2
	Defect	2,−2	1,1

and Sefton, 2001). When the decision is made repeatedly but still anonymously, the percentage of cooperative choices typically starts at the top end of this range and gradually falls to the lower value, but it never goes to zero.

It will be obvious how a Utilitarian preference could explain such cooperative behaviour because the joint benefit is greatest when both cooperate. The dislike of inequality can have the same effect. Specifically, individual i's utility function representation of their preferences in an interaction with 'j' now takes the form of (1), where $\$_i$ refers to the financial return to 'i'. Thus person 'i' likes to have $s for him or herself, the first term, but dislikes *any* difference between his or her $s and those enjoyed by 'j', the second/third term where 'c' is the parameter capturing the weight attached to this dislike for inequality.

$$U_i = \$_i - c.\max(0, \$_i - \$_j) - c.\max(0, \$_j - \$_i) \tag{1}$$

In particular, suppose 'c' has the value 0.5. The game in Table 28.1 is now transformed into the one given by Table 28.2.

There are two Nash equilibria in this transformed game: [cooperate, cooperate] and [defect, defect]. Hence if acting rationally on one's preferences (with common knowledge of this rationality and common priors) licenses actions that are in a Nash equilibrium, it would no longer be surprising to find that people sometimes chose to cooperate in the interaction depicted in Table 28.1.

One explanation of why the level of cooperation falls when interactions of this sort are repeated is that there are three broad types of people. There are the selfish (who always defect), the unconditionally nice (who cooperate all the time) and the conditional cooperators (who cooperate initially but only continue if this cooperation is reciprocated). On this account what happens in repeated play is that the conditional cooperators increasingly come across defectors and so switch from being cooperators to being defectors, eventually leaving only the hardcore of unconditional cooperators.

The thought that some people might be conditional cooperators is plausible not just because of the experimental evidence (see Clark and Sefton, 2001). There appear to be examples of such reciprocation in history, like the 'live and let live' norm at the beginning of World War 1 (see Axelrod, 1984). It is also an idea with a long pedigree in economics.

Adam Smith (1976[1759]), for example, famously argued that people obtained a very special pleasure from sharing judgements regarding what was appropriate (moral) behaviour. The origin of this special pleasure for Smith is the 'sympathy' we feel for others. He treats this as a psychological fact and suggests it is the basis for our moral judgements. It is, in effect, no different from the kind of feeling that the altruist has: it is unconditional and does not depend on what the other feels. What makes Smith's account different is his further argument that '*mutual* sympathy' is a very special pleasure: 'nothing pleases us more than to observe in men a fellow feeling with all the emotions of our own breast'. So when Rose acts and Max sympathises or approves and Rose knows that Max sympathises in this way, she gets a very special pleasure. This is very different from the reflective effect among altruists because they take their character from the initial experience: if this is good then others feel it as good; if it is bad then others feel it as bad. With mutual sympathy, when Rose experiences something bad, Max's initial sympathy will also experience the badness, but when Rose knows that Max has sympathised, she derives a positive pleasure (see Sugden, 2002). Since moral ideas encode feelings of sympathy in Smith, the sharing of these ideas, so that they become moral norms, becomes a guide to the actions that will generate the special pleasure of mutual sympathy. In other words, the shared rules of moral conduct create an expectation that one should act in a particular way and acting in accord with this expectation creates the special pleasure of mutual sympathy.

The first formal, 'modern' model of decision making where preferences have this reciprocal quality is Geanakoplos et al (1989). It is probably best known through Rabin (1993) and is set out in equations (2) and (3) below. (2) has a similar form to (1) in the sense that it comprises of two parts. The first is the 'material' pay-offs that 'i' receives from some outcome O: that is the utility value of whatever are the material aspects of the outcome for 'i' ($=M(O)$). So in the game of Table 28.1, this would be the utility value of the $ outcome. The second part is what is often called in the economics literature the 'psychological' pay-off associated with this outcome ($=P(O)$). Or to make a connection to the wider social science literature and the earlier observation on the axiomatic approach, the 'psychological' pay-off arises because outcomes have symbolic as well as material properties: that is, they mean something and these meanings motivate people to act. There is a similar 'psychological' element in (1) that comes from people valuing equality, but in (3) it now has a more complicated form to take account of its reciprocal character.

$$U_i(O) = (1 - v) M_i(O) + vP_i(O) \qquad (2)$$

Where 'v' is a parameter that weights the 'material' and 'psychological' aspects of an outcome.

$$P_i(O) = f_i(O)[1 + f_j(O)] \qquad (3)$$

Where 'f' is a function that identifies the fairness (i.e. $f > 0$) or unfairness (i.e. $f < 0$) of each person's action.

Here 'i' enjoys positive 'psychological' pay offs when the outcome involves either *both* people acting 'fairly' ($f > 0$) or *both* acting 'unfairly' ($f < 0$): that is, it depends on reciprocation. The positive effect of both behaving badly is sometimes controversial but can explain why people punish each other when each expects the other to breach whatever is the reigning norm of fairness. It is not an essential part of this theory. Equally Rabin's original expression for how 'fairness' might be judged is controversial, but can easily be amended.

Another example of a conditional preference that marks a departure from the indi-

Table 28.3   Prisoner's dilemma with team reasoning

		Person B	
		Cooperate	Defect
Person A	Cooperate	3,3	2,2
	Defect	2,2	1,1

vidualism of the dominant model, but not its instrumental form of rationality, comes from the work on 'we' or 'collective' intentionality (see Sugden, 2000; Tuomela, 1995). When a central defender in a soccer match tackles and wins the ball in the penalty area and decides to pass the ball promptly to a colleague in midfield, there is a natural question. Why didn't he or she try to beat a few of the opposing players before passing or shooting at the opposition goal? Anyone who has played football will know that the 6m pass is humdrum, whereas the pleasure of taking the ball past an opponent is second only to scoring a goal. One explanation is that the defender discounts this pleasure by the risk of failure and the attendant threat of being dropped from the team or worse, transferred. Alternatively, when he or she puts on a number 5 shirt, it could be said that they become a member of a team and they now decide what to do with reference to the team's interests and not their own. This is the idea behind 'collective' or 'we' intentionality: when we belong to a team we reason using a different set of collective preferences. This reasoning is sometimes called 'team reasoning'.

To see how it might work, consider again the dilemma in Table 28.1. When A and B belong to the same team, the team's interests might be defined by the average pay-off with the result that the pay-offs become those of Table 28.3.

A team thinker then considers what action each member of the team should take in order to maximise the average pay-off, with the result that each team member decides to cooperate. Reciprocation is crucial in this account because the transformation from Table 28.1 to Table 28.3 only occurs when team members play with each other (see Bacharach, 1999, where this is explicit). One team player interacting with a non-team player would have no reason to use 'team reasoning' because he or she is not in a team as such.

SOME DIFFICULTIES WITH THE INSTRUMENTAL MODEL

When psychological pay-offs depend on reciprocation in the manner of Geanakoplos and Rabin above, the judgement of the 'fairness' or 'rightness' of someone's action often depends on knowing what they were expecting you to do. For example, 'cooperate' may be the 'right' action in a prisoner's dilemma when the other person expects you to 'cooperate', but if they expect you to 'defect', then 'defect' might be the 'right' action in the sense that this is what the prevailing norm within that group dictates. This can complicate the usual chain of causation in game theory whereby beliefs about what others will do are derived from knowledge of the pay-offs and the assumptions of rationality, common knowledge of rationality and common priors. Instead in this case, one would need to fix beliefs about what people will do before the pay-offs can be determined.

To place some restriction on the admissible beliefs for this purpose and so bring some determinacy to the analysis, it is natural to require that beliefs are equilibrium ones. But once this is done, there is a sense in which the whole apparatus of game theory becomes strangely irrelevant since, once one knows equilibrium beliefs, one knows the actions that are to be undertaken. In which case, there is no real need to calibrate pay-offs in their light in order to show that the actions are, indeed, in equilibrium relative to these pay-offs (see Hargreaves Heap and Varoufakis, 2005; Gintis, 2009). One might as well say that people followed the norm that is captured by these equilibrium beliefs and in this way the rational choice model gives way to a model of 'rule' or 'norm' governed behaviour. Since the 'rules' or 'norms' also often encode shared beliefs about why an action is appropriate, behaviour of this kind is assimilable to a model of 'expressive' rationality (see Hargreaves Heap, 1989).

In much the same way, one might wonder whether there is a troubling issue in the team reasoning model of reciprocation concerning how people come (or do not come to be members of the team). In other words, as in the case of norm based reciprocation, much of the work in explaining behaviour seems to be done by something external to the instrumental model of rational action. One possible answer to these types of concern that preserves the essentials of the instrumental account involves an appeal to the idea of 'bounded rationality' and evolution.

Let us suppose that people are 'boundedly' rational in the sense that they simply choose actions initially without optimisation and then adjust behaviour in the light of experience, moving to those that secure better outcomes and away from those that do not. In other words, people grope towards the action that best satisfies their preferences (through learning or some other evolutionary mechanism) rather than achieving it all the time through careful calculation of what will serve them best. This is an appealing amendment to the instrumental model because we have limited cognitive capacities, and given the complexity of some decisions, it seems quite unlikely that we could always consider all the options and calculate exactly what to do for the best (see Simon, 1978). It also has interesting implications when such learning occurs over interactive decisions: social conventions can arise spontaneously (see Sugden, 1986; Gintis, 2009). That is, it appears to supply an instrumental account of the origins of the shared rules that govern behaviour.

To see this consider a version of the crossroads game where two people come across an unclaimed or disputed resource: there is a $10 note and a $5 note on the sidewalk. If these types of encounter occur repeatedly and some people start to use a rule that assigns priority to one of the parties when they meet (so that this person gets the $10 note), then those using the rule will achieve a mutually superior outcome in the sense that one goes away with $10 and the other enjoys the $5, whereas a free for all would produce a fight first over the $10 and then, when this is destroyed, they would jointly turn to the $5, causing its destruction. This advantage encourages others to use the same rule until it spreads within a population.

Since the shared rule is, in effect, a coordinating device and there is no reason to expect any particular rule to emerge. Any of a number are possible provided they are shared and at the 'crossroads of life', one is as likely to find rules like 'give way to the male/female' or 'give way to the old/young' emerging with consequent interesting effects on social stratification. This, in turn, makes the details of history matter because 'who' chose 'what' and 'when' influences the actual selection of a rule and typically the character of the rule will affect the distribution of the gains from coordination in society.

The difficulty, however, with this evolutionary model is that it explains the emergence of a convention, a simple shared rule; it does not explain how such a rule comes to have normative appeal: that is, how it comes to be seen not just as the pragmatically sensible thing to do, but also the 'right' thing. In other words, what is lacking, to return to the earlier discussion, is an explanation of how actions come to have symbolic properties so that they become the source of a distinct 'psychological' payoff for the individual.

So far I have been considering how well the instrumental model of individual rationality can accommodate philanthropic and reciprocal behaviour through the introduction of 'other regarding' or 'social' preferences. The instrumental model is consequentialist in the sense that it is the consequences of action that matter for the individual and which motivate him or her to act and, in effect, I have been considering how the domain of 'consequences' can be plausibly expanded to include the philanthropic and reciprocating aspects of what happens. I leave this discussion here and turn to what some regard as a more fundamental difficulty with the instrumental model: its consequentialism.

There are two concerns that I will mention. The first is the behaviour of the unconditional cooperators in the prisoner's dilemma games. Surely, they cannot be motivated in any meaningful way by the consequences of their action. They cooperate both with other cooperators and with defectors despite the differences in the consequences. Of course, it is possible to make the action itself its own consequence and so defeat the objection, but this is to miss the point. There is something different going on here and Kant supplies a possible key (Kant, 1949[1788]; see van Staveren, 2001, on virtue ethics; Hargreaves Heap, 1989, on expressive reason).

While the instrumental model takes preferences, the objectives of action as given (*de gustibus est non disputandum*) and makes reason calculative, Kant argued that reason had an additional and more important role in deliberating on what objectives one should pursue. It is only through taking one's objectives to be one's own in this sense that one can achieve a state of autonomy. What does reason tell us in this regard? Famously, Kant observes that if an action results from reason in this sense, then, since reason is a universal human characteristic, only those actions that are universalisable could be candidates. There are, however, some doubts over whether this categorical imperative will ever deliver much concrete advice because either too much or too little passes this test (although see O'Neill, 1989, for a counter view). Nevertheless, it would seem to point in the direction of cooperation in the prisoner's dilemma and it yields actions that can be indifferent to consequences in the manner of the unconditional co-operators in the prisoner's dilemma games.

The second trouble with the consequentialism of the instrumental model is that some valued outcomes seem to be intrinsically the by-products of action that is instrumentally undertaken. They may be valued but they cannot be pursued as an objective without undermining their attainment. One may value 'spontaneity', for example, but one cannot act to be 'spontaneous' because the action would as a result become planned (and not 'spontaneous'). Could 'love' and 'friendship' be similarly valued but difficult to pursue for the same reason? If they are, then this may be important for understanding reciprocity because both 'friendship' and loving relationships involve reciprocation but this cannot be a condition upon entering these relationships otherwise they would become a mere transaction. This is not to argue that consequences do not matter (they plainly do, for instance, when love is unrequited), but a model of individual agency seems to need to allow some space for actions that are not motivated in this sense. Some action is an expression of what one values, of what might be and not what is.

CONCLUSION

The power of the rational choice model is not in dispute: there are too many examples of actions that are sensitive to their relative price (which is, in effect, the key prediction of the model). What is in doubt is whether the concept of a preference can always be coherently expanded to cover many cases of philanthropic and reciprocating behaviour. In particular, are the 'social' or 'other regarding' preferences that might perform this task genuinely exogenous, really the properties of an individual or always amenable to being pursued in the manner of the instrumental model?

NOTE

1. There is no connection, therefore, despite the shared name, to the philosophy of Utilitarianism because these 'utility' numbers are not interpersonally comparable and so cannot be summed across individuals.

REFERENCES

Axelrod, R. (1984) *The Evolution of Cooperation*. New York: Basic Books.
Bacharach, M. (1999) 'Interactive team reasoning: a contribution to the theory of cooperation', *Research in Economics*, 53, 117–47.
Clark, K. and Sefton, M. (2001) 'The sequential prisoner's dilemma: evidence on reciprocation', *Economic Journal*, 111, 51–68.
Davidson, D. (1980) *Essays on Actions and Events*. Oxford: Clarendon Press.
Dawes, R. and Thaler, R. (1988) 'Anomalies: Cooperation', *Journal of Economic Perspectives*, 2, 187–97.
Fehr, E. and Schmidt, K. (1999) 'A theory of fairness, competition and cooperation', *Quarterly Journal of Economics*, 114, 817–868.
Geanakoplos, J., Pearce, D. and Stacchetti, E. (1989) 'Psychological games and sequential rationality', *Games and Economic Behaviour*, 1, 60–79.
Gintis, H. (2009) *The Bounds of Reason: Game Theory and the Unification of the Behavioral Sciences*. Princeton: Princeton University Press.
Green, H. (1971) *Consumer Theory*. Harmondsworth: Penguin.
Hargreaves Heap, S. (1989) *Rationality in Economics*. Oxford: Basil Blackwell.
Hargreaves Heap, S. and Varoufakis, Y. (2005) *Game Theory*. London: Routledge.
Kant, I. (1949[1788]). *Critique of Practical Reason*, trans and ed. L.W. Beck, *Critique of Practical Reasoning and Other Writings in Moral Philosophy*. Cambridge: Cambridge University Press.
O'Neill, O. (1989) *Construction of Reason*. Cambridge: Cambridge University Press.
Rabin, M. (1993) 'Incorporating fairness into economics and game theory', *American Economic Review*, 83, 1281–302.
Simon, H. (1978) 'Rationality as process and as product of thought', *American Economic Review*, 68, 1–16.
Smith, A. (1976[1759]) *The Theory of Moral Sentiments*. Oxford: Clarendon Press.
Staveren, I. van (2001) *The Value of Economics: an Aristotelian Perspective*. London: Routledge.
Sugden, R. (1986) *The Economics of Rights, Cooperation and Welfare*. Oxford: Basil Blackwell.
Sugden, R. (2000) 'Team preferences', *Economics and Philosophy*, 16, 175–204.
Sugden, R. (2002) 'Beyond sympathy and empathy: Adam Smith's concept of fellow feeling', *Economics and Philosophy*, 18, 63–87.
Tuomela, R. (1995) *The Importance of Us: a Philosophical Study of Basic Social Notions*. Stanford: Stanford University Press.

29. Regard[1]
Avner Offer

In economics it is assumed that individuals form their preferences independently of each other. In contrast, the concept of 'regard' implies that they form their preferences in response to each other. 'Regard' is the approbation of others. It takes many forms: acknowledgement, attention, acceptance, respect, reputation, status, power, intimacy, love, friendship, kinship, sociability (Offer, 1997). The idea goes back to Adam Smith, where it motivates his first book, *The Theory of Moral Sentiments* (1976[1759]). In a memorable passage, he states that economic activity is driven 'chiefly from this regard to the sentiments of mankind':

> What is the end of avarice and ambition, of the pursuit of wealth, of power, and preheminence? Is it to supply the necessities of nature? The wages of the meanest labourer can supply them . . . what are the advantages which we propose by that great purpose of human life which we call bettering our condition? To be observed, to be attended to, to be taken notice of with sympathy, complacency, and approbation, are all the advantages which we can propose to derive from it. (Smith, (1976[1759], 50)

Man is driven by self-interest, he says, but also has an innate capacity for sympathy. The book opens with a heart-warming affirmation, that 'How selfish soever man may be supposed, there are evidently some principles in his nature, which interests him in the fortune of others.' (Smith, (1976[1759], 9) That is not what it seems. Sympathy is not separate from self-interest. What really matters is not the sympathy *for* others, but rather the sympathy *of* others. This need for acknowledgement by others is an innate motivator which is comparable in its intensity with selfishness. Hence, self-interest and sympathy are one and the same. But in order to be worth having, regard has to be genuine. The regard of other people can be thought of as a signal, which needs to be authenticated. For the signal to be credible, the sender must be known to be capable of disinterested, unilateral, and authentic regard. And if the senders have such capacity, recipients need to have it too. That is why *The Theory of Moral Sentiments* opens with such a resonant affirmation of the capacity for 'sympathy'.

But an innate capacity for sympathy is not in itself sufficient to authenticate every instance of regard. Smith provides another device, which he calls 'the impartial specta-tor'. It is important: *The Theory of Moral Sentiments* invokes it 66 times. The approba-tion of other people may be regarded as authentic, if the recipient has done something to merit it. The recipient knows that he deserves the approbation only if he complies with the norms of virtue. He applies the best norms of society to his own behaviour, as if he were an 'impartial spectator'.[2] If he satisfies the standards of such a disinterested observer, if he judges himself to be *praiseworthy*, then he can be content. Indeed, he remains satisfied even if praise is not forthcoming. But the norms of the impartial spec-tator can only bind the virtuous. So in order for the model to work, Smith states that a capacity for virtue is also innate in human nature. This does stretch credibility, and even Smith had a sense that it might be a step too far: 'It seldom happens, however, that human nature arrives at this degree of firmness' (Smith, (1976[1759], 310–11). The model did not achieve the broad acceptance of Smith's other resonant term, 'the invisible hand', which is only mentioned once in *The Wealth of Nations*.

Nevertheless, Smith's idea of approbation as the 'governing principle of human nature' is intuitively appealing. We can also reconcile the impartial spectator with the 'invisible hand' model, in which the only motivator is self-interest. The apparent contradiction of the two is the once-notorious 'Adam Smith Problem' (Montes, 2003). Taking a cue from Offer (1997), this problem can be resolved as follows: the invisible hand applies in impersonal markets, while sympathy affects interpersonal exchange. Smith illustrates this in the 'Digression on the Corn Trade' chapter in *The Wealth of Nations*. The grain business is so extensive that no single merchant may hope to corner it. If any supplier raises the price above market-clearing levels, then somebody else will offer a lower price. Hence the grain market requires no regulation, despite the questionable virtue of many of its participants. In contrast, the incentives of approbation and sympathy operate when exchange requires a personal interaction. It is only when people interact directly with each other that inter-personal obligation can be said to exist.

Two questions remain: is it possible to improve on the authentication method of Smith's model, and how relevant is it to of economic exchange in modern societies?

THE ECONOMY OF REGARD

Reciprocal exchange is a feature of pre-modern societies. The potlatch, a periodic feast of reciprocal giving by Indian tribes in the Pacific Northwest, was a status competition in generosity and waste. The Solomon islanders undertook long sea voyages to trade decorative sea shells in the kula system of gift exchange. Hospitality to strangers remains the norm in many parts of the Mediterranean, Arab, Iranian and Indian worlds. The ethnographic record indicates that exchange begins with a unilateral transfer, for which reciprocity is expected. It is usually delayed and voluntary. Both value and timing are left to discretion, though often regulated by convention and custom. When the exchange is completed, a new sequence can begin. Reciprocity can also be indirect, with no return from the beneficiary (who may be unknown), but a credit notched up with the community, to be reciprocated at some future time and place.

In neo-classical market exchange, acquaintance is immaterial. The gains from trade are all there is. Every sale is simultaneously a purchase. Any delay incurs a discount. In contrast, in the gift exchange, the price is indeterminate. 'Delivery' and 'payment' are separated by discretion and delay. Over and above the gains from trade, exchange is also a good in itself, a 'process benefit', which takes the form of personal interaction.

The ultimate benefit is self-worth. As Smith made clear, self-worth requires the validation of others. The term 'regard' has two meanings: The first is 'to be noticed'. The second is 'to be valued'. It is this benefit of exchange, the warm glow of acknowledgement, which constitutes the authentication device in 'the economy of regard' (Offer, 1997). Validation needs to be independent and impartial. But instead of relying on self-validation by the 'impartial spectator', it is achieved by evaluating the approbation signal. Any unilateral signal of approbation can be defined as a 'gift'. A good signal, in theory, is one that is difficult to make and difficult to fake. Hence, the recipient should be able to evaluate signal quality (Camerer, 1988). The gift can be dear or cheap, substantive or symbolic. It is not costless. At the very least, 'regard' is a grant of attention, and attention is a scarce resource. Withholding regard signifies indifference and rejection. To convey authentic regard, a genuine signal requires discrimination and effort. A handwritten letter counts for more than an e-mail, although finding the right words (perhaps even more difficult) might achieve the same effect. Getting it right is not easy (Belk and Coon, 1991, 1993). The use of money to communicate regard is not efficient: a credible financial signal is costly, whereas approbation can be conveyed cheaply with an appropriate signal. Unlike the impartial spectator, for signalling to work does not require the assumption of innate virtue, or any virtue at all, except for the capacity to signal genuine regard.

The exchange of regard has the formal property of allocative efficiency. This can be shown by analogy with economic model of perfect price discrimination under monopoly (Frank, 1994, 393–95). In this model, the law of one price does not apply: the supplier is able to charge each recipient as much as she is willing to pay. There is no marginal price, and no consumer surplus: for each recipient of regard, exchange value equals use value. For this to happen, two conditions must be satisfied: the monopolist must know the recipient's maximum price, and there can be no arbitrage: recipients cannot trade with each other. These conditions are unusual in impersonal exchange, but are normal in reciprocity. Every provider is a monopolist of her own regard. No one else can supply it. Hence it cannot be traded among recipients. Under perfect price discrimination, demand and supply curves are identical to those of a competitive market: both total output and surplus are the same as in the competitive market, i.e. production is just as efficient (Offer, 1997).

In economics, self-interest provides sufficient motivation for driving an efficient market economy. But this assumption is inconsistent with two large facts. One is the game-theoretical result that rational choice gives rise to suboptimal deadlocks like prisoner's and social dilemmas. The second is that such deadlocks are routinely overcome, and that cooperation and trust are achieved at every level of economic activity. In standard theory this happens because reputations for honesty can be achieved by repetition. However, such reputation can only be credible if authentic virtue is possible, and that would violate the assumption of unbridled self-interest. The miracle of cooperation, a central feature of the market economy, is inexplicable in terms of standard theory.

It is sometimes argued that selfishness persists because it has been selected in evolution for its survival value; but the reciprocal motivation of regard must have a similar survival value, which justifies its identification by Smith as a fundamental motivation of similar power. 'Reciprocal altruism' is widely observed in animal species. It is easy to imagine the capacity for regard as being selected in human evolution for its survival benefits. Computer tournaments suggest that positive regard confers an evolutionary advantage, that 'nice' is better than 'nasty'. In the social experiments 'ultimatum' and 'dictator', people repeatedly demonstrate a unilateral propensity to give and reciprocate (Bowles and Gintis, 1998; Henrich, 2004; Fehr and Fischbacher, 2005).

Hunting-gathering involves foraging over large areas, with occasional large windfalls (e.g. a large mammal), which are more than a single hunter could either capture or consume. It is reasonable to assume that the capacity for regard, like the capacity for language, is innate, even if the forms that it takes are culturally specific. On this interpretation regard arises from a propensity which is satisfied by means of giving and receiving. The positive emotions (unlike the negative ones) are easy to fake (Ekman, 1985, 36, 86, 126). The ability to fake regard facilitates gift exchange, but it also places a premium on material authentication, i.e. on gifts.

In recent years, several economists have developed alternatives to *homo economicus*, which are becoming known as *homo reciprocans* (Bowles and Gintis, 1998; Dohmen et al, 2009). Regard promotes sociability, and sociability facilitates cooperation. It breaks the deadlock of the prisoner's dilemma with a norm of first-mover cooperation. Trust resembles a gift: a unilateral transfer with the expectation, but no certainty, of reciprocity. Regard provides an incentive for trust, and trust is efficient: it economizes on the transaction costs of monitoring, compliance and enforcement (Hollander, 1990; Kranton, 1996; Gérard-Varet et al, 2000; Bénabou and Tirole, 2006; Kolm, 2006; Kolm and Ythier, 2008). There is also model of one-sided approbation, i.e. without reciprocity, 'the economy of esteem' (Brennan and Pettit, 2004). It is more attractive for its consistency with neoclassical theory, than for its inherent plausibility.

SOCIALLY UBIQUITOUS

Regard pervades human interaction. Conversation is a gift economy, loaded with cues of acceptance or disdain. Non-verbal cues communicate intensities and qualities of regard; the smile, like many other gestures, is universally understood. Ostracism and exclusion are painful.

Reciprocity produces 'bads' as well as goods. Giving incurs obligation and debt: the giver notches up an emotional and material credit, in the form of a bond on the recipient. The term bond can signify a repeated exchange of regard. Like a financial bond, it has some features of contractual obligation. Like the human bond, it is an emotional link. The term bond is also used in the sense of a fetter, as a form of oppression. The obligation to reciprocate can be a burden, which needs to be relieved by means of a return gift. Asking for help is psychologically difficult, and so is the obligation to reciprocate. Excessive intimacy can be stressful. A gift without reciprocity vexes both giver and receiver, as in beggary. The gift signal can be rejected or misconstrued. It can initiate a spiral of insult, hate and retribution, like the duel, the blood feud, the crime of passion, and the spiral of divorce. The anonymity of the market confers immunity from such bonds; it 'economizes on love'.

Even unilateral or asymmetric transfers are not entirely disinterested. The giver hopes for regard from the younger generation, or aspires to an enduring reputation. Such transfers may also have insurance attributes: treating others with consideration upholds the norm of mutual support. 'Giving by stealth' confirms the capacity for unilateral regard which Smith identified as necessary for sympathy to be credible.

ECONOMICALLY UBIQUITOUS

Shopping is satisfying, but there is also an aversion to market trading (Frey, 1986). In advanced economies, most welfare (measured in real or imputed money) is not provided through markets, whether impersonal or relational. Exchange within the household is not mediated by money. Its scale is captured in 'extended national accounts', which assign a shadow price to household production which is extrapolated from women's paid labour. In these estimates, domestic output amounts to between one quarter to more than one third of national product. In affluent societies, governments allocate between one third and one half of national income. The non-profit sector typically allocates more than 5 per cent of income, and at least a similar share of employment. In market exchange as well, regard is often required to lubricate the wheels of commerce. The persistence of non-market exchange on such a scale indicates that gifting may be, if not always 'efficient' in the formal sense, at the very least a viable alternative to the market system. As Smith suggested, this preference arises out of the intrinsic benefits of social and personal interaction, from the satisfactions of regard.

Prices facilitate exchange when information is scarce and co-ordination difficult, when goods are standardized and cheap. The market works best when the efficiency of production runs ahead of the efficiency of cognition and communication. It economizes on costly information (Hayek, 1945). Conversely, reciprocal exchange is preferred when trade involves a personal interaction, and when goods or services are unique, expensive, or have many dimensions of quality. Such contexts give rise to mutual obligation. The demand for regard exceeds the capacity for voluntary provision, and the market steps in to provide the feigned pseudo-regard that is a hallmark of service in the retail and hospitality sectors.

In pre-industrial societies, the intensity of obligation is inversely related to kinship. Family formation was often a contract between parents, formalized by ritual. The family can provide good protection because of the low risk of default. Today, the family retains a grip over migrants, who send remittances home for extended periods. In the world as a whole, it is estimated that 60 per cent of workers, and 70 per cent of old people still rely on family support for social security. In affluent societies, families remain the wellspring of regard. They are held together by two bonds: between spouses and between generations. Modern family formation is discretionary, and hence conforms more closely to the voluntary model of gift exchange. In modern courtship and romantic attachment, the road to intimacy is a spiral of mutual self-disclosure, an exchange of information and gifts. It leads to erotic interaction, another potent form of bonding. The greater economic independence of women within the family has been offset by higher expectations of emotional intimacy, which are accordingly difficult to satisfy (Offer, 2006, ch. 13).

Shifting the gaze from women to men, history traces a withdrawal from the market and into the household. Male working hours have fallen drastically since the nineteenth century and most of this time has been transferred into the home. Time spent in paid employment in a 17-country 'world' between the 1960s and the 1980s, for women as well as men, amounted to only 21 per cent of the total available. A further 2 per cent were spent shopping. The vast bulk of the time is spent outside the market, in various forms of social interaction, in domestic work, or alone.

Children have also shifted out of the market and into the gift economy. Before affluence, children were able to bring in a current income, and were counted on for support in hardship, and in old age. In the transition to affluence, they lost their economic value, and gained a large affective value, becoming 'economically worthless, but emotionally priceless' (Zelizer, 1994, 209). Childrearing is a large economic cost, amounting to the value of a medium priced dwelling house, or almost half of women's potential lifetime earnings. Parental care is an unmeasured but vital input into human capital. When marriages break down, the probability of educational, behavioural and emotional disorders rises substantially, even after controlling for socio-economic factors.

Bequests are an anomaly: in orthodox theory, self-interest ends at death. Estimates of their scale range widely, from 20 to 80 per cent of all assets in the United States. Likewise, a good deal of life insurance cover is reciprocal or altruistic transfers. In return for care and attention, children provide parents with a sense of worth and pleasure. In North America, at least, offspring get more than they return. In the aggregate, this asymmetry may be an instance of delayed or indirect reciprocity. Offspring and kin reciprocate by caring for the old, the infirm, and the disabled. In the UK, caring extended beyond the family circle: 28 per cent of those cared for were friends or neighbours. The shadow wage of unpaid care in the UK came to about 7.5 per cent of national income in 1992, about the same as the total spent on the National Health Service.

There is an element of discretionary gift in any fixed wage, when intensity and quality of effort are difficult to observe. Wages persist above market clearing levels; this is taken as evidence of 'efficiency wages', an implicit contract which constitutes a reciprocal gift relation between employers and workers. Surveys have shown that those paid more respond with a greater effort, and that those with reciprocal preferences feel better about themselves as well (Dohmen et al, 2009). Even in large anonymous workplaces, there have been recurrent fashions for team production and other relational incentives. Academic tenure is a gift of lifetime income, subject only to minimal contractual obligations. The recipient repays in the time and quality of their own choosing. What keeps academics honest are the bonds of regard. The professor is under scrutiny by students, colleagues, and also the 'invisible college' of peers. Similar regard incentives are found in most professions. During the last two decades, the Open Source movement in information technology has innovated such salient public goods as Linux and Wikipedia, as well as a myriad of lesser products, whose production appears to be motivated by little more than the economy of regard (Dalle et al, 2004).

In agriculture, farming remains an extension of the household form of production, and continues, in the most advanced countries, to be dominated by family firms, with a little hired help. Individual farm acreage has risen with better technology, and the number of farms and their owners has declined, but farm work is still largely a family (or very small business) affair. The face-to-face methods of household task allocation are used to incentivize production for the market.

The basic problem of selling is to ascertain the preferences of others. That is also the problem of gifting. Some goods are useful mainly as gifts, e.g., greeting cards, toys, decorated wrapping paper, flowers and wedding rings. Retailing has a large peak at Christmas. Advertising attempts to apply mass production to personal suasion. Marketers endow their goods with a 'personality', by means of branding. An ad can simulate a smile and reproduce it by the million. Between the 1940s and the 1960s American magazine advertising usually incorporated an element of direct interpersonal appeal, in the form of 'endorsements'. Price information was almost never included. This simulated regard was designed to bypass the filter of reason, in order to evoke a reciprocal obligation in the customer's mind. Companies recruited women to convene house-parties, where the conventions of reciprocity were mobilized to sell crockery, cosmetics or sexual accessories. In the last two decades marketing has increasingly aimed to escape 'the law of one price', to discriminate among different market segments, in order to push prices up the demand curve. As information becomes cheaper, marketers attempt to personalize their appeal, and to collect information about individual clients in so-called 'database marketing'. The goal is to target promotions at the smallest possible market niche – the individual – in order to simulate a personal relationship between sellers and buyers.

In a competitive market of affluent consumers, any difference in quality, delivery, service etc. can be competed away by the price, which theory says will be shaved of all profit. Hence a residual source of market advantage is often the quality of regard. Almost half of American GNP (in 1970) could be described as transaction costs, i.e. as the measured extent of the divergence from the ideal of costless transactions. Of this, more than half was incurred between firms. The proportion of sales workers in the American labour force rose from 4 per cent in 1900 to 7.5 per cent in 1970, while in Britain it was higher still, 8.8 per cent in 1981. On this measure as well, the impersonal market has (until recently) retreated, not expanded.

The standard negotiating fixture in commerce is the 'business lunch', which uses the gift-exchange trappings of food and hospitality to create an emotional setting for trade. That part of the hospitality industry which does not cater primarily to courtship, kinship or friendship, relies on the businessman, who is travelling in pursuit of personal contact.

The mix of regard and of salesmanship is uneasy. Many employees find fulfilment in genuine exchanges of regard, using time and goods provided by their employer. But because money is involved, and authenticity is suspect, it belongs to the category of pseudo-regard. Rapport with customers is often driven, back at the office, by output quotas. In the web of commerce, every human bond is open to defection.

Entrepreneurship depends on the ability to attract reciprocal transfers from investors, lenders, suppliers and customers. The same applies to politics and political economy: a field too vast to more than mention here. A common identity can substitute for face-to-face relations. Communal cultures make the penalty of exclusion too costly to incur. Faith and ethnic bonds have facilitated trading among entrepreneurial communities: the Quakers in Britain, the Parsis in India, the overseas Chinese. The diamond trade in Israel, one of its three world centres, relies on handshake contracts, sealed by a blessing, and dominated by Orthodox Jews. Business credit is essentially a form of delayed reciprocity. In its first century, British industrialization relied primarily on funds raised locally from family, friends and business contacts, who based their trust on personal knowledge. The family firm or the partnership were typical forms of ownership. They remained so until the scale of economic projects (such as the railways and overseas enterprises) exceeded the resources of personal networks.

Chinese culture subscribes to Guanxi, a set of norms of reciprocity and gifting, which promote trust among initiates, and exclude others. In the People's Republic Guanxi was necessary to obtain goods and services. Overseas Chinese had the cultural equipment to connect into these pre-existing webs, often by going back to their village or town of origin, and taking on a local partner. In the absence of secure property rights in the People's Republic, reciprocity has fulfilled a similar function of securing expectations and underpinning trade and investment.

Loyalty and reciprocity can also work effectively for anti-social ends. Italy has its Cosa Nostra, the Chinese their Triads. A Russian Mafia, with roots in the past, re-emerged at the end of the Soviet Union. Small groups collude more effectively than large ones. Reciprocal communities of businessmen, professionals and workers often organize for rent seeking. A strong gift economy can crowd out the market if exchange depends entirely on reciprocal inclusion. This is an argument for liberalism, for the impersonality of the market, the law, the public service and the vote. Some forms of gifting are used to subvert the 'rules of the game'. Even law-abiding societies, with traditions of public integrity, are not immune to 'old boy networks'. Illegal gift economies subvert the effectiveness of government; sometimes due to a general ethos of reciprocity, or the activities of organized crime. But corruption can also be beneficial. Like the market economy, the planned economies in Eastern Europe also depended on networks of 'fixers', who acted as brokers in a gift economy ('blat' in Russia) mediated by their access to resources, relationships and reputations.

The economy of regard operates wherever incentives are affected by personal relations. Its core is in the household, but it extends whenever people work in small groups or bargain face to face. Gift exchange is sensitive to the cost of information and the cost of time. As market incomes rise, so does the cost of time. On the other hand, the cost of information is declining. These trends work in opposite directions. As the cost of time increases, regard-intensive exchanges like childcare become more expensive. Men, for a long time, have sacrificed wage income in return for more time at home, except for high earners, who have sought their regard in the workplace. This choice was starker for women, and those with the best careers have forgone children and marriage more frequently than lower earners (Offer, 2006, ch. 11). For women, market work provides additional choice and a new measure of regard. The redirection of regard (by both men and women) is creating a wake of social consequences, ranging from marriage breakdown at the personal end, to the fiscal crisis of the welfare state at the societal one.

Regard is difficult to measure because the yardstick of price is explicitly rejected. When regard and goods are traded together, 'revealed preferences' will therefore not measure accurately the welfare produced. Individuals are likely to choose what is best for them, whether traded for money or not. In public policy, however, there is an inclination to maximize only what is measurable, and also a movement towards simulated market forms of provision. Such policies (the 'New Public Management') have often failed, because (a) quantitative measures are often unable to capture quality, which is more easily monitored in face-to-face interaction with peers and clients (b) quantitative sanctions replace approbation with fear, and informal monitoring with costly evaluation, and lead to neglect of unmeasured but vital tasks, and (c) there are unmeasured losses of regard, goodwill, and trust. Regard is a good in itself, quite apart from its instrumental value, especially where personal interaction dominates exchange, as in education and medical care.

In the market sector, transactions legitimized by market impartiality, and justified as market-clearing, may actually be driven by pseudo-regard. One suspect is the rise of executive pay in the United States and Britain. Remuneration bears little relation to economic performance, and is influenced by the reciprocal gifting motives of compensation committee members, and by status competition among traders, managers, and owners.

Adam Smith placed mutual obligation on a par with self-interest. In the modern world, reciprocity and approbation continue to motivate exchange on the largest scale. The price system is not sufficient on its own. A substantial proportion of welfare is obtained in the context of personal interaction, and is affected by the payoffs of regard. The boundaries between impersonal markets and relational exchange are affected by the cost of information, and the relative price of providing goods interactively or impersonally. Reciprocal exchange, with its personalized gift and discretionary delay, is required to authenticate regard. It motivates gains from trade in ways that are similar to the market. It persists because regard is an abiding need, perhaps 'wired in', which impersonal markets are not equipped to gratify.

NOTES

1. This chapter is substantially new, but incorporates some verbatim passages from (Offer, 1997), which is also the source for all unreferenced quantitative statements, and which contains additional references. Slightly updated in (Offer, 2006, ch. 5).
2. Smith uses the masculine form throughout.

REFERENCES

Belk, R.W. and G.S. Coon (1991). 'Can't Buy me Love: Money, Dating and Gifts.' *Advances in Consumer Research* **18**: 521–527.

Belk, R.W. and G.S. Coon (1993). 'Gift Giving as Agapic Love: An Alternative to the Exchange Paradigm Based on Dating Experiences.' *Journal of Consumer Research* **20**(3): 393–417.

Bénabou, R. and J. Tirole (2006). 'Incentives and Prosocial Behavior.' *American Economic Review* **96**: 1652–1678.

Bowles, S. and H. Gintis (1998). 'Is Equality Passe? Homo Reciprocans and the Future of Egalitarian Politics.' Amherst, MA, Department of Economics, University of Massachusetts.

Brennan, G. and P. Pettit (2004). *The economy of esteem: an essay on civil and political society*. Oxford, Oxford University Press.

Camerer, C. (1988). 'Gifts as Economic Signals and Social Symbols.' *American Journal of Sociology* **94**: S180–214.

Dalle, J.-M., P.A. David, Rishab Aiyer Ghosh and Frank A. Wolak (2004). 'Free & Open Source Software Creation and "the Economy of Regard".' Contribution to the Third EPIP Workshop: "What Motivates Inventors to Invent?" at Scuola Superiore Sant'Anna, Pisa, Italy, 2–3 April 2004.

Dohmen, T., A. Falk, D. Huffman and U. Sunde (2009). 'Homo Reciprocans: Survey Evidence on Behavioural Outcomes.' *Economic Journal* **119**(536): 592–612.

Ekman, P. (1985). *Telling lies: clues to deceit in the marketplace, politics, and marriage*. New York, Norton.

Fehr, E. and U. Fischbacher (2005). 'The Economics of Strong Reciprocity.' *Moral Sentiments and Material Interests: The Foundations of Cooperation in Economic Life*. H.E.A. Gintis (ed.). Cambridge, Mass., MIT Press, pp. 151–191.

Frank, R.H. (1994). *Microeconomics and behavior*. New York; London, McGraw-Hill.

Frey, B. (1986). 'Economists Favour the Price System – Who Else Does?' *Kyklos* **39**(4): 537–63.

Gérard-Varet, L.A., S.-C. Kolm and J. Mercier Ythier (eds.) (2000). *The economics of reciprocity, giving, and altruism*. Basingstoke, Macmillan.

Gintis, H. (ed.) (2005). *Moral sentiments and material interests: The foundations of cooperation in economic life*. Cambridge, Mass., MIT Press.

Hayek, F.A. (1945). 'The Use of Knowledge in Society.' *American Economic Review* **35**(4): 519–530.

Henrich, J.P. (ed.) (2004). *Foundations of human sociality: economic experiments and ethnographic evidence from fifteen small-scale societies*. Oxford, Oxford University Press.

Hollander, H. (1990). 'A Social Exchange Approach to Voluntary Cooperation.' *American Economic Review* **80**(5): 1157–1167.

Kolm, S.-C. (2008). *Reciprocity: an economics of social relations*. Cambridge; New York, Cambridge University Press.

Kolm, S.-C. and J. Mercier Ythier (eds.) (2006). *Handbook of the economics of giving, altruism and reciprocity*. Amsterdam, Elsevier.

Kranton, R.E. (1996). 'Reciprocal Exchange: A Self-Sustaining System.' *American Economic Review* **86**(4): 830–851.

Montes, L. (2003). 'Das Adam Smith Problem: Its Origins, the Stages of the Current Debate, and One Implication for Our Understanding of Sympathy.' *Journal of the History of Economic Thought* **25**(1): 63–90.

Offer, A. (1997). 'Between the Gift and the Market: the Economy of Regard.' *Economic History Review* **50**(3): 450–476.

Offer, A. (2006). *The challenge of affluence: self-control and well-being in the United States and Britain since 1950*. Oxford, Oxford University Press.

Smith, A. (1976[1759]). *The theory of moral sentiments*. Oxford, Clarendon Press.

Zelizer, V. (1994). *Pricing the priceless child: the changing social value of children*. Princeton, NJ, Princeton UP.

30. Relational goods
Benedetto Gui

Imagine an economy where children have at their disposal agreeable gardens, where adults own comfortable houses, and jobs are well-paid. Does it make any difference if children play alone or with mates, adults have good or bad relationships with relatives and neighbours, and the social climate on the job is pleasant or detestable? No difference, according to conventional national accounting. Instead, not only introspection, but also empirical research indicates that people value such details considerably.

How can this inconsistency be reconciled? One possible strategy is to recognize that GDP or aggregate consumption measure amounts of goods (respectively, produced and consumed), not citizen well-being. Another is to observe that those considered in national accounting, and more generally in economic analyses, are only a subset of the goods people draw benefit from; so new categories of goods must be taken into consideration, beside conventional ones. The concept of *relational good* fits into the latter scientific strategy. The expression first appeared in contemporary social sciences literature in the late 1980s in the writings of a few authors, apparently unconnected and belonging to different disciplines – Pierpaolo Donati, a sociologist, and Martha Nussbaum, a philosopher, in 1986; Benedetto Gui, an economist, in 1987; Carole Uhlaner, a political scientist, in 1989.

FIVE FEATURES OF RELATIONAL GOODS: FROM UHLANER TO MORE RECENT CONTRIBUTIONS

We take as a starting point Uhlaner's work, the first to provide an accurate economic analysis of the new concept. The instance of relational good that inspires her contribution is the sense of belonging to a valuable social group that is enjoyed by political activists – an intangible reward, she argues, for their efforts.

Following Uhlaner, relational goods have the following features:

1. they spring out of relationships between two or more people;
2. but only on the condition that these act appropriately (see below);
3. they are personalized, in the sense that the identity of people involved matters;
4. they are local public goods, as they confer non-rival benefits to two or more people, but not to everybody;
5. they are a special category of local public goods, as they can only be enjoyed if shared with others.

The examination of these features will give us the opportunity for offering a brief account of the theoretical debate that has followed.

Feature 1 means that a good should not be considered relational just because it has something to do with personal interactions, as it could be the case of a dinner with friends. A dinner is better viewed as a package including ordinary goods, such as the food prepared by the cooks, the service by waiters in white gloves, plus some entities that spring out of the interaction among participants (the company they may enjoy, the feeling of friendship they may experience. . .). It is only the latter that should be called relational goods. In other words, the adjective *relational* is intended to specify what these goods are made of, not just one of their qualities. Indeed, too loose an acceptation would end up rendering the concept useless.

Feature 2 points out that it is not enough that some people have a meal close to each other for the relational goods mentioned above to be created, as a look at the cafeteria of an airport crowded with businessmen travelling alone immediately shows. The syntax of interpersonal communication has subtle rules. Circumstances matter a lot. For instance, if a delay in departures has just been announced dialogue becomes easier because everybody shares the same concerns.

Uhlaner indicates reciprocity as a crucial condition for the generation of relational goods within a group of interactants. An interesting development in this regard is proposed by Sugden (2005), who shifts the requirement from the level of actions to that of sentiments. Indeed, in his view relational goods follow from mutual awareness of a correspondence of sentiments. Sugden's position enlightens two aspects of relational goods. First, they spring from the communication of attitudes. So, what matters for an interactant is often not so much the objective content of another's action, but what that action reveals about his disposition (e.g. if he is passing me an information, does he feel superior thanks to his knowledge, or would he happily accept a role reversal tomorrow?). Secondly, relational goods do not require the symmetry of actions or conditions that prevailed in the examples of political activists or diners. For a correspondence of sentiments to be created, it is not necessary that a patient takes reciprocating actions similar or in any way corresponding to those performed by a nurse. A thank you or a smile can be enough for communicating recognition of the nurse's beneficial action, or favourable disposition, thus triggering mutual awareness of favourable sentiments.

However, while reciprocity makes full-blown relational goods, unilaterally valuable affective communication can still take place even in its absence. An extreme case is a therapist and a child with behavioural disturbances, but situations in which one person is made the object of caring attention for a long time before sending back positive replies, are numerous.

The identity of the interactants – feature 3 – is often of no lesser weight in personal interactions than circumstances. Who the others are (in terms of sex, age, job, role played, nationality. . .), who am I, what do we know of each other, which experiences have we shared, all these are key factors impinging on what can be done and said in a personal interaction, and how each act is interpreted by others.

Feature 4 concerns non-rivalry of relational goods. Sports fans know well that the greater the crowd attending a match, the stronger participants' emotions are. Examples such as this support Uhlaner's statement that relational goods are public goods, a statement that has been largely accepted since. Some authors have gone farther and stated that with relational goods, unlike roads that are subject to congestion, increasing the number of consumers increases the benefit obtained by each; so, relational goods could be called *anti-rival* (Becchetti and Santoro 2007, 245). However, this does not seem to be a general rule. First of all, relational goods such as feelings of intimate friendship tend to dilute as the number of guests at a home dinner party increases beyond a certain threshold – an instance of congestion. More importantly, relational goods may be rival. An example is the moral support received by a sick person from her relatives. Were another family member in similar need, time and psychic energies devoted to the former could not be addressed to the latter.[1] The other characteristic usually taken into consideration when discussing public goods is excludability. With relational goods it can be present (think of a social event – for simplicity with no food or beverages served – by invitation only), but not necessarily (after the local team has won an important match, anybody can rally in the streets and share the enthusiasm of other fans).

Feature 5 points out an often-mentioned peculiarity of relational goods: their creation cannot be separated from their enjoyment, as both take place during the same interaction. This has led a few authors to state that relational goods do not fit well into the category of public goods: these can be enjoyed by several people, but typically each can enjoy them on his own (I can visit a park in the afternoon, while you do it in the morning). Neither are they private goods – the argument continues – so they are better viewed as a 'third genus' (see for instance Magliulo 2010, 145).

Indeed, jointness of production and consumption has implications for incentives. For enjoying the sense of collective identity brought about by membership in a political group, you must participate in its activities, but you are also contributing to its existence. Examples like this – or like sport events, mentioned above – have led most of the literature to conclude that relational goods are not subject to free-riding. Unfortunately, this is not the general rule. The life of political groups is not only made up of exciting events with thousands of supporters, but also of unpleasant organizational work to be done during weekends, while others relax at the seaside. And an amateur choir can only be successful and gratifying for its members if they show up not only at concerts, but also at rehearsals, despite these possibly being boring and on those nights when there are more attractive things to do. In other words, the creation of relational goods often entails costly actions that are quite distinct from those required for enjoying them, and individual incentives do not play in favour of the former being performed. This is the theme of the fragility of relational goods. They only come into existence if several people freely choose to behave in appropriate ways. Fragility was less much of a problem when people had few individual alternatives, but in modern societies the opportunity cost of time is prohibitively high, so we risk to be caught in a 'relational poverty trap' (Antoci et al 2007).

HOW ARE RELATIONAL GOODS CREATED? THE MODEL OF THE 'ENCOUNTER'

An attempt at connecting the creation and enjoyment of relational goods with conventional economic activities is Gui's (2005) model of the 'encounter'. This expression indicates any personalized interaction. The prototypes are face-to-face interactions; however, telephone conversations, teleconferences, or even communication via e-mail or letter can also be seen as encounters, with decreasing degrees of personalization. Obvious examples of encounters are: a seller and a buyer negotiating a contract, a professional serving a client, two technicians repairing a piece of equipment, two friends sipping a drink in a bar.

An encounter can be viewed as a productive process having various outputs. In each example above, one output is quite obvious: the signing of a sales contract, the provision of a service, the repair of the equipment, and the refreshment, respectively. Relational consumption goods are a second category of outputs of encounters. This is particularly evident in the case of hairdressing, as the process is well known for leaving ample room for talk – and therefore for affective communication – between provider and customer (and possibly other people in the room). However, affective communication occurs, and matters for interactants, in virtually all personalized interactions: those between friends, by definition; certainly also those between colleagues (the social environment on the job is systematically reported as a principal determinant of worker satisfaction); but one should not underestimate the relational potential of casual or recurring trades, as each is an opportunity for contact with another human, for receiving consideration, for being listened to, for telling and hearing jokes, even for expressing one's personal concerns. A simple test for determining whether an encounter also produces a noteworthy output of relational consumption goods consists in comparing it with a process that is identical in all aspects apart from personal communication. Is there a significant difference between being instructed by a software package, rather than by a colleague worker? Or being nursed in a hospital bed by a smart robot, rather than by a human? Or getting an equally good coffee from a machine, also programmed to give information about nearby shops, rather than by a barman? The answer may depend on circumstances. In the example of coffee it may depend on whether you are chatting with a group of colleagues during a break, so you are already socializing, or instead you are stopping in the night at a gas station while driving alone in a snow storm, so the mere fact of exchanging a few words with a living person can be reassuring. And, secondly, it may also depend on whether the two are strangers to each other, or if instead the traveller is a regular client with a positive relationship with the barman.

The last sentence, by making reference to interactants having met before, points out that encounters have a third type of output: the change in the state of the relationship between the interactants themselves. This is better understood if we first move the attention to the encounter's inputs.

To begin with, there are ordinary inputs, such as (with reference to the examples above): transportation, so seller and buyer can meet; the use of the hairdresser's premises; spare parts for the repair; and two bottles of juice on the bar's table.

However, the most important inputs of encounters are human inputs: the presence, the characteristics, the actions, the skills and knowledge of interactants themselves. In economic-theoretical language, these human inputs are a function of interactants' human capital (both general and relation-specific) and of its intensity of use (time devoted to the encounter and effort exerted). An example can clarify this point. Let us consider the case of a doctor visiting a patient, so the service provided – the first type of output of the encounter – is a diagnosis. The human capital the doctor brings and puts to use for the duration of the visit includes first of all her theoretical knowledge and the professional experience accumulated over years of practice; these are helpful in visiting any patient. However, depending on how many times the doctor has visited that patient before, her human capital may include more or less *relation-specific* information that is only helpful in dealing with him: in our example, knowledge of his medical history, or of a possible tendency to overemphasize the pain he suffers. The doctor's human capital specific to that patient may also include knowledge of which team he is a fan of, which can be of some use in relieving his tension (think of a frightened child). Notice that not only the doctor's human capital has a bearing on the visit, as the patient's ability to describe his symptoms clearly, and in correct language, is also helpful.

Relation-specific human capital – or, more simply, *relational capital* – does not only comprise information. Another component is to be taken into consideration: the state of feelings of one party towards the other. Indeed, reciprocal feelings impinge significantly on how an interaction unfolds (e.g., reciprocal resentments make decision-making processes in organizations lengthy and controversial). And, furthermore, feelings they have a certain inertia. These two remarks make it legitimate to view reciprocal feelings as a capital variable. Reciprocal feelings are also largely determined by previous interactions. For instance, long-lasting mutual hostility between colleagues is typically created by violent quarrels. Such events cause a deterioration of the state of feelings between the persons involved, that is a decumulation of relation-specific human capital.

Summarizing, according to the model of the encounter, personalized interactions also generate relational goods, which comprise relational consumption goods and relational capital goods. In brief, the concept of *relational good* catches what makes personalized different from non-personalized interaction.

Taking it explicitly into consideration helps accounting for important economic phenomena. Just to mention a few: the misery of recent migrants usually concerns relational consumption goods, and is largely explained by scarcity of relation-specific capital in the destination country; relational goods consumed in interactions with other volunteers and beneficiaries rank high among the most-cited rewards of volunteering; research teams develop a specific jargon that facilitates internal communication – a typical example of relational capital; while standard financial transactions are conducted anonymously (that is without the assistance of relation-specific capital), the financing of new ventures in the Californian computer industry (which are highly non-standard contracts) was typically agreed in the restaurants of Palo Alto, so over repeated meals the parties could learn more about each other (or, in our language, accumulate relation-specific capital).

Relational goods enter the evaluation of an encounter that is made by interactants, both *ex-post* and *ex-ante*. The *ex-ante* perspective is relevant for understanding which interactions are initiated. Sometimes, were it not for relational goods they expect to consume during the interaction, customers would prefer a cheaper unknown service provider (think of hairdressing, but also of computer assistance). It is not infrequent that people spend their leisure time at golf clubs, despite feeling uneasy with other members and hating playing golf (that is, the balance of the encounter is in red as far as both relational and conventional consumption is concerned), but still they do it for the sake of social networking (that is for accumulating relation-specific capital with VIPs).

Two criticisms have been raised against the encounter approach. A few authors (in particular Donati and Solci 2011) refuse the idea that relational goods are the result of a productive process, and regard them instead as an 'emerging entity', out of the control of each interactants and therefore unpredictable; this leads them to depict personalized interactions as a source of novelties. Their view has a value. However, it is not at odds with the idea of a 'productive' process, at least if this is not restrictively described as the execution of pre-programmed actions within a fully controlled manufacturing context. Productive processes also include the development of innovative products. This typically proceeds following suggestions by various members of a team (possibly inconsistent with each other) and under the influence of random events, so it walks a unique path that nobody can forecast. Indeed, the most appropriate theoretical framework for studying such processes is a dynamic game of cooperation and conflict, with exogenous uncertainty and a large strategy set, one whose complexity players hardly control. One danger of Donati and Solci's position, preoccupied that admitting intentional actions may lead back to methodological individualism, is to downplay the role of individual decisions in initiating and conducting personalized interactions.

According to Julie Nelson, instead, describing the effects of encounters in terms of consumption and investment entails the risk of disregarding that relationships do not just bring about comfort, social acceptance or the accumulation of information. She affirms that we are 'in very large degree constituted by our relationships. [. . .] [W]e are continually *created and shaped by* the encounters in which we participate.' Actually, she admits, the fact that '[o]ur social interactions form our capacities, preferences, and usual modes of response to stimuli' can be expressed in terms of changes of interactants' human capital (Nelson 2005, my italics). Still, she is afraid that recourse to customary economic language may prevent a much needed discontinuity with the traditional reductionism of the economic science.

ARE RELATIONAL GOODS AUTHENTIC GOODS?

Proponents of relational goods are doubtless stretching the notion of a good towards its limits. Mann (2007), who goes back to 19th-century discussions on whether relationships can be considered economic goods, agrees with Austrian authors that they are not, at least in general. He focuses on 'relationships', loosely defined, not on goods springing out of them, and bases his conclusions on the disputable criterion of whether they lend themselves to application of the demand–supply logic.[2]

Granting the attribute of goods to entities of the interpersonal sphere comes quite naturally within Becker's *economic approach to human behaviour*, thanks in particular to the concept of 'household production'. For instance, Cauley and Sandler (1980), with reference to a couple of spouses, include warmth among the 'commodities' produced. Indeed, the traditional criteria for warmth being recognized as an economic good are easily met: firstly, it satisfies a need and, secondly, it entails an opportunity cost – some resources with alternative uses must be devoted to making it come into being (for instance, time to accompany the partner to a show he/she likes). Observe that these conditions require neither the existence of prices, nor the embracing of a market logic. The most delicate issue here is to draw a neat enough distinction between the candidate good and the benefits it confers to the parties in the relationship, as both pertain to the subjective sphere of the latter. This has precedents within the *Beckerian approach*, that treats as separate variables, for instance, the ability to appreciate music (an element of personal capital, accumulated over time) and the pleasure derived from a concert, that is enhanced by that ability – both of them inner phenomena as well.

As pointed out by several authors, relational goods do not lend themselves to the application of the demand and supply logic: the company of a hired person does not have the same characteristic as that of a genuine friend. However, this observation does not imply that people cannot display a willingness to pay (WTP) for genuine relational goods in a market system. In fact, people manifest significant WTP for the inputs of encounters that are supposed to yield relational goods (air tickets for meeting family members or friends, rental of premises for hosting social events, food to be offered to guests. . .). One can even think of experiments for identifying which share of the WTP (in terms of travel cost, plus the value of time devoted) for participating in a party is to be attributed to relational goods, rather than, for instance, to the music being played there. To be sure, sometimes the opposite occurs, and people have a WTP for avoiding interactions in which affective communication appears as undesirable: there also exist 'relational bads'.

RELATIONAL GOODS VS. SIMILAR CONCEPTS

Attention for the relational aspects of economic interaction has been growing in the recent economic literature. In the writings of a few authors one can find references to concepts bearing some similarity with relational goods. Among these are: *attention* (the socio-emotional resources a manager or a colleague devotes to a worker, see Dur 2009, p. 551; see also Robison et al, 2002, who speak of 'socio-emotional goods'); *regard* (an attitude of approbation that is communicated primarily in face-to-face settings and represents a source of satisfaction for the receiver; see Offer 1997, p. 452); *esteem* (an intangible good a person obtains from others by virtue of what they think and feel about her; see Brennan and Pettit 2004). What these concepts do not adequately express, however, is the interactive nature of affective communication (Gui and Stanca 2010).

The most important comparison, however, is with the concept of *social capital* that has gained wide acceptance in social sciences in the last three decades. Although one can find here or there different acceptations, social capital is usually employed at a *meso* level of analysis: neither the level of individual actors, nor that of a nation, but an intermediate one – that of a village or a neighbourhood. It refers to aspects of social relationships within a community (the respect of norms of cooperation, mutual familiarity, trust towards others. . .) that allow it to obtain better results (for instance, maintain an irrigation system successfully) than in their absence. Social capital is then an asset of a community. The concept of *relational capital* presented above refers instead to pairs (or small groups) of individuals, according to a micro perspective. Still the two are related, as the strength and density of micro level relationships among the members of a community also has a bearing at meso level.

EMPIRICS

Due to their intangible and interpersonal nature, relational goods do not lend themselves easily to empirical investigation. Still a few studies intended to assess their significance are found in the economic literature.

One relevant strand is characterized by the inclusion of explanatory variables of a relational nature – such as time spent with friends, relatives, or fellow volunteers – into happiness equations. The results of these studies confirm those obtained by psychologists and other social scientists (for instance Kahneman et al, 2004): interpersonal relations appear to be an important determinant of subjective well-being. What these studies tell us is that people who, *ceteris paribus*, devote more time to social activities, are more satisfied (Becchetti et al. 2008, 2011; Bruni and Stanca 2008). If people are free to choose their lifestyle, the result above admits two alternative interpretations: in terms of opportunities, or in terms of preferences (*ex-ante*). According to the former some people have better social opportunities than others, which allow them, *ceteris paribus*, to secure a more satisfactory baskets of goods, richer in relational goods. According to the latter interpretation, people who assign low priority to relational goods adopt relationally poor lifestyles, which turn out to be less satisfactory *ex-post*. The latter interpretation requires that some people be misled by systematically wrong visions of the world, or be conditioned by some psychological mechanism (as in Pugno 2007). All this is at odds with the traditional rational choice approach of economic theorists. Turning to empirical evidence, there are longitudinal studies suggesting that people who display stronger materialistic orientation when leaving college will end up richer but less happy than their colleagues with a more humanistic orientation (Diener and Biswas-Diener 2002, 142). The two alternative explanations come closer to each other if we acknowledge the presence of relational assets. Some materialistically oriented youths might realize after some time that having purely instrumental relationships, merely aimed at obtaining income and career advancements, leads to relational poverty, but starting new genuine friendship relationships may be quite hard at an age when professional life leaves little time available for investing in relation-specific capital in one's private life (an instance of near irreversibility). If this holds true, just a bit of irrationality in early adulthood choices suffices to explain the adoption of lifestyles that later reveal themselves to be regrettable.

A few authors use the results of happiness equations to quantify the value of relational goods. For instance Powdthavee (2008) computes the implicit subjective price of interactions with friends and relatives for individuals participating in the British Household Panel Survey. He finds that respondents value such interactions up to seven times more than their yearly household income. (A brief survey of the above strands of empirical literature can be found in Gui and Stanca, 2010.)

The literature mentioned so far refers to encounters occurring in private life, so the only connection with the economic sphere is that the two spheres compete for limited available time. A few papers focus instead on encounters occurring at work. Among them Borzaga and Depedri (2005), who find that relationships with clients, colleagues and superiors have a significant effect on both job satisfaction and intentions to quit – evidence that intangible goods derived from interpersonal relations have economic value, for both workers and firms.

SOME IMPLICATIONS

What are the consequences of taking relational goods seriously?

The first order of consequences concerns choices, at individual, organizational, and societal level.

In principle, nothing prevents individuals from taking relational goods into consideration when deciding about a job, or a house. However, as each needs to give reasons for his choices, to both oneself and others, lack of widespread understanding and recognition of these intangible entities may bias choices towards those yielding more tangible benefits, such as pay increases or greater prestige. Another domain of choices where their significance is little understood is consumption, which is usually viewed and measured in terms of conventional goods, despite these being often just an excuse or a precondition for the creation and enjoyment of relational goods; to say the least, the two categories of goods are usually strong complements.

As mentioned above, relational goods have an impact not only on employee satisfaction but also on organizational effectiveness. This statement has far reaching implication for organizational design. Despite the study of relational goods still far from being included in economics and management education, numerous managers and organization leaders are well aware of their importance. In the business literature the expression *relational capital* is becoming more and more fashionable. Although sometimes it is given restrictive meanings (so it boils down to goodwill and little more), some authors adopt definitions close to the one proposed here (for instance St-Pierre and Audet 2011).

The third level of choices concerns public policy. Human interaction is too delicate an issue for public intervention to play a direct role. Still public decisions can create an environment more conducive to the accumulation of relational capital – which, as we saw, often has the nature of a public good. Its accumulation requires repeated opportunities for informal interactions among the members of not too large communities. Apart from places of worship, schools and jobs, neighbourhood shops have traditionally played this part, but less and less so in modern cities, as residential mobility, commuting, and personal transport facilities extend the number of potential partners in casual interactions to the hundreds of thousands, thus breeding anonymity. Of course, city planning can do a lot to grant residents opportunities to meet (think of pedestrian areas, parks, playgrounds, spaces for newborn associations. . .). Many other sorts of decisions have a bearing on the patterns and frequency of personal interactions, and therefore on relational goods. An example, discussed by Merz and Osberg (2009), is the synchronization of working time, as staggered days off reduce opportunities for groups to meet.

The second order of consequences following from recognition of the existence and relevance of relational goods concerns our perception of what the economic system is and which logics of behaviour are most appropriate in economic interactions. Consideration of the relational dimension brings new attention to intentions and motivations. These have largely been disregarded by economic theory, which prefers to focus, instead, on objective variables. However, if the quality of life depends significantly on the relational quality of encounters, the traditional instrumental view of human action, apart from being disputable on moral grounds, is also ill-advised on efficiency grounds.

NOTES

1. Interestingly, with reference to such entities as receiving deference, sympathy, or approval, Corneo and Jeanne (1999, 711–712) speak of 'socially provided *private goods*'.
2. Incidentally, the connections between the current debate and Böhm-Bawerk's 'relationship-goods' are also investigated by Magliulo (2010), who reaches a more positive conclusion as to the legitimacy of the concept of *relational good*.

REFERENCES

Antoci, A., P.L. Sacco and P. Vanin (2007), 'Social capital accumulation and the evolution of social participation', *The Journal of Socio-Economics*, **36** (1), 128–143.

Becchetti, Leonardo and Marika Santoro (2007), 'The wealth-unhappiness paradox: a relational goods/ Baumol disease explanation', in Luigino Bruni and Pier Luigi Porta (eds), *Handbook on the Economics of Happiness*, Cheltenham, UK, and Northampton, MA, USA: Elgar, pp. 239–262.

Becchetti, L., A. Pelloni and F. Rossetti (2008), 'Relational goods, sociability, and happiness', *Kyklos*, **61** (3), pp. 343–363.

Becchetti, L., G. Trovato and D.A. Londoño Bedoya (2011), 'Income, relational goods and happiness', *Applied Economics*, **43** (1–3), pp. 273–290.

Borzaga, Carlo and Sara Depedri (2005), 'Interpersonal relations and job satisfaction', in Benedetto Gui and Robert Sugden (eds), *Economics and Social Interaction*, Cambridge: Cambridge University Press, pp. 125–149.

Brennan, Geoffrey and Phillip Pettit (2004), *The Economy of Esteem*, Oxford: Oxford University Press.

Bruni, L. and L. Stanca (2008), 'Watching alone: relational goods, television and happiness', *Journal of Economic Behavior and Organization*, **65** (3–4), pp. 506–528.

Cauley, J. and T. Sandler (1980), 'A general theory of interpersonal exchange', *Public Choice*, **35**, pp. 587–606.

Corneo, G. and O. Jeanne (1999), 'Social organization in an endogenous growth model', *International Economic Review*, **40** (3), pp. 711–725.

Diener, E. and R. Biswas-Diener (2002), 'Will money increase subjective well-being?', *Social Indicators Research*, **57**, pp. 119–169.

Donati, Pierpaolo (1986), *Introduzione alla Sociologia Relazionale*, Milano: Angeli.

Donati, Pierpaolo and Riccardo Solci (2011), *I Beni Relazionali. Che Cosa Sono e Quali Effetti Producono*, Torino: Bollati Boringhieri.

Dur, R. (2009), 'Gift exchange in the workplace: money or attention?' *Journal of the European Economic Association*, **7** (2–3), pp. 550–560.

Gui, B. (1987), 'Eléments pour une definition d'économie communautaire', *Notes et Documents*, pp. 19–20, 32–42.

Gui, B. (2005), 'From transactions to encounters: The joint generation of relational goods and conventional values', in Benedetto Gui and Robert Sugden (eds), *Economics and Social Interaction*, Cambridge: Cambridge University Press, pp. 23–51.

Gui, B. and L. Stanca (2010), 'Happiness and relational goods: well-being and interpersonal relations in the economic sphere', *International Review of Economics*, **57** (2), pp. 106–118.

Kahneman, D., A.B. Krueger, D.A. Schkade, N. Schwarz and A.A. Stone (2004), 'A survey method for characterizing daily life experience: the Day Reconstruction Method (DRM)', *Science*, **306**, pp. 1776–1780.

Magliulo, A. (2010), 'The Austrian theory of relational goods', *International Review of Economics*, **57** (2), pp. 143–162.

Mann, S. (2007), 'Beyond Böhm-Bawerk: Searching for a place for relations in economic theory', *Review of Social Economy*, **65** (4), pp. 445–457.

Merz, J. and L. Osberg (2009), 'Keeping in touch – A benefit of public holidays using time use diary data', *International Journal of Time Use Research*, **6** (1), pp. 131–166.

Nelson, Julie A. (2005), 'Interpersonal relations and economics: comments from a feminist perspective', in Benedetto Gui and Robert Sugden (eds), *Economics and Social Interaction*, Cambridge: Cambridge University Press, pp. 250–261.

Nussbaum, Martha (1986). *The Fragility of Goodness: Luck and Ethics in Greek Tragedy and Philosophy*, Cambridge and New York: Cambridge University Press.

Offer, A. (1997), 'Between the gift and the market: The economy of regard', *Economic History Review*, **50** (3). pp. 450–476.

Powdthavee, N. (2008), 'Putting a price tag on friends, relatives, and neighbours: Using surveys of life-satisfaction to value social relationships', *Journal of Socio-Economics*, **37** (4), pp. 1459–1480.

Pugno, Maurizio (2007). 'The subjective well-being paradox: A suggested solution based on relational goods', in Luigino Bruni and Pier Luigi Porta (eds), *Handbook on the Economics of Happiness*, Cheltenham, UK, and Northampton, MA, USA: Elgar, pp, 263–289.

Robison, L.J., A. Schmid and P. Barry (2002), 'The role of social capital in the industrialization of the food system', *Agricultural and Resource Economics Review*, **31** (1), pp. 15–24.

St-Pierre, J. and J. Audet (2011), 'Intangible assets and performance: Analysis on manufacturing SMEs', *Journal of Intellectual Capital*, **12** (2), pp. 202–223.

Sugden, Robert (2005), 'Correspondence of sentiments: An explanation of the pleasure of social interaction', in Luigino Bruni and Pier Luigi Porta (eds), *Economics and Happiness: Framing the Analysis*, Oxford: Oxford University Press, pp. 91–115.

Uhlaner, C. (1989), 'Relational goods and participation: Incorporating sociability into a theory of rational action', *Public Choice*, **62**, pp. 253–285.

31. Social and civil capital
Paolo Vanin

Distingue frequenter!

INTRODUCTION

The broad idea that economies and societies may work better if they can rely on an abundant 'capital' of trust, civic norms, associational networks and well functioning institutions has been inspiring for a great number of social scientists. The concept of 'social capital' has provided a useful lexicon for some of these ideas. Yet no consensus has been reached on the definition of this concept. While this has led some scholars to question social capital as an analytical tool, its popularity in social sciences has kept rising, both because it provides a bridge between different social sciences, and because different empirical measures of social capital have proved to be powerful explanatory factors for a wide array of relevant phenomena. I first discuss some of the most popular definitions of social capital, then turn to the empirics of its measures, effects and accumulation, with the aim to tackle some crucial issues, but without any ambition of exhaustiveness. In particular, I will pay less attention to theoretical models of social capital, as well as to policy implications, because the theoretical literature mostly looks for finer distinctions than the broad category of social capital, and policy implications are hard to draw at a general level.

Since the notion of social capital is much more established in the literature than that of 'civil capital', I concentrate most of my attention on the former (with a special focus on the economic literature). In my view, the notion of 'civil capital' may serve two main purposes with respect to social capital studies: from the point of view of the history of economic thought, it connects them to the tradition of 'civil economy', as documented by Bruni and Zamagni (2007); and from the point of view of current and future research, it connects them to the analysis of institutions, as developed, among others, by North (1990), Ostrom (1990), Platteau (2000) and Tabellini (2010). At the same time, vague unifying labels face the risk of introducing more confusion than clarity in social sciences and I will argue that 'unpacking' social and civil capital is currently a more productive research exercise than trying to provide a unifying treatment (hence the opening Jesuitic motto, *distingue frequenter!*).

DEFINITIONS

Table 31.1 offers an introductory taxonomy of social capital, based on the distinction between social norms and social networks and on the aggregation level, which helps present the main definitions of the concept.

Table 31.1 An introductory taxonomy of social capital

Forms of social capital			Aggregation level
Social norms	Social networks	Trust	Individual
Cooperation	Bonding connections	Preferences	Family
Coordination	Bridging connections	Beliefs	Neighbourhood
External sanction	Linking connections	Equilibrium	Peers
Internalized values	Strong and weak ties		Civil society
Equilibrium beliefs	Association density		Government

What is Social Capital?

The term 'social capital' has appeared several times in social sciences over the last century (Hanifan, 1916; Seely et al, 1956; Banfield, 1958; Homans, 1961; Loury, 1977; Bourdieu, 1980, 1986), but its popularity started to rise in the last decade of the 20th century, mainly thanks to the contributions by Coleman (1988 and 1990), Putnam et al (1993) and Putnam (1995, 2000). The World Bank (2011), which in the 1990s launched an initiative on social capital (see Grootaert and van Bastelaer, 2001), defines it as 'the norms and networks that enable collective action', a broad idea which encompasses five more specialized dimensions: groups and networks, trust and solidarity, collective action and cooperation, social cohesion and inclusion, and information and communication.

While such a definition is so broad that it identifies an entire field of studies, Coleman (1988, 1990) tries to give a still broad but more precise definition of social capital, conceived as long lasting patterns of relations, brought about by social interaction, which constitute a resource available to individual actors. Such a resource may be accumulated or depleted over time and it is 'productive' in the sense that it allows actors to reach goals otherwise not reachable – or it diminishes the cost of reaching them. These characteristics justify the use of the term 'capital'. As physical and human capital are incorporated in physical goods and in single human beings, respectively, social capital is incorporated in social relations.[1]

Putnam, Leonardi and Nanetti (1993), in an investigation of the determinants of economic and political performance in Italy, offer a narrower perspective on social capital, conceived in terms of horizontal associational networks. In particular, they argue that civic engagement is strongly related to the presence of horizontal associational networks, that local public administrations are more efficient where civic engagement is stronger, and that historical differences in civic engagement can explain a great part of the difference in development between Southern and Northern Italy. In light of these results, Putnam's (1995 and 2000) subsequent findings that various forms of social participation in the US have been declining in the late 20th Century have raised many worries.

After these popular contributions, the literature on social capital has grown exponentially. Some authors, especially economists, look at social capital from an individual point of view. Glaeser, Laibson and Sacerdote (2002) for instance define social capital as an individual's social skills, which are partly innate ('e.g., being extroverted and charismatic'), but partly cultivated (e.g., popularity), i.e., they are the result of an investment. Social skills enable one to 'to reap market and non-market returns from interaction with others. As such, individual social capital might be seen as the social component of human capital.' DiPasquale and Glaeser (1999) define social capital as an individual's connections to others, and argue that it matters much for private provision of local amenities and of local public goods, and that it may be reduced by individual mobility.

At a more aggregate level, Fukuyama (1995), followed by a huge literature (e.g., Paldam and Svendsen, 2000), identifies social capital with trust and argues that it determines the industrial structure of an economy. Collier (1998) in turn focuses on connections and distinguishes social capital at the firm, family, civil society and government level, emphasizing both the potential for positive and for negative externalities. Social capital at the firm level is the easiest one to study. As already noticed by Coleman, both the internal organization of a firm and inter-firm linkages are intentionally designed to make profits; yet, collusive connections within and among firms may have negative external effects. Family connections are a valuable resource in many contexts; yet, Fukuyama (1995) and Banfield (1958), among others, emphasize the possible contrast between strong family ties and aggregate levels of social capital (although Banfield does not use such term). At the civil society level, Narayan (1999) observes that social capital tends to exert positive aggregate effects when trust, norms and networks that foster cooperation extend beyond primary, ethnic, linguistic or even income groups and form 'bridges' across different groups, whereas it may have negative effects when groups form along social cleavages and not across them. He thus distinguishes between 'bonding' and 'bridging' social capital, characterized by intra-group and inter-group connections, respectively. Woolcock and Narayan (2000) emphasize the crucial role of the connections between common people and individuals and groups with political and economic power – what the subsequent literature calls 'linking' social capital. Bowles and Gintis (2002) consider that 'well-designed institutions make communities, markets and states complement, not substitute', whereas 'with poorly designed institutions, markets and states can crowd out community governance' (along similar lines, see also Narayan, 1999). More recently, Guiso, Sapienza and Zingales (2010) propose 'a definition of social capital as *civic* capital, i.e. 'those persistent and shared beliefs and values that help a group overcome the free rider problem in the pursuit of socially valuable activities'.

Critiques and Discussion

Sobel (2002) provides a critical review of the literature on social capital developed in the 1990s, arguing that the term is a vague keyword, which might be better to avoid altogether for analytical purposes, although the topics under its umbrella are vey interesting. Among other things, he argues that the literature has often failed to distinguish social capital from its desirable effects, as well as to provide convincing measures of its stock and of its accumulation. Moreover, he argues that its value and uses depend on the institutional environment, as illustrated, for instance, by Ostrom's (1999) analysis of different local arrangements to solve collective action problems. Manski's (2000) analysis of the economics of social interaction and Bowles and Gintis' (2002) investigation of community governance are just two examples of a growing literature that focuses on specific aspects of social capital without necessarily using such term. In their accurate review of the theoretical and empirical literature on social capital, Durlauf and Fafchamps (2005) still find that theoretical definitions are often ambiguous and confused, and that 'much of the empirical literature is at best suggestive and at worst easy to discount'.

To clarify some of the sources of confusion, it is useful to focus in isolation on the three prominent concepts in the definitions of social capital: networks, norms and trust.

Sociologists have been developing social network analysis for over half a century (see, e.g., Wasserman and Faust, 1994). The economic analysis of social networks is more recent, but it has been a very active field of research for the last fifteen years (see, e.g., Goyal, 2007). Definitions of social capital in terms of social networks are among the least controversial ones. Yet, the literature on social networks often avoids reference to a general and unitary concept of social capital, and rather focuses on several specific characteristics of network structure and of network dynamics.

While social norms have always been at the heart of sociological analysis, economists have often avoided invoking them as explanatory factors, partly for the fear of incurring *ad hoc* explanations (see, e.g., Cole et al, 1992). Young (2008) presents social norms as 'customary rules of behavior that coordinate our interactions with others', which, once established, 'continue[ ] in force because we prefer to conform to the rule given the expectation that others are going to conform' (Lewis, 1969). Social norms are therefore seen as (customary) Nash equilibria of coordination games, which can be sustained through different mechanisms, ranging from pure coordination motives to external sanction and to norm internalization (see, e.g., Bicchieri and Ryan, 2011). The idea that social capital consists of a specific set of social norms (cooperative norms, in many treatments) poses a few relevant challenges. First, while it is a convenient simplification in many contexts to assume that each individual takes customs (and expectations of other people's behavior) as exogenously given, to the extent that these are instead equilibrium variables the term 'capital' as referred to social norms may not be the most appropriate one.[2] Second, coherent theories of social norms enforced by external punishment must explain the incentives to punish (see Elster, 1989). Third, if enforcement comes through norm internalization, such internalization process should also be explained, clarifying whether and how it affects preferences, values and beliefs. This is done for instance in the literature on cultural transmission and socialization surveyed by Bisin and Verdier (2010).[3]

Social capital is often defined in terms of trust, which is a less obvious concept than it looks. Among the most recent studies on this topic, Fehr (2009) proposes a behavioral definition based on Coleman (1990): an individual displays trust when she puts herself in a vulnerable position involving social risk, so that she is better off (than if trust were not placed) if the trustee is trustworthy, but worse off if the trustee is not trustworthy. Fehr points out that an important determinant of trust is betrayal aversion, captured by the fact that 'people are more willing to take risk when facing a given probability of bad luck than to trust when facing an identical probability of being cheated'. This adds to a long list of determinants of trust, including risk aversion, altruism and beliefs about other people's trustworthiness.[4]

To the extent that we regard beliefs as endogenous, it may be misleading to look at trust as a capital stock, although it may be empirically justified when beliefs and behavior are rather stable.[5] Indeed, Guiso, Sapienza and Zingales (2010) develop a model of beliefs transmission, which shows how certain beliefs may persist for a very long time. Yet, their definition of 'civic capital' is problematic in its reference to 'socially valuable' goals, because what is socially valuable for one group can be detrimental for other groups. From Olson's (1982) analysis of rent-seeking groups to Gambetta's (1993) account of the Sicilian mafia, one could multiply the examples of situations in which the same links, values and beliefs that keep together the members of a group also exclude or harm the non-members. A general implication is that it is intrinsically difficult to aggregate social capital.

EMPIRICS

Measures

Knack and Keefer (1997) can be used as a guide to a vast part of the literature on the empirical measures of social capital, since, using data from the World Value Survey, they try to distinguish the different aspects of trust, social norms and association density.

As a proxy for trust (TRUST), Knack and Keefer take the percentage of respondents that most people can be trusted (after deleting the 'don't know' answers) to the following question: 'Generally speaking, would you say that most people can be trusted, or that you can't be too careful in dealing with people?' The same variable is also used by La Porta Lopez-de-Silanes and Shleifer (1997) and by a huge literature thereafter. Glaeser et al (2000) combine survey and experimental data to assess whether TRUST provides a better measure of the level of trustworthiness in a society rather than of trusting behavior. Sapienza, Toldra and Zingales (2007) document that TRUST mainly reflects beliefs rather than preferences. Yet Fehr (2009) contends that trust, both in surveys and in experiments, also reflects risk aversion and social preferences (in particular, altruism and betrayal aversion) and not only beliefs.

To capture the strength of norms of civic cooperation, Knack and Keefer construct a variable (CIVIC) on the base of the answers to various questions about how individuals evaluate some anti-civic behaviors.[6] Guiso, Sapienza and Zingales (2010) are among the many subsequent contributions that use such questions to construct a measure of social capital.[7] Putnam, Leonardi and Nanetti (1993) rather rely on outcome-based indicators of civic engagement, namely voter turnout at referenda, newspaper readership and the diffusion of preference vote at political elections. Referenda turnout is also used, among others, by Guiso, Sapienza and Zingales (2004), who in addition propose blood donations as a new measure.

As a proxy for the density of horizontal networks (GROUPS), they consider the average number of groups cited per respondent when faced with the question of whether they belong to any of a list of groups of ten kinds. Knack and Keefer separately focus on 'Putnamesque' and on 'Olsonian' groups, i.e., on groups that 'involve interactions that can build trust and cooperative habits' and on groups with redistributive goals, respectively. Allcott et al (2007) and the literature on social networks emphasize the relevance of community size and network density, but a deeper account of the measures used in this literature is out of the scope of the present discussion.

The experimental literature has also provided a substantial contribution to the measurement of trust, especially through variants of the trust game (Berg et al, 1995). In particular, it has allowed to identify the determinants of trusting behavior both in preferences (risk and betrayal aversion, altruism) and in beliefs. Karlan (2005) discusses experiment-based measures of social capital and Fehr (2009) presents results both from economics and from neurobiology. The recent intersection of economics and neurobiology appears very has highlighted the fact that trust also has physiological determinants, such as the mammalian neuropeptide oxytocin (Kosfeld et al, 2005), and that prosocial behavior is driven by the moral sentiments of fellow feeling, or empathy, which can be manipulated physiologically in experiments, and which are affected by personal history, institutions and organizations (Zak, 2011).

Effects

The empirical literature on the effects of social capital is huge. Sabatini's (2011) webpage offers an excellent overview. I limit myself to a small selection of some illustrative contributions. My choice is driven in part by substantive interest and in part by methodological implications.

An old argument, already emphasized by Loury (1977) and Coleman (1988), is that social capital favors the accumulation of human capital, since individual skills are cultivated and developed better in a socially rich environment. Goldin and Katz (1999) use the proportion of a county population living in small towns as a proxy for closed and cohesive social networks and show that 'smaller towns of Iowa had the highest rates of secondary school attendance' at the beginning of the 20th century. Interestingly, they also provide evidence that social capital has a double role of condition for accumulation of human capital and of handmaiden of human capital.

Putnam, Leonardi and Nanetti (1993) find that local public administrations are more efficient where civic engagement is stronger, and that historical differences in civic engagement can explain a great part of the difference in development between Southern and Northern Italy. To mention just two subsequent studies on the topic, Hall and Jones (1999) show that a relevant part of countries' productivity is explained by institutions and government policies (what they call 'social infrastructures');[8] and La Porta et al (1999) find that explanations of the quality of governments based on trust, social norms of tolerance and work ethic cannot be rejected.[9]

Coming to growth, Knack and Keefer (1997) find that, in a sample of OECD countries, controlling for institutional quality, one standard deviation change in TRUST is associated with a change in growth of more than half of a standard deviation, whereas 'associational activity is not correlated with economic performance – contrary to Putnam et al's (1993) findings across Italian regions'. To tackle the possible endogeneity of TRUST, they instrument social capital with ethno-linguistic diversity (and the past share of law students). Algan and Cahuc (2010) use immigrants' cultural inheritance to construct an exogenous and time-varying measure of trust, assessing its sizable impact on growth.

Two studies by Guiso et al (2004 and 2009) illustrate the relationship between social capital and financial development and trade, respectively. In the former, they show that in areas with high social capital in Italy, 'households are more likely to use checks, invest less in cash and more in stock, have higher access to institutional credit, and make less use of informal credit'; in the latter, they find that bilateral trust between European countries is significantly related to trade. To tackle omitted variable and endogeneity problems, they exploit movers' social capital in the area of living and in the area of origin in the former study, whereas in the latter they use common religion and somatic distance as instruments.

Buonanno, Montolio and Vanin (2009) find that history-predicted association density and altruistic norms, proxied by blood donations, significantly reduce property crime; and Buonanno, Pasini and Vanin (2011) find that the density of social interaction, proxied by the population share living in small towns, significantly reduces property crimes, possibly because social sanctions are stronger in small and closed communities.[10] To tackle endogeneity, the former study uses historical instruments, whereas the latter exploits demographic and geo-morphological information. Importantly, these studies also carefully control for spatial externalities.

Discussion

The empirical measures of social capital and of its effects deserve some comments. The first broad message is that the different dimensions of social capital can be measured. Much progress has been made in determining what exactly each measure captures, although much remains to be understood. In my view, empirical effort towards distinguishing and separating the different dimensions of norms, trust and networks should be encouraged, whereas the use of synthetic and all-capturing indicators should be discouraged, because they are hard to interpret and the literature on social capital has already suffered too much from vagueness and from a lack in precision and rigor.

A second broad comment is that the measures of social capital should be clearly distinguished from those of its outcomes. Moreover, efforts to determine the effects of social capital should tackle a number of methodological problems, with omitted variables and endogeneity in a prominent position, as discussed by Durlauf and Fafchamps (2005). Their review of the empirical literature leads them to conclude that individual-level studies are more promising than cross-country studies, and that more effort should be devoted to 'differentiate social capital effects from the presence of other group effects such as information spillovers, or the presence of common factors such as legal or political institutions', or, as emphasized by Fehr (2009), informal institutions. For instance, Knack and Keefer's (1997) instruments (ethno-linguistic homogeneity and the past share of law students) are certainly correlated with TRUST, but there can be plausible arguments to think that they also have a direct impact on growth. In light of the difficulty to find valid instruments, Fehr correctly suggests that experimental studies may allow to make significant progress. At the same time, creative and rigorous use of datasets to identify exogenous sources of variation in social capital, for instance along the lines of Guiso et al (2004 and 2009) or of Algan and Cahuc (2010), is another promising way, but again the challenge is to identify which dimensions of social capital or of institutions have which effect (and through which channel), and to persuade the reader that the proposed measure is indeed capturing what it is intended to capture and not some omitted variable.

ACCUMULATION

If social capital is defined at the individual level, either in terms of social skills or of social connections, as in Glaeser et al (2002) and in DiPasquale and Glaeser (1999), a standard economic model of investment can be applied to study its accumulation. Yet, if positive and negative externalities are present over different groups, the aggregate social capital stock may be hard to determine and its dynamics need not be related to aggregate investment.[11]

If social capital is defined in terms of cooperative social norms or trust, to the extent that such norms and trust represent Nash equilibria, and provided that multiple equilibria exist, sudden jumps are possible, as argued above. Yet the literature on cultural transmission and socialization surveyed by Bisin and Verdier (2010) shows several mechanisms by which norms and beliefs may persist and be stable over time.[12] For instance, Tabellini (2008) studies the interaction between the transmission of cooperative values and the endogenous determination of external enforcement, finding that historical shocks may have persistent effects. Guiso et al (2008) in turn investigate how distrusting beliefs may persist over time. Durante (2009) finds evidence supporting the idea that trust norms were affected by weather variability in the distant past and then persisted for a long time. Analogous results in terms of gradual change and persistent effects of initial conditions are also found by Antoci et al (2007), who study the co-evolution of social participation and social capital accumulation, taking the view that the former contributes to the latter, and both contribute to socially enjoyed leisure: in particular, they emphasize the potential existence of 'social poverty traps'.

From the empirical point of view, a common result, found, e.g., by Knack and Keefer (1997), Alesina and La Ferrara (2000 and 2002) and Glaeser et al (2000), is that, broadly speaking, trust, civic norms and social participation tend to be higher in more homogeneous societies, along dimensions such as income distribution and ethnicity. Another widely debated question is whether there is a decline in social capital in affluent societies (especially the US). Costa and Kahn (2003) for instance argue that the decline in social capital has been overestimated by Putnam. Finally, the long persistence debate, initiated by Putnam, Leonardi and Nanetti's (1993) argument that the process of social capital accumulation takes centuries, is taken up, among others, by Guiso et al (2008), who show that current differences in social capital across Italy can be traced back to the free-city experience enjoyed by some cities and not by others at the turn of the first millennium (which can themselves be instrumented by Etruscan origin of the city and by the presence of a bishop in the year 1,000).

CONCLUSION

I argued at the beginning that a 'civil capital' perspective may be useful to connect social capital studies to the analysis of institutions. Let me simply conclude with three examples of how the most recent literature is taking this direction. Tabellini (2010) captures the effects of history on culture through the effect of literacy rates in the 19th century, and of the political institutions in place in the regions of Europe over the past several centuries, on current values and beliefs, and assesses the effect of history-predicted culture on current economic development. Aghion et al (2010) show that government regulation is higher where trust is lower and argue that distrust raises demand for regulation, and in turn regulation discourages the formation of trust, so that multiple equilibria are possible.[13] Along similar lines, Aghion, Algan and Cahuc (2011) document a negative relation between state regulation and the quality of labor relations, and they interpret it as reflecting the contrast between labour market regulation through the state or through the civil society. This recent literature on the interplay between social capital and institutions appears as the beginning of a very promising stream of research.

NOTES

1. See Granovetter (1973 and 1985) for an analysis of the strength of weak ties and of the embeddedness of economic action in social structure.
2. Indeed, social norms have both the potential for long term persistence and for sudden changes, and although coordinated changes are difficult and rare, one might argue that coordinating expectations in the presence of multiple equilibria is one of the most fundamental roles of policy.
3. See Cervellati and Vanin (2010) for a theory in which the incentive to internalize moral values comes from their role as commitment devices.
4. Khalil (2003) collects the main perspectives on trust developed by economists since the late 1970s, organizing them according to whether trust is seen as an equilibrium strategy in a repeated game or as a result of a preference trait (which may itself be the result of social selection and cultural evolution).
5. If social capital is a set of values (or of norms sustained by internalized values), it has to do with the goals that individuals want to reach, whereas if it is a set of beliefs, it is rather part of the constraint function.
6. Such questions concern the degree of disapproval for the following behavior: 'claiming government benefits which you are not entitled to'; 'avoiding a fare on public transport'; 'cheating on taxes if you have the chance'; 'keeping money that you have found'; 'failing to report damage you've done accidentally to a parked vehicle'.
7. They use the first principal component among the first and the third question used for CIVIC and the analogous one on 'someone accepting a bribe in the course of their duties'.
8. To tackle endogeneity, they propose different measures of Western European influence (based on spoken language and distance from the equator) as instruments.
9. As an instrument for such cultural characteristics they use religion and find essentially that 'predominantly Protestant countries have better government than either predominantly Catholic or predominantly Muslim countries'. La Porta et al (1997) find that, controlling for GNP in 1994 in a cross-country regression, 'a standard deviation increase in trust raises judicial efficiency by 0.7, the anticorruption score by 0.3, bureaucratic quality by 0.3, and tax compliance by 0.3 of a standard deviation'.
10. To support this interpretation, they complement the empirical analysis with a theoretical model of social sanctions, based on moral hazard.
11. Dynamic network formation games focus on the connections aspect of social capital, showing the articulated interplay between incentives, behavior and emerging networks. I have discussed some of these issues in my review (Vanin, 2008) of Goyal (2007).
12. See Bowles (1998) for the interaction between endogenous preferences and market and non market institutions, and Bergstrom (2002) and Sacco et al (2006) for a discussion of economic and cultural selection mechanisms.
13. A similar argument is developed by Pinotti (2011).

REFERENCES

Aghion, Philippe, Yann Algan, Pierre Cahuc and Andrei Shleifer (2010), 'Regulation and Distrust', *The Quarterly Journal of Economics* 125(3), 1015–1049.
Aghion, Philippe, Yann Algan and Pierre Cahuc (2011), 'Civil Society and the State: The Interplay Between Cooperation and Minimum Wage Regulation', *Journal of the European Economic Association* 9(1), 3–42.
Alesina, Alberto and Eliana La Ferrara (2000), 'Participation in Heterogeneous Communities', *The Quarterly Journal of Economics* 115, 847–904.
Alesina, Alberto and Eliana La Ferrara (2002), 'Who Trusts Others?', *Journal of Public Economics* 85(2), 207–234.
Algan, Yann and Pierre Cahuc (2010), 'Inherited Trust and Growth', *American Economic Review* 100(5), 2060–2092.

Allcott, Hunt, Dean Karlan, Markus M. Möbius, Tanya S. Rosenblat and Adam Szeidl (2007), 'Community Size and Network Closure', *American Economic Review* 97(2), 80–85.

Antoci, Angelo, Pier Luigi Sacco and Paolo Vanin (2007), 'Social Capital Accumulation and the Evolution of Social Participation', *Journal of Socio-Economics* 36(1), 128–143.

Banfield, Edward G. (1958), *The Moral Basis of a Backward Society*, New York: Free Press.

Berg, Joyce, John Dickhaut and Kevin McCabe (1995), 'Trust, Reciprocity, and Social-History', *Games and Economic Behavior* 10(1), 122–142.

Bergstrom, Theodore C. (2002), 'Evolution of Social Behavior: Individual and Group Selection', *Journal of Economic Perspectives* 16(2), 67–88.

Bicchieri, Cristina and Muldoon, Ryan (2011) 'Social Norms' in Edward N. Zalta (ed.), *The Stanford Encyclopedia of Philosophy* (Spring 2011 edition), available at http://plato.stanford.edu/archives/spr2011/entries/social-norms/ (last accessed November 2012).

Bisin, Alberto and Thierry Verdier (2010), 'The Economics of Cultural Transmission and Socialization', NBER Working Paper 16512.

Bourdieu, Pierre (1980), 'Le capital social', *Actes de la Recherche en Sciences Sociales* 31, 2–3.

Bourdieu, Pierre (1986), 'The Forms of Capital', in J. Richardson (ed.), *Handbook of Theory and Research for the Sociology of Education*, New York: Greenwood Press, pp. 241–258.

Bowles, Samuel (1998), 'Endogenous preferences: The cultural consequences of markets and other economic institutions', *Journal of Economic Literature* 36 (1), 75–111.

Bowles, Samuel and Herbert Gintis (2002), 'Social Capital and Community Governance', *The Economic Journal* 112(483), 419–436.

Bruni, Luigino and Stefano Zamagni (2007), *Civil Economy. Efficiency, Equity, Public Happiness*, Bern: Peter Lang.

Buonanno, Paolo, Daniel Montolio and Paolo Vanin (2009), 'Does Social Capital Reduce Crime?', *Journal of Law and Economics* 52(1), 145–170.

Buonanno, Paolo, Giacomo Pasini and Paolo Vanin (2012), 'Crime and Social Sanction', *Papers in Regional Science* 91(1), 193–218.

Cervellati, Matteo and Paolo Vanin (2010), '"Thou Shalt Not Covet . . .": Prohibitions, Temptation and Moral Values', FEEM Working Paper N. 54.

Cole, Harold L., George J. Mailath and Andrew Postlewaite (1992), 'Social Norms, Savings Behavior, and Growth', *Journal of Political Economy* 100(6), 1092–1125.

Coleman, James (1988), 'Social Capital in the Creation of Human Capital', *American Journal of Sociology* 94S, 95–120.

Coleman, James (1990), *Foundations of Social Theory*, Cambridge, MA, and London, England: The Belknap Press of Harvard University Press.

Collier, Paul (1998), 'Social Capital and Poverty', The World Bank Social Capital Initiative Working Paper 4.

Costa, Dora L. and Matthew E. Kahn (2003), 'Understanding The American Decline In Social Capital, 1952–1998', *Kyklos* 56(1), 17–46.

DiPasquale, Denise and Edward L. Glaeser (1999), 'Incentives and Social Capital: Are Homeowners Better Citizens?', *Journal of Urban Economics* 45, 354–384.

Durante, Ruben (2009), 'Risk, Cooperation and the Economic Origins of Social Trust: an Empirical Investigation', MPRA Paper 25887, University Library of Munich, Germany.

Durlauf, Steven N. and Marcel Fafchamps (2005), 'Social Capital', in Philippe Aghion and Steven Durlauf (eds), *Handbook of Economic Growth*, Edition 1, Volume 1, Chapter 26, pp. 1639–1699, Amsterdam: Elsevier.

Elster, Jon (1989), 'Social Norms and Economic Theory', *The Journal of Economic Perspectives* 3(4), 99–117.

Fehr, Ernst (2009), 'On The Economics and Biology of Trust', *Journal of the European Economic Association* 7(2–3), 235–266.

Fukuyama, Francis (1995), *Trust. The Social Virtues and the Creation of Prosperity*, London: Penguin.

Gambetta, Diego (1993), *The Sicilian Mafia*, London: Harvard University Press.

Glaeser, Edward L., David Laibson, José A. Scheinkman and Christine L. Soutter (2000), 'Measuring Trust', *The Quarterly Journal of Economics* 115, 811–846.

Glaeser, Edward L., David Laibson and Bruce Sacerdote (2002), 'An Economic Approach to Social Capital', *The Economic Journal* 112(483), 437–458.

Goldin, Claudia and Lawrence F. Katz (1999), 'Human Capital and Social Capital: The Rise of Secondary Schooling in America, 1910–1940', *Journal of Interdisciplinary History* 29(4), 683–723.

Goyal, Sanjeev (2007), *Connections: An Introduction to the Economics of Networks*, Princeton and Oxford: Princeton University Press.

Granovetter, Mark (1973), 'The Strength of Weak Ties', *American Journal of Sociology* 78(6), 1360–1380.

Granovetter, Mark (1985), 'Economic Action and Social Structure: The Problem of Embeddedness', *American Journal of Sociology* 91(3), 481–510.

Grootaert, Christian, and Thierry van Bastelaer (2001), 'Understanding and Measuring Social Capital: A

Synthesis of Findings and Recommendations from the Social Capital Initiative', The World Bank, Social Capital Initiative Working Paper 24.

Guiso, Luigi, Paola Sapienza and Luigi Zingales (2004), 'The Role of Social Capital in Financial Development', *American Economic Review* 94(3), 526–556.

Guiso, Luigi, Paola Sapienza and Luigi Zingales (2008), 'Long Term Persistence', NBER Working Paper 14278.

Guiso, Luigi, Paola Sapienza and Luigi Zingales (2009), 'Cultural Biases in Economic Exchange?', *The Quarterly Journal of Economics* 124(3), 1095–1131.

Guiso, Luigi, Paola Sapienza and Luigi Zingales (2010), 'Civic Capital as the Missing Link', NBER Working Paper 15845.

Hall, Robert and Charles Jones (1999), 'Why do some countries produce so much more output per worker than others?', *Quarterly Journal of Economics* 114(1), 83–116.

Hanifan, Lyda J. (1916), 'The Rural School Community Centre', *Annals of the American Academy of Political and Social Sciences* 67, 130–138.

Homans, George C. (1961), *Social Behavior: Its Elementary Forms*, New York: Harcourt, Brace and World.

Karlan, Dean (2005), 'Using Experimental Economics to Measure Social Capital and Predict Financial Decisions', *American Economic Review* 95(5), 1688–1699.

Khalil, Elias (ed.) (2003), *Trust*, Cheltenham: Edward Elgar.

Knack, Stephen and Philip Keefer (1997), 'Does Social Capital Have an Economic Payoff? A Cross-Country Investigation', *Quarterly Journal of Economics* 112(4), 1251–1288.

Kosfeld, Michael, Markus Heinrichs, Paul J. Zak, Urs Fischbacher and Ernst Fehr (2005), 'Oxytocin Increases Trust in Humans', *Nature* 435, 673–676.

La Porta, Rafael, Florencio Lopez-de-Silanes and Andrei Shleifer (1997). 'Trust in Large Organizations', *American Economic Review* 87(2), 333–338.

La Porta, Rafael, Florencio Lopez-de-Silanes, Andrei Shleifer and Robert Vishny (1999), 'The Quality of Government', *Journal of Law, Economics and Organization* 15(1), 222–279.

Lewis, David (1969), *Convention: A Philosophical Study*, Cambridge MA: Harvard University Press.

Loury, Glenn C. (1977), 'A Dynamic Theory of Racial Income Differences', in P. Wallace and A. LaMond (eds), *Women, Minorities and Employment Discrimination*, Lexington, MA: Lexington Books.

Manski, Charles (2000), 'Economic Analysis of Social Interactions', *Journal of Economic Perspectives* 14, 115–136.

Narayan, Deepa (1999), 'Bonds and Bridges: Social Capital and Poverty', *Poverty Group, PREM, The World Bank.*

North, Douglas (1990), *Institutions, Institutional Change, and Economic Performance*, New York: Cambridge University Press.

Olson, Mancur (1982), *The Rise and Demise of Nations*, New Haven, CT: Yale University Press.

Ostrom, Elinor (1990), *Governing the Commons: The Evolution of Institutions for Collective Action*, Cambridge University Press.

Ostrom, Elinor (1999), 'Social Capital: A Fad or a Fundamental Concept', in Partha Dasgupta and Ismail Serageldin (eds), *Social Capital: A Multifaceted Perspective*, pp. 172–214, Washington, DC: World Bank.

Paldam, Martin and Gert T. Svendsen (2000), 'An Essay on Social Capital: Looking for the Fire Behind the Smoke', *European Journal of Political Economy* 16, 339–366.

Pinotti, Paolo (2011), 'Trust, Regulation and Market Failures', *Review of Economics and Statistics* 94(3), 650–658.

Platteau, Jean-Philippe (2000), *Institutions, Social Norms and Economic Development*, Amsterdam: Harwood Academic Publishers.

Putnam, Robert (1995), 'Bowling Alone: America's Declining Social Capital', *Journal of Democracy* 6(1), 65–78.

Putnam, Robert (2000), *Bowling Alone: The Collapse and Revival of American Community*, New York: Simon and Schuster.

Putnam, Robert, Robert Leonardi and Raffaella Nanetti (1993), *Making Democracy Work: Civic Traditions in Modern Italy*, Princeton: Princeton University Press.

Sabatini, Fabio (2011), *Social Capital Gateway*, www.socialcapitalgateway.org (last accessed November 2012).

Sacco, Pier Luigi, Paolo Vanin and Stefano Zamagni (2006), 'The Economics of Human Relationships', in S-C. Kolm and J. Mercier Ythier (eds), *Handbook of the Economics of Giving, Altruism and Reciprocity*, Volume 1, pp. 695–730, Amsterdam: Elsevier North Holland.

Sapienza, Paola, Anna Toldra and Luigi Zingales (2007), 'Understanding Trust', CEPR Discussion Papers 6462.

Seely, John R., Alexander R. Sim and Elizabeth W. Loosley (1956), *Crestwood Heights: A Study of the Culture of Suburban Life*, New York: Basic Books.

Sobel, Joel (2002), 'Can We Trust Social Capital?', *Journal of Economic Literature* 40, 139–154.

Tabellini, Guido (2008), 'The Scope of Cooperation: Values and Incentives', *The Quarterly Journal of Economics* 123(3), 905–950.

Tabellini, Guido (2010), 'Culture and Institutions: Economic Development in the Regions of Europe', *Journal of the European Economic Association* 8(4), 677–716.

Vanin, Paolo (2008). 'Goyal, S.: Connections: An Introduction to the Economics of Networks', *Journal of Economics* 95(1), 83–86.

Wasserman, Stanley and Katherine Faust (1994), *Social network analysis. Methods and applications*, Cambridge: Cambridge University Press.

Woolcock, Michael and Deepa Narayan (2000), 'Social Capital: Implications for Development Theory, Research, and Policy', *World Bank Research Observer* 15(2), 225–249.

World Bank (2011), Social Capital, http://go.worldbank.org/VEN7OUW280 (last accessed November 2012).

Young, H. Peyton (2008) 'Social norms', in Steven N. Durlauf and Lawrence E. Blume (eds) *The New Palgrave Dictionary of Economics*, 2nd Edition, Palgrave Macmillan.

Zak, Paul (2011), 'The physiology of moral sentiments', *Journal of Economic Behavior & Organization* 77(1), 53–65.

32. Social enterprise
Carlo Borzaga

The term *social enterprise* was used for the first time in the 1980s to identify the innovative private initiatives established in Italy by volunteer groups that had formed to deliver social services or provide economic activities designed to facilitate the integration of disadvantaged people. At about the same time, organizations sharing similar goals were developing in a number of other European countries. These initiatives were initially set up using the not-for-profit legal forms made available by national legal systems (associations, foundations or cooperatives), which were in some cases modified to allow them to combine entrepreneurial activities with the pursuit of social aims. As a result, in some countries such as France and Belgium, most of these organizations adopted associative forms, while in other countries, such as Italy, organizations adopted the cooperative forms, giving rise to *social cooperatives.*

Since the 1990s, the concept of *social enterprise* has been increasingly used to qualify entrepreneurial initiatives operating in a number of diverse sectors of general interest. The defining features of social enterprises are the goals pursued and the production modalities adopted, and not simply the goods and services produced. As a consequence, various types of initiatives of different kinds are currently defined as social enterprises, including those promoting ethical financing, micro-credit, fair trade, and generally those initiatives producing goods and services with goals other than profit, such as those that aim to combat poverty and undernourishment (Yunus and Weber 2008). This evolution underlines the need to develop a general and shared definition of *social enterprise* that goes beyond specific and diverse cultural and legal contexts.

A variety of terms has been used to refer to these types of enterprises, sometimes interchangeably and often creating confusion. Although the literature in this field is not yet consolidated, the time is ripe for a tentative clarification.

The terms *social enterprise*; *social entrepreneurship*; and *social entrepreneur* all refer to initiatives that aim to generate social value through the private use and management of human and financial resources that are partially generated by market and quasi-market exchanges. As such, these initiatives are not designed to pursue the maximization of profits, but rather to use market mechanisms to underwrite the provision of social goods. These three terms have been widely employed to refer to initiatives in the social, health, and educational spheres. However, it is increasingly recognized that such initiatives could in principle concern any type of activity, provided that it is of general social interest.

The main differences between the terms can be understood by contrasting *social enterprise* (when enterprise is used as a noun) and *social entrepreneurship*. *Social enterprise* refers to a production unit fully belonging to the universe of enterprises, and it produces general-interest services in a continuous and stable way. *Social entrepreneurship*, on the other hand, encompasses a broad range of activities and initiatives that fall along a *con-*

tinuum, including a range of non-conventional entrepreneurial initiatives with a social goal. Another crucial difference between these two terms is the emphasis that *social enterprise* often places on the collective dimension and social entrepreneurship places on the individual dimension. In Europe, the social enterprise is normally conceived as a collective enterprise, whose background is rooted in long-lasting tradition of associations and cooperative enterprises, engaged in the provision of general-interest services. In the US two main roots regard the debate around *social enterprise* and *social entrepreneurship*. The first root refers to the use of commercial activities by non-profit organizations in support of their mission. The second root highlights the crucial role played by social entrepreneurs who are conceived as 'extraordinary individuals' driven by philanthropic aims (Defourny and Nyssens 2010).

The term *social business* (and *social business enterprise*) falls somewhere between the other two concepts, though it is closer to the definition of *social enterprise*. This term was proposed by Yunus (Yunus and Weber 2008) to distinguish his initiatives from the broader spectrum of social entrepreneurship activities. For him more precisely, 'a social business is a non-loss, non-dividend company designed to address a social objective'. Similar to the concept of *social enterprise*, *social business* thus refers to production units that are formally established and organized to ensure continuous production, although in fields of activity other than welfare (such as mass production of milk products sold at very low price to undernourished people). Similar to *social entrepreneurship*, however, *social business* often disregards the collective dimension, by emphasizing the entrepreneurial qualities of the founders of the enterprise.

Social enterprise has a narrower focus than the other two terms, but nevertheless it more precisely and usefully identifies the main features of the diverse voluntary bottom-up organizations that have been established over the last three decades to produce general-interest services.

DEFINITION

The most comprehensive definition of *social enterprise* has been elaborated by the EMES European Research Network (Borzaga and Defourny 2001; Defourny and Nyssens 2008). This definition is broadly accepted by academics working in this field although other definitions can be found in specific contexts (for instance the British policy to promote social enterprises under the Blair government). It has also inspired several pieces of legislation designed to regulate these forms of enterprises. The definition was initially elaborated along two dimensions (the economic-entrepreneurial and social dimensions). Following the scientific debate and the introduction of recent laws on social enterprises, this definition can be more precisely structured along three axes: the economic–entrepreneurial, the social, and the ownership–governance.

The economic–entrepreneurial dimension presupposes that social enterprises fulfil three criteria:

1. continuous activity producing goods or providing services;
2. at least the partial use of costly production factors (e.g. paid work);
3. a high degree of autonomy and hence a significant level of economic risk.

The social dimension presupposes that social enterprises fulfil two additional criteria:

1. an explicit social aim of serving the community or a specific group of people;
2. the production of goods/services that are characterized by a general-interest or meritorial nature.

The ownership–governance dimension presupposes that social enterprises are characterized by:

1. collective dynamics involving people belonging to a community or to a group that shares a certain need or aim;
2. a decision-making process not based on capital ownership;
3. representation and participation of customers, stakeholder orientation, and a democratic management style;
4. a total non-distribution constraint or a partial non-distribution constraint such that the organization distributes profits only to a limited extent, thus avoiding profit-maximizing behaviour.

Rather than being strict prescriptive criteria, these indicators constitute a tool, somewhat analogous to a compass, which helps the observer locate the position of social enterprises relative to one another (Borzaga and Defourny 2001).

This definition does not refer to any specific national legal system or to precise legal forms. It conceives the social enterprise as a private and autonomous entity that operates productive activities according to entrepreneurial criteria. Differently from conventional enterprises, social enterprises pursue an explicit social goal, which implies the production of goods and services that generate direct benefits for the entire community or specific groups of disadvantaged people. This definition excludes profit maximization as a goal pursued by investors. By contrast, it implies the search of balance between the fair remuneration of labour and capital and the by-products generated to the advantage of users. Social enterprises involve various types of stakeholders – such as volunteers and funders – in its ownership and governing bodies; and they usually rely on a plurality of income sources, including public funds when the services delivered are recognized as merit goods by public authorities; monetary and work donations; as well as market and private payments.

As such, social enterprises can be distinguished from other types of enterprises and organizations. They differ from public enterprises because they are managed by private entities according to an entrepreneurial logic. They differ from conventional for-profit enterprises because they are characterized by goals, ownership assets, constraints, and governance modalities that exclude the maximization of owners' monetary advantages. They also differ from traditional cooperatives, which are enterprises owned by non-investors that are principally aimed to promote the interests of their owners. Nevertheless, social enterprises are close to cooperative enterprises in terms of their ownership of assets, democratic governance structures, and common origins. This explains why social enterprises often decide to adopt cooperative forms.

This definition also helps to locate social enterprises vis-à-vis nonprofit organizations. Organizations that mainly engage in advocacy activities, civic participation, or resource re-distribution may have a beneficial impact on society, but they are not social enterprises. Moreover, some social enterprises could in principle be excluded from the universe of non-profit organizations on the grounds of their legal framework or because they are partially allowed to distribute profits.

The definition proposed here delineates the boundaries of social enterprises more precisely than alternative terms, but nevertheless there are still grey areas both with respect to the nonprofit sector and those conventional enterprises that are formally expected to generate profits but in practice decide not to.

EVOLUTION AND DIFFUSION

The development of social enterprises has occurred in heterogonous ways. In some countries, social enterprises have expanded widely and rapidly, whereas in other countries they have emerged later or have yet to take root. The analysis of the socio-economic factors favouring or preventing their emergence provides a useful basis for understanding social enterprises (Borzaga and Ianes 2006).

When looking at the context of development of social enterprises, several initiatives developed to respond to new needs that were ignored by for-profit enterprises and could not be adequately addressed by public policies. Social enterprises were initially started as self-help groups of local communities. These new initiatives were not limited to advocating more effective interventions by local authorities. Social enterprises self-organized concrete responses by instigating entrepreneurial initiatives and mobilizing a mix of resources. They have responded to new and unmet needs, often relying also on voluntary work, especially in the start-up phases. Moreover, social enterprises are bottom up institutional innovations promoted by groups of citizens unsatisfied by the services provided by both for-profit enterprises and public agencies. Some of these initiatives were established mainly to combat increasing unemployment of people who were difficult to employ (Borzaga and Becchetti 2011).

The subsequent diffusion of social enterprises was influenced by decentralization policies in the sphere of social and educational services in contexts of growing pressures on public finances. Responding to fiscal crises and the declining legitimacy of welfare systems, social enterprises offered an appealing alternative to the provision of services by public agencies. The resulting decentralization generated new spaces for intervention by, and public resource flows to, social enterprises. These developments contributed to consolidating the organizational models of social enterprises under construction and stimulated a progressive concentration of social enterprises in public markets, particularly welfare markets. The increasingly high percentage of incomes generated from public contracting accelerated the diffusion and consolidation of social enterprises, but simultaneously had the unintended consequence of increasing the dependency of social enterprises on public resources and policies, thereby reducing the propensity of social enterprises to innovate. As a result the use of community resources (voluntary work above all), which was one of the main characteristics of the first social enterprises, decreased and the employment of paid work increased significantly.

This situation is not the terminal stage in the evolution of social enterprises (Borzaga and Fazzi 2011). The search for new and diversified forms of relationships among social enterprises, public institutions, and private enterprises is widening and deepening. One important issue is whether contracting mechanisms can better combine the general-interest goals that characterize the mission of social enterprises and the nature of the goods and services that social enterprises produce. At the same time, social enterprises are increasingly engaged in those structures, especially at the local level, where socio-economic development policies are discussed and defined.

There have also been new trends in investing for product and process innovation. Social enterprises appear to be especially eager to identify new products and fields of activity. These new fields border the traditional core activities of social enterprises, such as social services, health and education, but also involve completely new spheres, including culture, environment, social tourism, and social housing. Process innovation has also occurred as social enterprises have increasing networking through company groups and agreements. These include consortia, groups, product societies, project partnership, and temporary enterprise associations that aim to clarify and coordinate the roles and interdependency among the various actors in production chains. These initiatives have involved social inclusion initiatives targeting disadvantaged people by means of agreements between social and for-profit enterprises. Finally, investment for innovation has occurred in activities that aim to qualify human capital, which occurs mainly through life-long education for employees.

LEGAL RECOGNITION

Since the 1990s, the diffusion of social enterprises has been linked to the introduction of a set of regulations that have resulted in institutionalization. Regulations have had a role in defining the social enterprise sector. From an international perspective, although they share similar identity connotations, social enterprises are extremely diversified as far as fields of activity and legal-organizational forms used are concerned.

National legislatures have generally followed one of two paths in regulating this sector (Galera and Borzaga 2009). The first involves the creation of new legal forms designed specifically for social enterprises, and these have generally been created by adjusting existing legal forms, usually those for cooperatives. The new regulations have specified goals, activities, constraints, governance assets, and incentives. Italian Law 381 of 1991 on social cooperatives was the first to be adopted and it was subsequently regarded as a reference point by other countries that followed a similar route, such as France, Korea, Portugal, and Poland.

The main characteristics of these laws are the definition of a general-interest goal that social cooperatives are expected to pursue, including the focus on the types of services;[1] the assignment of both collective ownership and democratic governance according to open-door and one-person, one-vote cooperative principles; the possibility of engaging a plurality of stakeholders (including paid workers, beneficiaries, and volunteers); and the imposition of severe constraints on the distribution of profits.

The second path does not link social enterprises with a specific legal form, pinpointing instead a number of structural and mission characteristics that could be in principle satisfied by any type of private legal form. Among the countries which adopted this approach are Belgium with the *enterprise à finalité sociale*, the United Kingdom with the

Community Interest Company, and Italy with the Law 118/05 (and subsequent decrees) on the Social Enterprise. These three laws are quite similar and follow the definition provided by the EMES Network. All three identify as the main goal of the enterprise the pursuit of the general interest. All three involve precise and severe profit distribution constraints.

There are, however, two main differences among the three laws: the fields of activity where social enterprises are entitled to engage and the collective and participatory dimension. In terms of activities, Italian law identifies the sectors where social enterprises are allowed to operate, while the UK law leaves it up to the enterprise to choose which general-interest activities to carry out. In terms of participation, the Italian and Belgian laws admit only collective social enterprises and governing bodies in which workers and clients participate. Individual social enterprises are not envisaged by Italian and Belgian laws. Conversely, the UK law allows for the establishment of individual social enterprises.

INTERPRETATION

The emergence and diffusion of social enterprises challenge both the dominant model of welfare systems, which is based on the state and market, and neoclassical economic theory, which assumes that enterprises promote only the interests of their owners thus minimizing production costs. From this perspective, social enterprises are considered to be 'degenerative forms' of enterprises owing to the privileges granted (including fiscal benefits and protected markets) or alleged opportunistic behaviours adopted (such as the unfair exploitation of workers). Some authors contest the sustainability of social enterprises. On the opposite side, other authors are concerned about the commercialization of social enterprises, claiming that their productive ends could endanger their original social missions (Díaz 2002).

In order to address these concerns, it is necessary to acknowledge the limits of the traditional definition of *enterprise* and revise it accordingly. Enterprises that are created and managed on the basis of profit maximization can contribute to the general well-being only if the markets where they operate are perfect or almost perfect; in other words markets have to be sufficiently developed to avoid high transaction costs, provided that all agents have the resources needed to purchase goods and services that can meet their needs. As it can easily be ascertained, situations of perfect or at least sufficiently high competition are not as diffused as usually asserted. Most importantly, these situations rarely occur in several specific parts of the economy, including welfare services and, more generally, personal and community services. Depending on the specific case, these services are often characterized by one or more of the following limitations:

- the existence of non-paying demand, namely people who are characterized by fundamental needs, but are unable to earn the resources required to purchase the necessary goods and services at market prices;
- situations of market power in which competition is limited and one or a few enterprises can influence price levels to the disadvantage of users;
- the difficulty of users assessing the real quality of the service supplied. Given the

lack of adequate information, it is impossible to previously agree and verify important characteristics of the service both *ex-ante* and *ex-post*; hence, it is unfeasible to assess the correspondence between the price demanded and the utility or value of the service;

- the difficulty or even impossibility of preventing that part of the value produced by the enterprise turning into positive externalities, namely benefits for non-paying users, and thus undermining the possibility of achieving profit margins that can attract for-profit entrepreneurs;

- the difficulty that enterprises have in identifying the actual level of demand, as well as verifying and monitoring consumer behaviour; consumers can, in turn, influence the efficiency of the enterprise – and hence, its survival – and the quality of services, especially when it latter depends also on the type of relationship established between users and workers.

When goods and services are influenced by one or more of these limitations, the production and exchanges carried out according to market logic and self-interest turn out to be insufficient, with respect to either the quantity or the quality of needs. As a result, part of the population will unavoidably be left unsatisfied.

According to mainstream economic theory, public authorities can solve these problems by regulating markets and enterprises; redistributing resources to the advantage of those who would not otherwise be able to satisfy their needs; or arranging for the direct production of services by public agencies.

These strategies, however, have proved to be increasingly ineffective. Over the last three decades, public interventions have been often unable to confront those problems. Over the same period, social enterprises have autonomously emerged as an alternative actor. Their development is *per se* a confirmation of the shortcomings of the dominant interpretation.

A different interpretation of the enterprise and its functioning must be based on a more in-depth analysis of both enterprises and human behaviour. Enterprises are best conceptualized as institutional mechanisms coordinating the activity of a plurality of stakeholders whose aim is to solve a specific problem, usually of a collective nature, through the continuous production of goods or services. In contrast to the claims made by conventional economic theory, both individuals and the enterprise make their own decisions – including those related to production, work, and consumption – not simply with the goal of gaining maximum individual advantage, but with a plurality of motivations, including intrinsic ones (the interest in the action *per se*) and social ones (the interest in other people's well-being).

The enterprise can be defined as a coordination mechanism of individuals, who are driven by different motivations. As a result, it will tend to structure itself as an incentive mix aiming at attracting human and financial resources. Attracted resources contribute to achieving the goal set, although they do not exclusively benefit the owners.

Against this backdrop, a more compelling interpretation of the social enterprise can be proposed. The social enterprise can be regarded as an incentive structure, which is consistent with the goal of producing a good or service to the advantage of the community (a 'common good') or of a group of citizens. Through a consistent coordination of goals, ownership structure, and constraints, this incentive structure helps to overcome problems generated by monopolist action and the insufficient or asymmetric distribution of information. Indeed, given the impossibility of distributing profits to the owners and the circumstance that social enterprises are often managed by users, social enterprises are not interested in exploiting market power or information advantages in order to achieve a higher profit. At the same time, it can stimulate the involvement of stakeholders with social or other-regarding preferences. These include workers that commit themselves to the enterprises' goal and accept lower remuneration when compared to that paid by conventional enterprises, and funders who are happy with a remuneration of capital under market rate or profit. As a consequence, social enterprises can also manage to distribute part of the product to users who do not have the resources needed to purchase goods and services at market prices, but who are not acknowledged as needy people by the public administration. In these cases social enterprises, compared to for-profit enterprises, distinguish themselves by their 'distributive' nature (Bacchiega and Borzaga 2003), because they manage to combine the production function with that of voluntary and systematic distribution of part of the value produced to people who would not otherwise be able to satisfy their needs. Although they are private entities, social enterprises fulfil functions that are traditionally ascribed to the state. At the same time, they are also more flexible in activating responses and addressing the new needs of small groups of citizens.

This approach to interpreting social enterprises challenges conventional assumptions that are mainly centred around the action of private enterprises and the state. Conventional assumptions regard private enterprises exclusively as responsible for the production and allocation of private goods (because they promote the interests of producers) and the state, and only marginally nonprofit organizations, as responsible for redistributing the income generated. Production and distribution that benefit marginal groups can both be managed by social enterprises. Acknowledging the existence of social enterprises implies that private citizens should not simply be regarded as philanthropists, who can use part of their income to the advantage of third parties; they can also organize enterprises that perform totally or partially in the market, and as a consequence operate according to allocation logics other than that of equivalence.

CONCLUSIONS

Social enterprises constitute a complex and multi-sided phenomenon, which remains difficult to interpret. However, their characteristics, specificities, and behaviour can be better understood when they are regarded as mechanisms through which a group of people can autonomously manage production activities that benefit groups of disadvantaged people or, more generally, the entire community. This approach can explain why such enterprises have developed so quickly and will continue to spread. Moreover, it provides insights into the specific conditions under which social enterprises develop, especially in a historical phase when it is increasingly evident that both the production and redistribution actions of public authorities are unable to keep pace with the escalation of needs.

The suggested interpretation of social enterprises is not comprehensive and does not consider the broad range of products and services that that social enterprises can provide. It does not take into account, for instance, the important positive externalities generated by the action of social enterprises, such as their contribution to social cohesion and to the creation of social capital. However, the identification of salient issues can help to define strategies, contracting relations, membership, and policies towards recruiting and incentivizing employees. It can also help define appropriate public policies and legislative frameworks, since social enterprises can only thrive if their distinctive ownership and governance mechanisms are respected.

NOTE

1. With a distinction between social cooperatives providing social assistance, health and educational services and those that aim to integrate disadvantaged people to work.

REFERENCES

Bacchiega, A. and C. Borzaga (2003). *The Economics of the Third Sector: Towards a more Comprehensive Approach*, in Anheier, H. K. and Ben-Ner, A. (eds), *The Study of The Nonprofit Enterprise, Theories and Approaches*, Dordrecht: Kulwer.

Borzaga, C. and J. Defourny (eds) (2001). *The Emergence of Social Enterprises*, London: Routledge.

Borzaga, C. and A. Ianes (eds) (2006). *Economia della solidarietà: Storia e prospettive della cooperazione sociale*, Rome: Donzelli.

Borzaga, C. and L. Fazzi (2011). 'Processes of Institutionalization and Differentiation in the Italian Third Sector', *Voluntas* 22(3): 409–427.

Borzaga, C. and L. Becchetti (eds) (2011). *The Economics of Social Responsibility: The World of Social Responsibility*, London: Routledge.

Defourny, J. and M. Nyssens (eds) (2008). *Social Enterprise in Europe: Recent Trends and Developments*, EMES Working Paper 08/01.

Defourny, J. and M. Nyssens (2010). 'Conceptions of Social Enterprise and Social Entrepreneurship in Europe and the United States: Convergences and Divergences', *Journal of Social Entrepreneurship*, 1(1): 32–53.

Díaz, W. (2002). 'For Whom and for What? The Contributions of the Nonprofit Sector', in Lester M. Salamon (ed.), *The State of Nonprofit America*, Washington DC: Brookings Institution Press, 517–536.

Galera, G. and C. Borzaga (2009). 'Social enterprise: An international overview of its conceptual evolution and legal implementation', *Social Enterprise Journal*, 5(3): 210–228.

Yunus, M. and Karl Weber (2008). *Creating a world without poverty: social business and the future of capitalism*, New York: Public Affairs.

33. Social preferences
Samuel Bowles and Herbert Gintis[1]

Social preferences are motives such as altruism, reciprocity, intrinsic pleasure in helping others, inequity aversion, ethical commitments and other motives that induce people to behave more pro-socially (that is helping others and punishing those who hurt others) than would an own-material-payoff maximizing individual. Our use of the term is not restricted to cases in which the actor assigns some value to the payoffs received by another person, as in the utility functions of Fehr and Schmidt (1999), Rabin (1993) and Levine (1998). While this is a convenient way to model some of the motivations for pro-social behavior, we use the broader definition because moral, intrinsic, or other reasons unrelated to a concern for another's payoffs often motivate people to help others, adhere to social norms, and act in other pro-social ways even when it is personally costly to do so. A person, for example, may adhere to a social norm not because of the harm that a transgression would do to others, but because of the kind of person she would like to be; helping the homeless may be motivated by Andreoni's 'warm glow' of giving rather than a concern with the well being of the poor (Andreoni, 1990).

Social preferences are nicely illustrated in the ultimatum game, which is a one-shot, anonymous game in which one subject, called the 'proposer,' is allocated a sum of money, say $10, and is instructed to offer any number of dollars, from $0 to $10, to a second subject, called the 'responder.' The responder, who knows how much the proposer was given, can either accept the offer or reject it. If the responder accepts the offer, the money is shared according to the offer. If the responder rejects the offer, both players receive nothing, and the game ends. A self-regarding responder will obviously accept any positive amount of money. Knowing this, a self-regarding proposer will offer $1, and this will be accepted.

However, when actually played, in many replications of this experiment in more than 30 countries and in some cases with substantial amounts of money at stake, proposers routinely offer responders very generous shares, and responders frequently reject low offers. The fact that positive offers are commonly rejected shows that responders have social preferences, and the fact that the most frequent proposer offer is 50 percent of the pie, despite the fact that even 40 percent offers are almost never rejected, shows by that proposers too have social preferences. Considerable evidence supports the interpretation that those who reject positive offers are generally motivated a desire to punish the proposer for being unfair, even though it means giving up money to do so.

Here we survey several key findings from recent experiments that extend our understanding of social preferences.

STRONG RECIPROCITY IS COMMON

The ultimatum game is not atypical. In experiments, we commonly observe that people sacrifice their own payoffs in order to cooperate with others, to reward the

	H	D
H	$b - c, b - c$	$-c, b$
D	$b, -c$	$0, 0$

Note: We assume $b > c > 0$. Helping contributes b to the other player at a cost of c to the contributor.

Figure 33.1   A prisoner's dilemma: single-period payoff to help (H) and don't help (D)

cooperation of others, and to punish uncooperative players, even when they cannot expect to gain from acting this way. We call the preferences motivating this behavior *strong reciprocity*, the term 'strong' intended to distinguish this set of preferences from entirely amoral 'tit-for-tat' reciprocation that would not be undertaken by purely self-regarding individuals. Because the strong reciprocator would increase his game payoffs by not cooperating, the motives for behaving this way are, by the standard biological definitions, an altruistic preference and an important proximate cause of altruistic cooperation.

The key feature of the one-shot prisoner's dilemma game is that mutual cooperation maximizes the sum of the players' payoffs, but defecting maximizes a player's payoffs independently of what the partner does. This is illustrated in Figure 33.1, where each player contributes $b > 0$ to the other player by helping, at a cost $c > 0$ to himself. If $b > c$, then both players benefit by mutual helping. However, with self-regarding preferences, knowledge of the partner's strategic choice will make no difference in the outcome – the result will be mutual defection. The fact that a high level of cooperation results when subjects are assured that their partner has already cooperated and that their own decision to cooperate would be transmitted to their partners prior to the latter choosing what to do is an indication that subjects are motivated by strong reciprocity.

FREE-RIDERS UNDERMINE COOPERATION

In a social dilemma that is repeated for a number of periods, subjects tend to start with a positive and significant level of cooperation, but unless there are very few free-riders in the group, cooperation subsequently decays to a very low level.

The experimental public goods game is designed to illuminate such problems as the voluntary payment of taxes and contribution to team and community goals (Ledyard, 1995). The following is a common variant of the game. Ten subjects are told that $1 will be deposited in each of their 'private accounts' as a reward for participating in each of the 10 rounds of the experiment. For every $1 that a subject moves from his 'private account' to the 'public account' on a given round, the experimenter will add one half dollar to the final payoffs to each of the subjects. At the end of 10 rounds, the subjects will be given the total of their final payoffs, and the experiment is terminated.

The sum of individual payoffs will be maximized if, in each round, each puts the entire $1 in the public account, generating a public pool of $10. In this case, the experimenter adds $5 to the final payoff of each subject. At the end of the game, 10 rounds having been played, each subject would be paid $50 – in each round $1 contributed minus the $0.50 returned by the experimenter. However, every $1 a player contributes to the public account, while benefiting the nine others by a total of $4.50, costs the contributor $0.50. Therefore the dominant strategy for a self-regarding player is to contribute nothing to the pool, and if all subjects do this, each then earns just $10.

In fact, as in prisoner's dilemma experiments, in public goods experiments, only a fraction of subjects conform to the self-interest axiom, contributing nothing to the public account. Rather, subjects contribute on average about half their private account in round one, but in later rounds, contributions decay to a level close to zero.

This decay is significant for the following reason. A supporter of the self-interest axiom is inclined to interpret other-regarding behavior in experiments as confusion on the part of the subjects, who are not accustomed to anonymous interactions. Their behavior therefore reflects their beliefs, that is, their understandings of the effect of their actions on the probability of achieving various outcomes, not their preferences, namely their assessment of the value of these various outcomes. In everyday life, one's actions are normally seen by others, so even if not contributing is the dominant strategy in the game, a failure to contribute would entail a loss of reputation, and hence a loss of future profitable exchanges. The anonymity of the laboratory may be sufficiently extraordinary that subjects simply play by these prudent and self-regarding rules of everyday life. Accordingly, the initially substantiated and later decline in contributions in the public goods game might be seen as a confirmation of this belief-based interpretation: subjects are not altruistic; rather, they are simply learning how to maximize their payoffs through game repetition.

However, were this explanation correct, if the same subjects were permitted to play a second multi-round public goods game public goods identical to the first, they should to refuse to contribute on the very first round. This prediction has been tested and found to be wrong. When the public goods game is played with several groups and after every series of rounds group membership is reshuffled and the game is restarted, subjects begin each new series by contributing about half, but each time cooperation decays in the later rounds. If one believes that the decay in contributions within a game is due to learning how to maximize payoffs in the context of anonymity, one would also have to believe that subjects unlearn the money-maximizing behavior between series! In fact, the only reasonable explanation for the decay of cooperation is that public-spirited contributors want to retaliate against free-riders, and the only way available to them in the game is by not contributing themselves. Subjects often report this reason for the unraveling of cooperation retrospectively.

ALTRUISTIC PUNISHMENT SUSTAINS COOPERATION

In social dilemmas, strong reciprocators, by punishing free-riders, induce their cooperation in subsequent play, thereby allowing cooperation to be sustained over time. Experiments by Orbell et al (1986), Sato (1987), Yamagishi (1988a, 1988b, 1992), and Ostrom et al (1992) and many experiments since show that when subjects are given a direct way of retaliating against free-riders rather than simply withholding their own

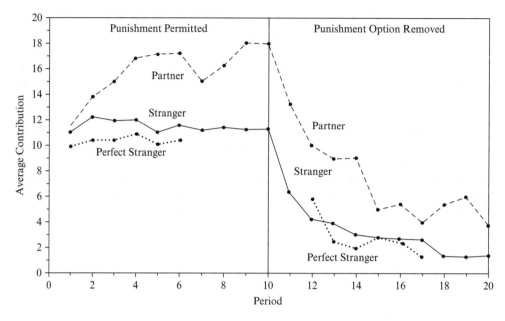

Note: Partner, Stranger, and Perfect Stranger treatments are shown when the punishment condition is played first (Fehr and Gächter, 2000). Results are similar when the punishment condition is played second.

Figure 33.2   *Public goods game with punishment, average contributions over time*

cooperation, they use it in a way that helps sustain cooperation. A particularly clear example of this was given by Fehr and Gächter (2000), who designed a repeated public goods game with an option of costly retaliation against low contributors in some treatments, called the *public goods with punishment* game.

Ernst Fehr and Simon Gächter used four-person groups, employing three different methods of assigning members to groups. Under the *partner treatment*, the four subjects remained in the same group for all 10 periods. Under the *Stranger treatment*, the subjects were randomly reassigned after each round. Finally, under the *perfect stranger treatment* the subjects were randomly reassigned in such a way that they would never meet the same subject more than once, so subjects knew that costly retaliation against low contributors could not possibly confer any pecuniary benefit to those who punish. Subjects were informed which treatment would obtain for their experiment.

Fehr and Gächter ran the experiment for 10 rounds with punishment and 10 rounds without. Their results are illustrated in Figure 33.2. The experimenters found that subjects were more heavily punished, the more their contributions fell below the average for the group. As a result, when costly punishment was permitted, cooperation did not deteriorate, and in the Partner treatment, despite strict anonymity, cooperation increased to almost full cooperation, even on the final round (top line, left panel). When punishment was not permitted, however, the same subjects experienced the deterioration of cooperation found in previous public goods games.

This result is telling because in the stranger and perfect stranger treatment, punishing free-riders is itself a public good, and is no different from contributing to the public good itself; both confer benefits on others at a cost to oneself. In both treatments, not contributing and not punishing are dominant strategies (they maximize payoffs regardless of the actions of the others). We term punishment in this setting altruistic for this reason. Yet as we saw subjects treat contribution and punishment differently. After the initial rounds in the standard public goods without punishment game, experimental subjects decline to contribute altruistically but once punishment is permitted they avidly engage in the altruistic activity of punishing low contributors.

Part of the reason for the difference is that people have an intrinsic motivation to punish shirkers, not simply an instrumental desire to alter their behavior or to affect the distribution of payoffs to either reduce unfairness or enhance one's own relative payoffs. This intrinsic desire to punish miscreants is retribution punishment. That subjects view punishment of shirkers also as retribution rather than simply as instrumental toward affecting behavior is consistent with the recent public goods with punishment experiment of Falk et al (2005). The game was one shot, ruling out behavior modification as a motive for punishing low contributors, and the punishment technology was such that punishment could not alter the difference in payoff between the punisher and the target (the cost to the punisher was the same as that inflicted on the target). Nonetheless, 60 percent of cooperators punished defectors.

PURELY SYMBOLIC PUNISHMENT IS EFFECTIVE

People are sensitive to others' evaluation of their moral worth or intentions and will cooperate in social dilemmas when the punishment for free-riding takes the form of criticism by peers rather than a reduction in material payoffs.

To test this idea, Masclet et al (2003) allowed the subjects in a public goods game to assign 'disapproval points' to the other group members after the subjects had been informed about each others' contributions. These disapproval points had no material consequences. They merely indicated the members' evaluation of one another. Allowing for the expression of disapproval raised the contributions to the public good relative to the baseline with no punishment opportunities.

In another experiment, Bochet et al (2006) compared the usual baseline public goods game with a 'chat-room' situation in which four group members communicated with one another through their computer terminals for several minutes before each round, and a 'face-to-face' situation in which group members engaged in face-to-face communication. These treatments are often called 'cheap talk' by game theorists, because any promises made cannot in any way be enforced. Nevertheless, the experimenters found that both forms of communication increased contributions considerably above the baseline level. Surprisingly, at least to the current authors' generation, chat-room communication was almost as effective in increasing contributions as face-to-face communication, and adding the option of material punishing (i.e., reducing the target's payoffs) increased contributions little more. Specifically, (a) face-to-face, face-to-face with punishment, chat room, and chat room with punishment all induced average contribution rates above 95 percent, and about 85 percent in the last of the 10 rounds; (b) punishment alone performed considerably less well, averaging about 70 percent, and 60 percent in the last period; (c) the baseline (no communication, no punishment) treatment performed worst of all, starting at 60 percent cooperation and declining to 20 percent in the final period, for an average contribution of about 48 percent.

Gächter and Fehr (1999) also found that, given some minimal social contact among strangers, making individual contributions publicly observable raises contributions to the public good substantially. Beyond this, Gächter and Fehr asked subjects to fill out questionnaires to measure the strength of their emotional responses toward cooperation and free-riding on the part of others. They show that free-riding elicits extremely strong negative emotions among the other group members. Moreover, in the post-experiment group discussions the other group members verbally insulted the free-riders.

These experiments and those by Falk et al (2005) and Fudenberg and Pathak (2009) described earlier make two things clear. First, the objective of punishment is not simply behavior modification but punishment per se. And second, the target's positive response to punishment cannot be explained by a desire to maximize payoffs in subsequent play, but as the shirker's attempt to right a wrong in the eyes of fellow group members. Thus the self-interest axiom explains neither the frequency nor the effectiveness of punishment.

SOCIAL PREFERENCES ARE NOT IRRATIONAL

The desire to contribute, to punish shirking, and otherwise to act on the basis of social preferences, like the desire to consume conventional goods and services, can be represented by preferences that conform to standard definitions of rationality (Savage, 1954; Hechter and Kanazawa, 1997; Gintis, 2009). These preference imply observable trade-offs, depending on the costs, and experiments confirm that the higher the cost of pro-social behavior, the less its frequency.

Many observers of experimental games have interpreted the fact that people sometimes sacrifice material gain in favor of moral sentiment as an indication of irrationality, the term 'rationality' being misused as a synonym for 'consistent pursuit of self-interest.' But subjects appear to be no less rational when deciding to cooperate and punish than when they compare prices to decide what to cook for dinner. This suggests that the preferences that lie behind their social behavior are consistent with the basic axioms of rationality, namely on transitivity (consistency) and completeness.

Andreoni and Miller (2002) tested the 'rationality' of pro-social choices by asking 176 subjects to play a version of the dictator game. Recall that in the dictator game, Bob is given a sum of money by the experimenter, and asked to transfer whatever proportion of the money that he wishes to another (anonymous) subject Alice. After Bob makes his decision, the money is transferred, and the game is over. In the Andreoni-Miller version of the game, the cost of giving was varied by the experimenter. Bob is given a sum m, a price p, and is asked to keep an amount ps, while transferring an amount po to Alice, such that $ps + ppo = m$. Thus, for instance, if $m = 40$ and $p = 3$, Bob could keep all 40 for himself or could keep 10 and transfer 10 to Alice, thus satisfying the equation $10 + 3 \times 10 = 40$. This p is the price of generosity. By varying m and p, the experimenters could see if the subjects responded to changes in the price of generosity in the expected way, and thus had 'rational preferences.'

In this experiment, 75 percent of the 'dictators' gave away some money, showing other-regarding behavior, and the average amount given away was 25.5 percent when the price $p = 1$ (a dollar-for-dollar transfer), which is about the same as in other dictator games (Forsythe et al, 1994). Moreover, the higher the price of generosity, the less money was given. For instance, when each dollar transferred to the other person cost two dollars ($p = 2$), only 14.1 percent was given away, and when each dollar transferred cost four dollars, only 3.4 percent of the dictator's endowment was transferred. Thus the subjects' demand for generosity responded to prices in a way no different from the demand, say, for ice cream. Equally important for the status of social preferences as rational, only 18 of the 176 subjects violated the principle of *transitive preferences* that requires that if an individual prefers *A* over *B* and *B* over *C*, he then prefers *A* over *C*. Moreover, these violations were almost all very minor. Indeed, 98 percent of the individual choices were consistent with transitive preferences. Similarly, in a public goods with punishment experiment in which punishment cannot be motivated by self-regarding preferences similar to that of Fehr and Gächter (2000), Anderson and Putterman (2006) found that the level of altruistic punishment that subjects inflicted on others varied inversely with the cost of punishing.

The fact that other-regarding preferences support price-responsive behaviors conforms to our representation of social preferences as distinct motivations within the framework of transitive preferences rather than some *sui generis* irrational or non-rational mode of behavior requiring a special model of decision-making. The fact that for many experimental subjects virtue is its own reward is perfectly consistent with the fact that, as in the case of people with self-regarding preferences, they would consider the price.

CONCLUSION

Experimental evidence suggests the importance of additional dimensions of social preferences, not described here due to limitations of space. For example, the extent and even valence of social preferences often depends on whether those interacting are from the same ethnic or other group. Moreover, while social preferences are evident in every population that has been studied thus far (and these number well over 60), the nature of social preferences differ across cultures. Finally, our view that social preferences have a strong ethical dimension is suggested by the fact that people readily punish individuals who have been unfair to others but not to the punisher herself.

Many economists, biologists and others will assert, as they have for at least a century, that altruism beyond one's immediate family members is highly exceptional and ephemeral. The experimental evidence of the last two decades tells strongly against this view. But the belief that self-interest is unrivaled among human motives has never depended on empirical tests. Rather it has appeared self-evident because the evolution of the human species by a process of natural selection was bound to produce a selfish animal. In the absence of a plausible evolutionary explanation of the origin of altruistic preferences (excepting close genealogical kin), the self-interest axiom was commonly accepted by default. But, as we show in Bowles and Gintis (2011), the idea that selfish genes must produce selfish individuals is false.

The experimental evidence suggests two aspects of preferences that will affect the course of economics and public policy in the years to come. The first is that populations are heterogeneous, including not only a minority of purely selfish individuals, but also unconditional altruists, strong reciprocators, and fair-minded people. The second is that people are versatile, acting in self interested ways in some situations and motivated by social preferences in others. These insights are now being imported into the standard fields of labor economics (Akerlof, 1982; Oh et al, 2011), law and economics (Kahan 1997), development economics (Hoff 2005), and even international trade (Belloc and Bowles, 2011). Public economics is particularly ready for a behavioral revolution as the new view of preferences supports novel explanations of voting, citizen support for egalitarian redistribution, the sometimes disappointing and even counterproductive effects of incentives, and the normative evaluation of policy interventions (Frey, 1997; Fong et al, 2005; Fong, 2001; Bowles and Hwang 2008; Bowles 2008).

NOTE

1.   The nature and importance of social preferences is treated at greater length and full references are provided in Bowles and Gintis (2011), Chapter 3. We are grateful to the European Science Foundation and the Behavioral Sciences Program of the Santa Fe Institute for support of this research.

REFERENCES

Akerlof, George A., 'Labor Contracts as Partial Gift Exchange,' *Quarterly Journal of Economics* 97,4 (November 1982):543–569.

Anderson, Christopher and Louis Putterman, 'Do Non-strategic Sanctions Obey the Law of Demand? The Demand for Punishment in the Voluntary Contribution Mechanism,' *Games and Economic Behavior* 54,1 (2006):1–24.

Andreoni, James, 'Impure Altruism and Donations to Public Goods: A Theory of Warm-Glow Giving,' *Economic Journal* 100 (1990):464–477.

Andreoni, James and John H. Miller, 'Giving According to GARP: An Experimental Test of the Consistency of Preferences for Altruism,' *Econometrica* 70,2 (2002):737–753.

Belloc, Marianna and Samuel Bowles, 'International Trade and the Persistence of Cultural-Institutional Diversity,' (Santa Fe Institute Working Paper 09–03–005, 2011).

Bochet, Olivier, Talbot Page, and Louis Putterman, 'Communication and Punishment in Voluntary Contribution Experiments,' *Journal of Economic Behavior and Organization* 60,1 (2006):11–26.

Bowles, Samuel, 'Policies Designed for Self-interested Citizens may Undermine "the Moral Sentiments": Evidence from Economic Experiments,' *Science* 320,5883 (2008):1605–1609.

Bowles, Samuel and Sung-Ha Hwang, 'Social Preferences and Public Economics: Mechanism Design when Preferences Depend on Incentives,' *Journal of Public Economics* 92,8 (2008):1811–1820.

Bowles, Samuel and Herbert Gintis, *A Cooperative Species: Human Reciprocity and its Evolution* (Princeton: Princeton University Press, 2011).

Falk, Armin, Ernst Fehr, and Urs Fischbacher, 'Driving Forces behind Informal Sanctions,' *Econometrica* 73,6 (November 2005):2017–2030.

Fehr, Ernst and Klaus M. Schmidt, 'A Theory of Fairness, Competition, and Cooperation,' *Quarterly Journal of Economics* 114 (August 1999):817–868.

Fehr, Ernst and Simon Gächter, 'Cooperation and Punishment,' *American Economic Review* 90, 4 (September 2000):980–994.

Fehr, Ernst, Klaus M. Schmidt and Simon Gächter, 'Altruistic Punishment in Humans,' *Nature* 415 (10 January 2002):137–140.

Fong, Christina M., 'Social Preferences, Self-Interest, and the Demand for Redistribution,' *Journal of Public Economics* 82,2 (2001):225–246.

Fong, Christina M., Samuel Bowles, and Herbert Gintis, 'Reciprocity and the Welfare State,' in Herbert Gintis, Samuel Bowles, Robert Boyd, and Ernst Fehr (eds) *Moral Sentiments and Material Interests: On the Foundations of Cooperation in Economic Life* (Cambridge, MA: MIT Press, 2005).

Forsythe, Robert, Joel Horowitz, N. E. Savin, and Martin Sefton, 'Replicability, Fairness and Pay in Experiments with Simple Bargaining Games,' *Games and Economic Behavior* 6,3 (May 1994):347–369.

Frey, Bruno, 'A Constitution for Knaves Crowds Out Civic Virtue,' *Economic Journal* 107(443) (July 1997):1043–1053.

Fudenberg, Drew and Parag A. Pathak, 'Unobserved Punishment Supports Cooperation,' *Journal of Public Economics* 94,1–2 (February 2009):78–86.

Gächter, Simon and Ernst Fehr, 'Collective Action as a Social Exchange,' *Journal of Economic Behavior and Organization* 39,4 (July 1999):341–369.

Gintis, Herbert, *The Bounds of Reason: Game Theory and the Unification of the Behavioral Sciences* (Princeton: Princeton University Press, 2009).

Hechter, Michael and Satoshi Kanazawa, 'Sociological Rational Choice,' *Annual Review of Sociology* 23 (1997):199–214.

Hoff, Karla, 'The Kin System as Poverty Trap?' in Samuel Bowles, Karla Hoff, and Steven Durlauf (eds) *Poverty Traps* (Princeton: Princeton University Press, 2005).

Kahan, Dan M., 'Social Influence, Social Meaning, and Deterrence,' *Virginia Law Review* 83 (1997):349ff.

Ledyard, J. O., 'Public Goods: A Survey of Experimental Research,' in John H. Kagel and Alvin E. Roth (eds) *The Handbook of Experimental Economics* (Princeton: Princeton University Press, 1995) pp. 111–194.

Levine, David K., 'Modeling Altruism and Spitefulness in Experiments,' *Review of Economic Dynamics* 1,3 (1998):593–622.

Masclet, David, Charles Noussair, Steven Tucker, and Marie-Claire Villeval, 'Monetary and Nonmonetary Punishment in the Voluntary Contributions Mechanism,' *American Economic Review* 93,1 (March 2003):366–380.

Oh, Seung-yun, Yong-jin Park, and Samuel Bowles, 'Veblen Effects, Political Representation, and the Twentieth Century Decline in Working Time,' (Santa Fe Institute 2011).

Orbell, John M., Robyn M. Dawes, and J. C. van de Kragt, 'Organizing Groups for Collective Action,' *American Political Science Review* 80 (December 1986):1171–1185.

Ostrom, Elinor, James M. Walker, and Roy Gardner, 'Covenants with and without a Sword: Self-Governance Is Possible,' *American Political Science Review* 86,2 (June 1992):404–417.

Rabin, Matthew, 'Incorporating Fairness into Game Theory and Economics,' *American Economic Review* 83,5 (1993):1281–1302.

Sato, Kaori, 'Distribution and the Cost of Maintaining Common Property Resources,' *Journal of Experimental Social Psychology* 23 (January 1987):19–31.

Savage, Leonard J., *The Foundations of Statistics* (New York: John Wiley Sons, 1954).

Yamagishi, Toshio, 'The Provision of a Sanctioning System in the United States and Japan,' *Social Psychology Quarterly* 51,3 (1988a):265–271.

Yamagishi, Toshio, 'Seriousness of Social Dilemmas and the Provision of a Sanctioning System,' *Social Psychology Quarterly* 51,1 (1988b):32–42.

Yamagishi, Toshio, 'Group Size and the Provision of a Sanctioning System in a Social Dilemma,' in W. B. G. Liebrand, David M. Messick, and H. A. M. Wilke (eds) *Social Dilemmas: Theoretical Issues and Research Findings* (Oxford: Pergamon Press, 1992) pp. 267–287.

34. Spiritual capital
André Habisch

INTRODUCTION AND DEFINITION

The notion of 'spiritual capital' sounds like an oxymoron: 'spiritual' originates from the Latin *spiritus* (translated from Greek *Pneuma* and Hebrew *Ruach*) and has the implication of 'supernatural being' or 'essential principle'. In the Western-Christian tradition 'spirit or spirituality' expresses the living, creative, spontaneous, challenging character of God's ('Holy spirit') presence or the corresponding orientation of the human person or community. Spirituality grants orientation, 'inspiration' and sense making. On the other hand 'capital' in its classical economic context is one of three (the others are: labour, land) factors of production. As input in the production function of an individual or household (capital *stock*) it originates from previous production and enhances the ability to perform productive activities in the future (capital *flow*). Thus, while 'spiritual' has implications of a challenging, unforeseen reality, requiring an attitude of careful attention and questioning; 'capital' is something known and disposable whose wise usage requires rational calculation. For the basic economic activity of optimal capital usage all relevant information have to be known – while the spiritual dimension represents the essential non-availability of relevant factors.

Spiritual capital is defined here as those individual as well as collective endowments of sense making, inspiration and innovation, which allow for continuous economic effort and ensure successful business cooperation and integrated human development. Spiritual capital is often nurtured by but not necessarily linked with institutionalized religion.

ROOTS OF THOUGHT: ANTI-MATERIALISM IN MAX WEBER

Without explicitly coining the term the founder of the sociology of religion, Max Weber, might be named as the conceptual protagonist of spiritual capital. Weber's path breaking thesis of the 'Protestant Ethics and the Spirit of Capitalism' opposed the Marxist materialist analysis, in which capital accumulation is the basic driver of the modern economic system ('capitalism') while every notion of 'spirituality' would be rejected as illusionary and simply hiding the overall exploitative character of economic relations. Even in the liberal neoclassical economic literature spiritual aspects are – comparable to gratuity (Bruni and Zamagni 2008) – methodically excluded from the analysis. Economic research increasingly squeezed out spiritual aspects or research topics. The cutting of theological and philosophical roots in economics since the late 19th and early 20th centuries (Oslington 2010), as well as the dominance of extrinsic motivation in organizational studies (Frey and Jegen 2001) are other consequences of that tendency.

Against these materialist reductions Weber closed a theoretical gap of development theory asking the question: when capital accumulation is the overwhelming logic behind economic behaviour and every rational economic investment is motivated only by an even higher economic return, *how was it possible that the modern capitalistic system (including its supportive institutions) came into place at all?* The traditional rural economy was characterized by a pervasive absence of capital goods as well as strict scarcity of investment capital; the vast majority of people led a hand-to-mouth existence. In the context of such a socio-economic environment, thriftiness, diligence and renouncement were not at all a rational behaviour for the first generation of entrepreneurs. They contributed substantially to the accumulation of capital goods in society and enlarged the economic possibilities of their predecessors. However, as Clark (2008) has shown, they rarely profited personally from the results. Why then did they invest? Weber stated that this grounding entrepreneurial behaviour is not deductible theoretically without taking the spiritual capital of Protestant-reformist theology and culture into account. The Calvinist tradition had abolished the mediating role of the Catholic Church (confession practice) and left the single believer with a painful uncertainty about his personal redemption. Within the Calvinist culture living a successful life and contributing to the common prosperity was perceived (not as the condition but) as the indicator of being accepted from God. Thus, according to Weber it was what I might call the spiritual capital of the Calvinist tradition which laid the ground for industrialization and the emergence of a modern capitalist society.

Weber's theory has been criticized from an historical point of view (e.g. Iannaccone 1998). His perspective on the emergence of capitalist production was obviously a too narrow German-Protestant one – overlooking for example that Catholic Belgium was among the first industrialized regions in Europe. Moreover, a broader historical analysis would have demonstrated that spiritual capital has also been crucial for the creation of financial institutions and markets long before industrialization took place. Franciscan theologians had been a driving force behind the foundation of Montes Pietatis in Italy in the 15th century (Bazzichi 2008), which later triggered the emergence of regional saving banks. But Weber's influential analysis clearly demonstrates that spiritual capital embedded in different religious traditions enfolds important catalyst power on the emergence of the modern business world.

HUMAN CAPITAL, SOCIAL CAPITAL, RELIGIOUS CAPITAL

Despite this powerful initialization, there is only a small body of literature on issues related to spiritual capital in sociology, political and other social sciences. Following the secularization hypothesis, these disciplines are generally rather reluctant to highlight the influence of religious and spiritual traditions on the development of modern social and economic institutions. However, spiritual capital might be interpreted in the context of the extension of capital theory, which is observable since the 1960s. This theoretical development has strong ethical implications because whatever is perceived as 'capital' has a strong impact on developmental policies, public appreciation, etc.

It was Nobel Prize winning economists Theodore W. Schultz (1961) and Gary S. Becker (1964) who introduced the concept of 'human capital', which transformed concepts of economic development. Becker's model of human capital and household behaviour was very influential because it was adaptable to a wide range of phenomena.

Opposing merely technocratic development concepts of earlier theories the authors identified knowledge, motivation and education as an important factor for economic development (Schultz 1979).

Following the lines of 'extending capital theory' in the 1980s and 1990s the concept of social capital evolved. From an individual's perspective the French sociologist P. Bourdieu (1983) perceived prevailing cultural and educational institutions as mere instruments to reproduce prevailing class differences in society and differentiated between economic, cultural and social capital of elites classes in that respect. Adopting a more civil society perspective the US pedagogic and sociologist J. Coleman (1988) showed that networks of (voluntary) engagements serve as an important social capital that differentiates more successful elementary schools in the US from less successful ones. Political scientists R. Putnam (1993) and E. Ostrom (1990) – the latter became the first woman to be awarded with the Nobel Prize in economics in 2009 – elaborated empirically the importance of social networks as social capital for enabling collective action on a local/ regional level and resulting socio-economic development (see Ostrom and Ahn 2010). In the work of these authors social capital (as civil society networks of voluntary engagement) is understood as an instrument to overcome Prisoner's Dilemma situations (as modelled in Game Theory) and to effectively organize collective action. It could be shown that availability of social capital is a crucial factor to explain different social and economic performance of very similar social entities – for example Italian regions (Putnam 1993), developmental projects (Ostrom 1990), etc. – resulting in successful or less successful socio-economic development. Since then, social capital theory emerged as a fruitful interdisciplinary research topic (for an overview see www.socialcapital-gateway.org, last accessed November 2012).

Iannaccone and Klick (2003) introduced the term 'religious capital' to explain patterns of religious beliefs and behaviour, over the life cycle, between generations, and among family and friends etc. This analytical tool is however directed more towards religiosity as such and does not explicitly question the effects of religious believes on business activities. Moreover, the authors clearly differentiate spirituality from religion.

SPIRITUAL CAPITAL AS A PART OF HUMAN CAPITAL

First, spiritual capital covers aspects of individual personality and competencies. Psychological research documents a strong and stabile influence of religion on health (see McCullough and Willoughby 2009 for an overview). Very religious people have a 29 per cent higher probability of reaching the respective next year of life expectancy than unreligious contemporaries. Powell et al (2003) have shown a 25 per cent reduction in mortality – international studies have raised these numbers as high as 25–30 per cent – for those who are intensely religious. Religious people rarely suffer from depression and generally report a higher quality of life. They are often described as kind and conscientious.

These findings are ultimately rooted in different behavioural patterns. Religious people are less dependent on alcohol, nicotine or other drugs, they show less risk-inclined behaviour, have better networks of mutual support and can handle stress more successfully. However, these determinants can statistically explain only 35–50 per cent of better health and increased well-being of religious people.

McCullough and Willoughby stress another factor: namely, the higher self-control and self-binding capacity. Both are crucial for living a successful life. As Duckworth and Seligman (2006) have shown, self-control is an even better indicator for academic success than intelligence. Delaying reward in infancy increases future economic and social success. According to Iannaccone (1998) and the economic theory of religion, expectations towards the hereafter play an important role in instructing a rational choice calculus: it opens up a larger time horizon and push towards 'investment behaviour' – a model which confirms the above thesis of Max Weber about the connection between protestant ethics and the emergence of capitalism. Findings from other religions also confirm these relationships; for example Oner-Ozkan (2007) has shown that Muslim students from Turkey, who are very religious, consider more carefully future consequences of their decisions than their less religious peers do.

In what form does religion influence self-regulation concretely? Religiosity may influence the selection of personal goals. There is some empirical evidence that religious belief influences the selection of personal goals and strengthens the desire for their achievement. This is because religiosity reduces goal conflicts, because the goals are integrated into an overarching goal system which increases consistency and the motivation effect (McCullough and Willoughby 2009). Moreover, religion can increase *self-awareness* as a prerequisite for effective self-control. An inaccurate self-perception prevents effective control of goal attainment. Religious practice enhances effective self-perception in at least three ways: through prayer and meditation (or the consciousness of being watched by God), through involvement in self-reflexive religious groups and through institutionalized practices of religious conscience formation in the confessional practice of the Catholic Church or in the Yom Kippur of Judaism.

Perception studies show that religious contexts require a high level of self-discipline and the renouncement of spontaneous chatting, eating and drinking, laughing and crying etc. Frequent or regular stays in these contexts strengthens the potential of effective self-commitment. Like a muscle, it grows with frequent use and degenerates without. Religious exercise – for example by prayer and fasting, meditation as in Zen-Buddhism, reading religious texts in Christianity – strengthens the potential of self-commitment in professional life. The same holds true for the *integration in social networks*, which strengthen the will to self-commitment using collective approval and disapproval. Self-help groups like Alcoholics Anonymous or Weightwatchers organize themselves following these principles.

According to McNamara (2002) religious meditation triggers self-control. Brain physiology shows that subjects with meditative experience cannot be stimulated by external impulses (like film sequences) as easily as test subjects with less experience. Asian experiments also show that cognitive conflicts are more easily solvable for subjects with meditative experience. Effective self-control is facilitated through the spiritual company of priests, ministers and other religious experts; regular exchange and informal controls strengthens the potential of self-commitment.

Beyond those rather outside orientated considerations basic theological contents also play an important role. It is the experience of God's supportive grace and choosing which motivates and strengthens the believer's desire to self-commit. The connection of participation in God's people and the adherence to a certain set of norms is most obvious in the Jewish Decalogue, which locates the commandments in the context of the overarching covenant of God with Israel. However, it is not the self-commitment as such, which the spiritual person is aiming at – in the sense of a 'spiritual body building' – rather it is a personal relationship with God (in the theistic religions) or oneness with universal cosmic principles (as in Eastern philosophies), which motivates believers intrinsically.

Is spiritual capital a relevant factor for professional success in the real world? The widespread secularization theory implies that the more educated and wealthy a person is, the less she or he is devoted to religion. As an empirical hypothesis, however, secularization is not confirmed by corresponding studies. On the contrary, the economic theory of religion – summarizing US and international studies (Iannaccone 1998) – shows that the percentage of religious persons increases with the level of education. A remarkable exception is the academic elite in social sciences and the humanities, which as a group is the only below average adherent to a religious group. Engineers and natural scientists on the other hand see an above average percentage of religiously affiliated persons.

A recent study among German managers confirms the connection between professional success, religious spirituality and self-commitment. In his qualitative interviews with 61 top managers of the largest German Enterprises (DAX 30, German branches of largest international companies, large family firms) Buß (2007) has demonstrated a higher than average rate of religious affiliation. Nearly 70 per cent of interviewees underlined the importance of religious atmosphere in the family of origin for determining their own identity. Strong religious practice was linked to values of self-control and self-commitment, here. Every fourth German top manager had been actively involved in a church-related youth group in his childhood; one of five managers is actively religious in the traditional canon of the church. But even among the un-churched, the active discussion of religious issues is remarkably widespread: only 10 per cent describe themselves as atheists. A third of the managers have been developing their own spirituality beyond church doctrines. These findings confirm the theoretical hypothesis about spirituality and self-commitment mentioned above.

SPIRITUAL CAPITAL, INNOVATION AND ENTREPRENEURSHIP

According to the research so far the main capital characteristic of lived spirituality seems to lie primarily in self-discipline and a voluntary ban of unwanted activities. In that perspective religious spirituality appears predominantly as a 'restrictive' affair, which guarantees the protection of property rights, the abandonment of laziness and luxury, the maintenance of a work ethic, the absence of alcohol and drug abuse, uncontrolled sexuality, etc. The benefit of spiritual capital is expected from this disciplinary function and the resulting constant work ethics. The Nobel laureate in economics, J. Buchanan, legitimizes religious preaching exactly in this way: 'We should all pay the preacher' because his sermon encourages engagement, lowers control costs and stabilizes an equilibrium of pro-social behaviour (Buchanan 1994).

In the self-concept of the most important spiritual traditions, however, 'restrictive' implications appear only as a by-product. Renouncement is not a goal in itself but rather a consequence of a different choice in life and the realization of better alternatives. Within the Christian tradition, Paul's letters constantly talk about the fundamental liberty of a follower of Jesus towards all kind or religious or cultic regulations. In a similar way Islam calls for obedience towards Qu'ran not in order to demonstrate one's own strength of self-commitment but to unify oneself with God's will. Abraham left his home not as a renunciation but to head towards an unknown future, following what he perceived as the promise of God. In the Jewish tradition the Ten Commandments have to be understood in the context of God's covenant with His people and the donation of the Promised Land. The historical Jesus told parables of the treasure in the field, the prodigal son, etc., which do not postulate ascetic self-denial; rather the message of God's loving self-revelation is calling for a corresponding practice of the faithful. In all these traditions spiritual life is not perceived as a limitation of freedom but rather as heuristics, indicating the search direction for better individual and collective alternatives. It is an inspiring source of innovation and change.

From such a perspective spiritual capital is not so much pointing to the disciplined labourer but rather to the Schumpeterian entrepreneur, who is inspired by a search for more human alternatives. Indeed, many of the industrial revolution's technical and social innovations were ethically motivated: they should reduce the pain of labourers, augment the quality of life of costumers and their families, etc. This humanizing effort also inspired the evolution of process innovations such as the introduction of flat hierarchies, semi-autonomous groups, human resource policies, co-entrepreneurship of employees, etc. The concept of entrepreneurship as 'creative destruction' (J. Schumpeter) including contemporary forms of 'social entrepreneurship', 'corporate citizenship', 'ethical innovation', etc., is compatible with such a more proactive concept of spiritual capital.

SPIRITUAL CAPITAL AS A PART OF SOCIAL AND ORGANIZATIONAL CAPITAL

So far we have highlighted contributions which elaborate the individual 'human capital' implications of spirituality. Another body of literature focuses more on social and organizational implications of spirituality. How does spiritual capital motivate and enable communities, organizations and effective networks to overcome dilemmas of cooperation, strengthen a cooperative behavioural equilibrium and develop corresponding institutions?

The inspiring work of Emil Inauen and Bruno Frey (2008) starts from the astonishing longevity of Benedictine monasteries in Southern German and Swiss regions (on average about 500 years), which can be interpreted as an indicator of organizational success. Even if there were isolated cases of power-abuse in the Benedictine history, these remain surprisingly rare given the enormous wealth of the monasteries and moderate levels of cultivated life styles in the social environment. According to the authors, the reasons lie within the organizational consequences of the spiritual capital of Benedictine monasteries. For instance, the authority of the abbot and his governing body (officials) is tempered by wide-ranging democratic elements: the free election of the abbot in the assembly of monks, the consent of the assembly for strategic decision-making, etc. The Rule of Benedict allowed only for relatively flat hierarchies. It demands from the abbot to listen especially to young members of the Order, which are deemed to be expressions of the Holy Spirit. Other elements are a careful selection of candidates and the benchmarking practice of mutual visitations and the special attention to criticism expressed within (Rost et al 2010, 103).

In a similar way, practical institutions of spiritual capital in for-profit companies have been analysed elsewhere, for example for the US (Malloch 2008) or for 'civil' enterprises in the tradition of 'economia civile' in Italy (Bruni and Zamagni 2007). Based on empirical research data with entrepreneurs from the Catholic Entrepreneurial Union in Germany Hammann et al (2009) provide evidence from ethical strategies of for-profit entrepreneurs inspired by Christian spirituality.

SPIRITUAL CAPITAL: OBJECTIONS AND POLICY IMPLICATIONS

Similarly to the earlier notions of human and social capital (see Schultz 1961) spiritual capital may also be criticized as illegitimate instrumentalization of the spirit, 'who blows where He wants to blow'. The Aristotle tradition perceives something instrumentally used as inferior, because usage seems to deny the intrinsic value and uniqueness. Kant, however, objected that usage is legitimate as long as the user is aware of the intrinsic value. With spirituality this is evident. Capital in itself is not a moral category. Like any other capital (for social capital see Gambetta's 1996 seminal work on trust and the Mafia) even spiritual capital might be abused to avoid the uncomfortable confrontation with reality or to manipulate people for selfish or criminal reasons.

Objections from business practitioners will probably run in a rather different direction: successful entrepreneurs are not necessarily spiritual people and spiritual capital appears to be only of minor importance for business success. To estimate the true meaning of the spiritual dimension of entrepreneurship, however, one must consider that spiritual capital – like every capital good – can still shape a corporate culture subliminally, if the current leaders are no longer consciously aware of it or clearly invest actively in its renewal. In many Chinese companies the Confucian tradition of learning has survived suppression during the now 60-year rule of Chinese Communism and again reveals its strength (see De Bettignies et al. 2011). In many companies, the founder routed the corporate culture so deeply that even less value-conscious successors continue the 'style of the house' and invest in carrying on the spiritual capital.

Accounting for spiritual capital poses serious challenges for the further development of economic and managerial analysis and education. Most importantly performance measurement on a company as well as economy level must not just rely on short-term financial aspects but also include the spiritual tradition as a basic business asset of the company. Strategic innovations and frequent adaptations to changing market environments should reflect the fact that gains from certain short-term orientated strategies might be overcompensated by depreciating side-effects on the spiritual capital of the company. Within accounting and financial analysis, key performance indicators should be developed to include spiritual capital variations (for example employee satisfaction, creativity, stakeholder relationships). On an economy level the respective debate on searching indicators for collective well-being 'beyond GDP' (Jones and Klenow 2011) has to be mentioned. From such a perspective spiritual capital not only marks an additional category of (individual or collective) assets but also calls for a new paradigm of business economics.

BIBLIOGRAPHY

Bazzichi, P. (2008) *Dall'usura al giusto profitto. L'etica economica della scuola francescana*, Edizione Effatà.

Becker, G. (1964) *Human Capital: A Theoretical and Empirical Analysis, with Special Reference to Education*, Chicago University Press.

Bourdieu, P. (1986) 'The forms of capital' in J. Richardson (ed.) *Handbook of Theory and Research for the Sociology of Education*, New York, Greenwood, pp. 241–258 (originally in 'Ökonomisches Kapital, kulturelles Kapital, soziales Kapital' in *Soziale Ungleichheiten* (Soziale Welt, Sonderheft 2), edited by Reinhard Kreckel. Goettingen: Otto Schartz & Co. 1983, pp. 183–98).

Bruni, L. and Zamagni, S. (2007) *Civil Economy. Efficiency, Equity, Public Happiness*, Bern: Lang.

Buchanan, J.M. (1994) *Ethics and economic progress*, Norman: University of Oklahoma.

Buß, E. (2007) *Die deutschen Spitzenmanager – Wie sie wurden, was sie sind*, München und Wien: Oldenbourg.

Clark, G. (2008) *A Farewell to Alms: A Brief Economic History of the World*, Princeton University Press.

Coleman, James S. (1988) 'Social Capital in the Creation of Human Capital', *American Journal of Sociology* 94 Supplement: S95–S-120).

Dasgupta, P. and Serageldin, I. (eds) (2000) *Social Capital: A Multifaceted Perspective*, Washington, D.C.: World Bank.

De Bettignies, H.C., Habisch, A., Ip, D. and Lenssen, G. (2011) 'Practical Wisdom from the Chinese Spiritual Tradition', *Special Issue of the Journal of Management Development* 30(8).

Duckworth, A.L. and Seligman, M.E.P. (2006) 'Self-discipline outdoes IQ in predicting academic performance of adolescents', *Psychological Science* 16: 939–944.

Duriez, B. and Soenens, B. (2006) 'Religiosity, Moral Values and Moral Competence: A Critical Investigation of the Religiosity – Morality Relation', *International Journal of Behavioral Development* 30(1).

Ekelund, R.B., Herbert, R.F. and Tollison, R.D. (2006) *The Marketplace of Christianity*, MIT Press, Cambridge, MA.

Frey, B.S. and Jegen, R. (2001), 'Motivation crowding theory: a survey of empirical evidence', *Journal of Economic Surveys* 15(5): 589–611.

Gambetta, D. (1996) *The Sicilian Mafia. The business of private protection*, Harvard University Press.

Hammann, W., Habisch, A. and Pechlaner, H. (2009) 'Values that create value: Socially responsible business practices in SMEs – empirical evidence from German companies', *Business Ethics: A European Review* 18(1): 37–51.

Iannaccone, L.R. (1998) 'Introduction to the economics of religion', *Journal of Economic Literature* 36: 1465–1496.

Iannaccone, L.R. and Klick, J. (2003) 'Spiritual Capital: An Introduction and Literature Review' (available at http://www.spiritualcapitalresearchprogram.com/, last accessed 1 June 2011).

Inauen, E. and Frey, B. (2008) 'Benediktinerabteien aus ökonomischer Sicht', Center for Research in Economics, Management and the Arts, Working Paper No. 2008–17.

Inauen, E., Rost, K., Osterloh, M. and Frey, B.S. (2010) 'Back to the Future – A Monastic Perspective on Corporate Governance', *Management Revue* 21(1): 38–59.

Jones, C. and Klenow. P. (2011) 'Beyond GDP? Welfare Across Countries and Time', NBER Working Paper No. 16352.

Malloch, T.R. (2008) *Spiritual Enterprise. Doing Virtuous Business*, New York, London: Encounter Books.

McCullough, M.E. and Willoughby, B.L.B. (2009) 'Religion, Self-Regulation, and Self-Control: Associations, Explanations, and Implications', *Psychological Bulletin* 135(1): 69–93.

McNamara, P. (2002) 'The motivational origins of religious practices', *Zygon* 37: 143–160.

Milgrom, P. and Roberts, J. (1992) *Economics, Organization and Management*, Prentice Hall.

Oner-Ozkan, B. (2007) 'Future time orientation and religion', *Social Behavior and Personality* 35: 51–62.

Oslington, P. (2010) 'Christianity's Post-Enlightenment Contribution to Economic Thought', in I.R. Harper and S. Gregg (eds) *Christian Theology and Market Economics*, Edward Elgar, Cheltenham, pp. 60–73.

Ostrom, E. (1990) *The Tragedy of the Commons. The Evolution of Institutions for Collective Action*, Cambridge University Press.

Ostrom, E. and Ahn, T.K. (2010) *Foundations of Social Capital*, Edward Elgar, Cheltenham.

Powell, L.H., Shahabi, L. and Thoresen, C. E. (2003) 'Religion and spirituality: Linkages to physical health', *American Psychologist* 58: 36–52.

Putnam, R.D. (1993) *Making Democracy Work. Civic Traditions in Modern Italy*, Princeton University Press.

Rost, K., Inauen, E., Osterloh, M. and Frey, B. (2010) 'The corporate governance of Benedictine abbeys. What can stock corporations learn from monasteries?' *Journal of Management History* 16(1): 90–115.

Schultz, T.W. (1961) 'Investment in Human Capital', *American Economic Review* 51: 1–17.

Schultz, T.W. (1979) 'Nobel Lecture: The Economics of Being Poor', *Journal of Political Economy* 81: 2–13.

35. Spiritual humanism and corporate economics
Luk Bouckaert

The question 'What is humanism?' has many answers in history. In the first section we will explore briefly some of the answers but our aim is to focus on spiritual humanism as a postmodern search for humanity. The second section deals with personalism as a paradigm for spiritual humanism. In the last section I shall apply spiritual humanism to the field of corporate economics by elucidating the notion of spiritual capital.

FROM SECULAR TO SPIRITUAL HUMANISM

The term 'humanism' refers first of all to the *renaissance movement* of the 14th and 15th centuries which brought a renewed model of education through the study of classical texts from antiquity. Humanists were practitioners of the *studia humanitatis*. The *studia humanitatis* or liberal arts were grammar, rhetoric, poetry, history, moral philosophy and, to some extent, politics. Instead of preparing students for the practical disciplines of law, medicine, or theology on the basis of traditional textbooks, humanists wanted to create a new sense of *humanitas*, enabling people to participate fully in public and cultural life. Familiarity with the cultural and moral legacy of antiquity was the way to shape a culturally literate and emancipated citizenship. The movement started in Italy (Florence and Naples) but spread across Europe. It was not an anti-clerical or anti-religious movement; many humanists worked for the organized Church and were in holy orders like Petrarch or Erasmus 'the prince of humanists'. It was a period of tolerance, critical debate and cultural creativity which, according to Stephen Toulmin, was substituted in the 17th century under pressure of religious conflicts by the modern agendas of Newton and Descartes (Toulmin, 1990). However, during the 16th and 17th centuries, the Jesuit promotion of the *humaniora* as a model of education and cultural literacy for young people was deeply inspired by the renaissance humanism of the 14th and 15th centuries.

During the 18th century the term humanism gained a more secular and anti-religious meaning. The authors of the famous French *Encyclopédie* like Diderot and d'Alembert and other enlightened philosophers like Julien Offray de La Mettrie (1709–1751) and Auguste Comte (1798–1857) redefined humanism. They no longer interpreted humanism as an educational model of cultural literacy but as a secular worldview based on rational and scientific knowledge. The wisdom of antiquity gave way to the positive knowledge of modern science. Renaissance or Christian humanism did not disappear but gradually lost its dominant position. Modern, secular humanism developed different expressions such as rationalism, positivism, secularism, Marxism, pragmatic humanism, existential humanism or, more recently, 'new atheism'. Today, the British Association of Humanism defines humanists as non-religious people who share the belief:

that this life is the only life we have, that the universe is a natural phenomenon with no super-natural side, and that we can live ethical and fulfilling lives on the basis of reason and humanity. [Humanists trust] to the scientific method, evidence and reason to discover truths about the universe and place human welfare and happiness at the centre of their ethical decision making. (See humanism, www.humanism.org.uk, last accessed November 2012).

In the second half of the 20th century – after Auschwitz and other tragedies in the name of humanistic utopias – postmodern forms of humanism emerged. The term 'postmodern' is a very loaded and ambiguous term. Literally, it means: what comes 'after' and goes 'beyond' modernity, the cultural epoch in Western history characterized by a strong belief in the blessings of *reason* in science, moral philosophy, economics and politics. Just as modernity was driven by a critique of pre-modern, traditional assumptions, post-modernity is eager to criticize the assumptions of modernity. But a lot of postmodern discourse has a more far reaching agenda. It promotes an ideology of deconstructionism and relativism, an epistemology of 'everything goes' or a morality without normative content. Postmodernism runs the risk of undermining every genuine search for truth and morality, not least its own epistemological and moral claims. Spiritual human-ism while sharing the postmodern critique of modernity rejects its ideology of pure deconstructionism.

Postmodern criticism of science – or at least of scientism – has two different sources. Firstly, philosophers of science such as Kuhn, Lakatos and Feyerabend revealed during the 1960s the hidden dogmatic structure of a positivist conception of science. Pointing out that empirical observations are always theory-laden, they undermined the idea that science is based on the hard rock of positive facts and hence is immune for theory and value-laden prejudices. According to them, science has the epistemological structure of a problem solving narrative inspired by meta-scientific assumptions and supported by selective observations. The second front of criticism came from social philosophers and activists. They accused mainstream scientists and research institutes of sustaining the expansion of the capitalist industrial–military complex and of participating in the over-exploitation of planetary resources. As a result of this double criticism, science and reason lost their exclusive claims to truth and social progress. Today a growing stream of deep ecologists, new age adherents, religious and non-religious people exploring non-rational sources of knowledge such as traditional wisdom, emotional intelligence, intuition and meditation, try to find new perspectives for meaning and purpose in life. Some call it a 'spiritual revolution' shaping a new type of human civilization (Heelas & Woodhead, 2005; Tacey, 2004; Bouckaert, 2011a). It is important to remember that spirituality in this new context does not coincide with a particular, institutionalized form of religion. Spiritual humanism is a post-secular forum for religious and non-religious people in search of a deep, personal and transcendent meaning in life. It is committed to a pluralist and interreligious dialogue and is very sensitive to non-rational sources of knowledge and ethics. The rise of spirituality is remarkable since it contradicts the classic thesis of secularization which, though it predicted the decline of religion, failed to notice the diffuse emergence of spirituality.

Where modern humanists believe that the human ratio is the measure of all things, spiritual humanists explore new ways of self-transcendence and mysticism in history and cosmology (Capra, 1975; Wilber, 1996). Early philosophical expressions of the new sense of transcendence can be found in Bergson's idea of *L'Evolution Créatrice* (1907),

Heidegger's philosophy of *Sein und Zeit* (1927) and Whitehead's *Process Philosophy* (1929). Buddhism and Taoism opened Western people to a perspective of spiritual, non-theistic enlightenment that fitted very well with some aspirations of the deep ecology movement. What seems to be the core element in this spiritual eco-humanism is the experience of deep interconnectedness with all beings and with Being itself. This experience which discloses the human subject as a receptive and interconnected self fundamentally differs from modern perceptions of the subject as a rational and self-defining ego. As we will see in the next section, spiritual humanism must not be reduced to its ecological and cosmological expression. Another experience of deep interconnectedness is articulated by personalism defining human freedom as a gift from and to the other.

The experience of universal interconnectedness is not derived from empirical observation or conceptual representation. It is based on an intuitive, pre-conceptual awareness revealing interconnectedness as an *ontological condition*. The disclosure of the interconnected self enables us to take some distance from our self-constructed and active egos and to live in touch with our deeper intuitions. It generates a space of inner freedom which allows new meaning and purpose in life. It coincides with the experience of the *Spirit* as the ultimate driver of meaning in every being and in the cosmos as a whole. Believers will interpret the Spirit as the manifestation of the creative love of God, whilst non-believers will see it as a non-material source of creativity in the evolutionary process. What these different interpretations may be and what unites them is a rejection of scientific materialism reducing nature to a complex chain of causal and mechanistic relations, a respect for the non-instrumental value of all living beings and an openness for spirituality beyond the borders of a particular religion.

PERSONALISM AS 'HUMANISM OF THE OTHER'

Personalism has many faces. The American stream of personalism around *The Personalist*, a journal founded by Ralph Tyler Flewelling in 1920, is rooted in the idealism of Hegel and Kant, while the European movement with Emmanuel Mounier and the Journal *Esprit*, set up in 1932, was a response to the voices of existentialism (Nietzsche, Kierkegaard, Heidegger) and to the political debates on Fascism and Marxism. Although personalism is deeply inspired by Christian humanism, the argument and style of personalism is philosophical and therefore open for both religious and non-religious people. In *Humanisme Intégral* (1936) Jacques Maritain explained why modern humanism's shortcomings would lead to a renewed interest in spirituality, not as a return to the sacred spirituality of medieval society but as a quest for a *profane spirituality* that does not segregate the spiritual but integrates it as a component of our political, social, economic and scientific activities (Bouckaert, 2011a).

Like deep ecology, personalism does not accept the rational ego as the exclusive source of meaning, knowledge and morality. It prioritizes the relational over the rational self, the intuitive over the analytical mind. But whereas eco-humanism starts from the ecological experience to disclose the interconnected self, personalism is grounded in social interaction and social commitment. Its focus is not biocentrism as the sharing element of all beings and the ultimate source of transcendent meaning. Personalists make a distinction between personal and non-personal forms of interconnection. Relations between *persons*, i.e. between beings gifted with the capacity of self-awareness and moral responsibility, are characterized by forms of personal involvement that are not accessible in non-personal relations. Although a dog can feel a lot of empathy and affection for his master and vice versa, it will never be able to open a space of self-reflection, free choice and moral responsibility. In a similar way, nature may manifest itself as a transcendent source of life but, not being a person, it cannot be considered as accountable for its positive and negative manifestations. For a personalist, the ecological web of interconnection gets its orientation and full meaning from the moral web of social relations. For example, respect for the non-instrumental meaning of nature has to be related to our social responsibility for marginalized people and future generations.

The emancipation of a person cannot be isolated from the emancipation of a 'community of persons'. Human development does not end by installing formal rights of equal freedom or by offering conditions of material welfare. One of the most difficult tasks is to release the individual from his ego-obsession and to transform his mind from an ego- into an alter-centred intentionality. The ego-liberation gives the individual the opportunity to (re)connect to his deeper, relational self and to develop his full potential as a gift from and to other people. Emmanuel Levinas refers to this transformation as 'humanism of the other' contrasting it to the prevailing 'humanism of the ego': 'Man par excellence – the source of humanity – is perhaps the Other' (Peperzak et al, 1996).

The basic assumption of humanism of the other is the idea that the ego/self is always preceded by the presence of the Other (eventually perceived as an absence which is a particular modus of being present). My life, my education, my freedom, my capabilities were given before I could appropriate them as part of myself. No one can claim full ownership. Even my claim of ownership must be recognized by other people as a legitimate claim to be operational and effective. In this sense moral autonomy only exists as a gift from others eliciting me to give on my turn real freedom to other people. Being respected as a free and creative person, I am invited to respond to this gift by respecting other people's freedom and creativity. If this principle of gift and reciprocity is operative in all basic human and social relations, it is also a fundamental characteristic of our relation to life itself. Life in all its diversity and evolution originates from an unconditional source of gift preceding our claims of ownership and founding the social flow of reciprocity and gift relations. In his social encyclical '*Caritas in Veritate*' Benedictus XVI points out how the logic of gift as the most fundamental principle of civilization has the potential to transform from within not only the sphere of civil society but also the spheres of politics and economics (Benedict XVI, 2009, Chapter 3; Zamagni, 2009).

Deep ecology and humanism of the other do not exclude each other. They overlap in their postmodern perception of the human subject as a receptive and interconnected self. This idea has far reaching consequences in the way we relate to our environment and to other people. One of these consequences is an in-depth transformation of our economic concepts and business practices. More than any other discipline, economics has promoted the idea of rational choice and adulated the *homo economicus*. The logic of rational choice gradually expanded to many other domains of human activity and disconnected our activities from our spiritual and relational self. If we want to reconnect to our spiritual selves and to life as a meaningful gift, we have to build up a more spiritual-based theory and practice of economics. One of the key notions in this reconstruction of economics is the concept of spiritual capital. We may say that the cultural move from secular to spiritual humanism is reflected in the field of economics by the enlargement of the notion of capital from financial to spiritual capital. This transformation is emerging, not as a *deus ex machina*, but as a new response to the complexities and changes of our ecological and social environment.

FROM FINANCIAL TO SPIRITUAL CAPITAL

The physical and material capital of a company are measured in monetary terms. Therefore, most people associate capital with financial assets which enable people to create a surplus value in monetary terms. The essence of capitalism is to generate a continuous and growing flow of profit from the stock of capital. Other forms of capital such as human or social capital are relevant and even important as far as they contribute to the flow of profit-making and can be measured in monetary terms. Is there a kind of historical dynamic that can transform this capitalistic logic into a more spiritual concept of economic development?

In the 19th century Karl Marx believed that the intrinsic 'social nature' of technological progress would create the material conditions for a social revolution putting an end to the private ownership of the means of production and to the appropriation of profit by the capitalist class. But the Marxist idea of social revolution resulted de facto in a practice of state capitalism. Although state capitalism differs from private capitalism, the basic assumption that capital is primarily measured in monetary terms and driven by an unlimited ambition for accumulation remain intact. The Keynesian revolution in Western societies was more successful in its combination of public and private forms of capitalism. But also the primacy of financial capital over other forms of capital was not questioned. The Keynesian revolution created the conditions for an expansive growth of welfare in Western societies. However, the Western model of welfare has been realized by an overexploitation of the planetary resources (a cost which is mainly transferred to future generations) and driven by the overexploitation of human expectations and needs (a cost which is mainly paid by the growth of pathological symptoms of stress and frustration in highly developed societies). Within the more enlightened part of the business community, there is some awareness of the 'spiritual deficit' produced by conventional capitalism. This awareness is expressed by the interest for new ideas such as the formation of spiritual capital and spiritual-based leadership.

A short history of the notion of capital can be helpful in this perspective (Bouckaert, 2009). No-one will deny that people invest their money in a company but also in all sorts of *immaterial assets*, such as time, expertise, talent, creativity, imagination, trust and loyalty. As the environment in which we live and work becomes increasingly complex and subject to rapid change, the level of immaterial investment rises. The importance of routine, reproductive knowledge and control-management declines, whilst the importance of 'tacit knowledge', creative thinking, mutual trust, emotional intelligence and a willingness to embrace the unknown increases. In a similar way, the more fundamental our immaterial investment on the input side, the more we expect as output an attractive, immaterial return on that investment.

The most widely used concept of non-financial capital is *human capital*. The entire literature on human capital focuses primarily on knowledge, experience and skills, emphasizing permanent education and training. Investing in human capital is an absolute must in an expanding knowledge economy. But the perception that a modern economy is primarily a knowledge economy seems too one-sided. Many top companies have similar levels of expertise, technology and labour productivity. Often, the competitive difference lies instead in the *values* that companies reflect and generate. Today, public opinion and markets (consumer, labour and capital markets) are highly sensitive to the degree to which ecological, social and human values are incorporated into the quality of a product and into the production process. In other words, we live in a knowledge-and-values-based economy. Human capital as a concept is too narrowly focused on the functional expertise and skills of individual workers and too little focused on the quality of relationships and environment. The rapid dissemination of the concept of 'social capital', a term coined by James Coleman (1988), is a response to this blind spot.

According to the sociologist Robert Putnam, 'social capital refers to features of social organisation such as networks, norms and social trust that facilitate coordination and cooperation for mutual benefit' (Putnam, 2002). Putnam's main message is that in Western societies – and he is thinking particularly of the US – social capital, and thus the relationships of mutual trust, cooperation and volunteering, are in systematic decline. To support his argument he points *inter alia* to the decline in associational membership and in the numbers engaged in voluntary work, the decline in voter turnout in elections and the increasing lack of trust between people. This decline in social trust is not irrelevant for economic growth as was pointed out in Fukuyama's bestseller *Trust* (1995) and in empirical research showing how low levels of social trust can reduce the growth potential of an economy (Moesen et al, 2000). The new thing is that human and social capital are recognized today as specific forms of capital that need specific policy and management. They have their own *modus operandi*. What is not questioned in this research is the primacy of financial capital over human and social capital. The interest in human and social capital gets its drive from the instrumental use we can make of it to generate economic growth and higher profits.

Spiritual capital is the youngest scion in the capital family. On the occasion of the 100th anniversary of the publication of Max Weber's enduring work, *The Protestant Ethic and the Spirit of Capitalism* (1905), the John Templeton Foundation launched a $3-million research programme on *Spiritual* Capital.[1] Over 500 research groups submitted detailed proposals, a level of interest that exceeded all expectations since there were only 40 projects to be sponsored. Some authors (Finke, 2003) interpret the term spiritual in the sociological sense of 'participating in a religious practice' which may be helpful for the study of the impact of religion in economic life in the line of Max Weber's *The Protestant Ethic and the Spirit of Capitalism* (Weber, 1995[1905]). However by reducing spiritual capital to 'religious capital' one misses the post-modern notion of spirituality as a personal and experience-based search for meaning and interconnectedness. Sociological research into religious capital does not question the conventional idea of capitalism, while questions about spiritual capital prompt a discussion of the *raison d'être* and the meaning of capitalism.

Although spirituality is first of all related to the personal quest for meaning, spiritual hunger is not only a matter for individuals. Like individuals, organizations too need inspiration and an inner compass to avoid becoming a hostage to market pressure or to whatever happens to be in vogue. Corporate spirituality is this inner compass. We may call it the spiritual capital of a company. As a corporate characteristic, spiritual capital can be described as 'a company's ability and commitment to develop a deep value-driven meaning in its mission, in all its activities and in its relationships'. Business spirituality is the theory and practice of managing spiritual capital. This notion of spiritual capital is related to a cluster of other interesting concepts such as 'spiritual intelligence' and 'spiritual based leadership'.

Corporate spirituality is not intended to convert a company into a sort of religious or denominational community, or into a new sort of monastery. Of course, one can learn a great deal from all these communities, but a modern company is a secular organization focused on generating meaningful and profitable activities in competitive markets. Profane spirituality plays a role in modern companies because it has the potential to awake a sense of co-creativity and co-responsibility among stakeholders. It stirs up inspiration, driving people to embrace the unknown and to undertake the ordinary with a newly found motivation and enthusiasm. There is a Buddhist saying that nicely illustrates the meaning of spirituality in work: 'Before Enlightenment, chopping wood carrying water, after Enlightenment, chopping wood carrying water'. In other words, the material work is the same both before and after 'spiritual enlightenment'. What is different is the inner approach to our work, the meaning we ascribe to it, the joy we draw from it and the openness for the unexpected.

Organizations with a relatively strong hierarchical and technocratic structure and a management style based on control and systematic implementation are not exactly rushing to embrace spirituality. They rely on a culture of instrumental and analytical rationality. In such a context, spirituality is an inconvenience. Those however, who regard business as a *process of co-creation and co-responsibility* will be interested in developing operative concepts of spiritual capital and spiritual-based leadership. One of the pioneering authors in the spiritual capital literature is Danah Zohar. Together with her husband the psychiatrist Ian Marshall, she developed a conceptual framework to underpin the notions of spiritual capital and spiritual intelligence (Zohar & Marshall, 2000, 2004). In her vision spiritual capital reflects what an individual or an organization exists for, believes in, aspires to, and takes responsibility for. But this reference to people's deepest meanings, values and purposes yet remains an empty concept if we do not understand how to build this capital and make it productive in society.

According to Zohar, spiritual capital is build up by leaders using their own intelligence. But in this case we do need the use of spiritual intelligence rather than rational intelligence. While material capital is linked to the use of rational intelligence (IQ), social capital to emotional intelligence (EQ), spiritual capital is generated by spiritual intelligence (SQ). SQ is the ability of our mind:

> to access higher meanings, values, abiding purposes, and unconscious aspects of the self and to embed these meanings, values, and purposes in living a richer and more creative life. Signs of high SQ include an ability to think out of the box, humility, and an access to energies that come from something beyond the ego, beyond just me and my day-to-day concerns. SQ is the ultimate intelligence of the visionary leader. (Zohar & Marshall, 2004)

As is indicated in Zohar's quotation, there is close link between the organizational concept of spiritual capital and the practice of spiritual-based leadership. While the vision and value commitment of market driven leaders is predominantly caused by market imperatives and performances, the value commitment of Spirit-driven leaders is determined by personal experience, inner conviction and a search for meaning. Books such as *Spirituality and Ethics in Management* (Zsolnai, 2004), *Theory U* (Scharmer, 2007), *Presence* (Senge et al, 2004) and *Leading with Wisdom* (Pruzan and Kirsten, 2007) – just to mention a few – explore the new paradigm of spiritual-based entrepreneurship and leadership.

There is an important caveat. It would be misleading to suggest that market and spirit exclude each other. On the contrary, NGOs such as Greenpeace, Amnesty International and many others infuse a lot of moral sensitivity in global markets. Consumers today are mobilized to screen products and services on their ecological and social qualities. Capital markets greatly distrust companies involved in unethical behaviour. Hence, being ethical and value-driven is a sound reaction to market pressure and an asset in reputation management. The point is that this market driven pressure to be ethical is limited in its size and its impact. There is a selective blindness at work in the underlying motivation.

Markets are always a mix of ethical and unethical pressures. A lot of irresponsible greed, short-sightedness and opportunistic motivation – even masked by an ethical discourse – is often operative in market behaviour. The banking crisis clearly illustrates the lack of critical awareness and the selective blindness at work. We saw how many banking companies on the one hand created ethical funds for a sustainable economy and, on the other hand, highly speculative funds for short-term profits and unsustainable growth. Spirit-driven entrepreneurs do not withdraw from market pressure but they act from a second source as well: the values that are considered as a non-negotiable part of a company's identity or that constitute its spiritual capital.

CONCLUSIONS

One of the most fascinating phenomena of the late 20th and early 21st centuries is the emergence of spiritual humanism characterized by a personally driven, experience-based, trans-religious and democratic search for meaning. It has nothing to do with fundamentalism or religious sectarianism but aims at a deep and intuitive experience of interconnectedness as a personal, organizational and public good. Deep ecology and personalism as 'humanism of the Other' are just two contemporary expressions of spiritual humanism. Both contribute to the notion of spiritual capital: the former by introducing the ecological sense of being interconnected, the latter by promoting relations of co-responsibility and stakeholder democracy. The idea of the human person as an interconnected and relational being has to be defended against some claims of liberal individualism, technocratic rationalism and social or religious paternalism.

Spiritual humanism in the economic sphere not only implies a spiritual-based model of leadership but, simultaneously, a workable concept of corporate spirituality. The task of a business leader is to generate a positive return from an invested stock of capital. If we succeed in enlarging the notion of capital by focusing on its immaterial aspects, we shall be able to enlarge the notion of profit as well by unveiling an immaterial return on investment. While conventional capitalists stick to the priority of financial capital (without necessarily denying the role of social and spiritual capital as instrumental goods), 'spiritual capitalists' aim at prioritizing spiritual and social capital as intrinsic goods (without denying the importance of financial capital as necessary and instrumental good). To reduce the gap between these two 'priority' positions, we need to reconstruct the fundamental notions of business in order to integrate the spiritual search for meaning in the conceptual frame of corporate economics.

NOTE

1. See http://www.metanexus.net/spiritual_capital/ (last accessed November 2012). For an introduction to the new field of spiritual capital research, see the papers written for the planning meeting of the research programme, October, 2003: Roger Finke, 'Spiritual Capital: Definitions, Applications and New Frontiers'; Robert D. Woodberry, 'Researching Spiritual Capital: Promises and Pitfalls'; Peter L. Berger and Robert W. Hefner, 'Spiritual Capital in Comparative Perspective'; Theodore Roosevelt Malloch, 'Social, Human and Spiritual Capital in Economic Development'; Laurence R. Iannaccone and Jonathan Klick, 'Spiritual Capital: An Introduction and Literature Review'. All papers are available at http://www.metanexus.net/spiritual_capital/ (last accessed November 2012).

BIBLIOGRAPHY

Benedict XVI (2009), *Caritas in Veritate*, Liberia Editrice Vaticana.
Bergson, Henri (1907), *L'évolution Créatrice*. Paris, Presses Universitaires de France (translated as: *Creative Evolutions*, London, MacMillan, 1911).
Bouckaert, Luk (ed.) (1999), 'Is personalism still alive in Europe?' *Ethical Perspectives*, vol. 6, no. 1.
Bouckaert, Luk (2007), 'Spirituality in Economics', in Bouckaert, L. & Laszlo, Z. (eds), *Spirituality as a Public Good*. European SPES Cahier 1, Antwerp, Garant, pp. 11–25.
Bouckaert, Luk (2009), 'Business spirituality and the Common Good', in De Bettignies, Henri-Claude & Thompson, Mike J. (eds), *Leadership, Spirituality and the Common Good*. European SPES Cahier 4, Antwerp, Garant, pp. 13–27.
Bouckaert, Luk (2011a), 'The search for a 'profane spirituality', *Spiritus. Journal for Christian Spirituality*, vol 11, pp. 24–38.
Bouckaert, Luk (2011b), 'Personalism', in Bouckaert, Luk & Zsolnai, Laszlo, *Handbook for Business and Spirituality*, Hampshire, Palgrave MacMillan.
Bruni, L. and Zamagni S. (2007), *Civil Economy. Efficiency, Equity, Public Happiness*, Oxford, Peter Lang.
Capra, Fritjof (1975), *The Tao of Physics*, Boston, Shambhala.
Coleman, James (1988), 'Social Capital in the Creation of Human Capital', *The American Journal of Sociology*, 94 (Supplement: Organizations and Institutions: Sociological and Economic Approaches to the Analysis of Social Structure).
Finke, Roger (2003), 'Spiritual Capital: Definitions, Applications, and New Frontiers', Paper prepared for the Spiritual Capital Planning Meeting, October 10–11, 2003.
Fukuyama, Francis (1995), *Trust. The Social Virtues and the Creation of Prosperity*, New York, The Free Press.
Goleman, Daniel (1995), *Emotional Intelligence*, New York, Bloomsbury Publishing PLC.
Heelas, Paul and Woodhead, Linda (2005), *The Spiritual Revolution. Why religion is giving way to spirituality*, Oxford, Blackwell Publishing.
Heidegger, M. (1927), *Sein und Zeit*, Tübingen, Max Niemeyer Verlag.
Hoevel, Carlos (2009), 'Towards the paradigm of Gift', *Revista Cultura Economica*, no 75/76, pp. 89–97.
Levinas, Emmanuel (1972), *Humanisme de l'autre homme*, Montpellier, Fata Morgana.
Malloch, Theodore Roosevelt (2010), 'Spiritual capital and practical wisdom', in Naughton, M., Habisch, A. and Lenssen, G. (eds), *Practical wisdom in management from the Christian tradition*, *Journal of Management Development*, vol. 29, no. 7/8, pp. 755–759.
Maritain, Jacques (1936), *Humanisme Intégral*, Paris, Aubier.
Moesen, Wim, Van Puyenbroeck, Tom and Cherchey, Laurens (2000), 'Trust as societal capital: economic growth in European regions', Public Economics Working Paper Series, Centrum Economische Studies, K.U. Leuven, 2000.
Mounier, Emmanuel (1936), *Manifeste au service du personnalisme*, Paris, Montaigne.

Nandram, S. and Borden, M.E. (eds) (2010), *Spirituality and Business. Exploring Possibilities for a New Management Paradigm*, Heidelberg, Springer.

Peperzak, A.T., Critchley, S. and Bernasconi, R. (eds) (1996), *Emmanuel Levinas: Basic Philosophical Writings*, Indiana University Press, Indianapolis.

Pruzan, Peter and Pruzan, Mikkelsen Kirsten (eds) (2007), *Leading with wisdom. Spiritual-based leadership in business*, Greenleaf Publishing, Sheffield.

Putnam, Robert (ed.) (2002), *Democracies in Flux: The Evolution of Social Capital in Contemporary Society*, New York, Oxford University Press.

Scharmer, Otto C. (2007), *Theory U. Leading from the future as it emerges*, Cambridge, Massachusetts, Sol.

Senge, Peter M., Scharmer, C. Otto, Jaworski Joseph and Flowers, Betty Sue (2004), *Presence: An Exploration of Profound Change in People, Organizations and Society*, New York, Random House Inc.

Tacey, David (2004), *The Spirituality Revolution. The emergence of contemporary spirituality*, East Sussex, Brunner-Routledge.

Toulmin, Stephen (1990), *Cosmopolis. The Hidden Agenda of Modernity*, New York, The Free Press.

Vernon, Mark (2008), *Humanism*, London, Hachette Livre.

Weber, Max (1995[1905]), *The Protestant Ethic and the Spirit of Capitalism*, London, Penguin.

Whitehead, Alfred North (1929), *Process and Reality: An Essay in Cosmology*, Corrected edition, David Ray Griffin and Donald W. Sherburne (eds) (1979), New York Free Press.

Wilber, Ken (1996), *A Brief History of Everything*, Boston, Shambhala.

Zamagni, S. (2009), 'Fraternity, Gift and Reciprocity in *Caritas in Veritate*', *Revista Cultura Economica*, no. 75/76, pp. 20–30.

Zohar, Danah and Marshall, Ian (2000), *SQ: Spiritual Intelligence, The Ultimate Intelligence*, London, Bloomsbury.

Zohar, Danah and Marshall, Ian (2004), *Spiritual Capital*, London, Bloomsbury.

Zsolnai, L. (ed.) (2004), *Spirituality and Ethics in Management*, Kluwer, Springer.

36. Subsidiarity and new welfare
Pier Luigi Porta

THE NOTION AND ITS CURRENT USE

The notion of *subsidiarity* involves different aspects and several levels of analysis. A historical reconstruction probably affords the best route to understanding its meaning and the way it has come to be used today, mainly in support and defence of the institutional set up of the European Union.

It is well known that the principle of subsidiarity is a natural companion of all forms of federalism. In the American case the 10th amendment of the Constitution states that the 'powers not delegated to the United States by the Constitution, nor prohibited by it to the States, are reserved to the States respectively, or to the people' following the earlier provision of the Articles of Confederation that 'each state retains its sovereignty, freedom, and independence, and every power, jurisdiction, and right, which is not by this Confederation expressly delegated to the United States, in Congress assembled'.

The European Union is not of course a federal state in its present shape, which makes it perhaps curious that so much talk about subsidiarity today should be provoked by the European experience, rather than by the proper forms of federalism. This may be interpreted as a sign of a possible road to federalism. However, in most cases, the idea has been put to contrary use precisely in the European case, i.e. of denying or dismissing any federal project or intention.

The European Union can be conceived as an innovative institutional and political project having subsidiarity as its basic principle of functioning. In part that is a line of thinking that has been used instrumentally, since the start, with a view to rejecting the misgivings of those who were (and still are) scared of the prospect of a European super-state; but it also embodies a deeper political philosophy which still is, in many ways, at the root of the European project, as it has developed especially over the past 20 to 30 years. During Jacques Delors' Presidency (1985–95), in particular, the principle was emphasized and Delors himself – a typical figure of economist-politician endowed with a characteristic European charisma – would maintain that what can be decided at a regional or local level should not be decided at the national level and under no circumstances, where a decision can be made at a national level, should things be decided instead at Union level. That is in fact a formulation of a principle known as vertical subsidiarity, of which we shall now examine some of the roots and the implications. In Delors' own experience the principle was designed to act as a constant counterweight to the natural tendency of the centre to accumulate power, with obvious implications for the design of a European Constitution. At the same time, and beyond the immediate political purposes, it was often observed that exactly Delors' case could give important hints at what lay behind this construction in terms of political philosophy. Delors' European charisma appeared to be well entrenched in the French Catholic-socialist tradition with its personalist philosophical background. It is appropriate to anticipate here that the principle of subsidiarity has been looming large in debates and also in official documents of the European Union since the start but more particularly since the Maastricht Treaty on the European Union (1992) where subsidiarity is declared to be a foundational principle of the Union, in the wake of article 5 of the Treaty of Rome (1957) where the principle itself is stated to be the basis of action on the part of the Community then established.

SOME BASIC DISTINCTIONS

In the context of what is called a *relational theory* of society (as we shall see below), subsidiarity emerges in three ways, which have been termed vertical, horizontal and lateral. *Vertical subsidiarity* concerns the principle where the larger institutions have a subsidiary role, which however should not be interpreted nor exercised as a substitute for the power of action of the smaller ones. That also means that institutional tasks and objectives should be set in such a way as to ensure that they are assigned to the institutions which are closer to the individuals or communities involved. *Horizontal subsidiarity* implies a less bureaucratic or legal reading of the idea, as it concerns the relationship of the public authorities and the public institutions toward the network of the civil society, the general idea being that there should be no tendency of the former to invade the range of operation of the civil society. On the contrary it should be the specific aim of the public authorities to encourage and foster the action of the private associations and of all the intermediate bodies constituting the civil society. Finally there is a third level of subsidiarity which operates within the realm of civil society itself in the assignment of tasks to the different institutions, concerning, e.g., education or labour relations or other aspects of life. That level has been termed *lateral* (or sometimes 'circular') *subsidiarity* (Quadrio Curzio, 2002).

With the above distinctions in mind it is perhaps easier to seize the link of subsidiarity to welfare – which is the object of the present chapter – and also to imagine what forms of *new* welfare may be involved here. However, before going into that, it is necessary to proceed to the historical reconstruction of the idea, as a preliminary to understanding the fundamental unity of the concept, without of course denying at the same time the significance of the distinctions just outlined.

HISTORICAL ROOTS OF THE IDEA OF SUBSIDIARITY

One of the sources of the ideal of subsidiarity is generally acknowledged to lie in the social doctrine and the contributions of the Catholic Church, since 1891 when the first Papal Encyclical (The *Rerum novarum*, of Pope Leo XIII) on the social order was published. The most explicit document in the above sense is the Encyclical *Quadragesimo anno*, issued by Pope Pius XI in 1931:

> When we speak of the reform of institutions, the State comes chiefly to mind, not as if universal well-being were to be expected from its activity, but because things have come to such a pass through the evil of what we have termed *individualism* that, following upon the overthrow and near extinction of that rich social life which was once highly developed through associations of various kinds, there remain virtually only individuals and the State. This is to the great harm

of the State itself; for, with a structure of social governance lost, and with the taking over of all the burdens which the wrecked associations once bore, the State has been overwhelmed and crushed by almost infinite tasks and duties. (*Quadragesimo anno*, § 79)

It is thus clear, from this analysis, that the intellectual source of the idea of subsidiarity is strongly linked to what we have called *horizontal* subsidiarity. The Pope continues:

> As history abundantly proves, it is true that on account of changed conditions many things which were done by small associations in former times cannot be done now save by large associations. Still, that most weighty principle, which cannot be set aside or changed, remains fixed and unshaken in social philosophy: Just as it is gravely wrong to take from individuals what they can accomplish by their own initiative and industry and give it to the community, so also it is an injustice and at the same time a grave evil and disturbance of right order to assign to a greater and higher association what lesser and subordinate organizations can do. For every social activity ought of its very nature to furnish help to the members of the body social, and never destroy and absorb them. (§§ 80, 81)

The Latin text reads as follows: 'cum socialis quaevis opera vi naturaque sua *subsidium* afferre membris corporis socialis debeat, numquam vero eadem destruere et absorbere'. *Subsidium* (emphasis added) is the crucial term here, from which of course *subsidiarity* springs. The Pope goes on to argue:

> The supreme authority of the State ought, therefore, to let subordinate groups handle matters and concerns of lesser importance, which would otherwise dissipate its efforts greatly. Thereby the State will more freely, powerfully, and effectively do all those things that belong to it alone because it alone can do them: directing, watching, urging, restraining, as occasion requires and necessity demands. Therefore, those in power should be sure that the more perfectly a graduated order is kept among the various associations, in observance of the principle of *subsidiary function*, [servato hoc 'subsidiarii' officii principio] the stronger social authority and effectiveness will be the happier and more prosperous the condition of the State.

These simple statements have important roots in Catholic social thought which can be traced to the re-interpretation of the scholastic concept of *bonum commune*, the 'common good' or 'common weal'. Pope Leo was himself a great upholder of the Aquinas renaissance, especially in his early Encyclical *Æterni Patris* of 1879. Thomas Aquinas, in particular, had analysed the idea in various places, such as his comment on Aristotle's Nicomachean Ethics (Aquinas 1993).

Another source, however, is sometimes considered to be more appropriate. That is provided by Johannes Althusius (1563–1638) who, in his *Politica Methodice Digesta, Atque Exemplis Sacris et Profanis Illustrata*, of 1603, presents a theory of the building of a political system, where the polity and the allegiance emerge as the result of a compound of political associations arising from the free initiative of the citizens themselves, rather than being superimposed by an élite or a military-political ruler. Althusius was a Calvinist: he does not make much of Aquinas, although his thought in some definite sense parallels Aquinas, being a by-product of *jus naturale* as a philosophy of justice.

It must be said that Althusius' work has enjoyed some popularity of late, especially after the rediscovery of his thought in the late 19th century as a result of the research of Otto von Gierke, the famous German theorist of the *Genossenschaftsrecht*, a conception of public law based on association and cooperation. Gierke's work (1868) is predictably often described as 'monumental' and it includes a treatise on Althusius and the development of political theory, where he speaks of *naturrechtliche Staatstheorie* or natural-law State theory. Gierke describes Althusius as the most profound political thinker between Bodin and Hobbes. As a matter of fact, Althusius' stand on political theory is in fact often contrasted with Bodin's. Jean Bodin (or Baudin, or Bodinus, 1530–1596), his predecessor and in some ways his mentor, in his treatment on *res publica* or the commonwealth, had argued that what makes the commonwealth superior to any other individual or city or body inside the commonwealth is the *ruler* himself (von Gierke 1981[1880]). Althusius disagrees. The power at the centre is to Althusius nothing but the result of the symbiotic life of the associations from which it springs. The commonwealth is composed of cities and provinces and it is to the latter (joined together in sharing services and activities) that sovereignty belongs. The organized body of the commonwealth is the people, i.e. the latin *populus*.

As it is to be expected the above conception has to do both with the political significance of a variety of associations and of a full life of civil society as well as with the advantages and the superiority of a federal commonwealth. A political theorist, Daniel Elazar, spoke of Althusius' *Politica* as a 'Grand Design for a Federal Commonwealth':

> Althusius' *Politica* was the first book to present a comprehensive theory of federal republicanism rooted in a covenantal view of human society derived from, but not dependent on, a theological system. It presented a theory of polity-building based on the polity as a compound political association established by its citizens through their primary associations on the basis of consent rather than a reified state imposed by a ruler or an elite. (Althusius, 1995[1603], p. xxxv)

The whole body of the civil economy of the Italian tradition (Bruni & Zamagni, 2007) goes in the direction of emphasizing the same general principle. The Italian case is perhaps the most evident and clear expression of a form of spontaneous order which includes the institutions and the intermediate bodies. The explosive rise of the economic discipline during the Enlightenment (of which the Italian Schools of Naples and Milan are the most significant) develops in many cases the idea that State, market and civil society must be conceived as separate, but closely interacting spheres. Of course this is not limited to Italy, although the Italians develop and disseminate the view of civil society in an important way. One of their sources is for example Montesquieu, whose *corps intermédiaries* are a safeguard with respect to the overwhelming strength of State power (Montesquieu 1748). It is a line of thought where the *corps intermédiaries*, far from being a seat of corruption or 'familism', are in fact the contrary, i.e. the spur to a proper flourishing of all the latent energies of individuals and social bodies. Pietro Verri and Antonio Genovesi are the best masters of the Italian tradition in that perspective.

No wonder that such a conception would come to be rated among the early sources of liberalism. A certain imprint of Christian liberalism remains attached to the idea of subsidiarity. It belongs to the so-called 'negative' side of liberal thinking, which basically identifies with letting do, or letting go: what the Physiocrats had earlier dubbed *laissez-faire* with a special implicit reference to the market and exchanges on the market. It is a principle that emphasizes responsibility and spontaneous initiative in an environment which opens the way unfettered to the 'just' enterprises. At the same time *subsidium* can also be seen to lean toward a limited but effective support on the part of the State for the activities of the lower layers of the institutions. So, for example, when Hayek (1979, vol. 2, ch. 7, p. 7) discusses the role of the State in the economy he writes:

> While the comprehensive spontaneous order which the law serves is a precondition for the success of most private activity, the services which the government can render beyond the enforcement of rules of just conduct are not only supplementary or subsidiary [In this sense – he footnotes here – the 'principle of subsidiarity' is much stressed in the social doctrines of the Roman Catholic Church] to the basic needs which the spontaneous order provides for. They are . . . services which must be fitted into the more comprehensive order of private efforts which government neither does nor can determine, and which ought to be rendered under the restrictions of the same rules of law to which the private efforts are subject.

This is in line with the ordo-liberal view which in Hayek takes the following form: 'In a free society the general good consists principally in the facilitation of the pursuit of unknown individual purposes.' That all definitely leans toward the negative side of liberal thinking, with very little concern for personalism and personal relationality.

LATTER-DAY CONCEPT AND USES

In general terms the *subsidiarity perspective* provides a basic way of looking into the link of liberty and social order. It is a view on spontaneous order. The Catholic overtones around that view are nothing but the result of the traditional Christian conception, especially prominent in St. Augustin, of limiting the power, the functions and the scope of the activity of the State. That view was historically one of the powerful inducements to the liberal (or even libertarian) idea of limited government and to the retrenchment of State activity and power. It is a view which, especially after the Reformation, has generally remained more fully valid in the Catholic camp compared to the Reformed Confessions, which have in many cases given rise to National Churches, while Catholicism has invariably affirmed the universal character of the religious authority.

It is a perspective that has been applied to numerous contexts, thus acquiring a variety of meanings. Today it appears to be significantly adopted, in its *vertical* mood, as a regulative principle by the European Union. Especially in the wake of the current crisis of Europe, it would seem of particular interest to examine how the conception is applied today and how it could evolve in the near future.

This set of problems has been at the core of social market economy, otherwise called Ordoliberalismus, since the Second World War. The works of Wilhelm Röpke are among the best contributions. In his book *Civitas Humana*, of 1944, Röpke discusses the counterweights to the State and also takes up the diagnosis of the weaknesses and the illnesses of the State.

A prominent use of the subsidiarity perspective concerns, in the *horizontal* variety, the relation of the political organization and the market sphere. The subsidiarity perspective puts a great weight on the individual *person* as the origin and source of any kind of initiative or association. In his chapter on the counterweights to the State, the author maintains that we should keep in mind that a plea for pluralism does not mean a blanket endorsement for any kind of pressure group, say from the family to the mafia

(Röpke, 1944). The correct distinction puts on one side those *corps intermediaries* which do effectively counter the pervasive power of the State on one side, from the dire forms of pluralism on the other side, which – far from limiting the power of the State – do in fact make use of that power by making it subservient and instrumental to their specific aims and needs or purposes. The distinction is all-important here; and when we come to the market sphere, all that boils down to studying and practicing all the sound forms of regulatory activity which are in fact an important tenet of ordoliberalismus as a doctrine. Of course everyone is tempted to indict the others with trespassing in that field of thought and action, as often happens in the public arena when lay and religious forms of solidarity are competing, which is quite frequently the case in the Western world.

Röpke is adamant about putting forward the classic Liberal-Catholic argument in favour of Church religion, and Christianity more particularly, as an active force fostering both sociality and personal responsibility, while keeping at the same time State power at bay. That, in his view, is not mere historical accident. It is rather the consistent predictable result of the teachings and contents of the Christian doctrine, which – differently from the social conception of the old pagan world – puts the individual person at the centre of the stage as the main performer, so that the person comes first *before* the State, while, at the same time, *above* the power of the State there is the force of God's justice and love. There is thus a very great spiritual energy which relies on personal responsibility and personal initiative and which lurks behind the whole array of initiatives which take, in one way or another, the form of charities. Paganism, the Enlightenment and Christianity are three driving forces behind charitable activities. We may perhaps acknowledge that Christianity, especially in the West, has been and still is historically the major force. This view bears resemblance, for example, with de Tocqueville's analysis of the American democracy (1838).

Whatever the source of inspiration of the principle, especially in the present world after the demise of the various forms of totalitarianism, it becomes increasingly appreciated that the principle of subsidiarity needs to be associated in a complementary way with some form of solidarity.

It is proper to consider the problem in connection both with the vertical notion and with the horizontal one. As far as the *vertical* side of the conception is concerned, what the European experience shows is precisely that it is not particularly productive to make use of the notion of subsidiarity when a central political force is insufficiently defined or when it even comes to be substantially ruled out. This is simply a confirmation of the fact, mentioned above, that the principle of subsidiarity takes its proper place in a federal setting. This in turn can be read as a result of necessary combination of subsidiarity with solidarity in the form of a balance between decentralized and central powers. There cannot be a balance, in other words, if one or the other force in the balance is either absent of excessively weak. In the case of Europe the principle of subsidiarity has been invoked also as a defence of the Eurosystem as one of the forms of 'reinforced cooperation' within the Union itself. It now becoming evident, after less than 10 years' experience, that a loose system, simply based on decentralized powers, is not sustainable and the central side of it needs reinforcement, if the system is to become fully viable. It is a misuse of the idea of subsidiarity to make it instrumental to avoiding the problem of a central core authority.

As far the *horizontal* side of subsidiarity is concerned, a similar problem emerges. The best way to make this clear is to turn to the relational theory of society, of which the clearest example is provided by the present reconstruction of the notion of *economia civile*. *Economia civile* is a concept introduced by Antonio Genovesi (1713–1769) with a view to highlighting the process through which society achieves an orderly state of things (1765–67). The latter comes out of a balance of *forza concentriva* (self-centred competition) and *forza diffusiva* (cooperation). It is easy to show that Genovesi's *economia civile* is the parent stem of our current principle of subsidiarity and at the same time of the notion that the principle does not stand up by itself.

Economia civile conceives of the economy as a set of institutions designed to promote public wellbeing, through the efforts of individuals and groups toward improving their conditions. Civil life becomes the medium through which public happiness can be achieved. The basic institution here is the *market* and the basic mechanisms of the functioning of a civil economy are interest, trust, and reciprocity, through which the civil economy can work for public happiness. The general conception of 'invisible hand', so dear to Adam Smith, is a paradigm of what subsidiary actions mean. At the same time it would not be enough to disperse the centres of power. Such a process will produce positive results if, and only if, the market is conducive to civic virtues. There is a difference between pure greed and the pursuit of more complex relationships of reciprocity. This is a distinction that permits the distinction between the entrepreneur from the speculator: the former generates trust, the latter relies on existing trust only to consume and destroy it.

Economia civile is a view of a spontaneous order of society which, beyond the acknowledgement of role and power of the *invisible hand*, allows full space to the *visible fabric* of civil virtues, the producers of trust, leading to real development and public happiness. When we speak of economic development we invariably adopt the silent assumption that all those processes which uphold the civic virtues are the basis, of at least the bulk, of the set of actions that we have in mind and that we leave to the free choice of the agents of an economy. It is the civic humanist tradition which can make the concept clear. Mandeville's idea of a heterogenesis of ends continues to work perfectly well, even if it does not assume (as Mandeville does) that man is inescapably prone to vice. The heterogenesis-of-ends mechanism becomes subsidiary (and not opposed) to civic virtues. *Economia civile* as a notion thus lies between Mandeville and Smith. It can give a serious account of why, for Smith, exchange turns into the cement of society, embodying as it does both competitive and cooperative ingredients. 'Smith was keenly aware of the ways in which human sentiments are responsive to interpersonal relationships, just like Genovesi was in his civil economy' (Bruni & Zamagni, 2007, p. 104). The market cannot be 'a morally free zone', as is sometimes affirmed, even if it does not strictly require friendship. But it is based on acknowledged fraternity, which we can take as a different name for symphathy, the basic structure on which Smithian morality is built and also the foundation of his political economy.

The principle of subsidiarity needs to be extended beyond an impersonal representation of the relations it is taken to describe. This reflects the basis of Amartya Sen's idea of justice, which, through the capabilities and functionings approach, moves the focus of attention beyond the mere goods and services involved and gives primacy to the needs of the persons and their actual capability to function under the conditions supposed.

Thus, from the standpoint of the achievement of social order, the approach of subsidiarity goes beyond a pure theory of rights and leads us into the realm of the theory of reciprocity and interpersonal relations.

BIBLIOGRAPHY

Althusius, J. (1995[1603]), *Politica*, ed. F. S. Carney, Indianapolis: The Liberty Fund.

Aquinas, Thomas (1993), *Commentary on Aristotle's Nicomachean Ethics*, Aristotelian Commentary Series, St. Augustines Press Inc.

Bruni, L. and Zamagni, S. (2007), *Civil Economy. Efficiency, Equity, Public Happiness*, Oxford: Peter Lang.

Bruni, L. and Zamagni, S. (eds) (2009), *Dizionario di economia civile*, Roma: Città Nuova.

Genovesi, A. (1765–67), *Delle lezioni di commercio o sia di economia civile con Elementi del commercio*, 2 volumes.

von Gierke, O. (1868), *Das deutsche Genossenschaftsrecht*, 4 vols., Berlin: Weidmann.

von Gierke, O. (1981[1880]), *Johannes Althusius und die Entwicklung der naturrechtlichen Staatstheorien. Zugleich ein Beitrag zur Geschichte der Rechtssystematik*, 7th unaltered edition with a preface by Julius von Gierke, Aalen (first edition, 1880, no. 7 of *Untersuchungen zur Deutschen Staatsund Rechtsgeschichte*, Berlin: Duncker & Humblot).

Hayek, F. A. (1979), *Law, Legislation and Liberty*, London: Routledge.

Montesquieu (1748), *De l'esprit des lois*, Geneva.

Quadrio Curzio, A. (2002), 'Le fondamenta di una Costituzione economica europea: sussidiarietà, sviluppo, solidarietà', in *Sussidiarietà e sviluppo. Paradigmi per l'Europa e per l'Italia*, Ch. III, pp. 89–124, Milano: Vita & Pensiero.

Röpke, W. (1944), *Civitas Humana. Grundfragen des Gesellschafts-und Wirtschaftsreform*, Erlenbach-Zürich, Eugen Rentsch Verlag.

Rubbettino, Voce (ed.) (2011), '"Sussidiarietà" di Tommaso Edoardo Frosini', in *Dizionario del liberalismo italiano*, vol. I, pp. 1012–1018.

de Tocqueville, A. (1838), *De la démocratie en Amérique*, Paris.

37. The common good
Antonio Argandoña

INTRODUCTION

In current ethical and political discourse, the common good is often a rhetorical concept, defined in very diverse ways. It had a prominent place in the political and social philosophy of Aristotle and Thomas Aquinas, lost ground when Western philosophy took an individualistic turn (and with the predominance of multiculturalism, which excludes any unitary conception of the good) but continued to be one of the main pillars of Catholic social teaching (Pontifical Council for Justice and Peace, 2004, no. 160). It returned to relevance in view of the modern manifestations of totalitarianism and other developments in recent decades, as a response to questions such as: is it possible to have a politics founded on a universal morality? Can there be a univocal notion of good in a multicultural world? Is a welfare state that combines economic prosperity with equality viable?

In Catholic social teaching the common good is defined as 'the sum total of social conditions which allow people, either as groups or as individuals, to reach their fulfillment more fully and more easily' (Pontifical Council for Justice and Peace, 2004, no. 164). This is a widely accepted definition that we can take as a starting point.

In this article we shall focus on the doctrine of the common good in the personalist tradition (Maritain, 1966), which starts with Plato and Aristotle and continues with Thomas Aquinas and Catholic social teaching. Following a brief review of the historical background, we shall discuss the relationship between the common good and human sociability, and between private goods and the common good, in order then to explain how the common good is built in a society. After that, we shall describe other conceptions of the common good, ending with the conclusions.

THE COMMON GOOD IN THE HISTORY OF THOUGHT

In the classical or Aristotelian–Thomistic tradition, the notion of the common good relates the good of people, insofar as they are part of a community, to the good of the community, insofar as it is oriented toward the people that are its members. For Aristotle, the formation of any community requires a common good, because 'the end of the city is living well . . . It is to be assumed, therefore, that the object of the political community is good actions, not only life in common' (1984a, III, 9, 1280b–1281a). For that reason the common good is constituted first of all by virtue, that is, by that which in a positive and stable way develops human beings in accordance with their nature.

Thomas Aquinas (1981, 1997) revived Aristotelian theory. The common good acquires its meaning in governance: 'to govern is to lead what is governed to its appropriate end' (1997, Book II, c. 3). The purpose of man is to contemplate and enjoy the highest of goods: God. The common good therefore has both a supernatural dimension and a temporal dimension, which coincides with what society needs in order to live in a good way.

In modern times, the concept of the common good was cut off from that tradition, and so there appeared a range of positions, from individualistic liberalism (the good of society yields to that of the individual) to collectivism (society is an entity in its own right, with a collective good that is different from and higher than the good of its members).

In the 20th century, the flourishing of Thomism gave new prominence to the concept of the common good. Maritain (1966) contrasts his 'personalist' conception with 'bourgeois individualism', 'communist anti-individualism', and 'totalitarian or dictatorial anti-communist anti-individualism'. The human person is part of a community and, in that sense, is subordinate to the community; but the person is much more than a member of the community, because he has a transcendent dimension, so that society must have the person as its end.

In the second half of the 20th century, the Second Vatican Council (1965, no. 26) stated clearly that the person is the subject, the root, the beginning and the end of all social life and all social institutions. Within the personalist tradition, Karol Wojtyla (John Paul II) developed the thesis that the person is naturally social, not only by necessity but on account of his ontological plenitude. In *Sollicitudo rei socialis* (John Paul II, 1987), he proposed the articulation between solidarity and the common good, describing solidarity as 'the firm and persevering determination to commit oneself to the common good; that is to say, to the good of all and of each individual, because we are all really responsible for all' (*ibid* no. 38).

The Encyclical *Caritas in Veritate* (Benedict XVI, 2009) has prompted renewed consideration of the common good as an ordering principle of economic life. 'The exclusively binary model of market-plus-State is corrosive of society' (*ibid* no. 39); what is needed is 'increasing openness, in a world context, to forms of economic activity marked by quotas of gratuitousness and communion' (*ibid* no. 39). The introduction of the 'logic of gift', not only in civil society but also in the market and the State, thus opens new horizons for the role of the common good. 'This is not merely a matter of a "third sector", but of a broad new composite reality embracing the private and public spheres, one which does not exclude profit, but instead considers it a means for achieving human and social ends' (*ibid* no. 46). And this promotes consideration of the common good in the 'category of relation' (*ibid* no. 53), because 'relationality is an essential element' of the 'humanum' (*ibid* no. 55).

SOCIABILITY AND THE COMMON GOOD

Human beings always seek the good (Aristotle, 1984b, I.1) – goods of all kinds, material or otherwise – and that seeking takes place in society. They need society not only in order to satisfy their needs but, above all, in order to develop as persons. Sociability is not a whim, an instinct or a constraint, but a property that flows from the nature of the person.

Society does not arise from a contract by which individuals surrender part of their freedom to the group in order to guarantee their protection and avoid conflict. It is not a mere aggregate of persons; yet it has no nature of its own independent of that of its members. Society's members are like the parts of a whole, but not in the way the arm is part of the body, as the arm cannot survive if separated from the body, whereas man retains his personality intact when separated from society.

If society is not a mere aggregate of subjects, it must have an end, which is its common good, and which cannot be reduced to the particular goods of its members. The centrality of the person demands that the end of society include the good of individuals, each and every one. There is, therefore, a good of the person and a good of society, which do not coincide but are related to one another. A person seeks his personal good because he cannot desire anything that he does not see as a good for himself, but he seeks it in society. It would be a contradiction if he were able to achieve his own good at the expense of, or even outside of, the common good. Society, in turn, has its own good, which is common to all its members but is not the sum of their personal goods. Being common, it cannot be the good of some, nor even the majority; rather, it is the good of all and of each one, at the same time and for the same reason.

It is very unlikely, however, that the members of a diversified community will all have the same conception of what their common good is. Does this mean that the common good cannot be realized? Not if the members of that community are aware that they can achieve their particular good only within the community; that serving the good of the community is a precondition for achieving their personal good; and that, therefore, they must contribute to the good of the other members of society – not to the particular good of each one but to the good that the community provides to them. The cooperation and participation of each in the common good closes the gap between the pursuit of the good of each individual and the pursuit of the common good.

The common good is thus 'the aim of the 'good life' with and for others in just institutions' (Ricoeur, 1992, p. 202). The idea of the common good is close to that of the 'structures of living together' that provide the conditions in which individual lives can flourish. 'The common good is . . . the good of the relations themselves between people, bearing in mind that such relations are understood as a good for all those who participate in them' (Zamagni, 2007, p. 23).

The common good is indivisible because the good that benefits each person cannot be separated from the good of others. It cannot be appropriated by any one of society's members; all have access to it. The goods that make up the common good are present as the foundation of all the actions of society's members; but they transcend the immediate ends of each action. Society's members seek those goods, probably unconsciously, in all their actions, but the goods themselves are not the result of specific actions.

Earlier we defined the common good as 'the sum total of social conditions which allow people, either as groups or as individuals, to reach their fulfillment more fully and more easily' (Pontifical Council for Justice and Peace, 2004, no. 164). This is a widely cited definition, yet it is not entirely correct, as it presents the common good not as an end in itself but as an instrument for the good of individuals or groups. It does not reflect the fact that the common good is not only the good that is common to the people who live in a community but also the good of the community itself.

PRIVATE GOODS AND THE COMMON GOOD

Economists distinguish among three types of goods: private goods (they are excludable: one can prevent its use by another person, and rival: the use by one person can reduce or prevent the use by another: for example, an ice-cream), public goods (non excludable: they are available to several people, and non rival: the use by one person does not reduce the use by another: the national defense, for example), and common resources (non excludable but rival: the fish in a lake). What we call here the common good is not another category of economic goods, although it is related to them.

The relationship between the common good and private goods is often presented in terms of confrontation, as if the pursuit of the second were incompatible with the pursuit of the first, or as if the good of society were a burden to individuals. But that is not the case. The key to understanding their relationship is that 'the beginning, the subject and the goal of all social institutions is and must be the human person' (Second Vatican Council, 1965, no. 25). The goal of the political community is the good of the person, insofar as the person is a part of the community. Yet the good of the person is not opposed to the good of society but is part of it.

The common good therefore takes precedence over the particular good, where the goods are of the same or a higher kind (Aquinas, 1981, II–II, q. 152, a. 4 ad 2). This is not for any quantitative reason (e.g., because the common good is the good of more people), but because the common good is the good of the whole of which the individual is part. It is not opposed to the pursuit of private interests as such but to the pursuit of private interests at the expense of the common good, turning the common good into an instrument for the particular good. In short, the tension between personal good and common good is resolved dynamically: a person has a duty to achieve the good for himself; but he can only achieve his own good if he also achieves the good of society, which is oriented to the person. Moreover, this is not the good of 'others' – a good that a person must seek because of some altruistic imperative – nor, clearly, the good of the State.

Just as society is not given but is somehow 'constructed' by all its members, the common good also is built by the members of society. It arises from the common activity of all and is enjoyed by all. It is a shared good, not only because everybody shares in it but above all because it 'overflows' from each person to the rest.

HOW THE COMMON GOOD IS BUILT

The concept of the common good, as stated here, seems of little use if the aim is to specify the conditions of life that individuals and communities consider most appropriate to achieve their goal. And as the abstract good does not move people to act, it is important that we more clearly specify its content. Maritain (1966, pp. 52–53) states the issue as follows, first:

> (t)hat which constitutes the common good of a political society is not only: the collection of public commodities and services – the roads, ports, schools, etc. – which the organization of common life presupposes; a sound fiscal condition of the state and its military power; the body of just laws, good customs and wise institutions, which provide the nation with its structure;

the heritage of its great historical remembrances, its symbols and its glories; its living traditions and cultural treasures.

Here, Maritain identifies the sum of social conditions that make it possible for the members of society to realize their goals. Second:

> The common good . . . includes also . . . the sum or sociological integration of all the civic conscience, political virtues, and sense of right and liberty, of all the activity, material prosperity and spiritual riches, of unconsciously operative hereditary wisdom, of moral rectitude, justice, friendship, happiness, virtue and heroism in the individual life of its members. For these things all are, in a certain measure, communicable and so revert to each member, helping him to perfect his life of liberty and person. They all constitute the good human life of the multitude.

These sentences point to the sum of the aids that society provides to its members. Third:

> To the previous two sets of elements we must add the harmonious integration of all these elements in a whole. (Maritain, 1951, p. 10)

The common good therefore obviously cannot be defined statistically, in terms of a country's wealth, consumption or another economic variable. Material goods are part of the common good insofar as they make the common good possible, as well as other goods like truth, beauty, peace, art, culture, freedom, tradition . . . All these can be 'common goods' that define in some way the abstract and transcendent concept of the common good.

As Maritain suggests, the common good is not a single good but is made up of an interwoven set of goods of varying scope and on different levels. It is not a precise institutional project, nor is the result of a predetermined objective assessment of what is good for human nature. Nor is the common good a subsidy that society offers to its members (like the welfare state), much less a burden that is imposed on them.

It is the task of the State to enable and promote the common good, but not to define it nor, therefore, to impose specific content that might realize it. Nor is it the task of the market, through the impersonal forces of the 'invisible hand'.

What we have said here regarding the common good of the *polis* applies equally to the different types of communities, as:

> no expression of social life – from the family to intermediate social groups, associations, enterprises of an economic nature, cities, regions, States, up to the community of peoples and nations – can escape the issue of its own common good, in that this is a constitutive element of its significance and the authentic reason for its very existence. (Pontifical Council for Justice and Peace, 2004, no. 165)

Every community at every moment in history must find its common good. But this is not to say that there is no universal common good, because all individuals and all smaller communities are part of larger communities, up to the whole of humanity in time and space.

OTHER CONCEPTIONS OF THE COMMON GOOD

As we said earlier, the concept of the common good has been addressed from different philosophical positions. Here we shall discuss 1) philosophical and political liberalism, 2) welfare liberalism, 3) communitarianism, 4) totalitarianism, and 5) the capability approach.

1) With the advent of modernity, the individual became the center of attention of social and political ethics. The main characteristic of the self-sufficient individual is the ability to choose the means to achieve ends that are not an integral part of his 'self'. Here, society is a rational project – a social contract between subjects who have their own conceptions of what is good. Morality is a product of individual choices, which cannot be judged by external criteria. The organization of society therefore does not depend on the concept of good, which is replaced by the concept of rights. People's moral or religious points of view play no relevant role in this society.

   Classical political liberalism relies on the free market – ruled by self-interest – and a minimal State to achieve social goals. For its conservative and libertarian branches (Nozick, 1988), the common good or general interest is determined in a consensual way as the sum of the private goods chosen by the citizens according to their utility functions; in a utilitarian spirit, it is the greatest good for the greatest number. And the role of the State is to promote the well-being of citizens and protect their freedom.

2) Welfare liberals today form the dominant currents in Western political thought. They start from the individualistic assumptions of liberalism but note that the agents, in trying to put their life plan into effect in the context of the free market, have very different starting positions. It is the task of the ethically neutral State to guarantee and distribute equitably the freedoms and resources that individuals need in order to lead the lives they have freely chosen. Hence the centrality of the concept of justice (Rawls, 1971).

   Besides the realization of the personal good of the agents, the concept of the common good also includes certain social outcomes, in terms of equality, leveling of starting conditions, and provision of a universal welfare state. The market is the sphere of efficiency and wealth creation, whereas the State is the sphere of solidarity and redistribution; and as the two spheres are ultimately incompatible, there will always be clashes between the two.

3) In political debate, communitarians are above all critical of liberalism. The person is not a self-sufficient being, separated from the community, concerned only for his particular interest and endowed with certain basic rights and freedoms that are prior even to the definition of the social order; rather, his 'self' is made up of communal ties, which he cannot do without. The community is much more than an aggregate of individuals; it becomes a moral space in which things have value insofar as the prevailing culture gives them meaning.

   The common good is no longer the sum of particular goods: the community is a common good in itself and a source of common goods for individuals. There is no universal common good; rather, each community has its own conception of the common good, which takes precedence over the good of citizens, because citizens owe it loyalty and commitment. It is the good of the community, not the good of individuals as members of the community. The State cannot be neutral. Its mission goes beyond guaranteeing the rights and freedoms of individuals to having its own conception of what is good in accordance with the values it recognizes in the community.

4) The concept of the common good has also been used by different types of totalitarianism (communism, Nazism, fascism), but in a radically different sense from that given it in the personalist tradition, because in totalitarianism the person is seen as merely a part of society, to which he is subordinate; and also because the totalitarian desire to impose a certain specific content of the common good on citizens is opposed to the idea of a good that is both the good of the person and the good of society.

It is this desire that has led authors of various tendencies to oppose the concept of the common good on the grounds that it is incompatible with democracy and the freedom of people. And the risk of totalitarianism clearly exists where the State is assigned the task of defining and implementing the common good. That is why the personalist tradition affirms that the common good is not so much a duty of the State as a duty of all the members of society, and that the role of the State to promote it, but not to define or impose it.

5) In both the theory and the practice of economic development, growth has been synonymous with an increase in the material resources of a country. The results, however, have been frequently insufficient, even regrettable, prompting a search for alternative approaches. One of the most suggestive is that of Amartya Sen, for whom 'development can be seen . . . as the process of expansion of the real freedoms that people enjoy' (1999, p. 3). Poverty is rooted not so much in a lack of material means as in the absence of certain freedoms, because of the denial of certain 'abilities to do valuable acts or reach valuable states of being'.

Sen does not use the concept of the common good, but his focus on capabilities brings him close to it, albeit without coinciding. Sen understands capabilities as oriented to the freedom to choose, in line with liberal theories, so that the common good is not the good of the community as a whole and the good of its members, but only the good of the members.

Developing the theory of capabilities, Nussbaum (2000) identifies the good that is common to human life with the sum of human rights, or with a list of core human capabilities. In the Aristotelian–Thomistic tradition a list of human rights is not enough to define the common good, because those rights do not capture the full depth and wealth of the concept, although they are of course part of it.

CONCLUSIONS: WHAT ROLE DOES THE COMMON GOOD HAVE TODAY?

The concept of the common good is far from being universally accepted, and those who use the concept have very different conceptions of it. When the common good is identified with a set of democratic freedoms or human rights, or with the generic object of social and redistributive policies, it is widely accepted. But when it is presented as a good that not only is shared by citizens but also exists in its own right, the level of acceptance declines considerably. In this order of things, Deneulin (2006) cites five objections that social philosophers and political scientists raise nowadays when discussing the Thomistic concept of the common good:

1) It simply amounts to recognition of the need to reach institutional agreements in order to promote the well-being of citizens. In other words, it is instrumental to the good of individuals. We criticized this conception earlier.
2) If it is not instrumental, the common good becomes a tool of totalitarianism. However, if we accept that the common good is the good not only of society but also of individuals, that threat disappears.
3) In practice, the common good is simply another name for the public goods that we hear about from economists. But those public goods are exclusive: though in principle available to all, when allocated to a particular user, they become reserved for exclusively private use.
4) It is another way of talking about a good that is common to human life and so is reduced to a list of rights that are necessary for a good human life. However, if that life is only personal, it does not include the common good, which also encompasses life in common and the structural conditions that make it possible.
5) It is an unrealizable concept because in a multicultural society it is impossible to reach agreement on the goods of which it is composed. So either the concept of the common good is abandoned or else it is reduced to a discussion of the partial common goods of a particular community. But if there is no good that is shared by all humans by the fact of being human, we will end up separating some communities from others. The fact that the common good described here cannot be reduced to a list of realizations for politicians is, rather, a strength of this concept, because it can never crystallize in a defined set of structures, which would be the same negation of the dynamism of human good in society.

The concept of the common good, as understood in the classical social and political philosophy and the Catholic social teaching, does not have wide acceptance in 'secular' media. Nevertheless, we have already seen how the exclusive pursuit of self-interest, divorced from any consideration of the good of society, has bad results. This is perhaps why the common good is so much talked about today, albeit in a sense that is, to say the least, inadequate: as the sum of personal goods, as mere common interest, as the exercise of justice, as recognition of the need to account for the consequences of one's own actions on others (what economists call the externalities of action), as an instrument of social negotiation between adversaries, and so on. Against all this, consideration of a rich, well founded concept of the common good may help to redefine the role of politics.

But this does not mean that putting the common good in practice is an easy task in politics. It demands a broad vision of the problems and taking into account the effects of the policies on the people and the organizations – and not only on their private interests, but also on creating and preserving the conditions which allow people, either as groups or as individuals, to reach their fulfillment more fully and more easily. It does not allow a concrete and detailed description of the common good to be imposed to the citizens. It is not monolithic: the common good is realized in every community as well as in the global society, in a historical, specific and plural way. It cannot be warranted by any political, economic or technical structure, unless it is based on the responsibility of the persons and the institutions. It is, therefore, a calling to all to take on their common responsibilities (Benedict XVI, 2009, no. 17).

REFERENCES

Aquinas, T. (1981), *Summa Theologica*, New York, NY: Christian Classics.
Aquinas, T. (1997), *On the Government of Rulers: De Regimine Principum*, Philadelphia, PA: University of Pennsylvania Press.
Aristotle (1984a), 'Politics', in J. Barnes (ed.), *The Complete Works of Aristotle*, vol. 2, Princeton, NJ: Princeton University Press.
Aristotle (1984b), 'Nicomachean Ethics', in J. Barnes (ed.), *The Complete Works of Aristotle*, vol. 2, Princeton, NJ: Princeton University Press.
Benedict XVI (2009), *Encyclical Letter Caritas in veritate*, Vatican City: Libreria Editrice Vaticana.
Deneulin, S. (2006), 'Amartya Sen's capability approach to development and *Gaudium et spes*', *Journal of Catholic Social Thought*, **3**, 2.
John Paul II (1987), *Encyclical Letter Sollicitudo rei socialis*. Vatican City: Libreria Editrice Vaticana.
Maritain, J. (1951), *The Rights of Man and Natural Law*, New York, NY: Charles Scribner's Son.
Maritain, J. (1966), *The Person and the Common Good*, Notre Dame, IN: University of Notre Dame Press.
Nozick, R. (1988), *Anarchy, State and Utopia*, New York, NY: Basic Books.
Nussbaum, M. (2000), *Women and Human Development: A Study in Human Capabilities*, Cambridge, UK: Cambridge University Press.
Pontifical Council for Justice and Peace (2004), *Compendium of the Social Doctrine of the Church*, Vatican City: Libreria Editrice Vaticana.
Rawls, J. (1971), *A Theory of Justice*, Cambridge, MA: Harvard University Press.
Ricoeur, P. (1992), *One Self as Another*, Chicago, IL: University of Chicago Press.
Second Vatican Council (1965), *Pastoral Constitution Gaudium et Spes*, in *Acta Apostolicae Sedis*, 58.
Sen, A. (1999), *Development as Freedom*, Oxford, UK: Oxford University Press.
Zamagni, S. (2007), 'El bien común en la sociedad posmoderna: propuestas para la acción político-económica', *Revista Cultura Económica*, **25** (70), pp. 23–43.

BIBLIOGRAPHY

On the Common Good in General

Archer, M.S. and P. Donati (eds) (2008), *Pursuing the Common Good: How Solidarity and Subsidiarity Can Work Together*, Vatican City: The Pontifical Academy of Social Sciences.
Cahill, L. (2005), 'Globalization and the common good', in J.A. Coleman (ed.), *Globalization and Catholic Social Thought*, New York, NY: Orbis.
Hollenbach, D. (2002), *The Common Good and Christian Ethics*, Cambridge, UK: Cambridge University Press.
Riordan, P. (2009), *A Grammar of the Common Good: Speaking of Globalisation*, London, UK: Continuum.

Other Conceptions of the Common Good

Grasso, K., G. Bradley and R. Hurt (eds) (1995), *Catholicism, Liberalism and Communitarianism*, Lanham, MD: Rowan and Littlefield.
Stiltner, B. (1999), *Religion and the Common Good. Catholic Contributions to Building Community in a Liberal Society*, New York, NY: Rowman and Littlefield.

On the Common Good in the Economy and in Companies

Alford, H.J. and M.J. Naughton (2001), *Managing as if Faith Mattered*, Notre Dame, IN: University of Notre Dame Press.

Argandoña, A. (1998), 'The stakeholder theory and the common good', *Journal of Business Ethics*, **17**, pp. 1093–1102.

Cortright, S.A. and M.J. Naughton (eds) (2002), *Rethinking the Purpose of Business. Interdisciplinary Essays from the Catholic Social Tradition*, Notre Dame, IN: University of Notre Dame Press.

De Bettignies, H-C. and F. Lépineux (eds.) (2009), *Business, Globalization and the Common Good*, Oxford, UK: Peter Lang.

Kennedy, R.G. (2007), 'Business and the common good', in P. Booth (ed.), *Catholic Social Teaching and the Market Economy*, London, UK: Institute of Economic Affairs, pp. 164–189.

Naughton, M.J., H.J. Alford and B. Brady (1995), 'The common good and the purpose of the firm', *Journal of Human Values*, **1** (2), pp. 221–237.

38. The economics of corporate social responsibility
Lorenzo Sacconi

INTRODUCTION

Over the past two decades, corporate social responsibility (CSR) has been a focal subject for scholars in management studies, business ethics, and the law. More recently, however, economists have also started to pay attention to CSR in both popular newspapers and academic journals. As early as 2005, *The Economist* acknowledged the spectacular growth of company CSR initiatives throughout the world, involving companies, business associations, stakeholders representative groups, NGOs, universities, international organizations, and yet others. What struck *The Economist* as especially disturbing – in line with a famous Milton Friedman's dictum of the 1970s – was that Boards of Directors, insufficiently committed to making profits for their shareholders, were instead engaging in 'pernicious benevolence' by being philanthropic with money taken not from their own pockets but from those of the corporate shareholders.

What in fact this view indicated was that CSR is a philanthropic activity that 'altruistic' managers undertake by misusing corporate money, which as such, is in contrast with profit maximization. According to this view, CSR was a peculiar manifestation of managerial self-dealing: managers used company funds for the self-satisfaction of their own arbitrary moral preferences.

Barely three years later, however, *The Economist* took a very different view on CSR. It now stated that 'done badly, [it] is just a fig leaf and can be positively harmful. Done well, though, it is not some separate activity that companies do on the side, a corner of corporate life reserved for virtue. It is just good business' (*The Economist*, 19 January, 2008, p. 3, *Special Report*). Hence CSR was no longer deemed to be merely philanthropic, but rather a part of the core business strategy of any large company operating in the turmoil of the global economy. In fact, companies worldwide are engaged in a series of challenges with their stakeholders that may crucially affect their business and economic operations, with the consequence that CSR may be considered as the appropriate way to address those challenges. Once it was recognized that CSR was no longer alien to the proper business and economic operation of a company, however, the second tenet also had to be to changed: henceforth, CSR could be reduced to being just a tool (according to an *instrumental* view) for achieving the traditional objective of shareholder value maximization – which is the function of a corporation – namely, as an effective *tool* of the overall strategy of making as much profit as possible.

At the same time also academic economists began publishing papers on the subject matter. Baron (2007, 2009) viewed CSR as a rational supply of philanthropy in response to a market demand for 'private politics' required by consumers and to the pressure exercised by NGOs – which are not in principle antagonistic to profit maximization. This becomes clear once it is recognized that some consumers do not simply have a preference for material goods, as they press for product differentiation in terms of the 'moral' characteristics of companies' output.

Even more recently, renowned micro-economists Bénabou and Tirole (2010), drawing on recent developments in economic psychology, observed that pro-social behaviors at the individual level enable us to understand the increasing interest in CSR shown by company managers. This translates into corporate philanthropy initiatives for the benefit of stakeholders, even though the authors' conclusions reveal a certain skepticism about the efficiency of these corporate policies in relation to the economic function of the firm. By contrast, other authors have attempted to give a more substantial account of CSR in terms of environmental externality prevention and unfairness avoidance by showing that these CSR programs are consistent with the traditional aim of business corporations to maximize shareholder value, at least when it is conceived 'in the long run' (see Heal 2005, 2008).

It must be admitted that the explanations that economists are providing neither penetrate the surface of the long-standing CSR phenomenon, nor contribute significantly to the lively debate on the deep reasons why corporations should embrace socially responsible conduct, and why CSR is considered to be an increasingly important management standard for corporations. Reflecting either a preservationist attitude towards existing economic models, or attempts to make this new research topic acceptable to economists who persist with a 'normal science' view of the profession, they continue to believe that the standard micro-economic understanding of the firm's objective-function and corporate governance structure (the principal–agent model recognizing shareholders' priority) is correct. They then try to tame recalcitrant facts about the spread of the CSR movement throughout the world, and its emphasis on what companies are obliged to do for the benefit of stakeholders other than shareholders, in order to accommodate them within the mainstream view of the capitalist business company. To sum up, since the importance of CSR as a global phenomenon cannot be ignored, the recent wave of papers by economists tends to deal with it by reducing CSR to 'corporate philanthropy' or a strategic tool in line with, and instrumental to, profitability.

To gain a proper understanding of the global CSR movement would require questioning more in depth the nature of corporations as social and economic institutions. On the battleground of corporate governance models, 'corporate social responsibility' denotes a movement that affirms a social norm relating to the range of obligations owed by corporations to their stakeholders. It challenges rival social norms, such as the one which avows shareholder primacy and the principle of 'shareholder value', which has also emerged in the last three decades, and has progressively gained support. CSR struggles against these concepts, and strives to gains its own settlement through the continuing expansion of its level of acceptance in the behavior and self-organization of companies in response to the demands and actions of their stakeholders. CSR is thus an emerging social norm or convention which is shaping the mutual expectations and reciprocal behaviors that agents in the interaction domain of corporate governance tend to accept progressively.

This picture can easily be understood by anyone (but especially economists) that has even a superficial idea of the evolutionary dynamics taking place in games that are played repeatedly by populations of players. From this perspective, competing social norms (concerning corporate obligations) tend to establish themselves as regularities of behavior resulting from equilibrium selection dynamics that essentially reflect how many players (companies and stakeholders, in our case) adopt the corresponding behavior as a consequence of how many of them embrace mutual (descriptive and normative) beliefs consistent with that behavior (Schotter 1981; Sugden 1986; Young 1998; for an application to the evolution of corporate governance institutions as equilibrium conventions, see also Aoki 2010).

In order to understand this picture, however, it must be acknowledged that CSR is neither about philanthropy (although it may include corporate giving) nor is it a strategy with the narrow purpose of profit maximization. The lively debate on the range of fiduciary duties owed by corporations to their shareholders and stakeholders or to society at large dates back to the 1930s (recall the famous Dodd vs. Berle controversy). Widening the perspective from America to other national models of capitalism, the rationale for that debate was further confirmed by the persistence of various institutional models of corporate governance whereby many stakeholders, and certainly not shareholders alone, were deemed to be sources of obligations owed by entrepreneurs and managers. The German co-determination model and the Japanese management model, with its distinctive extensive interpretation of managers' fiduciary duties – first of all towards employees – are typical examples of this.

Here, however, we can confine our reconstruction of the knowledge that permits us to appreciate the true nature of CSR to more recent strands of literature, both outside and inside economics. First of all, the stakeholder approach to strategic management and business ethics (Freeman 1984; Freeman and Gilbert 1988; Donaldson and Preston 1995) provided the intuition that a proper normative and explanatory model of the corporation needed to include the idea that those in a position of authority in the firm must discharge various responsibilities to many stakeholders in order to elicit mutual cooperation. In parallel, Masahiko Aoki (Aoki 1984) developed a branch of the new institutional economic theory of the firm that provided a cooperative view of corporate governance based on bargaining game theory, and then developed a theory of institutional complementarity between corporate governance and other social institutions, within which 'external' social responsibility also has a place (Aoki 2010). Later, the heterodox law and economics model of the Board of Directors as a 'mediating hierarchy' among corporate stakeholders was suggested as an appropriate interpretation of how American corporate law traditionally responded to the problems of team production and incomplete contracts (Blair and Stout 1999).

Thus, by combining stakeholder thinking with insights from social contract theories developed by both philosophers and economists (Rawls 1971; Buchanan 1975; Gauthier 1986) and a critical reading of the new institutional economic modeling of the firm (Williamson 1975; Aoki 1984; Grossman and Hart 1986; Hart and Moore 1991; Kreps 1990a, 1990b), a social contract view of the firm was ready well before the recent wave of economists' explanations of what CSR is, and it was able to explain why corporations must fulfill an extended range of obligations toward their stakeholders (see Sacconi 1991, 2000, 2006b, 2007).

This chapter continues this line of institutional-economics reasoning, which sees CSR as the emergence of a social norm that backs forms of corporate governance that extend fiduciary duties from those owed to proprietors and shareholders to those ranging over an enlarged set of properly defined corporate stakeholders. CSR is an additional component of corporate governance that complements residual control – providing that owners or appointed managers make discretional decisions that support the appropriation of profits by financial capital investors – with the additional duty of enabling even non-controlling stakeholders to participate in the distribution of corporate surpluses created by the investments and cooperation of all stakeholders. Thus, CSR is what provides (or denies) the institution of corporate governance by its (moral and social) legitimation on the part of all the stakeholders affected by the exercise of corporate authority.

CSR embraces a multi-fiduciary perspective on corporate governance, and must, therefore, respond to criticisms leveled against the idea that fiduciary duties can indeed be multiple (Jensen 2001; Marcoux 2003). This chapter provides a restatement of the social contract foundation of the multi-stakeholder and multi-fiduciary model of corporate governance that also answers all these criticisms. First, it provides an operational model of the reasoning and decision-making processes of an impartial board of directors that may be employed for mediation among different stakeholders. In this way, 'impartial mediation' acquires a well-defined meaning.

Second, it explains how the governance structure of the firm, including both residual rights of control and social responsibilities, can be chosen from behind a 'veil of ignorance' in a decision position that precedes strategic interaction among corporate stakeholders. It specifies the distributive justice principle for surplus allocation among different stakeholders. In fact, a proper modeling of the social contract, employing both bargaining theory and non-cooperative repeated games, in accordance with Binmore's reinterpretation of the Rawlsian maximin principle (Binmore 2005), shows that stakeholders under a veil of ignorance would choose a 'socially responsible' principle of a corporate constitution that entailed an egalitarian surplus distribution. In this way, a corporate objective-function that includes a fair balance among different stakeholders is well-defined and perfectly calculable.

Moreover, based on the same formal analysis, a principle of fairness such as this proves to be a social norm that satisfies the typical stability property of game equilibria (and hence conventions), which emerges from an equilibrium selection process starting from an ex-ante impartial mode of reasoning (the veil of ignorance). Thus, what is fair is also stable: CSR cannot be accused of being wishful thinking, or of failing the test of incentive compatibility. Hence the CSR social norm supports the emergence of a self-sustaining institution in the domain of corporate governance. Finally, a two-step model of the firm's social contract also explains what fiduciary duties the Board of Directors owes to whom within the set of the relevant corporate stakeholders – shareholders included. This also provides a priority ordering of stakeholder claims that may be made against the company.

The chapter is organized as follows. Section that follows on pages 376–378 critically considers recent 'additional' and 'instrumental' economic explanations of CSR. Section from pages 378–380 contrasts them with a 'constitutive' definition of CSR as an extended model of corporate governance, and provides the related definitions of stakeholders and fiduciary duties. Section from pages 380–385 critically reviews the new institutional economics literature that, although it may not be normally related to CSR, is much more useful than standard microeconomic theorizing for the purposes of gaining deep understanding of CSR. This section suggests, therefore, that economists should draw from it in order to understand why fiduciary duties must be expanded even for mere economic reasons of efficiency, and also why corporate reputation cannot leave aside the explicit settlement of an ethical norm of CSR. Section which follows from pages 385–395 presents the full-fledged social contract theory of multi-stakeholder corporate governance, which entails multiple fiduciary duties and a fair distribution of corporate surpluses. It also provides an explanation of CSR as a self-enforceable social norm. This section replies to the main criticisms leveled against the stakeholder model of corporate governance, while at the same time developing analytically the model's foundation. The last section concludes by making this new view of corporate objective-function intuitive, and adds comments on the limitations of this approach, as well as further research that has not been reported here in detail.

'ADDITIONAL' AND 'INSTRUMENTAL' APPROACHES TO CSR

There are few views of Corporate Social Responsibility (henceforth CSR) put forward in economic theory. Some of them do not require any major change in the notion of the firm as an institution and in its objective function. One of these views has been developed in response to the classic criticism set out by Milton Friedman, who sought to discredit CSR by describing it as an improper form of philanthropy carried out by self-dealing managers arbitrarily using shareholders' money to satisfy their own philanthropic caprices (Friedman 1970). According to this first view, by contrast, CSR consists of policies adopted by managers and entrepreneurs which use part of the company profit in order efficiently to satisfy the philanthropic desires of consumers (Baron 2007, 2009).

The basic idea is that, alongside the market of commodities and the typical business activity of companies, there is a 'market for private politics' in which citizens/consumers decide how to allocate their supply of donations among initiatives for the common good that are left unimplemented by 'public politics' because of state failures. Citizens/consumers can choose whether to pay their donations directly to charities (nonprofits) or to pay companies (by buying their products) if these are committed to giving corporate donations to charities and to supporting campaigns for the common good, social welfare, environmental protection, etc. Under certain conditions (among which the assumption that consumers derive a 'warm glow' from financing charities through their market consumption of goods), at least some groups of citizens/consumers would rationally and efficiently use companies as means to maximize their satisfaction from charities.

From the point of view of companies, CSR would thus be seen as a policy of product differentiation such that, in addition to their standard supply of goods, at an additional cost, charities that satisfy the warm glow preferences of consumers would also be supplied. Although such companies can be seen as having *moral management* (as opposed to companies that pursue social performance for merely instrumental motives), the firm's behavior does not require any substantial deviation from profit maximization under the hypothesis of consumers' warm glow, insofar as a proportion of consumers prefer to buy from companies that support charities corresponding to their charitable preferences rather than make donations directly.

'Private politics' can thus be seen as entailing CSR as an addition to the traditional business activity. But it is an addition that does not change the overall objective function and nature of the business firm (i.e. maximizing profit) to any significant extent.

Although understanding the true meaning of 'moral management' (Baron 2009) seems difficult within this perspective (could it be a technology rather than a motivation?), it is clear that this line of thought assumes that private politics are compatible with the standard view of the firm as a profit maximizing machine. I call this perspective the *additional* view of CSR.

Another recent economic approach to CSR is the purely *instrumental* one (Heal 2005, 2008). The *additional* view sees CSR as a genuine additional activity by the corporation. CSR is costly and *per se* inconsistent with business objectives; nevertheless, it too can be reconciled with profit maximization through the disposition of consumers to pay more for a differentiated product (containing charities) because of their warm glow preferences. By contrast, the *instrumental* view seeks to reduce CSR to a strategy entirely *functional* to the traditional business goal of shareholder-maximization pursued within the corporation's core business activities (without seeing it as a parallel line of production added by product differentiation). According to this explanation, a wider set of policies and programs are incorporated into CSR – not just corporate charities or financial support for nonprofits. Such CSR programs consist in some level of externalities prevention and reduction of the economic and social unfairness engendered *prima facie* by the rational selfish conduct of business.

Thus, CSR seems to fall within the scope of the company's core business, rather than adding a further dimension of activity. And this seems to be a clear improvement. But the idea is basically that these programs or corporate policies can be accounted for without any change in the basic nature of the corporation as a shareholder-value maximization machine, and without any reference to diverse motives to act among consumers, managers or investors. The reason is that, in order to pursue the same selfish objective as usual, the company must change its strategies. The decisive conditions for this to come about are that business strategies are undertaken under the threat that new regulations may be enacted by public authorities concerned with environmental issues; or that activism by stakeholders may impinge on the company's reputation (related to both externalities or unfairness). If the strategic environment of the firm contains these more stringent constraints, it can maximize profit only by adopting a CSR strategy.

In fact, it is not clear whether – also according to this line of thought – it would not be better to state the point differently. The objective function of the company (as a normative principle of conduct concerning what the company aims to maximize) could be understood as having changed so as to include broader goals like unfairness and externality reduction, whereas the argument about profit could be seen as working at the different level of incentives compatibility, i.e. what induces owners and managers to carry out such an enlarged objective and institutional function. It is clear, however, that those who work within this perspective want to reverse the most logical order by maintaining the priority of profit-maximization as the corporate goal and reducing CSR to a means to achieve it, or at most to an external constraint on the firm's behavior.

However, it is quite obvious that one of the main incentives that the firm may have in carrying out a CSR strategy – i.e. reputation effects – would not be effectively pursued if CSR policies were recognized by the stakeholders concerned as purely instrumental means to capture their benevolence. Under conditions of imperfect information, where stakeholders are incompletely able to disentangle truly responsible behaviors from ones only apparently so, or to understand the true nature of the company's behavior, this form of strategic CSR would be open to many forms of opportunistic behavior.

As we shall see later in this chapter, an instrumental view of CSR is self-defeating; whereas a reformulation of the normative objective function, governance structure, and managerial strategy in line with CSR principles would give much more credibility to CSR commitments and hence would improve the company's reputation to a much greater extent. In one way or another, CSR seems to entail a broadening or a restatement of the traditional profit motive.

Hence, the instrumental doctrine seems to be a rhetorical argument offered to CEOs so that they can convince their shareholders that furthering CSR policies pays; much less does it seem to stem from a deep understanding of how CSR reshapes the corporation's view, nature and goals. Given that the instrumental perspective begins by recognizing the shareholders' priority for the justification of CSR as it is stated in the shareholders' model of corporate governance, then the model of governance itself cannot be at issue in this view of CSR.

A 'CONSTITUTIVE' VIEW OF CSR AS A MULTI-FIDUCIARY MODEL OF CORPORATE GOVERNANCE

The perspectives on CSR discussed in the previous section seem to be better explained as attempts of orthodox economics to regain control over a phenomenon – the CSR movement involving managers, corporations and many groups of concerned stakeholders – that has been growing rapidly for at least the past two decades without being convincingly accounted for by mainstream economics.

A much deeper understating of CSR however has been provided within new institutional economics, unorthodox law and economics, and the stakeholder approach to management studies and business ethics, that relate it to the very economic nature of the corporation (Aoki 1984, 2001, 2010; Blair and Stout 1999, 2006, Stout 2011b, Freeman 1984, Evan and Freeman 1993; Freeman and Velamuri 2006; Freeman et al 2010; Donaldson and Preston 1995; Donaldson 2012; Clarkson 1999; Sacconi 1991, 2000, 2006a, 2006b, 2007, 2010a, 2010b, 2011).

According to these views, CSR is a form of corporate strategic management; moreover, it is a model for governing transactions among the firm's stakeholders. It is clear that here 'governance' is no longer the set of rules simply allocating property rights and defining the owners' control over the company's management. Instead, it relates to the new-institutional economics view whereby firms, like contracts and other institutional forms, are 'governance structures' which establish diverse rights and related responsibilities in order to reduce 'transaction costs' (Coase 1937; Williamson 1975, 1985; Grossman and Hart 1986) and the negative externalities related to economic transactions so as to approximate social welfare (Coase, 1960).

This view is *constitutive* because it sees CSR as a trait inherent in how the corporation functions and to its goal: that is, it sees CSR as the governance model on the basis of which a company pursues as its objective-function the joint interest and mutual advantage of all its relevant corporate stakeholders. Insofar as CSR is defined as a governance model entailing a multi-stakeholder definition of the corporate goal, it concerns less the sphere of corporate *means* than the domain of corporate *ends (the corporation's goals)* and *constitutional rules*, i.e. it is *constitutive*.

I hence submit the following definition (see also Sacconi 2006a, 2006b, 2007, 2010):

> CSR is a model of extended corporate governance whereby those who run firms (entrepreneurs, directors, managers) have responsibilities that range from fulfillment of their fiduciary duties towards the owners to fulfillment of analogous fiduciary duties towards all the firm's stakeholders.

Two terms must be defined for the foregoing proposition to be clearly understood:

1. *Fiduciary duties*: it is assumed that a subject has a legitimate interest but is unable to make the relevant decisions, in the sense that she/he does not know what goals to pursue, what alternative to choose, or how to deploy his/her resources in order to satisfy his/her interest. She/he, the *trustor*, therefore delegates decisions to a *trustee* empowered to choose actions and goals. The trustee may thus use the trustor's resources and select the appropriate course of action. For a fiduciary relationship – this being the basis of the trustee's authority *vis-à-vis* the trustor – to arise, the latter must possess a claim (right) towards the former. In other words, the trustee directs actions and uses the resources made over to him/her so that results are obtained which satisfy (to the best extent possible) the trustor's interests. These claims (i.e. the trustor's *rights*) impose fiduciary duties on the agent who is invested with authority (the trustee) which she/he is obliged to fulfill. The fiduciary relation applies in a wide variety of instances: tutor/minor and teacher/pupil relationships, and (in the corporate domain) the relation between the board of a trust and its beneficiaries, or according to the predominant opinion, between the board of directors of a joint-stock company and its shareholders, and then more generally between management and owners (if the latter do not run the enterprise themselves). By the term 'fiduciary duty', therefore, is meant the duty (or responsibility) to exercise authority for the good of those who have granted that authority and are therefore subject to it (Flannigan 1989).

2. *Stakeholders*: this term denotes individuals or groups with a major stake in the running of the firm and who are able to influence it significantly (Freeman and McVea 2001). However, from an economist's point of view, most relevant to defining stakeholders is the following distinction between two categories:

    a) *stakeholders in the strict sense*: those who have an interest at stake because they have made specific investments in the firm (in the form of human capital, financial capital, social capital or trust, physical or environmental capital, or for the development of dedicated technologies, etc.) – that is, investments which may significantly increase the total value generated by the firm (net of the costs sustained for that purpose) and which are made specifically in relation to *that* firm (and not to any other) so that their value is idiosyncratically related to the completion of the transactions carried out by or in relation to that firm. These stakeholders are reciprocally dependent on the firm because they influence its value but at the same time – given the specificity of their investment – depend largely upon it for satisfaction of their well-being prospects (lock-in effect);

b) *stakeholders in the broad sense*: those individuals or groups whose interest is involved because they *undergo* the 'external effects', positive or negative, of the transactions performed by the firm, even if they do not directly participate in the transaction, so that they do not contribute to, nor directly receive value from, the firm.

One can thus appreciate the scope of CSR defined as an extended form of governance: it extends the concept of fiduciary duty from a mono-stakeholder setting (where the sole stakeholder relevant to identification of fiduciary duties is the owner of the firm) to a multi-stakeholder one in which the firm owes fiduciary duties to *all* its stakeholders (the owners included).

THEORIES OF THE FIRM BENIGN WITH A STAKEHOLDER APPROACH TO CORPORATE GOVERNANCE

To give more substance to the economic foundation of the idea that corporate governance (CG) consists in an extension of fiduciary duties to all stakeholders and the impartial mediation among them, it may be worthwhile recalling the economic analysis of the risk of 'abuse of authority' in business organizations (Sacconi 2000, 2006b, 2007, 2009, 2010a). One tenet of the agency view, which reduces corporate governance to the disciplining of the relation between manager and shareholders, is that whilst shareholders suffer from strong asymmetry of information due to the separation between ownership and control, other stakeholders are satisfactorily protected either by contracts or the law. However, were this thesis true we would not have the modern new institutional theory of the firm, which is based on the idea that most contracts are basically incomplete (Coase 1937; Williamson 1975, 1985, 2010; Grossman and Hart 1986; Hart and Moore 1990). It is no accident, in fact, that the most acute economists working on mathematical principal–agent models see incomplete contracts as a secondary phenomenon reducible to asymmetry of information – and hence treatable in agency models – and at the same time are doubtful about the stakeholder approach to CG (Tirole 1999, 2001).

On the contrary, according to Williamson and others, incompleteness is pervasive and irreducible. This is the *first* hypothesis of new institutional economics concerning the firm. It stems from many factors: (i) non verifiability by third parties – i.e. a law court called upon to assess a breach of a contract would be unable to ascertain whether the breach has effectively occurred because it may have happened in states of the world that it cannot observe or verify; (ii) unforeseen contingencies: cognitive limitations on forecasting genuine new future events, plus the limitedness of the logical and calculative ability of agents. To explain: given a knowledge base expressed in a given language – containing for example N individual variables such as $(x_1, x_2, \ldots x_n)$, and M predicates expressing possible properties of any individuals x_i such as $(P_1, P_2, \ldots P_M)$ – players may be unable to infer all the possible states of the world that are in principle describable by a joint affirmation or negation of any predicate about any individual variable contemplated in the knowledge base (this introduces bounded rationality in Simon's sense at the basis of incomplete contracts, see Kreps 1990b, 1997).

Firms are *loci* of joint (or team) production, where the cooperation of many agents renders the firm's production function super-additive – i.e. by coordination in joint production they generate a surplus with respect to how much they would globally produce by operating in separate units. The *second* assumption of the new institutional economic theory of the firm is that most of this cooperative surplus derives from successful specific investments, namely investments that are idiosyncratic to the firm or the team wherein they take place, or in relation to specific transactions that one stakeholder expects to complete with other members of the productive team (Williamson 1975, 2010).

The crucial aspect of specific investments is that they generate a potential surplus that the stakeholders responsible for them expect to appropriate at a later stage to the extent that the transaction has been completed within the team. But they lose much of their value if the stakeholders that made them in the past have been excluded from the team before completion of the transaction. Hence, realization of their expected value depends on the completion of transactions with other members of the team. If some of these control assets on the basis of which decisions are taken that are essential for realization of the investment's value (i.e. the completion of the transaction after the investment's date), these further members are termed 'essential' (see Hart and Moore 1990; and with reference to the essentiality of human cognitive assets see Aoki 2010).

A *Third* basic assumption is that economic behavior is opportunistic – i.e. in Williamson's words 'selfish with astuteness'. (This assumption is in fact too pessimistic. A weaker statement could be more acceptable: in non-cooperative contexts – without explicit agreements and reciprocal expectations of conformity with fair principles of justice – economic behavior tends to be opportunistic, that is, tends to circumvent any promise or contractual non-binding agreement if doing so is useful to the agent's material self-interest.)

Taken together, the three foregoing assumptions entail that, after specific investments have been made, when a gap in the contract occurs, renegotiation of the contract becomes possible; moreover, there is also a surplus at stake that gives incentive to renegotiation. Thus ex-post to investments a new bargaining situation materializes among the team's members involved in a transaction. Especially those who are essential for the realization of other players' specific investments will *hold up* agents possessing the invested asset (physical or cognitive assets, financial, human or social capital): that is, they will ask them to give up most of their investment's value in order at least to recoup the investment's sunk cost. But the prediction of such an eventuality will necessarily deter the team's members from undertaking their potentially beneficial investments at an efficient level (i.e. the level at which they would invest if hold-up were not possible).

The functional explanation of the firm's emergence is that it provides an institution able to prevent such inefficiency. Put briefly, the firm fills gaps in incomplete contracts by assigning to the party with specific investments at risk ownership of the physical assets of the firm required for completion of any transaction (and related investments). This party thus also acquires residual decision rights on variables that cannot be fixed and inserted ex-ante into the contract ('non-contractible' decisions), and hence is also allocated authority over other participants in the team concerning the execution of decisions that cannot be constrained ex-ante by the contract.

It is in fact a typical assumption of this approach that authority in the firm reduces to a control right over residual decisions if these are to be personally executed by participants different from the right-holder, so that this control right is enforced by the possibility to exclude from the firm (the use of physical assets) a participant declining to execute the ex-post required (non ex-ante contractible) decision (Grossman and Hart 1986). (Note that there is presumably something lacking in this account of authority, i.e. the positive reasons for acceptance by the subordinate of her/his position in the authority relation. In other words, what are lacking are the reasons for accepting the authority relation in general, not just the threat of exclusion that may support the demand for obedience in a single case but represents simple influence or brute bargaining power, not necessarily authority.)

Residual (ex-ante non contractible) decisions hinge on decision variables that are essential for the completion of transactions necessary to valorize specific investments. Assume that agent A, responsible for an investment even if she/he is not the essential co-party for the transaction to which his/her investment is related, has residual control over the firm. Then she/he also has authority to command execution of a decision essential to the end of guaranteeing the completion of the transaction relevant to his/her investment under the threat of excluding the non-compliant essential agent (admitted that this is separable from the essential asset). Thus specific investments are protected by taking on authority in the firm (Williamson 1985; Grossman and Hart 1986; see also Kreps 1990b).

But specific investments are normally multiple and relate to assets held by different stakeholders: human capital, skills and knowledge possessed by different workers and managers, financial capital by investors, dedicated instrumental services and technologies by suppliers, information by consumers, social capital by all of them plus the local communities surrounding a company's plants etc. (Blair and Stout 1999; Sacconi 2000). The most idiosyncratic of these assets are firm-specific human capital and skills.

Assume that such multiple investments are interdependent and mutually essential, or that they are symmetric in value. In these cases authority and residual control should be symmetric, i.e. equally shared among all the team's members (Hart and Moore 1990; Aoki 2010). But purely egalitarian sharing of all residual decision rights cannot be feasible, simply because of huge collective choice and coordination costs in a very large and internally differentiated class of owners (Hansmann 1996). Or because physical assets are not perfectly divisible; or because there is no precise measure of the contributions of each investment to the team's value, so that their representation by means of ownership shares may be imprecise or even mistaken.

Moreover, there are cases where one single investment is by far the most important, whilst investments by others are nonetheless relevant to value creation. Or some agent holding some cognitive human asset (knowledge) may be essential for many investments made by others but inseparable from his/her cognitive asset, so that it would be pointless to threaten his/her exclusion from the firm (Rajan and Zingales 1998; Aoki 2010), whilst some other agents may be not essential to the former's investment even though they have important specific investments at stake.

There are consequently many configurations of specific investments and asset essentiality that cannot be translated into a pure symmetrical sharing of control right and authority (of course, the complete sharing of authority would amount to a *perfect* partnership with no authority at all – not even democratically delegated authority.) In any case, assume that, as is legally reasonable, ownership of physical assets is an exclusive right which cannot be dispersed equally among all the stakeholders, and hence entails that someone does not control the firm and someone else is in the position of control and exerts authority.

To explain: there are capitalist firms which are not controlled by the workers. There are also workers' or consumers' cooperatives which capital investors do not control. But there are very few firms which all these stakeholders jointly control (see Hansmann 1996).

Then add the assumption that authority and residual control entail a right of legitimate appropriation of all the team's produced residual, after contracts have been honored and their costs have been paid. From this it follows that the party in the position of authority in the firm will not only be protected in regard to his/her investment but also able to expropriate all the surpluses resulting from specific investments by other stakeholders, who can be now held up under the threat of being excluded from the firm, given that the contract is incomplete and no proviso exists as to surplus sharing under unforeseen contingencies. This is what is called 'abuse of authority', which means the 'opportunistic use of authority' in order to hold up other members of the team with specific investments at stake and who are protected neither by a complete contract nor by residual control rights (Sacconi 1991, 2000, 2006a, 2007, 2010a).

Recall that the theory models authority as residual control on ex-ante non contractile but ex-post relevant decision variables essential for someone else's investments. Admit that stakeholder A, being given ownership, controls the residual decision essential for realization of his/her own investment. At the same time, in the ex-post renegotiation game that starts when unforeseen events occur (ones relevant for another participant B's investments), A can order 'by fiat' a pejorative status quo if B refuses to consent to all the surplus attributable to his/her investment being appropriated by A. Clearly, this enables A to appropriate ex-post all the team's produced surplus, and there is no reason ex-post for not doing so. Note, moreover, that by such an exercise of authority the controlling party is not blatantly breaching the law or a contract. Admitted that ownership gives him/her large discretion about variables not ex-ante contractible, she/he is only exploiting a gap in the law (this is the 'advantage of flexibility', see Kreps 1990c).

Bad effects of abuse of authority are obviously appreciable by taking the ex-ante perspective (before investments are carried out). Those who predict abuse of authority have a reduced incentive to undertake their investments. Assuming that abuse can be predicted (which is not always the case if one takes seriously the assumption that unforeseen contingencies open the way to wide discretional decisions), they will refrain from making their investment, exactly as in the case of opportunistic hold-up under incomplete market contracts.

The results are as follows: (a) when authority is concentrated in the hands of only one of the team members, even in order to guarantee his/her investment protection (for example the risk capital invested to buy sophisticated and costly equipment), but (b) at the same time other specific investments are at risk, given their imperfect protection due to incomplete contracts (for example labor contracts are subject to the authority of the entrepreneur, who may order the execution of actions that allow expropriation of the result of human capital investments under the threat of dismissing workers who do not comply with the orders); then (c) the governance structure reveals an important inefficiency in term of disincentives to investment (in workers' human capital).

One could argue that the employer's mere awareness of this risk could by itself deter him/her from abusing his/her authority. For example, when the non-controlling stakeholder's investment is also essential for, or interdependent with, that of the owner, by reducing incentives for the non-controlling stakeholder the owner would also reduce the value of his/her own investment. She/he should therefore rationally refrain from abusing authority ex-post (Aoki 2010). Moreover, the owner may understand that by threatening abuse of authority ex-post she/he may reduce the company's overall surplus in subsequent transactions with the same team members, since the owner's reputation is damaged and the latter consequently reduce their subsequent investments. This should induce the controlling party to commit him/herself ex-ante not to abuse ex-post.

But awareness of the bad consequences of abuse of authority is not sufficient to prevent abuse in general; nor is such awareness sufficient in situations where the hold-up of long-run market contracts is possible (outside of hierarchical organizations). It may be the case that refraining from appropriating the overall surplus, thus permitting greater value creation, nevertheless reduces the owner's share up to the point where the absolute amount appropriated by him/her is smaller than the amount she/he would have obtained by abusing other stakeholders. This may happen even though the disincentive of their investments would reduce total value creation. The total of a smaller quantity may be larger than a fair share of a larger quantity.

Moreover, the simple awareness that ex-post abuse of authority can be detrimental to the owner's reputation in repeated interactions with stakeholders, who will accordingly reduce their investment in the future, may not be sufficient to dissuade the owner from ex-post abuse when unforeseen contingencies make it difficult ex-post to recognize abuses (note that this holds in general when the firm is the subject under discussion, since incompleteness of contracts is a precondition for the firm's emergence as an institution). If ex-post abuse is not observable or recognizable against a term of reference (say the contract), because it occurs in an unforeseen state of the world wherein explicit non-abusive provisos are not pre-established, the owner does not lose his/her reputation. Therefore the prospective stakeholder may have no informational basis for reducing his/her investment in successive repetitions of the basic transaction. Or – even worse – reputation effects may be so imprecise that punishment by reducing subsequent investments may hit some entrepreneur who under unforeseen contingences did not really abuse, while leaving untouched those who gravely abused but were not recognized as doing so precisely because of the *vagueness* of the situation (unforeseen events).

Summing up, bad reputation may fail to deter abuse of authority both because (i) the value at stake in each case of abuse can be considerable, and the abuser's share may be larger than the owner's payoff if she/he does not abuse – favoring cooperation, and (ii) unforeseen states of the world make abuse too vague and too difficult to disentangle from non-abuse, revealing the cognitive fragilities of the reputation mechanism (see Kreps 1990a, 1990b; Sacconi 2000).

In these cases the aforementioned inefficiency can only be eliminated by an institutional CG framework. They may require that – without eliminating ownership and authority – the agent in the position to run the firm also has responsibility for preventing the owners' (for example shareholders') ownership/authority abuse of non-controlling stakeholders (for example employees, suppliers, or consumers). This responsibility can be made effective in terms of compliance with some general and abstract principle of ethics and preventive procedures of behavior whereby the agent is made accountable – as in the case of corporate codes of ethics and CSR management systems (again Kreps 1990a, 1990b; Sacconi 2000; Sacconi et al 2003).

This would explain the autonomy and primacy accorded to the board of directors in the model of impartial mediating hierarchy (Blair and Stout 1999). On the one hand, the authority attached to ownership is delegated to a board of directors that thus becomes the true residual decision maker. On the other hand, the board uses such power impartially (according to principles, values and procedures explicitly established as reference points and pattern recognition models for impartial mediation), in order to prevent reciprocal abuse of authority (from above) and opportunism (from below) among the team stakeholders. Of course, abstract and general ethical principles and preventive procedures of conduct are also needed to restrain the board itself from abusing its delegated authority, which otherwise might degenerate into mere self-dealing.

This economic analysis is not only analogous to that carried out by defenders of the mediating hierarchy model of corporate governance (CG) (Blair and Stout 1999); it also provides the efficiency basis for the multi-fiduciary model of CG put forward in pages 378–380, where CSR was defined as a principle of extended fiduciary duties owed to stakeholders.

SOCIAL CONTRACT JUSTIFICATION OF THE NORMATIVE MODEL OF MULTISTAKEHOLDER CORPORATE GOVERNANCE

Challenges

The previous section showed that the CSR model of CG addresses serious efficiency problems in the transaction cost analysis of the business company, and that by solving these problems it may constitute a significant improvement in terms of transactions costs efficiency. Thus, extending fiduciary duties to the protection of all the relevant corporate stakeholders (in both the strict and broad senses) – especially those responsible for specific investments or essential cognitive assets – may be a better CG form than the alternatives from an efficiency point of view. But this is true only if the normative model is defined in a sufficiently clear and convincing way, in terms of both logically consistent normative principles and implementation conditions. Firstly, it requires that fiduciary duties owed to each relevant stakeholder must be well specified, and it must be explained how they are to be balanced one against another if stakeholders claims' are different – maybe conflicting.

In fact, critics of the multi-stakeholder perspective in CG contend that CSR is too vague a notion to be translated into a clearly-defined model of multiple fiduciary duties. Being loyal to one stakeholder who wants a given objective to be pursued may clash with being equally loyal to another stakeholder who wants pursuit of a different, maybe conflicting, objective. Hence, the critics conclude, there is no unique objective function of the firm under the multi-stakeholder perspective. Moreover, there is no criterion that determines the scope of fiduciary duties of due care, and no conflict of interest owed to each stakeholder, under a multi-stakeholder perspective.

According to Michael Jensen, because stakeholders are diverse, the multi-stakeholder firm's objective function cannot but be multidimensional. However, multidimensionality and possible conflicts among stakeholders' claims make any attempt to maximize or pursue such an objective function inconsistent. Thus, the model becomes devoid of normative power and cannot provide managers and directors with a clear-cut bottom line able to impose a restraint on their discretion. But without the restraint of a clear normative principle or goal whereby managers and directors are required to be accountable, they are free to pursue whatever goal they wish, including their mere self-interest. Thus the multi-stakeholder approach opens the way to managerial opportunism.

Other critics (e.g. Marcoux 2003) have brought analytical arguments against extending fiduciary duties to all the company stakeholders. In brief, fiduciary duties are incompatible with a multi-stakeholder perspective because they entail (i) a *privileged relation* (in terms of no conflict of interest between trustor and trustee, due care, accountability etc.) with a *specific* beneficiary – i.e. to make sense of fiduciary duties, one stakeholder is to be privileged over others. (ii) *Vulnerability* (due to power and knowledge asymmetries) of the beneficiary in a contractual relationship is also required. One party has a legitimate interest but must be unable to pursue it. Then she/he enters an *asymmetrical relation* of trust with a trustee (as in professional authority) in the subordinate position of a trustor, enabling the former to make discretionary decisions about the behavior that the latter will be required to adopt or the use of his/her ownership. The trustor's control is weak, and discretion is *shifted* to the trustee so that the trustor (beneficiary) becomes vulnerable to behavior on the part of the trustor. (iii) No conflict of interest with the vulnerable, privileged beneficiary. But if different stakeholders' interests are in conflict, the trustor may not be loyal to one of them, granting him/her the privileged status of beneficiary without contradicting loyalty to another.

In the following subsections these criticisms are countered by developing a social contract justification for CSR as a multi-fiduciary model of CG. Note that the vulnerability problem is by no means a difficulty for the CSR theory of CG since both specific investments and the cognitive essentiality of assets under incomplete contracts render more than one stakeholder vulnerable to abuse of authority and opportunism in the corporate context. Moreover, human capital investments are maximally specific and hence the most vulnerable by managerial decisions in the corporate context under shareholders' ownership. Hence there is no reason on the basis of the above requisite (ii) to exclude stakeholders other than shareholders from fiduciary duties.

The Social Contract as Impartial Board of Directors' Mode of Reasoning

In the mediating hierarchy view of CG (Blair and Stout 1999), the board of directors is an arbiter of the cooperative interaction among the various stakeholders participating in team production. But how should directors mediate among different stakeholders? The suggestion is that they should devise the principle for impartial mediation by working out the social contract that all stakeholders would hypothetically accept as a fair term of agreement for the implementation of a corporate joint cooperative strategy and the consequent allocation of rights, duties and payoffs.

The board of directors may construe the stakeholders 'social contract' by the following procedure of impartial reasoning inspired by the Rawlsian 'veil of ignorance'. This is an operational decision procedure by which the decision-maker accounts for any personal perspective 'as if' she/he were unable to identify it with his/her own personal perspective on the problem (see Sacconi 2006a, 2006b). First, the preconditions for a fair agreement must be established. Hence (i) force, fraud and manipulation must be set aside, and (ii) the only features of each stakeholder accounted for are his/her capability to contribute to team production under different joint plans, and the utilities that she/he can derive from each of them. Since any reasonable agreement must grant some advantage to some stakeholder, a fair reference point for 'advantage' must be set. Thus (iii) the agreement *status quo* must keep each stakeholder immune from hold-up: that is, before discussing the agreement, each stakeholder is granted at least full reimbursement of his/her specific investment's costs.

Then (iv) in order to calculate the legitimate shares that stakeholders can claim, the impartial director will put him/herself in the position of each stakeholder in turn (impersonality) and will assign equal probability to each position (impartiality). Thus, (v) by an effort of sympathy, she/he will accept or reject any available agreement according to each stakeholder's preference. Hence the terms of agreement deemed acceptable are those that *each* stakeholder is willing to accept from his/her own personal point of view. But then (v) solutions acceptable to some stakeholder but not to others are discarded. Thus (vi) the process ends with the non-empty intersection of the allocations acceptable from *whichever* point of view.

Note that an agreement acceptable from whichever point of view must necessarily exist since team production is mutually advantageous with respect to an alternative organization of production where members would split into separate units. If an agreement were not possible, stakeholders would simply organize themselves into separate production units.

A Theoretical Frame for the Social Contract Choice of a Corporate Governance Structure and Objective Function

The solution of the impartial agreement problem, as it is seen by the impartial director, equates the solution of the stakeholders' social contract with the definition of the firm's objective function. i.e. the objective function according to which the firm will be run by the impartial director.

In order to determine a simply calculable solution of this problem (see also the next section), assume for simplicity that there are only two stakeholders – e.g. a worker and a financial capital owner – and that the set of their possible agreements define a convex and compact space of possible outcomes. To make sense of this outcome space, assume that the two stakeholders meet at first in a 'state of nature' structured as a non-cooperative game. Such a state of nature is understood as a formal representation of their interactions in a situation characterized not only by potential mutually advantageous cooperation, or team production, but also by acute incompleteness of contracts and hence by potential reciprocal opportunistic behaviors. The one-shot 'state of nature' precedes the institution of any legal artifice such as the 'corporation' under which they could form a regulated and successful cooperative team. As a one-shot game, it closely resembles an asymmetrical prisoner's' dilemma, so that only one suboptimal equilibrium solution can be reached in it.

But assume that the two stakeholders repeatedly play this game, and that the set of all the possible repeated plays results in a wide space of feasible outcomes. In Figure 38.1 the convex and compact payoff space X_{EA} represents the outcome set of the repeated game

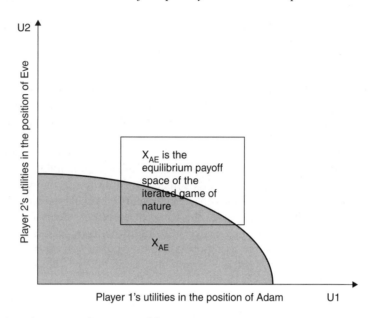

Figure 38.1   The repeated game equilibrium set X_{AE}

played by the poor worker (player 1 = Eve) and the rich proprietor of means of production and capital (player 2 = Adam).

Let these outcomes be all non-cooperative equilibria of the repeated game (i.e., when one player chooses his/her component of one of these repeated strategy combinations the other player has no incentive to deviate from it by changing his/her strategy component).

This statement can be interpreted as follows. By playing any compliance or non-compliance repeated strategy with potentially mutually advantageous incomplete contracts, players allow the emergence of whatever regularity (rule) of behavior in their contractual interaction. On adding *mutual expectations* (or shared *mutual knowledge*) to such regularity of behavior, the playing of any combination of repeated strategies corresponds to the emergence of a convention. Consider outcomes positioned on the Pareto frontier of the payoff space or near to it. These outcomes correspond to *conventions* that can be understood as 'corporate' constitutions dictating certain levels of cooperation and non-cooperation by means of a certain balance/imbalance in the powers, rights and responsibilities allocated to players.

For example, take an outcome splitting the cooperative surplus quite unevenly. It can be seen as reflecting a very asymmetrical exercise of authority by one of the two parties (e.g. the capital owner), who for many repetitions after having treated the other (the worker) fairly once in a while, 'abuse' his authority, while the other party (the worker) continues to abide by a contract requiring him to cooperate with the first party. As far as this convention (or repeated play of the game) is concerned, the worker accepts the proprietor's authority, since she enters the cooperation with him even though he does not symmetrically cooperate with her – which means that he repeatedly responds to her cooperation by reaping all the surplus and only a very few times by sharing it more evenly.

Thus we construe an outcome like this as not only a situation in which the proprietor of financial capital has ownership and control over the resource by means of which cooperation is carried out, but wherein he also exercises the related discretion in a quite extreme way – i.e. abusing it in order to appropriate the largest part of the surplus. This still allows the reaching of an efficient allocation (on the Pareto frontier or close to it) which nevertheless entails a strongly unequal distribution of the cooperative team's production surplus.

Other outcomes may on the contrary be understood as related to conventions that allow a less asymmetrical distribution of power between the parties, or less abuse of it, so that both players cooperate in a more symmetric way throughout the repetitions of the game, and neither of them resorts excessively to the possibility of defecting from cooperation by exploiting his discretion (abuse of residual decision power). These conventions result in a more even distribution of the cooperative surplus, also positioned on the Pareto frontier of the X_{AE} space. But the institutional interpretation of these regularities of behavior (much less abuse, much more mutual cooperation and less unequal distribution of the cooperative surplus) may be different.

These further outcomes may be interpreted as cases of constitution dictating a less asymmetric distribution of residual control rights and authority, so that both parties control some resource and neither of them can profit from abusing the amount of power allocated to him/her because the other party holds similar power. More interestingly, however, it may be understood as if the governance structure provided a bundle of rights and responsibilities such that even though one of the two parties is allocated authority and the full right to make residual decisions, he/she is nevertheless also constrained in the exercise of authority by a responsibility duty telling him/her that he/she cannot appropriate the entire surplus and is obliged to devolve a fair part of it to the compensation of the non-controlling second party. In other words, the fair payoffs distribution is implemented through a responsibility and accountability duty of the governing party. Also when the game is played in this way by the more powerful player (e.g. the financial capital owner), the weaker one (e.g. the skilled but poor worker) in equilibrium cooperates repeatedly, which means that he/she accepts this exercise of constrained authority.

Which of the two interpretations of the not-so-uneven-distribution-of surplus outcomes is correct is a question that goes beyond the formal representation of the outcome space. For the purposes of this chapter, it is sufficient to warrant that both interpretations (and many of their intermediate combinations) are admissible. This means that an even or nearly-even outcome, entailing a convention of symmetrical cooperation, does not necessarily entail that the constitution requires that all the members of the productive team hold a nearly even power and residual control rights – which might mean that the corporation has either a strictly democratic control structure whereby any residual decision is taken in common through some collective choice mechanism, or that there is no authority relation at all, since each player separately exercises control rights over some essential resource. This is a possibility for certain types of organization (for instance multi-stakeholder cooperatives or cooperative networks of nearly independent actors); but more often some hierarchical structure of control and asymmetric allocation of decision power may be necessary.

Thus symmetrical cooperation and even or nearly-even allocation of the cooperative surplus may also result from a constitution such that (i) one cooperating party exercises authority and full decision rights, but does not abuse them since she/he accepts a constitutional constraint not to do so and to share the fruits of cooperation evenly, while (ii) the second player, not being invested with control and residual decision rights but being nevertheless protected by the first party's responsibility rule and accountability, fully cooperates (which corresponds to her/his acceptance of the authority relation). Quite obviously, this corporate constitution regulating the stakeholders' cooperation may be seen as corresponding to a family controlled company whose CSR governance structure of extended fiduciary duties provides for the protection of non-controlling workers. The typical case of the large corporation run by a board of directors (Blair-Stout's case) which is impartial between dispersed shareholders holding very weak ownership rights, and other non-owner stakeholders, is a small move toward the other ('symmetric power') direction. Companies governed through the co-determination model (such as large German corporations), where shareholders elect the managing board but other stakeholders are also represented in the supervisory board, are located somewhere in between the above two typical cases (Osterloh et al 2010; Gelter 2009).

The Binmore-Rawls Egalitarian Solution

The frame set out in the previous section allows players entering the social contract to reason about the choice of the corporate constitution (i.e. selection of a particular convention under which the repeated game has to be played) and the objective function (i.e. choice of a solution function selecting a unique point within the outcome space of the possible ways of cooperation). Assume that before the players engage in the relevant interaction (e.g. any largely incomplete contract equipped with different allocations of residual decision rights and responsibilities), they want ex-ante to agree on the selection of one equilibrium point/outcome resulting from a possible convention of repeated plays. This may be seen as agreeing on a constitution stating to what they are entitled by playing their roles under a 'corporation' implementing team production. This distributive norm is a skeletal constitution for the corporation that the agents would be ex-ante prepared to enter.

There are many possible conventions, and the players want to avoid the risk of failing to coordinate on a combination of mutually optimal repeated strategies as good as possible for each of them. A cognitively convenient frame of reasoning (Denzau and North 1994; Bacharach 2006) suited to ex-ante agreeing on the same convention is that of looking for a 'fair' constitution, i.e. a constitution acceptable for all players independently of their personal perspectives. Hence, in order to accomplish the selection task, impartiality and impersonality are particularly fruitful modes of reasoning. Taken together with sympathy, these assumptions are the 'veil of ignorance' hypothesis. In other words, each agent makes his/her decision 'as if' he/she were ignorant about his/her true identity, so that he/she takes in turn the positions of each possible participant in the game and identifies the constitution whose acceptance is invariant under any personal position's replacement. This is the same as delegating choice of the constitution to the 'impartial director' presented at the beginning of the previous section, seen as an 'arbiter' for the corporate constitutional choice.

The foregoing construction allows resorting to Binmore's vindication of Rawls' maximin principle (Binmore 2005; Rawls 1971) in order to define the solution of the

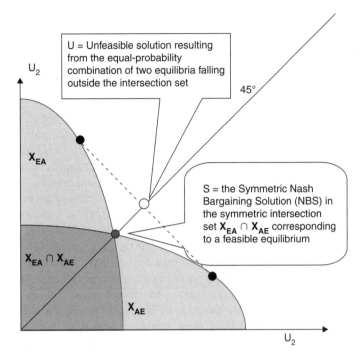

U = Unfeasible solution resulting from the equal-probability combination of two equilibria falling outside the intersection set

45°

X_{EA}

S = the Symmetric Nash Bargaining Solution (NBS) in the symmetric intersection set $X_{EA} \cap X_{AE}$ corresponding to a feasible equilibrium

$X_{EA} \cap X_{AE}$

X_{AE}

Figure 38.2   The Binmore-Rawls egalitarian social contract

corporate constitution selection problem. In this context, *impersonality* means that acceptance of the solution must not depend on personal and social positions. Thus, players – the poor but skilled worker (Eve) and the rich proprietor of means of production and capital (Adam) – should select a solution that cannot change under the symmetrical replacement of social roles and personal positions between individual players. Technically Figure 38.2 depicts any of these replacements by the symmetric translation of the initial payoff space X_{EA} with respect to the Cartesian axes representing the utility of player 1 and player 2, respectively. Thus, under the initial payoff space X_{EA}, player 1 will have all the possible payoffs of Eve and player 2 all the possible payoffs of Adam. But under the translated payoff space X_{AE}, roles are reversed and player 1 will then get Adam's possible payoffs and player 2 will get Eve's possible payoffs. Moreover, Figure 38.2 illustrates that each player, when taking the other's perspective, exercises perfect *empathetic* identification. That is, when player 1, who under X_{EA} was Eve thinks to be Adam under X_{AE}, this player is able to reproduce exactly the same payoffs that player 2 experienced when the player was Adam.

Impartiality means that the players must agree on an outcome under the hypothesis that the reciprocal replacement of positions works in such a way that each stakeholder has an equal probability of finding himself in the position of each of the possible two roles. Equal-probability explains *how* it is possible that the solution does not change under the symmetrical translation of the payoff space with respect to the players' utility axes. Take an outcome x_{EA} that by replacing personal positions may realize in two non-coinciding ways (x_{EA} itself and x_{AE}). To make this outcome acceptable requires taking the expected value of an equal probability distribution over the two realization ways: $\frac{1}{2}x_{EA} + \frac{1}{2}x_{AE}$. This would identify a point in the space that is invariant under the players' positions replacement (i.e., an egalitarian solution residing on the bisector).

However, this construction is not meant to be an excessive idealization. Agents retain awareness that the solution must be an equilibrium of the original game. That is, the solution must be a convention or a collective rule of behavior that the parties know is self-enforceable and incentive-compatible once they think that they all are playing it. This is a requirement of realism of the agreed solution: agents cannot afford to agree ex-ante on a solution if it is not incentive-compatible ex-post (beyond 'the veil of ignorance'). The reason is simple. Admit that the impartial solution proves ex-post not to be an equilibrium of the original game (does not belong to the original payoff space of the 'state of nature' game). Hence, the player who ex-post would be most favored by returning to a solution belonging to the initial equilibrium set would simply deviate to an equilibrium strategy.

Consequently, the stability condition requires that the ex-ante solution (agreed behind the 'veil of ignorance') must correspond to an outcome that under the players' place-permutation would nevertheless belong to the ex-post equilibrium set. In other words, the selected outcome must be an equilibrium (say) either if player 1 takes the position of Adam (and player 2 respectively the position of Eve) or in the opposite case when their identification is reversed (player 2 occupies Adam's position, whereas player B takes Eve's position), and all the more so when an equally probable combination of the two identifications is taken.

What has just been set is a more restrictive *feasibility* condition, replacing the initial one that stated as feasible all the outcomes represented in the equilibrium outcome set X_{AE}. Owing to the initial repeated game's assumptions, only equilibria of the original payoff space X_{EA} were feasible. Any further outcome – potentially subject to agreement – would be wishful thinking because no ex-post equilibrium would exist that could implement it (see point U in Figure 38.2). Adding the conditions of impersonality and impartiality further restricts feasible outcomes to the symmetric intersection $X_{EA} \cap X_{AE}$ of the two payoff spaces generated by symmetrical translation of the original space, which is a proper subset of the initial outcome (equilibrium) set X_{EA} as shown in Figure 38.2. This is a symmetrical payoff space wherein any bargaining solution necessarily falls on the bisector, which is the geometrical locus of egalitarian solutions (where parties share the bargaining surplus equally). Note that this result takes for granted an egalitarian status quo preceding the agreement, but this assumption too is a consequence of the veil of ignorance.

In particular, players resort to the Nash bargaining solution (NBS), which is the most widely employed solution for bargaining games (Nash 1950). It prescribes picking the point of the efficient (north-east) frontier of the payoff space (representing the outcomes set of possible agreements) where the product $\Pi(u_i - d_i)$ of the utilities u_i of players ($i = 1, 2$), net of utility d_i associated with their status quo, is maximal. Assuming that the players bargain according to the typical rationality assumptions of game theory (cf. Harsanyi 1977), and given that the feasible outcome set is the symmetric intersection sub-space $X_{EA} \cap X_{AE}$, the NBS is by assumption egalitarian and selects point S of Figure 38.2.

The striking result deriving from this construction is that the minimal requirements of social justice (impersonality, impartiality and empathetic identification) become compatible with realism and ex-post stability in an interaction where players are free to choose according to their preferences. In spite of Hayek (1973), freedom of choice and incentive compatibility does not require relinquishing the moral demands of social justice. On the contrary, it entails that the solution must be egalitarian and must coincide with the Rawls' *maximin* distribution, even within an originally asymmetrical set of possible outcomes. In fact, when the egalitarian solution is considered against the background of the initial equilibrium outcome space X_{AE}, it becomes evident that this solution coincides with the Pareto solution maximally preferable by the weak player E. Thus, given a real-life set of possible outcomes reflecting possible inequality between the participants, the solution falls on the equilibrium that most favors the worst-off. Thus Binmore vindicates the Rawlsian maximin rule (Binmore 2005). The so-called 'Rawlsian' view of corporate governance consists in adopting such a solution as basis for choosing the corporate objective function and corporate governance structure (see also Sacconi 2010a, 2010b, 2011).

Two-Steps Social Contract Derivation of the Multiple Fiduciary Structure

The social contract will be now employed to tell an hypothetical but simple story on how the multi-stakeholder corporation may have justifiably emerged, and its multiple fiduciary governance may have justifiably settled.

At the beginning all stakeholders face a 'state of nature' plagued by incomplete contracts and opportunistic behaviors. To put at an end to this mutually destructive interaction, they agree to form a multi-stakeholder productive association wherein all stakeholders have the same rights and duties, hence avoiding the situation where, by exclusive control, some may expropriate the fruits of other stakeholders' investments. In the productive association, therefore, all the stakeholders are confident that if any one of them makes a specific investment, nobody can hold up him/her with the threat of exclusion from the relevant transaction. This minimizes the 'contract costs' that would derive from incomplete contracts.

Assuming that the multi-stakeholder association is a possible form of team production, each stakeholder will rationally negotiate his/her adhesion to the association's plan of action, which requires adhesion by all of them. The association's joint plan is then selected by the *First Social Contract* (*pactum unionis*, since by this contract stakeholders decide to coalesce).

This agreement stipulates the following: (i) *rejection* of (or redress for) joint plans generating negative externalities for broad-sense stakeholders who in fact join the association in order to ensure that they will not victimized, (ii) *production* of the *maximum surplus possible* (i.e. the maximal difference between the value of goods and services for consumers, who also belong to the association, and the costs incurred by all other stakeholders to produce them), (iii) *'fair' distribution of the surplus* according to a rationally acceptable agreement reached among all the stakeholders in a bargaining process free from force or fraud and based on an equitable *status quo* insuring each stakeholder against hold-up.

The bargaining process is conducted by stakeholders under a veil of ignorance about their possible advantaged or disadvantaged positions in the productive association.

The solution is calculated according to maximization of the NBS within the symmetrical payoff space deriving from the association's possible outcomes, when all feasible personal payoffs are equally affordable to all stakeholders given the possibility of reciprocal replacement of their relative positions and roles (see the previous section).

However, once the first social contract has been accomplished, stakeholders immediately realize that the equally inclusive association is plagued by governance costs. Collective choice costs, coordination costs, and also free-riding costs in peer-group-managed teams may hugely reduce its actual output. They thus agree to devise an optimal authority structure in order to minimize governance costs.

By a further step in the process, they settle a *Second Social Contract* (called *pactum subjections* because by this contract stakeholders agree to submit to an authority) on the association's *governance structure*. This agreement stipulates that authority is delegated to the single stakeholder who is *most efficient* in governance. This problem has different solutions: either the typical public company with dispersed shareholders, or family-controlled companies, or partnerships or consumer cooperatives may be the most efficient governance solution according to contingencies (see Hansmann 1996).

The stakeholders' class invested with authority is remunerated with the *residual* and is authorized to appoint those who run the firm operationally (managing directors). But it is understood among the association's members that the authority of the corporate governance structure will be legitimated only in so far as it is *instrumental to* the first social contract. In other words, authority will be accepted by the prospective non-controlling members of the association if and only if the association's new ownership and control structure proves to be *the best way to implement* the first social contact of the firm – which pre-exists the authority relation and gives reasons for accepting it (Raz 1985; McMahon 1989). No constitution of the governance structure may be accepted if minimizing governance costs is not a means to improve the fair remuneration of the association's members. Of course, the remuneration of those delegated the association's governing role will impinge on the surplus recovered from reducing governance costs. But no governance structure could be accepted by the second social contract if it were not beneficial in an impartial way to all the stakeholders. Hence also a principle of accountability to non-controlling stakeholders – asking that they participate in some internal committee having supervisory powers – must be added, so that they may verify that corporate management does not significantly deviate from the principles settled by the first social contract. (The German system of co-determination, according to which representatives of non-controlling stakeholders – at least the workers – are entitled with a supervisory power, seems a desirable complement to the Blair-Stout impartial hierarch model of the board of director, at least when ownership is not extensively dispersed through the stock market.)

Accordingly, there is a two-step, agreement, and the directors' fiduciary duties ensue from each step. They owe special fiduciary duties to 'residual claimants' *via a narrow* fiduciary proviso replicating the typical duty of due care and non-conflict of interest. But this narrow proviso is obligating only under the constraint of respecting a *broader* fiduciary proviso owed to non-controlling stakeholders, which is more fundamental and overriding. In other words, once the three provisos of the first social contract have been met, if two or more courses of action indifferent in terms of broader proviso compliance are still feasible, the directors are obliged to choose the course of action more favorable to the residual claimant (owner or shareholders). But no priority of the shareholder value maximization principle over the stakeholders' common interests stated by the board's fiduciary proviso can be admitted.

To reconstruct this argument according to the Marcoux criterion of 'vulnerability' (Marcoux 2003), those suffering externalities are clearly vulnerable third parties. Once, however, externalities had been neutralized with a commitment to prevention or redress for them, strict stakeholders would come to the fore. Vulnerability due to incomplete contracts, specific investments and the risk of being subjected to *hold-up*, is actual for many of them. Moreover, the multiplicity of vulnerable stakeholders is not peculiar to the corporate case alone. Many fiduciary relations may involve multiple 'stakeholders' also in the same class of beneficiaries: i.e. a doctor's many patients, a lawyer's many clients etc. Partiality cannot be admitted in their treatment: rather, impartial and equal respect is required among them. Equal respect of the fiduciary duties owed to all beneficiaries requires a fair solution of the distributive justice problem among them (at least on the distribution of the professional's time and attention among their cases). In the enterprise case, the solution is given by the NBS of the symmetric bargaining game among stakeholders in the strict sense.

A clear priority order of stakeholders' claims thus follows, and (*contra* Marcoux) all vulnerable stakeholders thus are privileged in some respect. Broad-sense stakeholders are clearly the most vulnerable, and are thus assigned priority, but only in the weak sense of restricting the company's range of action to those joint plans that do not engender strong externalities detrimental to them. Second in priority are strict-sense stakeholders, who are granted privilege as the guiding principle in the discretion area of directors who must then protect their specific investments and arbitrate cooperation according to the symmetric NBS.

Last, in the subset of possible corporate decisions indifferent to the NBS, residual claimants are assigned privilege in order to allow (constrained) shareholder value maximization. Indeed, since the NBS is a uniquely determined solution, substantial discretion in choosing *shareholder value maximization* strategies that do not also entail improvement of the other stakeholders' positions is quite unrealistic.

CONCLUSIONS

The chapter has countered all the criticisms raised against the multi-stakeholder governance model and the constitutive interpretation of CSR. In particular, Jensen's criticism that a multi-stakeholder approach to strategic management and corporate governance would make the objective function of the firm either indefinite, too complex or unmanageable has been shown to be untenable. In fact, the objective function of the firm is univocally defined not as the maximization of shareholder value, but as the maximization of the Nash bargaining product of the stakeholders' utilities within a symmetrical payoff space, after having set the negative externality on other non-cooperating stakeholders at a minimum. This objective function is perfectly calculable as the Pareto efficient allocation of payoffs that maximizes the egalitarian distribution (viz. the symmetrical Nash bargaining product), which (in the case of an asymmetrical outcome space) equates with maximizing the worst-off strict-sense stakeholder's positions. Though abstract, this is by no means more detached from reality than the traditional 'maximization exercise' about profit. This objective function is the one to which stakeholders would have agreed in the case of a hypothetical contract whereby they could have decided to start up the firm as a cooperative venture to their mutual advantage under the veil of ignorance. The objective function is genuinely normative and can be translated into a set of practical prescriptions concerning a hierarchy of company's goals according to which managers are accountable (see Sacconi 2006a):

1. minimize the negative externalities engendered by the firm's operations and affecting stakeholders in the broad sense (perhaps by paying suitable compensation);
2. pursue the maximization of the joint surplus and its simultaneous fair distribution, as established by the impartial cooperative agreement among the stakeholders in the strict sense (i.e. maximizing the egalitarian distribution, or the worst-off stakeholder position);
3. if more than one option is compatible with the above defined agreement, then choose the one that maximizes the *residual* allocated to the owner (for example, the shareholder).

Besides the unique and calculable definition of the socially responsible corporation's objective function, the social contract theory also provides a practically implementable solution, so that the CSR model of CG may not be defined as 'wishful thinking'. In fact, pages 386–387 provided a well-defined board of directors' operational model that allows the solution to be reached through the 'veil of ignorance' mode of behavior and reasoning. Moreover, implementation is 'realistic' insofar as the impartial director focuses only on agreements implementable by stakeholders whose behavior ex-post rests on their individual incentives. Once the social contract has been identified, and admitted that stakeholders develop the mutual belief that all of them will abide by the agreement selected, none of them has an incentive to deviate because the corporate constitution selected corresponds to a convention of iterated play which is a Nash equilibrium point of the repeated game. There is no incentive to deviate from the agreed objective function and corporate conduct insofar as there is mutual expectation that all stakeholders will abide by it. The agreed solution is ex-post stable and compatible with individual motivations and incentives.

There is of course a limitation implicit in the assumption that players have developed such a system of mutually consistent beliefs in the ex-post perspective. Elsewhere I have argued that there is no logical necessity that this system of beliefs will ensue (Sacconi 2010a, 2011). It is for this reason that I have developed a behavioral theory of reciprocal beliefs and conformist preferences also evidencing that ex-post, after the agreement under the veil of ignorance, stakeholders will comply with the CSR model, since once they have agreed on the normative model of CSR they develop the reciprocal expectation of conformity and then also the desire to reciprocate conformity. This supports the prediction that stakeholders will comply with the normative model of CSR not just because of the ex-ante selection of a Nash equilibrium, but because they develop what can be called a 'sense of justice' which extends beyond purely self-interested rational behavior (Grimalda and Sacconi 2005; Sacconi and Faillo 2010; Sacconi 2011, Sacconi et al 2011).

REFERENCES

Andreoni, James (1990). 'Impure Altruism and Donations to Public Goods: A Theory of Warm-Glow Giving'. *Economic Journal* 100, 401, 464–477.

Aoki, Masahiko (1984). *The Cooperative Game Theory of the Firm*. Cambridge: Cambridge University Press.

Aoki, Masahiko (2001). *Toward a Comparative Institutional Analysis*. Cambridge MA: MIT Press.

Aoki, Masahiko (2010). *Corporations in Evolving Diversity*. Oxford: Oxford University Press.

Bacharach, M. (2006). *Beyond Individual Choice: Teams and Frames in Game Theory*. Princeton, NJ: Princeton University Press.

Baron, David P. (2007). 'Corporate Social Responsibility and Social Entrepreneurship'. *Journal of Economics & Management Strategy* 16, 3, 683–717.

Baron, David P. (2009). 'A Positive Theory of Moral Management, Social Pressure, and Corporate Social Performance'. *Journal of Economics & Management Strategy* 18, 1, 7–43.

Bénabou Roland and Jean Tirole (2010). 'Individual and corporate social responsibility'. *Economica* 77, 305, 1–19.

Binmore, Ken (2005). *Natural Justice*. Oxford: Oxford University Press.

Binmore, Ken and Adam Brandenburger (1990). 'Common Knowledge and Game Theory'. In Ken Binmore (ed.), *Essays in the Foundation of Game Theory*. Oxford: Basil Blackwell, 105–150.

Blair, Margaret M. and Lynn A. Stout (1999). 'A Team Production Theory of Corporate Law'. *Virginia Law Review* 85,2, 247–331.

Blair, Margaret M. and Lynn A. Stout (2006). 'Specific Investment: Explaining Anomalies in Corporate Law'. *Journal of Corporation Law* 31, 719–744.

Buchanan, James (1975). *The Limits of liberty. Between Anarchy and Leviathan*, Chicago: Chicago University Press.

Clarkson Center for Business Ethics (1999). *Principles of Stakeholder Management*. Toronto: Clarkson Center for Business Ethics, Rothman School of Management, University of Toronto.

Coase, Ronald H. (1937). 'The Nature of the Firm'. *Economica* 4, 1, 386–405.

Coase, Ronald H. (1960). 'The Problem of Social Cost'. *Journal of Law and Economics* III, 1–44.

Denzau, Arthur and Douglass C. North (1994). 'Shared Mental Models: Ideologies and Institutions'. *KIKLOS* 47, 1, 3–31.

Donaldson, Thomas (2012). 'The Epistemic Fault Line in Corporate Governance'. *Academy of Management Review* 37, 2, forthcoming.

Donaldson, Thomas and Lee E. Preston (1995). 'The Stakeholder Theory of the Corporation: Concepts, Evidence, and Implications'. *The Academy of Management Review* 20, 1, 65–91.

Evan, William M. and R. Edward Freeman (1993). 'A Stakeholder Theory of the Corporation: Kantian Capitalism'. In Tom L. Beauchamp and Norman E. Bowie (eds), *Ethical Theory and Business*, Englewood Cliffs, NJ: Prentice Hall, 97–106.

Flannigan, Robert (1989). 'The Fiduciary Obligation'. *Oxford Journal of Legal Studies* 9, 3, 285–294.

Freeman, R. Edward (1984). *Strategic Management: A Stakeholder Approach*. Boston: Pitman.

Freeman, R. Edward and Daniel, R. Gilbert (1988). *Corporate Strategy and the Search for Ethics*. New Jersey: Prentice Hall, Englewood Cliffs.

Freeman, R. Edward and John McVea (2001). 'A Stakeholder Approach to Strategic Management'. In Michael A. Hitt, R. Edward Freeman and Jeffrey S. Harrison (eds), *The Blackwell Handbook of Strategic Management*, Oxford: Blackwell, 189–207.

Freeman, R. Edward and S. Ramakrishna Velamuri (2006). 'A New Approach to CSR: Company Stakeholder Responsibility'. In A. Kakabadse and M. Morsing (eds), *Corporate Social Responsibility (CSR): Reconciling Aspiration with Application*, New York: Palgrave Macmillan, 9–2.

Freeman, R. Edward, Jeffrey R. Harrison, Andrew C. Wicks, Bidhan L. Parmar and Simone De Colle (2010). *Stakeholder Theory: The State of the Art*. Cambridge: Cambridge University Press.

Friedman, M. (1970). 'The Social Responsibility of Business is to Increase its Profit'. *New York Magazine*, 13 September.

Gauthier, David (1986). *Morals by Agreement*. Oxford: Oxford University Press.

Gelter, Martin (2009). 'The Dark Side of Shareholder Influence: Managerial Autonomy and Stakeholder Orientation in Comparative Corporate Governance'. *Harvard International Law Journal* 50, 1, 129–134.

Grimalda, Gianluca and Lorenzo Sacconi (2005). 'The Constitution of the Not-for-profit Organization: Reciprocal Conformity to Morality'. *Constitutional Political Economy* 16, 3, 249–276.

Grossman, Sanford J. and Oliver Hart (1986). 'The Costs and Benefit of Ownership: A Theory of Vertical and Lateral Integration'. *Journal of Political Economy* 94, 4, 691–719.

Hansmann, Henry (1996). *The Ownership of the Enterprise*. Cambridge, MA: Harvard University Press.

Hare, Richard M. (1981). *Moral Thinking*. Oxford: Clarendon Press.

Harsanyi, John C. (1977). *Rational Behavior and Bargaining Equilibrium in Games and Social Situations*. Cambridge: Cambridge University Press.
Hart, Oliver and John Moore (1990). 'Property Rights and the Nature of the Firm'. *Journal of Political Economy* 98, 6, 1119–1158.
Hayek, Fredrick A. (1973). *Law, Legislation and Liberty*. Chicago: University of Chicago Press.
Heal, Geoffrey (2005). 'Corporate Social Responsibility – An Economic and Financial Framework'. *The Geneva Papers* 30, 387–409.
Heal, Geoffrey (2008). *When Principles Pay, Corporate Social Responsibility and the Bottom Line*. New York: Columbia Business School Publishing.
Kreps, David (1990a). *A Course on Microeconomic Theory*. New York: Harvester Wheatsheaf.
Kreps, David (1990b). 'Corporate Culture and Economic Theory'. In J. Alt and K. Shepsle (eds), Perspectives on Positive Political Economy, Cambridge University Press.
Kreps, David (1990c). 'Static Choice in the Presence of Unforeseen Contingencies'. In P. Dasgupta, D. Rae, O. Hart and E. Maskin (eds), *Economic Analysis of Markets and Games*. Cambridge Mass: MIT Press.
Kreps, David (1997). 'Bounded Rationality'. In P. Newman (ed.), *The New Palgrave Dictionary of Economics and the Law*. London, Macmillan, 168–173.
Jensen, Michael C. (2001). 'Value Maximization, Stakeholder Theory, and the Corporate Objective Function'. *Journal of Applied Corporate Finance* 14, 3, 8–21.
Jensen, Michael C. and William H. Meckling (1976). 'Theory of the Firm: Managerial Behavior, Agency Costs and Ownership Structure'. *Journal of Financial Economics* 3, 4, 305–360.
Lewis, David (1969). *Convention. A Philosophical Study*. Cambridge, MA: Harvard University Press.
Marcoux, Alexei M. (2003). 'A Fiduciary Argument against Stakeholder Theory'. *Business Ethics Quarterly* 13, 1, 1–24.
McMahon, Christopher (1989). 'Managerial Authority'. *Ethics* 100, 1, 33–53.
Nash, John F. (1950). 'The Bargaining Problem'. *Econometrica* 18, 2, 155–162.
Osterloh, Margit, Bruno S. Frey and Hossam Zeitoun (2010). 'Voluntary Co-determination Produces Sustainable Productive Advantage'. In Lorenzo Sacconi, Margaret Blair, R. Edward Freeman and Alessandro Vercelli (eds), *Corporate Social Responsibility and Corporate Governance: The Contribution of Economic Theory and Related Disciplines*. Basingstoke: Palgrave Macmillan, 332–352.
Rajan, Raghuram G. and Luigi Zingales (1998). 'Power in a Theory of the Firm'. *Quarterly Journal of Economics* 113, 2, 387–432.
Rawls, John (1971). *A Theory of Justice*. Oxford: Oxford University Press.
Raz, Joseph (1985). 'Authority and Justification'. *Philosophy and Public Affairs* 14, 1, 3–29.
Sacconi, Lorenzo (1991). *Etica degli affari*. Milano: Il saggiatore.
Sacconi, Lorenzo (1999). 'Codes of Ethics as Contractarian Constraints on the Abuse of Authority within Hierarchies: A Perspective from the Theory of Firm'. *Journal of Business Ethics* 21, 2–3, 189–202.
Sacconi, Lorenzo (2000). *The Social Contract of the Firm: Economics, Ethics and Organization*. Berlin: Springer Verlag.
Sacconi, Lorenzo (2006a). 'CSR as a Model of Extended Corporate Governance, an Explanation Based on the Economic Theory of Social Contract, Reputation and Reciprocal Conformism'. In Fabrizio Cafaggi (ed.), *Reframing Self-regulation in European Private* Law. The Netherlands: Kluwer Law International, 289–346.
Sacconi, Lorenzo (2006b). 'A Social Contract Account for CSR as Extended Model of Corporate Governance (Part I): Rational Bargaining and Justification'. *Journal of Business Ethics* 68, 3, 259–281.
Sacconi, Lorenzo (2007). 'A Social Contract Account for CSR as Extended Model of Corporate Governance (Part II): Compliance, Reputation and Reciprocity'. *Journal of Business Ethics* 75, 1, 77–96.
Sacconi, Lorenzo (2010a). 'A Rawlsian View of CSR and the Game Theory of Its Implementation (Part I): The Multistakeholder Model of Corporate Governance'. In Lorenzo Sacconi, Margaret Blair, R. Edward Freeman and Alessandro Vercelli (eds), *Corporate Social Responsibility and Corporate Governance: The Contribution of Economic Theory and Related Disciplines*. Basingstoke: Palgrave Macmillan, 157–193.
Sacconi, Lorenzo (2010b). 'A Rawlsian View of CSR and the Game Theory of Its Implementation (Part II): Fairness and Equilibrium'. In Lorenzo Sacconi, Margaret Blair, R. Edward Freeman and Alessandro Vercelli (eds), *Corporate Social Responsibility and Corporate Governance: The Contribution of Economic Theory and Related Disciplines*. Basingstoke: Palgrave Macmillan, 194–125.
Sacconi, Lorenzo (2011). 'A Rawlsian View of CRS and the Game of Its Implementation (Part III): Conformism and Equilibrium Selection'. In Lorenzo Sacconi and Giacomo Degli Antoni (eds), *Social Capital, Corporate Social Responsibility, Economic Behavior and Performance*. Basingstoke: Palgrave Macmillan, 42–79.
Sacconi, Lorenzo and Marco Faillo (2010). 'Conformity, Reciprocity and the Sense of Justice. How Social Contract-based Preferences and Beliefs Explain Norm Compliance: The Experimental Evidence'. *Constitutional Political Economy* 21, 2, 171–201.

Sacconi, L., S. De Colle and E. Baldin (2003). 'The Q-RES Project: The Quality of Social and Ethical Responsibility of Corporations'. In J. Wieland (ed.), *Standards and Audits for Ethics Management Systems, The European Perspective*. Berlin: Springer Verlag, 60–117.

Sacconi, Lorenzo, Marco Faillo and Stefania Ottone (2011). 'Contractarian Compliance and the "Sense of Justice": A Behavioral Conformity Model and Its Experimental Support'. *Analyse & Kritik* 33, 1, 273–310.

Schotter, Andrew (1981). *The Economic Theory of Social Institutions*. Cambridge: Cambridge University Press.

Stout, Lynn A. (2006). 'Social Norms and Other-Regarding Preferences'. In John N. Drobak (ed.), *Norms and the Law*. Cambridge: Cambridge University Press, 13–35.

Stout, Lynn A. (2011a). *Cultivating Conscience*. Princeton, NJ: Princeton University Press.

Stout, Lynn A. (2011b). 'New Thinking On Shareholder Primacy'. Working paper, School of Law, UCLA. Law-Econ Research Paper No. 11–04

Sugden, Robert (1986). *The Economics of Rights, Co-operation and Welfare*. Oxford: Basil Blackwell.

Tirole, J. (1999). 'Incomplete contracts, where do we stand?' *Econometrica* 67, 741–781.

Tirole, Jean (2001). 'Corporate Governance'. *Econometrica* 69, 1, 1–35.

Wieland, Joseph (ed.) (2003). *Standards and Audits for Ethics Management Systems – The European Perspective*. Berlin: Springer Verlag.

Williamson, Oliver (1975). *Market and Hierarchies*. New York: The Free Press.

Williamson, Oliver (1985). *The Economic Institutions of Capitalism*. New York: The Free Press.

Williamson, Oliver (2010). 'Corporate governance, A Contractual and Organizational View'. In Lorenzo Sacconi, Margaret Blair, R. Edward Freeman and Alessandro Vercelli (eds), *Corporate Social Responsibility and Corporate Governance: The Contribution of Economic Theory and Related Disciplines*. Basingstoke: Palgrave Macmillan, 3–32.

Young, Peyton H. (1998). *Individual Strategy and Social Structure, an Evolutionary Theory of Social Institutions*. Princeton: Princeton U.P.

39. Third sector
Jacques Defourny

INTRODUCTION

The idea of a distinct third sector, made up of enterprises and organizations which are not part of the traditional private sector nor of the public sector, began to emerge in the mid-1970s. Such organizations were already very active in many areas of activity and were the subject of scientific works and specific public policies in some of these areas. But the idea of bringing these entities all together and the theoretical basis on which this could be done were not really put forward until the late 1970s.

In fact, without denying that the general public's view is still strongly characterized by the historical context of each country, it may be said that two conceptual approaches aiming to embrace the whole third sector gradually spread internationally, accompanied by statistical work aiming to quantify its economic importance. One is the US-based 'non-profit sector' approach; the other, mainly French in origin, forged the concept of the 'social economy' to bring together cooperatives, mutual societies and associations.

Other conceptualizations of the third sector have also been developed and have met with a positive response at the international level. This is particularly the case with approaches based on a 'tri-polar' representation of the economy, where the three 'poles' either represent categories of agents (private for-profit enterprises, the state, and households), or correspond to logics or modes of regulation of exchanges (the market, public redistribution and reciprocity), which in turn refer to the types of resources involved (market, non-market monetary and non-monetary resources). From such a perspective, the third sector is generally viewed as an intermediate space in which the different poles combine.

Our aim here is to focus on these three conceptual streams which try to capture the third sector as a whole. We want to show how they emerged in their respective contexts, what their specificities are and how they can be applied empirically to embrace a whole range of organizations. However, we do not pretend to provide any overview of the whole literature developed under those 'umbrella concepts' to analyse entities such as non-profit organizations, cooperatives or social enterprises.

Before reviewing these various approaches, let us stress that the 'third sector' notion as such today appears as the more 'neutral term', precisely allowing discussions to overcome region or stream specificities, not only among scientists but increasingly outside the academic community as well.

THE NON-PROFIT SECTOR

The concept of non-profit sector is deeply rooted in history, especially American history. As stated by Salamon (1997: 282):

[one of the factors which accounted for the early growth of the American penchant for voluntary association] was the deep-seated hostility to royal power and centralized state authority that the religious non conformists who helped populate the American colonies brought with them when they fled the Old World.

But it was only in the late 19th century that the idea of a non-profit sector began to take place. Non-profit organizations were then promoted not simply as supplements to public action but as superior vehicles for meeting public needs.

After the Second World War and more precisely in the 1960s and the 1970s, the expansion of the non-profit sector was strongly linked to partnership with government which increasingly supported these organizations. However, American perception of the latter remains marked by anti-state attitudes as shown by the growing use of the term 'independent sector' to refer to these entities.

Tax Exemption as a Key Criterion

It is mainly through the tax laws that the non-profit sector has come to be legally defined in the United States. In particular, the federal tax code identifies some 26 different categories of organizations that are entitled to exemption from federal income taxation. These organizations must be operated in such a way that 'no part of (their) earnings inures to the benefit of their officers or directors' and their founding document must stipulate this. Such a condition is known as the 'non-distribution (of profits) constraint' and it became the cornerstone of the conceptualization of the non-profit sector.

Although these tax-exempt organizations are of various kinds and include member serving organizations as well as primarily public serving organizations, much of the discussion of the non-profit sector in the recent American literature focuses on the second category, that is a subset of organizations that are tax-exempt and eligible to receive tax deductible gifts under Section 501 (c) (3) of the Internal Revenue Code. These organizations, which represent a very large range of public benefit activities (schools, colleges, universities, hospitals, museums, libraries, day care centers, social service agencies, etc.), are therefore thought of as the heart of the non-profit sector.

A Vast Literature on the Non-Profit Organizations

In the United States the work of the Filer Commission and, in 1976, the launch of the Yale University's 'Program on Non-profit Organizations', involving 150 researchers, marked a decisive step in the conceptualization of non-profit organizations (NPOs) and the non-profit sector. Since then, a vast scientific literature on NPOs has been developed, with contributions from disciplines as diverse as economics, sociology, political science, management, history, law, etc. It took place particularly in journals like the *Nonprofit and Voluntary Sector Quarterly*, published by the (mainly US) Association for Research on Nonprofit and Voluntary Action, and *Voluntas*, published by the International Society for Third Sector Research. Some major books also marked the early stages of this literature: Weisbrod (1977, 1988), Young (1983), James and Rose-Ackerman (1986), Powell (1987), James (1989), Anheier & Seibel (1990), among others.

It is often said that the bulk of theoretical contributions in this literature has been developed around one central question: how is it possible to explain the very existence and the role of non-profit organizations in contemporary economies dominated by for-profit enterprises on competing markets and by various degrees of public intervention? To explain the 'raisons d'être' of NPOs, key authors have stressed the role of NPOs as providers of public or quasi-public goods that the state is not willing to produce (Weisbrod, 1975) or the fact that NPOs are more able, through their strict constraint on profit distribution, to send trust signals to potential buyers who fear being exploited by for-profit providers because of important asymmetries of information on markets of non-standardized products or services (Nelson & Krashinsky, 1973; Hansmann, 1980). Apart from those most classical theories of state failure and market failure, other authors underlined factors which play as driving forces on the supply side. Among them, James (1983, 1986) suggests competition among religions fosters non-profit initiatives by religious entrepreneurs in fields like education, health and other major social services which are likely to attract members/believers. On their side, Ben-Ner and Van Hoomissen (1991) combine factors on the demand and supply sides: stakeholders on the demand side can best control the quality of the production they want by getting involved in the setting up and management of the organization, especially if expected benefits of all types they get from such an involvement are larger than all kinds of related costs.

A Definition for Cross-National Comparative Purposes

In spite of the very US-based roots of the non-profit sector concept, significant efforts have been made in the last two decades to allow cross-national comparative studies. Increasing reference is especially made to the conceptual framework established by the vast international study which has been coordinated by the Johns Hopkins University since 1990.

For all researchers involved in this project, the non-profit sector consists of organizations with the following characteristics:

- they are formal, i.e. they have a certain degree of institutionalization, which generally presupposes legal personality;
- they are private, i.e. distinct from both the state and those organizations issuing directly from the public authorities;
- they are self-governing, in the sense that they must have their own regulations and decision-making bodies;
- they cannot distribute profits to either their members, their directors or a set of 'owners'. This 'non-distribution constraint' lies at the heart of all the literature on NPOs;
- they must involve some level of voluntary contribution in time (volunteers) and/or in money (donors), and they must be founded on the free and voluntary affiliation of their members.

Although US researchers initially thought that the non-profit sector in their country would appear as the largest in the world, major statistical efforts based on that common definition and carried out in the late 1990s showed the workforce employed in the non-profit sector represented around 9 per cent of the active population in countries like the Netherlands, Belgium and Ireland while it only reached 6.3 per cent in the United States.

Among various other results of that outstanding international project, Salamon et al (2000) developed a 'social origins' theory which relates closely the size and key features of the non-profit sector to various country-specific characteristics such as the level of government social welfare spending and historical forces that shaped both the government regime and the civil society.

THE SOCIAL ECONOMY

In Europe, the broad diversity of socio-political, cultural and economic national circumstances has not allowed such a wide-ranging and rapid development of analytical works emphasizing the existence of a third sector. However, the economic entities that gradually came to be perceived through a third sector approach were already important in most countries: mutual organizations and cooperatives had existed almost everywhere for more than a century (Birchall, 1997), and association-based economic initiatives had also been increasing in numbers for some considerable time. As shown by Evers and Laville (2004), they were also rooted in solid and long-standing traditions: philanthropy (charities, community sector, etc.), has always been particularly influential in the UK and Ireland; civic commitment to the entire community towards greater equality and democracy clearly prevailed in Scandinavian countries; the principle of 'subsidiarity' has been central, especially with respect to Church-related initiatives, in countries such as Germany, Belgium, Ireland and the Netherlands; in various countries, the cooperative movement was closely linked to the development of the voluntary sector, either through a common civic background fostering participation and democracy (as in Denmark, Sweden, etc.), or through a common religious inspiration (as in Italy, Belgium, France, etc.); finally the role assigned to the family in countries such as Spain, Portugal, Greece and Italy also had a major influence on the pace of development of the third sector, especially as to the provision of personal services (child care, elderly care, etc.).

Cooperatives and Associations: Historical Divergence and Recent Convergence

During most of the 20th century, cooperatives developed their activities to meet their members' need to gain better access to markets (as consumers, savers, producers, etc.). Their specialization in specific fields, the pressure of market forces and their increasing size led most cooperatives to follow paths that differed from the evolution of most other components of the third sector, which were generally oriented to non-market activities, such as the delivery of services outside market channels, material assistance and advocacy. This is one of the key reasons why several countries have been reluctant to develop conceptions of the third sector encompassing both cooperative enterprises and community or voluntary organizations.

In the last decades, many associations have started to adopt some business-like behaviours and strategies (through professionalization, communication methods, some degree of market orientation, etc.) while new forms of cooperatives have appeared in fields such as personal services, which do not solely rely on market resources. Therefore, social cooperatives and, more broadly, social enterprises operating on the basis of public subsidies or contracts as well as market resources, may be seen as bridging at least partly the gap between cooperatives and associations (Borzaga and Defourny, 2001). More generally, a new generation of initiatives appeared in the final quarter of the 20th century, often dealing with new challenges, which were not usually addressed by traditional organizations: these challenges included the fight against unemployment (worker-owned firms, work integration social enterprises, female worker cooperatives, etc.), the need to combat social exclusion (housing and urban revitalization initiatives, new services to the poorest and people at risk in many respects), local development of remote areas, etc. Acknowledging the public benefit dimension of many activities undertaken by associations and social enterprises of all kinds, public authorities designed specific programmes and schemes to support them. As a result, various types of initiatives have become registered, labelled and identified with such public schemes, especially in the field of work integration. In some countries, legislation was even passed to create new legal forms for 'social enterprises', better suited to some types of organizations; in several cases, these new legal forms have been associated to general frameworks designed for cooperatives (this was the case in Italy, France, Portugal, Spain and Greece), while in others, they have tended to encompass various types of enterprises pursuing a community interest or a social aim (Belgium, United Kingdom, Italy), sometimes narrowly focused on work integration of disadvantaged groups (Finland, Poland).[1]

Such recent evolutions have paved the way for a rediscovery of the historical parenthood among associations and cooperatives as well as for a renewal of the concept of social economy which had been used in the 19th century along similar lines by authors like Smiley[2] in 1875 and Gide[3] around 1900.

Defining the Social Economy

Although deeply rooted in history, the concept of social economy was first revitalized in France at the end of the 1970s and subsequently in various countries like Belgium, Spain, Italy, Sweden and in an increasing number of other European and non-European countries (Canada, Argentina, Japan, South Korea, etc.). Although there is no universally accepted definition of the social economy, it is generally agreed that the social economy includes cooperatives and related enterprises, mutual societies as well as associations, which share a number of principles that can be summarized as follows:

- the aim of serving members or the community, rather than generating profits;
- independent management;
- a democratic decision-making process;
- the primacy of people and labour over capital in the distribution of income.

With the purpose of service, emphasis is placed on the fact that activities are not primarily carried out to achieve a financial return on capital investment. The possible generation of a surplus may thus be a means of achieving goals, but not the main motivation behind the activity.

Management independence is principally a means of distinguishing the social economy from public entities producing goods and services. The economic activities carried out by public authorities do not in general benefit from the wide-ranging autonomy which provides an essential impetus in voluntary initiatives.

The need for a democratic decision-making process derives from the 'one member, one vote' principle which is a key one in cooperative thought. Although this may be expressed through a great variety of actual practices, there is at least a strict limit placed on the number of votes per member in the body which holds the ultimate decision-making power.

Finally, the fourth principle covers a wide range of practices: limited remuneration of capital, distribution of surplus among the workforce or members/users in the form of bonuses or discounts, the creation of reserve funds for further development, the immediate use of surpluses for social purposes, etc.

Major comparative analysis of the social economy in Europe started in the early 1990s under the auspices of CIRIEC (Defourny and Monzón, 1992) as well as the European Economic and Social Committee (Chaves and Monzón, 2007). Among other results, such studies show that cooperatives represent a larger part of the third sector's paid workforce than associations (NPOs) in countries like Italy, Spain, Finland as well as in former socialist economies like Poland, Hungary, the Czech Republic and Slovakia. As to mutual societies, their overall weight is generally smaller but they are quite important in France, Germany and Portugal.

Journals promoting the social economy approach include the French *Revue internationale de l'économie sociale*, formerly *Revue des études coopératives, mutualistes et associatives* (*RECMA*) as well as *Economie et Solidarités* in French-speaking Canada, the *Annals of Public and Cooperative Economics* and the *Revista de economia publica, social y cooperativa* in Spain and Latin America.

Although the notion of social economy is more used in regions speaking languages from the Latin tradition, it is interesting to note the British government, which is at the forefront in the promotion of the third sector, recently adopted a definition of the latter which embraces all components of the social economy: 'The Government defines the third sector as non-governmental organizations which are value driven and which principally reinvest their surpluses to further social, environmental or cultural objectives. It includes voluntary and community organizations, charities, social enterprises, cooperatives and mutuals' (Cabinet Office, 2007:6).

The Social Economy Versus the Non-Profit Sector

Although these two approaches of the third sector clearly converge or are quite close on various points, they also diverge on a few key points, especially the control over the organization and the use of profits (Defourny and Develtere, 2009).

Firstly, the social economy has at its heart the requirement of a democratic decision-making process which, in addition to giving weight to members' involvement and voice, represents a structural procedure to control the actual pursuit of the organization's goals. In the NPO approach, such a control also comes from inside the organization through its governing bodies but without any formal democratic requirement.

Secondly, the non-profit approach prohibits any profit distribution and therefore excludes the entire cooperative component of the social economy, since cooperatives may redistribute part of their profits to their members. It also excludes some mutual societies, for instance mutual insurance companies which return part of their surpluses to members in the form of fee (premium) reductions.

Another way of summing up these differences would be to say that the conceptual basis of the non-profit approach is the non-distribution constraint which underlines its particular relevance for public benefit associations; whereas the notion of the social economy owes much to the cooperative tradition which of course gives clearer space to mutual interest organizations, (limited) distribution of profits to owners/members and a central place to democratic control over the organization's goals and functioning.

Let us stress however that these differences are only quite significant from a theoretical point of view; they might reveal much less significance when checked by empirical research. Especially, a democratic decision-making process should not be taken for granted in all social economy organizations. Moreover foundations, which are increasingly mentioned as a fourth component of the social economy, are not necessarily concerned about democratic rules.

Finally, at a worldwide level including developing countries, it is not difficult to stress the higher flexibility of the social economy approach: community-based economic organizations which play key roles in rural areas often distribute profits among members in various ways since improvement of the latter's living conditions is their major objective. More generally, many practices that draw on the 'not-for-profit but for service' principle take on a very wide variety of organizational forms. Some of them resemble cooperative models (credit unions, for example), while others look more like non-profits (NGOs and trusts) or mutuals (for instance community-based health insurance systems).

THE THIRD SECTOR IN THE WELFARE MIX

According to the literature on non-profit organizations and the social economy, while the state and private for-profit companies do of course provide certain services, the latter either will not be of the desired quality for some groups, as is often the case with uniformed public services, or they will not be affordably priced to satisfy total demand, as often is the case with market provision. Thus, third sector organizations (TSOs) generally provide either a necessary complement to both public and private for-profit provision of basic welfare services or they may deliver the bulk of some specific services.

Tools for Conceptualizing a Third Sector with Blurred Frontiers

Several European third sector scholars have discussed the growing 'welfare mix' made of those shared responsibilities among various types of providers and some have proposed a welfare triangle to better understand the relations between sectors (Evers, 1995; Laville, 1994; Pestoff, 1998; Evers and Laville, 2004). Figure 39.1 below depicts these relations.

As stated earlier, the role of organizations with social and service related purposes

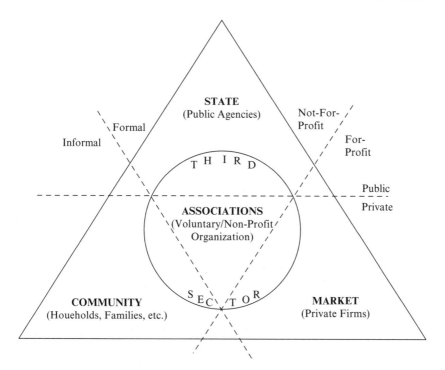

Source: Pestoff, 1998, 2005

Figure 39.1   The third sector in the welfare triangle

varies according to the historical and political traditions. Following Evers (1995), the characteristics of the third sector are simultaneously shaped by and shape the respective influences of state institutions, the market actors and the informal sector of families, etc. Thus, there is a constant tension at the border between the central triangle on one hand, and the market, state and informal areas, on the other. In the figure, these 'behavioural' tensions are represented by the three dotted lines crossing the large triangle.

The first type of tension concerns the conflict between the instrumental rationality of the market oriented to the maximization and distribution of profits and the soli-daristic, social and democratic values of both the third sector and the state. The next type of tension is related to state institutions and their universalistic values, which are contrasted by the particularistic logic of most private actors. Finally, there is the tension between formal organizations and the informal worlds of the family, personal relation-ships, neighbourhoods, and social networks, etc., which make it harder to draw a clear line between the latter and the third sector in areas of help and self-help. This gives a polyvalent and hybrid nature to TSOs, which must act under the multiple influence from and dependence on the other sectors and in extreme cases it may result in organizational transformation. Thus, TSOs often pursue multiple goals simultaneously, i.e., provid-ing service to members and others, lobbying for changes in the law or regulations, etc. Balancing various activities can be very difficult, and also requires greater transparency between the managers of TSOs and their strategic stakeholders.

Overlapping Areas as a Tool to Accommodate Diversity in TSOs' Logics and Behaviours

In relation to those tensions, let us now try to interpret and illustrate more precisely those areas in the figure where there is an overlap between the third sector and the other spheres of the economy. Indeed such overlapping areas are crucial to accommodate the current blurring of the third sector's borders. Even more importantly, they allow diverse conceptions of the third sector's place and role in Europe to co-exist while stressing that such views still have a lot in common (Defourny and Pestoff, 2008).

Taking them one by one, we find an area of overlap between *the third sector and the market* that suggests some third sector enterprises, like cooperatives, do fully operate on the market and make profits while adopting other rules than typical capitalist companies. The fast development of so-called social enterprises can also be analysed with the help of such blurred frontiers in the welfare triangle. Many social enterprises are clearly market-oriented while having a primary social aim, so they may be found in this overlapping area as well, especially if they distribute part of their surplus to their owners. In other cases, especially when promoted by state programmes which strongly support professional integration of long term unemployed or unskilled people, social enterprises may also appear in the upper zone of the circle (Nyssens, 2006).

This latter case leads us to organizations found in the overlap between *the state and the third sector*, where we can note the increased blurring between public and private results in new or hybrid organizations. One example is found in quasi-public organizations, or what Streeck and Schmitter (1985) refer to as 'private interest government', where the division between public and private almost disappears. Private non-profit organizations are explicitly given official public responsibilities in terms of defining, deciding and implementing public policy. Such quasi-public organizations often comprise the nexus of networks of public and private bodies with strong mutual interest in regulating a certain field (Kenis, 1992). This overlapping area also integrates the increasingly important partnerships between TSOs and public authorities. For instance, in the fields of education and health as well as various others, it is quite common for the state to prefer to delegate the provision of social services and to have contractual arrangements with private non-profit schools, hospitals or mutuals that it heavily finances. The strict regulation and supervision it imposes on them explain why such TSOs appear closer to the public sector than at the very centre of the third sector.

Finally, when examining the overlap between *the community and the third sector*, we note numerous examples of mixed organizations. A formal non-profit organization may attract the support of numerous individuals who are not necessarily members of an organization, but who nevertheless contribute their time and/or money to support the activities of an organization and to help achieve its goals. Another example is found in a variety of mutual-aid and self-help groups. Here the 'members' either have not yet created a formal association or the associations do not restrict their activities to 'dues-paying members'. Rather, they are open to all relevant persons in the community served by such mutual aid or self-help groups. This also reflects the fact that a great deal of new local non-profit initiatives start without any legal framework as 'de facto' associations relying exclusively on the work of volunteers. Although they choose to remain informal, do not register or adopt any legal status, they actually provide some services. They most often represent the early stage of organizations which may later choose to register and develop as formal non-profit organizations. This type of overlap helps avoiding a strict frontier between stages in organizations' trajectories.

To conclude, let us stress that this last conceptualization of the third sector as an intermediary area does not rule out the two former approaches. On the contrary, it can be fruitfully combined with them in order to provide a more dynamic and a less clear-cut conception of the third sector.

NOTES

1. For more details, see Defourny and Nyssens (2008) and the various works of the EMES European Research Network: www.emes.net (last accessed November 2012).
2. As explained by Malcolm Lynch (1995).
3. See Gueslin (1987).

BIBLIOGRAPHY

Anheier, H. and W. Siebel (eds) (1990), *The Third Sector. Comparative Studies of Non-profit Organizations*, W. de Gruyter, Berlin.

Ben-Ner, A. and T. Van Hoomissen (1991), 'Nonprofit Organizations in the Mixed Economy: A Demand and Supply Analysis', *Annals of Public and Cooperative Economics*, vol. 62, 519–550.

Birchall, J. (1997), *The International Cooperative Movement*, Manchester: Manchester University Press.

Borzaga, C. and J. Defourny (eds) (2001), *The Emergence of Social Enterprise*, London and New York: Routledge.

Cabinet Office (2007), 'The Future Role of the Third Sector in Social and Economic Regeneration: Final Report', HM Treasury, London.

Chaves, R. and J.-L. Monzón (2007), 'The Social Economy in the European Union', CRIEC and the European Economic and Social Committee, Brussels.

Defourny, J. and P. Develtere (2009), 'Social Economy: The Worldwide Making of a Third Sector', in J. Defourny, P. Develtere, B. Fonteneau and M. Nyssens (eds) (2009), *The Worldwide Making of the Social Economy*, Acco, Leuven and The Hague, pp. 15–40.

Defourny, J. and J.-L. Monzón Campos (eds) (1992), *Economie sociale – The Third Sector*, Brussels: De Boeck.

Defourny, J. and M. Nyssens (2008), 'Social Enterprise in Europe: Recent Trends and Developments', *Social Enterprise Journal*, vol. 4, no. 3, pp. 202–228.

Defourny, J. and V. Pestoff (2008), 'Images and Concepts of the Third Sector in Europe', EMES Working Papers, no 08–02, Liege: EMES European Research Network.

Desroche, H. (1976), *Le projet coopératif*, Les Editions Ouvrières, Paris.

Evers, A. (1995), 'Part of the Welfare Mix. The Third Sector as an Intermediate Area', *Voluntas*, vol. 6, no. 2, pp. 159–182.

Evers, A. and J.-L. Laville (eds) (2004), *The Third Sector in Europe*, Cheltenham: Edward Elgar.

Gueslin, A. (1987), *L'invention de l'économie sociale*, Paris: Economica.

Hansmann, H. (1980), 'The Role of Nonprofit Enterprise', in S. Rose-Ackerman (ed.), *The Economics of Nonprofit Institutions: Studies in Structure and Policy*, Oxford: Oxford University Press, pp. 57–84.

Hansmann, H. (1996), *The Ownership of Enterprise*, Cambridge: Harvard University Press.

James, E. (1983), 'How Nonprofits Grow: A Model', *Journal of Policy Analysis and Management*, vol. 2, pp. 350–365.

James, E. (1986), 'The Private Nonprofit Provision of Education: A Theoretical Model and Application to Japan', *Journal of Comparative Economics*, vol. 10, pp. 255–276.

James, E. and S. Rose-Ackerman (1986), *The Nonprofit Enterprise in Market Economies, Fundamentals of Pure and Applied Economics*, London: Harwood Academic Publishers.

James, E. (ed.) (1989), *The Nonprofit Organizations in International Perspective. Studies in Comparative Culture and Policy*, New York: Oxford University Press.

Kenis, P. (1992), *The Social Construction of an Industry*, Frankfurt am Main and Boulder, CO: Campus Verlag & Westview Press.

Krashinsky, M. (1986), 'Transactions Costs and a Look at the Nonprofit Organization', in S. Rose-Ackerman (ed.), *The Economics of Nonprofit Institutions*, New York: Oxford University Press, pp. 114–132.

Laville, J-L. (ed.) (1994), *L'économie solidaire – une perspective internationale*, Paris: Desclée de Brouwer.

Lynch, Malcolm (1995), 'Economie Sociale or Social Economy – A French or British phrase?', *Social Economy*, no 33, pp. 6–7.

Nelson, R. and M. Krashinsky (1973), 'Two Major Issues of Public Policy: Public Policy and Organization of Supply', in R. Nelson and D. Young (eds) *Public Subsidy for Day Care of Young Children*, Lexington, Mass: D.C. Heath & Co.

Nyssens, M. (ed.) (2006), *Social Enterprise – At the crossroads of market, public policies and civil society*, London and New York: Routledge.

Pestoff, V. (1998), *Beyond the Market and State. Civil Democracy and Social Enterprises in a Welfare Society*, Aldershot, UK and Brookfield, NJ: Ashgate.

Powell, W.W. (ed.) (1987), *The Non-Profit Sector*, New Haven: Yale University Press.

Rose-Ackerman, S. (ed.) (1986), *The Economics of Nonprofit Institutions. Studies in Structure and Policy*, New York: Oxford University Press.

Salamon, L. (1997), 'The United States', in L. Salamon and H. Anheier (eds), *Defining the Nonprofit Sector: A Cross-national Analysis*, Manchester: Manchester University Press, pp. 280–317.

Salamon, L., Anheier, H. and Associates (1999), *Global Civil Society. Dimensions of the Nonprofit Sector*, Baltimore: The Johns Hopkins Center for Civil Society Studies.

Salamon, L., Sokolowski, W. and H. Anheier (2000), 'Social Origins of Civil Society: An Overview', Working Paper of the Johns Hopkins Comparative Nonprofit Sector Project, no. 38. Baltimore: The Johns Hopkins Center for Civil Society Studies.

Streeck, W. and P. Schmitter (1985), *Private Interest Government – Beyond Market and State*, Beverly Hills and London: Sage.

Weisbrod, B. (1977), *The Voluntary Nonprofit Sector*, Lexington, MA: D.C. Heath.

Weisbrod, B.A. (1988), *The Non-Profit Economy*, Cambridge: Harvard University Press.

Young, D. (1983), *If Not for Profit, for What?*, Lexington, Mass: Lexington Books.

40. Trust
Vittorio Pelligra

INTRODUCTION

Trust is central for human life in a variety of senses. It constitutes that *vinculum soci-etatis*, the 'bond of society', to which John Locke, in the last of his *Essays on the Law of Nature* (1660/1954), attributed a crucial role in the sustaining of a civil society. Also according to many contemporary scholars, trust is the basic foundation of every social relationship, a cooperative 'atmosphere' both among citizens and between citizens and institutions. As the philosopher Sissella Bok argues: 'Whatever matters to human beings trust is the atmosphere in which it thrives' (Bok, 1978, p. 31). And: 'we inhabit a climate of trust as we inhabit an atmosphere and notice it as we notice air, only when it becomes scarce or polluted' (Baier, 1986, p. 232).

Trust plays a fundamental role in every social interaction, be it direct or indirect, personal or anonymous, mediated or not. Clearly, trust is a crucial issue for social and political sciences as well as psychological and philosophical studies.

Coming to the economic sphere was John Stuart Mill, who noticed both the virtues and the pervasiveness of trust: 'The advantage of humankind of being able to trust one another, penetrates into every crevice and cranny of human life: the economical is perhaps the smallest part of it, yet even this is incalculable' (1848, p. 131). This intuition was developed further, in the last century, by Kenneth Arrow, who, defining trust as the 'lubricant of the social system', convincingly argued that 'much of the economic backwardness in the world can be explained by a lack of mutual confidence' (1974, p. 357).

Trust has also been an important category linking economic and sociological research, especially for its role in the study of 'social capital'. This later concept refers to a combination of trust, networks and information that is conductive of cooperative attitudes and influences the economic, but also the political and social performance of communities (Ostrom and Ahn, 2003).

In modern economic theory trust elements can be especially important in the analysis of inter- and intra-organisational relations, the theory of contracts, the economics of labour and incentives, development economics, institutional design, behavioural game theory and many other domains.

For the theoretical economist, the 'fiduciary phenomenon' is a sort of paradox: something like a 'conceptual bumblebee' that works in practice but not in theory (see Hollis, 1998). However, by now, a vast body of empirical literature proves, through experiments conducted in field and controlled lab environments, that human beings have a marked propensity to trust one another and not to betray the trust placed in them by others. We know that people trust each other and are trustworthy, but we still lack a good theory of why this happens. Studying trust is thus a dual challenge: on one hand we need to analyse the empirical relevance of fiduciary phenomena and their determinants; on

411

the other hand we need to devise theoretical models that can successfully describe such complex phenomena in all their relational, psychological and motivational dimensions. In this sense, the study of trust has proven to be a fertile domain that, in recent years, has offered a significant contribution to the definition of a more articulated, realistic and 'reasonable' model of economic agent than the standard *homo economicus*.

In this chapter we will first identify the defining elements of fiduciary interactions; we will then examine some of the experiments that have substantiated the trust phenomenon with empirical evidence and finally we will discuss the theories that have been proposed so far to explain observed behaviour.

FORMALISING A FIDUCIARY INTERACTION: THE TRUST GAME

Let us imagine a simplified social interaction containing all the elements that are common to every possible trust relationship. These elements are firstly the people who make up the relationship, then their possible choices and then the consequences that such choices can jointly determine. Hence we need at least two players: player A and player B; the former has the option of trusting the other or not, whereas the latter can choose whether to repay or betray this trust. Finally, the consequences of the two players' choices are ranked on the basis of the preferences of player A. The preferred outcome is the one where A trusts player B and the latter repays his trust; the second ranking outcome is the one where A chooses not to trust B and the third and least preferred option is the one of betrayal of the trust placed on player B.

For player B the best outcome is the opportunistic choice of having player A's trust and betraying it; the second best is being worthy of A's trust and the third is the outcome of a pair of trust and trustworthy choices.

Figure 40.1 shows a formal representation of the interaction we just described. The pay-off associated with each outcome (the number on the left for player A and that on the right for player B) represents an ordinal index of each player's preferences for every possible consequence produced by the various choice combinations.

Three fundamental elements characterise this interaction:

1. *Conditional Gain*: if player A (trustor) trusts player B (trustee) and B is trustworthy, then player A gets a better result compared to the result he would have obtained not trusting B;
2. *Exposure*: if player A trusts B and his trust is betrayed, then A obtains a worse result that what he would have got had he not trusted B;
3. *Temptation*: if player A trusts B and player B betrays his trust, then player B obtains a better result than what he would have obtained had he been trustworthy.

From an observational viewpoint, we can define the 'trusting' and 'trustworthy' choices as follows:

a) the interaction takes the form of a Trust Game;
b) player A plays 'trust';

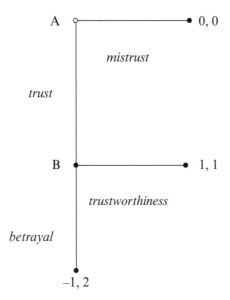

Figure 40.1   The basic trust game

The behaviour of player B, instead, is defined as 'trustworthy' when both a) and b) are true and:

c)   player B plays 'trustworthiness'.

Figure 40.2 generalises the same interaction, imposing the conditions of pay-off inequality, necessary to describe the defining elements of the trust relationship. Then the 'Conditional Gain' corresponds to condition $c > a$; 'exposure', is given by condition $a > b$, while 'temptation' is deduced from condition $e > f$. Note that these conditions imposing the relationship among pay-offs do not concern pay-offs f and d, that is, the pay-offs of player B associated with player A not trusting and with the combination (trusting, trustworthy). This in turn implies that the two values can be equal or the first greater than the second or the second greater than the first.

This is an important point because it tells us that there can be three types of fiduciary interaction. One in which both trustor and trustworthy trustee gain from cooperating; a second type whereby only the trustor gains from trustworthiness while the trustee does not gain anything relative to the status-quo; a third type where trustworthiness is expensive and implies a loss for the trustee compared to the initial situation.

Table 40.1 sketches the three different instances and gives each variant of the trust game a different name: basic, gratuitous and costly.

The basic elements of this type of relationship can be found in a vast array of social interactions, from family to work, in politics as well as in economics. Even the market, which appears to be conceived to minimise trusting, could not survive if there wasn't a large quantity of trust at its core on which to ground exchanges, property rights and the reliability of money.

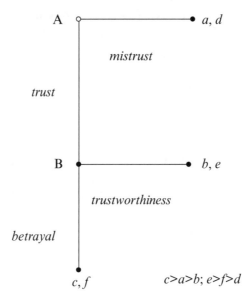

Figure 40.2   The generic trust game

Table 40.1   Fiduciary interactions: a taxonomy

Payoff conditions	Outcome	Cost of trustworthiness $(d - f)$	Name of the Game
$f > d$	mutual gain	negative	basic trust game
$f = d$	no advantage for B	null	gratuitous trust game
$f < d$	B's loss	positive	costly trust game

EXPERIMENTAL EVIDENCE

If we study this situation in terms of standard game theory (game theory is the discipline that studies strategic choices), we conclude that in a situation like the one described in the trust game, trust and trustworthiness should not exist. Indeed, before choosing whether to trust or not, player A should wonder, reasoning backward, what player B is likely to do. If player A believes that player B is self-interested and rational, the standard assumption of standard theory, then she will forecast that once B receives his or her trust, he or she would certainly betray it. This would allow B to achieve his or her preferred result, that is, the one characterised by a pay-off of 2. This outcome however is associated to a −1 pay-off for player A, less than what she would have had if she had not trusted (0). Hence, if player A is self-interested and knows that B is too, then she would maximise her own welfare by deciding not to trust. In the end, we would have a situation where a better outcome for both players exists (1,1) but it cannot be reached because they cannot trust each other or be trustworthy. This is what standard theory tells us.

A long series of lab experiments, however, has contributed to casting doubts on the realism of the standard conclusion. Starting from the seminal research by Berg, Dickhaut and McCabe (1995), empirical evidence has shown increasingly how real people tend to trust and be trustworthy to a much greater extent than assumed by standard theory.

In their pioneering work Joyce Berg and others observed the behaviour of real people, adequately incentivised, in a strategic situation known as 'Investment-Game'. In this game player A is given an amount of money. He can give some ($0 < i < e$) to the other player. The passed-on amount is tripled ($3i$) and given to player B, who in turn can return some of it ($0 < s < 3i$), if he wants, to player A. At the end of the game, A gets his initial endowment, less the amount he gave, plus the amount he was returned, while player B gets the amount he was sent by A, less the amount he chose to return to A. Standard theory says that since A knows that player B is rational and self-interested and would not return anything, A is not likely to send anything to B. Player A would keep his initial amount and player B would have nothing. Experimental observation, however, shows that normally A players invest part of their endowment, a third on average, and most of B players return at least as much as they received. This way the game is advantageous to both players, just as it often happens in real life. Martin Dufwenberg and Uri Gneezy (2000), in a second research, imagine this situation: player A finds a wallet on the street and can decide whether to return or keep it. If he returns it, there is a possibility (not a certainty) that player B, the owner, could reward him. Here too, standard theory would say that player A anticipates the fact that B will not reward him and is thus not likely to return the found wallet. Experimental data, on the contrary, highlight a few relevant elements. A players return the wallet less and less frequently as the amount contained in the wallet increases. B players frequently offer a reward, in a way that is correlated, above all, with their belief about As' expectation about the amount B should give as a reward. The more Bs think that As are trusting them, the more they become trustworthy. We can thus summarise some of the elements that came out from this and many other economic experiments on trust (see Camerer, 2003, for a comprehensive review): people trust and are trustworthy to a much greater extent than standard game theory predicts; trust is not blind and is subject to the calculation of expected cost–benefits; giving trust tends to generate trustworthy behaviour; in fiduciary interactions agents' intentions are as important as the consequence of their choices.

There exists a vast experimental literature that accumulated data in disagreement with standard theory. Without venturing any further in the methodological details of how observed data are interpreted, however important this may be, we can see that at this point an alternative theory is needed to explain the observations at hand.

A FEW REASONS TO BE TRUSTWORTHY?

If we want to build a theoretical model of trusting and trustworthy behaviour, we need to focus our attention mainly on the second aspect: trustworthiness. Once we manage to explain why a rational agent may decide to resist the temptation to be opportunistic, accounting for the fact that somebody will trust him becomes a lot easier, as this represents a mere problem of strategic thinking.

Enlightened Self-interest

The first possibility, occurring even to a rather conservative theorist, is what we could define as 'enlightened self-interest'. This is a really simple idea: if we consider each trust relationship not as an isolated instance, but rather as one application of a wider series of interactions that occur systematically and repeatedly with our partner, the considerations guiding our choices will change radically. The choice of not being trustworthy today, in fact, could have repercussions on my partner's inclination to trust me tomorrow, and if I include this consideration in my conceptual cost–benefit calculations, I will have to subtract from the immediate gain derived from the opportunistic choice all the gains I will miss as a consequence of my betrayed partner's decision not to trust me in the future. On the contrary, if I prove to be trustworthy today I will induce my partner to trust me again tomorrow.

In this case I will need to add to today's missed gain all the future gains deriving from a long-term cooperative relationship. It is easy to show that, if the players are patient enough, trusting and being trustworthy are the most rational courses of action. This explanation surely sheds light on an important aspect, the creation of a reputation, but it is not directly applicable to experimental observations, which in most instances consider non-repeated interactions. Also from a merely theoretical point of view, as Bowles and Gintis (2011) observe, this model is vulnerable to a series of criticisms based on the fact that even though logically coherent, it tends to produce a satisfactory result, in terms of equilibria, only in the presence of very restrictive assumptions and the dynamic properties of the equilibria are at best irrelevant. This particular problem affects all results based on the folk theorem, to a greater or lesser extent, by virtue of their own structure.

Altruism

A second possible explanation draws on the fact that, when taking decisions, economic agents take into consideration more complex objectives than just their mere personal interest. It could be, for example, that economic agents are sensitive to some form of 'altruism' (see Bergstrom and Stark, 1993). In this case, gains and losses suffered by my partner represent gains and losses for me, even though indirectly. If this is true, then an altruist player could be induced to behave in a trustworthy manner to avoid causing a loss to his partner, which would ultimately result in a loss for himself. On the contrary, a gain for his partner would cause an indirect gain for himself. By inserting this element of interdependence, the idea of altruism could be logically coherent with trustworthy and trusting behaviour. However, also in this instance the data does not agree with the theory. The behavioural model observed in reality seems to be more complex that that described by the principle of altruism.

Inequality-aversion

A further possible explanation assumes that humans have an innate sense of fairness guiding their social choices. This assumption is at the basis of the *inequality-aversion* theory (Fehr and Schmidt, 1999; Bolton and Ockenfels, 2000). This theory considers individuals who not only try to maximise their individual pay-offs, but also try to minimise the difference between their pay-off and that of others with whom they are interacting, be it advantageous or not. In the case of trust relationship, an inequality-adverse player B would be trustworthy, because he would avoid the choice producing the greatest difference in the distribution of wealth between himself and the other player. Within the trust game, this is actually the opportunistic choice, while the trustworthy choice is the one that offer simultaneously a high gain and no difference between one's own gain and that of the partner.

Reciprocity

Both altruism and inequality aversion theory consider individuals characterised by an extended utility function where a second psychological aspect is added to material gain. Beyond this complication of the utility function, however, these models share the same behavioural logic as the standard model: the two individuals make their choices on the basis of considerations that are only linked to the consequences of their joint actions. However, many experiments have demonstrated that in reality the logic of choice is definitely more complex and takes into account of the agents' intentions. The basic idea is that there can be very different reactions to the same action, depending on the intentions that have originated that action in the first place. This intuition is incorporated in the theories of *reciprocity*, which assume that individual A may be willing to sacrifice part of his material wealth to produce a material benefit for individual B, who in turn had benefited individual A. In much the same way A may be willing to punish B if he has damaged A. This reciprocity logic, whether positive or negative, poses a technical problem of formalisation. How are we to evaluate if an action has been fair or unfair, and hence capable of provoking a positive or a negative response? The answer is in the intentions of the agent. Standard game theory does not provide us with adequate instruments to formally describe the agent's intentions: in order to do this we need to recourse to the so-called psychological game theory (Geanakoplos et al, 1989). Within a psychological game, each player's utility depends not only on the choices made by him and the other players, but also on what the other players expect us to do and on what we believe the others expect us to do. This way it is possible to describe an action together with the intentions underlying it by taking into account what one does but also what one could have done but chose not to do. Matthew Rabin (1993) was the first author to propose a reciprocity model which, by adopting psychological game theory, introduces a reference point for every game (*equitable pay-off*) which allows the classification of each choice as either 'kind' or 'mean'. Players optimise their choices if they maximise a utility function in which a psychological element comes into play together with the material pay-offs component. The psychological value of the utility function will be positive when the individual responds kindly to a kind action and punishes a mean action; in the other cases it will be a cost. Going back to the issue of trust, it is easy to understand that this can be based on the expectation of a reciprocating behaviour, in the first place. If I trust you, I am kind, and in the logic of reciprocity this kindness brings about trustworthy behaviour.

Guilt-aversion

Another possibility, proposed to account for new experimental evidence, is linked to the assumption of *guilt-aversion* (Battigalli and Dufwenberg, 2007). The basic idea is that we tend to develop guilt when we frustrate the expectations of our partner. Empirical evidence does indeed show a positive correlation between the decision to resist the temptation to behave opportunistically and the belief regarding expected behaviour. In other words, the more we believe that others expect us to be trustworthy the more we will behave in a trustworthy manner, and this to avoid the psychological cost associated with guilt. This explanation is consistent with the observation that the possibility to communicate promises, intentions and other messages have a positive effect on the rate of trust and trustworthiness. The more explicit the expectation of trust, the higher the guilt associated with the opportunistic choice and hence the more frequently we will observe trustworthy choices.

Collective Rationality

A new line of explanation that drastically departs from the traditional economic approach is that which refers to the concept of *team-thinking* (Sugden, 1993, 2003; Bacharach, 2005). Here the basic idea is that once an individual identifies himself as a member of a given group, the group's objectives become his own, in the sense that he will be motivated to do his part to achieve the group's objective. Hence for a *team-thinker* any positive consequence of his choices is not by itself a reason for the action taken, but rather an incidental consequence produced by the joint individual plans of action which coordinate to achieve the group objective. In this sense a pair of trusting and trustworthy choices could be considered as a set of optimal actions within a group that is willing to achieve the objective of maximising overall welfare.

Trust Responsiveness

The last explanation for trusting and trustworthy behaviour that we will discuss here, takes on the previous idea of *guilt-aversion* and extends its application. In a situation similar to those described in a trust game, a trusting choice unequivocally drives some trustworthiness expectations: I would not trust you if I did not believe you are trustworthy. At this point player B knows with certainty what player A expects of her. The principle of *trust responsiveness* refers to the idea that, through this mechanism of expectations transmission, a genuine act of trust gives player B additional reasons to make a trustworthy choice (Pelligra, 2005, 2010). Taking a position initially elaborated by Adam Smith in his *Theory of Moral Sentiments* (1976[1759]), the idea of *trust responsiveness* is founded upon a complex motivational structure in which three independent forces are at play: on one hand we desire material gain, next to it, in Smith's words, is the 'desire to be approved' and finally the 'desire to be worthy of approbation'. The decision to behave in order to produce maximum gain, as an opportunistic choice maybe, is also evaluated in the light of the other two aspects: publicly betraying trust brings disapproval from any observer, whereas repaying trust is associated to social approval; but even in the event of absence of an external observer, even in the case of perfect anonymity of one's choices, there will always be an impartial observer, a judge within ourselves who will find us more or less worthy of praise, thus impacting on our self-esteem. These two additional mechanisms may account for the difference between conformism, the desire to do what others do or expect from us, and the self-esteem derived from doing what one believes it is right to do.

Whereas in the principles of enlightened self-interest, altruism and inequality-aversion the reasons leading to trust and trustworthiness are exogenous to the relationship, in the case of the reciprocity, guilt-aversion and trust responsiveness principles those reasons are endogenous, that is, they emerge and they develop within the trust relationship. In this sense, it is possible to speak of trust and trustworthiness as relational concepts.

CONCLUSIONS

We saw that the 'fiduciary phenomenon' is a crucial passage of civic life. It is however a difficult concept to understand and explain within the standard models of economic behaviour. Many explanations have been offered in recent years from long term interest to fiduciary responsiveness. Which of these models will offer the best explanation is something that needs to be established empirically by the work of future researchers, and which in turn will cause new theoretical developments and ever more sophisticated yet manageable models. The direction that appears to unfold is that of considering agents to be moved only by distributional considerations as well as attention towards other people's intentions and regret.

The discussion of the link between trust theory and institutional planning deserves a dedicated chapter. Indeed, if trust could be considered as an economic asset in its own right, then one should wonder how institutions and interaction patterns can be designed to favour the development of a high level of trust between agents. For reasons of space, we can only refer here to the work of Pelligra (forthcoming), Goodin (1996) and Brennan and Pettit (2004).

BIBLIOGRAPHY

Arrow, K. (1974), *The Limits of Organisations*, New York, W.W. Norton.
Bacharach, M. (2005), *Beyond Individual Choice*, Gold, N. and R. Sugden (eds), Princeton, N.J., Princeton University Press.
Baier, A. (1986), 'Trust and Antitrust', *Ethics* 96, pp. 231–60.
Battigalli, P. and Dufwenberg, M. (2007), 'Guilt in Games', *American Economic Review, Papers & Proceedings* 97, pp. 170–76.
Berg, J., Dickhaut, J. and K. McCabe (1995), 'Trust, Reciprocity and Social History', *Games and Economic Behaviour* 10, pp. 122–142.
Bergstrom, T. and Stark, O. (1993), 'How Altruism Can Prevail in an Evolutionary Environment', *American Economic Review* 83, pp. 149–155.
Bok, S. (1978), *Lying*, New York: Pantheon Books.
Bolton, G.E. and A. Ockenfels (2000), 'ERC – A Theory of Equity, Reciprocity and Competition', *American Economic Review* 90, pp. 166–93.
Bowles, S. and H. Gintis (2011), *A Cooperative Species: Human Reciprocity and Its Evolution*, Princeton: Princeton University Press.

Brennan, G. and P. Pettit (2004), *The Economy of Esteem. An Essay on Civil and Political Society*, Oxford: Oxford University Press.

Camerer, C. (2003), *Behavioral Game Theory*, Princeton: Princeton University Press.

Dufwenberg, M. and U. Gneezy (2000), 'Measuring Beliefs in an Experimental Lost Wallet Game', *Games and Economic Behavior* 30, pp. 163–82.

Fehr, E. and K.M. Schmidt (1999), 'A Theory of Fairness, Competition, and Cooperation', *Quarterly Journal of Economics* 114, pp. 817–68.

Geanakoplos J., Pearce D. and E. Stacchetti (1989), 'Psychological Games and Sequential Rationality', *Games and Economic Behavior* 1, pp. 60–79.

Goodin, R. (ed.) (1996), *The Theory of Institutional Design*, Cambridge: Cambridge University Press.

Guala, F. (2005), *The Methodology of Experimental Economics*, Cambridge: Cambridge University Press.

Guala, F. (2006), 'Has Game Theory Been Refuted?' *Journal of Philosophy* 103, pp. 239–63.

Hollis, M. (1998), *Trust within Reason*, Cambridge: Cambridge University Press.

Locke, J. (1954[1660]), *Essays on the Law of Nature*, Oxford: Clarendon Press.

Mill, J.S. (1848), *Principles of Political Economy*, London: John W. Parker.

Ostrom, E. and T.K. Ahn (2003), *Foundations of Social Capital*, Cheltenham: Edward Elgar.

Pelligra, V. (2005), 'Under Trusting Eyes: The Responsive Nature of Trust', in R. Sugden and B. Gui (eds), *Economics and Social Interaction: Accounting for the Interpersonal Relations*, Cambridge: Cambridge University Press.

Pelligra, V. (2010), 'Trust Responsiveness: On the Dynamics of Fiduciary Interactions', *Journal of Socio-Economics* 39(6), pp. 653–60.

Pelligra, V. (forthcoming), 'Promoting Trust Through Institutional Design', in S. Bartolini, L. Bruni and P.L. Porta (eds), *Policies for Happiness*, Oxford: Oxford University Press.

Rabin, M. (1993), 'Incorporating Fairness into Game Theory', *American Economic Review* 83, pp. 1281–1302.

Smith, A. (1976[1759]), *The Theory of Moral Sentiments*, Indianapolis: Liberty Classics.

Sugden, R. (1993), 'Thinking as a Team; Towards an Explanation on Non-selfish Behaviour', *Social Philosophy and Policy* 10, pp. 69–89.

Sugden, R. (2003), 'The Logic of Team Reasoning', *Philosophical Explorations* 6, pp. 165–81.

41. Values based organizations
Alessandra Smerilli

INTRODUCTION

The underlying motivations of actions have an important value in civil and economic life, and in those of organizations as well. Human beings are the only animals capable of attributing a meaning and a value to their own and others' motivations, and not only to the material results and objectives derived from a certain behavior. For as long as, and to the extent in which, organizations and markets remain human places, motivations will matter, including the most complex motivation of the simple search for profit (Bruni and Zamagni 2009).

Nevertheless, economics does not consider, or at least did not consider until recent times, the motivations underlying actions. Rather, and for uncommon reasons, economics considers it dangerous to include them in economic analyses. This is because the principal characteristic of modern economy, that which is most rooted and profound, is the definition of the market as a place where we can meet and exchange, without having to consider 'why' each party is undertaking a given action or trade. Analyzing the 'why', in fact, calls into play the identity, history, caste, class, religion – all the elements which during the *ancient regime* (and to a certain extent even at present, in some parts of the world) were a cause of limitations to economic and social development. These elements relegated and confined human interaction only within the strong bonds of the clan, groups, families, in the network of relatives and friends. In the past centuries, the market has had an extraordinary development, as we know, precisely because it has created a new system of relations, a new ethos, which ends on the surface of motivations of individuals, and limits itself to the 'secular' and anonymous choices. When we go into a store to buy wine, we are not asked 'why' we make that purchase (if it's to celebrate with friends or to sustain dependence in alcohol). As the market's mechanism, it is sufficient that who buys has the purchasing power and observes the commanded price. We are not asked if we are Muslims, Jews or Christians: market interactions happen beyond these diversities and are unaware of the motivations of different people.

The market evens out proper identities precisely so as not to enter into people's motivations. And thanks to this evening-out, the market relationship has proven an extraordinary capacity which renders interaction between people who otherwise would not have met possible. Had the market been dependent on motivations and therefore on identities, then these people would have never met.

The great English economist P. Wicksteed, pastor of the Unitarian Church, conceived this characteristic of the modern economy the most. He affirmed that economists should 'only be interested in the "what" and "how" and not the "why"' (1933)[1910], p.165) of actions, and that they remain free of any analysis of motives:

the objects and the actions which economic analysis deals with, will therefore include everything that enters in the circle of trade – which means everything that people can offer each
other, or can do for each other, where we see a sort of *impersonal capacity*. Or, in other words,
the things that a person can give or do for another person, *regardless of any form of personal and
individual consideration*, with him or with his motivations or his reasons. (Ibid pp. 4–5)

From this point of view, however, in the past decades, thanks to the development of
dialogue between economics and psychology, and to the growing consequences used
in the experimental methods in economy, scholars of economic science have noticed
that motivations have an important effect on people's choices and on who observes the
accomplishment of such choices. They are discovering 'experimentally' (other than from
the observation of the lives of real people) that if we do not take into account the motivations during the economic analysis, we will not understand that many important choices
(how to trust, to positively or negatively respond to an act of trust, to exchange reciprocity, to choose or to commit to work, to pay taxes, to respect the laws, etc.) depend on
how the subjects read and interpret the motivations of the others who they interact with.[1]

This recent motivational opening of economics is important because it is only within
the realm of an economic science open to the motivations that one can study and
understand the dynamics of values based organizations (VBOs).

In what follows, I present a definition of a VBO and then I show some dynamics that
can arise in a VBO when motivations deteriorate among members.

DEFINITION OF A VBO

No organization could work exclusively on the basis of contracts; all organizations need,
to some extent, motivation that goes beyond profit and material incentives. An example
is sit-down strikes, situations where organizations collapse because everyone does only
what is written in his/her job description. Another way to affirm the same reality is to say
that contracts are incomplete. Incomplete contracts in their turn generate space for what
is not negotiable and of course for conflicts. Even though perfect and complete contracts
could be created, we would still observe space in the organizations for non-instrumental
actions and gratuitousness.

There are, however, some organizations where the presence of intrinsically motivated people, with a particular 'vocation' linked to the specific activity or profession,[2]
is a key element for their success and growth (Heyes 2005). These are the so-called
VBOs. An analysis (basically empirical) of VBOs' characteristics is present in Mitroff
and Denton (1999). Other expressions can be found in the literature (mainly managerial and business literature: in economics the topic is actually missing): 'values-driven
organizations'(Barrett 2006) and 'ideological organizations' (Davies 1989).

In the literature there is no shared definition of the characteristics of a VBO. A key
element on which all definitions agree is the presence in such organizations of an ideal
mission and identity that, on the one hand, is not the maximization of profit or wealth
and, on the other, creates a strong link between the activity carried on and the values of
the VBO.

According to Molteni (2009) the ideal motive of these organizations can take on different forms: it can be present in the kind of activity that it undertakes, in the motiv-

ations for which an organization comes to be (for example, an enterprise that is formed to engage the most disadvantaged members of society in the production process) or in the 'way' of doing business, which has to do with the choice of the governance structure or the organizational structure. In our opinion, these characteristics should be simultaneously present in a VBO, though in varying levels and combinations. It is difficult to imagine, for example, ideal motivations that do not correspond with an adequate governance or organizational structure. 'New wine' of the ideal mission normally needs 'new wineskins' which are properly fit to contain that wine and to allow them to mature in time.

In general, the expression is used to refer to religion or spirituality based organizations (such as confessional educational institutions or spiritual organizations).[3]

Our use of the VBO category is much broader. In this chapter by VBO we mean any organization that presents three basic elements, one related to the organization and two to its members:

1. The activity carried out *is an essential part* of its identity, because the activity the VBO implements is engendered by a 'vocation' that represents the values, the identity and the *mission* of the organization; While the owners of a capitalistic enterprise can normally change the sector of their business should they deem it necessary, a VBO is born for a specific purpose, which is deeply bound to the organization itself. In other words, the undertakings within an VBO can be neither practically nor logically separated from the results one hopes to achieve. In other words, *the business is a constitutive part of the purpose for existence.*
2. The identity of the organization is deeply linked to a *core of members* with share, and in a certain sense *embody*, the 'vocation' and the ethical values of the VBO.[4]
3. These intrinsically motivated 'core members' are less reactive to price signal (i.e. wage) with respect to the other non (or less) intrinsically motivated members. They are the 'guardians' of the identity and ideal quality of the VBO; therefore they are the most ready to 'voice' in case of the deterioration of that ideal quality and values.[5]

To understand the peculiarities of a VBO, one should think of what it is not: businesses, for example, that have the pursuit of profit as their primary purpose, where the business is only an instrument to optimize something external, clearly distinct from the business itself and is therefore void of any intrinsic value, but by definition, is purely instrumental; an organization where the employees respond only to material incentives and where there is no call for a particular 'vocation' to its members, apart from their technical skills.

Examples of these VBOs are nonprofit organizations, charities, NGOs, environmental, educational or cultural organizations, among others.[6] The main objective of any VBO is to evolve and grow without losing its *identity*, to which its survival is linked in the middle and long run.[7]

In fact, if on one hand, an organization 'cannot survive unless it tends towards development, which is always qualitative but also often dimensional. . .[because] without tension towards development, as a rule, there can be no stability but retrogression' (Molteni 2009, p. 72); on the other hand, development should coincide with the faithfulness to the ideal mission, which means *dynamic* faithfulness to the identity of the organization.

Anyone operating in the field of social economy or in organizations characterized by a mission that goes beyond profits (as the authors of this chapter) knows very well that in such organizations the success and the harmonious growth chiefly depend on a few key persons (often some of the founders of the organization) who are intrinsically motivated. These core members affect the culture of the organization directly and *indirectly* through the imitation of their behavior by other less intrinsically motivated members. Once some of these core members leave the organization (because, for example, the new management does not sufficiently appreciate the ideal instances of the founders), cumulative effects often occur and can start a huge deterioration process within the organization. One important remedy against this deterioration process is the loyalty of the core members, which can be fostered by a participative and pluralistic governance.

The ideal type of VBO we have in mind is a primary school founded and run by a congregation of nuns (i.e. a typical case of VBO literature) that intends to continue the activity only if the core teachers (the nuns) see the ideal quality school in line with their spirituality. In such a school the transition of the management from the nuns to lay teachers (maybe for a reduction of the number of nuns) is always a critical moment in the life cycle of this VBO, because the identity of the school can be challenged by the typical price signals. An identity conflict at this stage between the nuns (intrinsically motivated) and the new managers can occur. Another example is an environmental NGO born from a small group of people who are lovers of a particular endangered species of bird: when the NGO grows the key issue is to keep the original 'vocation' that originated the NGO embodied, especially in the culture of the core intrinsically motivated founder members.

In the following section, we shall analyze the dynamics operating in VBOs when conflicts between the intrinsically or ideally motivated people and other members, basically interested in standard market incentives, occur. These moments of crisis are important passages in every organization, but they are absolutely crucial in VBOs. In particular, we shall examine the mechanism that can lead the intrinsically motivated people, the more interested in the mission of the organization, to abandon ('exit') the organization when they see their voice unlistened to and, as a consequence, the ideal quality of an organization falls into a process of deterioration.

EXIT, VOICE AND LOYALTY

The analysis starting point is the classical essay 'Exit Voice and Loyalty' by Albert O. Hirschman (1982[1970]).[8] In particular, Hirschman's hypothesis that 'competition of quality' and 'competition of prices' can be mirror-like.

A domain to which Hirschman dedicates special attention in his book is education – a field where VBOs are usually present. In the competition among educational institutions the distinction between quality competition and price competition is relevant. In the US during the 1960s, there was a discussion about Milton Friedman's proposal to introduce vouchers in the education system. Vouchers give families the 'exit' option, a tool for inserting the market mechanism into the management of the educational institutions. If they did not like the services, they could choose the 'exit' option and move to a higher quality school.

Hence, the 'exit' option offers a signal to the organization to improve the quality of services in order to maintain customers. According to Hirschman, the introduction of vouchers creates a typical case of *quality competition*. In the case of quality competition, however, the market works in a fundamentally different way from the classical case of *price competition*. In particular, in the case of quality competition the 'exit' option can generate a sort of adverse selection.

In mainstream economics, consumer demand is a function that links quantity, income and price. A change in quality is considered equivalent to a change in prices or quantities:

> [A]n article of poor quality can often be considered to be simply less in quantity than the same article of standard quality; this is the case, for example, of the automobile tire which lasts on the average only half as long, in terms of mileage, as a high quality tire. (Hirschman 1982[1970], p. 44)

Therefore, neoclassical economics considers quality competition and market competition as similar phenomena. A quality decline is considered equivalent to a fall in price (or in quantity) that, in Hirschman's words, 'is uniform for all buyers of the article' (ibid p. 48).

There are, however, snares hidden in this non-distinction. This is one of the main messages of *Exit, Voice and Loyalty*. In fact, in the traditional analysis of competition, when the price rises, the marginal consumer who exits from the market is the one who, to say, 'cares less' about that specific good; that is, the one who has the lowest reservation price.[9] So, the consumer who exits the market for a particular good can be defined the 'worst,' in the sense that she does not value the good, i.e. a particular school, as much. In this case, the rise in price is similar to the rise of the bar in a high-jump race: those who remain in the competition are the *best* and the global efficiency and quality of the system increases.

What about quality competition? Quality is a multidimensional concept. As mentioned, for many market goods there is no significant distinction between price and quality in terms of competition and efficiency. There is, however, a kind (or dimension) of quality that, according to Hirschman, operates in an antipodal fashion with respect to the standard competition. It is the case in which quality is not an objective and fully observable characteristic of a good, being quality associated to intrinsic dimensions of that particular good.

In the event of a deterioration in *this dimension* of quality, price being equal, the subject who tends to exit first *can be the one most sensitive to quality*. This consumer, then, normally does not correspond to the marginal consumer who exits in the event of a rise in price. This is because the deterioration in quality is 'frequently different for different customers of the article because appreciation of quality differs widely among them' (ibid).

In this kind of competition, therefore, the customer's *order could be reversed*: the subject who reacts first to a deterioration in quality is the same one who evaluates it highly:

> Those customers who care *most* about the quality of the product and who, therefore, are those who would be the most active, reliable, and creative agents of voice are for that very reason also those who are apparently likely to exit first in case of deterioration. (Ibid p. 47)

It is important to note that this analysis based on the distinction between price and quality competition is not suitable for all kinds of goods. Hirschman limits the analysis to the so-called 'connoisseur goods', which have two main features (that are *necessary* conditions for the 'reversal phenomenon'): 1) the price-increase equivalents into which a quality decline can be translated are different for different consumers; 2) such equivalents are positively correlated with the corresponding consumer surpluses. A typical example is the market of high quality wine (a Chianti from a particular area in Tuscany). The 'best consumers' (those who appreciate more the wine, i.e. who have the highest reservation price) are not very reactive to an increase of price given, however, the high level of quality. If, instead, the wine loses quality, they are the first who tend to abandon the good.

Coming back to the example of vouchers, what are the consequences of this scenario? If a drop in quality causes the 'exit' of the most sensitive parents, who will choose schools of better quality, the result could be a continuous deterioration of the school's level of quality because the supply might be recalibrated on the basis of the lowest standards of those who remain.[10]

In light of the above analysis, it is easier to grasp how this model fits in with the dynamics of VBOs.

Let us consider, for example, a VBO that faces a crisis of identity when, due to a dimensional growth and/or a generational change, a conflict arises between the new managers, the *novatores*, less interested in ideal quality and more in market prices, and the *veteres*, the intrinsically motivated or 'ideal quality conscious' founders.

Hirschman's model tells us that in such cases we enter into a situation in which (ideal) quality is deteriorating. The focus of the analysis in such situations will now be on the organization and its governance policies. According to Hirschman, in fact, in this case 'quality deterioration must therefore be redefined in subjective terms: from the member's view-point, it is equivalent to increasing disagreement with the organization's policies' (ibid p. 87). In the light of this theory, in what follows we hold that the quality conscious members will be first to voice when they see a deterioration of the VBO values and its ideal quality. 'Ideal quality' corresponds to the 'connoisseur good' in Hirschman's definition. Ideal quality, in fact, respects the two key characteristics of the connoisseur goods: a) the 'price increase equivalent' is different for different people (intrinsically and not-intrinsically motivated); b) The first to react to an ideal quality deterioration are those with the higher consumer surplus in terms of price, i.e. the intrinsically motivated people are the less sensitive to variations in price – effort, wage, etc. – but the most sensitive to ideal quality deterioration: a case analogous to the one mentioned about the special Chianti wine market. It is the case, for example, of ideological consumers or investors who are prone to paying a higher price (or to earn a lower interest rate) on the condition that the organizations they support by their choices are ethical and responsible; at the same time, these people are the first who give voice and threaten to exit in the case of deterioration of ethical quality of products and/or organizations.

Thus, if the 'voice' of the *veteres* is considered by the *novatores* only as organizational costs and is not listened to, then leaving the VBO ('exit') becomes the only available option to those who protest. There is an underlying hypothesis of our analysis, namely the 'core members' must have the option of finding a higher quality good if they leave the VBO. Nonetheless, the relationship between loyalty and job outside options is not simple or linear. In empirical research on workers' responses to dissatisfaction in organization 'there was not consistent evidence that possessing poor alternatives promotes loyalty behaviour' (Farrel and Rusbult 1992, p. 213). In some cases, these authors note, 'strong loyalty is exhibited by employees with good alternatives' (ibid).

A first consequence of the exit of the core members (or of some of them) can be on the consumer side. The deterioration of the ideal quality may in fact lead to an exit of some 'ideological' customers, who are the first to threaten to exit. Most VBOs, in fact, attract customers and sponsors because of their specific identity and ideal quality. Most of the people fostering VBOs perceive them as a sort of 'merit good'. After the exit of the core members, the VBO can lose the customers relatively more interested in the ideal scope of the organization – those customers who are, in the Hirschman's theoretical framework, the 'best' ones in terms of fidelity and moral support.

However, for the analysis at stake, the 'internal' side of the VBO is the most relevant mechanism that can be activated by the exit of the intrinsically motivated members, where that exit is caused because they have not been listened to. Although these two effects – internal and external – strengthen one another and can lead the organization into a kind of poverty trap, in what follows we'll deal only with the internal side of the crisis.

Our hypothesis is that the presence of intrinsically motivated people in a VBO is important not only because these people directly contribute to and preserve the 'ideal quality' of the organization, but also because their presence *indirectly* influences the behavior of other workers *via* imitation.

How to Prevent such Poverty Traps?

Hirschman's suggestion in this case is *loyalty*, which we have intentionally left in shadow up to now. In order to understand the role of 'loyalty' we have to start from the 'voice' option, that is defined as:

> any attempt at all to change, rather than to escape from, an objectionable state of affairs, whether through individual or collective petition to the management directly in charge, through appeal to a higher authority with the intention of forcing a change in management, or through various types of actions and protests, including those that are meant to mobilize public opinion. (Hirschman 1982[1970], p. 30)

In fact, in order to avoid that core members, who are the first who threaten to leave the organization in the case of loss of quality, selecting the 'loyalty' option instead of 'exit', it is necessary that those members foresee 'improvements to occur as a result of actions to be taken by himself or by others with him or just by others' (ibid p. 37).

When members (or stakeholders, such as financial supporters) are loyal, the voice option becomes an alternative to leaving. The possibility of selecting the loyalty option by the intrinsically motivated members is, then, subordinated to the hope of recuperation of the lost ideal quality. Then, loyalty requires the 'listening to' of voice: 'the decision whether to exit will often be taken in the light of the prospects for the effective use of voice' (ibid p. 39).

In other words, for intrinsically motivated subjects, leaving is an extreme decision taken only when there is no more room for voice in the organization. Loyalty, then, helps the organization to avoid cumulative deterioration. How to foster, then, loyalty in organizations and in particular in VBOs?

Pluralistic and participative governance that gives room to voice fosters the intrinsically motivated people's hope of retrieving that ideal quality that makes sense to the cost of their voice without leaving, i.e. their loyalty.

Thus, if, to keep the intrinsically motivated people inside the VBO is the key factor that determines the organization's culture, then the most important art of the managers of a VBO is the art of listening to the voice of those interested in ideal quality.

Finally, it is important to notice that the argument presented in this chapter could have a broader field of application than just VBOs. We chose VBOs as the subject of our analysis because in this kind of organization the intrinsic motivation element (the 'vocation') is immediately evident as a key ingredient in the existence and success of the organization. But without people with 'vocations' the whole of civil society fails to flourish. Then, all organizations, regardless of their specific values, have to foster higher motivations in its members. For this reason, the *value of vocation* is certainly high in VBOs, but it is also relevant in all other organizations and in our societies.

NOTES

1. See Stanca et al (2009) for a survey.
2. On the economic role of intrinsic motivation see Frey (1997), Le Grand (2003) and Deci (2005).
3. Mitroff and Denton (1999) identified five different VBO models all founded on religion or spirituality.
4. We use here the terms 'vocation,' 'ideal motivation,' and 'intrinsic motivation' synonymously. In fact, between ideal motivation or vocation and intrinsic motivation there is a very strict link. There is no ideal motivation without intrinsic motivation for the activity engendered.
5. In order to understand VBOs' peculiarities, it can be useful to think about what a VBO *is not*: organizations, for example, whose only purpose is to maximize profit, or organizations in which the activity is just instrumental to optimizing something else, and where the employees react only to wage or material incentives and no particular 'vocation' (apart from technical skills) is requested of its members.
6. It is easy to understand that not *all* nonprofit or civil society organizations are VBOs.
7. In this broader sense, many organizations can be included in the category of VBO. This list can include, for example, small, family-based for-profit firms whose development and survival are seriously challenged after the first generation of founders (which happens nowadays in the Italian districts which comprised 'Made in Italy' brands). Once the first generation retires, these small firms tend to encounter huge difficulties finding within the market new managers who are able to preserve the identity and business culture impressed by the entrepreneur. This specific and people-based culture represents the main competitive power of such firms, embodying the tacit know-how of the entrepreneurs.
8. There was much enthusiasm for Hirschman's book when it was first published, but after a few years the enthusiasm waned and in the last two decades his work has seldom been spoken of in economics. To the best of our knowledge, his model has never been applied to VBOs. It is therefore worth re-examining that small but inspiring book and retracing his line of argument in order to analyze the object of our study.
9. We are dealing now with non-perfect competition, which means sellers have the power to increase or decrease quality or prices because the products, for example different schools, are non-perfect substitutes.
10. In this case there would be a strong polarization: on the one hand, a few elite schools, and on the other, a large number of mediocre schools. A cost–benefit analysis would show a net loss of efficiency, measured on the basis of quality.

REFERENCES

Barrett, R. (2006), *Building a Values-Driven Organization: A Whole System Approach to Cultural Transformation*, Butterworth Heinemann, Oxford.
Bruni, L. and Zamagni, S. (2009), *Dizionario di economia civile*, Città Nuova, Roma.

Davies, L. (1989), 'The Institution as an Ideological System: How Morals Make the Organization', *Systemic Practice and Action Research*, 2, pp. 287–306.

Deci, E. (2005), 'The Relation of Intrinsic and Extrinsic Goals to Well-Being', Paper Presented at the Conference 'Capability and Happiness', Milano-Bicocca, 17 June 2005.

Farrel, D. and Rusbult, C.E. (1992), 'Exploring the Exit, Voice, Loyalty, and Neglect Typology: the Influence of Job Satisfaction, Quality of Alternatives, and Investment Size', *Employee Responsibilities and Rights Journal*, 5, pp. 201–218.

Frey, B. (1997), *Not Just for the Money: An Economic Theory of Personal Motivation*, Edward Elgar, Cheltenham.

Heyes, A. (2005), 'The Economics of Vocation, or "Why is a Badly-Paid Nurse a Good Nurse?"', *Journal of Health Economics*, 24, pp. 561–569.

Hirschman, A. (1982[1970]), *Exit, Voice and Loyalty. Response to Decline in Firms, Organizations and States*, Harvard University Press, Cambridge (MA).

Le Grand, J. (2003), *Motivation, Agency, and Public Policy. Of Knights & Knaves, Pawns & Queens*, Oxford University Press, Oxford.

Mitroff, I.I. and Denton, E.A. (1999), 'A Study of Spirituality in the Workplace', *Sloan Management Review*, 40, 4, pp. 83–92.

Molteni, M. (2009), 'Aziende a movente ideale', in Bruni, L. and Zamagni, S. (eds) *Dizionario di economia civile*, Città Nuova, Roma.

Stanca, L. Bruni, L. and Corazzini, L. (2009), 'Testing Theory of Reciprocity', *Journal of Economic Behavior and Organization*, 71, 2, pp. 233–245.

Wicksteed, P.H. (1933)[1910]), *The Common Sense of Political Economy*, Macmillan, London.

42. Virtue ethics and economics
Jean Mercier Ythier

ECONOMICS AS A MORAL SCIENCE

If ethics is the branch of knowledge that evaluates human action in terms of the good and the evil, than economics is, to a large extent and for essential parts of it, a branch of ethics.

Joseph Stiglitz's recent essay, *Freefall* (2010), displays a characteristic example of the interweaving of *ethical* and *analytic* considerations in the evaluation of a major economic crisis. Much of the argument concentrates on the perverse large-scale consequences of *cupidity* (that is, in analytic terms, profit-maximizing behavior) in ill-regulated financial markets.[1] On the *analytic* side of the thesis, the crisis is interpreted as a global ('systemic') market failure, and explained by the interplay of two types of imperfections of financial markets, namely, information imperfections and market incompleteness. It is shown how the race for financial and accounting innovation, sustained by the (partly illusory) benefits of financial development (i.e. the benefits of the endless efforts for completing incomplete capital markets), resulted in the massive under-evaluation of risk premiums for some financial products (pooled 'subprime' mortgage loans, principally); hence in severe deviations of the corresponding market prices from their 'fair' or 'efficient' values. On its *ethical* side, the chapter pictures the vivid portrait of professionals of finance who, blinded by the immediate prospect of enormous individual gains, opportunely lose sight of the longer-run prospect of enormous losses for themselves and, as a consequence of non-pecuniary externalities (an aspect of market failures), of still larger losses for society.

Stiglitz's analysis shares many common features with Keynes's analysis of the Great Depression.[2] The latter's distinction between the enterprise motive and the speculation motive of investors, in particular, displays an analogous combination of ethical appraisal and analytic explanation, closely intermingled. The economy according to Keynes's *General Theory* (1936) is locked in long-term unemployment by the bearish self-fulfilling prophecies of investors, driven mainly by irrational 'animal spirits'.[3] The focal point of Keynes's criticism is investors' irrationality. Speculation (the evil motive), construed as 'the activity of forecasting the psychology of the market', tends to predominate over enterprise (the good motive), defined as 'the activity of forecasting the prospective yield of assets over their whole life', because most investment decisions 'can only be taken out of animal spirits [. . .] and not as the outcome of a weighted average of quantitative benefits multiplied by quantitative probabilities' (Keynes 1936, Chap. 12: VI, VII). The whole analysis of this part of the *General Theory* implies, simultaneously, an *analytic* definition of investor's rationality as the maximization of carefully calculated expected profits, the expression of the author's deep skepticism about the validity of the former as a *description* of actual investors' behavior,[4] and the *ethical* appraisal of investors' motives on the basis of their overall human consequences (mass unemployment versus full employment).

The interweaving of the ethical evaluation of action motives (or consequences), on the one hand, and the analytic explanation of economic functioning, on the other, shows up in the history of economic analysis from its very beginnings, and notably in the economics of Aristotle (*Politics*: I, 8–11; *Nicomachean Ethics*: V, 5). The *Nicomachean Ethics* is of particular importance for the topic of this chapter, as one of the founding works of the virtue ethical tradition in normative ethics.[5] Chapter 5 of book V notably characterizes *commutative justice* as, essentially, an appropriate balance in the contractual relationships of market exchange; it also analyzes the role of *money* in exchange (an analysis that includes remarks on the conventional origin of money as a legal institution, and on the stability of its value over time). Joseph Schumpeter thus identifies Aristotle's economics as the first recorded contribution to analytic economics in his *History of Economic Analysis* (1954); and he discusses the relations of the two topics of economics of the *Ethics* above with their considerable posterity, namely, competitive market equilibrium as full-fledged analytic development of commutative justice, and macroeconomics as modern development of monetary theory.[6] Aristotle also applied his conceptual apparatus to his well-known ethical appraisal of economic activities. Economics, as the norm (nomos) of satisfaction of the needs of the community (oïkos), was distinguished from chrematistics, as the art of acquiring wealth; and the former was designated as the valuable ethical end of economic action. Commercial chrematistics, understood as the accumulation of money and wealth for its own sake, was criticized accordingly. Commercial profits and interest-bearing loans were assimilated to commercial chrematistics.

Schumpeter notes that Aristotle's criticism of interest and commercial profits is not implied by his analytic economics, and relates this observation to the weaknesses of Aristotle's conceptual apparatus as an economist, considered from the standpoint of the later developments of economic analysis (in Schumpeter's words, Aristotle's criticism is 'pre-analytic' on this matter: Schumpeter 1954, footnote 8, p. 61). Much of the progress in economic analysis that Schumpeter attributes to the scholastic doctors (*ibid*: I, 2) consisted of a progress in the understanding of the reasons why commercial profits and interest exist (why interest is paid *actually*, in particular). That is, it consisted of an accurate description of the *actual practices* of commerce and of its financing, and their *explanation* (*and justification*) through a conceptual framework consistent with these facts. A nice illustration is given by Schumpeter's transcription of St Thomas Aquinas's list of justifications, several of which can be understood as explanations, of commercial gains:

> (a) by the necessity of making one's living; or (b) by the wish to acquire means for charitable purposes; or (c) by the wish to serve *publicam utilitatem*, provided that the lucre be moderate and can be considered as a reward of work (*stipendium laboris*); or (d) by an improvement of the thing traded; or (e) by intertemporal or interlocal differences in its value; or (f) by risk (*propter periculum*). (*Ibid*, p. 87)

This enumeration is remarkable by its comprehensiveness, including the list of specifically economic reasons (d)–(f), which could be endorsed as such by any modern economic analysis of commercial profits.[7] The moral depreciation of commerce that St Thomas still expresses,[8] compared with the list above, appears as the expression of a moral (theological) sensibility detached, in the main, from any practical (social and ethical) criticism of commercial business. Concerning interest-bearing loans, the task of the scholastic doctors was made more difficult, but was also stimulated, by the ban on usury imposed by the Church (in 1311): 'the normative motive, so often the enemy of patient analytic work, in this instance both set the task and supplied the method for the scholastic analysts' (*ibid*, I, 2, p. 98). Schumpeter refers here to the necessity confronting scholastic doctors, in the context of their activities of directors of individual consciences, to elaborate a moral jurisprudence from the careful examination of the practices of commercial credit of their time. The accomplished analytic product of this (morally and theologically motivated) attention paid to this aspect of commercial practices was St Antonin's explanation (*and* justification) of interest in commercial loans by the *fact* that commercial credit is *normally productive*, that is, makes a positive contribution to commercial profits in the usual conditions of business.[9]

We may summarize the discussion above with a few general remarks, setting a first tentative framework for the discussion of moral issues in an economic context. Aristotle's view that the valuable ethical end of economic activities is the satisfaction of needs, as opposed to the accumulation of wealth, is not seriously disputed. It is usually complemented with a particular attention paid to the condition of labor, that is, employment and fair wage, for the simple reason that labor sustains the subsistence and welfare of most people (e.g. points (a) and (c) of Thomas Aquinas's list above). Fair wage is part of a general notion of commutative justice, the modern formulation of which is the (perfect) competitive equilibrium of general equilibrium theory. The latter is, jointly, an *ethical* and an *analytic* concept. As an ethical notion, it describes an ideal process of satisfaction of (subjective) individual needs in scarce resources, through individual transactions based on fair (that is, Pareto-efficient) prices. As an analytic notion, it describes the interdependence of individual decisions (demands and supplies of market commodities) through the formation of equilibrium prices in the ideal conditions above. Departures from these ideal conditions are the so-called market failures of economic theory. Capital markets are a major (potential) source of market failure, due notably to their incompleteness, and possibly also to price-manipulability (see note 7 above on the latter). Capital market failures involve the joint perturbation of value (deviations from efficient prices), money (credit crisis) and time (capital destruction), the severest form of which is a global crisis.

SELF-INTEREST VERSUS BENEVOLENCE: THE POSSIBILITY OF ALTRUISM[10]

Thomas Aquinas's list above is not only analytically comprehensive. It also points to the conception of a comprehensive social order, carefully balancing the relative positions of the sacred ((b): charity), the political ((c)), and the economic ((d)–(f)), through their ranks in the enumeration. This notion of a comprehensive social order, balancing appropriately the intellectual and the moral modes of understanding, is lost in the work of Adam Smith, if not as an intention, at least as a fact. His two main books, the *Theory of Moral Sentiments* (1759) and the *Inquiry into the Nature and Causes of the Wealth of Nations* (1776) are 'blocks cut out from a larger systematic whole' (Schumpeter 1954, I, 2, p. 137) that was never completed. The first one contains Smith's ethical theory, and the second one develops his economic analysis. The sharp contrast between the representations of human psychology and conduct conveyed by the two works fed a long lasting controversy about the so-called 'Adam Smith problem'.

The position that Smith occupies relative to our topic (normative ethics, economic analysis, and their relations) appears as singular as Aristotle's. He is a man of the Enlightenment. His work of moral philosophy was a significant, although not a decisive, contribution to the Enlightenment's re-founding of ethics on the precepts of universal reason. His work as an economist was recognized as the point of departure of economics as an autonomous social science. We very briefly situate, below, Smith's *Moral Sentiments* relative to the Enlightenment's revolution in ethics, and proceed next to a brief review of the posterity of *homo economicus* as an analytic device.

Moral Sentiments and the Ethics of the Enlightenment

Smith's ethical theory is built upon two main concepts, *sympathy* and the *impartial spectator*, the latter derived from the former. Sympathy consists of the disposition of human beings to imagine themselves in the shoes of others and experience to some extent the corresponding feelings: 'we enter as it were into his body, and become in some measure the same person with him' (Smith 2000[1759], I, 1, p. 4). These facts of imaginative empathy follow from the observation of the (moral) situation of others (say, the observation of somebody's grief, or joy) or from the observation of the (moral) relations between others (say, the observation of an act of beneficence). The impartial spectator is the moral self of individuals. It builds up progressively in the subjective conscience of everyone, through (what may be named) a converging learning process, which follows from the repeated exercise of sympathy in the various circumstances of moral life:

> As their sympathy makes them look at it [the individual's situation] in some measure with his eyes, so his sympathy makes him look at it, in some measure, with theirs [. . .] and, as the reflected passion which he thus conceives is much weaker than the original one, it necessarily abates the violence of what he felt [. . .] before he began to recollect in what manner they would be affected by it, and to view his situation in this candid and impartial light. (*Ibid*, I, 4, p. 24)

The *Moral Sentiments* were written in a critical period for the history of normative ethics. They followed the writings of Locke (1690), Hutcheson (1725) and Hume (1739) and preceded those of Rousseau (1762a, 1762b) and Kant (1785, 1788). The first exact formulations of the utilitarian principle as the greatest happiness of the greatest number appeared in Hutcheson (1725), Beccaria (1764) and Priestley (1768), before their complete development by Bentham (1789).[11] At the time of the French Revolution, the two main contributions of the Enlightenment to ethical theory had reached maturity, namely, *Kantian deontology*, which emphasizes duties and universal rules of conduct derived from the exercise of formal reason, and *utilitarianism*, which evaluates actions on the sole basis of their consequences on the total sum of individuals' pleasures and pains. The two of them stood in sharp contrast with the virtue ethics inherited from the Greek and Roman antiquity, and with the Christian moral theology elaborated by the Doctors of the Church.[12]

The *Theory of Moral Sentiments* occupies a singular and complex position in this spectrum of ethical theories, considered retrospectively. Its subject matter (the moral *sentiments* experienced by individuals in their sympathetic interactions) relates it closely to the British (actually, Scottish) sentimentalism of Hutcheson and Hume, and it appears, in this respect, poles apart from the formalism of Kant. But Smith's ethics also distinguishes sharply from Hutcheson's and Hume's (particularly from Hume's) by its dismissal of utility as a major (a fortiori as the unique) basis of moral approval, and by its overall distant appreciation of the emerging utilitarianism of his time.[13] Important aspects of the ethics of Adam Smith are, moreover, explicitly deontological, that is, they bestow a positive moral value upon duty-abiding and rule-following *per se*, independently of their consequences on the welfare of individuals or society.[14] Summing up, the impartial spectator of Adam Smith, born from sympathetic interactions, evaluates the propriety of actions on a pluralistic basis, which combines deontological, consequential and virtue-ethical criteria, in a balanced but predominantly deontological way.[15]

Homo economicus as an Analytic Device

Adam Smith's well-known observation that it 'is not from the benevolence of the butcher, the brewer, or the baker, that we can expect our dinner, but from their regard to their own interest' (Smith 1776, I, 2) was developed by subsequent economic analysis into an abstract representation of firms' and households' *rational* demand and supply of market commodities, summarized notably in households' demand functions that verify the following set of characterizing properties: (i) the determinants of individual demand and supply (that is, the arguments of demand functions) are market prices and individual wealth; (ii) households are not subject to monetary illusions (demand functions are homogeneous of degree 0); (iii) they spend their whole budget (demand functions are 'additive'); (iv) their demands and supplies of market commodities verify the *law of demand* (the matrix of coefficients of substitution of Slutsky is symmetric negative semi-definite). It was shown that households' market behavior verifies the four properties above *if and only if* this behavior results from the maximization, subject to the household's budget constraint, of an individual preference relation which is reflexive, complete and transitive (Antonelli 1886; Hicks 1939, I).[16] This abstract representation of rational market behavior serves two main purposes in economic analysis. As a *categorizing device*, it yields definitions of the substitution effects and income effects of variations in relative prices, and implies systematic relations between them. These substitution and income effects are measurable, by means of price and income elasticities notably, and their systematic relations can be tested empirically on microeconomic data. They play a central role in the description of actual market functioning. As a *theoretical device*, rational market behavior is, with competition assumptions, one of the two main building blocks of the theory of economic equilibrium, that is, of the (joint) explanation of the allocation of scarce resources and of the formation of market prices.[17]

Rational market behavior, as a hypothesis, has very few implications concerning the sympathetic interactions of individuals outside market exchange, if it has any. This point found its best expression in Wicksteed's *Common Sense of Political Economy* (1910). Contemporaneous works of Pareto (1913, 1916) reintroduced sympathy in the hardcore of economic analysis by extending his notion of optimum to (altruistic) interdependent utilities. I reviewed these and related contributions, and many of their modern extensions (Mercier Ythier 2006, 4). Two recent articles of mine (2010, 2011) provide a formal synthesis in the setup of the theory of competitive equilibrium with interdependent preferences of individuals. The latter defines a normative framework for an altruistic redistribution of individual wealth in a (competitive) market economy. Individuals have (ordinal, rational) preferences on: (i) their own consumption of market commodities, whose utility representation yields a notion of individual 'private' welfare (individual 'ophelimity', in Pareto's words); and (ii) the distribution of private welfare in society, whose utility representation yields a notion of individual 'social' welfare (individual 'utility', in Pareto's terms). An individual's social welfare may be increasing, constant or decreasing in another's private welfare. These forms of interdependence of individual utilities are interpreted as expressing, respectively, the benevolence, indifference and malevolence of the former individual, relative to the latter individual. Other-regarding concerns are thus conveyed by and captured through concerns relative to the distribution of private wealth and welfare (*distributive concerns*, in short). The distribution of private wealth and welfare is, in particular, a public good, as a common object of concern of the individual members of society (Kolm 1968, 1969; Hochman and Rodgers 1969). A *liberal social contract* (Kolm, 1985) relative to the distribution of private wealth and welfare is defined, from these premises, as a Pareto optimum relative to individuals' distributive preferences, which is unanimously preferred, in terms of the latter preferences, to the market equilibrium achieved prior to social contract transfers. One of the basic properties of this social contract bears direct relation to the topic of the present section, namely, the separability property, which states, essentially, that the allocation of resources of the social contract is a competitive market equilibrium (Mercier Ythier 2011, 4). In other words, the invisible hand of market exchange, driven by the *unsympathetic* motives of rational market behavior, contributes to the achievement of a social (Pareto) optimum determined from the *sympathetic* (altruistic) motives embodied in individuals' social preferences. That is, the efficiency gains that stem from competitive market exchange, properly distributed, contribute to the satisfaction of (distributive) altruism in society. The conditions that underlie this solution to the Adam Smith problem are outlined in Mercier Ythier (2010, 3; 2011, 4.4). Let us briefly mention those that pertain to altruism. It is shown, firstly, that social contract redistribution, if any, follows from distributive benevolence (non-benevolent 'transfer paradoxes' are banned, by construction, from social contract redistribution: *ibid* 2010, 3). And it is recalled, secondly, that social optimum entails competitive market equilibrium only if malevolence, if any, is not so strong and widespread as to induce the disposal of some fraction of aggregate resources at social optimum (*ibid* 2011, 4.4). In particular, civil peace appears as a common foundation and/or joint consequence of market exchange and social contract redistribution in this construct.

A considerable economic literature, originating notably in contributions of Olson (1965) and Becker (1974), studies the implications of utility-maximizing behavior in *non-market* environments such as the family, charities or the workplace. Many of these works are reviewed and evaluated in Kolm and Mercier Ythier (2006). The main characteristics of their representation of individual behaviors and interactions may be briefly outlined as follows: (i) individuals are utility-maximizers; (ii) individual preferences exhibit some type of *common concern*, which may follow, notably, from the existence of institutional public goods (as in Olson 1965), from distributive altruism in the sense above (as in Becker 1974), or from interactions per se (as in the reciprocity games considered in Kolm (2006), 13, or reviewed in Fehr and Schmidt 2006, 3.3); (iii) individuals interact notably through *voluntary transfers*; (iv) social equilibrium is a *non-cooperative Nash equilibrium* of the transfer game (subgame perfect equilibrium, when appropriate). Models' predictions are tested on empirical data produced from statistical surveys, from behavioral experiments, and also, more recently, from brain imaging techniques. The main findings of this literature relate to *individual motives*, and notably to: the elicitation of other-regarding motives and the demonstration of their determinate influence on individual behaviors, relative to alternative determinants such as (self-interested) strategic sophistication, or social norms; the assessment of the respective influence of various other-regarding motives such as altruism, fairness, malevolence or envy; the assessment of the respective influence on individual decisions of transfer (and punishment), of instrumental motives, versus intrinsic motives such as a joy or 'warm glow' of giving (or pleasure of punishing).[18] In spite of a common foundation in utility-maximizing behavior, the abstract representation of human conduct conveyed by these studies is not anymore a *homo economicus*, clearly, for reasons which follow jointly from the wide array of individual motives invoked and from the fact that the studied interactions take place, in the main, outside market exchange. The new (conceptual) specie was baptized *homo reciprocans*. We wish it a nice evolution.

NOTES

1. The title of the French translation *Le triomphe de la cupidité* (the triumph of cupidity) is more explicit still than the original in this respect.
2. There are important differences also, which notably follow from the differences between the two global crises. Stiglitz strongly emphasizes the large bonuses paid to traders in the worst of the financial crisis. Some lessons were drawn from the Great Depression: proactive economic policies (and the robustness of the economies of the new industrialized countries) prevented the transformation of financial collapse into general economic breakdown. In some sense, the financial system benefitted from a form of public insurance that consolidated a part of its large incomes, so opening the way to the (moral and political) criticism of the latter. During the Great Depression, there were no large bonuses to deplore, only large (financial and 'real') losses to regret. Attention concentrated, accordingly, on the devastating 'real' consequences of financial panics.
3. Animal spirits was a technical term of the vocabulary of the psychiatry of the 18th Century, used in essentially the same sense as the modern 'nerve impulse' (e.g. Michel Foucault (1972), II, 3). Keynes's own definition of animal spirits as 'a spontaneous urge to action rather than inaction', while broadly consistent with this former use of the notion, clearly suggests much more. It resonates, metaphorically, with at least three possible dimensions of irrationality: madness (through the connection with psychiatry), animal behavior, and also religious beliefs (animism, for example).
4. An aspect of Keynes's criticism, namely, the idea that the practical 'basis for such calculations [of expected profits] does not exist', stimulated subsequent progresses in decision theory, particularly the theory of expected utility with subjective probabilities of Savage (1954), which showed that rational decision making under uncertainty can dispense with the calculation of the objective probabilities of events. The criticism of the descriptive validity of the theory immediately rebounded with the Allais paradox (1953), displaying the contradiction between the independence axiom of the theory and the choices performed actually by individuals in experimental lotteries. This historical sequence is a case of fructuous confrontation of agents' *motives*, *rationality assumptions*, and *facts*. Elster's *Traité Critique de l'Homme Economique* (2009, 2010) is a nice recent example of a work built on this same basic epistemic pattern. It is divided into two (equal) volumes, *Le Désintéressement* (*The Disinterestedness*, 2009) that discusses the substantive motives of action, and *L'Irrationalité* (2010) that assesses the rationality assumptions of economic theory.
5. The other founding work is Plato's, as far as the Western philosophical tradition is concerned. The (considerable) Chinese tradition of virtue ethics originates in the *Analects* of Confucius (see (1998) for a recent edition in English). Virtue ethics distinguishes from other approaches of normative ethics by its grounding of the moral evaluation of conduct on the substantive virtues (such as honesty, generosity,

courage etc.) that motivate action. See, for example, the virtue ethics entry of the *Stanford Encyclopedia of Philosophy* (2012) for a concise introduction.

6. Schumpeter (1954, I, 1) clearly endorses the genetic relation between Aristotle's notion of commutative justice (and related notions of economic value) and the modern theory of competitive equilibrium, but seems more reluctant to acknowledge the most modern aspects of Aristotle's conception of money, in particular the latter's clear recognition of the conventional character of the monetary institution (the 'social contrivance of money', to use a famous phrase of Paul Samuelson (1958)). Schumpeter confines, too restrictively it may be argued, the Aristotelian conception of money to its role as a physical medium of exchange (a useful substitute for barter exchange), that is, to the conception of money that prevailed in the economic analysis of the eighteenth and nineteenth centuries (Schumpeter 1954, note 6).

7. Reason (e) occupies a singular position in this list, and may be viewed as a valid *analytic* reason to consider that the commercial (and financial) incomes proceeding from this source should be submitted, more than other types of incomes, to social, political or ethical evaluation and control. It refers to the so-called *arbitrage* activities (that is, the activity of purchasing commodities at some price, place and time, in order to sell them at a larger price at some other place or time). Arbitrage plays an essential role in the actual process of price formation. *Profitable* arbitrage is excluded, *by construction*, in the ideal representation of market functioning conveyed by competitive equilibrium theory: The making of equilibrium prices is performed, in the latter, by a *fictitious* agent (Arrow and Debreu 1954), the 'Walrasian auctioneer' or simply the 'Market', selecting prices in order to maximize the value of aggregate excess demand, and making no profit out of this 'activity' since excess demand vanishes by definition at equilibrium and out-of-equilibrium states are 'suspended', so to speak, that is, (should) last vanishingly short lapses of time. A critical *normative* aspect of competitive equilibrium is the *non-manipulability* of market prices, be it for individual profit or for any other *non-consensual* reason or 'interest' (e. g. political or otherwise; see Mercier Ythier (2010), p. 3, for an informal discussion of the public good characters of market prices and of non-manipulability as a normative feature of competitive equilibrium). Stiglitz's and Keynes's criticisms of financial markets mentioned above can be interpreted as a contention that *actual* (hence imperfect) capital market prices *are* manipulated, for *short-run profit*.

8. '*Negotiatio secundum se considerate quandam turpitudina habet*', *Summa Theologica*, II, 2, quaest. LXXVII, art. 4, quoted from Schumpeter (1954), p. 87.

9. This short summary does not render justice, of course, to the wealth and subtlety of Schumpeter's historical account. One aspect, among many, which is overlooked here is the link that he emphasizes between the development of economic activities on the one hand (the expansion of commerce and commercial credit, for the period under consideration), and the progresses in their intellectual understanding and moral acceptance on the other. Schumpeter clearly suggests a causal influence of the evolution of economic practices on the evolution of their mental representations in economic analysis and in moral discourse. Our chapter, conditioned by the topic of this section, focuses on the last two terms of these three-dimensional dynamics (the intellectual and moral comprehension of practices). Note that the word 'progress' can be understood here in two compatible senses: normatively, as improvement, or positively, as a fact of historical evolution. While Schumpeter obviously endorses the normative interpretation as far as his main object is concerned (economic analysis), his overall conception does belong to the wide family of (positive) evolutionary theories.

10. The title of this section paraphrases Thomas Nagel's influential *Possibility of Altruism* (1970).

11. See Schumpeter (1954), I, Chap. 3, notably 7-(b), 7-(c) and 7-(g).

12. The latter distinguishes: on the one hand, *cardinal* or human virtues, mainly Prudence, Justice, Fortitude and Temperance; and, on the other hand, the three *theological* virtues of Faith, Hope and Charity, which have God as their object (Aquinas II, 2).

13. See notably *Moral Sentiments*: Part II, Section II, Chap. III, pp. 129–132: 'But though it commonly requires no great discernment to see the destructive tendency of all licentious practices to the welfare of society, it is seldom this consideration which first animates us against them. . .'; and Part IV, Chap. II, pp. 271–277: 'But still I affirm, that it is not the view of this utility or hurtfulness which is either the first or principal source of our approbation or disapprobation. . .'. Smith views utility as a major source of *esthetical* (rather than ethical) value (Smith 1759).

14. *Ibid*, Part III, Chap. VI, pp. 249–254, and Part VI, Section III. Alasdair MacIntyre (1981) emphasizes the flavor of stoicism of Smith's ethics, and the corresponding differences between his and Hume's lists of virtues (Smith's praise of the virtue of self-command, particularly) in his influential contribution to the contemporary revival of virtue ethics (MacIntyre 1981, pp. 234–235). The marked deontological features of Smith's ethics explain also, presumably, why Michael Slote omits him as a source of inspiration of his own sentimentalist virtue ethics: he only refers to Hutcheson, Hume and Martineau (Slote 2001, p. 20). Slote's virtue ethics is remarkable notably by its homogeneity and consistency. It is similar to utilitarianism in almost all respects, except for a single (albeit, of course, essential) feature: it grounds its appraisal of actions on the benevolent *motive* that drives them (its presence (or not), and the quality of the motive

(its authenticity, spontaneity etc.)), whereas utilitarianism grounds it on the welfare enhancements that (may) result from the benevolent action. The ethics developed by Hume, Smith and Slote from a common sentimentalist origin may be characterized, respectively, as mainly (utilitarian) consequentialist, predominantly deontological, and fully (agent-based) virtue-ethical.

15. Sen makes use of the deontological aspects of the Smithian ethics of the impartial spectator that underlies his *Idea of Justice*, particularly in his development on the obligations of power (Sen 2009, II, 9, pp. 205–207).

16. See Mas-Colell (1985, 1, 2; Mas-Colell et al 1995, I) for one of the best contemporary accounts of demand and supply theory. Following a standard usage, we name *rational* preference relation any (binary) preference relation R over a set of alternatives X, which is reflexive (that is, xRx for all $x \in X$), complete (that is, either xRy or yRx for all $(x,y) \in X \times X$) and transitive (xRy and yRz imply xRz). xRy reads 'x is at least as good as y'. For the sake of brevity, we name *utility-maximizing behavior* the behavior (that is, agent's choice in a context) which follows from the maximization of a (context-independent) rational preference relation over any set of accessible acts (agent's context of choice, subset of X). Utility refers here to any (ordinal) utility representation of the preference relation, that is, to any real-valued function $u:X \to \mathbb{R}$ such that $u(x) \geq u(y) \Leftrightarrow xRy$. It is trivial to show that utility representations exist (actually, infinitely many of them) whenever the set of alternatives is finite. Existence extends to infinite sets of alternatives provided that the preference relation verifies, in addition, suitable properties of continuity and non-satiation (Debreu 1959, 4.6).

17. The symmetry of the Slutsky matrix is more difficult to interpret and justify, in behavioral terms, than the other characteristic properties of rational market behavior. It is also usually rejected in empirical tests on household data, except for single person households (Browning and Chiappori 1998). Symmetry means that the effect of a marginal increase of the price of any commodity (say, commodity j) on the (compensated, if applicable) demand or supply of any other commodity (say, commodity i, $i \neq j$) is equal to the effect of a marginal increase of the price of commodity i on the demand or supply of commodity j. Dropping symmetry is equivalent, in terms of implied rationality assumptions, to replacing the strong axiom of revealed preference by the weak variant of this axiom (Mas-Colell 1985, 2.9). The strong axiom of revealed preference, applied to consumer's budget sets, is logically equivalent to consumer's utility maximization (subject to consumer's budget constraint; see Mas-Colell et al 1995, 3.J). The weak axiom of revealed preference remains, nevertheless, equivalent to utility maximization if it is applied to any subset of up to three elements of the set of alternatives (see Mas-Colell et al 1995, 1.D). An alternative theory of market behavior would qualify as unambiguously better than the theory of rational market behavior (including the variants briefly evoked above) if it could serve the same general purposes in a more accurate and comprehensive way than the latter. This has not been achieved yet, as far as I know.

18. Other-regarding individual motives are discussed pervasively throughout Kolm and Mercier Ythier (2006), but more extensively and systematically in the chapters by Schokkaert (2), Elster (3), Mercier Ythier (5), Kolm (6), Lévy-Garboua et al (7), Fehr and Schmidt (8), Sacco et al (9), Bardsley and Sugden (10), Laferrère and Wolff (13), Arrondel and Masson (14), Docquier and Rapoport (17), Andreoni (18), Rotemberg (21), Putterman (22), and Fong et al (23). See also Elster 2009, I, on the same topic.

REFERENCES

Allais, M. (1953). 'Le comportement de l'homme rationnel devant le risque, critique des postulats et axiomes de l'école Américaine', *Econometrica* 21: 503–46.

Andreoni, J. (2006). 'Philanthropy', in S.-C. Kolm and J. Mercier Ythier (eds), *Handbook of the Economics of Giving, Altruism and Reciprocity*, Amsterdam: North-Holland, Chapter 18, pp. 1201–70.

Antonelli, G.B. (1886). *Sulla teoria matematica della economia politica*, Pisa: Tipografia del Folchetto (translated as Chapter 16 in J. Chipman, L. Hurwicz, M. Richter and H. Sonnenschein (eds) (1971). *Preferences, Utility and Demand*, New York: Harcourt Brace Jovanovich, pp. 336–64.

Aquinas, Thomas (1981). *Summa Theologica*, Notre Dame, IN: Christian Classics.

Aristotle (2005). *Nicomachean Ethics*, Cambridge: Cambridge University Press.

Aristotle (1996). *Politics*, Cambridge: Cambridge University Press.

Arrondel, L. and A. Masson (2006). 'Altruism, exchange or indirect reciprocity: What do the date on family transfers show?', in S.-C. Kolm and J. Mercier Ythier (eds), *Handbook of the Economics of Giving, Altruism and Reciprocity*, Amsterdam: North-Holland, Chapter 14, pp. 971–1054.

Arrow, K.J. and G. Debreu (1954). 'Existence of an equilibrium for a competitive economy', *Econometrica* 22: 265–290.

Bardsley N. and R. Sugden (2006). 'Human nature and sociality in economics', in S.-C. Kolm and J. Mercier

Ythier (eds), *Handbook of the Economics of Giving, Altruism and Reciprocity*, Amsterdam: North-Holland, Chapter 10, pp. 731–70.

Beccaria, C. (1995[1764]). *Dei Delitti e delle Pene* (English translation *On Crimes and Punishments*, Cambridge: Cambridge University Press).

Becker, G.S. (1974). 'A theory of social interactions', *Journal of Political Economy* 82: 1063–93.

Bentham, J. (1996[1789]). *Introduction to Principles of Morals and Legislation*, reprint Oxford: Oxford University Press.

Browning, M. and P.-A. Chiappori (1998). 'Efficient intra-household allocations: A general characterization and empirical tests', *Econometrica* 66, 1241–78.

Confucius (1998). *The Analects*, New York: Ballantine Books.

Debreu, G. (1959). *Theory of Value*, New York: Wiley.

Docquier, F. and H. Rapoport (2006). 'The economics of migrants' remittances', in S.-C. Kolm and J. Mercier Ythier (eds), *Handbook of the Economics of Giving, Altruism and Reciprocity*, Amsterdam: North-Holland, Chapter 17, pp. 1371–1408.

Elster, J. (2006). 'Altruistic behaviour and altruistic motivations', in S.-C. Kolm and J. Mercier Ythier (eds), *Handbook of the Economics of Giving, Altruism and Reciprocity*, Amsterdam: North-Holland, Chapter 3, pp. 183–206.

Elster, J. (2009). *Le Désintéressement. Traité Critique de l'Homme Economique I*, Paris: Seuil.

Elster, J. (2010). *L'Irrationalité. Traité Critique de l'Homme Economique II*, Paris: Seuil.

Fehr, E. and K.M. Schmidt (2006). 'The economics of fairness, reciprocity and altruism-Experimental evidence and new theories', in S.-C. Kolm and J. Mercier Ythier (eds), *Handbook of the Economics of Giving, Altruism and Reciprocity*, Amsterdam: North-Holland, Chapter 8, pp. 615–94.

Fong, C. M., S. Bowles and H. Gintis (2006). 'Strong reciprocity and the welfare state', in S.-C. Kolm and J. Mercier Ythier (eds), *Handbook of the Economics of Giving, Altruism and Reciprocity*, Amsterdam: North-Holland, Chapter 23, pp. 1439–64.

Foucault, M. (1972). *Histoire de la Folie à l'Age Classique*, Paris: Gallimard.

Hicks, J.R. (1939). *Value and Capital*, London: Oxford University Press.

Hochman, H.M. and J.D. Rodgers (1969). 'Pareto optimal redistribution', *American Economic Review* 59: 542–57.

Hume, D. (1978[1739]). *A Treatise of Human Nature*, reprint Oxford: Oxford University Press.

Hutcheson, F. (2001[1725]). *An Inquiry into the Original of Our Ideas of Beauty and Virtue*, reprint Boston, MA: Adamant Media Corporation.

Kant, I. (2002[1785]). *Groundwork of the Metaphysics of Morals*, reprint Oxford: Oxford University Press.

Kant, I. (2003[1788]). *Critique of Practical Reason*, reprint Cambridge: Cambridge University Press.

Keynes, J.M. (1936). *The General Theory of Employment, Interest and Money*, London: Macmillan.

Kolm, S.-Ch. (1966), 'The optimal production of social justice', in H. Guitton, and J. Margolis (eds), *Proceedings of the International Economic Association on Public Economics*, Biarritz; Economie Publique, CNRS: Paris, 1968, pp. 109–177; Public Economics (Macmillan: London, 1969) 145–200.

Kolm, S.-Ch. (1985). *Le Contrat Social Libéral*, Paris: Presses Universitaires de France.

Kolm, S.-Ch. (2006). 'Reciprocity: Its scope, rationales, and consequences', in S.-C. Kolm and J. Mercier Ythier (eds), *Handbook of the Economics of Giving, Altruism and Reciprocity*, Amsterdam: North-Holland, Chapter 6, pp. 371–541.

Kolm, S. Ch and J. Mercier Ythier (2006). *Handbook of the Economics of Giving, Altruism and Reciprocity*, Amsterdam: North-Holland.

Laferrère, A. and F.-C. Wolff (2006). 'Microeconomic models of family transfers', in S.-C. Kolm and J. Mercier Ythier (eds), *Handbook of the Economics of Giving, Altruism and Reciprocity*, Amsterdam: North-Holland, Chapter 13, pp. 889–970.

Lévy-Garboua, L., Meidinger, C. and B. Rapoport (2006). 'The formation of social preferences: Some lessons from psychology and biology', in S.-C. Kolm and J. Mercier Ythier (eds), *Handbook of the Economics of Giving, Altruism and Reciprocity*, Amsterdam: North-Holland, Chapter 7, pp. 545–613.

Locke, J. (1960[1690]). *Second Treatise of Government*, reprint Cambridge: Cambridge University Press.

MacIntyre, A. (2007[1981]). *After Virtue*, reprint Notre Dame, IN: University of Notre Dame Press.

Mas-Colell, A. (1985). *The Theory of General Equilibrium. A Differentiable Approach*, London: Cambridge University Press.

Mas-Colell, A., M.D. Whinston and Jerry R. Green (1995). *Microeconomic Theory*, New York, Oxford: Oxford University Press.

Mercier Ythier, J. (2006). 'The economic theory of gift-giving: Perfect substitutability of transfers and redistribution of wealth', in S.-C. Kolm and J. Mercier Ythier (eds), *Handbook of the Economics of Giving, Altruism and Reciprocity*, Amsterdam: North-Holland, Chapter 5, pp. 227–339.

Mercier Ythier, J. (2010). 'Regular distributive efficiency and the distributive liberal social contract', *Journal of Public Economic Theory* 12: 943–78.

Mercier Ythier (2011). 'Optimal redistribution in the distributive liberal social contract', in M. Fleurbaey, M. Salles and J.A. Weymark (eds), *Social Ethics and Normative Economics. Essays in honor of Serge-Christophe Kolm*, Berlin, Heidelberg: Springer-Verlag, pp. 303–26.

Nagel, T. (1970). *The Possibility of Altruism*, Princeton, NJ: Princeton University Press.

Olson, M. (1965). *The Logic of Collective Action*, Cambridge, MA: Harvard University Press.

Pareto, V. (1913). 'Il massimo di utilità per una colletività', *Giornale degli Economisti* 3: 337–341.

Pareto, V. (1916). *Traité de Sociologie Générale*, Genève: Droz.

Priestley, J. (2009[1768]). *Essay on the First Principles of Government*, reprint Michigan: University of Michigan Library.

Putterman, L. (2006). 'Reciprocity, altruism and cooperative production', in S.-C. Kolm and J. Mercier Ythier (eds), *Handbook of the Economics of Giving, Altruism and Reciprocity*, Amsterdam: North-Holland, Chapter 22, pp. 1409–38.

Rotemberg, J.J. (2006). 'Altruism, reciprocity and cooperation in the workplace', in S.-C. Kolm and J. Mercier Ythier (eds), *Handbook of the Economics of Giving, Altruism and Reciprocity*, Amsterdam: North-Holland, Chapter 21, pp. 1371–1408.

Rousseau, J.-J. (2001[1762a]). *Du Contrat Social*, reprint Paris: Garnier-Flammarion.

Rousseau, J.-J. (1966[1762b]). *Emile ou De l'Éducation*, reprint Paris: Garnier-Flammarion.

Sacco, P.L., P. Vanin and S. Zamagni (2006). 'The economics of human relationships', in S.-C. Kolm and J. Mercier Ythier (eds), *Handbook of the Economics of Giving, Altruism and Reciprocity*, Amsterdam: North-Holland, Chapter 9, pp. 695–730.

Samuelson, P.A. (1958). 'An exact consumption-loan model with or without the social contrivance of money', *Journal of Political Economy* 66: 467–82.

Savage, L. (1954). *The Foundations of Statistics*, New York: Wiley.

Schokkaert, E. (2006). 'The empirical analysis of transfer motives', in S.-C. Kolm and J. Mercier Ythier (eds), *Handbook of the Economics of Giving, Altruism and Reciprocity*, Amsterdam: North-Holland, Chapter 2, pp. 127–82.

Schumpeter, J.A. (1954). *History of Economic Analysis*, New York: Oxford University Press.

Sen, A. (2009). *The Idea of Justice*, London: Penguin Books.

Slote, M. (2001). *Morals from Motives*, Oxford: Oxford University Press.

Smith, A. (2000[1759]). *The Theory of Moral Sentiments*, reprint New York: Prometheus Books.

Smith, A. (1976[1776]). *An Inquiry into the Nature and Causes of the Wealth of Nations*, reprint Oxford: Clarendon Press.

Stanford Encyclopedia of Philosophy (2012). http://plato.stanford.edu/entries/ethics-virtue/ (last accessed March 2012).

Stiglitz, J.E. (2010). *Freefall*, New York: W.W. Norton & Company.

Wicksteed, P.H. (1910). *The Common Sense of Political Economy*, London: Macmillan.

43. Voluntary organizations
Dennis R. Young, Lewis Faulk and Jasmine McGinnis

OVERVIEW

People create organizations for a wide variety of reasons. At one end of the spectrum, communities or whole societies form governments in order to provide essential public goods such as defense, public safety, justice, environmental protection or a social safety net that would not otherwise be provided efficiently by the free market. In these cases, government is a solution to the free rider problem because it has the power of coercion to require people in a jurisdiction to contribute to the public good through taxation (Olson, 1965). In this instance, formal organizations such as government service bureaus or regulatory bodies are mandated to carry out the statutory provisions established in law by government. Within these organizations, people work under employment contracts in exchange for compensation packages specified by administrative law, influenced by labor markets and sometimes determined through negotiated union agreements.

At the other end of the formal organization spectrum is the private business corporation. Businesses are designed to carry out commercial activity more efficiently than a regime of individual contractual obligations by economizing on transactions costs. As initially developed by Coase (1937) in his theory of the firm, organizations will form and continue to grow in scope and size as long as the marginal cost of bringing an additional transaction inside the firm is less than the marginal cost of an equivalent market-based transaction with contractors outside the organization. People who work in for-profit organizations do so basically for economic reasons and are bound by quid pro quo contracts that require certain work to be done in exchange for material compensation as specified in their contracts.

Between the government organization and the business corporation, there is a vast array of other kinds of organizations that have attributes of both government organizations and profit-making corporations, but also substantially entail other motivations and mechanisms not specifically related to the quest for profits or the implementation of statutory mandates. These organizations can be driven substantially by altruism or a desire to achieve a public good and may operate through a regime of reciprocity wherein participants respond to mutual expectations without formal contracts. Altruism can drive the formation of organizations in which individual interests in public goods are sufficiently strong to overcome free rider effects. In particular, altruism can lead to organizations that form where government fails to provide the desired public goods either at all or in sufficient quantity to satisfy those with very strong demands (Weisbrod, 1975). Altruistic organizations can be held together through a combination of formal contractual obligations and reciprocity. That is, just as in government organizations or business corporations, individuals can be employed through quid pro quo market-based contracts to carry out the intent of the contributing altruists. Typically, this would take the form of a nonprofit organization that hires a staff to carry out its work. But altruistic organizations may also depend primarily on reciprocity where contributors benefit from each others' efforts and there is no formal contract to ensure a particular exchange of value for work, or even any paid staff to do the work. Democratically organized cooperatives of various kinds would fit this description, as would a variety of partnership arrangements and associations among individuals and organizations that operate without formal contracts and depend on mutual expectations, social obligations and goodwill.

The present chapter considers the latter classes of organizations that depend to a substantial degree on altruistic motivations and reciprocity. We use the term 'voluntary organization' to describe this class of organizations and apply this frame of reference in a cross-cutting manner that largely encompasses nonprofit organizations, cooperatives, partnership arrangements and membership associations. It is especially important to note that there are no clean boundaries between voluntary organizations and commercial and statutory organizations. Indeed, so-called 'hybrid' organizations that combine elements of these organizational types in various ways are increasingly common and require explicit recognition and attention (Billis, 2010).

In the next section, we review definitions and classifications of voluntary organizations in the literature. We follow this with a description of alternative scenarios through which voluntary organizations develop and take their place in the ecology of organizations. We then consider how voluntary organizations work in different circumstances, according to the kinds of goods or functions they provide, and the various strategies available to them to ensure cooperation. We conclude by identifying research issues for future study.

DEFINITIONS AND CLASSIFICATIONS

There is no single accepted definition of a 'voluntary organization.' Indeed this term is widely applied to nonprofit organizations, associations, cooperatives and other noncommercial, nongovernmental forms. Is there a pure form of voluntary organization, or is this simply a broad category encompassing a spectrum of related forms? With the focus on the nature of individual participation, Smith (1982) distinguishes between *volunteer* organizations whose goals are mainly accomplished by volunteers rather than paid staff and *voluntary* organizations that are driven substantially by paid staff. In later work, Smith (1997a; 1997b; 2000) describes a large but previously understudied segment of the nonprofit sector composed of volunteer organizations, which he terms 'grassroots associations.' His distinction between grassroots associations and the rest of the nonprofit sector is premised on a definition of a grassroots association as being 'locally based, significantly autonomous, volunteer-run, formal, nonprofit groups that have an official membership of volunteers and that manifest significant voluntary altruism' (Smith, 1997, p. 115). Wilderom and Miner (1991) make the distinction more sharply between 'voluntary groups', operating with volunteers only, and 'voluntary agencies' that engage at least one paid employee, citing various literature claiming that inclusion of paid staff reduces the vitality of volunteers as an organization's primary driving force. Enjolras (2000) cites four mechanisms – markets (prices), hierarchies, civic (coercion) and reciprocity – through which different kinds of organizations 'coordinate' themselves. The pure voluntary (or volunteer) organization depends solely on reciprocity, which involves 'a mutually contingent exchange of gratifications between two or more units' (Enjolras, p. 352 citing Gouldner, 1960). Less 'pure' voluntary organizations involve a mix of coordinating mechanisms; indeed, Enjolras argues that (impure) voluntary organizations, specifically democratically governed nonprofit organizations, are essentially a response to market, civic *and* reciprocity failures.

Van Der Meer, Te Grotenhuis and Scheepers (2009), in their international survey, find that voluntary organizations, broadly conceived, address three general purposes: recreational purposes, representing/advocating the interests of their members and advocating broad societal interests. Their analysis shows that voluntary organizations operating in these different spheres of activity also differ along the lines of membership, participation, volunteering and donation of money. These organizations and associations may be formally incorporated or informally organized, and they often operate in formal or informal networks of organizations and individuals with common interests, especially in pursuing advocacy within broader social movements (Rucht, 2010).

Researchers have also developed generic taxonomies within broad sub-classifications of voluntary organizations. For example, Spear (2000) distinguishes between consumer and producer cooperatives. Hansmann (1980; 1996) further distinguishes cooperatives from member-controlled nonprofits (which do not distribute profits to members) and differentiates among nonprofit organizations on the basis of their financing (commercial vs. donative) and governance (democratic vs. entrepreneurial). While these various forms of voluntary organizations differ in many respects, scholars also cite their similarities. For example, Spear (2000) identifies common theoretical reasons for the emergence of cooperatives and nonprofit organizations, more generally understood as 'social enterprises,' that form in response to market and government failures, social entrepreneurship and contextual (historical) factors. And Ben-Ner argues that the efficacy of nonprofit organizations in addressing market failure is related to their similarity to consumer cooperatives (Ben-Ner, 1986; Rose-Ackerman, 1996). In general, Enjolras (2000) argues that voluntary organizations are able to address market failures because they can combine reciprocity with hierarchic and market mechanisms in various ways under a system of democratic governance.

EVOLUTION AND THEORY OF VOLUNTARY ORGANIZATIONS

No one really knows how human beings began to form organizations. Anthropological studies suggest that hunter-gatherer bands dispersed their young members to mate with members of other bands, thus creating familial foundations for tribes that embraced internal cooperation. This process could give such tribes an evolutionary advantage when threatened (Wade, 2011b; Chapais, 2008). A new analysis suggests that tribes developed around religious ideas deriving from worship of common ancestors, and that warfare among tribes ultimately led to the development of states which were more efficient in providing defense or undertaking aggression (Wade, 2011a; Fukuyama, 2011).

However it all began, voluntary organizations appear to have been essential to human societal development. After tribes, the first organizations might have been voluntary ones, resulting from an exchange of gifts or favors between tribes to address a common problem or opportunity, such as a threat from another tribe, need for a more reliable food supply or protection against animal predators. New pursuits are often first undertaken in a voluntary framework and sometimes later commercialized or assumed as a function of government. For example, Lakdawalla and Philipson (2006) argue that nonprofits are the first to enter an industry and last to exit; these authors also show that nonprofits have higher rates of entry but that learning-by-doing leads to greater economic profits and higher rates of conversion from nonprofit to for-profit industries over time (Lakdawalla and Philipson, 1997). In modern times, care for ill or less fortunate members of society developed first through voluntary organizations, settlement houses and immigrant societies. In ancient Greece, Socrates' academy was essentially a voluntary organization, though schools have since developed in both commercial and governmental forms.

The actual evolutionary sequence through which voluntary organizations have emerged is probably not terribly relevant. We can just as well accept that states evolved directly from tribes because tribes needed protection, and strong states led by coercive leaders were best positioned to impose that protection. Or we can imagine the first organizations to be commercial because tribes found it worthwhile to trade goods with one another, on an explicit quid pro quo basis. If voluntary organizations emerged first, they were certain to be displaced by states and commercial organizations where the latter were more efficient. And if states or businesses evolved first, they were certainly not successful in serving all human needs, leaving ecological space for voluntary organizations to emerge. The latter scenarios largely reflect contemporary theory on why voluntary organizations exist in modern societies. Modern theory of nonprofit organizations is essentially one of government and market failures, wherein information asymmetries and public goods characteristics of various products and services in a market economy and democratic society require voluntary organization supplementation and/or substitution for commercial or governmental provision (Rose-Ackerman, 1996). Indeed, the same argument is made for the cooperative form by Spear (2000), who also adds excessive market power by private operators as another aspect of market failure that cooperatives help to moderate.

Essentially theories of voluntary organization stipulate that under particular circumstances, these organizations enjoy certain competitive advantages compared to other forms. Thus, over time, they emerge to occupy important niches in the ecology of organizations. For nonprofit organizations, Rose-Ackerman (1996) summarizes these advantages as greater trustworthiness deriving from a non-distribution of profits constraint, from decision-making structures that permit greater consumer control and from a looser accountability from investors that permits entrepreneurs to pursue ideological and value-based agendas. This greater trustworthiness gives nonprofits a competitive advantage where consumers or funders are poorly positioned to judge the quality or efficiency of services. Similarly, Enjolras (2000) argues that nonprofits that are democratically governed can overcome the coordination failures of hierarchies, markets and pure reciprocity, and hence are better positioned to succeed where governments, businesses and pure volunteer groups are likely to fail. Lakdawalla and Philipson (2006) also argue that by operating for altruistic rather than profit motives, nonprofits hold a competitive cost advantage over for-profit firms, allowing them to set their prices lower than for-profits.

HOW COOPERATION WORKS IN VOLUNTARY ORGANIZATIONS

Perhaps owing to the diversity of scenarios under which voluntary organizations may form, and certainly due to the variety of purposes they serve, these organizations require a range of structural mechanisms and management strategies to maintain cooperation and perform their work. Economic theory explains how cooperation works in diverse circumstances, primarily relating to the nature of the good and/or service produced and the externalities that may result from their production.

Voluntary organizations, broadly defined, produce a variety of economic goods and services along a spectrum ranging from pure private goods to pure public goods (see Figure 43.1). *Purely private goods* are fully rival and excludable such that two individuals cannot consume the same unit of the good, and individuals can easily be prevented from consuming the good if they fail to pay for it. A typical example is ice cream, but many consumer goods fall into this category. At the other extreme, *purely public goods* are both non-rival and non-excludable. Multiple individuals can consume the same unit of the good at once, and no one can be (easily) barred from its consumption. A classic example is national defense, but other examples include fireworks displays, mosquito spraying and scientific discovery.

Other goods that contain a mix of public and private attributes are called quasi-public goods. Within the realm of quasi-public goods there are two distinct types: rival but non-excludable goods are commonly referred to as *common pool resources*, which include public water sources, common grazing fields and the like. Without cooperation to limit the use of these goods, common pool resources are at risk of over-consumption – the classical problem of the commons (Hardin, 1968). Non-rival but excludable goods are often referred to as *club* or *toll goods*. Many people can consume the same unit of such a good without diminishing each other's enjoyment (up to a point of congestion), but people can be excluded from consuming it. Examples of toll or club goods include theater, toll roads, golf clubs and amusement parks.

Voluntary organizations produce goods within each of these categories. For example, producer cooperatives produce private goods for sale and private consumption. Many

	Rival	Non-rival
Excludable	Pure Private Goods	Club Goods
Non-excludable	Common Pool Goods	Pure Public Goods

Figure 43.1   Classification of economic goods

recreation associations and leagues produce club goods for member benefit. Regional agricultural associations protect common pool irrigation channels. Community associations maintain parks, public gardens and other pure public goods. Additionally, many voluntary organizations produce several different varieties of public and private goods as delineated in the boxes of Figure 43.1. For example, cooperative grocery stores or day care cooperatives produce private goods for consumers while providing benefits in the form of club goods for their members. Below, we discuss problems typically encountered and strategies used to address issues of cooperation that arise in production of these various kinds of goods.

Private Goods

Producer cooperatives, cooperative artisan markets and cooperative farmers' associations produce and sell consumable private goods and services, just as for-profit firms do. By joining together, members of cooperatives benefit from scale economies, allowing them to purchase inputs at lower prices, market their products on a larger scale and share the work of selling their goods. However, these organizations are challenged by several issues. Sharing revenues evenly among members may lead to shirking and free-riding behavior. Additionally, individual members can leave the group and compete directly in the market. Economic incentives must therefore be structured to fairly and efficiently compensate individual members for their contributions. Dues are often required as a form of membership tax to compensate for non-excludable benefits in order to cover operating costs. And regular updates on the progress and success of the cooperative can help members appreciate both the private and collective benefits of their cooperation.

Voluntary organizations also produce trust-related private goods (Hansmann, 1980). In this case, the quality of the product is difficult to evaluate because of information asymmetries between producers and buyers. An example is childcare. Parents may form voluntary organizations and commit to providing childcare on a rotating basis. In this way, parents who are directly involved in providing the service can directly monitor the quality of care. However, there is an incentive for parents to shirk their duties by receiving more childcare than they voluntarily provide. Therefore, member dues are often structured to include both fees and volunteer hours, with fee reductions for greater volunteer involvement. Similar to club goods, the quality of the service depends on the qualifications and commitment of the members producing them. Therefore, barriers to enter the cooperative, such as the level of fees charged and voluntary commitment required, are often combined with an extensive application and interview process to ensure that only committed and qualified members can join. Members will only sustain cooperation if the quality of the services is evident and complaints are promptly resolved. Hence, these organizations routinely engage their full memberships in meetings and group events, such as fundraisers, to demonstrate the quality of the care and to facilitate the resolution of any issues. Since quality is likely to be more important than price for members, prices charged by such organizations can be higher than by for-profits in the same industry. However, since these organizations often serve individuals with a range of incomes, price discrimination based on ability to pay is often employed (Hansmann, 1996).

Club Goods

A common feature of club goods is that the level of benefits and the quality of the experience depends on who is in the club (Buchanan, 1965; Hansmann, 1996; Gugerty and Prakash, 2010). For example, in a recreation association, the level of play depends on the skills of the members. In a social club, the value of the networks, membership status and other benefits accrued by the relationships formed depends on the social status and social connections of the members. Organizations providing club goods are predominantly structured as nonprofits rather than for-profit firms since high quality members would be less likely to join if someone else profited from their status (Hansmann, 1996). These organizations also offer varying degrees of exclusivity. Since they set dues to cover costs, clubs offering the same services may not differ much on member costs (Hansmann, 1996). However, higher quality clubs are more exclusive, structuring the admissions process to exclude all but the most desirable individuals. Organizations that value higher levels of involvement, such as sports organizations interested in more frequent games or broader participation in the sport, have less exclusive admissions. Both membership criteria and management policies are used in these organizations to ensure that each member can associate with other members of desired quality or status. Gugerty and Prakash (2010) create a typology of four varieties of nonprofit clubs: those with strict or lenient standards of admission and with strong or weak mechanisms for enforcement of those standards. In order to maintain cooperation among members, the enforcement mechanisms must match the standards. For example, clubs that have strict standards of admission must uphold those standards with strong enforcement. In general, Gugerty and Prakash (2010) show that different kinds of clubs choose different combinations of strong or lenient standards and strong or weak enforcement mechanisms as a result of trade-offs between the costs and benefits of these alternatives in particular circumstances.

Common Pool Resources

Managing voluntary cooperation to maintain common pool resources is fraught with a number of problems. Incomplete information among actors leads to situations where individuals may either (1) make mistakes when choosing strategies intended to accomplish their goals or (2) act opportunistically when they have information unavailable to others (Ostrom, 2000a). Since common pool resources, such as common water sources or grazing fields, are rival but not excludable, they suffer from the 'problem of the commons' in which rational individuals have incentives to consume inefficient amounts of the resource before it is exhausted, leading directly to the demise of the good (Ostrom, 1990). Lab experiments strongly support the predictions of overuse of common pool resources, particularly when appropriators fail to share information (Ostrom, 2007).

However, policymakers and scholars have long been interested in how democratic governance systems enable individuals to solve problems associated with common pool resources. Research on this issue largely rests on economic assumptions that no self-interested person would contribute to the production of a collective good unless the number of individuals in a group is small, there are coercion or reputation penalties, or there is some other mechanism used to induce individuals to act in their common interest. Yet examples that challenge the assumptions of the so-called 'free rider problem' are abundant (see Ostrom 2007, p. 52 for a list of published studies). Ostrom's (1990, 2000a, 2000b, 2007) work cites numerous examples of how groups throughout the world voluntarily come together to overcome these problems.

Various strategies exist to overcome depletion of common resources. For example, when people are allowed to communicate in lab settings, jointly beneficial outcomes are more likely to result (Ostrom, 2000). Research suggests that individuals engage in cooperation as a result of learning strategies where, over time, they acquire a greater understanding of their situations and adopt strategies that result in higher returns. Much of this learning occurs through the development of social norms of reciprocity and sanction (Bardhan, 1993). The cooperation of individuals also becomes a critical component of enhancing solidarity in communities, as norms of fairness and reciprocity directly inform individuals' goals and strategies (Elster, 1989; Axelrod, 1986). Instead of an emphasis on formal rules or external monitoring of common pool resources, communities' own informal cooperative groups can generate better outcomes. For example, during a drought, an environmentally conscious community may succeed in reducing its water consumption simply through an educational effort of its neighborhood association, informing its members about water conditions and the voluntary conservation efforts of local citizens.

Public Goods

Voluntary organizations that produce pure public goods, such as public radio or neighborhood safety, commonly face free-riding behavior because of the inability to exclude non-payers or to easily demonstrate that failure of any individual to support the good will result in its diminution.

These organizations must cover their costs without being able to directly charge for consumption. Even though the rational choice for consumers in these situations is to free-ride, studies, including lab experiments, generally find people contribute to public goods at higher levels than rational choice models would predict (Fischbacher and Gächter, 2010; Vesterlund, 2006). People are motivated to support public goods by a number of factors, including private self-interest, an interest in helping others and social pressure (Vesterlund, 2006), leading to a variety of strategies to increase giving. Because giving is in part motivated by perceived public benefits, common strategies to overcome free-riding are donation drives and public appeals, often making the case for the value they bring to the community. These strategies include advertising to potential donors the measureable difference their donation makes, as well as other objective indicators of the potential impact of their gift, such as the ratio of organizational expenses on program activities rather than administration (Vesterlund, 2006). Advertising the contributions of others can also lead to increased giving, in part by other donors signaling organizational quality (Shang and Croson, 2009; Vesterlund, 2003). Cooperation to support a public good is often conditional on other factors, such as reciprocity and the level of support others provide (Fischbacher and Gächter, 2010), supporting the strategy of advertising others' donations. Announcing gifts also rewards donors with recognition, appealing to the private benefits of giving, including 'warm glow' and social prestige. Other strategies include coupling private goods with public goods, creating 'selective incentives' such as 'member-only' benefits and 'exclusive' merchandise (Olson, 1965). In smaller communities, social norms and pressures may also be effective and in cases where a few individuals derive a disproportionate share of the collective benefits, those individuals may have sufficiently strong personal incentives to provide the good, despite the potential free-riding of others (Olson, 1965). For example, a voluntary group of 'privileged' (wealthy) individuals may find it in their interest to preserve large areas of a pristine landscape through their own purchasing power but still allow open access because of the costs associated with trying to exclude others.

Some voluntary organizations that primarily produce private or club goods, such as community gardens which supply members with plots of land to grow fresh produce, also produce pure public benefits in the form of positive externalities, such as more attractive public space, ecological awareness and education about healthy lifestyles. For such organizations, public or private land and resource donations can create incentives for cooperation and community buy-in, while private benefits, such as the fresh produce and cost-sharing, can sustain cooperation, hence maintaining the public benefits.

ISSUES FOR FUTURE RESEARCH

Research on voluntary organizations continues to be fertile territory for scholars. Definitional issues remain as the boundaries between different types of organizations become increasingly blurred in contemporary society. The definitional issues also complicate research since organizations like grassroots associations (which are volunteer-based) or actors within social movements (where formal and informal organizations are embedded within loosely structured networks) are extremely difficult to identify or count. Instead, much of the empirical research on voluntary organizations is based on studying formal organizations usually with paid staff, despite evidence that informal voluntary organizations are more numerous than formal ones (Smith, 1997a). A rich research agenda remains on the less visible or less well-defined areas of voluntary organization activity, including informal or grassroots voluntary organizations, hybrid organizations and social movements.

Moreover, many practical issues associated with effective management and governance of voluntary organizations remain to be well understood and resolved, especially in light of the increased complexity of organizational structures and blurring of organizational types (Billis, 2010). The same applies to policy issues associated with the proper role and functioning of voluntary organizations. Understudied aspects of the latter include measurement of the societal impacts of voluntary organizations, as well as the role these organizations play in a participatory democracy, especially in light of the modern revolution in communications technology and the growing influence of money in the public policy advocacy process.

Another research question is why the types and uses of voluntary organizations vary so much across national borders. In any given country, the choice to purposely establish a membership organization, association, nonprofit organization or cooperative is not solely based on the type of good being produced, as economic theories suggest. Rather, these choices appear also to be influenced by prior patterns of historical development (Salamon and Anheier, 1998). For example in France the concept of *economie sociale* (emphasizing values of solidarity and reciprocity) underlies the emphasis on associations, cooperatives and mutual organizations as the primary voluntary form. By contrast, in Sweden, Australia and New Zealand, long histories of public sector provision for the basic needs of most citizens appear to have resulted in voluntary action largely taking place through membership and recreational groups. In the United States, the strong focus on free markets seems to have influenced the development of the nonprofit corporation. And so on. The transnational variation in the employment of different forms of voluntary organization offers a natural experiment for researchers. Such a research agenda could address such questions as how different legal systems and cultural traditions result in alternative forms of voluntary organizations, and how prominent and effective these voluntary organizations are within the context of the economies in which they are embedded.

REFERENCES

Axelrod, Robert (1986). 'An Evolutionary Approach to Norms', *The American Political Science Review*, 80:4, pp. 1095–1111.
Bardhan, Pranab (1993). 'Symposium On Management of Local Commons', *The Journal of Economic Perspectives*, 7: 4, pp. 87–92.
Ben-Ner, Avner (1986). 'Nonprofit Organizations: Why Do They Exist in a Market Economy?', in Susan Rose-Ackerman (ed.), *The Economics of Nonprofit Institutions*, New York: Oxford University Press, pp. 94–113.
Billis, David (ed.) (2010). *Hybrid Organizations and the Third Sector*, Houndsmill, Basingstoke: Palgrave Macmillan.
Buchanan, James M. (1965). 'An Economic Theory of Clubs', *Economica*, 32, pp. 1–14
Chapais, Bernard (2008). *Primeval Kinship*, Cambridge MA: Harvard University Press.
Coase, Ronald (1937). 'The Nature of the Firm', *Economica*, 4, pp. 386–405, reprinted in Louis Putterman (ed.) (1986). *The Economic Nature of the Firm: A Reader*, New York: Cambridge University Press.
Elster, Jon (1989). 'Social Norms and Economic Theory', *The Journal of Economic Perspectives*, 3:4, pp. 99–117.
Enjolras, Bernard (2000). 'Coordination Failure, Property Rights and Non-Profit Organizations', *Annals of Public Cooperative Economics*, 71:3, pp. 347–374.
Fischbacher, U. and Gächter, S. (2010). 'Social Preferences, Beliefs, and the Dynamics of Free Riding in Public Goods Experiments', *The American Economic Review*, 100(1), pp. 541–556.
Fukuyama, France (2011). *The Origins of Political Order: From Prehuman Times to the French Revolution*, New York: D & M Publishers.
Gouldner, Alvin W. (1960). 'The Norm of Reciprocity: A Preliminary Statement', *American Sociological Review*, 25:2, pp. 161–178.
Gugerty, Mary Kay and Aseem Prakash (eds) (2010). *Voluntary Regulation of NGOs and Nonprofits: An Accountability Club Framework*, New York: Cambridge University Press.
Hansmann, Henry (1980). 'The Role of Non-Profit Enterprise', *Yale Law Journal*, April, 89, pp. 835–898.
Hansmann, Henry (1996). *The Ownership of Enterprise*, Cambridge, MA: Harvard University Press.
Hardin, Garrett (1968). 'The tragedy of the commons', *Science*, 162, pp. 1243–1248.
Lakdawalla, Darius and Tomas Philipson (1997). 'Nonprofit Production and Competition', *NBER Working Paper Series*, Working Paper 6377.
Lakdawalla, Darius and Tomas Philipson (2006). 'The Nonprofit Sector and Industry Performance', *Journal of Public Economics*, 90, pp. 1681–1698.
Olson, Mancur (1965). *The Logic of Collective Action*, Cambridge, MA: Harvard University Press.
Ostrom, Elinor (1990). *Governing the commons: The evolution of institutions for collective action*, Cambridge: Cambridge University Press.
Ostrom, Elinor (2000a). 'Collective action and the evolution of social norms', *The Journal of Economic Perspectives*, 14(3), pp. 137–158.
Ostrom, Elinor (2000b). 'The danger of self-evident truths', *PS: Political Science and Politics*, 33(1), pp. 33–44.
Ostrom, Elinor (2007). 'Institutional Rational Choice: An Assessment of the Institutional Analysis and Development Framework', P. Sabatier (ed.) *Theories of the Policy Process*, Boulder, Colorado: Westview Press.
Rose-Ackerman, Susan (1996), 'Altruism, Nonprofits, and Economic Theory', *Journal of Economic Literature*, June, Vol.XXXIV, pp. 701–728.

Rucht, Dieter (2010). 'Collective Action', in S. Immerfall and G. Therborn (eds) *Handbook of European Societies*, London: Springer, pp. 111–138.

Salamon, L.M. and H.K. Anheier (1998). 'Social Origins of Civil Society: Explaining the Nonprofit Sector Cross-Nationally', *Voluntas: International Journal of Voluntary and Nonprofit Organizations*, 9:3, pp. 213–248.

Shang, J. and R. Croson (2009). 'A Field Experiment in Charitable Contribution: The Impact of Social Information on the Voluntary Provision of Public Goods', *The Economic Journal*, 119(540), pp. 1422–1439.

Smith, David Horton (1982). 'Altruism, Volunteers and Volunteerism', in J. Harman, *Volunteering in the Eighties: Fundamental Issues in Voluntary Action*, Washington, DC: University Press of America, pp. 23–44.

Smith, David Horton (1997a). 'The rest of the nonprofit sector: Grassroots associations as the dark matter ignored in prevailing "flat earth" maps of the sector', *Nonprofit and Voluntary Sector Quarterly*, 26(2), p. 114.

Smith, David Horton (1997b). 'Grassroots associations are important: Some theory and a review of the impact literature', *Nonprofit and Voluntary Sector Quarterly*, 26(3), p. 269.

Smith, David Horton (2000). *Grassroots Associations*, Thousand Oaks, California: Sage Publications.

Spear, Roger (2000). 'The Co-operative Advantage', *Annals of Public and Cooperative Economics*, 71:4, pp. 507–523.

Toepler, Stefan and Helmut Anheier (eds) (2009). *International encyclopedia of civil society*, New York, NY: Springer, Vol. 3: P–Z.

Van Der Meer, Tom W.G. Manfred Te Grotenhuis and Peer L.H. Scheepers (2009). 'Three Types of Voluntary Associations in Comparative Perspective', *Journal of Civil Society*, 5:3, pp. 227–241.

Vesterlund, L. (2003). 'The Informational Value of Sequential Fundraising', *Journal of Public Economics*, 87(3–4), pp. 627–657.

Vesterlund, L. (2006). 'Why Do People Give', in W.W. Powell and R. Steinberg (eds), *The Nonprofit Sector: A Research Handbook*, 2nd ed., New Haven: Yale University Press, pp. 168–190.

Wade, Nicholas (2011a). 'From "End of History" Author, a Look at the Beginning and Middle', *The New York Times*, Tuesday, March 8, p. D3.

Wade, Nicholas (2011b). 'New View of How Humans Moved Away from Apes', *The New York Times*, March 11, p. A3.

Weisbrod, Burton A. (1975). 'Toward a Theory of the Voluntary Non-Profit Sector in a Three Sector Economy', in Edmund Phelps (ed.), *Altruism. Morality and Economic Theory*, New York: Russell Sage.

Wilderom, Celeste P.M. and John B. Miner (1991). 'Defining Voluntary Groups and Agencies within Organization Science', *Organization Science*, 2:4, November, pp. 366–378.

Index